P9-CDT-642

ALSO BY THE EDITORS AT AMERICA'S TEST KITCHEN

The America's Test Kitchen Healthy Family Cookbook
The America's Test Kitchen Family Baking Book
The America's Test Kitchen Family Cookbook
The Complete America's Test Kitchen TV Show Cookbook
The Best Simple Recipes
Slow Cooker Revolution

AMERICA'S TEST KITCHEN ANNUALS:
The Best of America's Test Kitchen
(2007–2011 Editions)
Cooking for Two
(2009–2011 Editions)
Light & Healthy
(2010 and 2011 Editions)

THE COOK'S COUNTRY SERIES:
Cook's Country Blue Ribbon Desserts
Cook's Country Best Potluck Recipes
Cook's Country Best Lost Suppers
Cook's Country Best Grilling Recipes
The Cook's Country Cookbook
America's Best Lost Recipes

THE BEST RECIPE SERIES:
Soups, Stews & Chilis
More Best Recipes
The New Best Recipe
The Best Skillet Recipes
The Best Slow & Easy Recipes
The Best Chicken Recipes
The Best International Recipe
The Best Make-Ahead Recipe
The Best 30-Minute Recipe
The Best Light Recipe
The Cook's Illustrated Guide to Grilling & Barbecue
Best American Side Dishes
Cover & Bake
Steaks, Chops, Roasts, and Ribs
Baking Illustrated
Restaurant Favorites at Home
Perfect Vegetables
Italian Classics
American Classics

For a full listing of all our books or to order titles:
http://www.cooksillustrated.com
http://www.americastestkitchen.com
or call 800-611-0759

PRAISE FOR THE BEST RECIPE SERIES AND OTHER AMERICA'S TEST KITCHEN TITLES

"Further proof that practice makes perfect, if not transcendent. . . . If an intermediate cook follows the directions exactly, the results will be better than takeout or Mom's."
NEW YORK TIMES on THE NEW BEST RECIPE

"Expert bakers and novices scared of baking's requisite exactitude can all learn something from this hefty, all-purpose home baking volume."
PUBLISHERS WEEKLY on THE AMERICA'S TEST KITCHEN FAMILY BAKING BOOK

"Scrupulously tested regional and heirloom recipes."
NEW YORK TIMES on THE COOK'S COUNTRY COOKBOOK

"An instant classic."
CHICAGO SUN-TIMES on AMERICA'S BEST LOST RECIPES

"This tome definitely raises the bar for all-in-one, basic, must-have cookbooks. . . . Kimball and his company have scored another hit."
PORTLAND OREGONIAN on THE AMERICA'S TEST KITCHEN FAMILY COOKBOOK

"A foolproof, go-to resource for everyday cooking."
PUBLISHERS WEEKLY on THE AMERICA'S TEST KITCHEN FAMILY COOKBOOK

"The strength of the Best Recipe Series lies in the sheer thoughtfulness and details of the recipes."
PUBLISHERS WEEKLY on THE BEST RECIPE SERIES

"One of the best books of the year."
MINNEAPOLIS STAR-TRIBUNE on THE BEST INTERNATIONAL RECIPE

"These dishes taste as luxurious as their full-fat siblings. Even desserts are terrific."
PUBLISHERS WEEKLY on THE BEST LIGHT RECIPE

"Like a mini-cooking school, the detailed instructions and illustrations ensure that even the most inexperienced cook can follow these recipes with success."
PUBLISHERS WEEKLY on BEST AMERICAN SIDE DISHES

"Makes one-dish dinners a reality for average cooks, with honest ingredients and detailed make-ahead instructions."
NEW YORK TIMES on COVER & BAKE

"[Steaks, Chops, Roasts, and Ribs] conquers every question one could have about all things meat."
SAN FRANCISCO CHRONICLE on STEAKS, CHOPS, ROASTS, AND RIBS

"The best instructional book on baking this reviewer has seen."
LIBRARY JOURNAL (STARRED REVIEW) on BAKING ILLUSTRATED

"A must-have for anyone into our nation's cooking traditions—and a good reference, too."
LOS ANGELES DAILY NEWS on AMERICAN CLASSICS

WELCOME TO AMERICA'S TEST KITCHEN

THIS BOOK HAS BEEN TESTED, WRITTEN, AND edited by the folks at America's Test Kitchen, a very real 2,500-square-foot kitchen located just outside of Boston. It is the home of *Cook's Illustrated* magazine and *Cook's Country* magazine and is the Monday-through-Friday destination for more than three dozen test cooks, editors, food scientists, tasters, and cookware specialists. Our mission is to test recipes over and over again until we understand how and why they work and until we arrive at the "best" version.

We start the process of testing a recipe with a complete lack of conviction, which means that we accept no claim, no theory, no technique, and no recipe at face value. We simply assemble as many variations as possible, test a half-dozen of the most promising, and taste the results blind. We then construct our own hybrid recipe and continue to test it, varying ingredients, techniques, and cooking times until we reach a consensus. The result, we hope, is the best version of a particular recipe, but we realize that only you can be the final judge of our success (or failure). As we like to say in the

test kitchen, "We make the mistakes, so you don't have to."

All of this would not be possible without a belief that good cooking, much like good music, is indeed based on a foundation of objective technique. Some people like spicy foods and others don't, but there is a right way to sauté, there is a best way to cook a pot roast, and there are measurable scientific principles involved in producing perfectly beaten, stable egg whites. This is our ultimate goal: to investigate the fundamental principles of cooking so that you become a better cook. It is as simple as that.

You can watch us work (in our actual test kitchen) by tuning in to *America's Test Kitchen* (www.americastestkitchentv.com) or *Cook's Country from America's Test Kitchen* (www.cookscountrytv.com) on public television, or by subscribing to *Cook's Illustrated* magazine (www.cooksillustrated.com) or *Cook's Country* magazine (www.cookscountry.com). We welcome you into our kitchen, where you can stand by our side as we test our way to the "best" recipes in America.

THE BEST ONE-DISH SUPPERS

A BEST RECIPE CLASSIC

THE BEST ONE-DISH SUPPERS

A BEST RECIPE CLASSIC

BY THE EDITORS OF

COOK'S ILLUSTRATED

PHOTOGRAPHY
KELLER + KELLER, CARL TREMBLAY, AND DANIEL J. VAN ACKERE

ILLUSTRATIONS
JOHN BURGOYNE

America's
TEST KITCHEN

BROOKLINE, MASSACHUSETTS

Copyright © 2011 by the Editors of *Cook's Illustrated*

All rights reserved. No part of this book may be reproduced or transmitted in any manner whatsoever without written permission
from the publisher, except in the case of brief quotations embodied in critical articles or reviews.

America's Test Kitchen
17 Station Street
Brookline, MA 02445

ISBN-13: 978-1-933615-81-3
ISBN-10: 1-933615-81-8

Library of Congress Cataloging-in-Publication Data
The Editors of *Cook's Illustrated*

The Best One-Dish Suppers: Do you want to get dinner on the table without dirtying an arsenal of pots and pans?
Here is a collection of more than 175 foolproof recipes for full-flavored, complete meals.

1st Edition
ISBN-13: 978-1-933615-81-3
ISBN-10: 1-933615-81-8
(hardcover): U.S. $35
1. Cooking. 1. Title
2011

Manufactured in the United States of America

10 9 8 7 6 5 4 3 2 1

Distributed by America's Test Kitchen, 17 Station Street, Brookline, MA 02445

Editorial Director: Jack Bishop
Executive Editor: Elizabeth Carduff
Executive Food Editor: Julia Collin Davison
Senior Editors: Lori Galvin and Suzannah McFerran
Associate Editor: Louise Emerick
Test Cooks: Christie Morrison, Adelaide Parker, and Dan Souza
Design Director: Amy Klee
Art Director: Greg Galvan
Designer: Beverly Hsu
Staff Photographer: Daniel J. van Ackere
Additional Photography: Keller + Keller and Carl Tremblay
Food Styling: Marie Piraino and Mary Jane Sawyer
Illustrator: John Burgoyne
Production Director: Guy Rochford
Senior Production Manager: Jessica Lindheimer Quirk
Senior Project Manager: Alice Carpenter
Traffic and Production Coordinator: Kate Hux
Asset and Workflow Manager: Andrew Mannone
Production and Imaging Specialists: Judy Blomquist, Heather Dube, and Lauren Pettapiece
Copyeditor: Cheryl Redmond
Proofreader: Debra Hudak
Indexer: Elizabeth Parson

Pictured on front of jacket: Dutch Oven Chicken Pot Pie (page 73)
Pictured on back of jacket: Lemon-Herb Cod Fillets with Crispy Garlic Potatoes (page 18), Roasted Chicken Breasts with
Red Potatoes, Fennel, and Cauliflower (page 48), and Dutch Oven Chicken Pot Pie (page 73)

Contents

PREFACE

ONE OF MY FAVORITE STORIES IS ABOUT A clock and a cow. A Vermonter, Harry Skidmore, was milking a cow in his barnyard when a stranger stopped by to get directions to the next town. Harry told him the way. The stranger said, "By the way, do you happen to have the right time? My watch has stopped."

Harry reached under the cow's udder, lifted one of the nipples, studied it for a second and said, "It's twenty-two minutes past four."

The stranger gave a skeptical look and said, "You wouldn't be pulling my leg now, would you?"

"Nope," said Harry. "That's the exact time, not a minute more, not a minute less."

Puzzled, the stranger asked, "Okay, but tell me how you do that."

"Easy," said Harry. "Just sit down on this milk-stool and I'll show ya." The stranger, curious, complied.

"Now, with your right hand grab that left teat and raise it an inch-and-a-quarter." The stranger did.

"All right," Harry concluded. "If you bend down just so and look straight ahead, you'll see the town clock over yonder."

That goes to show that sometimes things in life are simpler than they appear, but in the case of one-dish suppers, the finished recipes are quite the opposite—they look simpler than they really are. The problem is always the same; how does one combine foods—meat, chicken, or fish and a side, for example—all in the same cooking vessel (Dutch oven, roasting pan, broiling pan, skillet, or sheet pan) and get everything to turn out just right? Sometimes we simply roast different foods together at the same time, such as snap peas and chicken thighs. Or we make a quick Bolognese and then cook the pasta right in the sauce. Or we cook fish fillets on a bed of crispy potatoes. We also figured out how to do a stir-fry in the oven using a sheet pan for a hands-off cooking method.

We also roasted a bacon-wrapped pork loin alongside potatoes that were then dressed to make a warm potato salad. We roasted chicken on top of bread cubes and then used the bread as the base for an Italian panzanella salad. For a quick and easy chicken pot pie, we put the lid on upside down and then baked the biscuits on top, dropping the finished biscuits into the filling just before serving. And we updated the classic chicken and rice by adding toasted sesame seeds and oil, scallions, and ginger to make a new classic, Chicken and Sesame Rice with Edamame and Carrots.

We also give you plenty of updated and per-fected one-dish classics including Dutch Oven Shepherd's Pie, Chicken and Shrimp Jambalaya, Baked Ziti with Ricotta, Modern Baked Manicotti, Creole-Style Gumbo, Classic Chicken Stew with Winter Vegetables, and imaginative slow-cooker offerings such as Slow-Cooker Moroccan Chicken Stew and Slow-Cooker Pork Stew with Fennel and Prunes.

This collection of recipe makes one-dish suppers a whole lot more intriguing. In fact, that reminds me of a story. A Bostonian was driving through Chester, Vermont, on his way to his weekend place, when he spotted an unusual sight, an elderly man on the front porch of a country store, holding a fishing pole with the line trailing into a bucket of water. Remembering that he had some supplies to buy, the flatlander stopped. As he entered the store, he decided to have a little fun with the obviously addled native.

"Hey, old-timer," he said, "catch any big ones?"

"Ayuh," replied the fisherman. "You're the third one I got today."

Hope that *The Best One-Dish Suppers* catches you too, as it did me. It's a collection of recipes that are fresh, practical, and perfectly suited for the way most of us cook today.

Christopher Kimball
Founder and Editor,
Cook's Illustrated and *Cook's Country*
Host, *America's Test Kitchen* and
Cook's Country from America's Test Kitchen

1
SHEET PAN DINNERS

Sheet Pan Dinners

FLANK STEAK WITH CORN AND BLACK BEAN SALAD

LIKE OTHER CUTS FROM THE CHEST AND SIDE of the cow, flank steak has a rich, full, beefy flavor. It is particularly well suited to the grill, which has plenty of surface area to accommodate this large, flat cut. But what about those times when cooking outdoors isn't possible? Flank steak is typically too long to fit neatly in a skillet, making pan-searing troublesome. We wanted to find a reliable way to cook flank steak indoors and wondered if we might find our solution beyond the stovetop: If we could find a way to cook flank steak in the oven, we could use a sheet pan, which would be large enough to hold the steak and a side dish as well.

Since we love the dark, browned crust a flank steak develops from the intense heat of the grill, we decided to try and replicate that using the oven's broiler. The heat of the broiler did succeed in browning the exterior of the meat, but this didn't occur until the steak's interior was overcooked. Additionally, between flipping the steak and checking for doneness, we ended up having to monitor the steak constantly. Hanging outside while you grill is one thing, but hovering by the oven door was not what we had in mind.

Switching gears, we gave up trying to mimic the grill by using the broiler and instead decided to take advantage of the even heat of the oven. Roasting the steak on the pan until it reached a perfect medium-rare was an improvement. On the inside, the steak was great—evenly cooked and tender. But the color was drab and gray and our steak was missing the deep flavor and textural contrast of a crust. What if we started with a hot pan? For our next test, we put the sheet pan in the oven while it preheated, then quickly added the steak and cooked it as before. We were getting closer, but we wanted a better crust still.

We wondered if a spice rub might improve the flavor, appearance, and texture of the exterior of the steak. The bold flavor and deep red color of a Southwestern chili-based rub filled the bill; in addition to chili powder, coriander, cumin, cinnamon, and red pepper flakes added just the right amount of heat and complexity to our rub.

Pulling our spice-rubbed steak from the oven, we were impressed with the results: While the bottom of the steak was moist from resting in the collected juice, the top of the steak, exposed to the heat of the oven, formed an attractive and flavorful dark mahogany crust. To promote caramelization and boost flavor even further we added a little dark brown sugar to the rub.

With our basic method set, we focused on the details. Adding oil to the pan before preheating it caused a mess—the oil smoked and scorched the pan, making it difficult to handle. Brushing the sheet pan with oil just before adding the steak was an easier and safer alternative. As for oven temperature, 475 degrees was ideal—the steak cooked evenly and this was hot enough to allow the spice rub to develop flavor without burning.

Even with a large flank steak, we had space on our roomy sheet pan for a side dish. Keeping with the Southwestern flavor profile, we settled on a black bean and corn salad. Roasting the corn alongside the steak allowed the natural sugars in the corn to caramelize, giving it an appealing nuttiness and slight crunch. We tested frozen corn, canned corn, and fresh corn, but only the fresh corn browned properly, and its superior flavor was worth the small amount of additional preparation.

In addition to the black beans (canned worked fine for this recipe) tasters liked the sweetness, crunch, and color of red bell pepper. Minced onion was too harsh; scallions were favored for their milder flavor as well as visual appeal.

For the dressing, we found that the typical ratio of 1 part acid to 3 parts oil was much too mild for our hearty salad. Equal parts lime juice and oil delivered the right amount of brightness. A little honey balanced the citrus kick and adding the scallions to the dressing further mellowed their oniony flavor. To keep things efficient, we tossed all the salad ingredients but the corn with the dressing, while the corn and beef were in the oven. Then we stirred the corn in once it was all done.

Rather than concoct a complicated mix of spices and chiles to flavor the salad, we found that a simple combination of minced canned chipotle chile and fresh cilantro was all it needed. The salad's subtle, smoky heat and bright, refreshing flavor was an ideal complement to the spice-rubbed steak. This was by far the best steak dinner that never saw the grill.

KEYS TO SUCCESSFUL SHEET PAN DINNERS

When preparing our sheet pan dinner recipes, you of course need to have the proper ingredients and follow the recipe directions, but the real key to success is having the proper piece of equipment—not just any old sheet pan will do. While developing the recipes in this chapter, we found there were a few critical attributes to look for in your sheet pan (for our favorite brand, see page 26):

Large Size
We use a large, 18 by 13-inch sheet pan (also known as a half-sheet) for every recipe. This size fits perfectly in a standard-size oven and provides enough surface area for an entire roast plus vegetables, or for smaller pieces of food (like in our sheet pan stir-fries) to spread out and thus cook through evenly. And because a large sheet will allow food to spread out and have ample direct contact with the hot surface, moisture will evaporate quickly and foods will brown well. In some recipes, like our Crunchy Parmesan-Crusted Pork Chops with Glazed Winter Squash, the size is critical because the sheet pan needs to be large enough to accommodate a wire rack in order to elevate the chops and ensure a crunchy coating.

Rimmed Sides
To contain any liquid released by the food during cooking, rimmed sides are a must. But sides that are too high will trap moisture; lower sides (we prefer about 1-inch height) means easier moisture evaporation and thus very good browning and even cooking.

Heavy Duty, Solid Construction
When used in a high-heat oven, a lightweight, flimsy pan is likely to warp. A heavy, solidly constructed pan will stay flat and even. Another problem with lightweight pans is that the heat will transfer too quickly. A heavyweight sheet pan will still heat more quickly than a roasting pan (a trait we used to our advantage in developing these recipes) but not so fast as to burn the food.

Spice-Rubbed Flank Steak with Roasted Corn and Black Bean Salad
SERVES 4 TO 6

We prefer this steak cooked to medium-rare, but if you prefer it more or less done, see our guidelines in the chart on page 45. Be sure to use fresh corn here; canned or frozen corn will not roast well.

SPICE RUB
1	tablespoon ground cumin
1	tablespoon chili powder
1	tablespoon dark brown sugar
1½	teaspoons ground coriander
1	teaspoon salt
1	teaspoon ground black pepper
¼	teaspoon ground cinnamon
⅛	teaspoon red pepper flakes

STEAK AND SALAD
1	(2- to 2½-pound) flank steak, trimmed
3	ears corn, kernels cut from the cob (see the illustration on page 5) (see note)
5	tablespoons vegetable oil
	Salt and ground black pepper
2	tablespoons juice from 1 lime
2	scallions, sliced thin
2	teaspoons minced chipotle chile in adobo sauce
2	teaspoons honey
1	(15-ounce) can black beans, drained and rinsed
1	red bell pepper, stemmed, seeded, and chopped fine (see the illustrations on page 226)
¼	cup minced fresh cilantro leaves

1. **FOR THE SPICE RUB:** Combine all the ingredients in a bowl.

2. **FOR THE STEAK AND SALAD:** Adjust an oven rack to the lower-middle position, place a large rimmed baking sheet on the rack, and heat the oven to 475 degrees. Pat the steak dry with paper towels and rub evenly with the spice rub. Toss the

corn with 1 tablespoon of the oil and season with salt and pepper to taste.

3. Working quickly, brush 2 tablespoons more oil evenly over the hot baking sheet. Lay the steak on one side of the baking sheet. Spread the corn on the baking sheet, opposite the steak. Roast until the steak registers 125 degrees on an instant-read thermometer (for medium-rare), 15 to 20 minutes, stirring the corn halfway through roasting.

4. Meanwhile, whisk the remaining 2 tablespoons oil, lime juice, scallions, chipotles, and honey together in a large bowl. Stir in the black beans, bell pepper, and cilantro; set aside.

5. Transfer the steak to a carving board, tent loosely with aluminum foil, and let rest for 10 minutes. Return the corn to the oven and continue to roast until lightly browned, 5 to 10 minutes.

6. Stir the roasted corn into the bowl of black beans and season with salt and pepper to taste. Slice the steak into thin strips against the grain on the bias and serve with the corn and bean salad.

CUTTING CORN OFF THE COB

To cut the kernels off a cob without having them fly all over the kitchen counter, hold the cob on its end inside a large wide bowl and use a paring knife to cut off the kernels.

PORK LOIN WITH WARM POTATO SALAD

WHEN MOST AMERICANS THINK OF A PORK roast, it is usually a boneless center-cut loin roast that comes to mind. The practical advantages of this supermarket cut are many: It is affordable, widely available, and relatively quick-cooking. With its uniform shape and little connective tissue, one roast yields a good quantity of meat that is easy to slice and attractive to serve. Plus the mild, sweet flavor of roast pork pairs well with most any side dish. However, today's lean pork is prone to being overcooked, dry, and flavorless.

To mitigate this problem, the test kitchen typically brines the meat to keep it moist. After being tied with twine to promote even cooking, the pork is seared in a skillet to give it a flavorful, attractive crust, then it is transferred to the oven. Although this method is tried and true, we wanted to develop a recipe for a pork roast dinner that was easier. Could we skip the brining, tying, and searing and cook the pork, plus a side dish, in the oven from start to finish with one pan?

Without brining, we would have to find a way to keep the pork moist during cooking. Our thoughts turned to other pork roasts that stay naturally juicy. In addition to having more fat marbled into the meat, a pork rib or shoulder roast has a protective cap of fat that melts during cooking and essentially bastes the meat, adding flavor as well as ensuring juiciness. What if we mimicked this effect by wrapping the pork loin in bacon? We reasoned this could be the solution to two problems: in addition to protecting the pork and providing moisture during cooking, a crisp browned shell of bacon would serve, both visually and flavor-wise, in lieu of a seared crust.

We rubbed a pork loin with salt and pepper, then layered bacon slices crosswise over the entire roast, overlapping them slightly and tucking the ends underneath. We set it on a baking sheet and roasted it in a 375-degree oven until it registered 140 degrees. After pulling our roast out of the oven, the test appeared to be a total failure: The bacon was flabby and soggy while the rendered fat and juices pooled around the roast. Tasting the meat, however, told a different story—the pork roast was incredibly moist and juicy throughout and had a slight smoky flavor imparted by the bacon.

As we considered ways we could get crispier bacon, we recalled a technique the test kitchen has used for bacon-wrapped filets mignons, in which the bacon is precooked for a few minutes in the microwave before being wrapped around the meat. We gave it a shot here and found that three minutes

INGREDIENTS: Nitrate-Free Bacon

Nitrite has long been a controversial food additive, with studies showing it forms carcinogenic compounds called nitrosamines when heated in the presence of proteins, like those in bacon. Regular bacon is cured with nitrite or a virtually identical chemical, nitrate, both of which act as preservatives, though only nitrite has the potential to form nitrosamines. Bacon labeled "nitrate- or nitrite-free," on the other hand, is brined with salt, a bacterial lactic acid starter culture, and celery juice (sometimes listed as "natural flavor").

But here's the catch: Celery juice naturally contains a high level of organic nitrate, which is converted to the problematic nitrite by the bacteria in the starter culture and also by saliva during chewing. Despite this fact, it's technically correct to label the bacon "no nitrates or nitrites added," since the compounds are formed during production, not added as ingredients.

To quantify the nitrite and nitrate levels in both cured and uncured bacons, we sent three samples—Farmland Hickory Smoked, Farmland All-Natural Uncured Bacon (labeled "no nitrate or nitrite added"), and Applegate Farms Uncured Sunday Bacon (labeled "no nitrites added")—to a lab for testing. As we expected, all of the bacons contained nitrite and nitrate, and the nitrite levels were well within U.S. Department of Agriculture guidelines of no more than 120 parts per million (ppm). But to our surprise, the uncured bacons actually had higher levels of nitrite than the cured meat, and the Applegate Farms Uncured Sunday Bacon averaged more than three times the level of the regular bacon.

The bottom line? All bacon is likely to contain nitrite and nitrate, whether added at the outset or formed naturally during processing. If you want to avoid these compounds, you'll have to avoid bacon—and any other processed meats containing celery juice—altogether.

was enough time to allow some of the bacon fat to render, while still leaving the bacon pliable enough to wrap easily around the pork.

Giving the bacon a jump-start in the microwave had gotten us closer. However, it still wasn't as brown as we wanted. Cooking the pork at higher oven temperatures browned the bacon but dried out the pork. What if we cooked our roast at 375 degrees until it was almost done and then broiled it for the last few minutes to brown the bacon? This worked great; the meat remained juicy while the bacon became beautifully crisp and brown under the heat of the broiler. The last improvement was to rub some ground fennel seed on the roast along with the salt and pepper. The anise flavor of the fennel (a classic pork seasoning) added a little complexity and some higher aromatic notes to balance the bacon-pork combination.

Inspired by the bacon, we decided a warm, German-style roasted potato salad would be an appropriate side dish. Taking advantage of the large surface area of the baking sheet, we could simply roast the potatoes right alongside the pork, where they would absorb flavor from the juices and rendered bacon fat. We halved small red potatoes (our favorite for roasting because they hold their shape) and arranged them cut side down around the pork to maximize browning. As an added bonus, the small-sized potatoes also cooked in the same time as the pork, so we could throw everything on the sheet pan at the same time.

While the pork rested, we tossed the roasted potatoes with a simple Dijon vinaigrette made with white wine vinegar, olive oil, and minced shallot that we had warmed in the microwave. We covered the salad and let it sit for a few minutes, hoping the potatoes would absorb the dressing. It worked, but too well: by serving time, the potatoes had completely absorbed the dressing and the salad was dry. The flavor, however, was just right, so we didn't want to increase the vinaigrette. A splash of chicken broth added the desired moisture without affecting the dressing's careful balance of flavors. This dinner needed only one last touch; a generous handful of chopped parsley, stirred into the salad, provided a fresh counterpoint to the richness of the potatoes and pork.

Potatoes 101

Think all potatoes are the same? Think again. Until recently, most markets sold potatoes under generic names, such as "baking potato" or "boiling potato," which helped shoppers choose the right potato for each recipe. But now many markets sell potatoes by varietal name, such as Yukon Gold and Red Creamer. So what is the best use for each? Potato varieties can be divided into three major categories that guide their use.

NEW VERSUS OLD POTATOES

Potatoes can be categorized as "new" or "early" potatoes and "old" or "main crop" potatoes. Both new and old potatoes can come from any variety of potato. New potatoes are thin-skinned, less mature potatoes harvested in the late spring and summer. They are less starchy than "old" potatoes, because they haven't had time to convert their sugar into starch. These potatoes should be used as firm, waxy potatoes, regardless of variety. Old potatoes are fully mature and are harvested in the fall. They are usually starchier and have thick skins. These potatoes are often held in cold storage, or cured, in order for their skins to toughen, which helps protect their flesh for better storage. Most potatoes sold in supermarkets have been cured and can be considered "old" potatoes.

POTATO VARIETIES

DRY, FLOURY POTATOES

WHAT YOU NEED TO KNOW: Also known as "baking" potatoes, this group contains more total starch (20 percent to 22 percent) and amylose than other categories, giving these varieties a dry, mealy texture.

HOW TO USE THEM: The best choice when baking and frying, they are also great potatoes for mashing, because they can drink up butter and cream. Good when you want to thicken a stew or soup but not if you want distinct chunks of potatoes.

COMMON VARIETIES:
Russet, Russet Burbank, Idaho

"IN-BETWEEN" POTATOES

WHAT YOU NEED TO KNOW: These potatoes contain less total starch (18 percent to 20 percent) and amylose than dry, floury potatoes but more total starch and amylose than firm, waxy potatoes. Although they are "in-between" potatoes, their texture is more mealy than firm, putting them closer to dry, floury potatoes.

HOW TO USE THEM: They can be mashed or baked and they can be used in salads and soups but won't be quite as firm as waxy potatoes.

COMMON VARIETIES:
Yukon Gold, Yellow Finn, Purple Peruvian, Kennebec, Katahdin

FIRM, WAXY POTATOES

WHAT YOU NEED TO KNOW: Also known as "boiling" potatoes, these contain a relatively low amount of total starch (16 percent to 18 percent) and very little amylose, which means they have a firm, smooth, waxy texture. Freshly dug potatoes, which are often called "new" potatoes, fall into this group.

HOW TO USE THEM: Perfect when you want the potatoes to hold their shape, as with potato salad; also a good choice when roasting or boiling.

COMMON VARIETIES:
Red Bliss, French Fingerling, Red Creamer, White Rose

SCRUBBING POTATOES

Recipes in which the potatoes are not peeled usually instruct the cook to "scrub" the potatoes. Here's a quick and easy way to get the job done. Buy a rough-textured bathing or exfoliating bath glove and dedicate it for use in the kitchen. The glove cleans away dirt but is relatively gentle and won't scrub away the potato skin.

TIPS FOR BUYING AND STORING POTATOES

BUYING

Look for firm specimens that are free of green spots, sprouts, cracks, and other blemishes. We generally prefer to buy loose potatoes, so we can see what we are getting. Stay away from potatoes in plastic bags, which can act like greenhouses and cause potatoes to sprout, soften, and rot.

STORING

If stored under unsuitable heat and light circumstances, potatoes will germinate and grow. To avoid this, keep potatoes in a cool, dark, dry place. Although some experts warn that refrigerating potatoes can dramatically increase the sugar level, we've never encountered this problem in the test kitchen. Store potatoes in a paper (not plastic) bag and away from onions, which give off gases that will hasten sprouting. Most varieties should keep for several months. The exception is new potatoes—because of their thinner skins, they will keep no more than one month.

WHY DO MY POTATOES TURN GREEN?

The green patches found on some potatoes are caused by prolonged exposure to light or improper storage. This discoloration is produced by chlorophyll and is usually an indication of increased levels of a naturally occurring toxic alkaloid called solanine. Ingesting solanine can lead to illness, so if you discover green patches when peeling your potatoes, simply cut off the affected areas.

Bacon-Wrapped Pork Loin with Warm Dijon Potato Salad

SERVES 4 TO 6

If your pork roast has a thick layer of fat on top, trim the fat until it measure just ⅛ inch thick. We prefer to use small red potatoes measuring about 1 inch in diameter in this recipe, but you can substitute larger red potatoes, cut into ¾-inch chunks.

12	ounces (about 12 slices) bacon
1	(2½- to 3-pound) boneless pork loin roast, trimmed (see note)
2	teaspoons ground fennel seed
	Salt and ground black pepper
2½	pounds small red potatoes (about 15), scrubbed and cut in half
6	tablespoons olive oil
½	cup low-sodium chicken broth
1	medium shallot, minced (about 3 tablespoons)
1½	tablespoons white wine vinegar
2	teaspoons Dijon mustard
	Pinch sugar
¼	cup minced fresh parsley leaves

1. Adjust an oven rack to the upper-middle position and heat the oven to 375 degrees. Lay the bacon on a large microwave-safe plate and weigh it down with a second plate. Microwave the bacon on high power until it is slightly shriveled but still pliable, 1 to 3 minutes. Transfer the bacon to a paper towel–lined plate and let cool slightly.

2. Line a large rimmed baking sheet with aluminum foil. Pat the pork dry with paper towels, rub evenly with the ground fennel, and season with salt and pepper. Lay the roast in the center of the prepared baking sheet. Following the illustrations at right, shingle the bacon attractively over the top of the pork, tucking the ends underneath the roast.

3. Toss the potatoes with 1 tablespoon of the oil and season with salt and pepper to taste. Brush the baking sheet around the pork loin with 1 tablespoon more oil. Lay the potatoes, cut side down, on the baking sheet around the pork. Roast the pork and potatoes until the pork registers 130 degrees on an instant-read thermometer, 40 to 60 minutes, rotating the baking sheet halfway through roasting.

4. Remove the pork and potatoes from the oven, position the oven rack 6 inches from the broiler element, and heat the broiler. Broil the pork and potatoes until the bacon is crisp and browned and the pork registers 140 to 145 on an instant-read thermometer, 3 to 5 minutes.

5. Meanwhile, whisk the remaining ¼ cup oil, broth, shallot, vinegar, mustard, and sugar together in a large microwave-safe bowl. Microwave the dressing (uncovered) on high power until very hot, 1 to 2 minutes. Cover and keep warm until needed.

6. Transfer the pork to a carving board and let rest for 10 minutes. Whisk the warm dressing to recombine, then stir in the roasted potatoes and parsley. Season the potato salad with salt and pepper to taste, cover, and let sit until the potatoes have absorbed the dressing, 5 to 10 minutes. Cut the pork into ½-inch-thick slices and serve with the warm potato salad.

PREPARING A BACON-WRAPPED PORK LOIN

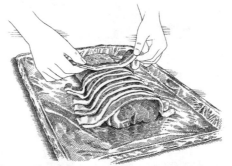

1. Shingle the bacon slices attractively over the top of the pork, overlapping them slightly.

2. Tuck the ends of the bacon slices underneath the roast to secure them.

Parmesan-Crusted Pork Chops with Winter Squash

WHEN DONE RIGHT, BAKED BREADED PORK chops are the ultimate comfort food: tender, moist pork surrounded by a crunchy coating that crackles apart with each bite. But all too often, these chops fall short of that ideal. Opt for the convenience of a packaged product from the supermarket for your breading and the result is a thin, sandy crust. Making your own breading with fresh crumbs can be problematic as well—often you end up with a soggy, patchy crust that won't stick to the meat. Our goal was to cook a juicy, flavorful chop with a crisp, substantial crust that would stay on the meat from fork to mouth. We weren't going to resort to a box of Shake 'N Bake, but we still wanted the chops to be quick and easy weeknight fare.

Our first task was choosing the pork chops. For ease of preparation we decided on boneless chops, which gave us two options: sirloin or center-cut chops. We settled on center-cut, which are widely available and cook more evenly. Chops that were between ¾ and 1 inch thick provided the best ratio of pork to coating.

For the moment, we decided to use the test kitchen's standard breading method (dusting with flour, dipping in beaten egg, and rolling in toasted bread crumbs) while we determined the best cooking technique. Simply breading the chops, tossing them on a sheet pan, and baking made the bottoms soggy. Placing the chops on a wire rack set over the baking sheet definitely helped, as did increasing the oven temperature from 350 to 425 degrees. The coating was now crisp all over.

Up until now we had been making our own bread crumbs in the food processor and toasting them on a baking sheet in the oven until dry and brown. These crumbs produced a good crust, but we wondered if there was an even easier option. Potato chips or crackers are a common shortcut breading; they are already crunchy and are easy to crush by hand or with a mallet. We tested all the usual suspects but found them all to be soggy, bland, greasy, or insubstantial.

Then we thought of panko, Japanese-style bread crumbs. The chops made with panko straight from the bag were pale and didn't have much flavor, but tasters were immediately impressed by the ultra-crisp, coarse but lightweight texture. Toasting the panko would improve color and flavor, for sure, but was there a faster way to do it? Recently in the test kitchen, we've used the microwave to dry and toast bread. We gave it a shot here, tossing the panko with some olive oil, salt, and pepper. After just a few minutes in the microwave, the panko was dark golden brown. A little Parmesan cheese added to the bread crumbs after they had cooled contributed a welcome boost of flavor.

We now needed something more substantial than our plain egg wash to get these thick, coarse crumbs to adhere to the chops. We recalled a recipe that uses mustard instead of eggs; although Dijon gave the chops good flavor, a straight swap was too intense. Keeping the eggs and adding a few tablespoons of Dijon thickened the mixture nicely and contributed just enough mustard flavor to our breading. A little thyme was a welcome final addition. Our coating was now crisp and tasted great—and best of all, it stayed on the chops.

With space on the sheet pan next to the chops, we could round out the dinner with a side. Winter squash came to mind; its creamy texture and sweetness would pair nicely with the pork's crisp coating. We chose small, round acorn squash, which is easy to prep and cut into uniform pieces. We experimented with halving the squash as well as cutting it into 1-inch pieces, but in the end we found it best to quarter the squash. This shape was attractive as well as easy to portion (one quarter per person). Since the squash would take longer to cook than the pork, we gave it a head start in the microwave (a trick we often use for longer-cooking vegetables), cooking the wedges until they just began to soften. Now when the pork was finished cooking, the squash was tender and starting to brown and had a sweeter, more pronounced flavor. To accentuate this sweetness, we brushed the flesh with melted butter and brown sugar before roasting. This mixture caramelized and browned in the oven, giving the squash a burnished, glazed appearance.

Crunchy Parmesan-Crusted Pork Chops with Glazed Winter Squash
SERVES 4

Be sure to leave the bread crumbs uncovered when micro-waving them in step 2 or they will not toast well.

- 2 cups panko bread crumbs
- 2 tablespoons olive oil
  Salt and ground black pepper
- 2 ounces Parmesan cheese, grated (1 cup)
- ¼ cup unbleached all-purpose flour
- 2 large eggs
- 3 tablespoons Dijon mustard
- ½ teaspoon minced fresh thyme leaves or ¼ teaspoon dried
- 4 (6- to 8-ounce) boneless center-cut pork chops, ¾ to 1 inch thick, trimmed and scored (see the illustration on page 241)
- 1 medium acorn squash (about 1½ pounds), quartered lengthwise and seeded (see the illustrations at right)
- 3 tablespoons unsalted butter, melted
- 3 tablespoons dark brown sugar
  Pinch cayenne pepper
  Lemon wedges, for serving

1. Adjust an oven rack to the middle position and heat the oven to 425 degrees. Line a large rimmed baking sheet with aluminum foil. Spray a wire rack with vegetable oil spray and set it in the prepared baking sheet.

2. Toss the bread crumbs with the oil in a shallow microwave-safe dish and season with salt and pepper to taste. Microwave the crumbs on high power, stirring often, until the crumbs are a deep golden brown, 3 to 5 minutes. Let the crumbs cool, then stir in the Parmesan.

3. Spread the flour into a separate shallow dish. In a third shallow dish, whisk the eggs, Dijon, and thyme together. Pat the pork chops dry with paper towels and season with salt and pepper. Working with one chop at a time, dredge in the flour, then dip into the egg mixture, and finally, coat with the toasted crumbs, pressing on them to adhere. Lay the breaded pork chops on one side of the prepared wire rack, spaced at least ½ inch apart.

4. Meanwhile, place the squash, cut side up, on a large microwave-safe plate, brush with 1 tablespoon of the melted butter, and season with salt and pepper to taste. Microwave the squash on high power until it begins to soften but still holds its shape, 8 to 10 minutes.

5. Arrange the squash, cut side up, on the prepared wire rack opposite the pork. Stir the remaining 2 tablespoons melted butter, sugar, and cayenne together, then brush over the squash.

6. Bake the pork chops and squash until the chops register 140 to 145 degrees on an instant-read thermometer and the squash is lightly browned and tender, 18 to 25 minutes. Let the chops and squash rest on the rack for 5 minutes, then serve with the lemon wedges.

CUTTING ACORN SQUASH SAFELY

1. Hard squash can be difficult (and dangerous) to prep. To cut the squash open safely, place it on a damp kitchen towel (which will hold it in place) and position the knife on top.

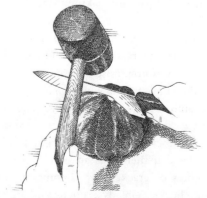

2. Strike the back of the knife with a rubber mallet to drive it into the squash. Continue to hit the knife with the mallet until the knife cuts through the squash. Once halved, you can easily remove the seeds and continue to cut up the squash as desired.

STUFFED CHICKEN BREASTS WITH ROASTED CARROTS

WHILE WE LOVE BREADED AND STUFFED chicken breasts, sometimes we yearn for similar results from an easier approach—a recipe that can be assembled quickly on a weeknight rather than saved for a special occasion. We wanted a no-fuss cheese filling and a simple method for stuffing the chicken—without butterflying and pounding chicken breasts or even breading them. And while we were at it, we planned on roasting a side dish along with the chicken to make a complete meal.

First we needed to figure out how to fill the chicken breasts. Although chicken breasts are commonly boned before being stuffed, research yielded a fair amount of bone-in recipes. It seemed worth a try since using bone-in chicken had great potential for moist, flavorful meat and we love the crisp, roasted skin of bone-in chicken. We had come across several recipes that called for cutting a pocket into the breasts just above the bone and others that stuffed the filling under the skin. First, we tried cutting a pocket into the breast and packing our working filling inside. The results were acceptable, but making a hole big enough to hold a decent amount of stuffing without tearing apart the breast was difficult, and packing the stuffing in was awkward. Moreover, a significant amount of the filling oozed out.

Still with high hopes, we tried the under-skin option—after all, there is already a natural pocket in place. Working carefully, we loosened the skin and fit about 1½ tablespoons of the cheese mixture underneath. The skin held the filling in place, and when the chicken emerged from the oven it was moist and tender, with a creamy, tangy, saucelike filling. And while we normally brine bone-in, skin-on chicken breasts to further ensure moist meat, we found that with the creamy filling, which basted the breasts as they cooked, this step wasn't necessary—the meat was perfectly moist and juicy. Our results were near flawless, but one problem remained—the skin was flabby and inedible.

We wondered if increasing the oven temperature would help to crisp up the skin. We had been baking the chicken breasts at 375 degrees, so next we tried cooking the chicken at 400 degrees, 425 degrees, and 450 degrees. The skin on the chicken cooked at 450 degrees was golden brown and crisp and the meat was perfectly cooked. We also tried brushing both oil and melted butter on the skin. Both encouraged browning, but butter was the clear winner for flavor.

With our method in place, we could focus on perfecting the flavor of the stuffing. Traditional recipes stuff the chicken with butter or cream cheese spiked with nothing more than parsley. Tasters preferred cream cheese for its creaminess and tang, but its flavor is mild so we tried adding a variety of ingredients, including other cheeses. We quickly discovered that melting cheeses such as cheddar tended to ooze out from under the skin, even when combined with the cream cheese. Goat cheese and Parmesan, however, were winners, in terms of both flavor and binding ability. As for other ingredients, tasters favored bold additions—chopped kalamata olives and heady oregano paired well with the goat cheese, while olive oil and a generous quantity of basil complemented our Parmesan filling.

Next, we looked for a side dish to pair with the chicken; we decided on roasted carrots, thinking that their earthy sweetness would be an excellent counterpoint to the potent flavors of the filling. Baby carrots offered convenience, but once cooked, these carrots were shy on both flavor and good looks. Instead, we peeled regular carrots and cut them on the bias into ovals; not only did this look elegant, but the shape allowed all the pieces to cook evenly. The ½-inch ovals also cooked more quickly than larger chunks, so the carrots finished cooking at the same time as the chicken. Tossed with a little butter and brown sugar for added sweetness, these simple roasted carrots were the perfect match for our stuffed chicken breasts.

Olive and Goat Cheese Stuffed Chicken Breasts with Roasted Carrots

SERVES 4

It is important to buy chicken breasts with the skin still attached and intact, otherwise the stuffing will leak out. Try to buy chicken breasts of similar size so that they will cook at the same rate.

3	ounces goat cheese, softened (¾ cup)
2	ounces cream cheese, softened (¼ cup)
¼	cup pitted kalamata olives (see the illustration on page 289), chopped fine
2	teaspoons minced fresh oregano leaves
1	small garlic clove, minced or pressed through a garlic press (about ½ teaspoon)
	Salt and ground black pepper
4	(10- to 12-ounce) bone-in, skin-on split chicken breasts, trimmed (see the illustration on page 48) (see note)
2	tablespoons unsalted butter, melted
1½	pounds carrots (about 9 medium), peeled, trimmed, and sliced ½ inch thick on the bias
1	tablespoon dark brown sugar
	Lemon wedges, for serving

1. Adjust an oven rack to the middle position and heat the oven to 450 degrees. Line a large rimmed baking sheet with aluminum foil. Mix the goat cheese, cream cheese, olives, oregano, garlic, ⅛ teaspoon salt, and ⅛ teaspoon pepper together in a small bowl.

2. Pat the chicken dry with paper towels, season with salt and pepper, then gently loosen the center portion of skin covering each breast following the illustrations at right. Using a spoon, place a quarter of the goat cheese mixture underneath the skin over the center of each chicken breast. Gently press on the skin to spread out the goat cheese.

3. Arrange the chicken, skin side up, on one side of the baking sheet. Brush the chicken with 1 tablespoon of the melted butter. Toss the carrots with the remaining 1 tablespoon melted butter and sugar and season with salt and pepper to taste. Spread the carrots in an even layer on the baking sheet, opposite the chicken.

4. Bake until the chicken registers 160 to 165 degrees on an instant-read thermometer and the carrots are browned and tender, 30 to 35 minutes, rotating the pan and stirring the carrots halfway through baking. Let the chicken and carrots rest on the baking sheet for 5 minutes, then serve with the lemon wedges.

➤ VARIATION

Parmesan and Basil Stuffed Chicken Breasts with Roasted Carrots

Follow the recipe for Olive and Goat Cheese Stuffed Chicken Breasts with Roasted Carrots, omitting the goat cheese, olives, and oregano. Add 2 ounces grated Parmesan cheese (1 cup), ¼ cup chopped fresh basil leaves, and 2 tablespoons extra-virgin olive oil to the cream cheese mixture in step 1.

FLAVORING CHICKEN BREASTS UNDER THE SKIN

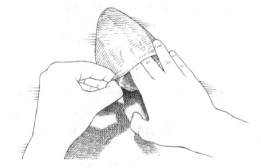

1. Using your fingers, gently loosen the center portion of the skin covering each breast, making a pocket for the filling or flavored butter.

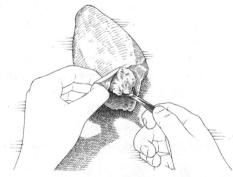

2. Using a spoon, place the filling or flavored butter underneath the loosened skin, over the center of each chicken breast. Gently press on the skin to spread out the filling or butter.

"Un-Stuffed" Chicken Breasts with Broccoli

HAVING DEVELOPED A RECIPE FOR SIMPLE stuffed bone-in chicken breasts (see page 12), we wondered if we could develop a similarly easy recipe using boneless breasts; after all, boneless, skinless chicken breasts are a weeknight staple—they require little in the way of prep and they cook quickly. Before heading to the kitchen, we laid out a general game plan for our streamlined recipe: Instead of stuffing the chicken breasts, we decided to top the breasts with the stuffing—an inside-out approach—to keep the work to a minimum. The chicken and stuffing would have to be flavorful enough to stand on their own, without a pan sauce. We also wanted a crisp, appealing coating (without the fuss or mess of breading and frying). Finally, since we hoped to turn this dish into a complete meal without using multiple pans, we needed to find a vegetable that would cook in the same amount of time as the chicken.

Having settled on boneless, skinless chicken breasts, we first turned our attention to the "stuffing," or topping. Taking a cue from classic chicken cordon bleu, we zeroed in on a topping of thin-sliced ham and Gruyère cheese and added Dijon mustard for its peppery tang.

To make our topping, we brushed the chicken with the mustard, then added layers of ham and Gruyère cheese. We first tried slices of Gruyère, but they tended to slide off the chicken; shredded cheese adhered better. For the crisp coating, we only briefly considered homemade bread crumbs. They require pulsing in a food processor and toasting in the oven, and we hoped to find a less fussy alternative. We wanted something that was already crisp and flavorful, so we considered convenience products that we could crush and use as is. Potato chips, Melba toast, and Ritz crackers all filled the bill, so we gave them each a shot. The potato chips were too greasy and the Melba was too dry, but the Ritz crackers were perfect, with a buttery flavor and just the right amount of crunch. We mounded the crushed cracker crumbs on top and pressed down to help them stick. The crumbs added the flavor (and visual appeal) of a breaded and fried stuffed chicken breast.

We found it easiest to arrange the breasts on the sheet pan before topping them. We nestled the breasts side by side on one half of the sheet pan (alternating their orientation, thicker end to thinner end, so they fit together like puzzle pieces). This method made the least mess and ensured that the topping stayed put—and perhaps more importantly, it also left space for the side dish.

We tested oven temperatures ranging from 400 to 475 degrees and quickly discovered that a higher oven temperature of 475 was best. Initially, we were concerned that the chicken would dry out at such a high temperature, but the nestled arrangement of the breasts and the insulation from the toppings kept it moist.

As for a side dish, we thought that broccoli would be a good match. Broccoli stands up well to roasting, and the high heat we were using to cook the chicken was just right for caramelizing the natural sugars in the broccoli and concentrating its flavor. Contact with the hot pan would be the key to browning, so we made sure to cut the broccoli in a way that would maximize its surface area. Starting with a large bunch of broccoli, we sliced each crown in half, and then cut each half into uniform wedges. Turning our attention to the stalk, we sliced off the tough exterior then cut the stalk into long ½-inch-thick pieces to help promote even cooking. We then tossed the broccoli with olive oil, salt, and pepper before spreading it out in a single layer next to the chicken.

By the time the chicken had reached 160 degrees and was ready to come out of the oven (about 20 minutes later), both the stalk pieces and crown wedges were tender and evenly cooked through. However, the broccoli hadn't browned quite as much as we had hoped. Raising the oven temperature or preheating the baking sheet could help, but we didn't want to interfere with the cooking of the chicken. We wondered if a scant amount of sugar sprinkled over the broccoli would promote browning. This simple step resulted in the best broccoli yet: blistered, bubbled, and browned stalk pieces that were sweet and full-flavored, along with crisp-tipped crowns that tasted even better.

For a variation, we incorporated some Italian-inspired flavors, swapping in prosciutto and sharp provolone for the ham and Gruyère, and a sage-flavored mayonnaise for the Dijon. Paired with the roasted broccoli, both versions are easy, full of flavor, and bound to become staples in your weekly repertoire.

Ham and Gruyère "Un-Stuffed" Chicken Breasts with Roasted Broccoli

SERVES 4

Swiss cheese can be substituted for the Gruyère. Nestle the chicken breasts close together on the baking sheet and alternate their orientation (thicker end to thinner end) so that they fit together nicely like puzzle pieces. This will help the toppings stay in place, prevent the chicken from overcooking, and allow a little extra space for the broccoli.

3	tablespoons olive oil
1½	pounds broccoli (1 large bunch), crown and stalk separated, crown cut into large wedges (see the illustrations at right), stalk peeled and sliced into ½-inch-thick planks about 3 inches long
½	teaspoon sugar
	Salt and ground black pepper
4	(6-ounce) boneless, skinless chicken breasts, trimmed
2	tablespoons Dijon mustard
4	slices (about 4 ounces) deli ham
4	ounces Gruyère cheese, grated (1 cup)
15	Ritz crackers, coarsely crushed (about ¾ cup)
	Lemon wedges, for serving

1. Adjust an oven rack to the lower-middle position and heat the oven to 475 degrees. Brush a large rimmed baking sheet with 1 tablespoon of the oil.

2. Toss the broccoli with the remaining 2 tablespoons oil and sugar and season with salt and pepper to taste. Pat the chicken dry with paper towels and season with salt and pepper.

3. Arrange the chicken breasts, side by side (and alternating thicker end to thinner end) on one side of the baking sheet. Spread the mustard over the top of the chicken, then top each breast with a slice of ham and ¼ cup of the cheese. Sprinkle the cracker crumbs over the cheese and press on the crumbs to adhere.

4. Lay the broccoli, cut side down, in an even layer on the baking sheet, opposite the chicken. Bake until the chicken registers 160 to 165 degrees on an instant-read thermometer and the broccoli is well-browned and tender, 20 to 25 minutes, rotating the pan halfway through baking. Let the chicken and broccoli rest on the baking sheet for 5 minutes, then serve with the lemon wedges.

PREPARING A BROCCOLI CROWN FOR ROASTING

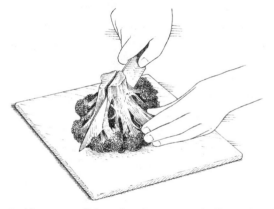

1. After cutting off the stalk and setting it aside (do not discard), place the broccoli crown upside down, then cut it in half through the central stalk.

2. Cut each half of the broccoli crown into 3 or 4 wedges if it measures 3 to 4 inches in diameter, or into 6 wedges if it measures 4 to 5 inches in diameter.

➤ VARIATION

Prosciutto and Sage "Un-Stuffed" Chicken Breasts with Roasted Broccoli

Follow the recipe for Ham and Gruyère "Un-Stuffed" Chicken Breasts with Roasted Broccoli, substituting 2 tablespoons mayonnaise for the mustard, 8 thin slices (about 2 ounces) prosciutto for the ham (use 2 slices of prosciutto per chicken breast), and 4 ounces shredded sharp provolone (1 cup) for the Gruyère. Sprinkle 1 tablespoon minced fresh sage leaves on top of the mayonnaise-coated chicken before adding the prosciutto.

GLAZED CHICKEN WITH SWEET POTATOES

GLAZED CHICKEN IS STANDARD WEEKNIGHT fare for many families, but more often than not, it's a mediocre affair consisting of candy-sweet glaze, dry meat, and flabby skin. We hoped to update this classic dish and develop a flavorful, super-easy glazed chicken dinner (side included) that would appeal to the entire family.

Right off the bat, we decided to give the customary glazed chicken breast a rest. In addition to being more flavorful, dark meat is very forgiving, remaining moist even when cooked beyond doneness. Although drumsticks are sometimes overlooked in favor of the meatier (and more skillet-friendly) thighs, we thought they would be perfect for this recipe since they are readily available in bulk, affordable, and—with their built-in handle—kid-friendly.

For the glaze, we hoped to rely strictly on pantry ingredients. A combination of honey, yellow mustard, and soy sauce was pleasantly sweet and tangy; adding a little cornstarch and heating it in the microwave thickened our glaze just enough to ensure it would cling to the chicken instead of collect in a pool on the pan.

The simplest recipes for glazed chicken we uncovered in our research were "dump-and-bake" versions. The glaze (often a jar of fruit preserves) is poured over the raw chicken and baked. This approach seemed dubious but we gave it a shot, coating the drumsticks with the glaze and throwing them in the oven. Not surprisingly, they emerged with skin that was flabby and pale. It was clear the skin needed to render and brown before the glaze was applied, so we gave the chicken a head start in the oven. But no matter how crisp the skin became, it turned flabby once the glaze was added. Then it struck us: One bonus of keeping the skin on is that it protects the meat from the heat of the oven and prevents it from drying out. But since a glaze does the same thing, should we get rid of the skin entirely?

For our next test, we skinned the drumsticks before coating them with the glaze and baking. This method produced promising results; the glaze had insulated the meat and kept it moist. Although some of the glaze ran off as the chicken cooked and released its juices, a thin coating had hardened into a crust directly on the meat—a perfect "primer" to which another application of glaze could adhere.

While some recipes call for continually basting the chicken at the end of cooking, after some experimentation we were happy to find that a single additional layer, brushed over the chicken halfway through cooking, was all it needed; the glaze now clung to the crust to form a glossy, thick coating.

With our glazing technique settled, we tested oven temperatures. Starting at a modest 325 degrees, we tested incrementally higher temperatures, and found that 450 gave us the best results. The high heat concentrated the glaze, resulting in deep browning and caramelization, and yet the chicken, protected by the glaze, stayed juicy. To make cleanup easy (given the sticky glaze), we lined the baking sheet with foil.

With our drumsticks ready to go, we turned our focus to an accompaniment. We liked the idea of sweet potatoes—roasting gives them a caramelized exterior and a smooth, creamy interior, and their earthy sweetness needs little enhancement.

Potatoes are commonly cut into wedges for roasting, which allows many pieces to fit on a rimmed baking sheet. But we found wedges less than ideal since they cooked through unevenly. Slicing peeled sweet potatoes into rounds was the best way to ensure perfectly even cooking, since we made each round the same width. In addition, this shape maximized contact with the hot pan, promoting further caramelization.

When we put the sweet potatoes in the oven at the same time as the chicken, they were still starchy and fibrous in the center by the time the chicken was ready. Covering them with foil helped speed up cooking, but they failed to brown or develop a crust, even when the foil was removed halfway through. The solution turned out to be parcooking the sweet potatoes in the microwave to give them a head start before roasting them uncovered the whole time. Now, when the chicken was done, the sweet potatoes were perfectly tender, with a slightly crisp, caramelized exterior. Aside from a sprinkling of salt, pepper, and cayenne, these sweet spuds needed no adornment. Served with our burnished chicken, this is an easy weeknight dinner that will earn rave reviews from diners of all ages.

Honey Mustard–Glazed Chicken Drumsticks with Sweet Potato Coins

SERVES 4

Chicken drumsticks come in various sizes; if your chicken drumsticks are smaller than 6 ounces each, you may need to adjust the baking time. If you opt not to peel the sweet potatoes, be sure to scrub them well before slicing.

2	pounds sweet potatoes (about 4 small), peeled, trimmed, and sliced into ¾-inch-thick rounds (see note)
2	tablespoons vegetable oil
¼	teaspoon cayenne pepper
	Salt and ground black pepper
½	cup honey
¼	cup soy sauce
¼	cup yellow mustard
2	teaspoons cornstarch
8	(6-ounce) chicken drumsticks, skin removed

1. Adjust an oven rack to the middle position and heat the oven to 450 degrees. Line a large rimmed baking sheet with aluminum foil and spray with vegetable oil spray (or use nonstick foil).

2. Toss the sweet potatoes with the oil and cayenne, season with salt and pepper to taste, and arrange in a single layer on a large microwave-safe plate. Microwave the potatoes on high power until they begin to soften but still hold their shape, 6 to 8 minutes, flipping them halfway through cooking.

3. Whisk the honey, soy sauce, mustard, and cornstarch together in a large microwave-safe bowl. Microwave the glaze on high power, whisking occasionally, until slightly thickened, 3 to 5 minutes. Let the glaze cool slightly.

4. Pat the chicken dry with paper towels, season with salt and pepper, and toss with half of the glaze. Arrange the chicken on one side of the baking sheet. Spread the sweet potatoes in a single layer on the baking sheet, opposite the chicken. Roast the chicken and sweet potatoes for 20 minutes.

5. Brush the chicken with the remaining glaze and carefully flip the sweet potatoes over with a spatula. Continue to roast the chicken and potatoes until the glaze is well browned, the chicken registers 175 degrees on an instant-read thermometer, and the sweet potatoes are lightly browned, 15 to 20 minutes longer. Let the chicken and sweet potatoes rest on the baking sheet for 5 minutes before serving.

LEMON-HERB COD FILLETS WITH CRISPY GARLIC POTATOES

THE COMBINATION OF COD AND POTATOES seems like a natural candidate for a sheet pan dinner; the duo is a classic pairing and cooking both fish fillets and potatoes on a sheet pan is standard practice in the test kitchen. Cooking them together on the same pan at once, however, presents a challenge: Fish cooks quickly while potatoes take quite a bit more time. Try to cook them together and the result is rubbery fish and rock-hard potatoes. And while the clean flavor and lean nature of cod is much of its appeal, it runs the risk of tasting plain. Could we find a way to boost the flavor of mild cod and cook both the fish and potatoes using just one pan?

Putting aside flavor for the moment, we focused on finding a cooking method that would deliver perfectly cooked potatoes and fish. We already knew that just throwing them in the oven together wouldn't work. And since chunks of potato would need a significant amount of time in the oven to become tender and spotty brown before the fish fillets could be added, we figured that slicing the potatoes thin would speed up the process. Additionally, slicing the potatoes would allow us to take advantage of the large surface area of the baking sheet, exposing more of the potatoes' flesh to the dry heat of the oven and the hot pan. We hoped this would result in some browning and crisping.

After a few tests, we settled on ¼-inch-thick potato slices—thin enough to cook quickly but thick enough to cut by hand without the aid of special equipment. Instead of spreading the potatoes across the oiled baking sheet in a single layer, we shingled them into four individual piles that would serve as a bed for each piece of cod. When the potatoes were tender and starting to brown (which took about 30 minutes in a 425-degree oven), we placed the fish on top and put the sheet pan back in the oven. Cod is a relatively wet fish, so it stands up well to high heat; 10 minutes later it was perfectly cooked and moist.

In an effort to speed up the cooking time of the potatoes (and thus save time overall), we tried covering them with foil during the initial stint in the oven. This method did cut the cooking time, but it also inhibited browning, so we ditched it. Tasters preferred the textural variation of the uncovered potatoes, which resulted in a combination of crisp golden potatoes that remained exposed to the heat of the oven and the creamy, soft potatoes that were under the fish.

Up to this point, russets had been our potato of choice, but we were curious to see if other varieties might be better. We tried red potatoes and Yukon Golds, but tasters found both a bit waxy. The traditional russet, with its tender bite and earthy flavor, was the unanimous favorite. Russets also formed tighter, more cohesive layers owing to their higher starch content. This allowed us to slide a spatula under the potatoes and fish and serve the whole thing intact for an attractive presentation.

EQUIPMENT: Spatulas

Few people give much thought to choosing a good turner-style spatula. Because spatulas are fairly cheap, most people own a drawer full of assorted styles and brands. But wouldn't it be better to own just two perfect spatulas—metal as well as plastic for nonstick pans—that feel natural and make cooking easier?

To this end, we scooped up nearly two dozen tools costing between $2 and $38: traditional short order–style squared-off metal turners, thin-bladed fish spatulas with long heads and short grips, even a spatula made entirely of wires. We ran them through a battery of tests—maneuvering fried eggs, sliding them under fresh-baked cookies, and then on to pans of lasagna, fluffy pancakes, and oversize hamburgers.

We came to several conclusions. A good spatula must have a slim—but not too narrow—front edge that can slip under any food with ease. A rectangular, well-proportioned head offers support without compromising dexterity. Handles measuring roughly 6 inches and a total length of about 11 inches provided enough distance to keep us safe while letting the spatula maneuver as a natural extension of our hands. We preferred only a slight offset to the grip; in fact, the handles on our top-rated spatulas extended nearly straight out from the head. Steeper angles limited our movement, especially in small or deep pans.

In general, we liked models with flexible heads, which can bend slightly and slide under foods in any kind of pan. The slotted metal head on the Wüsthof Gourmet Turner/Fish Spatula was a bit stiffer but sported a gentle curve that yielded the same result. Besides, a little stiffness could actually be a good thing; spatulas that were too flexible threatened to drop their cargo. In the end, we flipped for the fish spatulas, in particular the sleek agility and gently cradled heads of the metal Wüsthof and plastic Matfer Bourgeat Pelton, which both performed well beyond their job descriptions and vastly outperformed the others.

THE BEST SPATULAS

WÜSTHOF   MATFER BOURGEAT

The maneuverability, surgical precision, and crisp, high-end construction of the Wüsthof Gourmet Turner/Fish Spatula ($29.95) simply could not be beat. The Matfer Bourgeat Pelton Spatula ($7.50) was our favorite plastic spatula; comfortable from any angle, this spatula boasts a thin front edge and moderately flexible head with a slight upward tilt that kept food secure.

Now that our fish and potatoes were cooked to perfection, it was time to focus on infusing them with flavor. We kept the potatoes simple: a little olive oil, garlic, salt, and pepper were all they needed. The lean fish, however, could benefit from a more substantial preparation. We decided that a compound butter would add plenty of flavor and richness. We stirred minced thyme and lemon juice into softened butter and rubbed it on the fish before baking. This kept the fish moist and added flavor, but the thyme didn't spend long enough in the oven to mellow; tasters thought it overwhelmed the mild cod. Nevertheless, they liked the flavor combination, so we just needed an alternate method of incorporating it. Backing up, we considered the layered arrangement of fish and potatoes. What if we took each component of the herb butter—butter, thyme, and lemon—and layered them on top of the fish? After placing the cod on the potatoes, we scattered pieces of butter on top, then topped each fillet with a sprig of thyme, followed by a few slices of lemon. This technique was a success: the butter and lemon basted the fish as it baked, as the thyme gently flavored the fish. This method not only worked better than the compound butter, it was much easier; no chopping herbs or waiting for the butter to soften. Best of all, the rustic, layered appearance of the dish was impressive—an elegant presentation for an extremely simple one-dish meal.

Lemon-Herb Cod Fillets with Crispy Garlic Potatoes

SERVES 4

Halibut or haddock can be substituted for the cod.

3	tablespoons olive oil
1½	pounds russet potatoes (about 3 medium), scrubbed and sliced into ¼-inch-thick rounds
3	medium garlic cloves, minced or pressed through a garlic press (about 1 tablespoon) Salt and ground black pepper
4	(6-ounce) skinless cod fillets, 1 to 1½ inches thick
3	tablespoons unsalted butter, cut into ¼-inch pieces
4	sprigs fresh thyme
1	lemon, sliced thin

1. Adjust an oven rack to the lower-middle position and heat the oven to 425 degrees. Brush a large rimmed baking sheet with 1 tablespoon of the oil.

2. In a large bowl, toss the potatoes with the remaining 2 tablespoons oil and garlic and season with salt and pepper to taste. Following the illustrations below, shingle the potatoes into 4 rectangular piles that measure roughly 4 by 6 inches. Roast the potatoes until they are spotty brown and just tender, 30 to 35 minutes, rotating the baking sheet halfway through roasting.

SHINGLING POTATOES FOR LEMON-HERB COD

1. Shingle potato slices in 3 tight rows, measuring roughly 4 by 6 inches.

2. Gently push the rows together so that the potatoes are tidy and cohesive.

3. Carefully place a cod fillet, skinned side down, on top of each set of parcooked potatoes. Top the fish with the butter pieces, thyme springs, and lemon slices.

3. Pat the cod dry with paper towels and season with salt and pepper. Carefully place a cod fillet, skinned side down, on top of each potato pile. Top the fish with the butter pieces, thyme sprigs, and lemon slices. Continue to bake the fish and potatoes until the fish flakes apart when gently prodded with a paring knife, about 15 minutes.

4. Slide a spatula underneath the potatoes and fish and gently transfer to individual plates and serve.

Oven-Roasted Salmon and Vegetables

SALMON HAS BECOME ONE OF AMERICA'S favorite fish. The reason for its popularity is simple: Salmon is rich-tasting and flavorful without being aggressively fishy. Pan-searing is a favorite cooking method for restaurants, as the salmon's flesh cooks up tender with a flavorful, caramelized crust, giving you a final result with great textural contrast. But achieving the same professional-level results in a skillet on the stovetop can be a challenge for the home cook. We wondered if swapping the skillet for a sheet pan and the stovetop for the oven might make the process easier and more foolproof but still give us the same perfectly cooked, golden-crusted fish.

We knew that roasting at a high temperature (from 400 to 475 degrees) can create browning on the exterior of the fish, but by the time that point is reached, you've got a well-done piece of salmon. Slow-roasting at a very gentle oven temperature, between 250 and 300 degrees, seemed like a better place to start. To ensure uniform pieces that would cook evenly, we began by buying a whole center-cut fillet, dividing it into four pieces, and cooking them at 275 degrees for about 20 minutes. This method resulted in moist, near-translucent flesh through and through, but the fish was a little mushy, and there was no contrast in texture whatsoever. Cranking the temperature higher would definitely create a more golden exterior, but it would also sacrifice some of the medium-rare flesh inside.

Perhaps a hybrid cooking technique combining high and low heat would work. After a bit of experimentation, we settled on a starting temperature of 500 degrees, which we reduced to 275 degrees immediately upon placing the fish in the oven. The initial blast of high heat firmed the exterior of the salmon and helped render some of the excess fat that had made the slower-roasted fish mushy. To prevent the oven temperature from dropping too rapidly, we also preheated the baking sheet. This necessitated cooking the fish with its skin on, so the fillets could be placed skin side down in the pan to protect the flesh. The fish tasted a little too fatty on the first try with this new approach, but making several slits through the skin before placing it in the pan allowed most of the fat residing directly beneath the skin to render onto the baking sheet.

MAKING A FOIL PACKET

1. Spread the moistened, seasoned vegetables over half of a large piece of aluminum foil that measures roughly 18 by 24 inches.

2. Fold the foil over the vegetables, then fold the edges several times to seal the vegetables inside a large, flat packet.

PREPARING A WHOLE SALMON FILLET FOR OVEN-ROASTING

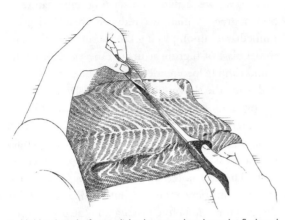

1. Hold a sharp knife at a slight downward angle to the flesh and cut off the whitish, fatty portion of the belly.

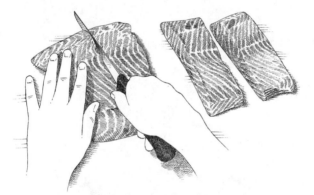

2. Cut the salmon fillet into 4 pieces of equal size to help ensure that they cook at the same rate.

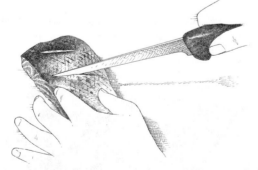

3. Using a sharp knife (or serrated knife), make 4 or 5 shallow slashes along the skin side of each piece of fish, being careful not to cut into the flesh.

The fish then gently cooked while the oven temperature slowly dropped. Though the temperature was never really in a range that we would consider true slow-roasting, this technique did rely on the declining ambient temperature, as opposed to constant heat, to slowly cook the fish. It worked beautifully; we now had salmon with a little firmness on the outside and a lot of moist, succulent meat on the inside.

Next we set out to dress up our perfectly cooked salmon and add a side dish to make it a complete meal. We dismissed spice rubs and glazes, which require sustained high heat to fully flavor the fish. We tried several marinades, but their impact was too subtle. A quick, bright Asian-flavored vinaigrette was the answer. After testing a few different ingredient combinations, we found that a vinaigrette with a strong acidic presence, a generous amount of fresh herbs, and a touch of heat worked best to balance the richness of the fish. In addition to soy sauce, we settled on a sweet-sour combination of rice vinegar, sugar, Asian chili paste, ginger, minced cilantro, and scallions.

For our side dish, we wanted something simple and clean. Snow peas dressed up with a few elegant matchsticks of carrot sounded appealing and were in keeping with the Asian theme of the vinaigrette. We tried tossing the snow peas directly on the sheet pan with the salmon, but they were army green, limp, and sitting in a pool of rendered salmon fat by the time the salmon was done. To preserve their color and texture, we decided to cook the snow peas and carrots in a foil packet (sometimes called a hobo pack). We scattered the vegetables over half of a large piece of foil and folded it in half, tightly crimping the edges to make a flat rectangular packet that fit perfectly on the sheet pan next to the salmon. Tossing the vegetables with water facilitated steaming so that by the time the salmon was done, the snow peas were cooked through but still crisp-tender. A touch of sesame oil and a sprinkle of sesame seeds were all that the vegetables required before serving.

Oven-Roasted Salmon with Soy-Herb Vinaigrette, Snow Peas, and Carrots

SERVES 4

To ensure uniform pieces of salmon that cook at the same rate, buy a whole center-cut fillet and cut it into 4 pieces. It is important to keep the salmon skin on during cooking; however, you can remove it before serving if desired.

SALMON AND VEGETABLES

12	ounces snow peas, tips and strings removed (see the illustration on page 50)
2	carrots, peeled and cut into 2-inch-long matchsticks
¼	cup water
	Salt and ground black pepper
1	(1¾- to 2-pound) skin-on salmon fillet, about 1½ inches thick (see note)
2	teaspoons vegetable oil
1	teaspoon toasted sesame oil
1	teaspoon toasted sesame seeds (optional)

VINAIGRETTE

¼	cup minced fresh cilantro leaves
2	scallions, minced
3	tablespoons rice vinegar
3	tablespoons vegetable oil
1	tablespoon soy sauce
2	teaspoons sugar
1	teaspoon sambal oelek chili paste (see page 230)
¼	teaspoon minced or grated fresh ginger (see the illustrations on page 216)

1. FOR THE SALMON AND VEGETABLES: Adjust an oven rack to the lowest position, place a large rimmed baking sheet on the rack, and heat the oven to 500 degrees. Toss the snow peas and carrots with the water and season with salt and pepper to taste. Following the illustrations on page 19, seal the vegetables inside a large flat aluminum foil packet.

2. Following the illustrations on page 20, trim the salmon fillet, cut it into four equal pieces, and make several shallow slashes through the skin of each piece. Pat the salmon dry with paper towels. Rub the fillets evenly with the vegetable oil and season with salt and pepper.

3. Reduce the oven temperature to 275 degrees. Working quickly, lay the salmon, skin side down, on one side of the hot baking sheet. Lay the foil packet of vegetables on the baking sheet, opposite the salmon. Roast the salmon and vegetables until the salmon is translucent in the very center when cut into with a paring knife and registers 125 degrees on an instant-read thermometer, 9 to 13 minutes.

4. FOR THE VINAIGRETTE: Whisk all the ingredients together in a small bowl.

5. Transfer the salmon to individual plates and spoon some of the vinaigrette over the top of each piece. Carefully open the foil packet (watch for steam), transfer the vegetables to a serving bowl, and toss with the sesame oil and sesame seeds (if using). Serve the salmon and vegetables, passing the remaining vinaigrette separately.

BROILED SALMON BURGERS WITH ASPARAGUS

SALMON BURGERS MADE WITH FRESH SALMON are an appealing alternative way to enjoy this popular fish. While they are often pan-fried or grilled, we wondered if moving them to the oven would give us room to cook up a side dish at the same time. We were after a complete meal featuring burgers that were packed with salmon, not binders, and were perfectly cooked through.

The first issue was how to chop the salmon. We tried cutting it into fine pieces, and this salmon packed together well—too well. The result was dense burgers. But chopping the salmon into larger pieces resulted in burgers that didn't hold together. Instead, we turned to the food processor. Processing the salmon gave us a mix of fine and larger pieces that held together but cooked up tender, not tough. Dividing the salmon into two batches gave us greater control over the texture and prevented overprocessing.

As for a binder, we wanted as little as possible. Most of the recipes we found used some combination of mayonnaise, egg, and bread crumbs, but these recipes yielded soggy, mushy burgers. The mayonnaise was adding much-needed moisture, but the egg seemed less helpful—it only made the burgers wet, requiring more bread crumbs. We made a batch of burgers without the egg, which allowed us to decrease the bread crumbs to a single slice of bread. Despite the minimal binder, these burgers had no trouble staying together.

For seasonings, we wanted to enhance the salmon but not overwhelm it. In addition to minced shallot and parsley, tasters liked the piquancy of a little Dijon mustard and some minced capers to balance the richness of the salmon.

When it comes to cooking, salmon burgers don't need much of it. Broiling was clearly the best option; the direct heat would brown the exterior as much as possible without overcooking the interior.

Before we could cook the burgers, we needed to take care of the side dish. Given the main course and the cooking method, asparagus was a no-brainer. Asparagus is a classic accompaniment to salmon, and broiling is an ideal way to cook it. The intense dry heat concentrates the flavor of the asparagus and gives it a slightly crisp, caramelized exterior. One bunch of asparagus was just enough for four people and fit perfectly in a single layer next to the burgers.

The only question left was how far to place the oven rack from the broiler. We decided to start at a somewhat conservative distance of five inches and work our way up. As we anticipated, there was little browning on either the asparagus or the burgers at this distance. Four inches was better; the burger was spotty brown and the spears had just started to color by the time both were cooked through. Three inches was the best; after 10 minutes (flipping the burgers and turning the spears halfway through) the burgers and asparagus were lightly browned on the outside and perfectly cooked inside. Fast and simple yet flavorful and satisfying, our one-dish salmon burgers with asparagus make quick work of dinner any night of the week.

Broiled Salmon Burgers with Asparagus
SERVES 4

Be sure to use raw salmon here; do not substitute cooked or canned salmon. Don't overprocess the salmon in step 2 or the burgers will have a pasty texture. Lay the salmon burgers close together on the baking sheet so that the asparagus has a little extra space for browning.

1	slice high-quality white sandwich bread, torn into 1-inch pieces
1	pound skinless salmon, cut into 1-inch chunks (see note)
1	medium shallot, minced (about 3 tablespoons)
2	tablespoons mayonnaise
2	tablespoons minced fresh parsley leaves
1	tablespoon Dijon mustard
2	teaspoons capers, rinsed and minced
	Salt and ground black pepper
1	pound asparagus (about 1 bunch), tough ends trimmed
1	teaspoon olive oil
	Lemon wedges, for serving

1. Position an oven rack 3 inches from the broiler element and heat the broiler. Pulse the bread in a food processor to coarse crumbs, about 4 pulses, and transfer to a large bowl (you should have about ¾ cup crumbs).

REMOVING SKIN FROM SALMON

Starting at one end of the fillet, slide the knife between the skin and flesh, until you can grab hold of the skin with a paper towel. Holding the skin firmly, continue to cut the flesh from the skin until it is completely removed.

2. Wipe the food processor clean, add half of the salmon, and pulse until there is an even mix of finely minced and coarsely chopped pieces, about 4 pulses; transfer to the bowl with the bread crumbs. Repeat with the remaining salmon, then transfer to the bowl and toss to combine.

3. Whisk the shallot, mayonnaise, parsley, mustard, capers, ½ teaspoon salt, and ⅛ teaspoon pepper together in a small bowl, then gently fold the mixture into the salmon until well combined. Divide the salmon mixture into 4 equal portions and gently pack each into a 1-inch-thick patty.

4. Arrange the salmon burgers on one side of a large rimmed baking sheet. Toss the asparagus with the oil and season with salt and pepper to taste. Spread the asparagus in a single layer on the baking sheet, opposite the burgers.

5. Broil the burgers and asparagus until the burgers are lightly browned on both sides and the asparagus is lightly browned and tender, 8 to 12 minutes, flipping the burgers and turning the asparagus halfway through broiling. Serve with the lemon wedges.

SHEET PAN STIR-FRIES

A STIR-FRY IS A GREAT CHOICE FOR A QUICK weeknight meal. In their most basic form, protein and vegetables, cut into small pieces, are rapidly cooked separately over high heat, then tossed together with a sauce and served over rice. Although the cooking time is relatively fast (the vegetable prep is the most time-consuming part of the process), it is still for the most part hands-on. We don't mind this stovetop approach most of the time (see our stir-fry recipes pages 211–234), but still, we wondered, could we find an approach to preparing this one-dish meal in the oven on a sheet pan, which would allow us some time to walk away from the stove?

Most stir-fries start with some sort of protein. For our three distinct stir-fries, we decided to go with flank steak, chicken breasts, and shrimp. Although we usually marinate the protein in a simple combination of soy sauce and Chinese rice cooking wine for traditional stir-fries, we opted to skip this step—without intense stovetop heat to

rapidly drive off liquid, we knew we would need to keep moisture to a minimum for our oven stir-fry.

Because everything would go in the oven at once, we made sure to choose vegetables that would cook at the same rate as the protein with which we were pairing them. How we cut the vegetables was also important; after a few preliminary tests we found that quartered shiitake mushrooms were easier to distribute on a sheet pan and more likely to brown than thin slices. Slicing asparagus on the bias increased its surface area, allowing it to cook faster. We also incorporated some vegetables that require almost no prep work. Canned sliced water chestnuts and bamboo shoots and frozen shelled edamame are great in stir-fries and ready to use after a quick rinse or a thaw.

With the protein and vegetables ready to go, we tackled the cooking. Broiling would provide plenty of intense heat, but it would also require almost as much hands-on time as a traditional stir-fry; since the heat comes mostly from the top, we would need to stir every few minutes to ensure even cooking. Instead we tossed the protein and vegetables with oil, salt, and pepper, spread the mixture on a sheet pan, and slid it into a very hot (500-degree) oven. While the stir-fry ingredients cooked through in less than 15 minutes, the moisture hadn't fully evaporated in that time, resulting in limp vegetables and pale meat sitting in a pool of liquid.

What if we started with a hot pan? We set an oven rack to the lowest position and put the sheet pan on the rack while the oven heated. When the pan was hot, we carefully but quickly scattered the vegetables and meat and were met with an encouraging sizzle. This batch was a huge improvement— the direct contact with the hot surface drove off some moisture immediately and jump-started the cooking. The vegetables and meat were nicely cooked, with no pools of liquid.

However, we wondered if there was a way to reduce steaming further. Since some of the ingredients we were using—such as water chestnuts, bamboo shoots, and edamame—don't benefit from the high heat of cooking and really just need to be warmed through, we realized there was no need to cook them on the sheet pan when we could just heat them with the sauce. This opened up valuable real estate on the pan without having to skimp on vegetables. With more space to spread out, the meat and vegetables on the sheet pan had more contact with dry heat, resulting in the best texture yet and, finally, a little browning.

Next we considered the aromatics. In our traditional stir-fry technique, aromatics (typically minced garlic, ginger, and scallions) are added toward the end of cooking and briefly sautéed. To mimic this process, we tried tossing the aromatics with the hot stir-fries as soon as they came out of the oven. The residual heat wasn't sufficient to tame the garlic and ginger, and tasters found their flavors raw and harsh. We had better luck adding them to the stir-fry before cooking. The scallions, however, were best when added at the end as a garnish.

Finally we tackled the sauce. Since our goal was to avoid using the stove, we turned to the microwave. After putting the stir-fry in the oven, our plan was to microwave the sauce until it was hot and just the right glazy consistency, then stir in the cooked meat and vegetables as soon as they came out of the oven. After microwaving several of our existing stir-fry sauces, we realized we would need to make some adjustments—tasters described these microwaved sauces as muddied at best and off-flavored at worst. We ran a few more tests to figure out what worked and what didn't. Our usual sauce base, chicken broth, was replaced with water. The bright flavor of orange juice was dulled in the microwave; we turned to grated zest for orange flavor and stirred a little juice into the cooked sauce for freshness. Bold ingredients such as soy sauce, oyster sauce, hot chili sauce, and sesame oil contributed complexity and using such potent components helped us to streamline our ingredient lists. To thicken the sauces enough to coat the protein and vegetables, we added a little bit of cornstarch, adjusting the amount as needed.

Our components and process were finally set: protein, vegetables, and aromatics are spread on a hot sheet pan and put in the oven; the accompanying sauce is cooked in the microwave; then everything is quickly combined while hot. With just a sheet pan and a large bowl, these incredibly quick and simple sheet pan stir-fries are as easy to clean up as they are to make.

Sheet Pan Stir-Fried Beef with Snap Peas, Water Chestnuts, and Oyster Sauce

SERVES 4

To make the beef easier to slice thin, freeze it for 15 minutes. Be sure to rinse and dry the water chestnuts thoroughly, as their packing liquid can easily overpower the flavor of the sauce. This dish comes together quickly, so be ready to start cooking the sauce as soon as you put the meat and vegetables into the oven. Serve with Simple Steamed White Rice (page 220).

1	pound flank steak, trimmed and sliced thin across the grain on a slight bias (see the illustrations on page 215)
12	ounces snap peas, stems and strings removed (see the illustration on page 50)
1	red bell pepper, stemmed, seeded, and sliced into ¼-inch-wide strips (see the illustrations on page 226)
2	tablespoons vegetable oil
3	medium garlic cloves, minced or pressed through a garlic press (about 1 tablespoon)
1	teaspoon minced or grated fresh ginger (see the illustrations on page 216)
	Salt and ground black pepper
¼	cup water
¼	cup oyster sauce
3	tablespoons mirin
2	tablespoons soy sauce
1	tablespoon light brown sugar
2	teaspoons cornstarch
1	teaspoon toasted sesame oil
1	teaspoon sambal oelek chili paste (see page 230)
1	(8-ounce) can sliced water chestnuts, drained, rinsed, and thoroughly patted dry (see note)
2	scallions, sliced thin on the bias (see the illustration on page 25)

1. Adjust an oven rack to the lowest position, place a large rimmed baking sheet on the rack, and heat the oven to 500 degrees. Toss the beef, snap peas, bell pepper, oil, garlic, and ginger together in a large bowl and season lightly with salt and pepper.

2. Working quickly, spread the beef and vegetables in an even layer on the hot baking sheet. Roast until the beef is just cooked through and the vegetables begin to brown, 8 to 12 minutes, stirring halfway through roasting.

3. Meanwhile, whisk the water, oyster sauce, mirin, soy sauce, sugar, cornstarch, sesame oil, and chili paste together in a large microwave-safe bowl. Microwave the sauce on high power, whisking occasionally, until the sauce has thickened, 3 to 5 minutes. Stir the water chestnuts into the hot sauce and cover to keep warm until needed.

4. Transfer the cooked beef and vegetables to the bowl of sauce and toss to combine. Sprinkle with the scallions and serve.

Sheet Pan Stir-Fried Chicken with Shiitakes, Bamboo Shoots, and Teriyaki Sauce
SERVES 4

To make the chicken easier to slice thin, freeze it for 15 minutes. Be sure to rinse and dry the bamboo shoots thoroughly, as their packing liquid can easily overpower the flavor of the sauce. This dish comes together quickly, so be ready to start cooking the sauce as soon as you put the meat and vegetables into the oven. Serve with Simple Steamed White Rice (page 220).

I	pound boneless, skinless chicken breasts (about 3 medium), trimmed and sliced thin (see the illustrations on page 219)
12	ounces shiitake mushrooms, wiped clean, stemmed, and halved if small or quartered if large
I	red bell pepper, stemmed, seeded, and cut into ½-inch pieces (see the illustrations on page 226)
2	tablespoons vegetable oil
3	medium garlic cloves, minced or pressed through a garlic press (about I tablespoon)
2	teaspoons minced or grated fresh ginger (see the illustrations on page 216)
	Salt and ground black pepper
5	tablespoons mirin
5	tablespoons soy sauce
¼	cup water
3	tablespoons sugar
2	teaspoons cornstarch
⅛	teaspoon red pepper flakes
I	(8-ounce) can sliced bamboo shoots, drained, rinsed, and thoroughly patted dry (see note)
2	scallions, sliced thin on the bias (see the illustration below)

1. Adjust an oven rack to the lowest position, place a large rimmed baking sheet on the rack, and heat the oven to 500 degrees. Toss the chicken, mushrooms, bell pepper, oil, 2 teaspoons of the garlic, and 1 teaspoon of the ginger together in a large bowl and season lightly with salt and pepper.

2. Working quickly, spread the chicken and vegetables in an even layer on the hot baking sheet. Roast until the chicken is just cooked through and the vegetables begin to brown, 8 to 12 minutes, stirring halfway through roasting.

3. Meanwhile, whisk the mirin, soy sauce, water, sugar, cornstarch, red pepper flakes, remaining 1 teaspoon garlic, and remaining 1 teaspoon ginger in a large microwave-safe bowl. Microwave the sauce on high power, whisking occasionally, until the sauce has thickened, 3 to 5 minutes. Stir the bamboo shoots into the hot sauce and cover to keep warm until needed.

4. Transfer the cooked chicken and vegetables to the bowl of sauce and toss to combine. Sprinkle with the scallions and serve.

SLICING SCALLIONS ON THE BIAS

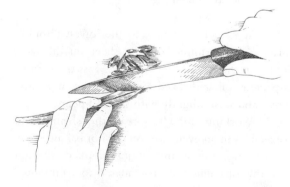

Slicing scallions on the bias makes for an attractive presentation. Simply hold the scallion at an angle, then slice it thin.

Sheet Pan Stir-Fried Shrimp with Asparagus, Edamame, and Spicy Orange Sauce

SERVES 4

To make this dish easier to eat, we suggest peeling the shrimp completely. This dish comes together quickly, so be ready to start cooking the sauce as soon as you put the meat and vegetables into the oven. Serve with Simple Steamed White Rice (page 220).

1	pound extra-large shrimp (21 to 25 per pound), peeled and deveined (see the illustration on page 145)
1	pound asparagus (about 1 bunch), tough ends trimmed, sliced on the bias into 2-inch lengths
2	tablespoons vegetable oil
3	medium garlic cloves, minced or pressed through a garlic press (about 1 tablespoon)
1	teaspoon minced or grated fresh ginger (see the illustrations on page 216)
	Salt and ground black pepper
6	tablespoons water
3	tablespoons soy sauce
¼	teaspoon grated zest plus 2 tablespoons juice from 1 orange
2	teaspoons cornstarch
7	teaspoons sugar
¼	teaspoon red pepper flakes
1	cup (4 ounces) frozen shelled edamame, thawed
2	scallions, sliced thin on the bias (see the illustration on page 25)

1. Adjust an oven rack to the lowest position, place a large rimmed baking sheet on the rack, and heat the oven to 500 degrees. Toss the shrimp, asparagus, oil, garlic, and ginger together in a large bowl and season lightly with salt and pepper.

2. Working quickly, spread the shrimp and vegetables in an even layer on the hot baking sheet. Roast until the shrimp is just cooked through and the asparagus is crisp-tender, 6 to 10 minutes, stirring halfway through roasting.

3. Meanwhile, whisk the water, soy sauce, orange zest, cornstarch, sugar, and red pepper flakes in a large microwave-safe bowl, then stir in the edamame. Microwave the sauce on high power, whisking occasionally, until the sauce has thickened and the edamame are softened, 6 to 8 minutes. Stir the orange juice into the hot sauce and cover to keep warm until needed.

4. Transfer the cooked shrimp and vegetables to the bowl of sauce and toss to combine. Sprinkle with the scallions and serve.

EQUIPMENT: Rimmed Baking Sheets

Rimmed baking sheets are kitchen workhorses. We use them daily for everything from baking cookies, biscuits, and jellyroll cakes to roasting vegetables and large cuts of meat. And because of their large flat surface, we have found they are also great for preparing an entire meal. We tested eight sheet pans in a variety of materials and came to some interesting conclusions.

We found that solid construction is more important than the choice of materials. A too-flimsy pan warps under high heat. Aluminum sheet pans will soften slightly at temperatures of 400 to 500 degrees, and the metal will expand and contract. While steel won't soften significantly below 500 degrees, the combination of metals in aluminized steel can behave differently at high heat, leading to the warping we experienced with some brands.

A pan that is too lightweight also can transfer heat too intensely. The best pan turned out to be the Vollrath (formerly Lincoln Foodservice) Half-Size Heavy Duty Sheet Pan model 5314; its large size (18 by 13 inches) gave us plenty of space to cook an entire meal (and also ensures that standard cooling racks and parchment paper fit perfectly).

THE BEST RIMMED BAKING SHEET

VOLLRATH

The Vollrath (formerly Lincoln Foodservice) Half-Size Heavy Duty Sheet Pan model 5314 ($15.99) performed flawlessly, is one of the thickest pans we tested, and sells at a reasonable price.

2

WALK-AWAY ROAST DINNERS

WALK-AWAY ROAST DINNERS

Easy Old-Fashioned Roast Beef

ROASTING IS ONE OF THE SIMPLEST AND MOST basic ways to cook a large cut of beef; a moderate oven temperature and extended cooking time can build rich, concentrated flavor and yield tender, juicy meat. A beef roast is always a great choice for feeding a small crowd, and few cooking methods can beat roasting in terms of ease, as the process is largely unattended; you simply put the meat in the oven and walk away. But when most people think of a beef roast, cuts like prime rib or beef tenderloin typically come to mind—and while both are tender and delicious, they are also expensive and usually reserved for special occasions. We wanted a flavorful but inexpensive roast paired with root vegetables for an easy one-dish meal.

We knew the roast we picked should have enough marbling to keep it tender, but not so much that it would require liquid or an extra-long cooking time to break down fat. After testing a variety of inexpensive cuts, we decided that a sirloin roast was best; it has a big, beefy flavor, enough fat to stay juicy, and a tender texture. Cheaper round roasts were second best: not bad, but a little tougher, drier, and less flavorful than the sirloin, and we knew that, because it would require a fussier cooking method, it would be problematic to cook a side dish at the same time. Both sirloin and round roasts will sometimes be labeled "rump" roasts; this means that the roast was cut from the area near the dividing line between the round and the sirloin. As such, any kind of rump roast falls somewhere between the two in our ranking: better than a "bottom round" roast, for example, but not quite as nice as a "top sirloin."

With the cut settled, we needed a foolproof technique for roasting the meat, and we knew that a low oven temperature was the way to go. A roast cooked at 250 degrees until it reaches an internal temperature of 120 degrees is definitely more tender and juicy than meat cooked to the same internal temperature in a 500-degree oven. That's because lower oven temperatures allow sufficient time for the even conduction of heat to the center of the roast. At higher oven temperatures, the outside and the inside of the roast have a much larger temperature differential, so the outside is overcooked by the time the interior is done.

When cooked at a constant low temperature, however, our roast developed very little exterior flavor or color. To get the browned crust we wanted, we would need to crank up the heat, either at the beginning or end of the cooking time, or sear the roast on the stovetop—or possibly both. Starting the roast at a high oven temperature didn't work; even after turning the temperature down to 250 degrees, the oven retained enough extra heat to spoil the prospect of a slow, evenly cooked center. Turning the oven up toward the end of the cooking time was much more successful—the meat did not overcook at the edges—but the exterior was still not as dark as we wanted. Ultimately we found that a two-pronged approach was best. We began with a quick sear in the roasting pan on the stovetop, then moved the roast to a low oven, and finally turned up the temperature for the last 10 minutes. The meat had a crisp crust when it went into the oven, and it developed a deeper, more even color during the final blast of oven heat.

Now that we had a surefire approach to cooking a flavorful, inexpensive roast, we hoped to pair it with some vegetables for a complete walk-away roast supper. Carrots and potatoes are a classic accompaniment to savory roast beef, but would these dense root vegetables cook on the same timeline as a sirloin roast? We tossed the vegetables in oil and added them to the pan with the roast. Cranking the heat during the last few minutes of cooking caramelized the vegetables beautifully, but one bite revealed hard, undercooked interiors.

Clearly the vegetables would need a significantly longer roasting time to cook through than the beef, so we began to consider our options. Stovetop boiling or steaming was out of the question since

EQUIPMENT: Roasting Pans

When you need this large pan, nothing else will do. A roasting pan should promote deep, even browning of food; be easy to maneuver in and out of the oven; and it should be able to travel from oven to stovetop so you can deglaze the pan. Roasting pans can be made from stainless steel, enameled steel, nonstick-coated aluminum, or anodized aluminum, all of which we tested. We opted not to test pans lined with copper, which are expensive; cast-iron pans, which when loaded with food are too heavy to lift; and pans made from Pyrex, ceramic, or stoneware, all of which seem better suited to lasagna and casseroles because they can't be used on top of the stove.

We tested eight roasting pans and preferred the materials we like in other cookware—stainless steel and anodized aluminum. These materials are heavy (though not excessively so) and produce good browning. Although nonstick coatings made cleanup easier, roasting racks slid around in these pans.

Roasting pans generally come in two styles—they either have upright handles or they have side handles. Upright handles tend to be square, while side handles are generally oval loops. We found upright handles to be easier to grip. The problem with side handles is that their position, coupled with the large size of the pan, can cause you to bring your forearms perilously close to the hot oven walls. We tested one pan without handles, which was by far the most difficult to take out of the oven.

We tested pans ranging in length from 16 to 20 inches and in width from 11 to 14 inches. We preferred pans that measured about 16 inches long and 12 to 14 inches across. Larger pans made for an awkward fit in the oven and, because of their large surface area, tended to burn pan drippings more easily.

Our favorite is the Calphalon Contemporary Stainless Steel Roasting Pan. It has all the features of more expensive pans (including its own V-rack). It's hefty enough for even the biggest bird, is easy to get in and out of the oven, and is widely available.

THE BEST ROASTING PAN

CALPHALON

The Calphalon Contemporary Stainless Steel Roasting Pan with V-Rack ($129.99) is sturdy enough to support the weight of a large bird, has easy-to-grip upright handles, and has a bottom that is heavy enough to prevent burning.

either would require an additional pan and close monitoring—not part of our walk-away concept. We needed to find a way to give the vegetables a head start without using the stovetop, so we turned to the microwave. We put the carrots and potatoes in a bowl along with a little water, covered it, and cooked them until they were just tender. Now they were ready to hit the roasting pan. This easy step ensured that the vegetables were perfectly cooked by the time the roast was ready—tender and creamy on the inside and lightly caramelized on the outside. A variation with parsnips and Brussels sprouts worked equally well, giving us two streamlined roast beef dinners we could prepare for an easy family dinner or gathering.

Easy Old-Fashioned Roast Beef with Caramelized Carrots and Potatoes

SERVES 6 TO 8

Top sirloin is our favorite beef roast for this recipe, but any boneless roast from the sirloin will work well. If your carrots are very thick, slice them in half lengthwise first to ensure even cooking. We prefer this roast cooked to medium-rare, but if you prefer it more or less done, see our guidelines in the chart on page 45.

2	pounds carrots (about 12 medium), peeled and cut into 2-inch lengths (see note)
2	pounds red potatoes (about 6 medium), scrubbed and cut into 1½-inch chunks
1	(3- to 4-pound) boneless top sirloin beef roast, tied at 1½-inch intervals (see the illustrations on page 33)
	Salt and ground black pepper
¼	cup vegetable oil
1	tablespoon minced fresh thyme or 1 teaspoon dried

1. Adjust an oven rack to the lower-middle position and heat the oven to 250 degrees. Combine

the carrots, potatoes, and 3 tablespoons water in a microwave-safe bowl. Cover and microwave on high power, stirring occasionally, until the vegetables are nearly tender, 15 to 20 minutes.

2. Meanwhile, pat the meat dry with paper towels and season with salt and pepper. Heat 1 tablespoon of the oil in a large roasting pan over medium heat until just smoking (the pan may extend over two burners). Brown the beef well on one side, about 3 minutes. Remove the pan from the heat and turn the roast browned side up.

3. Drain the microwaved vegetables well, toss with the thyme and remaining 3 tablespoons oil, and season with salt and pepper to taste. Spread the vegetables into the roasting pan around the beef. Roast the beef and vegetables until the center of the meat registers 110 degrees on an instant-read thermometer, 45 to 60 minutes.

4. Increase the oven temperature to 500 degrees and continue to roast the beef and vegetables until the center of the meat registers 120 to 125 degrees (for medium-rare), 10 to 15 minutes longer.

5. Transfer the beef roast to a carving board, tent loosely with aluminum foil, and let rest for 20 minutes. Meanwhile, continue to roast the vegetables until nicely browned, 10 to 20 minutes. Remove the twine from the beef, slice it ⅛ inch thick, and serve with the vegetables.

➤ VARIATION
Easy Old-Fashioned Roast Beef with Caramelized Parsnips and Brussels Sprouts

If your parsnips are very thick, slice them in half lengthwise first to ensure even cooking.

Follow the recipe for Easy Old-Fashioned Roast Beef with Caramelized Carrots and Potatoes, substituting 2 pounds parsnips, peeled and cut into 2-inch lengths, and 2 pounds Brussels sprouts, trimmed and halved, for the carrots and potatoes; microwave the vegetables with the water as directed until just tender, 10 to 15 minutes.

PORK LOIN WITH SWEET POTATOES AND CILANTRO SAUCE

UNASSUMING AND SIMPLE TO PREPARE, A boneless pork roast is hearty fare for a casual family dinner. When cooked correctly, the meat is tender and juicy, its flavor sweet and mild—usually so mild that a spicy rub or tangy sauce is welcome. Our goals for roasted pork loin were simple: We wanted a foolproof method for cooking the meat without drying it out; we wanted a boldly flavored sauce that would complement the pork without overwhelming it; and we wanted a simple side dish that we could roast alongside the pork for an easy, no-fuss meal.

Since the flavor of the sauce would guide the rest of the dish, we decided to start there. We knew that we wanted to keep the sauce simple; just a few basic ingredients with minimal prep. A no-cook sauce sounded promising; something along the lines of a fresh salsa or pesto would be flavorful and easy and would give our meal some direction. While brainstorming ideas, one of our test cooks recalled a Cuban dish she particularly enjoyed: tender pork served with a tangy cilantro sauce. Her vivid memory of the pairing had everyone hungry to re-create it.

The sauce our colleague described was fresh and light, similar to a loose pesto. We started with some cilantro, extra-virgin olive oil, garlic, lime juice, and a touch of sugar to balance the tartness. A few seconds in a blender pureed the ingredients too much, yielding a muddy sauce of over-pulverized, soapy-tasting cilantro. We opted to use the food processor instead. After a dozen or so short pulses, the cilantro was minced fine but still retained some texture. However, the flavor, though no longer soapy, still had a bitterness that tasters disliked. Thinking that the extra-virgin olive oil might be the culprit, we substituted regular olive oil in our next test. Sure enough, the milder flavor was the ticket, and our sauce now had the bright, grassy flavor of cilantro with no trace of bitterness.

While we were pleased with our sauce, we knew that no matter how good it was, it could never disguise a dry, overcooked pork loin, so next we turned our attention to creating a juicy and flavorful pork roast. We started by brining the pork (soaking it in a saltwater solution), which is a technique we often use in the test kitchen to season and boost the juiciness of meat. And brining did indeed yield tender, juicy, well-seasoned pork, but we quickly learned that it didn't protect the pork from overcooking and drying out if roasted at too high a temperature. After much trial and error, we found we got the best results from cooking the roast in a moderate 375-degree oven until it registered 140 to 145 degrees. The temperature of the roast continued to rise out of the oven, and it reached its ideal serving temperature of 150 degrees while resting on a carving board before slicing.

INGREDIENTS:
Enhanced or Unenhanced Pork?

Because modern pork is remarkably lean and therefore somewhat bland and prone to dryness if overcooked, a product called "enhanced" pork has overtaken the market. In fact, it can be hard to find unenhanced pork in some areas. Enhanced pork has been injected with a solution of water, salt, sodium phosphate, sodium lactate, potassium lactate, sodium diacetate, and varying flavor agents to bolster flavor and juiciness, with the total amount of enhancing ingredients adding 7 to 15 percent extra weight. Pork containing additives must be so labeled, with a list of the ingredients. After several taste tests, we have concluded that while enhanced pork is indeed juicier and more tender than unenhanced pork, the latter has more genuine pork flavor. Some tasters detected unappealingly artificial, salty flavors in enhanced pork. Enhanced pork can also leach out juices that, once reduced, will result in overly salty sauces. In the test kitchen, we prefer natural pork, but the choice is up to you. It should be noted, however, that if you buy enhanced pork you should not brine it, as it has essentially already been brined.

We had found when developing our beef roast recipe (see page 29) that browning the roast first on the stovetop helped develop flavor, and while a similar technique would surely be successful here, we wondered if we couldn't streamline our pork recipe by skipping the browning and instead using a dry rub that would complement our Cuban-inspired sauce and lend visual appeal. A mixture of ground coriander (the seed of the cilantro plant), cumin, salt, and pepper gave the pork's exterior color and flavor, and also complemented our lively cilantro sauce.

With our pork loin and sauce perfected, we could look at rounding out the meal. For this to be a walk-away roast dinner, the vegetable we chose would need to roast alongside the pork, so cooking time was an issue. In keeping with our Cuban-inspired theme, our thoughts first turned to yucca. Typically served fried, yucca is a long, brown-skinned tuber with a waxy outer bark. But since yucca can be hard to find, we came up with a more accessible choice—creamy and rich sweet potatoes. We tossed sweet potato chunks with some oil and a pinch of cayenne pepper and roasted them with the pork. This gave us tender potatoes, but they weren't as browned as we would have liked. So in the time it took to let the pork roast rest, we turned up the oven temperature and gave the potatoes 10 more minutes in the high heat so that they were nicely browned. With that, both elements of our walk-away pork roast dinner were ready to be drizzled with the fresh cilantro sauce. Making a flavor-packed meal couldn't get much easier than this.

Roast Pork Loin with Sweet Potatoes and Cilantro Sauce
SERVES 6

A ¼-inch-thick layer of fat on top of the roast is ideal; if your roast has a thicker fat cap, trim it back accordingly. To use kosher salt in the brine, see page 34 for conversion information. If the pork is "enhanced" (see page 32 for more information), skip step 1, don't rinse the pork in step 2, and season the roast with salt in step 2. This sauce uses two entire bunches of cilantro, including the stems. Do not substitute extra-virgin olive oil for the regular olive oil because it will impart a bitter flavor to the sauce.

PORK AND POTATOES

½ cup sugar
 Table salt (see note)
1 (3-pound) boneless pork loin roast, trimmed and tied at 1½-inch intervals (see the illustrations at right)
1 teaspoon ground coriander
1 teaspoon ground cumin
 Ground black pepper
3 pounds sweet potatoes (about 6 small), peeled, quartered, and cut into 2-inch chunks
3 tablespoons vegetable oil
⅛ teaspoon cayenne pepper

CILANTRO SAUCE

2 bunches cilantro, stem ends trimmed (about 2½ lightly packed cups) (see note)
½ cup olive oil (see note)
4 teaspoons juice from 1 lime
2 medium garlic cloves, minced or pressed through a garlic press (about 2 teaspoons)
½ teaspoon sugar
 Salt and ground black pepper

1. **FOR THE PORK AND POTATOES:** Dissolve the sugar and ½ cup salt in 2 quarts water in a large container. Submerge the pork in the brine, cover, and refrigerate for 1½ to 2 hours.

2. Adjust an oven rack to the lower-middle position and heat the oven to 375 degrees. Remove the roast from the brine and rinse. Pat the roast dry with paper towels and season with the coriander, cumin, and ½ teaspoon pepper.

3. Toss the sweet potatoes with the oil and cayenne, season with salt and pepper to taste, and spread into a large roasting pan. Lay the pork on top of the potatoes. Roast the pork and potatoes until the center of the pork registers 140 to 145 degrees on an instant-read thermometer, 50 to 70 minutes, turning the roast over halfway through roasting.

4. **FOR THE CILANTRO SAUCE:** Pulse all the ingredients together in a food processor until the cilantro is finely chopped, 10 to 15 pulses, scraping down

HOW TO TIE A ROAST

Tying a roast not only yields more attractive slices, but also ensures that the roast will have the same thickness from end to end so that it cooks evenly.

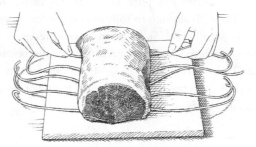

1. Cut pieces of heavy-duty butcher's twine that are at least 8 inches longer than the girth of the roast. Slide the pieces of twine underneath the roast at even intervals (as directed in the recipe).

2. Tightly tie each piece of twine around the roast, starting with a piece in the very center, followed by pieces at both ends, then finally the remaining pieces in between.

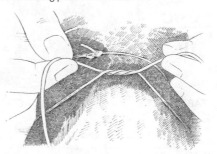

3. We think it's best to use a surgeon's knot when tying a roast. To make a surgeon's knot, simply wrap the twine around twice when making the first knot; this will hold the initial knot securely in place.

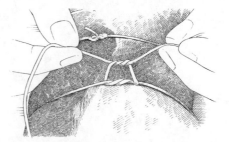

4. Top the first knot with a regular knot, tightening it securely against the meat.

the bowl as needed. Season the sauce with salt and pepper to taste. (The sauce can be refrigerated in an airtight container for up to 2 days.)

5. Transfer the pork to a carving board, tent loosely with aluminum foil, and let rest for 15 minutes. Meanwhile, increase the oven temperature to 450 degrees and continue to roast the potatoes until nicely browned, about 10 minutes. Slice the pork ¼ inch thick and serve with the potatoes and cilantro sauce.

TWO TYPES OF SALT FOR BRINING

You can use either kosher or regular table salt for brining. Kosher salt is ideal because its large, airy crystals dissolve quickly in water. Unfortunately, the salt crystals of the two major brands of kosher salt—Morton and Diamond Crystal—are not equally airy, and therefore measure differently. This inconsistency between the two brands makes precise recipe writing a challenge. Because we don't know which brand of kosher salt you might have on hand, we list table salt in our brining recipes. If you use kosher salt in your brine, keep the following in mind when making the conversion from table salt in our brining recipes.

TABLE SALT   KOSHER SALT

¼ cup table salt =	½ cup Diamond Crystal Kosher Salt
	or
	¼ cup plus 2 tablespoons Morton Kosher Salt

EASY STUFFED PORK LOIN WITH ACORN SQUASH WEDGES

WANT TO KNOW THE EASIEST WAY TO MAKE ordinary pork roast extraordinary? Stuff it! Contrary to popular belief, stuffing a pork roast does not have to be an all-day production, nor does it have to involve advanced knife skills or the knot-tying ability of an America's Cup captain. What it does require is a knockout stuffing. In addition to providing an unexpected burst of flavor in each bite, the stuffing also serves to keep the meat moist and juicy; in fact, stuffing makes brining—the tried and true method of preventing dried-out pork—unnecessary. Our challenge would be to create a stuffing that could be stuffed uncooked into our roast before it went into the oven, or made entirely in the microwave, eliminating the need for a skillet on the stovetop. In addition, we wanted to be able to roast a vegetable with our stuffed pork roast to make it a complete meal.

Simplifying the stuffing process was going to be our first—and most important—hurdle. A survey of existing recipes yielded some interesting and complicated methods. We decided to try an approach that would fall somewhere between two of these methods. We started by making a deep cut lengthwise down the center of the roast (much like a pocket method we had seen, but cutting through at both ends), being careful not to cut all the way through to the cutting board. The second step was to make two more cuts, horizontally through each half, but again not cutting all the way through. The pork loin could then be opened like a letter into a single, flat piece. We mounded stuffing (a test recipe for now) down the center of the roast and sealed it by wrapping the sides of the pork loin up and around the filling. Finally, we tied the roast with twine at 1-inch intervals. This simple method took about five minutes and allowed for just the right balance of pork to stuffing in each bite.

With our process hurdle cleared, we could move on to the stuffing. Given our limited one-pot guidelines, we ruled out cooked bread or rice mixtures and any stuffing that would require sautéing meats or reducing liquids. Fresh fruit seemed like the best bet for achieving our goals of simplicity and flavor. We tried putting a simple uncooked stuffing of chopped apple, dried cranberries, and shallots in our roast before it went in the oven. Though tasty, this mixture lacked cohesiveness; one slice of the knife scattered cranberries and barely cooked apples across the cutting board. Microwaving the mixture didn't solve the problem either; partially cooking the apples caused them to break down too much during roasting, leaving us with a stuffing resembling applesauce.

While we wanted to stick with fruit, perhaps relying on dried fruit that we plumped would give our stuffing the consistency we wanted. We substituted chopped dried apples for fresh. To soften and plump the dried fruit (apples and cranberries) in the microwave, we would need to add some liquid, so we tried a combination of apple cider and cider vinegar. We also added fresh ginger for a warm, spicy note and a little brown sugar for sweetness. Less than 10 minutes' time in the microwave yielded a cohesive, soft fruit chutney with great flavor, perfect for stuffing our pork.

The only nagging problem with the stuffing now was the texture; it needed some kind of crunch to contrast the softness of the fruit. We immediately thought of nuts, which frequently appear in chutneys and fruit relishes. The idea of using raw, untoasted nuts was unappealing, but we were holding fast to our one-dish-for-cooking mantra, so the oven and the stovetop were off the table. Could we toast nuts in the microwave? Skeptical but willing to give it a shot, we spread a quarter cup of walnuts on a plate and set the microwave for three minutes. After the time elapsed, the nuts were hot and beginning to release their aroma, but we could not yet detect any browning. We returned the nuts to the microwave after a quick stir and cooked them in one-minute intervals, watching for signs of toasting. After about five minutes, the walnuts were perfectly browned and ready to be chopped. After rubbing a combination of chopped rosemary and thyme and a little coriander over the roast, we now had a stuffed pork loin ready for the oven.

PREPARING EASY STUFFED PORK LOIN

1. Slice the pork open down the middle, from end to end, cutting about two-thirds of the way through the meat.

2. Gently press the pork loin open. Carefully slice into the sides of the roast starting from the initial cut, being careful not to cut through, and press the pork flat.

3. Season the inside of the pork with salt and pepper, then mound the filling evenly down the center of the roast.

4. Wrap the sides of the pork around the filling, then tie the roast closed with butcher's twine at 1-inch intervals. Don't tie the roast too tight or you may squeeze out the filling.

However, we still needed one last thing to complete the dish: the perfect vegetable to roast with the stuffed pork. Since we already had an intense flavor combination in our main dish, we knew we needed to keep the side dish simple. We liked the idea of a no-fuss vegetable that we could slice and season simply with a little oil, salt, and pepper. Acorn squash, with its subtle sweetness, thin skin, and visually appealing shape, quickly came to mind. We cut the squash in half to remove the seeds and membrane and then followed the natural curves of the squash to cut it into 1-inch wedges—no peeling necessary. The squash was tender by the time the pork finished roasting, but we returned the squash to a hotter oven to promote caramelization while the pork rested.

We held our breath as we sliced into the pork, but there was no need to fear: the filling remained in place, a colorful splash of flavor and texture in each circle of rosy pork. The delicate wedges of squash, now slightly browned, made our dinner complete—and far from ordinary.

Easy Stuffed Pork Loin with Acorn Squash Wedges
SERVES 6

A ¼-inch-thick layer of fat on top of the roast is ideal; if your roast has a thicker fat cap, trim it back accordingly. The moist stuffing for the pork loin makes brining unnecessary. Handle the cooked squash carefully, as it will be quite delicate.

¼	cup walnuts, chopped coarse
1½	cups dried apples (about 4 ounces), chopped fine
¾	cup apple cider or apple juice
½	cup dried cranberries (about 2½ ounces)
1	medium shallot, minced (about 3 tablespoons)
1	tablespoon cider vinegar
1	tablespoon light brown sugar
1	tablespoon minced or grated fresh ginger (see the illustrations on page 216)
	Salt and ground black pepper

1	(3-pound) boneless pork loin roast, trimmed
2	teaspoons minced fresh thyme or ½ teaspoon dried
1	teaspoon minced fresh rosemary or ¼ teaspoon dried
1	teaspoon ground coriander
3½	pounds acorn squash (about 2 large), halved (see the illustrations on page 10), seeds removed, and cut into 1-inch-thick wedges
¼	cup olive oil

1. Adjust an oven rack to the lower-middle position and heat the oven to 375 degrees. Spread the walnuts out over a large microwave-safe plate and microwave on high power until lightly toasted, about 5 minutes; set aside.

2. Combine the dried apples, cider, cranberries, shallot, vinegar, brown sugar, and ginger in a microwave-safe bowl. Cover and microwave on high power until the apples are soft and the liquid is absorbed, 7 to 10 minutes. Stir in the toasted walnuts and season with salt and pepper to taste.

3. Pat the pork dry with paper towels. Following the illustrations on page 35, slice the roast open and flatten it with your hands. Season the inside of the roast with salt and pepper, mound the dried apple mixture evenly down the center, then tie the pork around the filling with butcher's twine into a tidy roast.

4. Combine the thyme, rosemary, coriander, ¼ teaspoon salt, and ⅛ teaspoon pepper, then rub the mixture evenly over the outside of the roast. Lay the roast in a large roasting pan. Toss the squash wedges with the olive oil, season with salt and pepper to taste, and spread in the roasting pan around the pork. Roast the pork and squash until the center of the meat registers 140 to 145 degrees on an instant-read thermometer, 50 to 70 minutes.

5. Transfer the pork to a carving board, tent loosely with aluminum foil, and let rest for 15 minutes. Meanwhile, increase the oven temperature to 450 degrees and continue to roast the squash until tender, about 15 minutes. Remove the twine from the pork, slice it ½ inch thick, and serve with the squash.

SPICE-RUBBED PORK TENDERLOIN

WHEN DONE RIGHT, NOTHING CAN MATCH the fine-grained, buttery-smooth texture of pork tenderloin. And because of their size—they are relatively long and thin—they cook quickly, allowing you to put dinner on the table in less than 30 minutes. But generally speaking, since most of the flavor in a cut of meat comes from the fat that surrounds and marbles the muscles, lean cuts like pork tenderloin have a tendency to be bland. As such, they benefit from bold seasoning, often in the form of a dry rub, marinade, or sauce. We decided we would first need to determine how to flavor our pork, and then we could focus on selecting a complementary side dish—one that would cook quickly, in the same amount of time as the pork tenderloins. We wanted to find a combination that was big on flavor, but low on prep time, for an easy yet satisfying weeknight meal.

Pork tenderloin couldn't be easier to prepare—it requires a minimal amount of trimming and because it is naturally so tender, in the test kitchen we have found that brining isn't necessary. When cooking pork tenderloin, we typically start by searing it on the stovetop to brown the exterior and add flavor. But inspired by the spice rub used in our roast pork loin recipe (see page 36), we wondered if a dry rub once again might allow us to skip the step of browning, adding both flavor and color to our tenderloins without the extra work. Seasoning with salt and pepper would provide a solid base, but we wanted a distinct flavor profile to guide the rest of the dish. Herbes de Provence, a dried herb blend that usually includes thyme, fennel, savory, marjoram, and lavender, would give a distinctively Mediterranean flavor to our pork without requiring a number of different herbs and spices. After a very potent first test, we learned that a little of this blend goes a long way; a mere 2 teaspoons was sufficient to flavor and coat two tenderloins without overwhelming the pork.

Because pork tenderloins tend to be long, thin, and lean, a relatively brief stay in a hot oven works best to avoid overcooking. The high temperature aids in browning the outside of the meat, while the short cooking time ensures a tender, moist interior. We found that roasting the tenderloins at 450 degrees for about 30 minutes was all we needed to bring the interior of the pork to a rosy 140 degrees. To optimize browning on the exterior of the pork, we turned the tenderloins over halfway through the cooking time.

Finding a vegetable accompaniment for such a quick-cooking meat would prove to be tricky; after just 30 minutes of roasting time, most root vegetables would still be raw yet more delicate vegetables, such as green beans or asparagus, would be overcooked. Thinking again about our Mediterranean-inspired rub, we wondered if fennel might work—its sweet, delicate flavor would be the perfect complement to our pork tenderloin. We began with three fennel bulbs and cut them into ½-inch-thick slices. After tossing them in olive oil, we placed them in the roasting pan with the pork. After 30 minutes of roasting, the pork was done, but the fennel was still partially raw. We transferred the pork tenderloins to a carving board and returned the fennel to the oven, but in the 10 to 15 minutes the pork rested, the fennel still didn't finish cooking.

The fennel needed a jump start—and perhaps some company in the roasting pan. While tasters liked the mild flavor of the fennel, they also thought this dish could handle some bolder, brighter additions. We decided to reduce the amount of fennel we were using and supplement it with artichoke hearts, niçoise olives, and cherry tomatoes. After parcooking the fennel in the microwave, we tossed it with the artichoke hearts, olives, and a little olive oil. We spread the mixture into the roasting pan and placed the tenderloins on top. This time, the vegetables were almost perfectly cooked when the pork was done. We removed the pork, stirred in the cherry tomatoes and some lemon zest, and returned the vegetables to the oven to finish cooking. When we retrieved the vegetables 10 minutes later, the fennel was tender, the tomatoes had softened and begun to release their juice, and the bright aroma of lemon filled the kitchen.

In less than an hour, we were transported to Provence with a weeknight dinner that was low on fuss but high on flavor.

PREPARING FENNEL

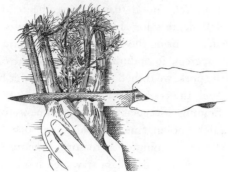

1. Cut off the stalks and feathery fronds (the fronds can be minced and used for a garnish).

2. Trim a very thin slice from the base and remove any tough or blemished outer layers from the bulb.

3. Cut the bulb in half through the base. Use a small, sharp knife to remove the pyramid-shaped core.

4. Lay the cored fennel flat on the cutting board and slice into ½-inch-thick strips.

Spice-Rubbed Pork Tenderloin with Fennel, Tomatoes, Artichokes, and Olives

SERVES 4 TO 6

Be sure to thoroughly thaw and pat dry the frozen artichokes; otherwise, their moisture will inhibit the browning of the roasted vegetables. Herbes de Provence, a blend of dried herbs such as rosemary, basil, marjoram, bay leaves, thyme, and lavender, is available in the spice aisle of supermarkets.

2	(12- to 16-ounce) pork tenderloins, trimmed
2	teaspoons dried herbes de Provence
	Salt and ground black pepper
2	large fennel bulbs (about 2 pounds), trimmed of stalks, cored, and cut into ½-inch-thick strips (see the illustrations at left)
12	ounces frozen artichoke hearts, thawed and patted dry
½	cup pitted niçoise or kalamata olives (see the illustration on page 289), halved
3	tablespoons extra-virgin olive oil
3	cups cherry tomatoes (about 1 pound), halved
1	tablespoon grated zest from 1 lemon
2	tablespoons minced fresh parsley leaves

1. Adjust an oven rack to the lower-middle position and heat the oven to 450 degrees. Pat the pork dry with paper towels, then season with the herbes de Provence, salt, and pepper.

2. Combine the fennel and 2 tablespoons water in a microwave-safe bowl. Cover and microwave on high power until softened, about 5 minutes. Drain the fennel well, toss with the artichokes, olives, and oil and season with salt and pepper to taste.

3. Spread the vegetables into a large roasting pan. Lay the pork on top of the vegetables. Roast the pork and vegetables until the center of the meat registers 140 to 145 degrees on an instant-read thermometer, 25 to 30 minutes, turning the tenderloins over halfway through roasting.

4. Transfer the pork to a carving board, tent loosely with aluminum foil, and let rest for 10 minutes. Meanwhile, stir the cherry tomatoes and lemon

zest into the vegetables and continue to roast until the fennel is tender and the tomatoes have softened, about 10 minutes.

5. Stir the parsley into the roasted vegetables. Cut the pork into ½-inch-thick slices and serve with the vegetables.

WALK-AWAY ROAST CHICKEN WITH POTATOES

WITH ITS HALLMARK CRISP, BROWNED SKIN and tender, juicy meat, roast chicken is an eminently satisfying and comforting dish. But as simple as it may look, it is usually a complicated entrée to prepare. The main problem is that roasting a chicken requires constant attention. The chicken is typically turned multiple times during roasting to ensure even cooking and the signature crisped skin, and basting the chicken every few minutes to guarantee juicy meat is likewise a time-consuming task. Could we streamline the process and still get a really great roast chicken, one that didn't require constant monitoring while in the oven? We aimed to develop a true hands-off walk-away roast chicken and wondered if oven temperature might play a role—would a low, slow roasting time keep the meat moist without all the fuss? And while we were at it, could we add a side dish of potatoes or vegetables to make yet another complete walk-away roasted one-dish meal?

If we were going to give our chicken little to no attention while it roasted, we would need to concentrate our efforts on creating optimal flavor before the bird even went into the oven. Over the years, the test kitchen has learned that brining chicken in a sugar and salt solution produces a superior roast. Brining ensures that the meat is seasoned through to the bone and also adds moisture that is retained when the chicken is cooked, resulting in a more flavorful, juicy piece of meat. Meanwhile, the sugar in the brine helps produce perfectly browned skin.

EQUIPMENT: Roasting Racks

A roasting rack (also known as a V-rack) raises poultry and roasts out of the drippings, while giving the oven's heat easy access to the whole surface—a good start toward a well-rendered exterior and even cooking. If your roasting pan doesn't come with a V-rack, you'll need to purchase one separately. We recommend fixed V-racks (as opposed to adjustable) because we've found that the adjustable V-racks are not as sturdy as the fixed ones and are prone to collapse, especially after turning the bird. But which brand of V-rack is best? We brought several into the test kitchen to find out.

Right away, we noted that not all V-racks are actually V-shaped. The slight bend on some roasting racks barely qualifies as a "V" and leaves no room for roasting vegetables underneath. The innovative Cuisipro Roast and Serve ($28.95) is shaped like a trough with a hinge at the center. Remove the dowel from the hinge and the rack comes apart, dropping the roast onto a platter or cutting board. While it worked fine, this rack was another that didn't elevate the roast enough, and its size (15 inches by 11½ inches) makes it a tight squeeze in all but the largest pan.

In addition to shape, handles were a decisive factor. Tall, vertical handles make removing the rack easy, even with bulky oven mitts. Horizontal handles, or no handles at all, make removal nearly impossible. In our tests, we also noticed that handle position matters. When located on the short sides of a rectangular rack they can get in the way of the roasting pan's handles. We prefer handles positioned on the long side of the rack.

The All-Clad Nonstick Roasting Rack ($24.95) is our top choice. It's large enough to hold two small chickens and has the features we like. With its handles on the short side, the Norpro ($9.75) is a distant runner-up. If you're also in the market for a new roasting pan, you should consider our favorite roaster, the Calphalon Contemporary Stainless Steel Roasting Pan ($129.99), which includes a rack that's just as good as the All-Clad model.

THE BEST ROASTING RACK
All-Clad's Nonstick Roasting Rack ($24.95) is our favorite for its large capacity and easy-to-grasp handles.

ALL-CLAD

PREPARING WALK-AWAY ROAST CHICKEN

1. With your fingers, carefully loosen the skin over the breast.

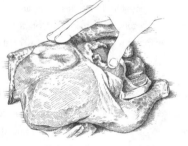

2. Spoon 1 tablespoon of the butter under the skin on each side of the breast.

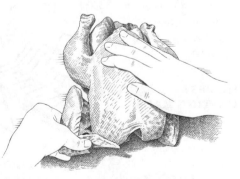

3. With your fingers on top of the skin, work the butter to distribute it evenly over the breast.

4. Tuck the wings by simply twisting them back behind the back and closing the joints of the wing tightly. The tension of the closed, tucked wing will help to keep it in place.

A typical recipe for roast chicken calls for roasting the chicken at 375 degrees for about one hour. But these recipes also call for turning the chicken multiple times. Could we lower the temperature and get away with leaving the bird untouched once it went into the oven? Roasting the chicken at a much lower temperature—250 degrees—without turning it did indeed produce moist, evenly cooked meat, but it also resulted in pale, flabby skin. Since we wanted a classic roast chicken, crisp skin was a must. We reasoned that cranking the heat toward the end of roasting—after the fat from the skin had a chance to render—would brown and crisp the skin.

We knew the chicken would need to roast at a higher heat for a fair amount of time to achieve the crisp skin we were after, so we would need to turn the heat up well before the chicken was done. We tried turning the oven temperature up to 425 degrees once the chicken registered an internal temperature of 130 degrees. This gave the bird about 30 minutes of high heat, and the results were impressive—tender, juicy meat, with crisp golden skin.

Most recipes brush the bird with either butter or oil to help brown and crisp the skin, so we tried both. Butter produced poor results due to the low oven temperature; despite a nice brown color, the skin was chewy and greasy. Brushing the bird with oil was much better and the result was crispier skin and a beautiful golden brown color.

We also knew from test kitchen experience that separating the skin from the meat allows hot air to circulate more freely under the skin, which in turn renders more fat and produces crispier skin. And since we were separating the skin from the meat anyway, we slipped a little butter between the skin and meat—this would help keep the delicate breast meat juicy while adding flavor.

Trussing is another technique that is often recommended when roasting a whole bird, as it is said to promote more even cooking. However we found quite the opposite. We trussed a bird according to the best French method and found that in the one and a half hours it took to cook the dark meat through, the white meat became overcooked. We realized that trussing actually makes it more difficult to cook the inner part of the thigh properly—because it was less exposed to the heat, it needed more oven time. Meanwhile, when we roasted an untrussed bird, we found the white and dark meat cooked through more evenly.

We were happy to discover that a variety of vegetables worked well with the timing and oven temperature required for the chicken. For our master recipe we kept things simple with a combination of potatoes and shallots, both of which roasted nicely alongside the chicken and benefited from the flavorful drippings. We included a mixture of root vegetables in one variation and made another with spring vegetables. We continued to roast the vegetables while the chicken rested, which allowed everything to be ready at the same time.

Walk-Away Roast Chicken with Potatoes

SERVES 4

To use kosher salt in the brine, see page 34 for conversion information. If using a kosher chicken, skip step 1, don't rinse the chicken in step 3, and season with salt in step 4.

½	cup sugar
	Table salt (see note)
1	(4½- to 5-pound) whole chicken, giblets discarded
2½	pounds red potatoes (7 or 8 medium), scrubbed and cut into 1-inch pieces
8	medium shallots (about 8 ounces), peeled and halved
¼	cup olive oil
	Ground black pepper
2	tablespoons unsalted butter or flavored butter (see the recipes on page 49), softened

1. Dissolve the sugar and ½ cup salt in 2 quarts cold water in a large container. Submerge the chicken in the brine, cover, and refrigerate for 1 to 1½ hours.

2. Adjust an oven rack to the lower-middle position and heat the oven to 250 degrees. Coat a V-rack with vegetable oil spray and set inside a large roasting pan. Toss the potatoes and shallots with 3 tablespoons of the oil and season with salt and pepper

CARVING A CHICKEN

After brining and roasting the perfect bird, you still have one last task before bringing it to the table—carving it. While carving isn't difficult, there is definitely a way to approach it that will yield nicely portioned chicken parts and slices of boneless breast—portions that look attractive on a platter and are easy to serve. This method works for both whole and butterflied chickens (as well as turkey and duck, for that matter).

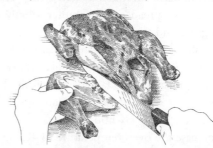

1. Cut the chicken where the leg meets the breast. For a whole bird, you may need to pull the leg out to help release the hip joint. For a butterflied bird, only a thin piece of skin is holding the portions together, so be gentle.

2. Cut through the joint that connects the drumstick to the thigh. Repeat on the second side to remove the other leg.

3. Cut down along one side of the breastbone, pulling the breast meat away from you as you cut.

4. Remove the wing from the breast by cutting through the wing joint. Slice the breast into attractive slices.

to taste. Spread the vegetables in the roasting pan underneath the V-rack.

3. Remove the chicken from the brine, rinse, and pat dry with paper towels. Following the illustrations on page 40, gently loosen the center portion of skin covering each side of the breast. Using a spoon, place the butter underneath the skin, then gently press the on the skin to spread out the butter. Gently tuck the wings behind the back.

4. Brush the chicken with the remaining 1 tablespoon oil, season with pepper, and place, breast side up, in the prepared V-rack. Roast until the breast registers 125 to 130 degrees on an instant-read thermometer, 1½ to 1¾ hours.

5. Increase the oven temperature to 425 degrees and continue to roast the chicken until the breast registers 160 to 165 degrees and the thighs register 175 degrees, about 30 minutes.

6. Transfer the chicken to a carving board and let rest for 10 minutes. Meanwhile, increase the oven temperature to 500 degrees and continue to roast the vegetables until fully cooked and golden, 5 to 10 minutes. Carve the chicken following the illustrations on page 41 and serve with the vegetables.

➤ VARIATIONS

Walk-Away Roast Chicken with Root Vegetables

If your parsnips and carrots are very thick, slice them in half lengthwise first to ensure even cooking.

Follow the recipe for Walk-Away Roast Chicken with Potatoes, substituting 1 pound carrots (about 6 medium), peeled and cut into 1-inch pieces, and 4 medium parsnips, peeled and cut into 1-inch pieces, for 1½ pounds of the potatoes.

Walk-Away Roast Chicken with Potatoes and Spring Vegetables

Follow the recipe for Walk-Away Roast Chicken with Potatoes, substituting 1 pound asparagus, tough ends trimmed and cut into 2-inch lengths, and 1 (9-ounce) box frozen artichokes, thawed and patted dry, for 1½ pounds of the potatoes.

HIGH-ROAST CHICKEN WITH POTATO GRATIN

A SIMPLE ROAST CHICKEN IS SATISFYING comfort food, as we learned with our Walk-Away Roast Chicken with Potatoes (page 41), but occasionally we want something with a bit more pizzazz, a bird that would really impress company. High-roasting, we agreed, was the answer. This technique, in which the bird is roasted at temperatures in excess of 450 degrees, promises perfectly cooked meat with exceptionally crisp, beautifully golden skin. If we could pair this entrée with ideally crisp and creamy potatoes, a presentation that was slightly more elegant than the simple potato pieces from our previous recipe, we would be all set. Our challenge would be to prevent the breast meat from overcooking at such a high temperature. Still, we thought this technique was worth a shot.

Brining the bird was our first step; we already knew that brining improves the flavor and texture of a roasted bird. The salt in a brine permeates the chicken so the meat is evenly seasoned, while sugar promotes caramelization of the skin. Brining also keeps the breast meat moist and tender—something that would be especially important here considering the intense heat of the oven.

We began by roasting three birds for about an hour at 425, 450, and 500 degrees. When the birds came out of the oven, the differences between them were marked. The 500-degree bird was a looker, with beautiful, deep brown, crisp skin. The other two were splotchy and only mildly attractive. Of course, the inevitable had also occurred: The breast meat on all the birds had been torched; as the thighs sauntered up to the finish line the more delicate breast meat overcooked. Worst of all, with 450- and 500-degree oven temperatures, everyone fled coughing and hacking out of the kitchen, which had filled with billows of smoke.

To remedy the uneven cooking, we tried several adjustments, from preheated roasting pans to different configurations of oven temperatures, all to no avail. The obvious solution was to flip the bird over so that the breast would spend some time shielded from the intense oven heat while the thighs would receive the exposure they needed to catch up. After trying this technique, however, we vetoed it. We were after deep browning and crisp skin, neither of which was produced by this method. For that, the bird needs to spend all, or at least most, of the roasting time breast up.

We suspected that the fix lay in butterflying the chicken—that is, removing the backbone, then opening and flattening the bird. This method would give the thighs greater exposure to the heat, increasing the odds that they would cook at the same rate as the breast. In addition, all areas with skin would be face up to facilitate even browning and crisping. We tried it, and it worked like a charm. The thighs actually raced ahead of the breast meat and finished cooking first (since thighs are fattier and more forgiving, this wasn't a problem). For super crisp skin and a beautifully browned bird, 500 degrees was the optimal temperature. We now had a juicy, perfectly cooked bird, but there was

still that smoking problem, caused by the rendered fat scorching.

Following in the footsteps of our walk-away roast chicken, we placed our potatoes underneath the roast to absorb the drippings. For a more elegant presentation, we looked to come up with a side that echoed the style of potatoes au gratin, with its contrasting textures. We cut the potatoes into mere ⅛-inch-thick slices, hoping their edges would beautifully crisp while their centers would remain creamy. Unfortunately, they burned in spots, dried out in others, and stuck to the pan. But, they showed great potential; tasters lined up for any stray morsel of crisp potato.

We assumed that the potatoes needed some protection as they cooked to keep them from burning and drying out, and switching from a roasting pan and rack to a broiler pan with a slotted top was the answer. With the chicken resting on the top, the potatoes in the broiler pan turned a deep brown and were crisp, almost like potato chips, but far tastier. A foil lining on the pan bottom, plus some vegetable

PREPARING A HIGH-ROAST BUTTERFLIED CHICKEN

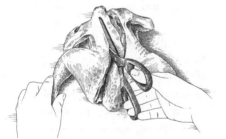

1. Using kitchen shears, cut along both sides of the backbone to remove it.

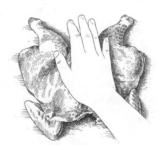

2. Flip the chicken over, use the heel of your hand to flatten the breastbone, and tuck the wings underneath.

3. Using your fingers, gently loosen the center portion of skin covering each side of the breast.

4. Using a spoon, place the butter underneath the skin.

5. Gently press on the skin to spread out the butter.

6. Transfer the chicken to a broiler-pan top and push each leg up to rest between the thigh and breast.

oil spray, helped with potato removal and cleanup. For a variation, we combined other root vegetables with the potatoes. Sweet potatoes, while offering great color and flavor, disintegrated under the high heat and extra fat, but celery root was a success.

With technique and our side dish resolved, it was time to work flavorings into the chicken. Clearly, anything on the surface of the chicken would burn at 500 degrees. Instead, we mixed garlic, herbs, and other bold flavors with some softened butter and placed it under the chicken skin before roasting. The flavored butter added subtle, welcome flavor, not only to the chicken but to the potatoes below as well (and we knew that butter under the skin also helps to keep the breast meat moist).

When all was said and done, we had roasted four dozen chickens and more than 60 pounds of potatoes, but we had accomplished what we had set out to do: We had five-star, perfectly browned roast chicken with spectacular skin—and a flavorful potato gratin too.

High-Roast Butterflied Chicken with Potato Gratin
SERVES 4

To use kosher salt in the brine, see page 34 for conversion information. Be sure to rinse the brined chicken thoroughly before cooking or the skin may burn. If using a kosher chicken, skip step 1, don't rinse the chicken in step 3, and season with salt in step 4. A food processor makes quick and easy work of slicing the potatoes.

½	cup sugar
	Table salt (see note)
1	(4½- to 5- pound) whole chicken, giblets discarded
2½	pounds russet or Yukon Gold potatoes (about 5 medium), peeled and sliced ⅛ to ¼ inch thick (see note)
2	tablespoons olive oil
	Ground black pepper
2	tablespoons unsalted butter or flavored butter (see the recipes on page 49), softened

1. Dissolve the sugar and ½ cup salt in 2 quarts cold water in a large container. Submerge the chicken in the brine, cover, and refrigerate for 1 to 1½ hours.

2. Adjust an oven rack to lower-middle position and heat the oven to 500 degrees. Line a broiler-pan bottom with aluminum foil and spray with vegetable oil spray (or use nonstick foil). Toss the potatoes with 1 tablespoon of the oil and season with salt and pepper to taste. Spread the potatoes evenly over the prepared broiler-pan bottom, and cover with the broiler-pan top.

3. Remove the chicken from the brine, rinse well, and pat dry with paper towels. Following the illustrations on page 43, butterfly the chicken, flatten the breastbone, and gently tuck the wings behind the back.

4. Gently loosen the center portion of skin covering each side of the breast. Using a spoon, place the butter underneath the skin, then gently press on the skin to spread out the butter. Place the chicken on the slotted broiler-pan top, brush with the remaining 1 tablespoon oil, and season with pepper. Push each leg up to rest between the thigh and breast.

5. Roast the chicken until the skin is crisped and deep brown and the breast registers 160 to 165 degrees and the thighs register 175 degrees on an instant-read thermometer, 40 to 45 minutes, rotating the pan halfway through roasting.

6. Transfer the chicken to a carving board and let rest for 10 minutes. Meanwhile, remove the broiler-pan top and, using paper towels, soak up any excess grease from the potatoes. Transfer the potatoes to a serving platter. Carve the chicken following the illustrations on page 41 and serve with the potatoes.

➤ VARIATION

High-Roast Butterflied Chicken with Potato and Celery Root Gratin
Follow the recipe for High-Roast Butterflied Chicken with Potato Gratin, substituting 1 pound celery root, peeled and sliced ⅛ to ¼ inch thick, for 1 pound of the potatoes.

Knowing When Meat and Poultry Are Done 101

While practiced chefs can often judge the doneness of meat and poultry by sight and/or touch, we find it is safer and a lot more accurate to use an instant-read thermometer. Here's what you need to know to make sure dinner is really ready.

A thermometer takes the guesswork out of knowing when meat or chicken is done. We always cook pork until it reaches 140 to 145 degrees, and we cook chicken until the breast registers 160 to 165 degrees and thighs register 175 degrees. Beef is more variable. The chart below presents the various ideal serving temperatures for meat and chicken. If food safety is your primary concern, cook all meat until well-done. As the meat rests before serving, the temperature will climb 5 to 10 degrees, with the temperature of smaller cuts climbing less than the temperature of larger roasts.

MEAT	COOK UNTIL	AFTER RESTING
CHICKEN AND TURKEY BREASTS	160 to 165 degrees	160 to 165 degrees
CHICKEN THIGHS	175 degrees	175 degrees
PORK	140 to 145 degrees	150 degrees
BEEF		
RARE	115 to 120 degrees	125 degrees
MEDIUM-RARE	120 to 125 degrees	130 degrees
MEDIUM	130 to 135 degrees	140 degrees
MEDIUM-WELL	140 to 145 degrees	150 degrees
WELL-DONE	150 to 155 degrees	160 degrees

CHOOSING AN INSTANT-READ THERMOMETER

Our test kitchen winner is fast (it registers temperatures from −58 to 572 degrees in seconds), accurate, and perfectly proportioned.

THE BEST INSTANT-READ THERMOMETER:
Thermoworks Splashproof Super-Fast Thermapen, $96

TAKING THE TEMPERATURE OF A STEAK OR CHOP

Hold the steak or chop with tongs and insert the thermometer through the side of the meat. You can also use this method with burgers and chicken.

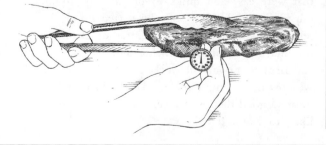

CARRYOVER EFFECT

When it comes to red meat and pork, judging doneness, even with a thermometer, involves some guesswork. That's because sometimes you aren't judging whether the food is ready to eat but whether it will be ready to eat once it has cooled or rested. For instance, to allow for juices to distribute themselves evenly, steaks, chops, and roasts should rest five to 20 minutes. (A steak needs less time than a big roast.) As meat rests, its temperature will climb. The thicker the cut, the more the temperature will rise. Also, food coming out of a very hot oven will have more residual heat than food coming out of a cooler oven.

TIPS FOR USING A THERMOMETER

• Regularly check accuracy by leaving the probe in a bucket of ice water for a minute or two. If the temperature doesn't register 32 degrees Fahrenheit, use the calibration button to reset the thermometer.

• Slide the probe deep into the center of foods, making sure that the tip does not exit the food.

• Avoid bones, cavities (say, in a turkey), and pan surfaces, all of which will throw off the reading.

• Take more than one reading, especially in large roasts and turkeys.

TAKING THE TEMPERATURE OF A ROAST

For many roasts, it's possible to slide the probe right through the meat and into the pan, which will give you a false reading. To make sure that the probe stays in the meat, insert the thermometer at an angle. Push the probe deep into the roast and then slowly draw it out, looking for the lowest temperature to find the center of the meat.

TAKING THE TEMPERATURE OF A CHICKEN OR TURKEY

Check the thickest part of the thigh and the breast. For a stuffed bird, insert the thermometer into the center of the cavity as well to make sure the stuffing has reached a safe temperature of 165 degrees.

ROASTED CHICKEN BREASTS WITH ROOT VEGETABLES

ROASTED BONE-IN, SKIN-ON CHICKEN breasts can be the ultimate simple-yet-elegant main course, especially when the meat is moist, tender, and well seasoned and the skin is crisp and golden brown. But the simplest dishes can also be the hardest—dry, chalky meat and rubbery skin are all too often the norm. Despite the demand, recipes for plain roasted chicken breasts are in short supply, and none we could find were flawless. We tested a half-dozen recipes, and it was clear that most of them use potent ingredients like herbs, spices, and citrus juice in an attempt to disguise the bland, dry meat. The skin on all of the breasts proved equally disappointing. Hints of crispness were overshadowed by mostly fatty, rubbery skin. Our goal was to create a recipe for simple roasted chicken breasts that would yield perfectly cooked meat and skin, along with a side of root vegetables for a homey and satisfying one-dish meal.

We started by simply roasting the breasts in the oven at a range of heat levels, from 350 degrees all the way up to 500 degrees, but the meat emerged bone-dry every time. Meanwhile, the visual difference among the chicken breasts from each test was glaring as soon as the breasts emerged from the oven. The skin on those roasted at 350 degrees was pale yellow and rubbery looking; the skin roasted at 500 degrees was burnt. The right temperature for perfect skin was clearly between these two extremes, but before we could think about crisp skin, we needed to find a way to keep the breast meat from turning to shoe leather.

As we found with our walk-away roast chicken (see page 39), brining the chicken in a solution of salt, sugar, and water ensured that the meat was moist and well seasoned throughout. The sugar in the brine also promotes caramelization of the skin, so our brine would help on several levels. Sure enough, the brined chicken retained its moisture, even when we increased the oven temperature. At 450 degrees, the highest temperature we could use without burning the skin, the brined meat was still juicy and the skin color improved, but the skin still wasn't as crisp as we wanted.

We knew from experience that cooking the chicken elevated on a wire rack over a rimmed baking sheet and separating the skin from the meat would allow hot air to circulate more freely, render more fat, and produce crispier skin. Now the color of the skin was appealing, but a crispy texture remained elusive.

We had been rubbing oil on the skin, as it helped with browning and crisping. Now we tried rubbing some under the skin as well. The results were even better. Next we tried butter instead of oil, and this was the best yet. The butter under the skin helped to keep the delicate breast meat juicy while adding flavor, and on top of the skin it helped encouraged better browning and also added flavor. Melting the butter for brushing over the skin's exterior ensured it was easy to work with.

Next we needed to address a familiar byproduct of the rendered fat from roasting chicken: smoke. The high temperature we were using to cook the chicken, as well as the additional butter used to crisp the skin, caused fat to drip into the baking sheet below our wire rack, where it burned and smoked up the kitchen. Putting root vegetables—potatoes, parsnips, and carrots—beneath the chicken absorbed any fat that dripped down. To better accommodate our vegetables, at this point we switched from a rimmed baking sheet to a 9 by 13-inch casserole dish. Roasting was now smoke-free, the meat was juicier, and we had a side dish for our meal. Since the vegetables didn't have quite enough time to cook through in the time the chicken was done, we gave them a head start in the microwave, as well as a little extra roasting time while the cooked chicken rested.

At last, we had perfectly roasted chicken breasts that were easy and quick to prepare. We found our recipe could also easily be varied simply by selecting a different flavored butter or changing the mix of vegetables (fennel, cauliflower, squash, and Brussels sprouts all worked well). Best of all, we now had a simple recipe that produced white meat so good that even lovers of dark meat were likely to take notice.

Roasted Chicken Breasts with Root Vegetables

SERVES 4

To use kosher salt in the brine, see page 34 for conversion information. If using kosher chicken, skip step 1, don't rinse the chicken in step 4, and season with salt in step 5. If your parsnips and carrots are very thick, slice them in half lengthwise first to ensure even cooking.

½ cup sugar
Table salt (see note)

4 (12-ounce) bone-in, skin-on split chicken breasts, trimmed (see the illustration on page 48)

1 pound red potatoes (about 3 medium), scrubbed and cut into 1-inch chunks

1 pound parsnips, peeled and cut into 1-inch lengths (see note)

1 pound carrots (about 6 medium), peeled and cut into 1-inch lengths

2 medium shallots (about 2 ounces), peeled and quartered

8 medium garlic cloves, peeled

2 teaspoons minced fresh rosemary leaves or ½ teaspoon dried

3 tablespoons olive oil
Ground black pepper

2 tablespoons unsalted butter or flavored butter (see the recipes on page 49), softened

2 tablespoons unsalted butter, melted
Lemon wedges, for serving

1. Dissolve the sugar and ½ cup salt in 2 quarts cold water in a large container. Submerge the chicken in the brine, cover, and refrigerate for 30 to 60 minutes.

2. Meanwhile, adjust an oven rack to the middle position and heat the oven to 450 degrees. Combine the potatoes, parsnips, carrots, and 3 tablespoons water in a microwave-safe bowl. Cover and microwave on high power, stirring occasionally, until the vegetables begin to soften, 10 to 15 minutes.

3. Drain the vegetables well, toss with the shallots, garlic, rosemary, and oil and season with salt and pepper to taste. Spread the vegetables into a 13 by 9-inch baking dish and top with a wire rack (the rack may overhang the dish slightly).

4. Remove the chicken from the brine, rinse, and pat dry with paper towels. Following the illustrations on page 12, gently loosen the center portion of skin covering each breast. Using a spoon, place the butter underneath the skin, then gently press on the skin to spread out the butter.

5. Lay the chicken on the wire rack, brush with the melted butter, and season with pepper. Roast the chicken and vegetables until the chicken registers 160 to 165 degrees on an instant-read thermometer, 30 to 35 minutes.

EQUIPMENT: Wire Racks

Here in the test kitchen, wire racks aren't reserved just for cooling cookies. We put wire racks to work day in and day out when making numerous savory recipes to turn a baking sheet into the perfect pan for broiling and roasting. Set inside a rimmed baking sheet, a wire rack will elevate food, allowing air to circulate fully around it and thus ensure even cooking and an exterior that doesn't become soggy from released juices.

A good rack should be sturdy, able to withstand a hot broiler, and clean up without warping or damage. It should also fit inside a standard 18 by 13-inch baking pan, which eliminated four of the six brands we purchased.

The two remaining products, the CIA Bakeware 12 x 17-Inch Cooling Rack ($15.95) and the Libertyware Cross Wire Cooking Rack Half-Sheet Pan Size ($5.25), performed well. The CIA rack offered extra support with a central brace and six feet rather than four. It also did not warp in the oven or dishwasher. It took top honors. But the more inexpensive rack from Libertyware is almost as good, and at one-third the price, it's our Best Buy.

THE BEST WIRE RACKS

CIA BAKEWARE

Our winner, the CIA Bakeware 12 x 17-Inch Cooling Rack ($15.95), fit perfectly inside a standard 18- by 13-inch rimmed baking sheet, and it offers extra support with a central brace and six feet rather than four.

6. Transfer the chicken to a carving board and let rest for 10 minutes. Meanwhile, continue to roast the vegetables until nicely browned, about 10 minutes. Serve the chicken and vegetables with the lemon wedges.

➤ VARIATIONS

**Roasted Chicken Breasts with
Red Potatoes, Fennel, and Cauliflower**
Follow the recipe for Roasted Chicken Breasts with Root Vegetables, substituting 1 fennel bulb (about 12 ounces), trimmed of stalks, cored, and sliced thin (see the illustrations on page 38), and ½ medium head cauliflower, trimmed, cored, and cut into 1-inch florets, for the carrots and parsnips. Omit the rosemary and sprinkle with 1 tablespoon minced fresh tarragon before serving.

**Roasted Chicken Breasts with Squash,
Carrots, and Brussels Sprouts**
Follow the recipe for Roasted Chicken Breasts with Root Vegetables, substituting ½ medium butternut squash, peeled, seeded, and cut into 1-inch chunks (about 2 cups), and 10 ounces Brussels sprouts, trimmed and halved, for the potatoes and parsnips. Substitute 1 tablespoon minced fresh thyme for the rosemary.

TRIMMING SPLIT CHICKEN BREASTS

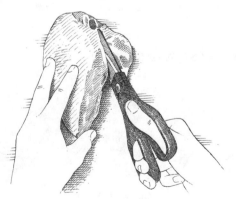

Using kitchen shears, trim the rib sections from each breast following the vertical line of fat from the tapered end of the breast up to the socket where the wing was attached.

CRISPY CHICKEN THIGHS WITH SNAP PEAS

WHEN IT COMES TO EASY WEEKNIGHT MEALS, chicken breasts are always quick to come to mind. Thighs, by contrast, are typically associated with dishes that spend hours simmering on the stove— think slow-cooked stews and braises. But roasted chicken thighs have moist, well-seasoned meat and crisp skin and, as a bonus, they are inexpensive and much less prone to drying out than lean breast meat. We thought chicken thighs would make a great centerpiece for a one-dish weeknight meal. Our goals were simple: We wanted crisp, golden skin; moist, tender meat; and a vegetable sidekick that would be done to perfection at the same time as the chicken.

We quickly discovered that the difficulties with roasting chicken thighs relate directly to the level of heat. If the oven is too hot, achieving crisp skin can be difficult because it doesn't have enough time to render its fat, but if the oven is too low, the meat will cook through before the skin is browned and crisped. Roasting the thighs at 450 degrees yielded the best results: the meat was perfectly moist and tender after just 30 minutes and the skin was golden brown, although it wasn't quite crisp enough for our liking. To solve this problem, we tried finishing the chicken under the direct heat of the broiler. We were definitely pleased with the crisp texture, but the skin still seemed a bit too thick and fatty. Remembering a technique we have used when cooking duck, we tried slashing the skin a few times before placing the thighs in the oven. This trick worked like a charm; the skin rendered even more fat, leaving it thin and crisp.

Although the roasted thighs were good seasoned with salt and pepper, we wanted them to really shine. From our testing with roasted chicken breasts (see page 46), we knew that rubbing a flavored butter under the skin was an easy way to add flavor and increase moisture. We simply rubbed the butter directly on the meat (under the skin) before slashing the skin.

Now it was time to complete our dish, and green beans seemed like the perfect accompaniment to this weeknight family meal. As with our High-Roast Butterflied Chicken with Potato Gratin (page 44), we tried spreading the beans in the bottom of the broiler pan and placing the chicken on the pan top. Since green beans can't withstand the entire cooking time, we added them, tossed with a tablespoon of oil, toward the end, just for the time the chicken went under the broiler. Unfortunately, this wasn't quite enough time. We wanted to keep our recipe simple so we wondered if snap peas, with their short cooking time, would be a better choice. The first test was promising. After five minutes under the broiler, the snap peas were perfectly cooked and crisp tender, but they were mired in a greasy mess of oil and rendered chicken fat. For our next test we eliminated the step of tossing the snap peas in oil before cooking, and we drained the rendered fat from the pan before adding the snap peas. This was a big improvement, and the peas still got plenty of flavor from the fat that rendered during the final

---

FLAVORED BUTTERS FOR ROAST CHICKEN

FLAVORED BUTTERS, ALSO CALLED COMPOUND BUTTERS, ARE AN EASY WAY TO ADD flavor to simple roast chicken. All of these recipes make enough for one recipe Walk-Away Roast Chicken with Potatoes (page 41), High-Roast Butterflied Chicken with Potato Gratin (page 44), Roasted Chicken Breasts with Root Vegetables (page 47), or Crispy Chicken Thighs with Snap Peas (page 50).

Orange-Rosemary Butter
MAKES ABOUT 2 TABLESPOONS

2   tablespoons unsalted butter, softened
2   medium garlic cloves, minced or pressed
    through a garlic press (about 2 teaspoons)
2   teaspoons minced fresh rosemary leaves
1   teaspoon grated zest from 1 orange

Combine all the ingredients in a small bowl.

Lemon-Thyme Butter
MAKES ABOUT 2 TABLESPOONS

2   tablespoons unsalted butter, softened
2   teaspoons minced fresh thyme leaves
1   medium garlic clove, minced or pressed
    through a garlic press (about 1 teaspoon)
1   teaspoon grated zest from 1 lemon

Combine all the ingredients in a small bowl.

Southwestern-Flavored Butter
MAKES ABOUT 2 TABLESPOONS

2   tablespoons unsalted butter, softened
2   teaspoons chili powder
1   medium garlic clove, minced or pressed
    through a garlic press (about 1 teaspoon)
1   teaspoon minced fresh oregano leaves
1   teaspoon ground cumin
¼   teaspoon cayenne pepper

Combine all the ingredients in a small bowl.

Asian-Flavored Butter
MAKES ABOUT 2 TABLESPOONS

2   tablespoons unsalted butter, softened
2   teaspoons minced or grated fresh ginger
    (see the illustrations on page 216)
1   medium garlic clove, minced or pressed
    through a garlic press (about 1 teaspoon)
½   teaspoon five-spice powder

Combine all the ingredients in a small bowl.

minutes of broiling, as well as from the compound butter that dripped down from the chicken. By immediately transferring the peas to a serving bowl, we stopped them from overcooking and preserved their wonderful, crisp-tender texture. A final toss with some rice vinegar gave the snap peas a bright splash of acidity.

Crispy Chicken Thighs with Snap Peas

SERVES 4

To use kosher salt in the brine, see page 34 for conversion information. If using kosher chicken, skip step 1, don't rinse the chicken in step 3, and season with salt in step 4. Be sure to transfer the cooked snap peas to a serving dish immediately to avoid overcooking.

½	cup sugar
	Table salt (see note)
8	(6-ounce) bone-in, skin-on chicken thighs, trimmed
2	tablespoons unsalted butter or flavored butter (see the recipes on page 49), softened
1	tablespoon olive oil
	Ground black pepper
1	pound snap peas, stems and strings removed (see the illustration at right)
2	teaspoons rice vinegar

1. Dissolve the sugar and ½ cup salt in 2 quarts cold water in a large container. Submerge the chicken in the brine, cover, and refrigerate for 30 to 60 minutes.

2. Adjust an oven rack to the middle position and heat the oven to 450 degrees. Line a broiler-pan bottom with aluminum foil and cover with the broiler-pan top.

3. Remove the chicken from the brine, rinse, and pat dry with paper towels. Gently loosen the center portion of skin covering each thigh. Using a spoon, place the butter underneath the skin, then gently press on the skin to spread out the butter. Lay the chicken, skin side up, on the broiler-pan top.

4. Following the illustration at right, make 3 diagonal slashes through the skin of each thigh with a sharp knife (do not cut into the meat). Brush the chicken with the oil and season with pepper. Roast until the chicken registers 165 degrees on an instant-read thermometer, 30 to 40 minutes.

5. Remove the chicken from the oven. Position an oven rack 6 inches from the broiler element and heat the broiler. While the broiler heats, remove the broiler-pan top with the chicken from the pan bottom and set aside. Drain the fat from the broiler-pan bottom, spread the snap peas into the pan, and season with salt and pepper to taste. Place the broiler-pan top with the chicken over the pan of peas.

6. Broil the chicken until the skin is crisp and the thighs register 175 degrees, 5 to 10 minutes. Transfer the chicken to a carving board and let rest for 5 minutes. Transfer the snap peas to a serving bowl, toss with the vinegar, and serve with the chicken.

STRINGING SNOW PEAS AND SNAP PEAS

Snap off the tip of the snow pea or snap pea while pulling down along the flat side of the pod to remove the string.

ENSURING CRISP-SKINNED THIGHS

Make 3 diagonal slashes in the skin of each piece of chicken to help render the fat.

3

DUTCH OVEN DINNERS

DUTCH OVEN DINNERS

CLASSIC POT ROAST WITH ROOT VEGETABLES

A GENUINELY GOOD POT ROAST ENTAILS the transformation of a tough (read cheap), nearly unpalatable cut of meat into a tender, rich, flavorful roast by means of braising. And since pot roast typically includes some vegetables and produces its own sauce, it's one of the all-time great one-pot suppers. It also, unfortunately, has garnered a rather dubious reputation for delivering stringy, dry meat, insipid flavor, and mushy vegetables. In the hope of earning this classic dish a place back on the dinner table, we set about determining the right cut of beef, proper cooking temperature, ideal braising liquid, and a superlative mix of vegetables.

The meat for pot roast should be well marbled with fat and connective tissue in order to provide the dish with necessary flavor and moisture. Recipes typically call for roasts from the sirloin (rump), round (leg), or chuck (shoulder). So we began by cooking a dozen cuts from these three sections in order to find the right one. From the sirloin, we tested the bottom-rump roast and top sirloin. These two lean cuts packed great beef flavor but lacked the richness we expect from pot roast. The round cuts—top round, bottom round, and eye round—had more fat running through them than the sirloin cuts, but the meat never quite achieved the fall-apart tenderness we were after. In the end, we found that the chuck cuts (boneless chuck-eye roast, seven-bone roast, and top blade roast) cooked up the most tender. The high proportion of fat and connective tissue in these cuts gave the meat much-needed moisture as well as a superior flavor. Ultimately, we crowned the boneless chuck-eye roast our winner because it is easy to find in supermarkets and it also requires minimal preparation.

But even with the right cut, we still had a problem. Following the direction of a few recipes, we braised our chuck-eye roast for four hours, and while the meat was certainly tender, there were still undesirable pockets of fat and connective tissue throughout. We wondered what would happen if we split the large cylindrical roast into two sleeker halves. Dividing the roast into two fairly equal pieces is easy, as the seam of fat that runs down the center of the roast acts as a built-in guide. We trimmed the obvious pieces of fat from each lobe, leaving a thin layer of fat on top, and tied each piece to keep it from falling apart during braising. With less extraneous fat, these two roasts definitely cooked up better than one.

To make the most out of our humble chuck-eye roasts, which would do most of their cooking at low temperature, we decided to first sear them on the stovetop. This step developed a well-caramelized exterior and left us with flavorful fond (the browned bits stuck to the bottom of the pot) we could use to build our braising liquid.

There were two main questions concerning the liquid: what kind and how much was needed to best cook the roast and create a flavorful sauce. We had started our testing with a modest ¼ cup of water, as suggested in a few recipes. This produced a roast that was fibrous, even after hours of cooking. After increasing the amount of liquid incrementally, we found that the moistest meat was produced when we added enough liquid to come halfway up the sides of the roast (3 to 3½ cups of liquid for a 3½- to 4-pound roast). Flipping the meat once during cooking ensured that the roast cooked evenly and became tender throughout.

Next we tested different liquids, hoping to give the roast and the sauce a flavor boost. In addition to the water, we tried chicken broth, beef broth, and red wine. Each broth failed to win tasters over when used on its own—the chicken broth was rich but gave the dish a distinct poultry flavor, while the beef broth made the dish taste a bit sour. We found that an equal amount of each did the job, and tasters also liked the addition of a little red wine after the roast was removed from the pot (added any earlier and its flavor penetrated the meat too deeply). Some sautéed onion, celery, and garlic added another layer of flavor to the braising liquid.

To go from braising liquid to sauce, many recipes use a thickener (either a roux or a slurry of cornstarch mixed with a little braising liquid). Both techniques made the sauce more gravylike than we preferred. We chose to remove the roast from the pot once it had finished cooking, then reduce the liquid until the flavors were concentrated and the sauce had thickened naturally.

Pot roast can be cooked either on the stovetop or in the oven, but after a few rounds of stovetop cooking, we felt it was too difficult to maintain a steady temperature and low simmer. Turning to the oven, we began pot-roasting at 250 degrees. This worked sometimes, but, as with the stovetop method, the results were inconsistent since it's difficult to maintain a constant simmer at such a low temperature. We then tested higher temperatures in the hope of achieving greater consistency and reducing the cooking time. Heat levels above 350 degrees boiled the meat to a stringy, dry texture as the exterior of the roast overcooked before the interior was cooked and tender. The magic temperature turned out to be 300 degrees—high enough to keep the broth at a bare simmer but low enough to prevent the meat from drying out.

Pot roast is well-done meat—it should be cooked to an internal temperature well above 165 degrees.

Up to this point, we had been bringing the meat up to an internal temperature of 200 to 210 degrees, the point at which the fat and connective tissue begin to melt. In a 300-degree oven, the roast hit that temperature in about 2½ hours, but the meat was still not fall-apart tender. We wondered what would happen if we cooked it even longer. Slowly increasing the cooking time, we found that between 3 and 3½ hours, the internal temperature of the roast was still 210 degrees, but the meat had a substantially different appearance and texture. The roast was so tender that it was starting to separate along its muscle lines. A fork poked into the meat met with no resistance and nearly disappeared into the flesh. We took the roast out of the pot and sliced into it. Nearly all the fat and connective tissue had dissolved into the meat, giving each bite a soft, silky texture and rich flavor. The conclusion? Not only do you have to cook pot roast until it reaches 210 degrees, but the meat has to remain at that temperature for a full hour. In other words, cook the pot roast until it's done—and then keep on cooking.

While we were more than happy with our unctuous, fall-apart roasts and intensely flavored sauce, our work wasn't finished. We wanted a mix of hearty vegetables that would complement the meat

PREPARING A POT ROAST

Chuck-eye roast has great flavor, but we found that the interior fat is best trimmed before cooking. Simply pull the roast apart at the natural seam and trim away large knobs of fat from each half.

1. Pull the roast apart at its major seams (delineated by lines of fat) into 2 halves. Use a sharp knife as necessary.

2. Using a knife, remove the large knobs of fat from each piece, leaving a thin layer of fat on the meat.

3. Tie 3 pieces of butcher's twine around each piece of meat to prevent them from falling apart as they cook.

and help round out this one-dish supper. Since pot roast is often served with either mashed or boiled potatoes, they seemed like a natural place to start. Yet, while we love russets mashed or boiled, they turned into a mushy mess when cooked in the braise. Skin-on red potatoes, on the other hand, held their shape beautifully and provided welcome creamy bites. To balance the rich, hearty flavors of the dish, we looked to some of the sweeter root vegetables, namely turnips, carrots, and parsnips. Tasters found turnips bland, but loved a combination of carrots and parsnips. By cutting the vegetables in half and adding them after the roast had cooked for two hours, we ensured that everything emerged tender at the same time.

After some minor kitchen alchemy, we had turned an inexpensive cut of beef and a handful of humble root vegetables into a hearty meal, complete with a side dish and sauce. Perhaps most remarkable is the fact that it was all created in just one pot.

EQUIPMENT: Slicing Knives

No other knife can cut with such precision in a single stroke as a carving knife, which is specially designed to cut neatly through meat's muscle fibers and connective tissues. We recently set out to find the best, and based on previous knife-testing experience, we were already aware of key attributes to look for: an extra-long, sturdy, tapered blade with a round tip for easy, trouble-free strokes; a granton edge, which means the knife has oval scallops carved into both sides of the blade, making a thinner edge possible without sacrificing the heft and rigidity carried by the top of the blade—perfect for producing thinner slices with little effort; and, finally, a comfortable handle. After we tested nine knives that fit these criteria, one knife came out in front, scoring top points in slicing, sharpness, and comfort.

THE BEST SLICING KNIFE

Our favorite model, the Victorinox (formerly Victorinox Forschner) Fibrox 12-Inch Granton Edge Slicing Knife ($39.95), produces thin, uniform slices of meat every time.

VICTORINOX

Classic Pot Roast with Root Vegetables

SERVES 6 TO 8

Use a good-quality, medium-bodied wine, such as a Côtes du Rhône or Pinot Noir, for this dish.

1	(3½- to 4-pound) boneless beef chuck-eye roast, pulled apart into 2 roasts, trimmed, and tied (see the illustrations on page 54)
	Salt and ground black pepper
3	tablespoons vegetable oil
1	medium onion, chopped medium
1	celery rib, chopped medium
4	medium garlic cloves, minced or pressed through a garlic press (about 4 teaspoons)
2	teaspoons sugar
1	teaspoon fresh minced thyme leaves or ¼ teaspoon dried
1	cup low-sodium chicken broth
1	cup beef broth
1	cup water
1½	pounds carrots (about 9), peeled and cut into 3- to 4-inch lengths
1½	pounds red potatoes (4 to 5 medium), scrubbed cut into 1½-inch pieces
1½	pounds parsnips, peeled and cut into 3- to 4-inch lengths
⅓	cup dry red wine (see note)

1. Adjust an oven rack to the lower-middle position and heat the oven to 300 degrees. Pat the beef dry with paper towels and season with salt and pepper. Heat 2 tablespoons of the oil in a large Dutch oven over medium-high heat until just smoking. Brown both roasts on all sides, 7 to 10 minutes; transfer to a large plate.

2. Add the remaining tablespoon oil, onion, and celery to the pot and cook over medium heat until softened, 5 to 7 minutes. Stir in the garlic, sugar, and thyme and cook until fragrant, about 30 seconds. Stir in the broths and water, scraping up any browned bits.

3. Add the browned roasts with any accumulated juice to the pot and bring to a simmer. Cover,

transfer the pot to the oven, and cook for 2 hours, turning the roasts over halfway through the roasting time.

4. Nestle the carrots into the pot around the meat and sprinkle the potatoes and parsnips over the top. Continue to cook, covered, until the meat and vegetables are very tender, 1 to 1½ hours longer.

5. Remove the pot from the oven. Transfer the vegetables to a large bowl, season with salt and pepper to taste, and cover to keep warm. Transfer the roasts to a carving board, tent loosely with aluminum foil, and let rest while finishing the sauce.

6. Defat the braising liquid following one of the methods on page 65 (if necessary, return the defatted liquid to the pot). Stir in the wine and simmer until the sauce measures 2 cups, about 15 minutes. Season with salt and pepper to taste.

7. Remove the twine from the roasts, cut the meat against the grain into ¼-inch-thick slices, and serve with the vegetables and sauce.

BEEF EN COCOTTE WITH CREAMY MUSHROOM BARLEY

A FEW YEARS AGO WE DISCOVERED A FRENCH cooking technique called *en cocotte* and were immediately drawn to its simplicity. Loosely translated as casserole-roasting, cooking en cocotte entails placing a seasoned, browned piece of beef (or other large roast) in a large Dutch oven, scattering in a handful of chopped aromatics, covering the pot, and baking it in a low oven. Without any additional liquid, juice is drawn from the meat into the pot where they concentrate and gently cook the meat. The result is an incredibly tender medium-rare roast and a flavorful jus. In a break from tradition, we decided to adapt cooking en cocotte to a one-dish supper by preparing a side dish in the same pot as the roast. While root vegetables seemed like an obvious choice for a beef roast, we wanted to see if we could take advantage of this method to prepare another complement to beef, creamy barley. If we were successful we would be adding a unique dish to our one-pot repertoire. We started our testing with the beef.

Two inexpensive roasts immediately came to mind as possibilities for this method: eye round roast (a lean cut from the leg) and top sirloin roast (a lean, beefy cut often used for grill-roasting). To determine which roast we liked best, we seared each in a large Dutch oven, then placed the covered pot in a 250-degree oven (our preferred temperature for cooking en cocotte). Cooked to medium-rare, the eye round roast was still tough despite its rosy interior. Top sirloin was far and away the best option as it was noticeably more tender, with concentrated beef flavor. Sticking with top sirloin, we settled on a 3- to 4-pound roast (enough to serve six to eight people), which we trimmed of excess fat and then tied prior to searing to help ensure even cooking. (To make the tied roast fit easily into the pot, we tied it just once around the middle to make it round; see illustration on page 58.) To our surprise, this roast hit 125 degrees in only 25 minutes. While certainly convenient, this short cooking time seemed insufficient for turning barley from a tough grain to a tender, creamy dish. Undeterred, we ordered some barley and started testing.

Similar to rice, barley is available in a few different forms, each of which represents a different level of processing. Hulled barley, which is sold with the hull removed and the bran intact, is the least refined, followed by pearl (or pearled) barley, which is hulled barley that has been polished to remove the bran. Then there is quick-cooking barley (similar to instant rice), which is parcooked and available as kernels or flakes. Again like rice, the level of processing dictates cooking time and, ultimately, texture. To determine which barley would produce the best creamy side dish, we cooked up a batch of each type using a modified risotto method. We added all of the broth in the beginning, simmered the barley gently until tender, and stirred vigorously at the end to achieve a creamy consistency.

Pearl barley quickly separated itself from the pack, cooking up into a satisfying dish, dotted with tender grains of barley. Hulled barley, on the other hand, retained its chew no matter how long we simmered it, and the protective bran prevented surface starch from dissolving into a creamy sauce. Quick-cooking barley was plagued by just the opposite problem, quickly dissolving into a porridgelike mush that seemed more appropriate for a hearty breakfast than a side dish for beef.

However, even with our preferred barley in hand, we still had a problem. The beef had cooked to medium-rare in about 25 minutes, while the pearl barley took about an hour to reach al dente. Unwilling to use a separate pot to cook the barley or add the beef partway through cooking, we went for the long shot and added them at same time. After searing the beef and sautéing the barley with some onion, we deglazed the pot with cognac (a natural choice for beef), stirred in some beef broth, and placed the browned roast on top. Following our en cocotte method, we pressed foil over the Dutch oven, popped on the lid, and slid it into a 250-degree oven. After 25 minutes, we temped the beef and were surprised to find that it barely registered 80 degrees. After another 25 minutes, it was a hair under 120 degrees, so we let it cook for five more minutes (making a full 60 minutes) to reach a perfect medium rare. And in that time the barley had become tender with a satisfying bite.

How was this drastic change in the meat's cooking time possible? It turns out that starchy barley absorbs and transfers heat much more slowly than water vapor. While our test roasts were left alone in a pot filled with hot steam, this roast was surrounded by a protective, insulating layer of barley. This slower transfer of heat meant the roast needed more than twice as long to cook, coincidentally the amount of time it took the barley to become tender. And since our roast needed 20 minutes to rest, we had plenty of time to stir the tender barley until its outer starch layer dissolved into a luxurious sauce.

Now we needed to add flavor to the meat and barley. A complementary ingredient to both ingredients is mushrooms, which lend meatiness and earthy undertones. For great mushroom texture and flavor, we sautéed both white mushrooms and dried porcini mushrooms with the onions. Tasters liked this barley but complained that it tasted overly beefy and a little one-note. To rein in the beefiness, we experimented with different ratios of beef broth, chicken broth, and water, finally settling on 2 cups of beef broth and 1 cup each of chicken broth and water. This cooking liquid provided rich meatiness without any of the sour beef flavor tasters disliked. To add depth, we looked to a few of our favorite aromatics: garlic, thyme, and tomato paste. Cooked until fragrant, this aromatic trifecta boosted the barley's flavor. Finally, a flourish of shredded Parmesan cheese stirred in at the end added complexity and creaminess. After all of our hard work adding depth and richness, tasters started to complain that the dish lacked brightness. When a simple squeeze of fresh lemon juice only served to detract from the beefiness of the dish, we took a different approach. Inspired by the South American herb and vinegar sauce chimichurri, often used to cut the richness of grilled steaks, we created a bright, complex sauce with parsley, sherry, oil, and garlic. Drizzled over the sliced beef, this final touch was the perfect accent to our elegant new one-pot supper.

RINSING RICE AND GRAINS

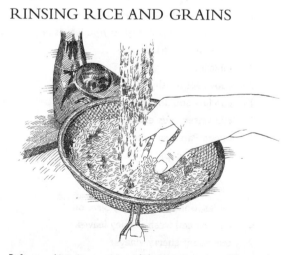

Before cooking rice or grains, it's best to rinse them. This washes away any excess starch and prevents the final dish from turning out sticky or gummy. Simply place the rice or grains in a fine-mesh strainer and rinse under cool water until the water runs clear, occasionally stirring the rice or grains around lightly with your hand. Set the strainer of rinsed rice or grains over a bowl and let drain until needed.

Beef en Cocotte with Creamy Mushroom Barley

SERVES 6 TO 8

To keep the barley from becoming greasy, trim the beef well. We prefer this roast cooked to medium-rare, but if you prefer it more or less done, see our guidelines in the chart on page 45. Be sure to use a Dutch oven with a tight-fitting lid.

BEEF

1	(3- to 4-pound) boneless top sirloin beef roast, trimmed and tied once around the middle (see the illustration below)
	Salt and ground black pepper
3	tablespoons vegetable oil
8	ounces white mushrooms, wiped clean, trimmed, and sliced thin
1¼	cups pearl barley, rinsed (see the illustration on page 57)
1	medium onion, chopped medium
½	ounce dried porcini mushrooms, rinsed and minced
3	medium garlic cloves, minced or pressed through a garlic press (about 1 tablespoon)
1	tablespoon tomato paste
1	teaspoon minced fresh thyme leaves or ¼ teaspoon dried
3	tablespoons cognac
2	cups beef broth
1	cup low-sodium chicken broth
1	cup water, plus extra as needed
1	ounce Parmesan cheese, grated (about ½ cup)

SAUCE

5	tablespoons extra-virgin olive oil
¼	cup minced fresh parsley leaves
2	teaspoons sherry vinegar
1	medium garlic clove, minced or pressed through a garlic press (about 1 teaspoon)
	Salt and ground black pepper

1. **FOR THE BEEF**: Adjust an oven rack to the lowest position and heat the oven to 250 degrees. Pat the beef dry with paper towels and season with salt and pepper. Heat 2 tablespoons of the oil in a large Dutch oven over medium-high heat until just smoking. Brown the beef on all sides, 7 to 10 minutes; transfer to a large plate.

2. Add the remaining tablespoon oil, white mushrooms, barley, onion, and porcini mushrooms to the pot and cook over medium heat until softened, 5 to 7 minutes. Stir in the garlic, tomato paste, and thyme and cook until fragrant, about 30 seconds. Stir in the cognac, scraping up any browned bits, and cook until almost completely evaporated, about 30 seconds. Stir in the broths and water and bring to a simmer.

3. Off the heat, add the browned beef with any accumulated juice to the pot. Place a large sheet of aluminum foil over the pot and press to seal, then cover tightly with the lid. Transfer the pot to the oven and cook until the center of the roast registers 120 to 125 degrees on an instant-read thermometer (for medium-rare), 60 to 80 minutes.

TYING TOP SIRLOIN FOR EN COCOTTE

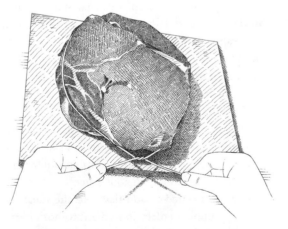

To help the roast fit easily into the round pot, and to ensure even cooking, tie a piece of butcher's twine around the center of the roast.

4. Remove the pot from the oven. Transfer the beef to a carving board, tent loosely with foil, and let rest 20 minutes. (If the barley is underdone, continue to cook over medium heat, adding additional water as needed, until tender.) Stir the Parmesan into the barley and cook over medium heat until creamy, 1 to 2 minutes. Season with salt and pepper to taste, and cover to keep warm.

5. FOR THE SAUCE: Whisk all the sauce ingredients together in a bowl and season with salt and pepper to taste. Remove the twine from the beef and cut against the grain into ¼-inch-thick slices. Serve the beef with the barley and sauce.

DUTCH OVEN BEEF POT PIE

WE LOVE BEEF POT PIE. WHEN TENDER HUNKS of slow-cooked beef, chunks of hearty root vegetables, and a rich, meaty gravy rendezvous under a buttery roof of flaky pie crust, there is little in this world that can stop us from grabbing our forks and digging in. As a result, we are always looking for ways to put this beefy, comforting dish on the dinner table more often. The reason it only shows up a few times year isn't so much the cooking time (which is largely hands-off) but rather the multitude of pots, pans, and dishes it requires. First, you need a pot or skillet to brown the beef and aromatics, a couple of pots for making the roux-thickened gravy and blanching vegetables, and ultimately a casserole dish in which to assemble and bake the pie. We wanted a recipe that could feed a crowd (or leave us with some leftovers) and produce a pot pie with all of the rich, beefy flavor of the classic, using only a Dutch oven.

Since beef pot pie is first and foremost about the beef, picking the right cut was an essential first step. Using prepackaged "stew meat" from the supermarket was a nonstarter; the jumble of scraggly bits and large chunks were impossible to cook evenly.

Cuts like tenderloin, strip, or rib eye turned mealy with prolonged cooking; they were better reserved for searing or grilling. More esoteric cuts like hanger or skirt steak offered great flavor, but their texture was too stringy. Well-marbled blade steaks and short ribs worked well, but in the end were deemed no better than chuck-eye roast. It's one of the cheapest, beefiest cuts in the supermarket, and it turns meltingly tender when it's properly cooked. With our star in the wings, we set about building a one-pot pie.

In our early tests, one taster noted that beef pot pie is a lot like beef stew with a layer of pastry on top. And while it can be argued that there are differences in consistency and ingredients between the two, the idea got us thinking. Since we build most of our stews in just one pot, maybe beef stew was a good place to begin. First, we browned cubes of chuck-eye roast in a large Dutch oven, which deepened the meat's flavor and also produced a dark fond that would form the foundation of the gravy. Continuing with our beef stew method, we then softened onion, stirred in flour to form a roux, and deglazed the pot with red wine and a combination of chicken and beef broth. Finally, we returned the beef to the pot, popped on the lid, and transferred the pot to a 300-degree oven. After about 2½ hours of gentle simmering (with 1-inch pieces of carrot added halfway through), we had tender meat and vegetables and richly flavored gravy. Feeling good about our beef stew approach up to this point, we focused on the pie dough topping.

In an ideal one-pot scenario, we would put raw pie dough (no parbaking required) directly on the partially cooked filling and bake the pie until the crust was golden and the meat and vegetables tender. With this goal in mind, we rolled out a recipe of our traditional pie dough to ¼-inch thickness, trimmed it to measure 11 inches across, and crimped the edge so that it would fit in the pot. But even with the right size dough round, we had a hard time lowering it into the pot. To make transferring possible, we froze the shaped crust until stiff, making it much easier to handle. With our crust in place we returned the pot to the oven until it developed a lovely golden patina, which, given such a low oven temperature, took about an hour and 20 minutes. Since we were already removing the pot from the oven halfway through cooking to add the carrots, this was a perfect time to add the crust as well. Having cleared the crust hurdle we moved on to fine-tuning our filling.

First, we added 1-inch chunks of celery root with the carrots to give the stew more hearty vegetable presence. To "beef up" our beef pot pie, we took another page from our beef stews and included a few umami-rich ingredients: mushrooms, anchovies, and tomato paste. We sautéed half a pound of white mushrooms with the onions and then stirred in a minced anchovy and a tablespoon of tomato paste. While the anchovy might seem out of place, it added rich meatiness (not fishiness) to the filling. Countless pounds of beef (but only one pot) later, we had arrived at our ultimate Dutch oven beef pot pie.

TOPPING A DUTCH OVEN POT PIE WITH PIE CRUST

Gently place the frozen Dutch Oven Pot Pie Crust on top of the filling in the pot.

Dutch Oven Beef Pot Pie
SERVES 6 TO 8

You can use either homemade or store-bought pie dough for the crust; see store-bought dough instructions in the Dutch Oven Pot Pie Crust recipe (page 61). Do not let the pie sit after stirring in the celery root and carrots; the filling must be hot when the frozen crust is placed on top.

1   (3-pound) boneless beef chuck-eye roast, trimmed and cut into 1-inch pieces (see illustrations on page 133)
    Salt and ground black pepper
3   tablespoons vegetable oil
8   ounces white mushrooms, wiped clean, trimmed, and quartered
1   medium onion, chopped medium
3   garlic cloves, minced or pressed through a garlic press (about 1 tablespoon)
1   medium anchovy fillet, rinsed and minced
2   teaspoons minced fresh thyme leaves or ½ teaspoon dried
⅓   cup unbleached all-purpose flour
1   tablespoon tomato paste
¾   cup dry red wine
1¾ cups low-sodium chicken broth
1¾ cups beef broth
1   pound celery root, peeled and cut into 1-inch pieces
3   carrots, peeled and cut into 1-inch pieces
1   recipe Dutch Oven Pot Pie Crust (page 61), frozen for at least 30 minutes

1. Adjust an oven rack to the lower-middle position and heat the oven to 300 degrees. Pat the beef dry with paper towels and season with salt and pepper.

2. Heat 1 tablespoon of the oil in a large Dutch oven over medium-high heat until just smoking. Add half of the beef and brown on all sides, 7 to 10 minutes; transfer to a large bowl. Repeat with 1 more tablespoon oil and the remaining beef; transfer to the bowl.

3. Add the remaining tablespoon oil, mushrooms, and onion to the pot and cook over medium heat until softened and lightly browned, 7 to 10 minutes. Stir in the garlic, anchovy, and thyme and cook until fragrant, about 30 seconds. Stir in the flour and tomato paste and cook for 1 minute.

4. Stir in the wine, scraping up any browned bits, and cook until almost completely evaporated, about 1 minute. Gradually whisk in the broths, smoothing out any lumps. Add the browned beef with any accumulated juice and bring to a simmer. Cover, transfer the pot to the oven, and cook for 1¼ hours.

5. Remove the pot from the oven. Season the filling with salt and pepper to taste, then stir in the celery root and carrots. Following the illustration on page 60, place the frozen crust directly on top of the filling in the pot. Bake until the crust is golden, about 80 minutes. Let the pot pie cool for 20 minutes before serving.

Dutch Oven Pot Pie Crust

MAKES 1 CRUST

We prefer the buttery flavor and flaky texture of homemade dough here; however, you can substitute store-bought pie dough if desired. If using store-bought pie dough, roll it into an 11-inch circle on parchment paper, then shape and freeze as directed in step 4. Before cutting and shaping the dough as directed in step 4, be sure to measure the width of your pot, so that the crust will fit nicely.

1¼	cups (6¼ ounces) unbleached all-purpose flour
1	tablespoon sugar
½	teaspoon salt
3	tablespoons vegetable shortening, cut into ½-inch pieces and chilled
5	tablespoons unsalted butter, cut into ¼-inch pieces and chilled
4–6	tablespoons ice water

1. Process the flour, sugar, and salt together in a food processor until combined. Scatter the shortening over the top and process until the mixture resembles coarse cornmeal, about 10 seconds. Scatter the butter pieces over the top and pulse until the

MAKING A DUTCH OVEN POT PIE CRUST

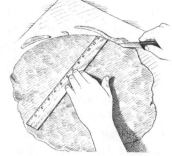

1. Roll the dough out to a ¼-inch-thick round on a large piece of parchment paper. Leaving the dough on the parchment, use a paring knife to trim the dough into a circle that is the same diameter as the width of the pot used to make the filling.

2. Fold back the outer ½-inch rim of the dough.

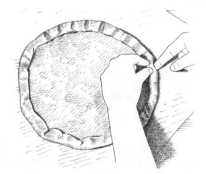

3. Using your knuckles and forefingers, crimp the folded edge of the dough to make an attractive fluted rim.

4. Using a paring knife, cut 4 oval-shaped vents, each about 3 inches long and ½ inch wide, in the center of the dough.

mixture resembles coarse crumbs, about 10 pulses. Transfer the mixture to a medium bowl.

2. Sprinkle 4 tablespoons of the ice water over the mixture. Stir and press the dough together, using a stiff rubber spatula, until it sticks together. If the dough does not come together, stir in the remaining water, 1 tablespoon at a time.

3. Turn the dough onto a sheet of plastic wrap and flatten into a 4-inch disk. Wrap the dough tightly in plastic wrap and refrigerate for at least 1 hour or up to 2 days. Before rolling the dough out, let it sit on the counter to soften slightly, about 10 minutes. Roll the dough out to a ¼-inch-thick round on a large piece of parchment paper.

4. Measure the width of the pot to be used for the pot pie filling. Following the illustrations on page 61, leave the dough on the parchment and trim it into a circle the same size as the width of the pot. Fold back the outer ½-inch rim of the dough, then crimp the folded edge. Cut four oval-shaped vents, each about 3 inches long and ½ inch wide, in the center of the dough. Slide the parchment paper and dough onto a baking sheet, cover loosely with plastic wrap, and freeze until firm, at least 30 minutes, or up to 24 hours.

PORK ROAST EN COCOTTE WITH KALE AND SHALLOTS

HAVING HAD GREAT SUCCESS WITH OUR recipe for Beef en Cocotte with Creamy Mushroom Barley (page 58), we set out on a mission to create an equally satisfying and interesting one-pot supper with a pork roast taking center stage. The process for cooking en cocotte is simple: Place a browned roast, along with a few aromatics, in a large Dutch oven, cover tightly, and bake in a low oven where it essentially steam-cooks in the contained, moist-heat environment of a large covered pot. As for vegetables to pair with the pork, we thought braised greens would add hearty flavor to complement the mild pork, and we guessed that sturdy kale might cook at about the same rate as the pork. In an ideal situation, the juice from the pork would flavor the kale as both cooked to a sublime tenderness, creating a unique one-pot supper. However, we knew it was equally likely that we'd end up with an unappetizing, dried-out pork roast sitting in a sulfurous pot of stewed kale. Determined to pursue the former while avoiding the latter, we started our testing with the pork to nail down the proper cut. We'd address the kale and seasonings later.

We knew we wanted a boneless pork cut, which would fit more easily into a Dutch oven and cook faster, than a bone-in roast, so we looked at our options. Big, fatty cuts from the shoulder (Boston butt for example) need to be slow-cooked for several hours to become tender, far longer than we were willing to wait. At the other end of the spectrum, pork tenderloin cooks so quickly that there is little time for developing a flavorful jus, which would be key to producing robustly flavored greens. Relatively lean and tender yet substantial, pork loin roasts seemed like our best choice. Following our traditional en cocotte method, we tested two readily available pork loin cuts. We tied a blade-end roast and a center-cut loin and browned them on the stovetop in large Dutch ovens, added a handful of aromatics, covered the pots, and cooked them slowly in a 250-degree oven. While both roasts were juicy and tender in about 45 minutes, tasters slightly preferred the blade-end loin to the center-cut loin for its extra flavor and juiciness. That said, both types of pork loin roasts will work in this recipe—we found that the size of the loin is what is most important. Pork loins can come in different shapes and sizes depending on how they've been butchered. Even if two roasts weigh the same, one can be long and thin while the other might be short and wide. For practical purposes, a shorter, wider piece (about 7 to 8 inches long and 4 to 5 inches wide) is ideal simply because it fits into the pot.

After browning the roast, we packed in one bunch of chopped kale leaves, covered the pot and cooked it just as before, thinking that the juice released from the pork would steam the leaves. Unfortunately, the kale was still tough and crunchy, even after the 45 minutes it took for the pork to reach 140 degrees. To see how long it would take for the kale to soften, we removed the pork and placed the pot back in the oven. To our surprise, even after 90 minutes in the 250-degree oven, the kale was still chewy. Stymied, we took another look at what was happening in the pot. Since our original en cocotte method uses no additional liquid, the steam created in the pot comes directly from the juice released from the meat as it cooks. While this amount of steam is sufficient to gently heat the pork through, it was clearly not enough to break down kale's tough fibers. While we could have increased the oven temperature to pull more juice from the pork and create more steam, we knew this would lead to dried-out meat. Hoping to bump up the amount of steam produced, we tried breaking slightly from the en cocotte tradition and added some chicken broth to help cook the kale, which would also help boost the pork's meatiness. This time we browned the roast, removed it to a plate, and added the kale and a cup of chicken broth to the pot. After five minutes of covered steaming, the kale had wilted slightly and turned bright green. We then placed the pork roast back into the pot and transferred it to the oven. Forty-five minutes later we removed the pork to rest and found a bed of tender kale sitting in a flavorful broth. The pork resting time gave us the opportunity to cook this liquid down to a concentrated sauce. With our pork and kale sorted out, we focused on some final touches.

To season the pork, we decided to try adding herbes de Provence, a heady combination of basil, fennel seed, lavender, marjoram, rosemary, sage, summer savory, and thyme. We seasoned the pork with this handy herb mixture, along with salt and pepper, before browning it. The hot oil bloomed the herbs, which then infused the broth as the pork cooked, providing flavor throughout the pot. To offer some sweetness and contrasting texture, we added quartered shallots to the pot with the kale. And finally, to round out the rich flavor of the sauce, we stirred in 1 tablespoon each of butter and whole grain mustard. The kale was now slightly sweet, bright, and rich, a perfect complement to our juicy herbed pork. It was hard to believe that we had created this elegant dish with just one pot and fewer than 10 ingredients.

Pork Roast en Cocotte with Kale, Shallots, and Mustard
SERVES 4 TO 6

This recipe works best with a pork roast that is about 7 to 8 inches long and 4 to 5 inches wide; we prefer a blade-end roast (see page 64). We prefer to leave a ¼-inch-thick layer of fat on top of the roast; if your roast has a thicker fat cap, trim it back to be about ¼ inch thick. Be sure to use a Dutch oven with a tight-fitting lid.

I   (2½- to 3-pound) boneless pork loin roast, trimmed and tied at 1½-inch intervals (see the illustration on page 33) (see note)

I   tablespoon herbes de Provence
    Salt and ground black pepper

3   tablespoons vegetable oil

I   pound shallots (about 12 large), peeled and quartered

I   cup low-sodium chicken broth

I   large bunch kale (about 1 pound), stemmed, leaves cut into 1-inch pieces (see the illustrations on page 150)

I   tablespoon unsalted butter

I   tablespoon whole grain mustard

1. Adjust an oven rack to the lowest position and heat the oven to 250 degrees. Pat the pork dry with paper towels and season with the herbes de Provence, salt, and pepper. Heat 2 tablespoons of the oil in a large Dutch oven over medium-high heat until just smoking. Brown the pork on all sides, 7 to 10 minutes; transfer to a large plate.

2. Add the remaining tablespoon oil and shallots to the pot and cook until softened and lightly browned, 5 to 7 minutes. Stir in the broth, scraping up any browned bits, and bring to a simmer. Stir in the kale, cover, and cook, stirring occasionally, until bright green and wilted, about 5 minutes.

3. Off the heat, nestle the browned pork with any accumulated juice into the pot. Place a large sheet of aluminum foil over the pot and press to seal, then cover tightly with the lid. Transfer the pot to the oven and cook until the center of the roast registers 140 to 145 degrees on an instant-read thermometer, 35 to 55 minutes.

4. Remove the pot from the oven. Transfer the pork to a carving board, tent loosely with foil, and let rest 20 minutes. Meanwhile, continue to simmer the kale over medium-high heat until it is tender and the liquid has nearly evaporated, 3 to 5 minutes. Stir in the butter and mustard, season with salt and pepper to taste, and cover to keep warm.

5. Remove the twine from the pork and slice against the grain into thin slices. Serve with the kale.

THE RIGHT ROAST

Buying the right pork loin will make all the difference in this recipe because the pork needs to fit inside the pot. Look for a 2½- to 3-pound pork loin roast that is wide and short and steer clear from those that are long and narrow. We prefer a roast cut from the blade end; however, a center-cut roast (which is more common) works just fine.

LONG AND NARROW
At 12 inches long and 3 inches wide, this pork loin will not fit in a large Dutch oven.

SHORT AND WIDE
At 8 inches long and nearly 5 inches wide, this pork loin fits comfortably in a large Dutch oven.

SPICY MEXICAN PORK AND RICE

THE SIMPLE TECHNIQUE OF COOKING RICE IN a flavorful liquid has been used to great effect by cultures the world over (think chicken and rice, paella, risotto, and pilaf). In these preparations, the rice acts like a sponge, absorbing richness and flavor from the broth. The resulting dish is often far greater than the sum of its parts, making it an ideal foundation for a unique one-pot supper. Wishing to take this classic method in a new direction, we decided to incorporate the flavors and textures of a test kitchen favorite, pork tinga. Spiced with chipotle chiles and bathed in a tomatoey sauce, pork tinga is a stewlike dish from Mexico. While it is traditionally cooked until thickened and spooned onto crispy tostadas, we would forgo the tortillas in favor of rice. Our challenges would be adapting the cooking method while maintaining the dish's bold essence, and determining the best way to cook the rice, all using just one pot.

The test kitchen's tinga recipe goes something like this: first, cubes of boneless pork butt are simmered in salted water until very tender. Next, the meat is drained, shredded, sautéed with chipotle chiles and oregano, and stewed in tomato sauce. Spread onto homemade tostadas and garnished with myriad Mexican accoutrements, the dish is spicy, smoky, sweet, and meaty. But with very little sauce left in the final dish, it's hardly the ideal place to cook 1½ cups of rice (enough for four to six people). To provide sufficient liquid for the rice, we tried saving and adding back the water in which we had cooked the pork. While this pork broth had good meatiness on its own, it only served to dilute our stew. It was clear that we needed to add far more zest to our broth if we had any hope of producing a flavorful pot of rice.

While authentic tinga (our recipe included) avoids browning the pork so as not to compete with the tang and smokiness of chipotle chiles, we felt our new dish might benefit from this added depth. After searing the meat in two batches to provide good color and fond (the meaty browned bits on the

Defatting 101

Defatting a broth, soup, stew, or braise is important if you don't want your final dish to look and taste greasy. Below we've compiled four different ways to defat a liquid. The method you choose will depend on the dish you are making and the equipment you have on hand. For the first three methods, it is important to let the liquid settle for 5 to 10 minutes before defatting; this allows all of the fat to separate out and float to the top.

SKIM WITH A LADLE OR WIDE SPOON

This is the simplest way to defat a liquid, and it works with broths, soups, stews, and braises. Let the liquid settle in the pot for 5 to 10 minutes, then skim the fat away with a ladle or wide spoon. The advantages of this method are that it's very easy and it doesn't dirty any extra dishes; however, some fat will remain in the broth.

USE A TALL, NARROW CONTAINER

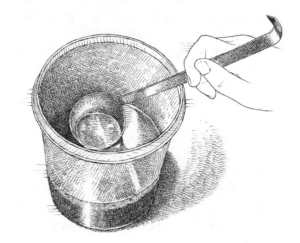

If you are using a large pot or have a large quantity of fat to skim, pour the broth into a tall, narrow container before defatting. This will create a deeper layer of fat that is easier to skim and remove. After letting the broth settle for 5 to 10 minutes, skim with a ladle or wide spoon. (Although some fat will remain behind, there will be less than if you simply defat the broth right in the pot.) This method also works with all kinds of broths, soups, and stews.

USE A FAT SEPARATOR

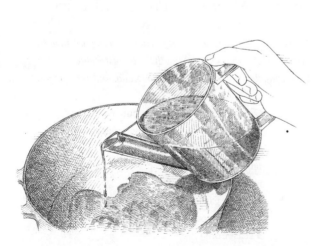

This technique works best with broths and braises that don't have much in the way of vegetables or garnishes taking up space in the pot. It requires a fat separator (as for size, we recommend buying the largest fat separator you can find). To use, simply pour the liquid into the fat separator and let it settle for 5 to 10 minutes. Then pour it back into your pot through the spout, leaving the fat behind in the separator.

REFRIGERATE OVERNIGHT

If you are making a stew or braise, you can simply refrigerate it without defatting—the fat will collect and solidify on the top as it chills. Upon removing it from the refrigerator, you can simply scrape the large solid pieces of fat right off the top before reheating and using. This also works for broths.

bottom of the pot), we added minced onion, dried oregano, and a full tablespoon of minced canned chipotle chiles in adobo sauce. Canned chipotles are not only easier to use (no soaking or charring required) and locate than their dried brethren, but the adobo sauce they are packed in adds additional smoke and depth.

Next, we substituted a combination of chicken broth and tomato sauce for the salted water. After about an hour and a half of simmering, the pork was very tender and had a subtle, appealingly sweet taste, but it was the intensely flavored broth that tasters raved most about. A few cloves of minced garlic and some minced thyme, while certainly not traditional, added even more complexity to the broth. Returning to tinga protocol, we removed the tender pork from the pot and shredded it into small pieces. Next, we set about adding rice to the dish.

Both medium-grain rice and long-grain rice are staples of the Mexican kitchen. To find our preference, we made two batches of our modified tinga stew, stirring medium-grain rice into one and long-grain rice into the other. After covering and simmering the pots until the rice became tender, we tasted and deliberated. To our surprise, neither variety of rice seemed quite right. Tasters felt the long-grain rice was too fluffy for this substantial, homey dish, while medium-grain rice turned out a pot of Mexican-style risotto (not a good thing). Stumped, we brainstormed ways to find a happy medium. We've learned over time that the amount of liquid used to cook rice can have a dramatic effect on its consistency.

Up to this point, we had been using a standard ratio of 1½ cups of broth to 1 cup of rice, but now we wondered if increasing the liquid might produce slightly denser long-grain rice (we knew going this route with the long-grain rice was an easier fix than trying to make medium-grain rice fluffier). We made another batch of stew, this time using 2 cups of liquid for every cup of rice. To our tasters' delight, this rice was the best of both worlds: substantial without being pasty, and fluffy

enough to balance the rich pork and sauce. Our rice conundrum solved, we moved on to some final touches.

Up to this point we had been shredding the cooked pork into bite-size pieces, just as we do for our classic tinga recipe (key for fitting onto a tostada), but with rice in the mix our tasters noted they would prefer the meat in more substantial chunks, so it would maintain a greater presence among the rice. So we decided to leave the pork in the 1-inch cubes.

True to its Mexican roots, tinga is always served with a wide range of garnishes. We wanted to keep this one-pot dish simple and find out which garnishes were imperative, and which could be optional. To cut the pork's richness, we found lime juice was a must, along with fresh cilantro, which provided citrusy brightness as well as unmistakable Mexican character. Finally, we added sliced scallions to the mix for clean, subtle onion flavor. Other options for topping this sweet, spicy, smoky mix of rice and pork are queso fresco, diced avocado, and sour cream. Anyway you choose to garnish it, our Mexican pork and rice is a one-pot pleasure.

Spicy Mexican Pork and Rice
SERVES 4 TO 6

Be sure to stir the rice gently when cooking in step 6; aggressive stirring will make the rice taste gluey. Serve with crumbled queso fresco, diced avocado, and sour cream.

1	(2-pound) boneless pork butt roast, trimmed and cut into 1-inch pieces
	Salt and ground black pepper
2	tablespoons olive oil
2	medium onions, minced
5	medium garlic cloves, minced or pressed through a garlic press (about 5 teaspoons)
1	tablespoon minced chipotle chile in adobo sauce
1	teaspoon minced fresh thyme leaves or ¼ teaspoon dried

½ teaspoon dried oregano

2 cups low-sodium chicken broth

1 (8-ounce) can tomato sauce

1½ cups long-grain white rice

½ cup minced fresh cilantro leaves

3 scallions, sliced thin

1 tablespoon juice from 1 lime

1. Adjust an oven rack to the lower-middle position and heat the oven to 300 degrees. Pat the pork dry with paper towels and season with salt and pepper.

2. Heat 1 tablespoon of the oil in a large Dutch oven over medium-high heat until just smoking. Add half of the pork and brown on all sides, 7 to 10 minutes; transfer to a large bowl. Repeat with the remaining tablespoon oil and remaining pork; transfer to the bowl.

3. Add the onion to the fat left in the pot and cook over medium heat until softened, 5 to 7 minutes. Stir in the garlic, chipotles, thyme, and oregano and cook until fragrant, about 30 seconds. Stir in the broth and tomato sauce, scraping up any browned bits.

4. Add the browned pork with any accumulated juice and bring to a simmer. Cover, transfer the pot to the oven, and cook until the pork is very tender, 75 to 90 minutes.

5. Remove the pot from the oven and increase the oven temperature to 350 degrees. Defat the braising liquid following one of the methods on page 65 (if necessary, return the defatted liquid to the pot).

6. Bring the defatted braising liquid to a simmer and thoroughly stir in the rice. Cover and continue to cook in the oven until all of the rice is tender and the liquid has been absorbed, 20 to 30 minutes, gently stirring the rice from the bottom of the pot to the top every 10 minutes.

7. Stir in the cilantro, scallions, and lime juice and season with salt and pepper to taste. Cover and let stand 5 minutes before serving.

DUTCH OVEN SHEPHERD'S PIE

A RICH LAMB STEW BLANKETED BY A MASHED potato crust, shepherd's pie is a hearty casserole from the cool climes of sheep-centric northern Britain. Best eaten on a blustery winter day, this lamb dish used to be a meal made on Monday with Sunday night's leftovers—the remnants of the roast, vegetables, and mashed potatoes. In this day and age, few of us have such delicious Sunday dinners, much less leftovers, so we aimed to create an assertively flavored shepherd's pie from scratch. We also wanted to put to work what we had learned from simplifying beef pot pie (see page 59); we wanted to cook this pie in just one Dutch oven.

To keep the prep work to a minimum, we started our testing with ground lamb, which required no trimming or cutting. We sautéed the meat in a large Dutch oven until just cooked through, but we were surprised at the amount of rendered fat that pooled around the meat. Because the fat is responsible for much of the gamy flavor of lamb (which tasters preferred in moderation), we decided to drain the meat before continuing. After transferring the cooked, drained lamb to a bowl, we starting building the stew.

First, we sautéed carrots, onions, and garlic until softened to form a rich aromatic foundation. As for the liquid in the stew, we settled on chicken broth thickened with ⅓ cup of flour. Chicken broth provided a neutral flavor that we liked; we did a few tests with beef broth, but tasters felt that it clashed with the lamb's earthy flavors. Peas, characteristic of many British-style meat stews, were a must for their bright color and sweetness. To keep their fresh flavor and color, we added them with the cooked lamb just before the dish went into the oven. While some tasters liked the clean, simple flavor of this filling, others thought it wan and lacking. Wishing to prove that British food need not be bland, we added tomato paste to bolster the lamb's sweet meatiness and Worcestershire sauce to boost overall richness. With the basic lamb flavors elevated, all the filling needed was a dose of minced thyme. At last, our shepherd's pie filling was meaty, robust, and full flavored.

With the filling assembled and cooked, we were ready to top it off with a mashed-potato crust. We quickly found out that simple mashed potatoes would not do; they crumbled and broke down while baking, leaving us with soggy mashed potatoes and muddled gravy. Needing some structure to keep the potatoes separate from the stew, we adopted a French technique used in duchess potatoes and stirred in an egg yolk with the dairy. This batch was better than the first, but it still needed more binder to keep from crumbling. To see if we simply needed more of the same, we went with two yolks. This did the trick; the potatoes retained their shape and texture and picked up a little more richness in the bargain. Plus, the yolks gave the potatoes a slight golden hue that complemented the deep brown of the stew beneath. Given the added richness from the yolks, the crust was too heavy when we used half-and-half, so we replaced it with whole milk, which tasters much preferred. We then placed dollops all over our filling, spreading them into an even layer, and popped the pot into the oven.

Because both the lamb and the mashed potatoes were already cooked, the baking time was conveniently short—all it needed was about 20 minutes. Once the potato crust turned golden brown, the shepherd's pie was done and ready to come out of the oven. From a few humble ingredients and just one Dutch oven, we had created a savory, ultra-comforting homage to the cool green pastures of northern Britain.

Dutch Oven Shepherd's Pie
SERVES 6 TO 8

We like the authentic flavor of ground lamb here, but you can substitute 90 percent lean ground beef if you prefer.

TOPPING

2   **pounds russet potatoes (about 4 medium), peeled and sliced crosswise into 1-inch-thick rounds**
     Salt

6   **tablespoons (¾ stick) unsalted butter, softened**
¼   **cup whole milk, warmed**
     Ground black pepper
2   **large egg yolks**

FILLING

2   **pounds ground lamb (see note)**
1   **tablespoon vegetable oil**
2   **medium onions, minced**
2   **carrots, peeled and cut into ¼-inch pieces**
2   **medium garlic cloves, minced or pressed through a garlic press (about 2 teaspoons)**
2   **teaspoons minced fresh thyme leaves or ½ teaspoon dried**
⅓   **cup unbleached all-purpose flour**
1   **tablespoon tomato paste**
3   **cups low-sodium chicken broth**
2   **teaspoons Worcestershire sauce**
1   **cup frozen peas**
     Salt and ground black pepper

1. FOR THE TOPPING: Adjust an oven rack to the middle position and heat the oven to 400 degrees. Put the potatoes and ½ teaspoon salt in a large Dutch oven and add water to cover. Bring to a boil then reduce to a gentle simmer and cook until the potatoes are tender when pierced with a skewer, 15 to 20 minutes.

2. Drain the potatoes well, return them to the pot over low heat, and mash thoroughly with a potato masher. Off the heat, fold in the butter until melted, then stir in the warm milk and season with salt and pepper to taste. Stir in the yolks, then transfer the mixture to a large bowl and cover until needed. Rinse and dry the pot.

3. FOR THE FILLING: Cook the lamb in the Dutch oven over medium heat, breaking up the meat with a wooden spoon, until no longer pink and the fat has rendered, about 3 minutes. Drain the lamb through a fine-mesh strainer, discarding the juice and fat.

4. Add the oil, onions, and carrots to the pot and cook over medium heat until softened, 5 to 7 minutes. Stir in the garlic and thyme and cook until fragrant, about 30 seconds. Stir in the flour

and tomato paste and cook for 1 minute. Gradually whisk in the broth and Worcestershire sauce, scraping up any browned bits and smoothing out any lumps. Bring to a simmer and cook until thickened, 3 to 5 minutes.

5. Off the heat, stir in the drained lamb and peas, season with salt and pepper to taste, and smooth the filling into an even layer. Dollop the potato topping over the filling, then spread it into an even layer, covering the filling completely and anchoring the potatoes to the sides of the pot.

6. Bake until the top is light golden, 20 to 25 minutes. Let cool for 20 minutes before serving.

Chicken en Cocotte with Potatoes and Carrots

THE BASIC METHOD FOR MAKING CHICKEN EN cocotte, a French bistro classic, is indeed simple: place a seasoned bird in a pot, scatter in some aromatics, cover, and bake. What emerges from this simple method is surprisingly special—a chicken that is incredibly tender and juicy, with a rich, soul-satisfying flavor. To make this a true dinner in a pot, however, we wanted to add vegetables to the mix, and we hoped we could cook the chicken and vegetables through in about an hour.

Before we could address vegetables, flavorings, or the sauce, we had to determine the ideal temperature at which to bake our bird. We seasoned half a dozen 4½- to 5-pound chickens (the largest we could fit in a Dutch oven), placed them in large Dutch ovens, popped on the lids, and baked them at temperatures ranging from 200 to 400 degrees, until the breast meat registered 160 degrees and the legs hit 175 degrees. There were drastic differences among these chickens. The birds baked at 375 degrees and 400 degrees cooked too rapidly, resulting in an overcooked, dry layer of breast meat just under the skin. Birds baked at the low end of the temperature range stayed moist and juicy, but took up to two hours to cook through—a nonstarter for what we hoped would be a weeknight chicken dinner.

Between these extremes we found our sweet spot, a moderate 350-degree oven. At this temperature, our bird emerged supremely juicy and tender, in just under an hour. With our oven temperature set, we addressed the vegetables.

Since we wanted our chicken in a pot to be a complete one-pot supper, we decided to include both red potatoes and carrots. We cut 1½ pounds of red potatoes and 1 pound of carrots into 1-inch pieces and scattered them around the chicken, covered the pot, and baked it just as before. Unfortunately, after an hour in the oven, a few of the potatoes and carrots were still raw in the middle. Up to this point we had been following traditional chicken en cocotte doctrine, which forbids adding liquid to the pot lest flavors become washed out. Suspecting that a little more braising liquid might help the vegetables cook more evenly, we broke with tradition and added ½ cup of chicken broth to the pot. Our suspicions were confirmed when we removed the lid from this test pot to a plume of steam and a mix of perfectly cooked vegetables. Having determined the best way to cook our chicken and vegetables, we focused on developing flavor and building our sauce.

While our cooking liquid was good, we had to admit that it wasn't as intensely flavored as the versions we made without any additional liquid. To add back some of the concentrated chicken flavor, we tested lightly browning the breast and back of the chicken on the stovetop before adding the vegetables and transferring it to the oven. Tasters liked this version better but still wanted more chicken richness. We tried browning both sides until very dark, but, while this bumped up the flavor considerably, it also dried out the top layer of breast meat. Instead, we chose to focus the heavy browning on the chicken back, which is composed entirely of fatty dark meat. This disparity in browning not only produced a rich, full-bodied braising liquid, it also gave the back meat a jump start so that it cooked at the same rate as the breast.

Since we were now browning the chicken on the stovetop, we wondered if the vegetables wouldn't benefit from the same treatment. After removing the browned chicken, we sautéed the potatoes and carrots, along with a halved onion, crushed garlic cloves, and thyme, until well browned. This was by far our best batch yet, boasting rich meatiness and complex flavor. It was time to attend to our sauce.

Having done our background work developing a boldly flavored braising liquid, we had an easy time turning it into a finished sauce. After removing the chicken to rest, we transferred the vegetables to a bowl and defatted the liquid in the pot (we also discarded the halved onion and garlic cloves). To our cup of concentrated braising liquid we added lemon juice for brightness and acidity and 2 tablespoons of butter to round out of the flavors and boost richness. After negotiating a veritable labyrinth of overly complicated recipes and questionable chicken-in-a-pot lore, we had brought this ingenious one-pot supper back to its simple roots.

Chicken en Cocotte with Potatoes and Carrots

SERVES 4

If using a kosher chicken, do not season with salt in step 1. Be sure to use a Dutch oven with a tight-fitting lid.

1	(4½- to 5-pound) whole chicken, giblets discarded
	Salt and ground black pepper
2	tablespoons vegetable oil
1½	pounds red potatoes (4 to 5 medium), scrubbed and cut into 1-inch pieces
1	pound carrots (about 6 medium), peeled and cut into 1-inch pieces
1	medium onion, peeled and halved, root end left intact
6	medium garlic cloves, peeled and crushed
1	teaspoon minced fresh thyme leaves or ¼ teaspoon dried
½	cup low-sodium chicken broth
1	bay leaf
2	tablespoons unsalted butter
2	teaspoons juice from 1 lemon

1. Adjust an oven rack to the lower-middle position and heat the oven to 350 degrees. Pat the chicken dry with paper towels, tuck the wings behind the back following the illustration below, and season with salt and pepper.

2. Heat the oil in a large Dutch oven over medium-high heat until just smoking. Add the chicken, breast side down, and cook until lightly browned, about 5 minutes. Flip the chicken and continue to cook until the back of the chicken is well browned, 6 to 8 minutes; transfer to a large plate.

3. Add the potatoes, carrots, onion, and garlic to the fat left in the pot and cook over medium heat until browned, 8 to 10 minutes. Stir in the thyme and cook until fragrant, about 30 seconds. Stir in the broth and bay leaf, scraping up any browned bits.

4. Off the heat, place the chicken, breast side up, on top of the vegetables. Place a large sheet of aluminum foil over the pot and press to seal, then cover tightly with the lid. Transfer the pot to the oven and cook until the breast registers 160 to 165 degrees and the thighs register 175 degrees on an instant-read thermometer, 50 to 60 minutes.

5. Remove the pot from the oven. Transfer the chicken to a carving board, tent loosely with foil, and let rest for 20 minutes. Using a slotted spoon, transfer the vegetables to a large bowl, discarding

PROTECTING THE WINGS

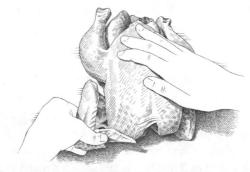

Tucking the wings of a chicken behind the back will keep them out of the way and prevent the wingtips from burning. Simply twist the wing back behind the back and close the joints of the wings tightly. The tension of the closed, tucked wing will help to keep it in place.

the onion. Season with salt and pepper to taste and cover to keep warm.

6. Defat the sauce following one of the methods on page 65 (if necessary, return the defatted liquid to the pot). Discard the bay leaf. Bring to a gentle simmer, whisk in the butter and lemon juice, and season with salt and pepper to taste. Carve the chicken following the illustrations on page 41 and serve with the vegetables and sauce.

➤ VARIATIONS

Chicken en Cocotte with Potatoes, Corn, and Bacon

Do not season the chicken with salt, as the bacon adds considerable salt to this dish.

Follow the recipe for Chicken en Cocotte with Potatoes and Carrots, omitting the carrots and lemon juice, and only seasoning the chicken with pepper in step 1. Before adding the vegetables to the pot in step 3, cook 4 ounces bacon (about 4 slices), chopped fine, over medium heat until rendered and almost crisp, 3 to 5 minutes; add the vegetables and continue to cook as directed. After the chicken has cooked for 30 minutes in step 4, add 4 ears corn, husks and silk removed, cut into 1-inch rounds, to the pot and continue to cook as directed for 20 to 30 minutes longer.

Chicken en Cocotte with Coconut Milk, Shiitakes, and Sweet Potatoes

Follow the recipe for Chicken en Cocotte with Potatoes and Carrots, omitting the potatoes, carrots, butter, and lemon juice. Add 1 pound shiitake mushrooms, wiped clean, stemmed, and quartered, to the pot with the onion and garlic. Substitute ½ cup coconut milk for the broth. After the chicken has cooked for 30 minutes in step 4, add 1½ pounds sweet potatoes (about 2 medium), peeled and cut into 1½-inch pieces, to the pot and continue to cook as directed for 20 to 30 minutes longer. Stir 2 teaspoons juice from 1 lime and 3 tablespoons minced fresh cilantro leaves into the sauce in step 6.

DUTCH OVEN CHICKEN POT PIE

MOST EVERYONE LOVES A GOOD CHICKEN POT pie—juicy chunks of chicken, fresh vegetables, and a full-flavored sauce, all topped with pie dough or biscuits—though few seem to have the time or energy to make one. Like a lot of satisfying dishes, traditional chicken pot pie takes time, not to mention a mess of dirty pots and pans. Before the pie even makes it into the oven, the cook must poach a chicken or chicken parts, take the meat off the bone and shred it, strain the stock, prepare and blanch the vegetables, make a sauce, and make or roll out pie dough or biscuits. That's fine for a Sunday supper when you can dedicate yourself to a few hours of cooking and cleanup, but what about dinner during the week? Hoping to land somewhere in the stratosphere, we shot for the moon: all the trappings of a classic chicken pot pie on the table in less than an hour and a half, dirtying just one pot. We started with the chicken.

Arguably the most time-consuming part of making chicken pot pie is cooking and shredding the chicken. Traditionally, a whole chicken is poached, shredded, and returned to the pot with the gravy and vegetables just before the topping goes on. This method poses a number of challenges. First, the white and dark meat do not cook at the same rate, resulting in dried-out breast meat. In addition, it can take over an hour to poach a whole bird, let it cool, and shred it into bite-size pieces—an absolute nonstarter.

Since tasters preferred the rich meatiness of the drumsticks and thighs to the breast meat, we tried substituting legs for the whole chicken in our bare-bones working recipe. These certainly cooked faster, but they still took too long to cool and shred. What if we cut up the chicken meat before cooking it? In stews we typically shred breast meat after it is cooked, rather than cube it raw, because it stays moister when cooked whole. Noting that dark meat (much like the chuck-eye roast we use in our beef pot pie) has considerable connective tissue and fat, we wondered if it would pose the same problem.

Taking a cue from our beef pot pie (see page 59), we cut boneless, skinless chicken thighs into 1-inch pieces and browned them in two batches in a Dutch oven. We then built a working filling and gently stewed the browned chicken until cooked through. This technique produced tender bites of chicken and a rich-tasting gravy (due to the fond developed during browning) far quicker than using a whole bird. With the meat of the matter settled, we addressed the vegetables and gravy.

Since we wanted the flavors of traditional chicken pot pie, that meant carrots and peas mingling in a flour-thickened gravy of chicken broth and white wine. To this mix we added minced onion, garlic, and thyme (sautéed in the fat rendered from browning the chicken) and chunks of celery root. To round out our filling, and give it classic pot pie character, we finished it with cream, fresh tarragon, and dry sherry. Successful thus far in meeting our stringent pot pie demands, we tackled what would be our biggest challenge yet, the topping.

While pie dough was a must for our beef pot pie, we wanted our homey chicken pot pie crowned with flaky biscuits. Adding biscuits to a pot pie typically means two things: getting out the stand mixer or food processor to make the dough and using a separate sheet pan to bake (or at least par-bake) the biscuits. Since we had no room for either of these in our master plan, we had to get creative. In the hope of ditching the power equipment, we cased our biscuit archives in search of something simpler. While most biscuit recipes require cutting cold butter into the flour (when the butter melts it produces steam, which creates flaky layers) we found one recipe that omitted the butter (and the mixer) entirely. Stirring together 2 cups of flour, 1½ cups of heavy cream, 2 teaspoons of baking powder, plus salt and sugar might sound like a recipe for biscuit disaster, but the result is a batch of flaky, rich biscuits. The trick to these easier biscuits is kneading the dough briefly to develop gluten, which then traps gas, helping the biscuits rise to lofty heights. However, easy and delicious as they were, we quickly discovered that these biscuits still needed to be baked separate from the filling to prevent soggy bottoms.

While pulling out a sheet pan to bake the biscuits certainly wouldn't have been the end of the world, we were committed to our efficiency-driven, one-pot goal. Since baking the biscuits on top of the filling hadn't worked, why not invert the Dutch oven lid and use it as a makeshift sheet pan? While a few in the test kitchen questioned our sanity, we were willing to see this idea through. After heating the oven to 425 degrees, we whipped up a batch of biscuits, cut them into rounds, and spaced them evenly on the inverted lid. We then placed the lid on the pot (over the simmering filling) and baked them until golden brown. Due to the lid's slight incline, these biscuits slid to the center, fused together, and remained raw in the middle. A sheet of parchment paper between the biscuits and lid solved the sliding issue (and made transferring to a cooling rack a snap), but still the biscuits in the center of the lid were baking slower than the ones on the sides. To resolve this problem, we pressed the dough into a round, cut it into eight sconelike wedges, and arranged the biscuits along the outer rim of the lid, with the thin point of each facing inward and the thicker ends closer to the edge. These biscuits cooked through evenly, leaving even the most skeptical tasters without complaint. With our one-pot goal finally in sight, we focused on a few lingering issues.

While 425 degrees is ideal for baking biscuits, it is far too hot to gently simmer pot pie filling. Our testing had shown that in the 35 minutes it took for the biscuits to turn a golden brown, our filling (which started at a simmer) had come to a rolling boil. We remedied this by placing the biscuit-laden lid on top of room temperature filling and allowing the 425-degree oven to bring it to a simmer. Then, once the biscuits were baked, we simply removed the lid and biscuits, reduced the oven to 300 degrees, and let the filling cook until the meat and vegetables were tender. Finally, we warmed the biscuits through by placing them on the cooked filling as it cooled for 10 minutes. A formidable battery of tests later, we had accomplished the impossible: a classic-tasting, soul-satisfying chicken pot pie, created entirely using one pot (and its lid).

Dutch Oven Chicken Pot Pie

SERVES 8

Do not substitute boneless, skinless chicken breasts for the thighs in this recipe or the meat will taste very dry.

BISCUITS

2	cups (10 ounces) unbleached all-purpose flour, plus extra for rolling out the dough
2	teaspoons sugar
2	teaspoons baking powder
½	teaspoon salt
1½	cups heavy cream

FILLING

3½	pounds boneless chicken thighs (about 14 thighs), trimmed and cut into 1-inch pieces
	Salt and ground black pepper
3	tablespoons vegetable oil
2	medium onions, minced
4	medium garlic cloves, minced or pressed through a garlic press (about 4 teaspoons)
1	teaspoon minced fresh thyme leaves or ¼ teaspoon dried
½	cup unbleached all-purpose flour
⅓	cup dry white wine
3½	cups low-sodium chicken broth
1	pound celery root, peeled and cut into ½-inch pieces
1	pound carrots (about 6 medium), peeled and cut into ½-inch pieces
1	cup frozen peas
¾	cup heavy cream
¼	cup minced fresh tarragon leaves
1	tablespoon dry sherry

1. FOR THE BISCUITS: Adjust an oven rack to the lowest position and heat the oven to 425 degrees.

2. Whisk the flour, sugar, baking powder, and salt together in a large bowl. Stir in the cream until a dough forms, about 30 seconds. Transfer the dough to a lightly floured counter, gather into a ball, and knead until smooth, about 30 seconds. Flatten the dough into a 7-inch circle and cut into 8 wedges.

3. Place a sheet of parchment paper on the upside down lid of a large Dutch oven and nestle it securely inside a nest of towels to hold it steady. Following the illustration below, arrange the biscuits on the parchment-lined pot lid; set aside while preparing the filling.

4. FOR THE FILLING: Pat the chicken dry with paper towels and season with salt and pepper. Heat 1 tablespoon of the oil in the large Dutch oven over medium-high heat until just smoking. Add half of the chicken and brown lightly, 6 to 8 minutes; transfer to a large bowl. Repeat with 1 tablespoon more oil and the remaining chicken; transfer to the bowl.

5. Add the remaining tablespoon oil and onions to the pot and cook over medium heat until softened, 5 to 7 minutes. Stir in the garlic and thyme and cook until fragrant, about 30 seconds. Stir in the flour and cook for 1 minute. Stir in the wine, scraping up any browned bits. Gradually whisk in the broth, smoothing out any lumps.

6. Stir in the celery root, carrots, and browned chicken with any accumulated juice. Off the heat, cover the pot with the upside down, biscuit-topped lid and transfer to the oven. Bake until the biscuits are dark brown, about 35 minutes, rotating the pot halfway through baking.

7. Remove the pot from the oven and reduce the oven to 300 degrees. Transfer the parchment

ARRANGING THE BISCUITS

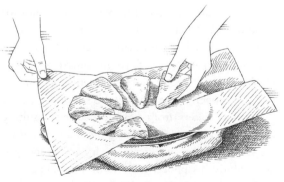

After cutting the biscuit dough into 8 wedges, arrange them on the inverted, parchment-lined pot lid with the wide end of the biscuits flush to the edge of the lid. To hold the inverted lid steady, nestle it into a nest of kitchen towels.

and biscuits to a cooling rack. Return the pot to the oven and continue to cook, uncovered, until the filling is thickened and the vegetables are tender, 20 to 25 minutes, stirring occasionally.

8. Remove the pot from the oven, stir in the peas, cream, tarragon, and sherry and season with salt and pepper to taste. Arrange the biscuits on the hot filling and let sit 10 minutes before serving.

➤ VARIATION

Dutch Oven Chicken Pot Pie with Bell Pepper, Corn, Zucchini, and Basil
Follow the recipe for Dutch Oven Chicken Pot Pie, omitting the celery root, carrots, and peas. Add 1 red bell pepper, stemmed, seeded, and cut into ½-inch pieces, to the pot with the onions. Add 1 teaspoon chili powder to the pot with the garlic. After removing the biscuits from the oven in step 7, stir 2 medium zucchini (about 1 pound), halved lengthwise, seeded (see the illustration on page 148), and cut into ½-inch pieces, and 2 cups fresh or frozen corn into the filling and continue to cook as directed. Substitute ¼ cup chopped fresh basil leaves for the tarragon.

CLASSIC CHICKEN AND RICE WITH CARROTS AND PEAS

CHICKEN AND RICE, IN ITS MANY FORMS, appears on dinner tables the world over—and for good reason. When this classic one-pot preparation is done well, it is a comforting melange of tender, juicy chicken and richly flavored, fluffy rice. If vegetables are included, it quickly becomes a satisfying one-pot supper. Unfortunately, this seemingly simple dish often suffers from poor execution, resulting in a multitude of unappetizing problems. Whether the rice is mushy and greasy or dry and crunchy, it consistently disappoints. Combine this subpar rice with dried out chicken and pallid flavors and you've got a recipe for disaster. Resolved to righting the many wrongs perpetrated against this dish, we set about developing a foolproof method that would deliver juicy chicken and tender, fluffy rice, every time. First, we tackled the chicken.

Chicken and rice typically falls into one of two camps. The first features a mix of bone-in chicken pieces (often cut from a whole bird) served on top of the rice, while the other, decidedly homier, version shreds the chicken and mixes it into the rice. While we have had good versions of both, we prefer the latter, as the shredded meat readily absorbs flavors and produces a more cohesive dish. We knew that dark meat, with its substantial connective tissue and fat, would provide more flavor than breast meat as well as added insurance against overcooking. In the name of convenience, we started with boneless, skinless chicken thighs, which are easy to shred once tender. Next, we had to make a decision about the rice.

While long-grain white rice is most common, we also found recipes calling for medium-grain rice and even basmati rice. We thought it prudent to test these different varieties, as each has its own unique characteristics and cooking requirements. For testing purposes, we made three batches of a basic working recipe. We browned our boneless, skinless chicken thighs in a large Dutch oven, then added aromatics and broth and brought everything to a simmer. Once the chicken was almost cooked through, we stirred in one of our rice options, popped on the lid, and simmered the pot gently until the rice became tender and the chicken was cooked through. Finally, we shredded the chicken and stirred it back into the pot along with salt and pepper to taste. Ignoring some glaring issues with this method, we focused on the taste and texture of the rice. Both the long-grain rice and medium-grain rice won points for their clean, neutral flavor. Basmati rice, a staple in Indian cuisine, proved far more fragrant, with a nutty flavor that tasters deemed out of place in this recipe. In terms of texture, we preferred long-grain rice (which cooked up relatively fluffy) to the risottolike pot of medium-grain rice. Having crowned long-grain rice our king, we focused on perfecting our method.

Producing a pot of fluffy long-grain rice is not difficult: Bring broth to a boil, add rice, cover, and simmer (untouched) for about 15 minutes; remove from the heat, let sit 15 minutes, fluff with a fork, and serve. In this scenario, each grain of rice has equal contact with the simmering broth, resulting in an evenly cooked pot of rice. Adding large pieces of chicken to the equation disrupts this even heat distribution, creating cooler pockets throughout the pot. If the rice in this pot is left untouched, some grains (those closest to the chicken) will cook more slowly than the rest, resulting in crunchy bites in your dish. The obvious solution to this problem is to stir the pot during cooking to break up the cooler spots and create a more consistent pot-wide temperature. Herein lies the problem: Stirring loosens starches (the same ones responsible for risotto's velvety sauce) on the surface of the rice, allowing it to mix with available liquid and thicken into a paste. While this is a desirable characteristic when building a risotto, it's a liability when trying to make fluffy rice. In the hope of achieving a more even cooking environment, so that we could stir as little as possible, we tried moving our pot of chicken and rice to the oven.

After building the base on the stovetop, we stirred in the rice, covered the pot, and transferred it to a 350-degree oven. We tested oven temperatures from 300 to 450 degrees and found that anything under 350 failed to produce significant steam (which was key to cooking any grains of rice that weren't directly in the broth), while temperatures over this caused an undesirable crust to form around the surface edge. This oven method produced more evenly cooked rice than our no-stir stovetop batch, but we still found crunchy bites throughout. Wary of making risotto, but resigned to the fact that stirring was necessary, we made another oven batch and stirred it twice during cooking. This quick adjustment did the trick, ensuring that no grain of rice was left stuck in a colder area of the pot. Now that we had a method that consistently produced fluffy rice, we took a closer look at our flavors.

Throughout our testing, tasters had complained that our rice lacked the rich chicken flavor they expect of this classic. Up to this point we had been using boneless thighs because they require little prep, but now we wondered if bone-in, skin-on thighs might provide more flavor. To find out, we made another batch using bone-in, skin-on thighs, removing and discarding the skin and bones before shredding the meat. The fat rendered from the skin and the gelatin eked from the bones lent this rice bold chicken flavor that tasters loved. To ensure that our rice didn't become greasy from the added fat, we drained off all but 2 tablespoons of fat from the pot before sautéing the aromatics. Next, we focused on adding vegetables and creating some interesting variations.

We wanted a classic pair of vegetables to go with our chicken and rice, and that meant peas and carrots. After a few tests, we found that ½-inch pieces of carrots cooked at the same rate as the rice, making them an easy addition. Once the rice was cooked we stirred in 1 cup of frozen peas, along with lemon juice, lemon zest, and parsley for a big hit of freshness. We were so pleased with this simple, easily amendable recipe, we created three internationally inspired variations. We paired sesame rice with edamame, chipotle rice with olives and scallions, and cardamom-spiked rice with caramelized onions. Having explored all of the comforting flavors and unique versatility of this humble dish, while perfecting some of its trickier elements, we could finally sit down to a big bowl of one of the world's greatest one-pot suppers, perfected.

SHREDDING MEAT

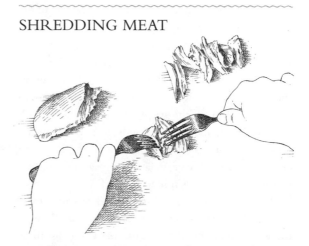

Using two forks, shred the cooked meat into bite-size pieces.

Classic Chicken and Rice with Carrots and Peas

SERVES 6

To keep the dish from becoming greasy, remove excess fat from the chicken thighs and trim the skin. Be sure to stir the rice gently when cooking in step 4; aggressive stirring will make the rice taste gluey.

2½	pounds bone-in, skin-on chicken thighs (about 10 thighs), trimmed
	Salt and ground black pepper
1	tablespoon olive oil
1	medium onion, minced
4	medium garlic cloves, minced or pressed through a garlic press (about 4 teaspoons)
1	teaspoon fresh minced thyme leaves or ¼ teaspoon dried
2½	cups low-sodium chicken broth
2	cups long-grain white rice
3	carrots, peeled and cut into ½-inch pieces
1	cup frozen peas
3	tablespoons minced fresh parsley leaves
½	teaspoon grated zest from 1 lemon
4	teaspoons juice from 1 lemon

1. Adjust an oven rack to the middle position and heat the oven to 350 degrees. Pat the chicken dry with paper towels and season with salt and pepper.

2. Heat the oil in a large Dutch oven over medium-high heat until just smoking. Add half of the chicken and brown lightly, 6 to 8 minutes; transfer to a large bowl. Repeat with the remaining chicken using the fat left in the pot; transfer to the bowl.

3. Pour off all but 2 tablespoons of the fat left in the pot, add the onion, and cook until softened, 5 to 7 minutes. Stir in the garlic and thyme and cook until fragrant, about 30 seconds. Stir in the broth, scraping up any browned bits. Stir in the browned chicken with any accumulated juice and bring to a simmer. Cover and simmer gently for 20 minutes.

4. Thoroughly stir in the rice and carrots. Cover, transfer the pot to the oven, and cook until all of the rice is tender and the liquid has been absorbed,

20 to 30 minutes, gently stirring the rice from the bottom of the pot to the top every 10 minutes.

5. Transfer the chicken to a carving board and replace the pot lid to keep the rice warm. Let the chicken cool slightly, then shred it into large chunks, following the illustrations on page 75, discarding the skin and bones.

6. Gently stir the shredded chicken, peas, parsley, lemon zest, and lemon juice into the rice, and season with salt and pepper to taste. Cover and let stand until the chicken is warmed through, about 5 minutes, before serving.

➤ VARIATIONS

Chicken and Sesame Rice with Edamame and Carrots

We like slicing the carrots on the bias, into ½-inch-thick pieces, for this Asian-style dish.

Follow the recipe for Classic Chicken and Rice with Carrots and Peas, omitting the peas, parsley, lemon zest, and lemon juice. Add 1 tablespoon minced or grated fresh ginger to the pot with the garlic. After the rice has cooked for 10 minutes in step 4, stir 1 cup frozen shelled edamame into the pot and continue to cook the rice as directed for 10 to 20 minutes longer. Stir 4 scallions, sliced thin on the bias, 2 tablespoons toasted sesame oil, 2 tablespoons toasted sesame seeds, 1 tablespoon rice wine vinegar, and 1 teaspoon sugar into the rice with the shredded chicken in step 6 and season with soy sauce to taste.

Chicken and Chipotle Rice with Tomatoes, Olives, and Scallions

Follow the recipe for Classic Chicken and Rice with Carrots and Peas, omitting the carrots, peas, parsley, lemon zest, and lemon juice. Add 2 teaspoons minced chipotle chile in adobo sauce to the pot with the garlic. Add 1 (14.5-ounce) can diced tomatoes, drained, to the pot with the rice. Stir ½ cup pitted green olives (see the illustration on page 289), chopped coarse, and 4 scallions, sliced thin, to the pot with the shredded chicken in step 6. Serve with lime wedges.

Chicken and Rice with Caramelized Onions, Cardamom, and Raisins

Follow the recipe for Classic Chicken and Rice with Carrots and Peas, omitting the carrots, peas, and parsley. Increase the amount of onions to 3 and slice them thin. In step 3, cook the onions with 1 teaspoon brown sugar and ½ teaspoon salt over medium heat, stirring frequently, until golden and caramelized, 25 to 35 minutes, before adding the garlic. Add 2 teaspoons minced or grated fresh ginger, ½ teaspoon ground cardamom, ½ teaspoon ground cumin, and ⅛ teaspoon crumbled saffron threads to the pot with the garlic. Add ⅓ cup raisins and 3 tablespoons minced fresh cilantro leaves to the pot with the shredded chicken in step 6.

SIMPLIFIED CASSOULET

EVERY ONCE IN A WHILE, A DISH COMES along that is so robust and satisfying to every sense that we deem it comfort food. Cassoulet is such a dish. An unctuous stew of creamy white beans, confit, tender pork, and garlic sausage, all capped with buttery bread crumbs, cassoulet can be divine. Yet for most cooks, the reasons to eat cassoulet greatly outnumber the reasons to make it. Cassoulet can take three days to prepare and often requires a formidable list of uniquely French ingredients. Making confit and garlic sausages, soaking and cooking dried beans, and spending a long weekend tied to the stove were just a few of the obstacles that stood between us and an easier pot of cassoulet. Luckily, our desire to enjoy an authentic-tasting cassoulet, without breaking our backs, was motivation enough to accept this challenge. We raided our shelves of French cookery tomes and did some required reading.

Cassoulet originated in southeast France, and each area of this region boasts its own recipe. The best known and most often replicated cassoulet hails from Toulouse. This cassoulet starts with the preparation of confit. Meat or poultry, most often goose legs, is placed in a large container, sprinkled heavily with salt, and cured for 24 to 48 hours. After this sojourn in salt, the meat is slowly simmered in its own fat, where it develops rich, concentrated flavor. Next, fresh pork and garlic sausages must be stuffed, and dried beans soaked and parcooked. Only then does the actual cooking begin: brown the sausage and pork, add aromatics and white wine and simmer until tender, then stir in the confit and beans, top with toasted bread crumbs and gently bake until the beans are tender, the flavors have melded, and the crust is golden brown. There was clearly some streamlining to do.

The first place to begin was obviously the confit. Preparing our own was out of the question, and store-bought confit wasn't a good option because it's expensive and inconsistent. While many variations (restaurant versions in particular) do include this deeply flavorful preserved meat, it's by no means essential. We decided to substitute readily available chicken thighs for the duck legs; we would look for other ways to bring rich meatiness to the dish.

For starters, we needed another source of preserved animal fat to compensate for the lack of confit fat in the pot. We tested salt pork and bacon, rendering each until crisp and using the fat to brown the chicken. Tasters preferred the smokiness of bacon to more subtle salt pork.

For the stewing pork, we needed a flavorful cut that had plenty of connective tissue so that it wouldn't dry out during prolonged cooking. Our options included shoulder, spare ribs, belly, and country-style ribs. We tested each and found little difference among the cuts—all stayed moist, tender, and flavorful after hours in the pot. We settled on country-style ribs since they are inexpensive and easy to find in small package sizes. To facilitate even cooking, we cut the ribs into 1-inch pieces.

After ruling out hard-to-find French sausages (and not willing to take the time to make our own), we found that both kielbasa and andouille sausages provided a nice balance of garlic and smoke. We found that the sausage lent the most flavor to the stew when cut into thin slices. With all of our meats in a row, we addressed the beans.

While dried beans are certainly de rigueur in traditional cassoulet, they also demand an overnight soak and a separate pot—two things we were unwilling to involve in our simplified stew. All cassoulets use some form of white bean, the most celebrated being the *tarbais*, a half-inch-long kidney-shaped bean with a very thin skin and a supremely creamy texture. As tarbais beans are only available dried, we needed a canned alternative that would offer comparable creaminess. We ran tests with cannellini, navy, butter, and great Northern beans, and we were pleased to find that readily available cannellini beans were a very close approximation. Added toward the end of cooking, these large beans held their shape well and maintained their creamy presence in the pot. After wading through an intimidating list of fussy ingredients, we finally felt ready to start cooking our stew.

Following standard flavor-building procedure, we first rendered the bacon in a large Dutch oven and used the fat to brown the chicken, pork, and sausage. Next, we added onion, garlic, thyme, and ground cloves to form a substantial aromatic base. We were originally skeptical of cloves, but we realized their power to add warmth and depth after tasting them in a few different recipes. After deglazing with white wine and store-bought chicken broth (chicken or pork broth is the traditional cooking liquid) we transferred the pot to a low oven and let it gently bubble away until the chicken and pork were tender. Finally, we stirred in the beans and crisped bacon (we removed it after rendering to prevent it from burning) and showered the pot with a few handfuls of store-bought bread crumbs (we didn't want to use a sheet pan or skillet to toast fresh crumbs). After a brief stint in a hot oven to brown the crumbs, we tucked into our simplified cassoulet. Despite being slightly greasy and watery, with a soggy raft of bread crumbs and overcooked bites of sausage, our stew actually tasted pretty good. Having gotten this far, we happily set about addressing these last issues.

In our efforts to replicate the rich flavor of confit, we had apparently gone overboard with the amount of fat in the pot. Instead of eliminating any one type of flavorful fat, we chose to drain off the excess prior to sautéing the aromatics. This quick fix worked pretty well, but the stew still tasted overly rich. While not authentic, we found that tomato paste and diced tomatoes, along with the white wine, provided just the right amount of acidity to counter the stew's richness. The wateriness, likely a result of using fully cooked canned beans (instead of moisture-absorbing dried beans) was easily remedied with a few tablespoons of flour. To prevent the sausage from overcooking, we chose to skip the searing step (we were already browning plenty of the ingredients) and stir it in at the end with the beans. Finally, we tackled the bread crumbs.

In traditional cassoulet, cooked in a wide-rimmed *cassole*, the top of the stew dries out and forms a skin upon which the bread crumbs sit and toast. But in a Dutch oven, where moisture is trapped by the tall sides of the pot, the surface stays moist and the bread crumbs become soggy. We thought using cubes of bread, with far less surface area than crumbs, might solve the problem, but we wondered how we would toast them without an extra sheet pan or skillet. One taster suggested using the microwave and, while we were highly skeptical, we gave it a shot. We tossed a cubed baguette (a naturally dry and crunchy bread) with butter in a large bowl and threw it in the microwave on high power. Miraculously, in less than 10 minutes we had perfectly toasted, golden croutons. Even more impressive was how crunchy this raft of buttery cubes remained once baked atop the stew. At last we had it: a simplified cassoulet that was worthy of the name.

Simplified Cassoulet

SERVES 8 TO 10

To keep the dish from becoming greasy, remove excess fat from the chicken thighs and trim the skin. The bacon and sausage add considerable salt to this dish, so make sure not to season the chicken and pork in step 3.

CROUTONS

1	(12-ounce) baguette, cut into ½-inch pieces (about 10 cups)
3	tablespoons unsalted butter, melted

STEW

6	ounces (about 6 slices) bacon, chopped fine
10	bone-in chicken thighs (about 3¾ pounds), trimmed (see note)
1	pound boneless country-style ribs, trimmed and cut into 1-inch pieces
1	medium onion, minced
4	medium garlic cloves, minced or pressed through a garlic press (about 4 teaspoons)
1	teaspoon minced fresh thyme leaves or ¼ teaspoon dried
¼	teaspoon ground cloves
3	tablespoons unbleached all-purpose flour
1	tablespoon tomato paste
1¾	cups low-sodium chicken broth
1	(14.5-ounce) can diced tomatoes, drained
¾	cup dry white wine
3	(15-ounce) cans cannellini beans, drained and rinsed
½	pound kielbasa sausage, halved lengthwise and sliced ¼ inch thick
	Salt and ground black pepper

1. FOR THE CROUTONS: Toss the baguette pieces and butter together in a large bowl. Microwave on high power until dry and light golden, 7 to 9 minutes, stirring often; set aside.

2. FOR THE STEW: Adjust an oven rack to the lower-middle position and heat the oven to 300 degrees. Cook the bacon in a large Dutch oven over medium heat until crisp and rendered, 5 to 7 minutes. Transfer the bacon to a paper towel–lined plate, leaving the fat in the pot.

3. Pat the chicken and pork dry with paper towels (do not season). Heat the fat left in the pot over medium-high heat until just smoking. Add half of the chicken and brown lightly, 6 to 8 minutes; transfer to a large bowl. Repeat with the remaining chicken using the fat left in the pot; transfer to the bowl. Remove and discard the chicken skin.

4. Add the pork to the fat left in the pot and brown lightly, 6 to 8 minutes; transfer to the bowl with the chicken.

5. Pour off all but 2 tablespoons of the fat left in the pot, add the onion, and cook over medium heat until softened, 5 to 7 minutes. Stir in the garlic, thyme, and cloves and cook until fragrant, about 30 seconds. Stir in the flour and tomato paste and cook for 1 minute. Whisk in the broth, scraping up any browned bits and smoothing out any lumps.

6. Stir in the tomatoes, wine, and browned chicken and pork with any accumulated juice and bring to a simmer. Partially cover the pot, transfer to the oven, and cook until the chicken and pork are tender, 60 to 70 minutes.

7. Remove the pot from the oven and increase the oven temperature to 425 degrees. Stir in the beans, sausage, and reserved bacon and season with salt and pepper to taste. Sprinkle the croutons evenly over the surface of the stew and bake until the croutons are deep golden brown, 10 to 15 minutes. Let cool for 10 minutes before serving.

SEAFOOD RISOTTO

AT ITS BEST, SEAFOOD RISOTTO SHOWCASES al dente rice and a thoughtful composition of sweet, tender seafood bathed in a simple yet elegant starchy sauce. Unfortunately, waxing poetic about seafood risotto is considerably easier than making a great pot of it. Traditional risotto demands 30 minutes of diligent attention and stirring to produce evenly cooked, ultra-creamy rice. Hot broth is ladled into the pot in small amounts while the cook provides near-constant stirring until the rice is tender but still maintains a slight bite. While certainly worth the effort, this method is out of reach for most of us for a weeknight meal. Tack on a labor-intensive seafood broth and the daunting task of choosing and cooking the right mix of seafood, and seafood risotto might appear to be more work than it's worth. We wanted a more hands-off method that required one pot and guaranteed rich flavor and perfectly cooked seafood. We decided to first establish a method for cooking the rice before addressing the other elements of the dish.

Stirring medium-grain rice (which is higher than both short- and long-grain rice in an important starch called amylopectin) in hot broth releases surface starches that dissolve into, and thicken, the broth. Since stirring is paramount to this technique, we knew eliminating it entirely wasn't an option, but were hopeful we could reduce the amount required. To see how infrequently we could add broth and stir (and still get the creamy results we desired) we made dozens of batches of

risotto. We were happy to find that batches stirred roughly half of the time were hard to distinguish from those stirred constantly. We also tested some almost no-stir methods. While these recipes often produced good results, their specific liquid requirements and cooking times made it difficult to add raw seafood directly to the rice (and poaching it in another pot was out of the question). In the end, we settled on a technique that adds almost half of the liquid at the beginning and stirs infrequently for the first 13 to 17 minutes. The remaining broth is then added in 1-cup increments and stirred frequently (not constantly) for the final 13 to 17 minutes. We found this shortened period of stirring still provided plenty of time to adjust the consistency of the sauce and cook the seafood right in the same pot. With our method nailed down, we turned our attention to the broth.

EQUIPMENT: Dutch Ovens

A good Dutch oven (variously called a stockpot, round oven, or casserole by manufacturers) is absolutely a kitchen essential. It is heavier and thicker than a real stockpot, allowing it to retain and conduct heat more effectively, and deeper than a skillet, so it can handle large cuts of meat and cooking liquid. Dutch ovens are the best choice for braises, en cocotte cooking, stews, and chilis, as they can go on the stovetop to sear foods and then into the oven to finish with steady, slow cooking. Their tall sides also make them useful for deep-frying, and many cooks press Dutch ovens into service for jobs like boiling pasta. After testing nine Dutch ovens at varying prices, we discovered we like a Dutch oven that is roughly twice as wide as it is tall, with a minimum capacity of 6 quarts, though 7 quarts is even better. The bottom should be thick so that it maintains moderate heat and prevents food from scorching, and the lid should fit tightly to prevent excess moisture loss. And while two of the more expensive pots we tested came out on top, we did find that one of the more inexpensive options could keep up with these winners in almost every facet. That's good news for the budget-minded cook.

THE BEST DUTCH OVENS

The All-Clad Stainless 8-quart Stockpot ($294.95) and the Le Creuset 7¼-Quart Round French Oven ($269) are our top choices. (The All-Clad is the best choice for cooks who prefer a lighter pot.) For those looking for a less-expensive alternative, the Tramontina 6.5-Quart Cast Iron Dutch Oven ($54.95) is a solid choice and our Best Buy.

ALL-CLAD   LE CREUSET   TRAMONTINA

During our research we came across one noted cookbook author who suggested that plain water was the best choice for seafood risotto, but our tasters were quick to disagree, arguing that the resulting risotto tasted incredibly thin and bland. Adding bottled clam juice to the water was more promising, offering a welcome briny hit, but the broth still lacked depth. Stepping away from the sea for a moment, we tried substituting store-bought chicken broth for the water. This was certainly our richest batch yet, but tasters were missing a certain seafood essence. Since we knew we wanted our risotto to include shrimp, we wondered if we could use their shells to flavor the broth. We tried simmering the broth in the microwave with the shells from ½ pound of shrimp, along with onion, bay leaves, and peppercorns (a few classic broth additions). Just 20 minutes in the microwave (no additional pot required) infused the broth with a light but distinct seafood flavor. After we made several batches of our working risotto recipe with this broth, we realized that we needed a little more depth and an acidic note for balance. Saffron, a classic complement to seafood, tied together the flavors and imparted a lush golden hue to the rice. For acidity, and additional color, we added a can of drained diced tomatoes. With our stage set, we introduced the seafood.

In addition to the shrimp, we included squid, which tasters liked for its mild flavor and gentle bite. We cut the bodies into rings but left the tentacles whole to showcase their unique texture and visual appeal. For a briny hit of flavor, we hoped to add shellfish like clams and mussels, but their inclusion posed a riddle: how to cook them without using a separate pot? They were certainly attractive nestled into the creamy rice, but it was nearly impossible to cook them in the gently simmering risotto. In the end, we excluded clams and mussels and used scallops for their gentle brininess and characteristic sweetness (they were also far less work than their shelled brethren). We chose small bay scallops over large sea scallops because they cooked quickly and fit on a fork with a bite

of rice. Now we needed to find the best way to cook the seafood.

We tested a number of recipes that called for adding the seafood to the rice as it stood off the heat (usually for about five minutes). We liked the theory behind this technique, which relies on residual heat to gently cook the seafood, but found it often produced rare shrimp and squid. In order to properly cook 1½ pounds of cold seafood we found it necessary to keep the pot on the heat for about three minutes before taking it off the heat. Stirring during this brief period ensured that every bite of seafood cooked at the same rate. With a richly flavored pot of perfectly cooked rice and seafood, we addressed a few final touches.

Except in the rarest situations, fish and cheese are never combined in Italian cooking—a tradition we wished to honor in our seafood risotto. To achieve the same richness and body that grated Parmesan would provide in other risottos, we added a minced anchovy with the aromatics and stirred in additional butter once the rice had finished cooking. The anchovy lent a savory character while the butter gave the rice a voluptuous feel. Using a few labor- (and pot-) saving techniques, we had managed to turn a couple cups of humble rice into a one-pot supper bordering on ambrosia.

REMOVING TENDONS FROM SCALLOPS

The small, rough-textured, crescent-shaped tendon that attaches the scallop to the shell will toughen when cooked. Use your fingers to peel the tendon away from the side of each scallop before cooking.

Seafood Risotto

SERVES 4 TO 6

Do not buy peeled shrimp; you will need the shrimp shells to order to make the broth. You can substitute ½ pound sea scallops, quartered, for the bay scallops.

BROTH

4	(8-ounce) bottles clam juice
4	cups low-sodium chicken broth
1	(14.5-ounce) can diced tomatoes, drained
	Shells from ½ pound shrimp (see below)
1	medium onion, chopped coarse
10	black peppercorns
2	bay leaves
½	teaspoon salt
⅛	teaspoon saffron threads, crumbled
	Hot water, as needed

RISOTTO

5	tablespoons unsalted butter
1	medium onion, minced
	Salt
5	medium garlic cloves, minced or pressed through a garlic press (about 5 teaspoons)
1	teaspoon minced fresh thyme leaves or ¼ teaspoon dried
1	medium anchovy fillet, rinsed and minced
2	cups Arborio rice
1	cup dry white wine
½	pound large shrimp (about 31 to 40 per pound), shells removed and reserved for the broth, and deveined (see the illustration on page 145)
½	pound small bay scallops, tendons removed (see the illustration on page 81) (see note)
½	pound squid, bodies cut crosswise into ½-inch rings, tentacles left whole
1	tablespoon juice from 1 lemon
2	tablespoons minced fresh parsley leaves
	Ground black pepper

1. FOR THE BROTH: Combine all the broth ingredients in a large bowl and microwave on high power until fragrant and flavorful, about 20 minutes. Strain the broth through a fine-mesh strainer into a large measuring cup, pressing on the solids to extract as much liquid as possible. (You should have 8 cups of broth; if not, add hot water as needed.) Cover to keep warm and set aside.

2. FOR THE RISOTTO: Melt 2 tablespoons of the butter in a large Dutch oven over medium heat. Add the onion and ¼ teaspoon salt and cook until softened, 5 to 7 minutes. Stir in the garlic, thyme, and anchovy and cook until fragrant, about 30 seconds. Stir in the rice and cook, stirring frequently, until the grains are translucent around the edges, about 3 minutes.

3. Stir in the wine and cook, stirring frequently, until fully absorbed, 2 to 3 minutes. Stir in 3½ cups of the warm broth. Bring to a simmer and cook, stirring about every 3 minutes, until the broth is absorbed and the bottom of the pot is dry, 13 to 17 minutes. Meanwhile, reheat the remaining broth in the microwave until hot.

4. Continue to cook the rice, stirring frequently and adding more hot broth, 1 cup at a time, every few minutes as the pan bottom turns dry, until the rice is cooked through but still somewhat firm in the center, 13 to 17 minutes.

5. Stir in the shrimp, scallops, and squid and continue to cook, stirring frequently, until the seafood is just cooked through, about 3 minutes. Remove the pot from the heat, cover, and let stand for 5 minutes.

6. Stir in the remaining 3 tablespoons butter, lemon juice, and parsley and season with salt and pepper to taste. If desired, add the remaining broth, ¼ cup at a time, to loosen the consistency of the risotto before serving.

CHICKEN AND SHRIMP JAMBALAYA

WITH CHICKEN, SAUSAGE, SHRIMP, RICE, tomatoes, and a laundry list of herbs and spices, the Louisiana classic known as jambalaya may sound more like a weekend project than a weeknight dinner. Yet with the right recipe, jambalaya is a one-pot meal that can be on the table in about an hour. Not to mention its bold flavor combination of sweet, spice, and smoke is a true crowd-pleaser. However, all too often we've encountered versions that are nothing more than a disappointing, bland pot of gummy rice, over- or undercooked shrimp, and tough, dry chicken. Determined to do justice to this New Orleans institution, we did some research and started cooking.

Following one of the more authentic-looking jambalaya recipes, we cut up a whole chicken into eight pieces and seared both sides in a large Dutch oven. After removing the chicken, we browned ½ pound of andouille and then transferred the sausage to the bowl with the chicken. We then stirred in the traditional Cajun aromatic trio of minced green bell pepper, onion, and celery and sautéed them until softened. Next, we stirred in chicken broth (the most common choice in the recipes we tested) and 2 cups of long-grain white rice, along with the browned chicken, sausage, and a can of drained diced tomatoes. We popped on the lid and gently simmered everything until the rice became tender, and finally we shredded the chicken and stirred it back in with the shrimp. After a five-minute rest to warm the chicken and cook the shrimp, we tasted. The result? Tasters had a laundry list of complaints, including dried-out chicken, unevenly cooked rice, wan flavors, and undercooked shrimp. We tackled the chicken first.

Although most jambalaya recipes call for a whole chicken cut up into parts, this inevitably leads to overcooked breast meat. Bucking tradition, we opted to use flavorful chicken thighs instead. This not only

guaranteed moist, not dry, chicken every time but also saved us the time it takes to cut up a whole chicken. Next, we took aim at the rice.

In our first test, some of the grains of rice were perfectly tender, while others remained stubbornly crunchy and raw—a problem we had encountered while developing our Classic Chicken and Rice with Carrots and Peas (page 76). Just as in that recipe, the large pieces of chicken disrupt even heat distribution, creating cooler pockets throughout the pot where rice gets trapped and fails to cook through. Transferring the pot to the even heat of a 350-degree oven and stirring just twice during cooking (more stirring produces pasty rice) solved the problem. This rice turned out fluffy and tender throughout. With the heart of the dish in place, we addressed our tasters' complaints regarding flavor.

While green bell peppers may be traditional for jambalaya, our tasters consistently found them bitter-tasting and drab. Instead, we switched to red bell peppers, which stayed sweet and colorful. To the pepper, onion, and celery, we also added garlic and thyme for more depth. Up to this point we had been using all chicken broth and, while our jambalaya certainly tasted rich and meaty, some tasters felt it lacked the requisite brininess of true Cajun cooking. One bottle of clam juice, substituted for a cup of the chicken broth, did just the trick. Tasters were also clamoring for more tomato flavor, but adding a second can of diced tomatoes overwhelmed the dish's other components. Instead, we tried stirring in a couple teaspoons of tomato paste with the other aromatics—a technique that quickly boosted tomato flavor and overall color. Finally, we spiced things up with ¼ teaspoon of cayenne pepper, ensuring that every bite would deliver subtle, persistent heat.

Our final challenge was achieving perfectly cooked shrimp. Given that five minutes off the heat wasn't enough to cook them through, we tried stirring in the raw shrimp right when we removed the chicken to shred it, giving them an additional five minutes of residual heat. When this method failed, we decided to place the pot back in the oven for five to seven minutes, while we shredded the chicken. After removing the lid from this batch to sprinkle on some parsley, we could see that the shrimp were perfectly cooked, tender and succulently sweet. This jambalaya was smoky and sweet, spicy and savory, with perfectly tender shrimp, moist chicken, rich flavor, and rice cooked just so. You'd never have guessed it was made in our Boston test kitchen and not on Bourbon Street.

Chicken and Shrimp Jambalaya

SERVES 6

To keep the dish from becoming greasy, remove excess fat from the chicken thighs and trim the skin. Be sure to stir the rice gently when cooking in step 5; aggressive stirring will make the rice taste gluey.

1¼	pounds bone-in, skin-on chicken thighs (about 4 thighs), trimmed
	Salt and ground black pepper
1	tablespoon olive oil
½	pound andouille sausage, halved lengthwise and sliced ¼ inch thick
1	medium onion, minced
1	celery rib, chopped fine
1	red bell pepper, stemmed, seeded, and chopped fine (see the illustrations on page 226)
5	medium garlic cloves, minced or pressed through a garlic press (about 5 teaspoons)
1	teaspoon minced fresh thyme leaves or ¼ teaspoon dried
¼	teaspoon cayenne pepper
2	teaspoons tomato paste
1½	cups low-sodium chicken broth
1	(8-ounce) bottle clam juice
1	(14.5-ounce) can diced tomatoes, drained
2	cups long-grain white rice
1	pound large shrimp (31 to 40 per pound), peeled and deveined (see the illustration on page 145)
3	tablespoon minced fresh parsley leaves

1. Adjust an oven rack to the middle position and heat the oven to 350 degrees. Pat the chicken dry with paper towels and season with salt and pepper.

2. Heat the oil in a large Dutch oven over medium-high heat until just smoking. Add the chicken and brown lightly, 6 to 8 minutes; transfer to a large bowl. Add the sausage to the fat left in the pot and brown lightly, about 5 minutes; transfer to the bowl with the chicken.

3. Pour off all but 2 tablespoons of the fat let in the pot, add the onion, celery, and bell pepper, and cook until softened, 5 to 7 minutes. Stir in the garlic, thyme, and cayenne and cook until fragrant, about 30 seconds. Stir in the tomato paste and cook for 1 minute. Stir in the broth and clam juice, scraping up any browned bits.

4. Stir in the tomatoes, browned chicken, and browned sausage with any accumulated juice. Bring to a simmer, cover, and simmer gently for 20 minutes.

5. Thoroughly stir in the rice. Cover, transfer the pot to the oven, and cook until all of the rice

INGREDIENTS:
Long-Grain White Rice

Higher-quality white rice offers a pleasing al dente texture and a natural, slightly buttery flavor. While most of this subtle variation comes from the variety of rice, processing also affects flavor. All white rice has been milled, a process that removes the husk, bran, and germ. The longer the rice is milled, the whiter it becomes. Many brands (except organic) are enriched to replace lost nutrients. Cooked long-grain white rice grains should be fluffy and separate. We tasted six national brands of long-grain white rice, plain (steamed in our favorite rice cooker) and in pilaf. Our favorite had subtle "buttery and toasty" notes reminding us of "nuts" or "barley." Even with the added flavors in rice pilaf, tasters preferred our winning brand for both taste and texture.

THE BEST LONG-GRAIN WHITE RICE
Lundberg Organic Long-Grain White Rice stood out for its nutty, buttery flavor and distinct, smooth grains.

LUNDBERG

is tender and the liquid has been absorbed, 20 to 30 minutes, gently stirring the rice from the bottom of the pot to the top every 10 minutes.

6. Transfer the chicken to a carving board. Stir the shrimp into the rice, cover, and continue to cook in the oven until the shrimp are bright pink, 5 to 7 minutes. Let the chicken cool slightly, then shred into large chunks, following the illustration on page 75, discarding the skin and bones.

7. Gently stir the shredded chicken and parsley into the rice and season with salt and pepper to taste. Cover and let stand until the chicken is warmed through, about 5 minutes, before serving.

SOUTH CAROLINA SHRIMP BOIL

WHILE NEW ENGLAND HAS ITS CLAMBAKES and New Orleans its crawfish boils, the coastal towns of South Carolina boast a unique seafood boil that features local shell-on shrimp, smoked sausage, corn on the cob, and potatoes simmered in a broth seasoned with Old Bay. When it's time to eat, the broth is discarded and the shrimp and vegetables are heaped onto newspaper-covered picnic tables cluttered with paper towels and buckets for spent cobs and shells. While the simple, one-pot aspect of this dish is a big part of its charm, it can also be its biggest downfall. Home cooks are apt to add everything to the pot at the same time, or let everything boil away madly, often resulting in blown-out potatoes, mealy corn, and rubbery shrimp. The seasonings are also hit-or-miss—sometimes the Old Bay hits you over the head; other times it's far too subtle. We set out to develop a foolproof version of the shrimp boil that would have well-balanced seasoning and properly cooked components.

The most promising recipe we tested started by browning smoky, spicy andouille sausage to render fat and boost flavor. It then instructed to set the browned sausage aside and add 16 cups of water and 1 tablespoon of Old Bay to the pot. The potatoes and corn went in next and, when the potatoes

were barely tender, the sausage was added back to the pot, followed five minutes later by the shrimp. The staggered cooking was key, ensuring intact potatoes, plump corn, and nicely cooked sausage and shrimp. Unfortunately, the flavors in this recipe were washed out.

While the broth is discarded in a shrimp boil, it is important for flavoring all the other ingredients in the pot. To boost our broth's flavor, we tested adding garlic, onion, celery, and bell pepper, but only the garlic added any flavor, given the short cooking time. And rather than increasing the amount of Old Bay, we tried to get the same effect by subtraction. We reduced the amount of water to 5 cups, barely enough to cover the 1½ pounds of potatoes, four ears of corn, 1½ pounds of sausage and 2 pounds of shrimp we were using. With less water to dilute the seasonings, the flavor of our broth was now more intense.

For even more flavor, we tried replacing a cup of the water with an equal amount of clam juice, chicken broth, or beer. Tasters preferred the clam juice, which reinforced the brininess of the shrimp. Figuring that two is often better than one, we substituted an additional bottle of clam juice and, as expected, tasters liked this version even more. Some recipes called for tomato, which added brightness and some complementary sweetness to the broth. We tested various canned tomato options and found that diced tomatoes infused the broth faster than whole, without overpowering the way tomato puree did. With a bold, flavorful broth in the pot, we set about streamlining and perfecting our method.

Looking for ways to shortcut the process, we wondered if it was necessary to remove the browned andouille from the pot, only to add it back in later. For our next batch, we tried leaving it in to cook with the other ingredients. After 20 minutes, the potatoes were tender, and the sausage was still perfectly moist. Best of all, the extra simmering time for the sausage imparted extra flavor to the corn and potatoes. Next, we examined the shrimp.

Up to this point we had been adding the shrimp to the simmering liquid during the last few minutes of cooking, but that gave them scant time to soak up flavor. To compensate, we tossed them with additional Old Bay before adding them to the pot, but the spice washed right off. To get it to adhere, we would need to keep the shrimp out of the broth. Unwilling to use a separate pot or pan to cook the shrimp, we looked around the kitchen for alternatives. A common piece of equipment in most home kitchens, a metal steamer basket, seemed promising. Again we tossed the shrimp with 2 teaspoons Old Bay and placed them in the basket, which we set directly atop the simmering vegetables and sausage. With the shrimp elevated above the liquid, the seasoning stayed put, and 10 minutes later we had juicy and robustly flavored shrimp. Plus, cooking them this way was foolproof and relaxed, right in the spirit of a casual, one-pot seafood boil.

South Carolina Shrimp Boil

SERVES 8

This recipe uses shell-on shrimp; if you substitute peeled shrimp, reduce the amount of Old Bay seasoning to ¼ teaspoon.

2	teaspoons vegetable oil
1½	pounds andouille sausage, cut into 2-inch lengths
2	garlic cloves, peeled and crushed
5	teaspoons Old Bay seasoning
3	cups water
2	(8-ounce) bottles clam juice
1	(14.5-ounce) can diced tomatoes
4	ears fresh corn, husks and silk removed, cut into 2-inch rounds
1½	pounds red potatoes (about 3 medium), scrubbed and cut into 1-inch pieces
1	bay leaf
2	pounds extra-large shell-on shrimp (21 to 25 per pound) (see note)
1	tablespoon minced fresh parsley leaves

1. Heat the oil in a large Dutch oven over medium-high heat until just smoking. Add the sausage and cook until well browned, about 5 minutes. Stir in the garlic and 3 teaspoons of the Old Bay and cook until fragrant, about 30 seconds. Stir in the water, clam juice, tomatoes with their juice, corn, potatoes, and bay leaf and bring to a boil. Reduce to a simmer, cover, and cook until the potatoes are barely tender, 15 to 20 minutes.

2. Toss the shrimp with the remaining 2 teaspoons Old Bay and transfer to a collapsible steamer basket. Nestle the steamer basket into the pot, cover, and continue to simmer, stirring occasionally, until the shrimp are just cooked through, 10 to 12 minutes.

3. Remove the steamer basket and transfer the shrimp to a large serving bowl. Strain the vegetables, discarding the liquid, garlic cloves, and bay leaf, and transfer to the serving bowl. Sprinkle with the parsley and serve.

INDOOR CLAMBAKE

A CLAMBAKE IS A RITE OF SUMMER ALL ALONG the East Coast. For this beach party classic, loads of shellfish and a variety of vegetables are steamed in a wide, sandy pit using seaweed and rocks warmed from a nearby campfire. This feast usually takes a day or more to prepare—digging the pit is no small chore—and hours to cook. We wanted to re-create the great flavors of the clambake indoors. Though some may mock the idea of a kitchen clambake, it is nonetheless a simple and efficient way (taking a mere half-hour) to prepare a fantastic shellfish dinner— complete with corn, potatoes, and sausage—using only one pot.

An indoor clambake is not a novel idea. We found dozens of recipes in our cookbook library. While the methods used to put together an indoor clambake vary dramatically, the ingredients, in keeping with tradition, are fairly consistent, including clams, lobsters, potatoes, corn, onions, and sausage. Some recipes tell the cook to partially cook each ingredient separately and then finish things together on the grill, while others recommend specific systems for layering the ingredients in a large pot. Some recipes use seaweed or corn husks for extra flavor, while others tout the importance of smoky bacon. The common goal of all these recipes, however, is to manage the process such that the various components are cooked perfectly and ready to serve at the same time. Taking note of these different clambake styles, we began our testing.

It soon became apparent which methods were worthwhile and which simply made a mess. Partially cooking the ingredients separately before combining them on the grill required a slew of pots and pans and far too many steps. Layering the various ingredients in a Dutch oven, on the other hand, was both easy to do and produced tasty results. With the pot set over high heat, the components steamed and infused one another with their flavors. This method was not without problems, however, as any aromatics in the pot turned out slimy, and half the ingredients wound up submerged in weakly flavored water. Using this one-pot method as a point of departure, we began to tinker with the method and the ingredients.

Although all of the recipes we uncovered called for adding water to the pot; to create steam for cooking, we found the shellfish released enough of their own liquid to make adequate steam. When placed over high heat, the shellfish took only a few minutes to release the moisture needed to steam the whole pot, with a cup or more left over to use as a sauce for the clams. We took advantage of those first few minutes when the pot was dry by lining it with sliced sausage, giving it a chance to sear before the steam was unleashed. We tested several kinds of sausage, and tasters preferred mild kielbasa. The light smoky flavor of this sausage works well with seafood, and its high fat content ensures that it browns without burning.

With the sausage layered on the bottom, we played with the order in which to add the remaining ingredients. We found it best to lay the clams right on top of the sausage because they provide most of the necessary liquid for the steam and needed to be close to the heat source. Although potatoes actually take the longest to cook, they were best laid on top of the clams, close to the heat source yet easily accessible so we could test their doneness with a knife. We shortened their cooking time by cutting the potatoes into 1-inch pieces.

We placed the corn, with a layer of husk left on, on top of the potatoes. The husk, we found, protects

PREPARING LOBSTER FOR AN INDOOR CLAMBAKE

1. Freeze the lobsters for 15 minutes (do not overfreeze). Holding the lobster firmly with a kitchen towel, firmly drive the tip of a large, heavy-duty chef's knife through the back of the upper portion of the lobster's head, then swing the knife down through the head to kill the lobster.

2. Once the lobster is cooked, use your hands to twist the tail free from the body. (If the lobster is too hot use kitchen towels to protect your hands.)

3. Twist the legs free from the body, and then twist the claws free from the body.

the delicate corn from becoming infused with too much shellfish flavor. Finally, we placed the lobsters on top of the corn. We decided to omit aromatics like onion, carrot, and celery, which no one ate; the bacon, which smoked out the delicate flavor of the shellfish; and the seaweed, which was hard to find and unnecessary for flavor.

Layered in this fashion, the clambake took just 17 to 20 minutes to cook through completely over high heat. Conveniently, the shellfish liquid is quite salty and naturally seasons all the ingredients. After taking a couple of minutes to remove the ingredients from the pot and arrange them attractively on a platter, we had a feast that had been made from start to finish with one pot in half an hour.

Indoor Clambake

SERVES 4

Be sure to use a large (8-quart) Dutch oven in which you can easily layer the ingredients.

2   (1- to 1¼-pound) live lobsters
1   pound kielbasa sausage, sliced ½ inch thick
2   pounds littleneck clams, scrubbed (see the illustration at right)
1   pound red potatoes (about 3 medium), scrubbed and cut into 1-inch pieces
4   ears corn, silk and all but the last layer of husk removed
8   tablespoons (1 stick) unsalted butter, melted, for serving

1. Freeze the lobsters for 15 minutes to sedate them (do not overfreeze). Following the illustration on page 87, cut through the head of the lobsters to kill them.

2. Lay the sausage, cut side down, over the bottom of a large Dutch oven. Layer the clams, potatoes, corn, and lobsters (in that order) on top of the sausage. Cover and cook over medium-high heat until the potatoes are tender and the lobsters are bright red, 17 to 20 minutes.

3. Off the heat, remove the lobsters and set aside until cool enough to handle. Using a slotted spoon, transfer the corn, potatoes, clams, and sausage to a large serving platter. (If desired, strain the cooking liquid left in the pot into individual dipping bowls.)

4. Twist and remove the lobster tails, claws, and legs (using a towel to protect your hands if hot). Arrange the lobster tails, claws, and legs on the platter and discard the lobster bodies. Portion the melted butter into individual dipping bowls. Serve the clambake with the melted butter and strained cooking liquid (if desired).

SCRUBBING CLAMS

Use a soft brush, sometimes sold as a vegetable brush, to scrub away any bits of sand trapped in the shell.

4

CASSEROLES

CASSEROLES

BEEF TACO BAKE

SO MAYBE THEY'RE NOT AUTHENTIC MEXICAN food, but ground beef tacos have earned a special place at the table for at least a couple of generations of Americans. As a quick crowd-pleasing, family-friendly weeknight meal, the ground meat taco's simplicity and comfort-food appeal is undeniable. But taco night can be messy, both when it comes to eating the tacos and in terms of serving, with bowls of toppings cluttering the tabletop (which in turn translates to more cleanup). And while supermarket taco kits make quick work of the cooking, their stale, dusty seasoning packets produce flat-tasting fillings, reeking of dried oregano and onion powder. We decided to give taco night a makeover. We not only wanted a beef mixture that surpassed the results you'd get from those dusty taco kits, but we also wanted to do away with the array of mismatched bowls and the assembly process. We wanted to take our tacos apart and reassemble the components, the filling, taco shells, and garnishes into a single layered casserole that would cook quickly and be simple to serve.

We started with the beef. Tests combining ground beef ranging from 80 to 93 percent lean with a handful of basic taco spices showed that there is such a thing as too much fat. Pools of orange oil seeped out of the beef mixture made with ground chuck (aka 80 percent lean beef). Even the 85 percent option, our favorite for ground beef chili, cooked up slick and oily. At the other end of the spectrum, the filling made with the 93 percent lean beef (extra-lean) was dry and sandy. Ultimately we chose the 90 percent lean beef, which was full-flavored without being greasy.

Most of the labels on the taco seasoning packets we looked at contained dehydrated onion and/or garlic, so we started our filling in a similar vein but with freshness in mind. We sautéed some minced onion and garlic to add some moisture to our meat mixture as well as flavor it. For 1½ pounds ground beef, one chopped onion was enough; as for garlic, we liked a generous tablespoon, minced.

As for other spices, the supermarket taco seasoning packets indicated a hodgepodge of ingredients, some impractical and unappealing (MSG), and some simply vague ("spices"). However, they all included chili powder, so that's where we started to fashion our own mixture. We began with 1 tablespoon and quickly increased it to 2 tablespoons for the right kick. A teaspoon each of ground cumin and ground coriander added savory, complex flavors. Dried oregano in a more modest amount—½ teaspoon—provided herbal notes. Instead of dumping the raw spices onto the meat, we first bloomed them with the onion and garlic in oil in a skillet to bring out their complex flavors, and then we added the beef.

Now our filling needed a sauce to bind it together. First we tested adding a can of tomato sauce. After a short simmer, it reduced to the saucy consistency we were after, but in terms of flavor we thought it needed more punch to carry a casserole. We tried swapping out the tomato sauce for canned Ro-Tel tomatoes (which incorporate green chiles), and it was a success. The green chiles provided a jolt without any extra work on our part, and the Ro-Tel tomatoes' chunky texture gave the filling some variety. A little cider vinegar and brown sugar provided the characteristic sweet and sour tang.

Happy with the beef, we moved on to the other layers. Beans are a common addition to tacos and seemed an obvious candidate to bulk up our casserole. After trying whole beans and refried beans in our working recipe, we settled on the refried because they provided a distinct, creamy layer that contrasted nicely with the beef. Homemade refried beans are best, of course, but were too much work for what was intended to be a quick weeknight dinner. We decide to start with canned refried beans and bump up their flavor by combining them with other classic taco ingredients. Another can of Ro-Tel tomatoes was a good start. Chopped cilantro brought a welcome brightness, and a good dose of hot sauce added heat and pungency. We found it difficult to spread the beans evenly on top of the meat layer, so we made the beans the first level of the casserole and spread the mixture over the bottom of an empty casserole dish.

While taco toppings vary a bit from table to table, shredded cheese is always a requirement. We tried both cheddar and Monterey Jack and, although neither was bad, when combined with the richness of ground beef, tasters found the cheddar a little greasy. The creaminess of the Monterey Jack was just what we were striving for, but the flavor was a bit too mild. We found our answer in Colby Jack, a blend of Colby and Monterey Jack cheeses. The flavor of the Colby (which is similar to cheddar), combined with the creaminess of the Monterey Jack, was ideal for this casserole. We spread a layer of Colby Jack on top of our beans, followed by the beef filling, then another smattering of cheese.

Finally, it was time to find the best way to incorporate the taco shells. We experimented with simply sticking the store-bought taco shells, both whole and halved, into the casserole before baking, but these casseroles were awkward to serve and eat. We wondered if tortilla chips would serve as a more user-friendly stand-in for the taco shells. Tasters agreed they were easier to eat but the chips lacked the hearty crunch and distinct flavor of the thicker store-bought taco shells from their childhood memories. So we tried the taco shells again, this time crushing them into bite-size pieces before scattering them on top of the beef, followed by just a touch more cheese. Just 15 minutes in a very hot oven was enough to heat everything through, meld the flavors, and brown the topping. This topping was exactly what we were after.

For a fresh finish, we sprinkled our casserole with sliced scallions before serving. Our taco bake packs all the texture and flavor expected from taco night into a one-dish meal that even adults (not to mention the cook) can enjoy.

Beef Taco Bake
SERVES 6

If you can't find Ro-Tel tomatoes, substitute one 14.5-ounce can diced tomatoes and one 4-ounce can chopped green chiles, reserving 6 tablespoons of the tomato juice and 2 tablespoons of the chile juice. You can substitute 4 ounces each of Colby and Jack cheeses for the Colby Jack cheese.

1	(16-ounce) can refried beans
2	(10-ounce) cans Ro-Tel tomatoes, drained with ½ cup juice reserved
¼	cup minced fresh cilantro leaves
1	tablespoon hot sauce
8	ounces Colby Jack cheese, shredded (2 cups)
1	tablespoon vegetable oil
1	medium onion, minced
	Salt and ground black pepper
4	medium garlic cloves, minced or pressed through a garlic press (about 4 teaspoons)
2	tablespoons chili powder
1	teaspoon ground cumin
1	teaspoon ground coriander
½	teaspoon dried oregano
1½	pounds 90 percent lean ground beef
2	teaspoons cider vinegar
1	teaspoon light or dark brown sugar
12	taco shells, broken into 1-inch pieces
2	scallions, sliced thin

1. Adjust an oven rack to the upper-middle position and heat the oven to 475 degrees. Mix the refried beans, half of the drained tomatoes, cilantro, and hot sauce together, then smooth the mixture evenly into a 13 by 9-inch baking dish. Sprinkle 1 cup of the cheese over the top.

2. Heat the oil in a 12-inch skillet over medium heat until shimmering. Add the onion and ½ teaspoon salt and cook until softened, 5 to 7 minutes. Stir in the garlic, chili powder, cumin, coriander, and oregano and cook until fragrant, about 1 minute.

3. Stir in the beef and cook, breaking up the meat with a wooden spoon, until no longer pink, 5 to 8 minutes. Stir in the remaining tomatoes, reserved tomato juice, vinegar, and brown sugar. Bring to a simmer and cook until the mixture is thickened and nearly dry, about 10 minutes. Season with salt and pepper to taste.

4. Spread the beef mixture in the baking dish and sprinkle with ½ cup more cheese. Scatter the taco shell pieces over the top, then sprinkle with the remaining ½ cup cheese.

5. Bake until the filling is bubbling and the top is spotty brown, about 15 minutes. Let the casserole cool for 10 minutes, then sprinkle with the scallions and serve.

TO MAKE AHEAD

Prepare the ground beef filling through step 3, then let cool to room temperature before continuing to assemble the casserole in step 4. Cover the casserole with plastic wrap and refrigerate for up to 2 days. Remove the plastic wrap and bake as directed in step 5, increasing the cooking time to 20 minutes.

Easy Chicken Enchiladas

WHEN YOU FIRST THINK OF CASSEROLES, YOU likely picture ingredients that are either layered into the dish or simply mixed together and poured in. It's easy to forget that enchiladas are, in fact, a casserole dinner. And while they might be an irresistible favorite, Mexican enchiladas made in the traditional manner certainly aren't easy. With softened tortillas rolled around a cheesy filling packed with slow-cooked meat and a long-simmered spicy chili sauce inside and out, they are one of the fussier casseroles to make. Could we streamline the preparation and still retain the authentic flavor of the real thing?

Sauce is so central to enchiladas that it often defines them, so we started there. While the red sauce used in *enchiladas rojas* is made with dried chiles and is robust and fiery, the green sauce used in *enchiladas verdes* is prepared with fresh chiles and tomatillos (a tangy little tomato-like fruit) and is more tart and vibrant. Store-bought canned sauce of either variety, with its tinny, harsh flavor, was a nonstarter. But homemade sauces aren't exactly easy to make. We agreed we wanted enchilada recipes using both options, but our sauces needed to be easy to prepare; we started with the red.

Not only are whole dried chiles difficult to find in some areas, but they also require substantial preparation time, including toasting, seeding, stemming, rehydrating, and processing in a blender. Our sauce would depend on store-bought chili powder in lieu of the traditional dried chiles, so we needed to augment its comparatively bland flavor. Our first thought was to bloom the spice, or heat it in oil, a technique that intensifies flavor. We began by sautéing onions and garlic in oil and then added the chili powder to the pan. This produced a fuller, deeper flavor as expected, and we built up our sauce's backbone further by adding ground cumin and sugar.

Many traditional red sauce recipes incorporate tomatoes. Keeping convenience in mind, we explored our canned tomato product options. We tried adding diced tomatoes to the pan and then pureeing the mixture, but the texture was too thick and the flavor too acidic. Canned tomato sauce—which has a very smooth, slightly thickened texture and a milder tomato flavor—was our best option. This red sauce hit the mark.

Next we tackled the green sauce. For the chiles, we tested poblanos, serranos, and jalapeños. Tasters preferred the poblanos, which have mild to moderate heat and a deep herbal flavor that is more complex than the other two. As for the tomatillos, we decided to use fresh rather than canned for their bright, tangy, and balanced flavor. (That said, fresh tomatillos can be difficult to locate, so canned can be substituted.)

Traditional verde sauce recipes dry-roast whole tomatillos and chiles on the stovetop until soft and charred using a flat cast-iron vessel known as a *comal*. These ingredients are then ground with a mortar and pestle to form a sauce. More modern recipes, and the route we would take, skip the comal in favor of similarly fast, intense cooking techniques such as sautéing, high-heat oven-roasting, or broiling, then use a blender or food processor to create the sauce.

We quickly eliminated sautéing and oven-roasting; neither added enough char or smokiness. Broiling seemed more promising, especially when we tossed everything with a little oil to promote the charring. One taste and we knew that we'd hit the jackpot: Broiling tempered the tartness of the tomatillos and brought an almost sweet richness to the poblanos. The tomatillos did fine left whole, but we found that slicing the poblanos in half and broiling them skin side up helped blacken them more evenly.

Onion and garlic enhanced the roasted flavor of the chiles and tomatillos, while cilantro added freshness, and a teaspoon of sugar deepened the sweetness of the tomatillos. Lime juice brought the bright sauce into focus. A quick whir in the blender made a puree that was too smooth; a few pulses in the food processor better approximated the coarse, rustic texture produced by a mortar and pestle, but now the sauce was a little too thick. Just ¼ cup of chicken broth lent a subtle richness and thinned the sauce while maintaining its body.

With the sauces in line, we moved on to the filling. We decided on chicken for its general appeal and its ability to work with both sauces for our master recipe. We tried roasting a whole chicken as well as chicken parts (for a speedier option), as roasting promised flavorful results, but both were too time-consuming. Poaching in broth or water is another common technique; while faster, it doesn't offer much in terms of enhanced flavor. Why not use boneless, skinless chicken parts and poach them right in the sauce? Both thighs and breasts cooked quickly using this method and were nicely seasoned, and also lent the sauce richness. Shredding the cooked chicken gave it the right texture to meld nicely with the other filling ingredients (chiefly sauce and cheese).

Picking the cheese was next on our list. It needed to add flavor as well as help bind our filling. Queso fresco, the traditional choice, is an unripened cheese with a creamy color, mild flavor, and crumbly texture. But because it is not readily available in many parts of the United States, we tried similarly semisoft farmer's cheese instead. Tasters liked this cheese for its creamy texture and mellow flavor, but it was Monterey Jack and sharp white cheddar that made the top of the list. In the end, tasters preferred the sharp flavor of the cheddar.

Looking for more heat, we tested the addition of fresh jalapeños, chipotles in adobo sauce, and

MAKING ENCHILADAS

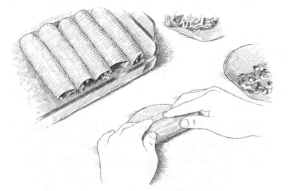

1. Working quickly with the warm, pliable tortillas, spread them out over a clean counter. Place ⅓ cup of the chicken mixture evenly down the center of each tortilla.

2. Tightly roll each tortilla around the filling, and lay them, seam side down, in a 13 by 9-inch baking dish. Repeat with the remaining tortillas and filling.

pickled jalapeños to several batches of enchilada filling. The fresh jalapeños were too mild. Chipotles added a distinctive, warm heat and smoky flavor that some tasters enjoyed but most found overwhelming. Everyone was surprised that the pickled jalapeños were the favorite. The vinegar pickling solution added appealingly spicy, bright, and sour notes to the filling.

When it came to assembling our enchiladas, we needed to make sure our tortillas were pliable enough to roll without breaking. We found that lightly spraying them with vegetable oil spray on both sides, then warming them in a moderate oven before filling and rolling them, was all we needed to do.

Once rolled, placed in the casserole dish, and topped with more sauce and cheese, our enchiladas need just 15 minutes in a hot oven. Finally, we had authentic-tasting enchiladas that didn't take all day to make.

Easy Chicken Enchiladas

SERVES 4 TO 6

You can substitute 8 ounces of shredded Monterey Jack, shredded pepper Jack, or crumbled queso fresco for the cheddar. Serve with sour cream, diced avocado, shredded romaine lettuce, and lime wedges.

1	pound boneless, skinless chicken breasts and/or thighs, trimmed
1	recipe Green or Red Enchilada Sauce (page 96)
8	ounces sharp cheddar cheese, shredded (2 cups)
½	cup minced fresh cilantro leaves
1	(4-ounce) can pickled jalapeños, drained and chopped (about ¼ cup)
	Salt and ground black pepper
12	(6-inch) corn tortillas
	Vegetable oil spray

1. Adjust an oven rack to the middle position and heat the oven to 350 degrees. Combine the chicken and enchilada sauce in a medium saucepan. Cover and simmer gently over medium-low heat until the breasts register 160 to 165 degrees and the thighs register 175 degrees on an instant-read thermometer, 8 to 12 minutes.

2. Remove the chicken from the pot and set the sauce aside. Let the chicken cool slightly, then shred the meat into bite-size pieces following the illustration on page 75. Combine the shredded chicken, ½ cup of the enchilada sauce, 1 cup of the cheese, cilantro, and jalapeños in a large bowl. Season with salt and pepper to taste and cover to keep warm.

3. Lightly coat both sides of the tortillas with vegetable oil spray. Spread 6 tortillas onto a baking sheet and bake until the tortillas are soft and pliable, 2 to 4 minutes.

4. Working quickly while the tortillas are still warm and pliable, spread them out over a clean counter. Following the illustrations on page 94, place ⅓ cup of the chicken mixture evenly down the center of each tortilla. Tightly roll each tortilla around the filling, and lay them, seam side down, in a 13 by 9-inch baking dish. Repeat with the remaining tortillas and filling.

5. Increase the oven temperature to 450 degrees. Pour 1 cup more sauce over the enchiladas and sprinkle with the remaining 1 cup cheese. Cover the enchiladas tightly with aluminum foil that has been sprayed with vegetable oil spray (or use nonstick foil).

6. Bake until the enchiladas are heated through, about 10 minutes. Remove the foil and continue to bake until the cheese is melted, 3 to 5 minutes longer. Let the casserole cool for 10 minutes, then serve, passing the remaining sauce separately.

➤ VARIATION
Easy Beef Enchiladas
Red enchilada sauce is the best match for beef; we don't recommend using the green sauce.

Follow the recipe for Easy Chicken Enchiladas, substituting 1¼ pounds top blade steaks, trimmed (see the illustrations on page 97) for the chicken. Add ½ cup water to the pan with the sauce and beef in step 1; cover and simmer the beef gently

ENCHILADA SAUCES

Green Enchilada Sauce

MAKES ABOUT 2½ CUPS

You can substitute two 11-ounce cans tomatillos, drained, rinsed, and patted dry, for the fresh tomatillos; broil as directed in step 1. If you can't find poblanos, substitute 5 jalapeños, stemmed and seeded.

1	pound tomatillos (about 12 medium), husks and stems removed, rinsed well, dried, and halved if larger than 2 inches in diameter
3	poblano chiles, halved lengthwise, stemmed, and seeded
1	tablespoon olive oil
¼	cup low-sodium chicken broth
1	medium onion, minced
2	medium garlic cloves, minced or pressed through a garlic press (about 2 teaspoons)
½	cup packed fresh cilantro leaves
1	tablespoon juice from 1 lime
1	teaspoon sugar
	Salt and ground black pepper

1. Position an oven rack 6 inches from the broiler element and heat the broiler. Line a rimmed baking sheet with aluminum foil. Toss the tomatillos and poblanos with the oil. Arrange the tomatillos (cut side down if halved) and poblanos, skin side up, on the prepared baking sheet. Broil until the vegetables blacken and begin to soften, 5 to 10 minutes, rotating the pan halfway through cooking.

2. Remove the vegetables from the oven, let cool slightly, then remove the skins from the poblanos (leave tomatillo skins intact). Process the broiled vegetables, broth, onion, garlic, cilantro, lime juice, and sugar together in a food processor until the sauce is almost smooth, 30 to 60 seconds. Season with salt and pepper to taste. (The sauce can be refrigerated in an airtight container for up to 1 week.)

Red Enchilada Sauce

MAKES ABOUT 2½ CUPS

Be sure to use canned tomato sauce, not jarred tomato sauce, in this recipe because it has a very smooth texture and few seasonings. One 15-ounce can of tomato sauce can be substituted for the two 8-ounce cans if necessary.

1	tablespoon vegetable oil
1	medium onion, minced
2	medium garlic cloves, minced or pressed through a garlic press (about 2 teaspoons)
3	tablespoons chili powder
2	teaspoons ground cumin
2	teaspoons sugar
2	(8-ounce) cans tomato sauce
½	cup water
	Salt and ground black pepper

Heat the oil in a medium saucepan over medium-high heat until shimmering. Add the onion and cook until softened, 5 to 7 minutes. Stir in the garlic, chili powder, cumin, and sugar and cook until fragrant, about 30 seconds. Stir in the tomato sauce and water, bring to a simmer, and cook until slightly thickened, about 5 minutes. Season with salt and pepper to taste. (The sauce can be refrigerated in an airtight container for up to 1 week.)

INGREDIENTS: Tomatillos

Tomatillos give our Green Enchilada Sauce its distinctive tart flavor and green color. Tomatillos are a fruit that resemble small green tomatoes (about the size of a walnut) and are covered by a thin papery husk. The husk should be dry and the fruit should be firm. Tomatillos are carried by some supermarkets and many Latin American markets.

until tender, about 1½ hours, before continuing with step 2.

TO MAKE AHEAD

Assemble the Easy Chicken Enchiladas or Easy Beef Enchiladas through step 4. Cover the enchiladas with plastic wrap, transfer the remaining sauce to an airtight container, and refrigerate for up to 2 days. Before continuing with step 5, remove the plastic wrap, spray the enchiladas lightly with vegetable oil spray, and bake, uncovered, until the tortillas are lightly toasted on top, 10 to 20 minutes. Continue to sauce and bake the enchiladas as directed in step 5.

TRIMMING BLADE STEAKS

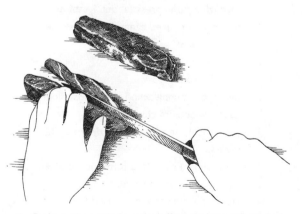

1. Halve each steak lengthwise, leaving the gristle on one half.

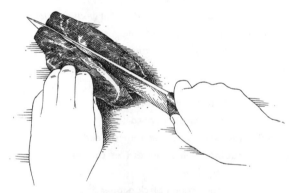

2. Cut away the gristle from the half to which it is still attached.

MEXICAN LASAGNA

WE HAD JUST DEVELOPED AN EASY RECIPE FOR enchiladas, but there's another casserole inspired by enchiladas that has an appeal all its own. At some point, time-pressed cooks came up with a one-dish supper with the flavor profile of enchiladas but simpler assembly. They started using ground meat and layering the enchilada ingredients rather than rolling. Down the line, they improvised additions such as tomatoes, bell peppers, and beans. Eventually this casserole become a Tex-Mex standard in its own right. We found countless recipes, most of which unfortunately insisted on disguising canned or jarred ingredients with cans of cream-of-something soups and gobs of cheese, then baking the whole mess until the flavors were lifeless. Our goal was to breathe some life and spice into this typically heavy dish. To accomplish that, we would have to eliminate the creamy sauce and drastically reduce the lengthy oven time. Our plan was to create a spicy filling, then spread it between layers of corn tortillas, the topmost of which would be covered with melted cheese.

We started with the meat. Most recipes we found used ground beef, but pork, chicken, and turkey were common as well. After testing each of our options, we decided on pork, which had a more subtle flavor in the final dish than the beef and a natural sweetness that paired well with the sweet and earthy corn tortillas. (Tasters thought the ground chicken tasted a little dry, but turkey can be a good substitute for the pork.)

Moving on to the sauce and remaining add-ins, off the cuff we knew what *not* to use— canned cream-of-anything soup. As for the rest of the ingredients, recipes varied widely. Tasters didn't care for more offbeat options such as olives, mushrooms, or green bell peppers, but they did like pinto beans, sweet corn, red bell peppers, and chipotle chiles, in addition to the ubiquitous tomatoes, onions, and garlic. They also liked chili powder, but not in the large quantities suggested by most recipes. Just 2 teaspoons contributed spice without masking the subtler beans and vegetables. For the cheese, we found Colby Jack added good flavor and melted well without becoming stringy or greasy. Cilantro and lime juice were the natural Southwestern choices to round out the filling.

Our first attempt at assembling the dish was a disaster in more ways than one. The middle layers of tortillas completely disintegrated, leaving behind a homely sort of cornmeal mush. Meanwhile, the top layer, instead of crisping up, withered and toughened into a leathery mess. The filling was dry, as all the moisture had soaked into the tortillas. And even though the dish had been in the oven for only 30 minutes, the fresh flavors of the cilantro, chiles, and lime juice were muddy and washed out.

We tackled the tortilla problem first. They acted like a sponge in our casserole, soaking up all the liquid. Our enchilada recipe (see page 93) solved this problem by spraying the tortillas with cooking spray and heating them briefly in a low oven, and we discovered this method helped here as well. The top layer was dramatically improved. The tortillas were crisp like nacho chips, even buried under a layer of melted cheese. And the inner layers were better— distinct rows of tortillas were visible—but overall they were still mushy.

We had been cooking the casserole in a 400-degree oven, thinking it would allow for the best balance between quick and even cooking. After experimenting with other temperatures, we found that increasing the heat to 450 degrees maximized the crispness of the topping and minimized the amount of time that the tortillas had to soak up liquid. At this temperature, the casserole was in and out of the oven in 15 minutes—just long enough to meld the flavors, melt the cheese, and crisp up the top layer of tortillas. But still, the inner layers of tortillas were breaking down too much, absorbing all of the liquid and leaving behind a dry filling.

How could we keep the liquid in the sauce and out of the tortillas? Thus far, we had not used any flour, as we had decided against a thick, creamy sauce. But perhaps by thickening the sauce with a small quantity of flour we could keep the tortillas drier, since water bound up in swollen starch granules is more difficult for foods to absorb. The addition of just 2 tablespoons of flour did the trick: The filling

remained saucy and the tortilla layers were soft but still intact.

Now just one problem remained. We had worked hard to produce a casserole that did not turn into a homogeneous mush, but we watched in horror as hungry tasters massacred the dish with spatulas and serving spoons. The crispy top layer of tortillas was difficult to cut through without mangling the layers beneath it. We resolved the issue by quartering the tortillas that made up the top layer so there would be no need to hack through a whole one. Finally, we had a full-flavored Tex-Mex casserole that was in perfect balance.

Mexican Lasagna with Pork, Corn, and Pinto Beans
SERVES 6 TO 8

Ground turkey can be substituted for the ground pork. You can substitute 8 ounces each of Colby and Jack cheeses for the Colby Jack cheese. Serve with salsa, diced avocado, sour cream, and/or scallions.

2	tablespoons vegetable oil
1	medium onion, minced
2	red bell peppers, stemmed, seeded, and cut into ½-inch pieces (see the illustrations on page 226)
	Salt and ground black pepper
3	medium garlic cloves, minced or pressed through a garlic press (about 1 tablespoon)
1	tablespoon minced canned chipotle chile in adobo sauce
2	teaspoons chili powder
1½	pounds ground pork
2	tablespoons unbleached all-purpose flour
2	cups low-sodium chicken broth
1	(15-ounce) can pinto beans, drained and rinsed
1	(14.5-ounce) can diced tomatoes, drained
2	cups frozen corn, thawed
¼	cup plus 2 tablespoons minced fresh cilantro leaves
2	tablespoons juice from 1 lime
18	(6-inch) corn tortillas
	Vegetable oil spray
12	ounces Colby Jack cheese, shredded (3 cups)

1. Adjust an oven rack to the middle position and heat the oven to 350 degrees. Heat the oil in a large Dutch oven over medium heat until shimmering. Add the onion, bell peppers, and ½ teaspoon salt and cook until softened, 8 to 10 minutes.

2. Stir in the garlic, chipotles, chili powder, and ¼ teaspoon pepper and cook until fragrant, about 30 seconds. Stir in the pork and cook, breaking up the meat with a wooden spoon, until no longer pink, 5 to 8 minutes. Stir in the flour and cook for 1 minute.

3. Gradually stir in the chicken broth and bring to a simmer. Stir in the beans, tomatoes, and corn and simmer until the mixture is slightly thickened and the flavors have blended, about 10 minutes. Off the heat, stir in ¼ cup of the cilantro and lime juice and season with salt and pepper to taste.

4. Meanwhile, lightly coat both sides of the tortillas with vegetable oil spray. Place 9 tortillas on a baking sheet (some overlapping is fine) and bake until the tortillas are soft and pliable, 2 to 4 minutes; transfer to a plate. Repeat with the remaining 9 tortillas and transfer to the plate. Increase the oven temperature to 450 degrees.

5. Spread one-third of the pork mixture in a 13 by 9-inch baking dish. Layer 6 of the tortillas on top of the filling, overlapping as needed, and sprinkle with 1 cup of the cheese. Repeat with a third more filling, 6 more tortillas, and 1 cup more cheese. Spread the remaining filling over the top. Cut the remaining 6 tortillas into quarters and scatter them over the filling. Sprinkle with the remaining 1 cup cheese.

6. Bake until the filling is bubbling and the topping is golden brown, about 15 minutes. Let the casserole cool for 10 minutes, then sprinkle with the remaining 2 tablespoons cilantro and serve.

TO MAKE AHEAD

Assemble the casserole through step 5, then cover with plastic wrap and refrigerate for up to 2 days. Before continuing with step 6, remove the plastic wrap, cover the dish with aluminum foil that has been sprayed with vegetable oil spray (or use non-stick foil) and bake until hot, about 30 minutes. Remove the foil and continue to bake as directed in step 6.

SAVORY CHICKEN COBBLER

FEW DISHES CAN WHET THE APPETITE LIKE chicken pot pie. Those three little words conjure images of buttery, flaky crust set atop moist chicken enveloped by rich, creamy sauce and surrounded by sweet peas and tender carrots. Who wouldn't want to serve such soul-satisfying fare? But the reality is, as homey as it sounds, this dish is a production. You've got to cook and break down a chicken, make a sauce, parcook vegetables, and at the same time prepare, chill, and roll out pie crust. Then, after all that work, there's still no guarantee the chicken won't be dry, the vegetables overcooked, the sauce pasty, and the crust more soggy than flaky.

A true, from-scratch pot pie is an all-day affair, but we saw no reason a chicken casserole full of tender, juicy chicken and bright vegetables and crowned with a crisp, buttery top should be out of reach for cooks short on time. With a traditional pot pie as inspiration, we set out to develop a flavorful chicken casserole that was streamlined and could be on the table without taking hours to prepare.

The first step was to figure out how to cook the chicken. Roasting a whole bird was too time-consuming. Poaching bone-in parts was quicker, but not quick enough. Using boneless, skinless parts was definitely a timesaver in terms of cooking and prep, though it did mean doing away with two prime sources of a bird's flavor. To help replace that lost flavor, we substituted chicken broth for water as the poaching liquid. Now even the thickest pieces were done in 12 minutes, at most, and because these smaller pieces required a relatively small amount of chicken broth in which to cook, the resulting liquid could provide the base for a velvety, full-bodied sauce that didn't need reducing. Plus, with the skin and bones already removed, the meat was easy to handle and shredded nicely into bite-size morsels.

Next we addressed the vegetables. Our tasters voted for a traditional medley of onions, carrots, celery, and peas. Cooking the chicken together with the vegetables, while undeniably efficient, resulted in meat and sauce that tasted like vegetable soup base, and vegetables that turned mushy and tasted like, well, nothing. Cooking the two elements separately—the chicken in broth, the vegetables in a little oil—was the only way to tease out and maintain their distinct flavors and textures in the pie. We then brightened the filling with a squirt of fresh lemon juice and minced parsley and added the frozen peas right before transferring everything to the baking dish.

As for the sauce, we tested a simple combination of a butter-and-flour roux, the poaching liquid, and milk. This sauce tasted clean and nicely chicken-y, but without the benefit of the fond from browning a chicken, which is typically incorporated into such a sauce, or the deeply concentrated jus of a roasted bird as a flavor base, it lacked a certain savory depth. What we needed were some powerhouse ingredients to give it a boost. In the test kitchen we have found that one key to maximum flavor in a hurry is to add foods rich in glutamates—naturally occurring flavor compounds that enhance savory qualities. Many of these are pantry items that we tend to keep on hand—tomato paste, red wine, soy sauce, and anchovies, as well as mushrooms and Parmesan cheese. Red wine was out of the question here, and the idea of salty little fish in our pie did not appeal. However, 1 teaspoon each of soy sauce and tomato paste (both cooked in the pan until browned and caramelized), along with some mushrooms, enhanced the savory character of our sauce. And because the amounts of soy sauce and tomato paste were so small, no one could pinpoint their presence.

With our filling finished, we focused on the topping. Since the laborious process of making a traditional pie dough was off the table, we considered our alternatives. Cream biscuits seemed like a good option, but we wanted something a little different, something that was as easy as the biscuits but with the flakiness of pie dough. Then a colleague mentioned a more rugged-textured topping she had recently stumbled across in a cookbook: The recipe was for a vegetable stew with a garlic-cheddar "cobbler" crust. Not quite biscuit, not quite pie crust, this savory topping sounded like a snap to prepare—just rub butter into flour, salt, and

leavening; toss in some grated cheese, pepper, and minced garlic; bind the lot together with cream; and crumble it over the filling. The idea was offbeat but worth trying.

And in fact, the crumble proved a huge hit, especially after some tweaking here and there: Out came the overly assertive garlic, along with the cheddar, which we replaced with glutamate-rich Parmesan. We also adapted the method. Since the chicken filling was already fully cooked, we decided to prebake the crumble before scattering it over the casserole, so that a brief stint in the oven would be all the pie needed. Prebaking would also ensure that the crumble didn't lose any of its wonderful crispness. Crumbling the mixture onto a sheet pan and baking it while we made the filling fit smoothly into our method. The crumble-topped casserole needed a mere 15 minutes to brown and start bubbling up the sides—just long enough for us to tidy up the dirty pots and utensils.

Our savory chicken cobbler wasn't traditional, but it won over even the traditionalists among us.

Savory Chicken Cobbler with Carrots, Mushrooms, and Peas
SERVES 6 TO 8

Prepare the Savory Cobbler Topping (page 102) first, then set it aside while assembling the filling. Do not omit the soy sauce or tomato paste; they don't convey their distinctive tastes but greatly deepen the savory flavor of the filling.

1½	pounds boneless, skinless chicken breasts and/or thighs, trimmed
3	cups low-sodium chicken broth
2	tablespoons vegetable oil
1	medium onion, minced
3	carrots, peeled and sliced ¼ inch thick
1	celery rib, chopped fine
	Salt and ground black pepper
10	ounces cremini mushrooms, wiped clean, trimmed, and sliced thin
1	teaspoon soy sauce
1	teaspoon tomato paste
4	tablespoons (½ stick) unsalted butter
½	cup unbleached all-purpose flour

1 cup whole milk
¾ cup frozen peas
2 teaspoons juice from 1 lemon
3 tablespoons minced fresh parsley leaves
1 recipe Savory Cobbler Topping (page 102)

1. Adjust an oven rack to the upper-middle position and heat the oven to 450 degrees. Combine the chicken and broth in a large Dutch oven, cover, and simmer until the breasts register 160 to 165 degrees and the thighs register 175 degrees on an instant-read thermometer, 8 to 12 minutes. Remove the chicken from the pot and pour the broth into a liquid measuring cup. Let the chicken cool slightly, then shred the meat into bite-size pieces following the illustration on page 75.

2. Wipe the pot dry, add 1 tablespoon of the oil and heat over medium heat until shimmering. Add the onion, carrots, celery, and ¼ teaspoon salt, cover, and cook, stirring occasionally, until softened, 5 to 7 minutes. Transfer to a bowl with the chicken; set aside.

3. Add the remaining 1 tablespoon oil to the pot and heat over medium heat until shimmering. Add the mushrooms, cover, and cook until the mushrooms have released their liquid, about 5 minutes. Uncover, increase the heat to medium-high, and stir in the soy sauce and tomato paste. Continue to cook, stirring often, until the mushrooms are dry and browned and a dark fond begins to form on the surface of the pan, about 5 minutes. Transfer to the bowl with the chicken and vegetables; set aside.

4. Add the butter to the pot and melt over medium heat. Stir in the flour and cook for 1 minute. Gradually whisk in the reserved chicken broth and milk. Bring to a simmer, scraping up any browned bits, and cook until the sauce thickens, about 1 minute. Off the heat, stir in the chicken-vegetable mixture, peas, lemon juice, and 2 tablespoons of the parsley. Season with salt and pepper to taste.

5. Spread the mixture into a 13 by 9-inch baking dish and scatter the cobbler topping evenly over the top. Place the casserole on a rimmed baking sheet and bake until the filling is bubbling and the topping is browned, 12 to 15 minutes. Let the casserole cool for 10 minutes, then sprinkle with the remaining 1 tablespoon parsley and serve.

TO MAKE AHEAD

Prepare the filling through step 4, then transfer to an airtight container and refrigerate for up to 2 days. (The topping can also be refrigerated in an airtight container for up to 2 days.) Before continuing with step 5, reheat the filling in the microwave on medium power, stirring often, until hot, about 5 minutes. Season the filling with additional lemon juice, salt, and pepper to taste, then assemble and bake the casserole as directed in step 5.

Savory Chicken Cobbler with Bacon, Bell Pepper, Corn, and Scallions

SERVES 6 TO 8

Prepare the Savory Cobbler Topping (page 102) first, then set it aside while assembling the filling. Do not omit the soy sauce or tomato paste; they don't convey their distinctive tastes but greatly deepen the savory flavor of the filling.

1½ pounds boneless, skinless chicken breasts and/or thighs, trimmed
3 cups low-sodium chicken broth
2 tablespoons vegetable oil
2 red bell peppers, stemmed, seeded, and cut into ½-inch pieces (see the illustrations on page 226)
1 medium onion, minced
1 celery rib, chopped fine
Salt and ground black pepper
1 teaspoon soy sauce
1 teaspoon tomato paste
4 ounces (about 4 slices) bacon, minced
½ cup unbleached all-purpose flour
1 cup whole milk
¾ cup frozen corn, thawed
2 teaspoons juice from 1 lemon
3 scallions, sliced thin
1 recipe Savory Cobbler Topping (page 102)

1. Adjust an oven rack to the upper-middle position and heat the oven to 450 degrees. Combine the chicken and broth in a large Dutch oven, cover, and simmer until the breasts register 160 to 165 degrees and the thighs register 175 degrees on an instant-read thermometer, 8 to 12 minutes. Remove the

chicken from the pot and pour the broth into a liquid measuring cup. Let the chicken cool slightly, then shred the meat into bite-size pieces following the illustration on page 75.

2. Wipe the pot dry, add the oil and heat over medium heat until shimmering. Add the bell peppers, onion, celery, and ¼ teaspoon salt, cover, and cook, stirring occasionally, until softened, 5 to 7 minutes. Uncover, stir in the soy sauce and tomato paste, and cook for 1 minute longer. Transfer to a bowl with the chicken; set aside.

3. Add the bacon to the pot and cook over medium heat until rendered and crisp, 5 to 7 minutes. Stir in the flour and cook for 1 minute. Gradually whisk in the reserved chicken broth and milk. Bring to a simmer, scraping up any browned bits, and cook until the sauce thickens, about 1 minute. Off the heat, stir in the chicken-vegetable mixture, corn, lemon juice, and 2 of the scallions.

Season with salt and pepper to taste.

4. Spread the mixture into 13 by 9-inch baking dish and scatter the cobbler topping evenly over the top. Place the casserole on a rimmed baking sheet and bake until the filling is bubbling and the topping is browned, 12 to 15 minutes. Let the casserole cool for 10 minutes, then sprinkle with the remaining scallion and serve.

TO MAKE AHEAD

Prepare the filling through step 3, then transfer to an airtight container and refrigerate for up to 2 days. (The topping can also be refrigerated in an airtight container for up to 2 days.) Before continuing with step 4, reheat the filling in the microwave on medium power, stirring often, until hot, about 5 minutes. Season the filling with additional lemon juice, salt, and pepper to taste, then assemble and bake the casserole as directed in step 4.

Savory Cobbler Topping

MAKES ENOUGH FOR ONE 13 BY 9-INCH CASSEROLE

Do not substitute milk or half-and-half for the heavy cream.

2	cups (10 ounces) unbleached all-purpose flour
2	teaspoons baking powder
¾	teaspoon salt
½	teaspoon ground black pepper
⅛	teaspoon cayenne pepper
6	tablespoons (¾ stick) unsalted butter, cut into ½-inch cubes and chilled
1	ounce Parmesan cheese, grated (½ cup)
¾	cup plus 2 tablespoons heavy cream

1. Adjust an oven rack to the upper-middle position and heat the oven to 450 degrees. Combine the flour, baking powder, salt, pepper, and cayenne in a large bowl. Sprinkle the butter pieces over the flour mixture and, using your fingers, rub the butter into the mixture until it resembles coarse cornmeal.

2. Stir in the Parmesan. Add the cream and stir until just combined. Crumble the mixture into irregularly shaped pieces, ranging from ½ to ¾ inch each, onto a parchment-lined rimmed baking sheet. Bake until fragrant and beginning to brown, 10 to 13 minutes; set aside until needed.

MAKING SAVORY COBBLER TOPPING

Crumble the mixture into irregularly shaped pieces, ranging from ½ to ¾ inch each, onto a parchment-lined rimmed baking sheet.

Savory Chicken Cobbler with Summer Squash, Zucchini, Tomatoes, and Basil

SERVES 6 TO 8

Prepare the Savory Cobbler Topping (page 102) first, then set it aside while assembling the filling. Do not omit the soy sauce or tomato paste; they don't convey their distinctive tastes but greatly deepen the savory flavor of the filling.

1½	pounds boneless, skinless chicken breasts and/or thighs, trimmed
3	cups low-sodium chicken broth
2	tablespoons vegetable oil
1	medium yellow summer squash (about 8 ounces), halved lengthwise and cut into ½-inch pieces
1	medium zucchini (about 8 ounces), halved lengthwise and cut into ½-inch pieces
1	medium onion, minced
1	celery rib, chopped fine
	Salt and ground black pepper
1	teaspoon soy sauce
1	teaspoon tomato paste
4	tablespoons (½ stick) unsalted butter
½	cup unbleached all-purpose flour
1	cup whole milk
2	cups cherry tomatoes (about 12 ounces), quartered
2	teaspoons juice from 1 lemon
¼	cup chopped fresh basil leaves
1	recipe Savory Cobbler Topping (page 102)

1. Adjust an oven rack to the upper-middle position and heat the oven to 450 degrees. Combine the chicken and broth in a large Dutch oven, cover, and simmer until the breasts register 160 to 165 degrees and the thighs register 175 degrees on an instant-read thermometer, 8 to 12 minutes. Remove the chicken from the pot and pour the broth into a liquid measuring cup. Let the chicken cool slightly, then shred the meat into bite-size pieces following the illustration on page 75.

2. Wipe the pot dry, add 1 tablespoon of the oil, and heat over medium heat until shimmering. Add the yellow squash and zucchini and cook until just softened, about 5 minutes. Transfer to a bowl with the chicken; set aside.

3. Add the remaining 1 tablespoon oil to the pot and heat over medium heat until shimmering. Add the onion, celery, and ¼ teaspoon salt, cover, and cook, stirring occasionally, until softened, 5 to 7 minutes. Uncover, stir in the soy sauce and tomato paste, and cook for 1 minute longer. Transfer to the bowl with the chicken and zucchini; set aside.

4. Add the butter to the pot and melt over medium heat. Stir in the flour and cook for 1 minute. Gradually whisk in the reserved chicken broth and milk. Bring to a simmer, scraping up any browned bits, and cook until the sauce thickens, about 1 minute. Off the heat, stir in the chicken-vegetable mixture, cherry tomatoes, lemon juice, and 3 tablespoons of the basil. Season with salt and pepper to taste.

5. Spread the mixture into a 13 by 9-inch baking dish and scatter the cobbler topping evenly over the top. Place the casserole on a rimmed baking sheet and bake until the filling is bubbling and the topping is browned, 12 to 15 minutes. Let the casserole cool for 10 minutes, then sprinkle with the remaining 1 tablespoon basil and serve.

TO MAKE AHEAD

Prepare the filling through step 4, then transfer to an airtight container and refrigerate for up to 2 days. (The topping can also be refrigerated in an airtight container for up to 2 days.) Before continuing with step 5, reheat the filling in the microwave on medium power, stirring often, until hot, about 5 minutes. Season the filling with additional lemon juice, salt, and pepper to taste, then assemble and bake the casserole as directed in step 5.

SPINACH AND FETA PHYLLO PIE

MOST TAVERNS IN GREECE AND LIKELY EVERY Greek-American restaurant in the States offer some version of *spanakopita* on their menu—*spanaki* meaning "spinach" and *pita* meaning "pie." Not necessarily a "pie" as we think of it in this country, but a casserole, spanakopita is made by layering sheets of phyllo dough in a baking dish with a blend of spinach, onions, and tangy feta cheese spiked with lemon, garlic, and herbs. The pie is then baked and cut into squares. Each piece should be the perfect marriage of crisp, flaky pastry and a savory filling.

On paper, spanakopita never fails to make the mouth water. Unfortunately, modern-day versions of this dish rarely taste as good as they sound, with dense, stringy layers of overcooked spinach; a thin, shattered crust of dried-out pastry; and sporadic chunks of feta cheese. And working with store-bought phyllo dough can test anyone's patience. After so much labor and an often-disappointing payoff, we had to wonder, is spanakopita really worth it? We wanted a spanakopita that lived up to its billing and didn't require help from a Greek grandmother to prepare.

We focused first on perfecting a spinach and feta filling with big, bold flavors. Since spanakopita means "spinach pie," we knew where to start—with the green stuff. Many of the recipes we found called for fresh spinach, which needs to be washed, cooked, drained, chopped, and squeezed dry. In a side-by-side tasting, we were happy to find tasters were equally pleased with filling made from frozen chopped spinach, which is more convenient than the fresh, as it only needs to be thawed and squeezed dry. Too many recipes we found skimped on the spinach, resulting in spanakopitas that were thin and greasy, with too much phyllo. We wanted a thick layer of spinach and feta that would stand up to the pastry crust. No less than three 10-ounce packages for a 13 by 9-inch dish would do.

As for the feta, we needed to ensure it was evenly distributed in our filling; in many of the recipes we tested we found big chunks of the salty cheese adrift in a sea of clumpy greens. Beaten eggs are a standard ingredient in spanakopita recipes—they serve to bind the filling ingredients together, add richness and flavor, and lighten the layer of spinach—and we realized we needed to use them to help distribute our cheese. By first crumbling the feta, then mixing it with the eggs, we were able to get a little feta into every bite.

Scallions, garlic, and herbs such as dill are traditional ingredients in spanakopita, but they are usually called for in such paltry amounts that their flavors simply disappear. We doubled the quantities of each, which allowed their presence to be known. Lemon juice and grated nutmeg were less commonly listed, but tasters approved of both. The flavors in our pie were now bright and clean, but the filling still seemed a little dry and, despite the eggs, it still lacked richness. A few recipes included ricotta cheese to balance the bite of the feta, and our tasters agreed it rounded out the flavors and gave the filling just the right creamy texture.

When spread into a 13 by 9-inch baking dish, our spinach filling stood a proud 1½ inches high, a marked improvement over the sad, sunken versions we had seen in earlier tests. A filling this thick needed more than a few paper-thin sheets of pastry to hold it all together. We found that 16 sheets of phyllo (eight on top and eight on the bottom) made crusts that were substantial but still tender. When we tried more than that above or beneath, the pastry was tough to bite through. We did find that adding a middle layer of four sheets of phyllo helped the pie keep its shape after it was sliced.

Almost every recipe utilizing phyllo calls for brushing each layer of pastry with some sort of fat, usually oil or clarified butter, to encourage flakiness. We preferred the flavor of olive oil, but tasters complained the pie was greasy, even when we used as little as a teaspoon of oil per sheet. Brushing each sheet was somewhat laborious as it was, and attempting to distribute less than 1 teaspoon evenly across the sheet of phyllo without tearing it would be mind-numbingly tedious, if not impossible. Remembering how we had used vegetable oil spray to lightly and evenly coat the tortillas in our Easy Chicken Enchiladas (page 95), we wondered if the same trick would work here. Switching to olive oil spray had a twofold benefit: it enabled us to coat the phyllo with a thinner (but still adequate) layer of fat than brushing, and it made the process quick and easy.

Phyllo is famous for its crisp, flaky layers, but it was this quality that gave us the most trouble once the pie hit the hot oven. In every test, the papery layers curled and separated from each other as they baked. Cutting into the pie sent shattered pieces of phyllo everywhere. Some dessert recipes involving phyllo advise sprinkling each layer with granulated sugar, which then melts in the oven and helps the layers stick together. Could grated cheese work the same way? A small quantity of grated Parmesan dusted across each of the top layer's sheets worked wonders, yielding a cohesive crust that was still crisp, and now with a nice boost in flavor.

Lastly, we wondered about the lengthy baking times specified by most recipes—typically an hour in the oven at 350 degrees. When we tried this, our bright flavors were washed out and flat, the spinach was well on its way to being mushy and overcooked, and the phyllo became dried out and was more prone to shattering. Increasing the temperature to 400 degrees and reducing the cooking time to about 35 minutes resulted in a filling and crust that were both done to perfection.

Phyllo pies are also often made with a meat filling, so we decided to make a variation using ground chicken, which was easy enough to do using the same basic method.

❧

Spinach and Feta Phyllo Pie

SERVES 6 TO 8

Make sure the phyllo is fully thawed before use; to thaw, let it sit in the refrigerator overnight or on the countertop for several hours (do not use the microwave). The most popular brand of phyllo, Athens, is available in boxes of 20 sheets measuring 14 by 18 inches and in boxes of 40 sheets measuring 14 by 9 inches. If you can only find the larger sheets, simply cut them in half widthwise.

1	pound feta cheese, crumbled into fine pieces (4 cups)
12	ounces whole-milk ricotta cheese (1½ cups)
4	large eggs, lightly beaten
1	bunch scallions, sliced thin
⅓	cup minced fresh dill leaves
3	tablespoons juice from 1 lemon
2	medium garlic cloves, minced or pressed through a garlic press (about 2 teaspoons)
1	teaspoon freshly grated nutmeg
¾	teaspoon salt
⅛	teaspoon ground black pepper
3	(10-ounce) packages frozen chopped spinach, thawed and squeezed dry
	Olive oil spray
20	(14 by 9-inch) sheets phyllo (about 8 ounces), thawed (see note)
1	ounce Parmesan cheese, grated (½ cup)

1. Adjust an oven rack to the middle position and heat the oven to 400 degrees. Mix the feta, ricotta, eggs, scallions, dill, lemon juice, garlic, nutmeg, salt, and pepper together in a large bowl. Stir in the spinach until uniform.

2. Spray the inside of a 13 by 9-inch baking dish liberally with olive oil spray. Following the illustrations on page 106, lay 1 phyllo sheet in the bottom of the prepared dish and coat thoroughly with olive oil spray. Repeat with 7 more phyllo sheets, spraying each with oil. Spread half of the spinach mixture evenly into the dish. Cover with 4 more phyllo sheets, spraying each with oil.

3. Spread the remaining spinach mixture evenly into the dish. Cover with 7 more phyllo sheets, spraying each with oil and sprinkling each with a generous tablespoon of Parmesan. Lay the final sheet of phyllo over the top and coat thoroughly with oil (do not sprinkle the final layer with Parmesan).

4. Working from the center outward, use the palms of your hands to compress the layers and press out any air pockets. Using a sharp knife, lightly score the pie into serving squares but do not cut through more than the top 3 sheets of phyllo.

5. Bake until the phyllo is golden and crisp, 30 to 35 minutes. Let the casserole cool for at least 10 minutes or up to 2 hours before serving.

TO MAKE AHEAD

Assemble the casserole through step 4, then cover the casserole with plastic wrap and refrigerate for up to 1 day. Remove the plastic wrap and bake as directed in step 5, increasing the cooking time to 35 to 40 minutes.

ASSEMBLING PHYLLO PIE

1. Liberally coat a 13 by 9-inch baking dish with olive oil spray. Lay 1 phyllo sheet in the bottom of the dish and coat thoroughly with olive oil spray. Repeat with 7 more phyllo sheets, spraying each with oil.

2. Spread half of the filling on top of the phyllo. Layer 4 pieces of phyllo on top of the filling, spraying each with oil. Spread the remaining filling over the top. Cover with 7 more sheets of phyllo, spraying each with oil and sprinkling each with 1 tablespoon of Parmesan.

3. Place 1 last piece of phyllo over the layer and spray with oil (do not sprinkle with Parmesan). Using a sharp knife, lightly score into serving squares, taking care not to cut through more than the top 3 pieces of phyllo.

Chicken and Feta Phyllo Pie

SERVES 6 TO 8

Make sure the phyllo is fully thawed before use; to thaw, let it sit in the refrigerator overnight or on the countertop for several hours (do not use the microwave). The most popular brand of phyllo, Athens, is available in boxes of 20 sheets measuring 14 by 18 inches and in boxes of 40 sheets measuring 14 by 9 inches. If you can only find the larger sheets, simply cut them in half widthwise. Do not use ground chicken breast here (also labeled 99 percent fat free) or the filling will be very dry.

1	tablespoon olive oil
2	pounds ground chicken (see note)
8	ounces feta cheese, crumbled into fine pieces (2 cups)
3	large eggs, lightly beaten
1	bunch scallions, sliced thin
½	cup pitted kalamata olives, chopped coarse
⅓	cup minced fresh mint leaves
3	tablespoons juice from 1 lemon
2	medium garlic cloves, minced or pressed through a garlic press (about 2 teaspoons)
1	teaspoon salt
¼	teaspoon ground black pepper
¼	teaspoon cayenne pepper
	Olive oil spray
20	(14 by 9-inch) sheets phyllo (about 8 ounces), thawed (see note)
1	ounce Parmesan cheese, grated (½ cup)

1. Adjust an oven rack to the middle position and heat the oven to 400 degrees. Heat the oil in a large skillet over medium heat until shimmering. Add the chicken and cook, breaking the meat into small pieces with a wooden spoon, until no longer pink, about 5 minutes. Transfer the meat to a strainer and let drain, about 5 minutes. Break apart any large clumps of meat with your fingers.

2. Mix the feta, eggs, scallions, olives, mint, lemon juice, garlic, salt, pepper, and cayenne together in a large bowl, then stir in the drained chicken.

3. Spray the inside of a 13 by 9-inch baking dish liberally with olive oil spray. Following the

illustrations on page 106, lay 1 phyllo sheet in the bottom of the prepared dish and coat thoroughly with olive oil spray. Repeat with 7 more phyllo sheets, spraying each with oil. Spread half of the chicken mixture evenly into the dish. Cover with 4 more phyllo sheets, spraying each with oil.

4. Spread the remaining chicken mixture evenly into the dish. Cover with 7 more phyllo sheets, spraying each with oil and sprinkling each with a generous tablespoon of Parmesan. Lay the final sheet of phyllo over the top and coat thoroughly with oil (do not sprinkle the final layer with Parmesan).

5. Working from the center outward, use the palms of your hands to compress the layers and press out any air pockets. Using a sharp knife, lightly score the pie into serving squares but do not cut through more than the top 3 sheets of phyllo.

6. Bake until the phyllo is golden and crisp, 30 to 35 minutes. Let the casserole cool for at least 10 minutes or up to 2 hours before serving.

TO MAKE AHEAD

Assemble the casserole through step 5, then cover the casserole with plastic wrap and refrigerate for up to 1 day. Remove the plastic wrap and bake as directed in step 6, increasing the cooking time to 35 to 40 minutes.

RUSTIC SAUSAGE AND SPINACH POLENTA CASSEROLE

POLENTA IS NOTHING MORE THAN DRIED, ground corn cooked on the stovetop with a liquid and typically finished with butter and cheese. It's served as a side, often cooked to a soft consistency and spooned onto a plate as a bed for a hearty topping, usually something ragout-like with tomatoes, vegetables, and/or meat. With that image in mind, we realized that a polenta-based casserole made perfect sense. We imagined a layer of soft polenta covered with savory toppings and cheese, each prepared separately then assembled and baked at fairly high heat until the layers were just heated through.

Before focusing on the toppings, we had to settle on the best way to make the polenta for our casserole. After testing a variety of traditional Italian recipes, we realized that making authentic polenta is a lot of work. Coarse cornmeal is slowly added to boiling salted water and stirred constantly, which prevents scorching, for 30 to 40 minutes. Within five minutes, you'll feel like you've been arm wrestling Arnold Schwarzenegger. After making several batches of traditional polenta, we wondered if instant polenta (also called quick-cooking polenta) could be our answer. Instant polenta, like quick-cooking grits and instant rice, has been partially cooked, then dried. All you need to do is reconstitute it with boiling water. After testing several brands we found at the supermarket (all imported from Italy), we found that instant polenta, while it doesn't taste quite the same as traditional polenta, nevertheless has good flavor and takes only 10 minutes to cook, making it a good choice for our easy casserole.

Although the instant polenta was quick to make on the stove, it still required constant monitoring. We were curious if we could simplify the cooking of the polenta by using the microwave, freeing up the stove—and our attention—to cook our topping. We combined the water and polenta in a large bowl before microwaving it, covered, on high. We were dubious about the results, but after 10 minutes, the water had been absorbed and we had perfectly cooked, lump-free polenta! Not only did this method cut out the saucepan, but we found we only had to stir the polenta once during cooking.

The polenta was creamy and properly cooked, but tasters thought it was a little bland. To bump up the flavor, we stirred in some grated Parmesan, along with salt and pepper. This was a start. With the addition of a little minced garlic and a couple tablespoons of butter, which helped keep it smooth and soft, the polenta was finally just right. Once transferred to a casserole dish, our polenta was ready for the topping.

While polenta is extremely versatile and works with any number of sautéed vegetables, meats, and cheeses, we were immediately drawn to the idea of sausage, which offers a heartiness that is an ideal foil to mild polenta. We sautéed some onion, then added sweet Italian sausage (removed from its casing), breaking up the sausage into substantial, bite-size chunks. When the sausage was lightly browned, we added garlic and red pepper flakes. Canned diced tomatoes contributed sweet bites of tomato as well as juice that cooked down into a sauce and kept our topping moist.

Looking for a vegetable to pair with the sausage, we tried red bell peppers. Tasters thought they were good but a tad too sweet. We tried baby spinach and, while its earthy flavor was a perfect match, it withered in the oven. We had better success with heartier curly-leaf spinach, especially when we kept the cooking time to a minimum by adding it to the skillet only in the last moment to let it wilt. Before spooning the topping over the cooked polenta, we stirred in a little red wine vinegar to cut through the richness of the sausage. A sprinkling of Parmesan before baking melted into an attractive topping and minced parsley, sprinkled on before serving, freshened the finished dish.

For a vegetarian version, we substituted sliced mushrooms for the sausage. After a few tries, we discovered that the key to achieving a good mushroom flavor, without spending a fortune, was to supplement regular supermarket mushrooms (we liked cremini) with dried porcini mushrooms (also widely available in supermarkets). The cremini had a meaty bite, while the dried porcini really helped to drive home a serious mushroom flavor. Sprinkled with a little fontina cheese, this duo of polenta and mushrooms was just as satisfying as our sausage version.

Rustic Sausage and Spinach Polenta Casserole

SERVES 6 TO 8

Be sure to use dried, instant polenta in this recipe; do not substitute traditional polenta or precooked polenta in a tube. Don't break up the sausage too finely in step 3; we liked it best when broken into ½-inch bite-size chunks. The skillet will be quite full after adding the spinach, but it wilts down substantially as it cooks.

POLENTA

5½	cups water
1½	cups instant polenta (see note)
	Salt and ground black pepper
3	ounces Parmesan cheese, grated (1½ cups)
2	tablespoons unsalted butter
1	medium garlic clove, minced or pressed through a garlic press (about 1 teaspoon)

TOPPING

1	tablespoon olive oil
1	medium onion, minced
	Salt and ground black pepper
1½	pounds sweet Italian sausage, removed from its casing
6	medium garlic cloves, minced or pressed through a garlic press (about 2 tablespoons)
¼	teaspoon red pepper flakes
1	(14.5-ounce) can diced tomatoes
8	ounces curly-leaf spinach, stemmed, washed, and chopped coarse
1	tablespoon red wine vinegar
2	ounces Parmesan cheese, grated (1 cup)
2	tablespoons minced fresh parsley leaves

1. Adjust an oven rack to the middle position and heat the oven to 400 degrees.

2. FOR THE POLENTA: Combine the water, polenta, and 1½ teaspoons salt in a large bowl, cover, and microwave on high power until most of the water is absorbed, 8 to 10 minutes. Stir the polenta thoroughly, then continue to microwave, uncovered, until it is creamy and fully cooked, 1 to 3 minutes longer. Stir in the Parmesan, butter, garlic, and salt and pepper to taste. Cover to keep warm; set aside.

3. FOR THE TOPPING: Meanwhile, heat the oil in a 12-inch skillet over medium-high heat until shimmering. Add the onion and ½ teaspoon salt and cook until softened, about 5 minutes. Add the sausage and cook, breaking the meat into large chunks with a wooden spoon, until lightly browned, about 10 minutes. Stir in the garlic and red pepper flakes and cook until fragrant, about 30 seconds.

4. Add the tomatoes with their juice, bring to a simmer, and cook, stirring occasionally, until the flavors have blended, about 5 minutes. Stir in the spinach, a handful at a time, and cook until wilted, about 2 minutes. Off the heat, stir in the vinegar and season with salt and pepper to taste.

5. Smooth the cooked polenta evenly into a 13 by 9-inch baking dish. Carefully spoon the sausage mixture on top of the polenta and sprinkle with the Parmesan.

6. Bake until the polenta is heated through and the cheese is melted and just beginning to brown, 15 to 20 minutes. Let the casserole cool for 10 minutes, then sprinkle with the parsley and serve.

➤ VARIATION

Rustic Mushroom and Spinach Polenta Casserole

Follow the recipe for Rustic Sausage and Spinach Polenta Casserole, omitting the sausage, red pepper flakes, and vinegar. In step 3, add 1½ pounds cremini mushrooms, wiped clean and sliced ¼ inch thick, 3 tablespoons more olive oil, and ¼ ounce dried porcini, rinsed and minced, to the skillet with the onions; cook over medium heat until the mushrooms have released their liquid and are well browned, about 20 minutes. Add 1 tablespoon minced fresh thyme leaves to the skillet with the garlic. Sprinkle 4 ounces fontina cheese, shredded (1 cup), over the casserole with the Parmesan in step 5; bake as directed.

TO MAKE AHEAD

Assemble the Rustic Sausage and Spinach Polenta Casserole or Rustic Mushroom and Spinach Polenta Casserole through step 5, then cover the casserole with plastic wrap and refrigerate for up to 2 days. Before continuing with step 6, remove the plastic wrap, cover the dish with aluminum foil that has been sprayed with vegetable oil spray (or use non-stick foil) and bake until hot, about 30 minutes. Remove the foil and continue to bake as directed in step 6.

BAKED ZITI

WHAT CHURCH SUPPER OR POTLUCK DINNER would be complete without baked ziti? This Italian-American dish sounds simple enough: Combine cooked pasta with tomato sauce, then add cheese and maybe sausage. But if it is so easy to prepare, why are most versions dry, bland, and downright unappealing? We wanted to develop a terrific recipe for baked ziti, with tender noodles, tasty tomato sauce, and gooey cheese.

We started with the noodles. Too many recipes we found overcooked the pasta on the stovetop, so by the time the noodles were assembled into the casserole and baked, the pasta had become soft and squishy. We made sure our ziti was slightly undercooked on the stovetop, knowing it would finish cooking through in the oven.

With the ziti boiled and set aside, we moved on to the other components. Mozzarella traditionally binds the noodles together and enriches this baked casserole. Twelve ounces of whole-milk mozzarella was just right for 1½ pounds of pasta. More made the casserole too gooey. Tasters, however, found the cheesy flavor a bit quiet—after all, mozzarella is very mild—so we added a few ounces of Parmesan for a flavor boost. To ensure that the cheese was evenly distributed throughout the casserole, we layered half the pasta into the baking dish, sprinkled it with half the cheeses, and then added the remaining pasta and cheeses.

While the mozzarella is the binder, it's the tomato sauce that keeps things moist. There are a lot of options among canned tomato products (canned being our choice for simplicity and year-round dependable quality). A few tests proved a smooth sauce made with crushed tomatoes had the best potential for keeping our casserole moist and appealing since it could coat the pasta evenly and thoroughly. Diced tomatoes were the runner-up, with good tomato flavor, but tasters did not like the chunks of tomato and the casserole tended to dry out in the oven. We agreed it was best to keep this casserole classic and simple, so for seasoning we added just some garlic and crushed red pepper, sautéed in olive oil. We then added the crushed tomatoes and brought the sauce to a simmer.

Long-simmered sauces, we found, produced a baked ziti that tasted dull and insipid. In a dish with so few components, the tomato flavor is best bright and fresh. We found that 15 minutes was all that was required to cook out any raw flavor from our sauce ingredients. We were surprised to find that, although our sauce was fairly loose, our casserole still needed more moisture. The solution was to dilute the tomato sauce with some of the pasta cooking water before tossing it with the pasta—1½ cups reserved water to 1½ pounds of pasta.

This baked ziti was good, but a little dull. While many recipes throw in the kitchen sink, adding vegetables, meatballs, and more, we wanted a solution that felt truer to its minimalist concept. Ricotta is a common ingredient in baked ziti recipes, so we tried stirring some cheese into the tomato sauce (as many recipes instruct). This was the worst of both worlds: the ricotta tasted chalky and deadened the tomato flavor without adding richness. Next we tried spooning the ricotta between the two layers of ziti in place of the mozzarella mixture. This produced a layer of ricotta in the center of the casserole, which kept the pasta moist and added enough interest to please everyone (we left the topping of mozzarella-Parmesan in place for its gooey, cheesy appeal). Two tablespoons of olive oil stirred into the ricotta gave it some additional richness and flavor.

We tested a variety of baking dishes and found that the conventional 13 by 9-inch baking dish was ideal, allowing the pasta to heat through quickly. More time in the oven only dried out the noodles or made them overly soft. With that in mind, we found that a hot 400-degree oven was best, yielding a casserole with tender pasta with just enough chew. About 30 minutes in the oven (not the hour called for in many recipes) did the trick.

A final step we wouldn't do without: A handful of chopped fresh basil, sprinkled over the top of the casserole, provided a burst of flavor and color. In addition to our classic version made with mozzarella, ricotta, and marinara, we developed a variation to please the carnivores with crumbled Italian sausage.

Baked Ziti with Ricotta

SERVES 6 TO 8

You can use any short tubular pasta in place of the ziti.

12	ounces whole-milk or part-skim ricotta cheese (1½ cups)
¼	cup olive oil
	Salt and ground black pepper
12	ounces whole-milk mozzarella cheese, shredded (about 3 cups)
3	ounces Parmesan cheese, grated (about 1½ cups)
1½	pounds ziti (7½ cups)
3	medium garlic cloves, minced or pressed through a garlic press (about 1 tablespoon)
½	teaspoon red pepper flakes (optional)
2	(28-ounce) cans crushed tomatoes
¼	cup chopped fresh basil leaves

1. Adjust an oven rack to the middle position and heat the oven to 400 degrees. Mix the ricotta, 2 tablespoons of the oil, ½ teaspoon salt, and ½ teaspoon pepper together in a medium bowl. In a separate bowl, toss the mozzarella and Parmesan together.

2. Meanwhile, bring 6 quarts water to a boil in a large Dutch oven over high heat. Add the ziti and 1½ tablespoons salt and cook, stirring often, until al dente. Reserve 1½ cups of the pasta cooking water, then drain the pasta. Transfer the pasta to a bowl; set aside.

3. Wipe the pot dry, add the remaining 2 tablespoons oil, garlic, and red pepper flakes (if using) and cook over medium heat until fragrant but not brown, 1 to 2 minutes. Stir in the tomatoes and simmer until slightly thickened, about 15 minutes. Off the heat, season with salt and pepper to taste, then stir in the cooked pasta and reserved cooking water.

4. Pour half of the pasta-sauce mixture into a 13 by 9-inch baking dish. Dollop large spoonfuls of the ricotta mixture evenly over the pasta, then pour the remaining pasta-sauce mixture over the ricotta. Sprinkle with the mozzarella mixture.

5. Bake until the filling is bubbling and the cheese is spotty brown, 25 to 35 minutes. Let the casserole cool for 10 minutes, then sprinkle with the basil and serve.

➤ VARIATION
Baked Ziti with Italian Sausage
Follow the recipe for Easy Baked Ziti with Ricotta, adding 1 pound sweet or hot Italian sausage, casing removed, to the pot before adding the oil, garlic, and red pepper flakes in step 3; cook the sausage, breaking up the meat with a wooden spoon, until no longer pink, about 4 minutes. Stir in the oil, garlic, and red pepper flakes, and cook until fragrant, about 30 seconds, before adding the tomatoes.

TO MAKE AHEAD
Assemble Baked Ziti with Ricotta or Baked Ziti with Italian Sausage through step 4, then cover the casserole with plastic wrap and refrigerate for up to 2 days. Before continuing with step 5, remove the plastic wrap, cover the dish with aluminum foil that has been sprayed with vegetable oil spray (or use nonstick foil), and bake until hot, about 30 minutes. Remove the foil and continue to bake as directed in step 5.

BAKED PENNE WITH CHICKEN

PENNE WITH CHICKEN AND BROCCOLI IS A well-loved and classic combination that we knew could be made into a crowd-pleasing casserole. There are plenty of recipes already out there: The cooked pasta, chicken, and broccoli are usually tossed in a rich cream sauce flavored with garlic and cheese. Our goal was to stick with this general concept but find a way to prevent the sauce from tasting overly heavy, as is typically the case, while keeping the chicken from drying out and the broccoli from turning cafeteria green. We wanted a baked penne casserole with components that were in balance and vegetables that tasted and looked fresh.

To start, we took a look at the traditional method for making a cream sauce. Generally, aromatics such as onions and garlic are sautéed, then cream is added and allowed to simmer, thicken, and reduce before the sauce is finished with cheese. Wanting to make the sauce less fatty and heavy, we tried replacing some of the heavy cream with chicken broth. This not only made the sauce lighter, but it boosted the chicken flavor. A little white wine also helped cut through the sauce's heaviness without lessening its flavor. These additions of broth and wine, however, made the consistency of the sauce a bit too loose. Unlike cream, chicken broth and wine don't become dramatically thicker as they reduce. In order to make the sauce thick enough to properly coat the chicken, penne, and broccoli, we found it necessary to add some flour.

Onion, garlic, and fresh thyme rounded out the sauce's flavor, as did some cheese. We tried several Italian cheeses, including Parmesan, fontina, and pecorino, but tasters far preferred the slightly sweet flavor of Asiago. But the sauce was still a little bit lackluster until we introduced yet another flavorful component: mushrooms. They paired well with the sauce and added a needed earthy depth. We used both fresh sautéed mushrooms and some dried porcini in order to achieve a decent mushroom flavor. (We also discovered that sun-dried tomatoes rounded out the sauce nicely, so we utilized them in a variation.)

Moving next to the chicken, we found it easiest to use boneless, skinless breasts and cut them into bite-size pieces that mirrored the size of the penne. Simply tossing raw chicken with the broccoli, penne, and sauce and baking it in the oven, however, didn't work. It took far too long for the chicken to cook through, by which time the pasta was overdone, the broccoli was limp, and the sauce was dried out. Testing a variety of ways to precook the chicken, we tried broiling, sautéing, and poaching. Broiling turned the edges of the chicken unappealingly crisp, and while the poached chicken was juicy and tender, it was also the blandest. Sautéing the chicken in a skillet with a little oil worked well, but it required an extra pan, which we didn't want to deal with. Going back to the poaching idea, we tried poaching the chicken right in the sauce to infuse it with flavor during cooking. This method worked like a charm and gave us chicken that remained tender and juicy and was well-seasoned. In order to prevent the chicken from overcooking in the oven, we found it best to cook it only partway in the sauce and let it finish in the oven.

Turning our attention to the broccoli, we decided right off the bat not to bother with the broccoli stems and to focus only on the florets, which eliminated issues with disparate cooking times and avoided the extra work of peeling stems. Often, the broccoli florets are cooked briefly in boiling water (blanched) then plunged into ice water (shocked) to keep them crisp and green. We found the shocking wasn't necessary since we were baking the casserole right away. One minute in boiling water took the raw edge off the broccoli, and by using the same water to cook both pasta and broccoli, we were able to eliminate an extra pot. We cooked the broccoli first and simply skimmed it out of the cooking water using a slotted spoon, then added the pasta to the pot. It was time to focus on the pasta, the topping, and the baking time.

INGREDIENTS: Panko

To see if there really is a difference between the brands of this light, Japanese-style bread-crumb coating, we picked up four samples at Boston-area supermarkets and tested them in two recipes: baked chicken Parmesan and pan-fried breaded pork cutlets. Each brand worked fine in both baked and fried applications, but with slightly different textural qualities. While three brands possessed a delicate crispness, the oil-free brand (purchased from a large natural foods supermarket) provided a much more substantial crunch. In the end, if a super-crunchy—rather than delicate and crisp—texture is what you're aiming for, choose our winner. Otherwise, brand doesn't really matter.

THE BEST PANKO
The oil-free bread crumbs from Ian's offered the most substantial crunch.

IAN'S

One pound of penne, although easy to measure, unfortunately made too much filling to fit in a standard 13 by 9-inch baking dish. Reducing the pasta to 12 ounces was our only answer. Undercooking the pasta slightly so that it retained a firm (al dente) center helped keep it from turning too mushy in the oven, and tasters approved of a sprinkling of cheesy bread crumbs over the top (using supercrisp store-bought panko saved us the effort of making homemade bread crumbs). Because all of the ingredients in the casserole were precooked, it took less than 15 minutes in a 450-degree oven for the bread crumbs to brown and the flavors to meld.

Baked Penne with Chicken, Broccoli, and Mushrooms

SERVES 6 TO 8

Be careful not to overcook the broccoli in step 2; it cooks very quickly. You can use any short tubular pasta in place of the penne. Because the chicken is only partially cooked before going into the casserole dish, for health and safety reasons we don't recommend making this casserole ahead.

¾	cup panko bread crumbs
3	ounces Asiago cheese, grated (1½ cups)
3	tablespoons olive oil
	Salt and ground black pepper
1½	pounds broccoli (1 large bunch), stems discarded, florets cut into 1-inch pieces
12	ounces penne (3¾ cups)
1	medium onion, minced
1¼	pounds cremini mushrooms, wiped clean, trimmed, and sliced ¼ inch thick
¼	ounce dried porcini mushrooms, rinsed and minced
8	medium garlic cloves, minced or pressed through a garlic press (about 8 teaspoons)
1	tablespoon minced fresh thyme leaves
5	tablespoons unbleached all-purpose flour
1	cup dry white wine
2	cups low-sodium chicken broth
1	cup heavy cream
1½	pounds boneless, skinless chicken breasts (4 to 5 medium), trimmed and sliced thin (see illustrations on page 219)

1. Adjust an oven rack to the middle position and heat the oven to 450 degrees. In a large bowl, toss the panko with ½ cup of the Asiago, 1 tablespoon of the oil, ¼ teaspoon salt, and ¼ teaspoon pepper.

2. Bring 4 quarts water to a boil in a large Dutch oven over high heat. Stir in the broccoli and 1 tablespoon salt and cook until the broccoli is bright green, about 1 minute. Using a slotted spoon, transfer the broccoli to a rimmed baking sheet; set aside. Return the water to a boil. Add the penne and cook, stirring often, until al dente. Drain the pasta and transfer it to a bowl; set aside.

3. Wipe the pot dry, add the remaining 2 tablespoons oil, and heat over medium heat until shimmering. Add the onion, cremini, porcini, and ¾ teaspoon salt, cover, and cook until the mushrooms have released their liquid, about 5 minutes. Uncover, increase the heat to medium-high, and continue to cook until the mushrooms are dry and beginning to brown, 5 to 10 minutes longer.

4. Stir in the garlic and thyme and cook until fragrant, about 30 seconds. Stir in the flour and cook for 1 minute. Slowly whisk in the wine, scraping up any browned bits, and simmer until nearly evaporated, about 1 minute. Gradually whisk in the broth and cream, smoothing out any lumps, and bring to a simmer. Add the chicken and cook, stirring occasionally, just until no longer pink, about 4 minutes.

5. Off the heat, stir in the remaining 1 cup Asiago and ¼ teaspoon pepper until the cheese has melted. Stir in the cooked pasta and broccoli. Pour the mixture into a 13 by 9-inch baking dish and sprinkle with the panko mixture. Bake until the filling is bubbling and the topping is browned and crisp, 12 to 15 minutes. Let the casserole cool for 10 minutes and serve.

➤ VARIATION

Baked Penne with Chicken, Broccoli, and Sun-Dried Tomatoes

Follow the recipe for Baked Penne with Chicken, Broccoli, and Mushrooms, omitting the cremini and dried porcini mushrooms; cook the onion and salt as directed in step 3 until softened, 5 to 7 minutes, before adding the garlic and thyme in step 4. Substitute 5 ounces of smoked mozzarella, shredded (1¼ cups), for the Asiago; toss ½ cup of the cheese with the panko in step 1, and stir the remaining ¾ cup cheese into the sauce in step 4. Add 1 cup oil-packed sun-dried tomatoes, rinsed, patted dry, and cut into thin strips, to the sauce with the cheese in step 5.

BAKED TORTELLINI

IN THE WORLD OF BAKED PASTA, WHERE hearty, traditional dishes such as lasagna dominate, more delicate baked tortellini offers a refreshing and potentially elegant change of pace. When done right, the result is a modern take on classic baked pasta, utilizing a choice of flavors and ingredients that are more upscale than what you'd find in most baked pasta casseroles. This dish should match the delicate flavor of tortellini with an equally sophisticated sauce and appropriate add-ins.

We started with the starring ingredient, the tortellini. We found several varieties sold at the supermarket—dried, frozen, and fresh—and began by tasting them side by side. The dried versions, usually found in the spaghetti aisle, were utterly unimpressive, with a stale and lifeless flavor. The frozen tortellini tasted a bit better and were more moist, but even they couldn't hold a candle to the clean flavor and fine texture of the fresh tortellini (found in the refrigerator case). Although the instructions for cooking fresh tortellini say to boil them for just a few minutes, we found it necessary (regardless of brand) to boil them for at least 10 minutes to ensure that all the folds of each piece of pasta were thoroughly cooked and tender. Unlike the unfilled pastas used in other pasta casseroles, tortellini won't continue cooking in the oven, so we found that they should be fully cooked on the stovetop.

Moving on to the sauce, we wanted something with an indulgent edge but wasn't too heavy. We started with a combination of chicken broth and heavy cream, which produced a respectable flavor that was neither too rich nor too lean. Thickening the sauce with a little flour was necessary to give it the ability to coat the tortellini and vegetables.

Onion, garlic, fresh thyme, and Parmesan lent robust flavor, but we were still not satisfied. Starting the sauce off by sautéing a little bacon before adding the onion to the pot gave the sauce some necessary oomph, but it wasn't until we added white wine that we knew we were getting somewhere. The wine added a mildly acidic note that helped cut through the richness of the bacon and cream without obscuring their flavors, and it gave our sauce a necessary hint of elegance.

With the tortellini and sauce figured out, we still needed to round out the casserole with some vegetables. We wanted to add some interesting flavors yet keep the prep work and cooking to a minimum. Fennel seemed appropriate for this flavor profile but was too much work to peel, chop, and core (we still wanted to keep this casserole simple). Slightly bitter radicchio came to mind. It took only moments to chop a head of radicchio into bite-size pieces, and it required no precooking—we simply stirred it into the tortellini and sauce before moving the casserole to the oven. There, it would braise in the sauce, and the combination of cream and chicken stock would mellow its bitterness. To offset the radicchio both in terms of flavor and color, we turned to an even more low-maintenance vegetable: peas. We tossed the peas, still frozen, into the pot with the radicchio (we have found frozen peas are a more reliable choice than fresh in terms of consistent quality).

We liked the idea of a bread-crumb topping to add textural contrast, but we felt the crumbs needed a flavor boost. Tossing them with some butter helped, plus it aided browning, eliminating the need for pretoasting the crumbs. We tried adding some Parmesan to the mix, but it tasted too sharp and not quite right. We set the cheese idea aside. Success came in the form of walnuts: crushed in the food processor, they lent the topping texture and savory richness. Although we've used panko bread crumbs as a shortcut topping in other casseroles, we found that for this casserole, the slightly sweet flavor of homemade bread crumbs was preferable to the more neutral panko. Moreover, making the bread crumbs wasn't additional work; we simply pulsed the bread with the walnuts in the food processor.

With its mix of savory flavors, slight richness, and upscale comfort-food appeal, this tortellini casserole would be a welcome addition to anyone's baked-pasta repertoire.

Creamy Baked Tortellini with Peas, Radicchio, and Bacon
SERVES 6 TO 8

For the best flavor and texture, be sure to buy fresh tortellini sold in the refrigerator case at the supermarket. Avoid buying tortellini that is either frozen or dried. However, because fresh tortellini are so tender, you can't prepare this casserole ahead because the pasta will become mushy.

½	cup walnuts
4	slices white sandwich bread, torn into quarters
2	tablespoons unsalted butter, melted
3	(9-ounce) packages fresh cheese tortellini
	Salt and ground black pepper
I	tablespoon olive oil
4	ounces (about 4 slices) bacon, minced
I	medium onion, minced
6	medium garlic cloves, minced or pressed through a garlic press (about 2 tablespoons)
2	teaspoon minced fresh thyme leaves
¼	cup unbleached all-purpose flour
I	cup dry white wine
2	cups low-sodium chicken broth
I	cup heavy cream
2	ounces Parmesan cheese, grated (I cup)
I	head radicchio (about 10 ounces), cored and chopped medium
I	cup frozen peas

1. Adjust an oven rack to the middle position and heat the oven to 400 degrees. Process the walnuts in a food processor until coarsely chopped, about 5 seconds. Add the bread and butter and process to uniformly coarse crumbs, about 6 pulses; set aside.

2. Bring 6 quarts water to a boil in a large Dutch oven over high heat. Add the tortellini and 1½ tablespoons salt and cook, stirring often, until tender.

Drain the tortellini, then transfer to a large bowl and toss with the oil. Cover to keep warm; set aside.

3. Wipe the pot dry, add the bacon, and cook over medium heat until brown and crisp, about 5 minutes. Stir in the onion and cook until softened, 5 to 7 minutes. Stir in the garlic and thyme and cook until fragrant, about 30 seconds. Stir in the flour and cook for 1 minute.

4. Slowly whisk in the wine, scraping up any browned bits, and cook until nearly evaporated, about 1 minute. Gradually whisk in the broth and cream, smoothing out any lumps, and bring to a simmer.

5. Off the heat, stir in the Parmesan and season with salt and pepper to taste. Stir in the cooked tortellini, radicchio, and peas. Pour into a 13 by 9-inch baking dish and sprinkle with the processed walnut mixture. Bake until the topping is brown and crisp, about 15 minutes. Let the casserole cool for 10 minutes and serve.

ULTIMATE CHILI MAC

SYNONYMOUS WITH SIMPLER TIMES AND simpler food, chili mac was once a favorite childhood comfort food and has an appeal that, for many of us, extends well into adulthood.

Initial testing prompted reminiscing, and the test kitchen was divided about which version of chili mac was best (mom's, of course). For some, it was a macaroni-and-cheese-like version with a bit of chili stirred in. For others, it was predominantly chili with a little macaroni added for heft. Still others insisted that there could be only one way to make the best chili mac: spicy chili, with elbows stirred in (no other pasta would do) and lots of gooey, melted cheese on top. We eventually settled on developing a recipe that would be a combination of the best spicy beef chili and creamy macaroni with cheese. We wanted a simple dish that would appeal to young and old alike. It couldn't be overly seasoned, or it would lose its kid appeal. And it couldn't be weighed down with too much cheese, or grownups wouldn't be happy.

Our first challenge was coming up with a chili with the correct heat and spice level. We sautéed onion, red bell pepper, and a generous amount of garlic to start. In lieu of fresh chiles (jalapeños added too much heat), we added chili powder, as well as some cumin. Based on experience, we knew the easiest way to tame the raw flavor of the dry spices was to briefly sauté them with the aromatics. This would help bloom their flavors and reduce their harshness. The ground beef went into the pot next, and we cooked it just until it was no longer pink. We now had a seasoned beef mixture that was waiting for the tomato component to transform it into chili. We felt that chunky diced tomatoes would be a good choice, as they would add texture and good brightness, so we stirred in a can, brought the mixture to a simmer, and partially covered the pot to allow the chili to slightly thicken. After 20 minutes of simmering, we had our first taste. With 1 tablespoon of chili powder and 2 teaspoons of cumin, the chili seemed spicy without being overbearing. The thickness also seemed ideal: spoonable and slightly thickened. Now it just needed the macaroni.

We started our testing by cooking a full pound of elbows only to al dente since we knew that, as with other baked pasta casseroles, the pasta would continue to cook in the oven and would absorb liquid as it baked. What we didn't count on was how much liquid it would soak up. After we stirred our pasta into the chili and transferred it to a baking dish, we popped it into the oven. This first try turned what seemed to be a promising casserole into bad cafeteria food. The macaroni took over, and the casserole was dry and bland.

We took a step back and evaluated all our components. We decided to try increasing the amount of tomato in the chili and added tomato puree (in addition to the can of diced tomatoes) figuring it would better coat the pasta. We also added a small amount of brown sugar to help tame the acidity of the tomato. We cut the amount of macaroni down to 8 ounces, and to boost the chili flavor that had been diluted by the pasta, we increased the chili powder to 2 tablespoons and the cumin to

1 tablespoon. With those changes, finally the spices were just right, but to our surprise the resulting dish was still too dry. Looking at other pasta recipes (not just casseroles), we homed in on the pasta cooking water, which often comes into play in stovetop pasta recipes to loosen the sauce. Could it do the same for our chili mac? We gave it a shot and in fact, it did. If we reserved some of the pasta cooking

INGREDIENTS: Diced Tomatoes

Unlike most kinds of canned produce, which pale in comparison to their fresh counterparts, a great can of diced tomatoes offers flavor almost every bit as intense as ripe in-season fruit. For this reason it's one of the most important staples we stock in our pantry. We rely on diced tomatoes for everything from tomato sauce to chili to soups and stews. But supermarket shelves are teeming with different brands of diced tomatoes. To make sense of the selection, we gathered 16 widely available styles and brands and tasted them plain and in tomato sauce, rating them on tomato flavor, saltiness, sweetness, texture, and overall appeal.

To our surprise, nearly half of the brands fell short. The lowest-rated tomatoes were flat-out awful, eliciting complaints like "mushy, gruel-like texture" and "rubbery and sour." We found that various factors, such as geography and additives, played into whether a sample rated highly. Our top-ranked tomatoes were grown in California, source of most of the world's tomatoes, where the dry, hot growing season develops sweet, complex flavor; the bottom-ranked brands came from the Midwest and Pennsylvania. We tasted tomatoes that were too sweet or too acidic (from not enough or too much citric acid) or bland from lack of salt. Tasters overwhelmingly favored those brands with more salt. In fact, the tomatoes with the least salt—125 mg per serving compared to 310 mg in the top-rated brand—ranked last. In the end, one can stood out from the pack. Hunt's Diced Tomatoes were our tasters' favorite, praised for being "fresh" and "bright," with a "sweet-tart" flavor and "juicy," "firm, crisp-tender chunks."

THE BEST DICED TOMATOES

Tasters chose Hunt's over all the others, praising the tomatoes for their "fresh," "bright" flavor.

HUNT'S

water and added it back to the chili and macaroni mixture before moving it to the oven, we were able to achieve the consistency we wanted. The tomato puree combined with the water to form a moist, flavorful coating for the pasta.

At this point, we needed to incorporate the cheese component. Colby Jack, which offers the flavor of Colby cheese with the creaminess of Monterey Jack, was ideal. The cheese was so good on top of the casserole, we also tried stirring some into the filling. This final touch was perfect, producing by far the most flavorful batch of chili mac yet.

After just 15 minutes in the oven, the topping turned a bubbly, golden brown. Better than what most remembered from mom's kitchen, this substantial chili mac still reminded us all of simpler times and the satisfying food of our youth. This was definitely a winner for the whole family.

Ultimate Chili Mac

SERVES 6 TO 8

Ground turkey can be substituted for the ground beef. You can substitute 5 ounces each of Colby and Jack cheeses for the Colby Jack cheese. Don't forget to reserve ¾ cup of the pasta cooking water in step 1; the water is used to thin out the chili in the casserole.

8	ounces elbow macaroni (2 cups)
	Salt and ground black pepper
2	tablespoons vegetable oil
2	medium onions, chopped medium
1	red bell pepper, stemmed, seeded, and chopped medium (see the illustrations on page 226)
6	medium garlic cloves, minced or pressed through a garlic press (about 2 tablespoons)
2	tablespoons chili powder
1	tablespoon ground cumin
1½	pounds 85 percent lean ground beef
1	(28-ounce) can tomato puree
1	(14.5-ounce) can diced tomatoes
1	tablespoon light or dark brown sugar
10	ounces Colby Jack cheese, shredded (2½ cups)

1. Adjust an oven rack to the middle position and heat the oven to 400 degrees. Bring 4 quarts water to a boil in a large Dutch oven over high heat. Add the macaroni and 1 tablespoon salt and cook, stirring often, until al dente. Reserve ¾ cup of the pasta cooking water, then drain the pasta. Transfer the pasta to a bowl; set aside.

2. Wipe the pot dry, add the oil, and heat over medium heat until shimmering. Add the onions, bell pepper, and ¾ teaspoon salt and cook until softened, 8 to 10 minutes. Stir in the garlic, chili powder, and cumin and cook until fragrant, about 1 minute. Stir in the beef and cook, breaking up the meat with a wooden spoon, until no longer pink, 5 to 8 minutes.

3. Stir in the tomato puree, diced tomatoes with their juice, brown sugar, and reserved pasta water and bring to a simmer. Cover the pot partially (leaving about 1 inch of the pot open), and continue to simmer, stirring occasionally, until the flavors have blended, about 20 minutes.

4. Off the heat, season with salt and pepper to taste. Stir in the cooked pasta, then stir in 1 cup of the cheese. Spread the mixture into a 13 by 9-inch baking dish and sprinkle with the remaining 1½ cups cheese.

5. Bake until the filling is bubbling and the cheese is spotty brown, about 15 minutes. Let the casserole cool for 10 minutes and serve.

TO MAKE AHEAD

Assemble the casserole through step 4, but let the filling cool to room temperature before sprinkling with the top layer of cheese. Cover the casserole with plastic wrap and refrigerate for up to 2 days. Before continuing with step 5, remove the plastic wrap, cover the dish with aluminum foil that has been sprayed with vegetable oil spray (or use non-stick foil), and bake until hot, about 30 minutes. Remove the foil and continue to bake as directed in step 5.

MEAT LASAGNA

MOST FAMILIES HAVE HOMEMADE LASAGNA once or twice a year, on holidays (especially if they are Italian) or birthdays. Lasagna is not enjoyed more frequently because it takes the better part of a day to boil the noodles, slow-cook the sauce, prepare and layer the ingredients, and then finally bake it. Although this traditional method does produce a superior dish, we were interested in an Americanized version, one that could be made in two hours or less from start to finish. We would have to sacrifice some of the rich flavors of a traditional recipe, but we were hoping to produce a lasagna good enough to still impress a family gathering. A bland, dry casserole just wouldn't do.

Previous test kitchen experience had led us to prefer no-boil lasagna noodles to regular dried. No-boil noodles are simply more convenient and they taste better too—their thin, delicate texture resembles fresh pasta. After a few initial tests, we discovered that the secret of no-boil noodles is to leave the tomato sauce a little on the watery side. The noodles can then absorb the excess liquid, resulting in a sauce with the perfect consistency, rather than drying out the dish. With this in mind, we got to work.

Italian cooks build meat sauce from the meaty browned bits left in the pan from the meatballs and Italian sausages they cook and later layer into the lasagna. By combining top-quality tomato products with a four-hour simmer, they make a rich, thick, and complex-tasting sauce. We were after the same depth of flavor, but, as time was of the essence, meatballs and a slow simmer were out of the question. We began by testing different kinds of ground meat.

Working with a base of sautéed aromatics (onions and garlic), an all-beef sauce turned out to be one-dimensional and dull. Adding ground pork was an improvement and certainly more interesting. Although the combination of beef and sweet Italian sausage (removed from its casing and browned with the beef) was even better, tasters were still left wanting. Finally, we turned to meatloaf mix, a combination of equal parts ground beef, pork, and veal sold in one package at most supermarkets. The flavor of the sauce made with this trio was robust and sweet. But still, we wanted something richer, creamier, and more cohesive. Our thoughts turned to Bolognese, the classic three-hour meat sauce enriched with dairy. We reduced a quarter cup of cream with the meat before adding the tomatoes. The ground meat soaked up the sweet cream, and the final product was rich and decadent. Even better, at this point we had been at the stove for only 12 minutes.

Because no-boil noodles rely primarily on the liquid in the sauce to rehydrate and soften, we had to get the moisture content of our sauce just right. If the sauce was too thick, the noodles would be dry and crunchy; too loose and they would turn flaccid, limp, and lifeless. Tasters found that a sauce made with two 28-ounce cans of pureed tomatoes was too heavy for the lasagna and overwhelmed the other flavors. Meanwhile, two 28-ounce cans of diced tomatoes yielded too thin a sauce. We settled on one 28-ounce can of each. The combination of pureed and diced tomatoes yielded a luxurious sauce, with soft but substantial chunks of tomatoes. We added the tomatoes to the meat mixture, warmed it through (no reducing necessary), and in just 15 minutes on the stove the meat sauce was rich, creamy, ultra-meaty, and ready to go.

Most Americans like their lasagna cheesy. It was a given that we would sprinkle each layer with mozzarella cheese, and after a test of whole-milk cheese versus part-skim we found that whole-milk mozzarella was the best for the job. It had a more intense flavor than its part-skim counterpart and a nicer melting quality. We also tested shredded, bagged mozzarella, but because it has a very low moisture content, it melted oddly and was somewhat dry. Shredding a 1-pound block of whole-milk mozzarella on a box grater or in a food processor was the ticket.

Ricotta was the next cheese up for scrutiny. It turned out that it made little difference whether we used whole-milk or part-skim ricotta. They were both characteristically creamy and rich, and tasters gave them both a thumbs-up. For added sharpness, we tested the ricotta mixed with Parmesan and Pecorino Romano cheeses. Tasters unanimously rejected the Pecorino for giving the lasagna a "sheepy" and "gamy" flavor. However, the grated Parmesan added a nice little kick to the mild, milky ricotta. An egg helped to thicken and bind the mixture, and some chopped basil added flavor and freshness. Tucked neatly between the layers of noodles, this ricotta mixture was just what the lasagna needed.

With all the components of the lasagna decided, it was time to concentrate on the layering procedure. Smearing the entire bottom of a 13 by 9-inch glass dish with some of the sauce was the starting point. Next came the first layer of no-boil noodles, which we topped with ricotta, then mozzarella, and, finally, more meat sauce. We built two more layers using this same process. For the fourth and final layer, we covered the pasta with the remaining meat sauce and the remaining mozzarella and then sprinkled the top with grated Parmesan.

In our tests, we found that covering the lasagna with foil at the outset of baking prevented a loss of moisture and helped soften the noodles properly. We then removed the foil for the last 25 minutes of baking to ensure the top layer of cheese turned golden brown. An oven temperature of 375 degrees proved ideal; by the time the top was browned, the noodles had softened.

Even though we found that our lasagna made with no-boil noodles took a little longer in the oven than a conventional lasagna, time saved in preparation more than made up for the difference. Start to finish, the meat and tomato lasagna took about an hour and a half to make: 40 minutes prep time, 40 minutes in the oven, and 10 minutes to rest. Finally, a lasagna we could make on a weeknight, or whenever the craving strikes.

Weeknight Meat Lasagna

SERVES 6 TO 8

We prefer Barilla no-boil lasagna noodles for their delicate texture that resembles fresh pasta. If you can't find meatloaf mix, you can substitute eight ounces each 85 percent lean ground beef and ground pork. Eight ounces each ground beef and sweet Italian sausage (casing removed) is also a good substitute for the meatloaf mix.

SAUCE

1	tablespoon olive oil
1	medium onion, minced
6	medium garlic cloves, minced or pressed through a garlic press (about 2 tablespoons)
1	pound meatloaf mix
¼	cup heavy cream
1	(28-ounce) can tomato puree
1	(28-ounce) can diced tomatoes, drained
	Salt and ground black pepper

FILLING AND NOODLES

15	ounces whole-milk or part-skim ricotta cheese (1¾ cups)
2½	ounces Parmesan cheese, grated (1¼ cups)
½	cup chopped fresh basil leaves
1	large egg, lightly beaten
½	teaspoon salt
½	teaspoon ground black pepper
12	no-boil lasagna noodles
1	pound whole-milk mozzarella cheese, shredded (4 cups)

1. Adjust an oven rack to the middle position and heat the oven to 375 degrees.

2. FOR THE SAUCE: Heat the oil in a large Dutch oven over medium heat until shimmering. Add the onion and cook until softened, 5 to 7 minutes. Stir in the garlic and cook until fragrant, about 30 seconds. Stir in the meatloaf mix and cook, breaking up the meat with a wooden spoon, until no longer pink, about 4 minutes.

3. Stir in the cream, bring to a simmer, and cook until the liquid evaporates and only the fat remains, about 4 minutes. Stir in the tomato puree and drained diced tomatoes, bring to a simmer, and cook until the flavors are blended, about 3 minutes. Off the heat, season with salt and pepper to taste. Cover to keep warm; set aside.

4. FOR THE FILLING AND NOODLES: In a medium bowl, mix the ricotta, 1 cup of the Parmesan, basil, egg, salt, and pepper together; set aside.

5. Spread ¼ cup of the meat sauce over the bottom of a 13 by 9-inch baking dish (avoiding large chunks of meat). Place 3 of the noodles on top of the sauce, and spread 3 tablespoons of the ricotta mixture evenly down the center of each noodle. Sprinkle with 1 cup of the mozzarella, then spoon 1½ cups of the meat sauce evenly over the top. Repeat the layering of the noodles, ricotta, mozzarella, and sauce two more times.

6. For the final layer, place the 3 remaining noodles on top of the sauce, then spread the remaining sauce over the noodles, and sprinkle with the remaining 1 cup mozzarella and remaining ¼ cup Parmesan.

7. Cover the dish tightly with aluminum foil that has been sprayed with vegetable oil spray (or use nonstick foil). Bake for 15 minutes, then remove the foil and continue to bake until the filling is bubbling and the cheese is spotty brown, about 25 minutes longer. Let the casserole cool for 10 minutes and serve.

TO MAKE AHEAD

Assemble the lasagna through step 6, cover with plastic wrap, and refrigerate for up to 2 days. Remove the plastic wrap and bake as directed in step 7, increasing the covered baking time to 25 minutes.

MODERN BAKED MANICOTTI

WE HAVE A LOVE/HATE RELATIONSHIP WITH manicotti. Well-made versions of this Italian-American classic—pasta tubes stuffed with rich ricotta filling and blanketed with tomato sauce—can be eminently satisfying. What we don't love so much is putting it all together. For such a straightforward collection of ingredients (after all, manicotti is just a compilation of pasta, cheese, and tomato sauce), the preparation is surprisingly fussy. Blanching, shocking, draining, and stuffing slippery pasta tubes require more patience (and time) than we usually have. In addition, a survey of manicotti recipes proved that most recipe writers don't get the filling right; too often the ricotta-based mixture turns out bland and runny. We wanted a recipe that was easier and tasted like the best of the classic versions.

Our testing started with the pasta component. Cheese-stuffed pastas have been consumed in Italy since medieval times, and traditional recipes use either homemade *crespelle* (thin, eggy, crêpelike pancakes) or rectangular sheets of homemade pasta as wrappers for the filling. Over time, most Italian-American recipes evolved to use ready-made dried pasta shells instead of homemade wrappers. For manicotti, pasta tubes are parboiled, shocked in ice water to stop the cooking, drained, and stuffed with ricotta filling. We focused our streamlining attention on this latter, modern method.

Some recipes require a pastry bag or a zipper-lock bag with the corner snipped off for filling the cylinders with ricotta. Others take a different approach, suggesting a small soupspoon for stuffing the tubes. With a bowl of basic ricotta filling at our side, we took a deep breath and gave each method a try. The pastry bag was messy but workable. However, many cooks don't own a pastry bag, and we didn't want to write a recipe requiring a specialty tool. Using a zipper-lock bag to force the ricotta into a slick parboiled pasta tube was equally messy; most of the cheese oozed out of the bag, with an embarrassingly small amount actually making it into the tube. The soupspoon was also frustrating; we eventually gave up on it and used our fingers instead. Noticing our impatience, a colleague suggested slitting a blanched noodle lengthwise, packing it with filling, and putting the stuffed tube into a casserole dish seam side down. Not bad, but this method still called for blanching, shocking, and draining the noodles.

On the back of one of the manicotti boxes, we found a "quick" recipe that seemed worth trying. It called for stuffing uncooked pasta tubes with ricotta, covering them with a watery sauce, then baking. Filling dried pasta tubes with cheese was marginally easier than stuffing limp parboiled noodles, but it wasn't without missteps: A few shattered along the

---

EQUIPMENT: Large Saucepans

Now that even low-cost manufacturers are offering fully clad cookware—a construction that features alternating layers of materials extending from the cooking surface up the sides, ensuring more even cooking—we wondered if we still needed to shell out $200 for our former favorite in this category, the All-Clad Stainless 4-Quart Saucepan. We rounded up eight models priced from $49.97 to $384.95 to see how much we needed to spend to get a great fully clad saucepan. In our testing, we found that the real differences came down to design and maneuverability. Pans that were particularly heavy or had poorly designed handles did not rate well, nor did those with sharp corner angles that prevented a whisk from getting into the corners. Happily, we found that a good-quality, fully clad, easy-to-maneuver pan could be had for just $69.99 (its biggest flaw was that its interior scratched easily), but in the end our old favorite still reigned supreme.

THE BEST LARGE SAUCEPANS

ALL-CLAD   CUISINART

The All-Clad Stainless 4-Quart Saucepan with Lid and Loop ($194.99) held on to its title as our favorite for heating slowly and evenly, but we found a good-quality, fully clad, easy-to-maneuver pan in the more affordable Cuisinart MultiClad Unlimited 4-Quart Saucepan ($69.99), which performed nearly identically to our winner.

way. Still, we followed the recipe through, watering down a jar of tomato sauce with a cup of boiling water and pouring it over the manicotti. After 45 minutes in the oven, this manicotti was inedible, with some of the pasta shells remaining uncooked and the pink, watered-down sauce tasting, well, like water.

Nearly at wit's end, we remembered the crespelle and fresh pasta sheets, which avoided the assembly problems associated with manicotti tubes. We scanned the ingredient list on a package of store-bought crêpes, hoping to use them instead of crespelle, but alas, they were far too sugary. Fresh pasta sheets aren't sold at many supermarkets. It was then that we thought of no-boil lasagna noodles. What if we softened the noodles in boiling water, turning them into pliable sheets of pasta, then spread the filling over the noodle and rolled them up, pinwheel-style? This method worked like a charm. After a quick soak, the no-boil lasagna noodles could be spread with filling and rolled up in a few minutes.

It was a given that ricotta would serve as the filling's base, but was whole-milk, part-skim, or even fat-free ricotta preferable? While in our lasagna (see page 117) the type didn't make much of a difference since it was just one layer among many, here it was much more in the spotlight. For our manicotti, the part-skim ricotta provided the ideal level of richness that still allowed the other flavors to shine. In addition to ricotta, shredded mozzarella and Parmesan are generally added to the filling, but we wondered if other cheeses might work better. After testing cream cheese, fresh mozzarella, fontina, Asiago, pecorino, and aged provolone, we decided none were as good as the classics. We would stick with tradition, opting for mozzarella and Parmesan.

Eggs are usually added to manicotti filling to prevent it from separating and becoming loose and watery. After experimenting with various amounts of whole eggs and yolks, we settled on two whole eggs. But eggs alone didn't completely prevent a runny filling. The proper amounts of mozzarella and Parmesan also proved key; a generous amount of mozzarella was necessary. For 16 manicotti we used a full 2 cups of mozzarella.

As for seasonings, a few specks of parsley plus salt and pepper are the norm. Looking for improvement, we explored other options, eventually settling on a combination of fresh parsley and basil (dried herbs were too harsh).

A slow-cooked tomato sauce didn't fit into our streamlining goal, so we were relieved when tasters preferred the bright, fresh flavor of a 15-minute sauce made with olive oil, garlic, and crushed tomatoes. We punched up our quick sauce with more fresh basil and a dash of red pepper flakes.

Finally, most baked pasta dishes benefit from a browned, cheesy topping. The best approach was to add a light sprinkling of Parmesan and pass the casserole under the broiler. This, at last, was manicotti that won our complete affection: great tasting *and* easy to prepare.

Modern Baked Manicotti

SERVES 6 TO 8

We prefer Barilla no-boil lasagna noodles for their delicate texture that resembles fresh pasta. Other brands of no-boil noodles contain only 12 noodles per package; note that this recipe requires 16 noodles.

SAUCE

2	tablespoons olive oil
3	medium garlic cloves, minced or pressed through a garlic press (about 1 tablespoon)
½	teaspoon red pepper flakes (optional)
2	(28-ounce) cans crushed tomatoes
2	tablespoons chopped fresh basil leaves
	Salt and ground black pepper

FILLING AND NOODLES

24	ounces part-skim ricotta cheese (3 cups)
4	ounces Parmesan cheese, grated (2 cups)
8	ounces whole-milk mozzarella, shredded (2 cups)
2	large eggs, lightly beaten
2	tablespoons minced fresh parsley leaves
2	tablespoons chopped fresh basil leaves
¾	teaspoon salt
½	teaspoon ground black pepper
16	no-boil lasagna noodles

1. Adjust an oven rack to the middle position and heat the oven to 375 degrees.

2. FOR THE SAUCE: Heat the oil, garlic, and red pepper flakes (if using) in a large saucepan over medium heat until fragrant but not brown, 1 to 2 minutes. Stir in the tomatoes and simmer until slightly thickened, about 15 minutes. Off the heat, stir in the basil and season with salt and pepper to taste. Cover to keep warm; set aside.

3. FOR THE FILLING AND NOODLES: In a medium bowl, mix the ricotta, 1 cup of the Parmesan, mozzarella, eggs, parsley, basil, salt, and pepper together; set aside.

4. Pour 1 inch of boiling water into a 13 by 9-inch broiler-safe baking dish and slip the noodles

ROLLING MANICOTTI

1. Using a spoon, spread ¼ cup of the ricotta cheese mixture evenly over the bottom three-quarters of each noodle.

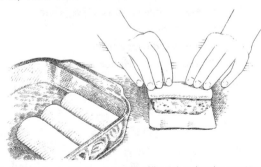

2. Roll each noodle up around the filling, then lay the manicotti, seam side down, in the baking dish.

into the water, one at a time. Let the noodles soak until pliable, about 5 minutes, separating the noodles with the tip of a knife to prevent sticking. Remove the noodles from the water and place in a single layer on clean kitchen towels; discard the water and dry off the baking dish.

5. Spread 1½ cups of the sauce over the bottom of the baking dish. Following the illustrations at left, spread ¼ cup of the ricotta mixture evenly over the bottom three-quarters of each noodle with a spoon. Roll the noodles up around the filling and lay them, seam side down, in the baking dish. Spoon the remaining sauce evenly over the filled manicotti, covering pasta completely.

6. Cover the dish tightly with aluminum foil that has been sprayed with vegetable oil spray (or use nonstick foil). Bake until bubbling, about 40 minutes. Remove the baking dish from the oven and remove the foil. Position the oven rack 6 inches from the broiler element and heat the broiler. Remove the foil, sprinkle with the remaining 1 cup Parmesan, and broil until the cheese is spotty brown, 4 to 6 minutes. Let the casserole cool for 10 minutes and serve.

➤ VARIATION

Modern Baked Manicotti Puttanesca

Follow the recipe for Modern Baked Manicotti, adding 3 anchovy fillets, rinsed and minced, to the pot with the garlic in step 2. Add ¼ cup pitted and quartered kalamata olives and 2 tablespoons capers, drained and rinsed, to the ricotta mixture in step 3.

TO MAKE AHEAD

Assemble the Modern Baked Manicotti or Modern Baked Manicotti Puttanesca through step 5, cover with plastic wrap, and refrigerate for up to 2 days. Remove the plastic wrap and bake as directed in step 6, increasing the covered baking time to 1 hour.

EGGPLANT CASSEROLE

EGGPLANT PARMESAN HAS A LOT OF APPEAL because it has the same Italian, tomato-sauced, comfort-food profile as manicotti or lasagna, but offers a break from the noodles and meat. But while it is essentially just eggplant, tomato sauce, and cheese, traditional recipes for eggplant Parmesan are notoriously tedious and messy. Typically, sliced eggplant is salted, breaded, and then deep-fried in several batches before being topped with sauce and cheese. Add to this the fact that most versions turn out disappointingly greasy and soggy after all that work. We understood why most people would rather not bother. Could we breathe some life into this classic combination and develop a streamlined technique for a modern, more in-balance take on eggplant Parmesan that was actually worth making?

We decided we needed to break from tradition and look toward a looser interpretation of eggplant Parmesan to meet our goals. Right off the bat we eliminated the breading process. It was simply too fussy, and all the oil the coating absorbed made the dish too greasy. Of course, we would still need to cook the eggplant before putting it in the casserole, so the question was how.

Sautéing or frying eggplant, breaded or unbreaded, is problematic because eggplant is essentially a sponge, ready to absorb anything, and it's packed with water. This one-two punch transforms raw eggplant into oil-soaked mush before it has a chance to caramelize. For this reason, eggplant is often salted before cooking to draw out liquid. While we weren't limiting ourselves to 30 minutes for this casserole, standing in the kitchen salting and drying slices of eggplant wasn't really appealing. For a more hands-off route, we wondered if the high heat of the oven could both evaporate the juices and concentrate the vegetable's flavor with a limited quantity of oil.

We tossed sliced eggplant with olive oil and salt, then spread the eggplant out on baking sheets and cooked it in the oven until browned (a good indicator that the bulk of the moisture was gone). This initial test was promising—excess moisture had evaporated and the eggplant had even browning—so we focused on fine-tuning details. For efficiency's sake, we chose globe eggplants since they are a decent size; we didn't want to multiply the number of slices we'd have to prepare by dealing with smaller varieties of eggplant. For the best appearance, taste, and texture, we settled on unpeeled, ¾-inch-thick rounds. These slices seemed a little on the thick side when raw, but once roasted they shrank to a manageable size for layering in a casserole dish and serving (thinner slices tended to disintegrate). Most eggplant Parmesan recipes we found called for 2 pounds of eggplant, but we found it was necessary to double this amount in order to achieve a proper balance of ingredients.

After some experimentation we found that roasting 4 pounds of eggplant required 3 tablespoons of oil: 2 tablespoons to coat all of the eggplant rounds and 1 tablespoon to coat the two baking sheets and prevent sticking. Rotating the pans and flipping the slices partway through ensured even cooking, and at 450 degrees, the slices became fully tender and golden brown in about 35 minutes.

With the eggplant roasting in the oven, we had time to grate some cheese and whip up a quick tomato sauce. For the cheese, Parmesan was a given, but mozzarella is standard in many eggplant Parmesan recipes as well, serving as the binder for the casserole. We agreed to use both.

A heaping tablespoon of minced garlic, sautéed in olive oil, started off our quick sauce, followed by a large can of crushed tomatoes. Ten minutes of simmering cooked out the raw tomato flavor but still left the sauce bright and fresh-tasting. After seasoning with salt and pepper, we finished the sauce with some chopped fresh basil and moved on to putting the casserole together.

In a 13 by 9-inch baking dish, we layered sauce, cooled eggplant, more sauce, then cheese, and repeated the process. The casserole went into a 375-degree oven, covered with foil to keep it from drying out. When the eggplant was hot throughout, we took the foil off so the top of the casserole could brown.

The result? Very close...but no cigar. Tasters were impressed by the flavor of this dish, but felt it wasn't hearty enough to stand alone as a main course. Thinking that perhaps our efforts to lighten the dish had gone too far, we considered some options for bulking it back up. We were trying to stay away from adding pasta or ground meat and/or sausage to this particular casserole, so we considered a layer of ricotta, which had added depth and interest to our Baked Ziti with Ricotta (page 110) without becoming overbearing or greasy. We mixed some ricotta with Parmesan, salt, pepper, and an egg for stability before spreading the mixture into two thin but distinct layers in our casserole.

To our surprise, understated ricotta was once again the solution, in this case imparting richness and body to the casserole while still allowing the eggplant to be the front-runner.

For a final touch, we decided the casserole would benefit from a crisp topping as a nod toward the traditional breaded and fried version of this dish. After the casserole was in the oven, we tossed together some panko, olive oil, Parmesan, and a clove of garlic, then when the foil came off the baking dish, we sprinkled on the panko topping so it could get crispy and brown in the oven.

Our streamlined take on eggplant Parmesan was just as satisfying as the old-fashioned comfort-food version, but with the additional benefit of being lighter and easier to prepare—traits that we have to admit are comforting all on their own.

Eggplant Casserole
SERVES 6 TO 8

Leaving the skins on the eggplant keeps the slices intact during roasting.

6   tablespoons olive oil
4   medium eggplant (about 4 pounds), sliced crosswise into ¾-inch-thick rounds
    Salt and ground black pepper
6   tablespoons olive oil

5   medium garlic cloves, minced or pressed through a garlic press (about 5 teaspoons)
1   (28-ounce) can crushed tomatoes
2   tablespoons chopped fresh basil leaves
15 ounces whole-milk or part-skim ricotta cheese (1¾ cups)
3   ounces Parmesan cheese, grated (1½ cups)
1   large egg, lightly beaten
1   pound whole-milk mozzarella cheese, shredded (4 cups)
1   cup panko bread crumbs

1. Adjust the oven racks to the upper-middle and lower-middle positions and heat the oven to 450 degrees. Line 2 large rimmed baking sheets with aluminum foil and brush each with 1½ teaspoons of the oil. Toss the eggplant with 2 tablespoons more oil and 1 teaspoon salt and arrange in a single layer on the prepared baking sheets.

2. Roast the eggplant until golden brown, 35 to 45 minutes, flipping the eggplant with a spatula and switching the baking sheets halfway through the roasting time. Let the eggplant cool until needed. Adjust an oven rack to the middle position and reduce the temperature to 375 degrees.

3. Meanwhile, heat 2 tablespoons more oil and 4 of the garlic cloves in a large saucepan over medium heat until fragrant but not brown, 1 to 2 minutes. Stir in the tomatoes and ¼ teaspoon salt and simmer until slightly thickened, about 10 minutes. Off the heat, stir in the basil and season with salt and pepper to taste. Cover to keep warm; set aside.

4. In a medium bowl, mix the ricotta, 1 cup of the Parmesan, egg, ½ teaspoon salt, and ½ teaspoon pepper together; set aside.

5. Spread ¾ cup of the sauce over the bottom of a 13 by 9-inch baking dish. Fit half of the roasted eggplant into the dish in a single layer, squeezing them together tightly as needed. Spread ¾ cup more sauce over the eggplant. Dollop half the ricotta mixture over the sauce, then gently flatten the dollops with the back of a spoon.

6. Sprinkle with 2 cups of the mozzarella then dollop ¾ cup more sauce over the cheese. Repeat the layering process with the remaining eggplant, the remaining ¾ cup sauce, the remaining ricotta mixture, and the remaining 2 cups mozzarella.

7. Cover the dish tightly with foil that has been sprayed with vegetable oil spray (or use nonstick foil). Bake until the filling is bubbling, about 25 minutes.

8. Toss the panko with the remaining ½ cup Parmesan, remaining 1 tablespoon oil, and remaining garlic clove together in a bowl and season with salt and pepper to taste. Remove the foil from the casserole, sprinkle with the panko mixture, and continue to bake until the topping is spotty brown and crisp, 20 to 25 minutes. Let the casserole cool for 10 minutes and serve.

TO MAKE AHEAD

Assemble the casserole through step 6, cover with plastic wrap, and refrigerate for up to 1 day. Remove the plastic wrap and bake as directed in step 7, increasing the covered baking time to 45 minutes.

PASTA ROLL-UPS WITH CHICKEN AND GOAT CHEESE

WE HAD ALREADY DEVELOPED A HOMESPUN manicotti recipe for our collection of classic casseroles, so for our final recipe in the group we agreed we wanted an Italian-style stuffed pasta, but one that was a little different, something a little more upscale. We decided to turn the manicotti on its head and swap the red sauce for a rich (but not heavy) white sauce and the simple cheese filling for a more substantial chicken filling, which we knew could work well with a variety of flavor profiles.

We started with the filling. While Italians typically use leftover meat to stuff their pasta (a recipe we'd seen called for a pound of any combination of cooked meat), we wanted to build our sauce from the ground up without requiring precooked ingredients. Considering our options, chicken seemed like the best choice: it's quick-cooking and mild enough to pair with a variety of ingredients. We had learned from our Savory Chicken Cobbler testing (see page 99) that poaching boneless, skinless chicken parts in broth was efficient and produced good results. In addition to being fast and easy (even the thighs were done in 12 minutes) this method gave us a flavorful mix of dark and white meat, which we could assemble into portions as we pleased. Another bonus of this method was that the leftover poaching broth, infused with flavor by the chicken, gave us the perfect base for our sauce.

But before we could jump ahead to the sauce, we had to finish the filling. For the cheese, we knew we wanted something more intensely flavored than ricotta to pair with the chicken, so we tested a few possibilities. Gorgonzola was too overpowering and fontina was too dull and grainy. Goat cheese, however, was perfect. It was more flavorful than ricotta but still creamy, and we found its flavor was nicely brightened by the addition of lemon zest and juice. A little Parmesan sharpened the goat cheese and lent some bite, as did briny olives. We tried black and green olives and quickly discovered that the black olives turned the filling an unappealing purple hue. Luckily, tasters were in favor of the cleaner flavor of the green olives anyway. A touch of minced garlic and a generous amount of fresh chopped basil finished the filling perfectly.

Next we addressed the sauce. With the reserved poaching broth ready to go, we had the base of a classic French sauce called *velouté*, which is basically roux-thickened broth. Deciding to start bare bones and build the flavor of the sauce as needed, we made a roux by cooking equal parts butter and flour. We then whisked in the reserved broth and a cup of heavy cream and simmered until thickened. The sauce was rich and appropriately clingy, but no surprise, it tasted a little dull. White wine cut the richness and started building depth. For more complexity, we added minced onion and garlic (sautéing them in the butter before adding the flour). A couple of bay leaves and freshly ground nutmeg imparted a delicate but noticeable enhancement. As a final addition, we stirred some Parmesan and chopped basil into the thickened sauce off the heat. Satisfied with the flavor of both the filling and sauce, we were ready to roll.

Just as we had done for our Modern Baked Manicotti (page 121), we soaked no-boil noodles in boiling water to make them pliable before spreading the filling over the softened noodles and rolling them up pinwheel-style. We spread some of the sauce in the bottom of a 13 by 9-inch baking dish, then nestled in the rolled pasta. After a few rounds, we decided to modify the manicotti rolling technique; spreading the chicken filling out over the noodle was turning the meat into unappealing small bits. So instead of rolling them up like pinwheels, we mounded the chicken filling on one end of the pasta and rolled the pasta around it (more like a sushi roll).

We then covered the pasta with the remaining sauce and baked it until the noodles were fully softened and the filling was hot throughout. Though the overall flavor was spot on, the filling was separated and loose. It lacked cohesion, and tasters thought it had more in common with warm chicken salad than a filling suitable to a pasta dinner. To make our filling more cohesive, we tried adding some mozzarella, which proved key to marrying the ingredients and transforming them from chicken salad territory to pasta filling.

Despite our progress, the filling was still a little loose and separating slightly, plus tasters found it a tad dry. In the next test, we incorporated some of our cream sauce, which contained a fair amount of flour, hoping it would add moisture as well as starch to bind the filling and prevent separation. We were thrilled to find that with that addition, our filling was moist and no longer curdled. Increasing the quantity of flour in the sauce (from ¼ cup to ⅓ cup) created a thick binder that provided enough heft to keep the filling together as well as set up around the rolled pasta.

Baking the casserole took some finesse, as the bright and subtle flavors of the filling were easily killed with extended stints in the oven. After some experimentation, the key proved to be using a low-heat/high-heat method. We baked the casserole, covered, at 350 degrees until it just started to bubble around the edges. We then removed the cover and quickly broiled the casserole to brown the top. This last technique was the final touch needed to perfect our fresh take on pasta casserole.

Pasta Roll-Ups with Chicken and Goat Cheese

SERVES 6 TO 8

We prefer Barilla no-boil lasagna noodles for their delicate texture that resembles fresh pasta. Other brands of no-boil noodles contain only 12 noodles per package; note that this recipe requires 16 noodles. It's important not to overbake this dish; be sure to remove the casserole from the oven once the sauce begins to bubble around the edges in step 8.

CHICKEN AND SAUCE

1	pound boneless, skinless chicken breasts and/or thighs, trimmed
2½	cups low-sodium chicken broth
4	tablespoons (½ stick) unsalted butter
1	medium onion, minced
4	medium garlic cloves, minced or pressed through a garlic press (about 4 teaspoons)
⅓	cup unbleached all-purpose flour
¼	cup dry white wine
1	cup heavy cream
2	bay leaves
½	teaspoon fresh grated nutmeg
1	ounce Parmesan cheese, grated (½ cup)
2	tablespoons chopped fresh basil leaves
	Salt and ground black pepper

FILLING AND NOODLES

10	ounces goat cheese (2½ cups)
6	ounces whole-milk mozzarella cheese, shredded (1½ cups)

2   ounces Parmesan cheese, grated (1 cup)

1   large egg, lightly beaten

1   teaspoon grated zest and 1 tablespoon juice
    from 1 lemon

1   medium garlic clove, minced or pressed
    through a garlic press (about 1 teaspoon)
    Salt and ground black pepper

½   cup plus 2 tablespoons chopped fresh basil
    leaves

⅓   cup green olives, chopped medium

16 no-boil lasagna noodles

1. FOR THE CHICKEN AND SAUCE: Adjust an oven rack to the middle position and heat the oven to 350 degrees. Combine the chicken and broth in a large saucepan, cover, and simmer over medium heat until the breasts register 160 to 165 degrees and the thighs register 175 degrees on an instant-read thermometer, 8 to 12 minutes.

2. Remove the chicken from the pot and pour the liquid into a measuring cup. Let the chicken cool slightly, then shred the meat into bite-size pieces following the illustration on page 75.

3. Wipe the pot dry, add the butter, and melt over medium heat. Add the onion and cook until softened, 5 to 7 minutes. Stir in the garlic and cook until fragrant, about 30 seconds. Stir in the flour and cook for 1 minute. Slowly whisk in the white wine and simmer until nearly evaporated, about 30 seconds.

4. Gradually whisk in the reserved broth and cream. Stir in the bay leaves and nutmeg, and simmer, whisking often, until the sauce is thickened and measures about 3½ cups, about 10 minutes. Off the heat, remove and discard the bay leaves. Whisk in the Parmesan and basil and season with salt and pepper to taste. Cover the sauce to keep warm; set aside.

5. FOR THE FILLING AND NOODLES: In a large bowl, combine the goat cheese, mozzarella, ½ cup of the Parmesan, egg, lemon zest, lemon juice, garlic,

½ teaspoon salt, and ½ teaspoon pepper until uniform. Gradually stir ½ cup of the sauce into the cheese mixture, then fold in the shredded chicken, ½ cup of the basil, and olives; set aside.

6. Pour 1 inch of boiling water into a 13 by 9-inch broiler-safe baking dish and slip the noodles into the water, one at a time. Let the noodles soak until pliable, about 5 minutes, separating the noodles with the tip of a knife to prevent sticking. Remove the noodles from the water and place in a single layer on clean kitchen towels; discard the water and dry the baking dish.

7. Spread 1 cup more sauce over the bottom of a 13 by 9-inch baking dish. Following the illustrations below, mound ¼ cup of the chicken-cheese mixture evenly over the bottom of each noodle

ASSEMBLING THE PASTA ROLL-UPS WITH CHICKEN

1. Using a spoon, mound ¼ cup of the chicken-cheese mixture evenly over the bottom of each noodle, then compact the filling into a tidy log.

2. Roll the noodle up and around the filling, then lay the roll-up, seam side down, in the baking dish.

and compact into a tidy log. Roll the noodle up around the filling, and lay seam side down in the baking dish. Spoon the remaining sauce evenly over the filled noodles, covering the pasta completely.

8. Cover the dish tightly with aluminum foil that has been sprayed with vegetable oil spray (or use nonstick foil). Bake until the edges are just bubbling, 25 to 30 minutes, rotating the pan halfway through the baking time.

9. Remove the baking dish from the oven and remove the foil. Position the oven rack 6 inches from the heating element and heat the broiler. Remove the foil from the dish, sprinkle with the remaining ½ cup Parmesan, and broil until the top is spotty brown, 4 to 6 minutes. Let the casserole cool for 10 minutes, then sprinkle with the remaining 2 tablespoons basil and serve.

➤ VARIATION

Pasta Roll-Ups with Chicken, Sun-Dried Tomatoes, and Pine Nuts

Follow the recipe for Pasta Roll-Ups with Chicken and Goat Cheese, substituting ½ cup oil-packed, sun-dried tomatoes, rinsed, patted dry, and chopped fine, for the olives. Add ¼ cup pine nuts, toasted, and 2 teaspoons minced fresh oregano leaves to the filling with the chicken in step 5.

TO MAKE AHEAD

Assemble the Pasta Roll-Ups with Chicken and Goat Cheese or Pasta Roll-Ups with Chicken, Sun-Dried Tomatoes, and Pine Nuts through step 7, cover with plastic wrap, and refrigerate for up to

1 day. Remove the plastic wrap and bake as directed in steps 8 and 9, increasing the covered baking time in step 8 to 45 to 55 minutes.

EQUIPMENT:
Broiler-Safe Baking Dishes

When it comes to casseroles, our favorite pan is the Pyrex Bakeware 13 x 9 Baking Dish. At just $8.99, this inexpensive workhorse is almost perfect. The flaw? Pyrex does not recommend its ovensafe tempered glassware go under the broiler because abrupt temperature changes **can** cause it to crack or shatter, a condition called thermal shock. We needed an alternative with roughly the same dimensions and capacity, since many recipes are sized to fit the Pyrex, but one that could handle the heat. We gathered seven rectangular broiler-safe baking dishes, priced between $37 and $125, and cranked up the heat. In the end, we preferred those that were lightweight, with large, easy-to-grip handles and straight sides, and comparatively inexpensive. Our winner, the HIC Porcelain Lasagna Baking Dish, has it all.

THE BEST BROILER-SAFE BAKING DISH

HIC

The lightweight HIC Porcelain Lasagna Baking Dish ($37.49) has the perfect depth and size to properly cook a variety of dishes, large handles for secure gripping, and straight sides for easy serving.

5

STEWS AND CHILIS

Stews and Chilis

BEST BEEF STEW

ONCE THE TEMPERATURE DROPS AND WINTER is on its way, the anticipation of hearty, stick-to-your-ribs beef stew looms large in our minds. Part of the thrill of making a successful beef stew is the challenge of turning a tough cut of beef tender in a Dutch oven full of vegetables and savory broth. And as beef stew simmers, its incredibly rich aroma fills the house—and intensifies our anticipation for a great meal ahead. But frankly, the taste of beef stew often isn't as complex as its aroma would have us believe, and while it doesn't taste bad in these cases, it's just not good enough to merit the hours it takes to prepare. We wanted a go-to recipe for beef stew that would live up to our expectations.

Of the dozen or so recipes we tried, ranging from quick-and-easy versions with store-bought beef broth, heavy thickeners, and tiny pieces of beef to better (but still disappointing) four-hour versions, the only one that delivered truly satisfying flavor came from the famed Michelin-starred chef Thomas Keller. The problem? It took four days, a dozen dirty pots and pans, and nearly 50 ingredients to make. There had to be a reasonable compromise between the dim, underdeveloped flavors in the shortcut recipes and Keller's no-holds-barred version.

The basic process for beef stew is straightforward: Brown chunks of beef in a Dutch oven, add aromatics and thickener, cover with liquid, and simmer until everything is tender and the flavors have melded. The key to developing complexity is to maximize flavor in every step. American beef stew is first and foremost about the beef—all other ingredients exist merely to support or complement it—so picking the right cut is essential. Using packaged "stew meat" from the supermarket was a nonstarter; the jumble of scraggly bits and large chunks was impossible to cook evenly. Cuts like tenderloin, strip, or rib eye turned mealy with prolonged cooking; they're better for searing or grilling. More esoteric cuts like hanger or skirt steak offered great flavor, but their texture was stringy. While well-marbled blade steaks and short ribs (favored by Keller) worked well, in the end they were no better than chuck-eye roast. It's one of the cheapest, beefiest cuts in the supermarket, and it turns meltingly tender when it's properly cooked.

The first key to rich, meaty flavor is proper browning, which means searing in two separate batches for a big pot of stew. Otherwise, the meat releases too much moisture and ends up steaming in its own juices. After browning the beef, we decided to caramelize the usual choices of onions and carrots to start the stew off with as much flavor as possible. Though at first we planned to remove the meat while sautéing the vegetables, we found that when we left it in the pot, its residual heat helped the onions and carrots cook faster and more evenly. A little flour lightly thickened the stew; we then deglazed the pan with some red wine, added chicken broth (favored over store-bought beef broth), and let the stew simmer for 2½ hours

INGREDIENT: **Salt Pork**

We often use salt pork to add meaty flavor to recipes, but buyer beware: confusion exists about the difference between fatback and salt pork, a confusion we experienced at several markets where these products were not correctly labeled.

Salt pork comes from the belly of the pig (like bacon), and it has been cured or preserved in salt. It has streaks of meat running through it and is often rendered to make cracklings. Salt pork is fattier and chewier than bacon, but the two can often be used interchangeably. (Note that bacon is usually smoked but salt pork is not.)

As its name implies, fatback comes from the back of the animal. Unlike salt pork, fatback is not smoked or cured; rather it is simply fresh fat. Fatback is generally used to lard meat—that is, to run strips of fat through lean meat to improve its flavor when roasted. Fatback doesn't contain meat and cannot be used as a substitute for salt pork or bacon, so make sure to check your package closely before leaving the grocery store.

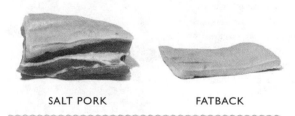

SALT PORK   FATBACK

Stews 101

While stews generally require a moderate amount of preparation and effort, time and gentle simmering really do most of the work. That said, we've all had (or made) stews with tough meat, listless vegetables, and dull, watery broth. Follow these tips for producing superior stew.

1. CUT YOUR OWN MEAT

Packaged stew meat is often made up of irregularly shaped scraps that cook at varying rates. Cut your own stew meat to guarantee same-size chunks that share the same flavor and cooking time. Use fatty, flavorful cuts (we like chuck-eye roast and pork butt) that will stay moist with extended cooking.

2. SKIP THE FLOUR BEFORE BROWNING

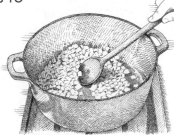

Contrary to popular belief, dusting meat with flour before searing it doesn't help it brown better. In fact, we have found just the opposite. The flour itself darkens a little, but the meat remains pale and doesn't develop the intense flavor compounds that are the goal of browning. Instead of flouring, pat stew meat dry and season it with salt and pepper before browning.

3. BROWN THE MEAT PROPERLY

Crowding the pan with too much meat or using inadequate heat can cause meat to steam (rather than brown) and ultimately lose flavor. To avoid this problem, add the meat only after the oil begins to smoke and leave plenty of space (about ½ inch) between pieces (this may mean browning in batches). Turn only when the first side is well seared and brown.

4. IF THE FOND BURNS, REMOVE IT

Browning meat in more than two batches can lead to a pan covered by burnt (rather than browned) fond that can impart a bitter flavor to the stew. If the fond is blackening, add a little water to the empty pot and scrape the fond to loosen it. Discard burnt bits and water and wipe the pot clean. Add fresh oil and proceed with the next batch of meat.

5. SAUTÉ THE AROMATICS TO ENHANCE FLAVOR

Recipes that call for dumping spices and aromatics, such as garlic and onion, into the pot at the same time as the liquid fail to maximize their flavor. So hold the liquid and sauté these flavor-enhancing ingredients first.

6. FLOUR AROMATICS TO THICKEN THE STEW

Many recipes call for thickening a stew by simmering with the lid off, but this method risks overcooking. Thicken stew at the beginning of cooking by sprinkling flour over the sautéed aromatics. Then cook the flour for a minute to remove any raw taste.

7. STAGGER THE ADDITION OF VEGETABLES

When vegetables are dumped indiscriminately into the pot at the outset of cooking, they not only lose flavor and turn mushy, but also water down the stew. Take into account the cooking time of individual vegetables and add them at the appropriate time.

8. SIMMER THE STEW IN THE OVEN

To ensure a steady, gentle simmer that allows the internal temperature of the meat to rise slowly and eliminates the risk of scorching the pot bottom, cook the stew in a covered Dutch oven at 300 degrees (for chicken) or 325 degrees (for beef and pork). This will keep the temperature of the stewing liquid below the boiling point (212 degrees) and ensure meat that is tender.

9. COOK THE MEAT UNTIL FALL-APART TENDER

When meat is undercooked, its fat and connective tissue have not had the chance to break down sufficiently, and it will taste rubbery and tough. Cook meat to the point where the collagen has melted down. This yields tender meat that separates easily when pulled apart with two forks.

10. DEFAT THE STEW BEFORE SERVING

Let the stew settle, then skim away the fat with a wide, shallow spoon or ladle, or pour the stew liquid into a tall, narrow container, which creates a thicker layer of fat that's easier to remove. If you have one, a fat separator make this step incredibly easy. Or, if there's time, refrigerate the stew overnight; when the fat solidifies, it can be lifted right off. For more information on defatting, see page 65.

in the oven, which we found provides a more even heat than the stovetop. Despite the little tweaks in the browning steps, our stew still lacked real meatiness. We decided to attack the problem in a more scientific manner.

We've long known that ingredients rich in glutamates—compounds that give meat its savory taste—can enhance the flavor of a dish. Tomatoes are one such ingredient. We experimented with various canned tomato products, finally landing on tomato paste, which lent just the right background note.

Thinking of other glutamate-rich ingredients, we wondered about cured meats; bacon was too smoky for the dish, but salt pork worked well, adding a subtle depth to the broth and the beef. Then we remembered another salted product that's packed with glutamates: anchovies. We mashed one up and incorporated it along with the garlic and tomato paste. It was a smashing success, with tasters praising the newfound beefiness—but not guessing its source. In fact, we found we could add up to four fillets with increasingly better results before the fishiness revealed itself. Finally, our stew was packed with the depth we sought. But one problem remained: texture.

Keller's stew, unlike most basic beef stew recipes, starts with homemade veal stock. As it cooks, collagen in the veal bones is transformed into gelatin, which gives the final stew rich, luxurious texture—something that our flour-thickened broth lacked. Theoretically, powdered gelatin should work, but once we removed the flour, we needed to add nearly ½ cup of gelatin powder to thicken the stew sufficiently. Flour or gelatin alone didn't work, but what about a combination? We made the stew with ¼ cup of flour just as before but added a single packet of gelatin softened in water after removing the stew from the oven. After just three minutes of simmering on the stovetop, the liquid developed a rich, glossy sheen that looked (and tasted) every bit as rich as the veal stock–based version.

With the base of our stew perfected, the rest of the recipe was simple: we added a handful of frozen pearl onions toward the end of cooking along with some frozen peas. As for potatoes, starchy russets broke down too easily, turning the stew grainy. Medium-starch Yukon Golds added halfway through cooking were the way to go. As we ladled steaming bowls of the supremely meaty and satisfying stew, we couldn't help but appreciate that, sometimes, the little things really do matter.

CUTTING BEEF STEW MEAT

You simply can't make good stew from bad meat. And to get the best stew meat possible (regularly shaped, evenly cut, and all from the chuck), you should really cut it up yourself. We like to use a beef chuck-eye roast, but any boneless beef roast from the chuck will work. The trick is not to cut the pieces of meat too small while trimming away the fat—the fat will render into the stew and be easy to skim off later. That said, don't be surprised if you have a good amount of trim—count on roughly ½ pound trim for every 4 pounds of meat.

1. Pull apart the roast at its major seams (delineated by lines of fat and silver skin); use a knife as necessary.

2. With a sharp, thin-tipped knife, trim off the excess fat and silver skin.

3. Cut the meat into pieces as directed in the recipe.

Best Beef Stew

SERVES 6

Use a good-quality, medium-bodied wine, such as a Côtes du Rhône or Pinot Noir, for this stew. Try to find beef that is well marbled with white veins of fat; meat that is too lean will come out slightly dry. Look for salt pork that is roughly 75 percent lean.

2	medium garlic cloves, minced or pressed through a garlic press (about 2 teaspoons)
4	medium anchovy fillets, rinsed and minced
1	tablespoon tomato paste
1	(3½- to 4-pound) boneless beef chuck-eye roast, trimmed and cut into 1½-inch pieces (see the illustrations on page 133)
2	tablespoons vegetable oil
2	medium onions, halved and sliced pole to pole into ⅛-inch-thick pieces (see the illustration below)
4	carrots, peeled and cut into 1-inch pieces
¼	cup unbleached all-purpose flour
2	cups red wine (see note)
2	cups low-sodium chicken broth
4	ounces salt pork, rinsed of excess salt
2	bay leaves
4	sprigs fresh thyme
1	pound Yukon Gold potatoes (about 2 medium), scrubbed and cut into 1-inch chunks
1½	cups frozen pearl onions, thawed
2	teaspoons (about 1 packet) unflavored powdered gelatin
½	cup water
1	cup frozen peas, thawed
	Salt and ground black pepper

1. Adjust an oven rack to the lower-middle position and heat the oven to 300 degrees. Combine the garlic and anchovies in a small bowl and press with the back of a fork to form a paste. Stir in the tomato paste; set aside.

2. Pat the meat dry with paper towels (do not season). Heat 1 tablespoon of the oil in a large Dutch oven over medium-high heat until just smoking. Add half of the beef and brown well on all sides, 7 to 10 minutes; transfer to a large bowl. Repeat with the remaining 1 tablespoon oil and the remaining beef (leave the second batch of meat in the pot).

3. Stir the first batch of browned meat with any accumulated juice, onions, and carrots into the pot. Reduce the heat to medium and cook, scraping up any browned bits, until the onions are softened, 5 to 7 minutes. Stir in the garlic mixture and cook until fragrant, about 30 seconds. Stir in the flour and cook for 30 seconds.

4. Slowly add the wine, scraping up any browned bits. Increase the heat to high and simmer until the wine thickens and reduces slightly, about 2 minutes. Stir in the broth, salt pork, bay leaves, and thyme and bring to a simmer. Cover, transfer the pot to the oven, and cook for 1½ hours.

5. Remove the bay leaves, salt pork, and thyme sprigs from the pot and stir in the potatoes. Continue to cook, covered, in the oven until the meat is tender, 1 to 1½ hours longer.

6. Remove the pot from the oven. Using a large spoon, skim any excess fat from the surface of the stew. Stir in the pearl onions and cook over medium heat until the potatoes and onions are cooked through and the meat offers little resistance when poked with a fork (the meat should not be falling apart), about 15 minutes. Meanwhile, sprinkle the

SLICING ONIONS

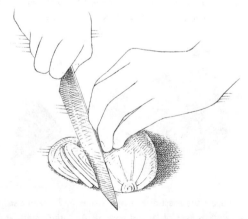

When slicing onions, be sure to slice them with the grain, from pole to pole. When sliced the opposite way, against the grain, the onions will have a stringy texture.

gelatin over the water in a small bowl and allow to soften for 5 minutes.

7. Stir in the gelatin mixture and peas and continue to simmer until the gelatin is fully dissolved and the stew is thickened, about 3 minutes. Season with salt and pepper to taste and serve. (The stew can be cooled and refrigerated in an airtight container for up to 2 days. Reheat gently, adding water as needed to loosen its consistency, before serving.)

HUNGARIAN GOULASH

THOUGH YOU'D NEVER GUESS IT FROM THE gussied-up versions served in this country, traditional Hungarian goulash is the simplest of stews, calling for little more than beef, onions, and paprika. Sour cream has no place in the pot, nor do mushrooms, green peppers, or most herbs. Instead, the best goulash features the simple heartiness of beef melded with the sweetness of long-cooked onions. But the real revelation is the paprika. Instead of being a mere accent, its fruity, almost chocolaty flavors infuse the meat and help transform the braising liquid into a rich, thick sauce. Ignoring the countless recipes with endless ingredient lists, we set out to bring a humble but delicious dish back to its roots.

The Hungarian herdsmen who developed this campfire stew used tough cuts of meat such as shin (a cross section from the front leg that includes both bone and meat), cooking it for hours over a low fire until tender. While many modern recipes still call for shin, it is not widely available in this country. Instead, we reached for chuck-eye roast, the test kitchen favorite for beef stew, and cut it into sizable chunks.

As for the paprika, tasters affirmed that the traditional sweet kind was best, preferring its floral, fruity qualities to the spiciness of hot paprika or the overwhelming smoky flavor of smoked paprika. Fresh, high-quality paprika is a must, but to achieve the desired level of intensity, some recipes call for as much as ½ cup per 3 pounds of meat. However, because this stew is nothing more than meat, onions, and sauce, we found that once we reached

3 tablespoons of paprika, the spice began contributing a gritty, dusty texture.

To eliminate the grittiness, we tried steeping the paprika in broth and then straining it through a coffee filter. This captured plenty of paprika flavor without a trace of its texture, but straining took nearly 30 minutes—a deal breaker. After consulting with chefs at a few Hungarian restaurants, we were turned on to a new idea: paprika cream, a condiment our sources said was as common in Hungarian cooking as the dried spice. We couldn't find it locally, so we ordered it online. "Paprika cream" turned out to be a deep red paste, packaged in a metal tube, that contained ground paprika camouflaged in a puree of red bell peppers. When we added it to our stew, it created vibrant paprika flavor without any offensive grittiness.

This convenience product was great, but we didn't want to have to hunt it down every time we made goulash. So why not create our own paprika cream? We began with a jar of roasted red peppers (their tender texture would be better for our purposes than fresh). We drained the peppers and pureed them in a food processor along with the paprika. To better approximate the lively yet concentrated flavors of the cream from the tube, we also added a couple of tablespoons of tomato paste and a little

INGREDIENTS: Sweet Paprika

Some cooks think of paprika as merely a coloring agent. But the best versions of this sweet Hungarian spice (made from a different variety of red pepper than hot or smoked paprika) pack a punch that goes beyond pigment. We sampled six brands, two from the supermarket and four ordered online. Our findings? It pays to mail-order your paprika—the supermarket brands had little flavor and even less aroma.

THE BEST PAPRIKA
The Spice House Hungarian Sweet Paprika outshone the competition with the complexity of its "earthy," "fruity" flavors and "toasty" aroma, making the slight inconvenience of mail-ordering it well worthwhile.

SPICE HOUSE

vinegar. Bingo! We were able to add up to ⅓ cup paprika without any resulting grittiness.

Up to now we had also been following the standard stew protocol: Sear the meat in batches, cook aromatics (in this case, just onions), return the beef to the pot along with broth and other ingredients, and cook until the meat is tender. But once we introduced the paprika paste into the mix, we found that the flavor of the seared meat competed with the paprika's brightness. Referring back to the many goulash recipes we had gathered in our research, we found an interesting trend: Many did not sear the meat. Instead, the onions went into the pot first to soften, followed by the paprika and meat, and then the whole thing was left to cook. That's it. There was no browning of the meat, and no additional liquids added.

Intrigued but dubious, we cooked the onions briefly in oil, added the paprika paste and raw meat, and placed the covered pot in the oven. Sure enough, the onions and meat provided enough liquid to stew the meat. As we cooked batch after batch using this no-sear method, we noticed something peculiar: The meat above the liquid actually browned during cooking. In effect, we were developing flavors that were similar to (though not quite as intense as) the flavor of seared beef. Toward the end of cooking, we added a little broth (store-bought beef broth worked best here) to thin out the stewing liquid and make it more saucelike.

In keeping with authentic goulash, the only vegetables in the pot were onions. But in deference to our American tasters, who wanted at least a few vegetables in their stew, we incorporated carrots into the mix, finding that we also appreciated the sweetness and textural contrast they provided. And even though sour cream is not traditional, some tasters did enjoy the goulash with a dollop of cool, tangy sour cream. Even with these slight adulterations, our Hungarian goulash was the real deal: a simple dish of tender braised beef packed with paprika flavor.

Hungarian Goulash
SERVES 6

Paprika is vital to this recipe, so it's best to use a fresh container; do not substitute hot or smoked paprika for the sweet paprika. A Dutch oven with a tight-fitting lid is crucial to the success of this dish since there is not much braising liquid; if necessary, place a sheet of aluminum foil over the pot before adding the lid to ensure a tight seal. Serve with sour cream and buttered egg noodles.

1	(3½- to 4-pound) boneless beef chuck-eye roast, trimmed and cut into 1½-inch pieces (see the illustrations on page 133)
	Salt and ground black pepper
1	(12-ounce) jar roasted red peppers, drained and rinsed (about 1 cup)
⅓	cup sweet paprika (see note)
2	tablespoons tomato paste
1	tablespoon white vinegar
3	pounds onions (about 6 medium), minced
2	tablespoons vegetable oil
4	carrots, peeled and sliced 1 inch thick
1	bay leaf
1	cup beef broth, warmed

1. Adjust an oven rack to the lower-middle position and heat the oven to 325 degrees. Pat the beef dry with paper towels, season with salt and pepper, and set aside. Process the roasted red peppers, paprika, tomato paste, and 2 teaspoons of the vinegar in a food processor until smooth, 1 to 2 minutes, scraping down the sides as needed.

2. Combine the onions, oil, and 1 teaspoon salt in a large Dutch oven, cover, and cook over medium heat, stirring occasionally, until the onions soften but have not yet begun to brown, 8 to 10 minutes. (If the onions begin to brown, reduce the heat to medium-low and stir in 1 tablespoon water.)

3. Stir in the processed roasted pepper mixture and continue to cook, uncovered, until the onions begin to stick to the bottom of the pan, about

2 minutes. Stir in the beef, carrots, and bay leaf until well coated. Using a rubber spatula, carefully scrape down the sides of the pot. Cover, transfer the pot to the oven, and cook, stirring every 30 minutes, until the meat is mostly tender and the surface of the liquid is ½ inch below the top of the meat, 2 to 2½ hours.

4. Stir in the beef broth until the surface of the liquid measures ¼ inch from the top of the meat (the beef should not be fully submerged). Continue to cook in the oven, covered, until the meat is tender, about 30 minutes longer.

5. Remove the stew from the oven and remove the bay leaf. Defat the braising liquid (see page 65; if necessary, return the defatted liquid to the pot and reheat). Stir in the remaining 1 teaspoon vinegar, season with salt and pepper to taste, and serve. (The goulash can be cooled and refrigerated in an airtight container for up to 2 days. Reheat gently, adding water as needed to loosen its consistency, before serving.)

INGREDIENTS: Beef Broth

Historically we've found beef broths short on beefy flavor, but with a few flavor additives, beef broth can pull off a deeply flavored beef soup or stew. We tasted 13 different beef broths, stocks, and bases to find out which one would suitably stand in for homemade. Generally, you should note the ingredients on the label; we found the best broths had flavor-amplifying ingredients, such as yeast extract and tomato paste, near the top of the list and included concentrated beef stock. Our winner, Rachael Ray Stock-in-a-Box All-Natural Beef Flavored Stock, elicited consistent praise from tasters.

**THE BEST
BEEF BROTH**
Rachael Ray Stock-in-a-Box All-Natural Beef Flavored Stock was described by tasters as having a "steak-y" and "rich" flavor.

RACHEL RAY

PORK STEW WITH FENNEL AND PRUNES

THOUGH LESS COMMON HERE IN THE UNITED States, pork stews are popular in many parts of the world. One of our favorites is a dish from France that combines braised pork with carrots, prunes, brandy, and a touch of cream. The pork is fall-apart tender, its flavor enhanced by the sweetness of the carrots and the prunes, balanced by the savory broth and rich cream sauce—a luxurious blend of flavors and textures. We wanted a satisfying pork stew with a careful balance of savory and sweet.

We already knew from our experience with stewing beef that the shoulder, or chuck, is the best cut for braising, so we assumed that pork shoulder would make the best, most flavorful pork stew. To test this proposition, we stewed various cuts of pork from both the shoulder and loin, including several kinds of chops. The shoulder cuts were indeed far superior to those from the loin. Like beef chuck, pork shoulder has enough fat to keep the meat tender and juicy during the long cooking process. Since the picnic roast, which comes from the shoulder, includes the skin and bone, it means more prep work. We opted for a boneless roast to avoid that extra work, but as with beef, we recommend buying a boneless roast and cutting it into pieces yourself. (You can use a picnic roast, but the bone, skin, and thick layer of fat will need to be removed with a knife and discarded).

So once our boneless pork roast was cut up and seasoned, we browned it to enhance its flavor. After setting aside the meat, we added leeks to the pot, cooking them until they softened, which provided a sweet, aromatic backdrop for the stew and kept with the French flavors of the dish.

Next we moved on to the braising liquid. We needed a full 5 cups of liquid to properly braise the pork and provide ample liquid for serving. Brandy would be the defining flavor of our braising liquid, complemented by chicken broth for a savory element and cream for richness. We knew this would require a careful balancing act. Starting with 1 cup of brandy (enough to generously deglaze the pan and shine through the other ingredients without overwhelming them), we added 2 cups each of the chicken broth and cream. But this was too heavy. And because this stew requires a significant amount of time in the oven, the sweetness of the cream was also now a bit cloying, which in turn dulled the flavor of the brandy. (Like our beef stews, this pork stew is started on the stovetop, but the bulk of the cooking happens in the oven for gentle, all-encompassing heat.) The

obvious fix was to decrease the amount of cream (to 1 cup) and increase the amount of chicken broth (to 3 cups). This was an improvement, but the cream still had that overly sweet, "cooked" flavor. The solution was easy: Holding the cream and adding it at the end of cooking retained its fresh flavor without overpowering the other ingredients.

We already knew prunes and carrots would play an integral role in our stew, but we thought another vegetable might further round out the flavors. We settled on fennel—with its subtle anise notes, it perfectly complemented the other flavors of the stew. Combined with the cream, brandy, and pork, it was a hit. Because fennel and carrots cook at a much faster pace than pork, we added them halfway through cooking so they could coast to the finish line together. The prunes were best added at the very end of cooking to prevent them from breaking down and disintegrating into the stew. And finally, freshly minced tarragon as well as some lemon juice added a welcome complexity and brightness to the finished dish.

PREPARING LEEKS

1. Trim and discard the roots and the dark green leaves.

2. Slice the trimmed leek in half lengthwise, then cut it into ¼-inch pieces.

3. Rinse the cut leeks thoroughly in a bowl of water to remove the dirt and sand.

Pork Stew with Brandy, Fennel, and Prunes

SERVES 6

Boneless pork butt roast is often labeled as boneless Boston butt in the supermarket. While 1 cup of brandy may seem like a lot for this recipe, we recommend using an inexpensive brand and not skimping on the amount; it provides just the right balance of flavors. For best flavor, do not substitute dried tarragon for the fresh.

1	(3½- to 4-pound) boneless pork butt roast, trimmed and cut into 1½-inch pieces
	Salt and ground black pepper
3	tablespoons vegetable oil
1	large leek, white and light green parts only, halved lengthwise, sliced ¼ inch thick, and rinsed thoroughly (see the illustrations at left)
3	medium garlic cloves, minced or pressed through a garlic press (about 1 tablespoon)
3	tablespoons unbleached all-purpose flour
1	cup brandy

3   cups low-sodium chicken broth

2   bay leaves

I   pound carrots (about 6 medium), peeled and
    sliced 1 inch thick

I   large fennel bulb (about 1 pound),
    trimmed of stalks, cored, and cut into
    ½-inch-thick strips (see the illustrations
    on page 38)

I   cup heavy cream

I   cup prunes, halved

2   tablespoons minced fresh tarragon leaves

I   tablespoon juice from 1 lemon

1. Adjust an oven rack to the lower-middle position and heat the oven to 325 degrees. Pat the pork dry with paper towels and season with salt and pepper.

2. Heat 1 tablespoon of the oil in a large Dutch oven over medium-high heat until just smoking. Add half of the pork and brown well on all sides, 7 to 10 minutes; transfer to a large bowl. Repeat with 1 tablespoon more oil and the remaining pork; transfer to the bowl.

3. Add the remaining 1 tablespoon oil to the pot and place over medium heat until shimmering. Add the leek and ¼ teaspoon salt and cook until wilted and lightly browned, 5 to 7 minutes. Stir in the garlic and cook until fragrant, about 30 seconds. Stir in the flour and cook for 1 minute.

4. Slowly whisk in the brandy, scraping up any browned bits. Gradually whisk in the chicken broth, smoothing out any lumps. Stir in the bay leaves and browned pork with any accumulated juice and bring to a simmer. Cover, transfer the pot to the oven, and cook for 1 hour.

5. Stir in the carrots and fennel and continue to cook in the oven, covered, until the meat is tender, about 1 hour longer.

6. Remove the stew from the oven and remove the bay leaves. Using a large spoon, skim any excess fat from the surface of the stew. (The stew can be cooled and refrigerated in an airtight container for up to 2 days. Reheat gently, adding water as needed to loosen its consistency, before continuing.) Stir in the cream and prunes, cover, and let stand for 5 minutes. Stir in the tarragon and lemon juice, season with salt and pepper to taste, and serve.

Brazilian Black Bean and Pork Stew

IN BRAZIL, THERE IS A BLACK BEAN AND PORK stew, known as *feijoada*, that has become so popular it is now considered one of Brazil's national dishes. Espousing the humble attitude of old-world frugality, feijoada originally used up every last bit of the pig, including the feet, ears, tail, and snout—nothing was off-limits. But not only do authentic recipes require a lot of pork, they also require a lot of time and can quickly become a daunting project. We sought a loose interpretation of feijoada using the basic flavor elements—creamy beans and smoky, tender pork—for a hearty but not ho-hum stew.

Typical recipes call for cooking the beans and meat on the stovetop for hours and hours, adjusting the heat as needed to maintain the proper simmer. While these recipes tried to take into account the various cooking times of all the contents of the pot, the result was often overcooked meat, mushy beans, and too much liquid. Luckily, we had a leg up on these recipes from the outset; previous testing had shown us that cooking in the low, slow heat of the oven results in optimally cooked meat stews (with tender meat and creamy beans) that require a lot less attention. We decided to start with the beans, then layer in the other elements of this stew.

Usually we prefer to soak beans in a saltwater solution (or brine them) prior to cooking, as this step softens the tough bean skins and evens out the cooking time so that fewer beans burst open. But a few broken beans wouldn't be a bad thing in this dish; we wanted a somewhat thickened stew and a portion of burst beans would only contribute to this desired consistency. After two hours in the oven, our beans were perfectly tender. The addition of sautéed onion and garlic complemented the earthy flavor of the beans, while some chili powder, cumin, and coriander added fragrance. We also discovered that adding a small amount of baking soda to the beans and water at the beginning of cooking produced a darker, more appealing color.

Now that we had achieved properly cooked and flavorful beans, we focused on selecting the meat. From the beginning, we decided that although many authentic recipes call for a wide assortment of pork products (pig ears, tails, and feet), we wanted to use ingredients that were easy both to find and to cook. With these obscure parts crossed off our list, we took a look at what was left: pork butt, slab bacon, spareribs, pork loins, and numerous varieties of sausages, ham hocks, and salt pork. We ultimately chose a combination of pork products that maintained some tradition but could easily be found and seemed more approachable to cook. We went with a ham hock for smoky flavor, chunks of pork butt for big, meaty bites, and pieces of linguiça, the Portuguese pork sausage, for its potent, garlicky bite.

The challenge now was to figure out how to layer the meat in with the beans so the flavors melded while getting all the elements of the stew to cook at the right rate. We knew it would take the pork about the same amount of time to cook in the oven as the beans, though the sausage wouldn't take nearly as long. With that in mind, we began by browning the pork, which we'd cut into substantial 1½-inch pieces, and cooking the aromatics, then adding the beans and cooking liquid (with so many other flavors in the pot, water was the best choice), and finally placing the pot in the oven. After an hour, we stirred in the sausage and allowed the stew to finish cooking. Tasting our first batch, we found that while the beans and pork were cooked properly after two hours in the oven, the sausage was still drying out. After a few more tests we found that 30 minutes was plenty of time for the sausage to cook and still remain juicy, so we adjusted our timing and added it to the stew later on.

Now that the method and time were settled, we had a new problem on our hands. We noticed that once all the pork and sausage were in the pot, real estate was at a premium. The ham hock, used to add depth and smoky flavor, was now crowding the pot. Could we get the same flavor using chopped bacon rather than the large ham hock? Tasters agreed that although the bacon resulted in a slightly stronger flavor, it got the job done and enabled us to comfortably fit all the meat and beans in the pot.

We had finally arrived at a flavorful yet streamlined black bean and pork stew. The beans were rich and creamy and the pork was tender and juicy. With an easy-to-make fresh Brazilian salsalike hot sauce ready and waiting to be spooned over the top, our hearty stew had the fresh, zesty finish it needed.

Brazilian Black Bean and Pork Stew

SERVES 6

Boneless pork butt roast is often labeled as boneless Boston butt in the supermarket. The baking soda added to the beans helps preserve their dark hue; without it, the beans will turn a muddy, grayish color. Be sure to serve this stew with the hot sauce; it adds important flavor. For more heat, include the jalapeño seeds and ribs when mincing.

STEW

1	(3½- to 4-pound) boneless pork butt roast, trimmed and cut into 1½-inch pieces
	Salt and ground black pepper
3	tablespoons vegetable oil
4	ounces (about 4 slices) bacon, chopped fine
1	medium onion, minced
4	medium garlic cloves, minced or pressed through a garlic press (about 4 teaspoons)
1	tablespoon chili powder
1	teaspoon ground cumin
1	teaspoon ground coriander
7	cups water
1	pound dried black beans, picked over and rinsed
2	bay leaves
⅛	teaspoon baking soda
1	pound linguiça sausage, cut into ½-inch pieces

HOT SAUCE

2	firm, ripe tomatoes, cored, seeded, and chopped fine
1	medium onion, minced
1	small green bell pepper, stemmed, seeded, and chopped fine
1	jalapeño chile, stemmed, seeded, and minced
⅓	cup white wine vinegar
3	tablespoons extra-virgin olive oil
1	tablespoon minced fresh cilantro leaves
½	teaspoon salt

1. FOR THE STEW: Adjust an oven rack to the lower-middle position and heat the oven to

325 degrees. Pat the pork dry with paper towels and season with salt and pepper.

2. Heat 1 tablespoon of the oil in a large Dutch oven over medium-high heat until just smoking. Add half of the pork and brown well on all sides, 7 to 10 minutes; transfer to a large bowl. Repeat with 1 tablespoon more oil and the remaining pork; transfer to the bowl.

3. Add the bacon to the pot and cook over medium heat until rendered and crisp, 5 to 7 minutes. Stir in the remaining 1 tablespoon oil, onion, and ¼ teaspoon salt and cook until the onion is softened, 5 to 7 minutes. Stir in the garlic, chili powder, cumin, and coriander and cook until fragrant, about 30 seconds.

4. Stir in the water, beans, bay leaves, ¼ teaspoon salt, baking soda, and browned pork with any accumulated juice and bring to a simmer. Cover, transfer the pot to the oven, and cook for 1½ hours. Stir in the linguiça and continue to cook in the oven, covered, until the meat and beans are fully tender, about 30 minutes longer.

5. FOR THE HOT SAUCE: Meanwhile, combine all the hot sauce ingredients in a medium bowl and let stand at room temperature until the flavors meld,

about 30 minutes. (The sauce can be refrigerated in an airtight container for up to 2 days.)

6. Remove the stew from the oven and remove the bay leaves. Season with salt and pepper to taste and serve with the hot sauce. (The stew can be cooled and refrigerated in an airtight container for up to 2 days. Reheat gently, adding water as needed to loosen its consistency, before serving.)

CLASSIC CHICKEN STEW WITH WINTER VEGETABLES

WHEN WE THINK OF CHICKEN STEW, WE imagine tender, moist chunks of chicken, accompanied by potatoes, carrots, and peas, all enveloped in a glossy, flavorful, thick sauce—the kind of supper our grandmothers would slave over when we were kids. Now that we're adults, we think a bowl of chicken stew should be every bit as hearty and comforting, but it shouldn't require a whole day spent in the kitchen. There had to be a quicker, but just as flavorful, way.

Researching chicken stew, we uncovered a variety of recipes with a range of complexity. Some started with a whole chicken that was cut up, browned, and then simmered in water to make broth. The liquid was then strained and the meat was removed from the bones before composing the rest of the stew. The results were pretty tasty, but this seemed like an excessive amount of work (and time). On the other end of the spectrum were recipes that simply poached cubed, boneless, skinless breasts and some vegetables in a quick "sauce" made of canned soup. These versions tasted like bad cafeteria food. We knew more simmering time would be needed to develop the rich flavor we were after. We decided to go for the middle ground.

Given our experience with stews, and having prepared a number of research recipes, we suspected the method would go something like this: Brown the chicken, remove it from the pan, build a sauce with the fond (the browned bits left from the chicken) and aromatics (onion and garlic), deglaze

---

EQUIPMENT: Chef's Knives

We ask a lot of chef's knives in the test kitchen. They have to be versatile enough to handle almost any cutting task, whether cutting tomatoes for salsa or slicing through meat and bones. The blade has to be sharp and slice easily with minimal force behind it, and the handle has to be comfortable and not get slippery when wet. We've tested many knives in recent years, and we keep coming back to the Victorinox (formerly Victorinox Forschner) Fibrox 8-Inch Chef's Knife. This knife is lightweight, has a blade that's just the right length (8 inches), and has a comfortable grip and nonslip handle (useful for cutting up messy chicken parts).

THE BEST CHEF'S KNIFE
The Victorinox Fibrox 8-Inch Chef's Knife ($24.95) has a comfortable grip and sharp blade.

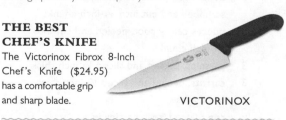

VICTORINOX

the pan with broth, and return the chicken along with vegetables to simmer in the flavorful broth until tender. Seeing as a whole chicken provided so much flavor, we started there. We cut a chicken into small pieces, browned it, made a simple sauce (we could refine the flavors later), and simmered away. But we quickly encountered several problems. The breasts cooked through more quickly than the thighs and drumsticks and became dried out, bland, and stringy—a far cry from the tender pieces of stew meat we had envisioned. But the dark meat, the thighs and drumsticks, produced wonderfully tender chunks of meat—perfect for stew.

We made the stew again using whole chicken legs, but this time it was clear that tasters preferred the meatier thighs to the drumsticks. However, they found the bones undesirable (and unattractive) in the finished stew. To remedy this, we tried removing the meat from the bones at the end of cooking and shredding it into large pieces. This made great-tasting stew, but fussing with the meat and bones was time-consuming and messy. Maybe we could save time by getting rid of the bones altogether and using boneless thighs that we cut into small pieces prior to cooking. This was a win-win situation: Tasters thought the stew tasted just as good and we liked the easy, streamlined process.

Now we could refine the cooking method. Chicken stew, we were finding, is best when it is gently simmered, which is easiest to do in a low oven. On the stovetop, the cooking time varied and even though we set the flame at the same heat level every time, the heat transfer was not uniform, leading to burnt pots. Stewing in a 300-degree oven was much more reliable, producing a predictably even, consistent level of heat. After 30 minutes in the oven, the thighs were cooked through and no longer pink. Unfortunately, they were not as tender as we wanted. After gradually increasing the cooking time, we ended up keeping the dish in the oven for about an hour. At this point, the meat was exceedingly tender and flavorful. During the longer stay in the oven the heat breaks down the connective tissue in the thighs, much as it does in a pot roast, yielding more tender meat. (White meat, on the other hand, contains little connective tissue,

so there's no benefit to cooking it longer—in fact, cooking white meat longer will result in drier, rubbery meat.)

Finally we could consider the other flavors and ingredients in our stew. Carrots and potatoes are classic additions, and tasters gave each one a thumbs-up. Other root vegetables also work well in hearty stews, so we chose to add parsnips and celery root to provide complexity of flavor and texture. Some white wine, added to the sauce, contributed an acidic note to an otherwise hearty flavor profile, and a bit of fresh thyme added depth. With a sprinkling of fresh parsley at the end, we had our ideal comfort food—a rich, satisfying stew that didn't take all day to make.

Classic Chicken Stew with Winter Vegetables
SERVES 6 TO 8

Do not substitute boneless, skinless chicken breasts for the thighs in this recipe. Turnips, rutabagas, or parsley root can be substituted for the carrots, celery root, or parsnips if desired.

3	pounds boneless chicken thighs (about 12 thighs), trimmed and cut into 1-inch pieces (see note)
	Salt and ground black pepper
3	tablespoons vegetable oil
2	medium onions, minced
4	medium garlic cloves, minced or pressed through a garlic press (about 4 teaspoons)
1	teaspoon minced fresh thyme leaves or ¼ teaspoon dried
¼	cup unbleached all-purpose flour
½	cup dry white wine
3½	cups low-sodium chicken broth
8	ounces red potatoes (about 2 medium), scrubbed and cut into ¾-inch chunks
8	ounces celery root, peeled and cut into ¾-inch chunks
3	parsnips, peeled and sliced ½ inch thick
3	carrots, peeled and sliced ½ inch thick
2	bay leaves
¼	cup minced fresh parsley leaves

1. Adjust an oven rack to the lower-middle position and heat the oven to 300 degrees. Pat the chicken dry with paper towels and season with salt and pepper.

2. Heat 1 tablespoon of the oil in a large Dutch oven over medium-high heat until just smoking. Add half of the chicken and brown lightly, 6 to 8 minutes; transfer to a large bowl. Repeat with 1 tablespoon more oil and the remaining chicken; transfer to the bowl.

3. Add the remaining 1 tablespoon oil to the pot and heat over medium heat until shimmering. Add the onions and ¼ teaspoon salt and cook until softened, 5 to 7 minutes. Stir in the garlic and thyme and cook until fragrant, about 30 seconds. Stir in the flour and cook for 1 minute. Stir in the wine, scraping up any browned bits.

4. Gradually whisk in the broth, smoothing out any lumps. Stir in the potatoes, celery root, parsnips, carrots, bay leaves, and browned chicken with any accumulated juice and bring to a simmer. Cover, transfer the pot to the oven, and cook until the chicken is very tender, 50 to 60 minutes.

5. Remove the pot from the oven and remove the bay leaves. Stir in the parsley, season with salt and pepper to taste, and serve. (The stew can be cooled and refrigerated in an airtight container for up to 2 days. Reheat gently, adding water as needed to loosen its consistency, before serving.)

CREOLE-STYLE GUMBO

PEEK INTO A POT OF GUMBO AND YOU'LL SEE the influence of the many groups who have settled in New Orleans. The base, a roux, arrived with the French; smoked sausage was brought by Germans and Acadians (from northeastern Canada); and the peppers that give gumbo its kick tagged along with the Spanish. Okra came from Africa and ground sassafras (filé powder) was used by Native Americans. Many Louisiana natives fondly remember waking up to the smell of roux (usually flour and lard), which the cook would stir over low heat until it was chocolate-colored. Aromatic vegetables were stirred in, then homemade fish or meat stock, and finally the meat: poultry, sausage, game, and seafood are all traditional. The process takes the better part of an afternoon—but time is not gumbo's only problem. There's also what New Orleans chef Paul Prudhomme refers to as "Cajun napalm."

To understand Prudhomme's comment, it helps to know how roux is prepared. It's made by cooking equal parts fat and flour until colored. Light roux is the base of many cheese sauces and gravies, but dark roux is used almost exclusively in Cajun and Creole cooking. To achieve the requisite deep, dark brown color and toasted flavor, the flour and fat (usually vegetable oil today) are cooked over low heat for a bare minimum of 30 minutes. To avoid burning the flour, the cook needs to stir constantly—but even over low heat, temperatures in the pot can reach 500 degrees, making any splattering a dangerous prospect. Worse, after a steady hour of slow stirring, the roux can go from toasty brown to burnt in seconds. We wanted to find an easier, safer, quicker way to make gumbo at home.

Our testing started with a handful of recipes for "faster" roux. Those that didn't give the roux time to darken made for insipid gumbo. Others, like Prudhomme's version, turned up the heat to accelerate the process, with explosive and scary results. We did find one recipe, though, that offered the promise of both ease and safety. Three-quarters cup each of flour and vegetable oil were mixed together in a large pot and moved to a 350-degree oven to cook—sans stirring—for just under two hours. This hands-off roux sounded too good to be true, but we had to try it. The same recipe called for homemade shrimp stock; while we ultimately hoped to avoid such a time-consuming step, we wanted to understand its flavor contribution to the gumbo, so we decided to stick with it for now. We peeled a pound of shrimp and simmered the shells with onion and peppercorns. When it was time to check on the roux, we were delighted to discover that it looked (and smelled) perfect. The closed lid and gentle heat had provided the perfect no-stir environment for the roux to brown. How would it hold up in the gumbo? We'd soon find out.

Traditional gumbos start with sautéing chopped onion, celery, green bell pepper, and garlic in the dark roux. The stock is added next, followed by the chicken (we preferred thighs here for their flavor). Tomatoes and okra are controversial additions to gumbo in Louisiana—gumbo lovers are passionately for or against. We decided to include both. Stirring in the spicy andouille sausage, okra, and shrimp at the end kept them from overcooking. When the gumbo was done, tasters were amazed at the rich, toasty, silky taste. The only downside: It wasn't as speedy as we'd hoped.

Cranking up the oven temperature shortened the cooking time, but at a cost: The roux required stirring or it scorched. Jump-starting the roux on the stovetop before transferring it to the oven would require high heat and constant stirring, so we ruled it out. What about toasting just the flour in a dry pot on the stove? After five minutes (yes, we had to stir) the flour began to brown, so we added the oil and put the pot in the oven. Forty-five minutes later, the roux was beautifully dark brown—but how would it taste? We added everything to the pot and waited anxiously as it finished cooking. Success! Our gumbo had the toasted, smoky flavor of a long-cooked roux and, its 45-minute cooking time gave us a perfect window to prepare the other ingredients. We fine-tuned the roux, which was a tad thin and greasy, by cutting back the oil by ¼ cup and adding an extra tablespoon of flour with the vegetables.

One sticking point remained: the homemade shrimp stock. We switched to store-bought chicken broth, but not surprisingly, tasters complained that it lacked the rich, briny depth of the shrimp stock. Would mixing the broth with clam juice do the trick? Nope—the resulting liquid also lacked complexity and punch. We needed something to enhance the shrimp flavor. Thinking of all the possibilities we suddenly had an idea we hoped just might be crazy enough to work: adding Asian fish sauce, which is complex, intensely flavored, and made from fish. We snuck some into our next batch without telling tasters, and they unanimously agreed that this gumbo was the best yet; the fish sauce added briny depth without being identifiable. Sure, some may view it as heretical to authentic gumbo. We prefer to look at it as yet another culture stirred in to an already diverse pot.

Creole-Style Gumbo
SERVES 6 TO 8

Fish sauce is an important flavoring in this stew; do not omit it. The roux cooking time in step 2 may be longer depending on the type of pot you use; the color of the finished roux should be that of an old, dark copper penny.

¾	cup plus 1 tablespoon unbleached all-purpose flour
½	cup vegetable oil
1	medium onion, minced
1	green bell pepper, stemmed, seeded, and chopped medium (see the illustrations on page 226)
1	celery rib, chopped fine
5	medium garlic cloves, minced or pressed through a garlic press (about 5 teaspoons)
1	teaspoon minced fresh thyme or ¼ teaspoon dried
¼	teaspoon cayenne pepper
1	(14.5-ounce) can diced tomatoes, drained
3¾	cups low-sodium chicken broth
¼	cup fish sauce (see note)
2	pounds bone-in chicken thighs (about 6 thighs), skin removed and trimmed Salt and ground black pepper
8	ounces andouille sausage, halved lengthwise and sliced ¼ inch thick
2	cups frozen okra, thawed (optional)
2	pounds extra-large shrimp (21 to 25 per pound), peeled and deveined (see the illustration on page 145)

1. Adjust an oven rack to the lowest position and heat the oven to 350 degrees. Toast ¾ cup of the flour in a large Dutch oven over medium heat, stirring constantly, until it just begins to brown, about 5 minutes.

2. Off the heat, whisk in the oil until smooth. Cover the pot, transfer it to the oven, and cook until the mixture is deep brown and fragrant, about 45 minutes. Remove the pot from the oven and whisk the roux to combine.

3. Stir the onion, bell pepper, and celery into the hot roux and cook over medium heat, stirring often,

until the vegetables are softened, about 10 minutes. Stir in the remaining 1 tablespoon flour, garlic, thyme, and cayenne and cook until fragrant, about 1 minute. Stir in the tomatoes and cook until they look dry, about 1 minute. Gradually stir in the broth and fish sauce, scraping up any browned bits and smoothing out any lumps.

4. Season the chicken with pepper, add it to the pot, and bring to a boil. Cover, reduce to a gentle simmer, and cook until the chicken is cooked through and tender, about 40 minutes.

5. Skim any fat that has collected on the top. Transfer the chicken to a plate, let it cool slightly, then shred into bite-size pieces, following the illustration on page 75, discarding the bones. Stir the shredded chicken, sausage, and okra (if using) into the stew, return to a simmer, and allow to heat through, about 5 minutes.

6. Stir in the shrimp and continue to simmer until cooked through, about 5 minutes. Season the gumbo with salt and pepper to taste and serve. (The gumbo can be cooled and refrigerated in an airtight container for up to 2 days. Reheat gently, adding water as needed to loosen its consistency, before serving.)

DEVEINING SHRIMP

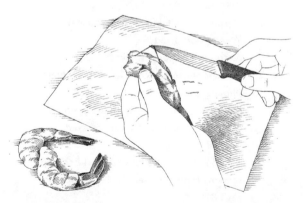

Hold the peeled shrimp between your thumb and forefinger and cut down the length of its back, about ⅛ to ¼ inch deep, with a sharp paring knife. If the shrimp has a vein, it will be exposed and can be pulled out easily. Once you have freed the vein with the tip of a paring knife, just touch the knife to a paper towel and the vein will slip off the knife and stick to the towel.

CIOPPINO

CIOPPINO IS A SAN FRANCISCO SEAFOOD STEW with roots that stretch to the shores of northern Italian fishing communities, where tomato and seafood stew was known as *ciuppin*. Bay Area lore is brimming with tales of Italian fishermen simmering the rich, red stew aboard small fishing boats as they headed back through the Golden Gate. On shore, cioppino was among the first signature dishes served in the city's earliest restaurants at Fisherman's Wharf.

As with many regional dishes, there is no one recipe for cioppino. Ingredients and technique vary radically among recipes. In fact, the stew is more a concept than a combination of specific ingredients. In our research, only one common thread surfaced—the stewing liquid is based on tomatoes. The rest of the ingredients depended entirely on the sea's daily bounty and the personal taste of the recipe's author. Armed with a collection of extremely different recipes, we set out to develop a streamlined cioppino recipe that any seafood lover could enjoy.

It soon became clear that many of the recipes, especially those from popular cookbooks, were unnecessarily complicated. Most boasted long lists of fish, shellfish, and aromatics, and had intricate and somewhat troublesome techniques for a stew that was said to have been "thrown together" on fishing boats and piers. Digging further and into more obscure territory, we turned up simpler, more straightforward recipes. These recipes were more appealing to us. We decided to make cioppino as simple as possible; consequently, we decided to eliminate fish stock and fillets from our cioppino and concentrate on quick-cooking shellfish.

The simpler, more homespun recipes we uncovered had their own problems—a handful called for every dried herb imaginable and some were nothing more than tomatoes and fish. We knew we wanted something fresher-tasting and more complex than fish in tomato sauce. We found four recipes that looked promising and got to work.

Three of the four contenders were universally panned. The procedures, while not difficult, proved to be time-consuming. And with overly thick sauces, it was nearly impossible to submerge and evenly cook the seafood. Tasters commented that these stews contained too many ingredients; they had to "fight their way" through them. And the extraneous ingredients—such as green peppers, leeks, carrots, and celery—competed entirely too much with the stew's tomato and seafood flavors.

These three recipes also called for native San Francisco Dungeness crabs. We did secure some of these crabs by mail order, but tasters actually found them extremely hard to eat in a stew and voted them out. For our shellfish, then, we settled on clams, mussels, shrimp, and scallops.

Of the four initial test recipes, one stood at the fore. It was a simple recipe that yielded a buttery, sweet tomato broth studded with a bounty of seafood—no excessive or unwanted embellishments. Aromatics included only garlic (of which tasters wanted more), onions, and parsley. The surprise ingredient was butter, which added a luxurious richness to the flavor and texture of the stew. With more testing, we found the butter was best incorporated at the outset so it had time to emulsify and blend with other ingredients, so we decided to sauté the aromatics in a combination of butter and oil.

Up to this point, we had been using store-bought chicken broth, along with clam juice and canned tomatoes, to make the liquid. The chicken broth now seemed out of place and we wondered: was it really necessary? We eliminated the chicken broth and were pleased to find that a simple combination of tomatoes and bottled clam juice tasted best. But with a relatively small amount of liquid in the pot, we were having a hard time properly cooking the seafood. We decided to try steaming open the clams and mussels in a combination of water and white wine before building the soup so we could use their juices as part of the broth. This preemptive step did the trick. The shrimp and scallops were best cooked at the last minute, right in the cioppino broth.

Next we concentrated on the garlic, the heat, and the herbs. Tasters wanted more of everything. We eventually settled on six cloves of garlic. We upped the heat by adding red pepper flakes to the sautéing onions and garlic in small increments until tasters cried uncle. As for herbs, fresh oregano and thyme

were favored over parsley and complemented the stew's basic flavors. Seasoned with a healthy amount of salt and pepper, the broth had arrived. It was rich and tomatoey, garlicky, with strong herbal accents and a good dose of heat. Best of all, this seafood stew can be on the table in less than one hour.

Cioppino
SERVES 6 TO 8

Note that this stew comes together rather quickly, so be sure to have all the ingredients prepped and ready to go before you begin cooking. Serve with crusty bread or Garlic Toasts (page 152).

1	cup dry white wine or dry vermouth
¾	cup water
24	littleneck clams, scrubbed (see the illustration on page 88)
24	mussels, scrubbed and debearded (see the illustration on page 147)
6	tablespoons extra-virgin olive oil
2	tablespoons unsalted butter
1	medium onion, chopped medium
6	medium garlic cloves, minced or pressed through a garlic press (about 2 tablespoons)
1	teaspoon minced fresh thyme leaves or ¼ teaspoon dried
1	teaspoon minced fresh oregano leaves or ¼ teaspoon dried
½	teaspoon red pepper flakes
2	tablespoons unbleached all-purpose flour
1	(8-ounce) bottle clam juice
1	(28-ounce) can whole tomatoes, tomatoes chopped medium and juice reserved
1	bay leaf
1	pound large sea scallops (10 to 12 scallops), tendons removed (see the illustration on page 81)
1	pound large shrimp (31 to 40 per pound), peeled and deveined (see the illustration on page 145)
	Salt and ground black pepper

1. Bring the wine and water to a boil in a large Dutch oven. Add the clams, cover, and cook for 3 minutes. Stir in the mussels, cover, and cook until

the clams and mussels have just begun to open, 2 to 4 minutes longer. As the clams and mussels open, transfer them to a large bowl. Discard any unopened clams or mussels.

2. Measure out and reserve 2½ cups of the steaming liquid, avoiding any gritty sediment that has settled on the bottom of the pot. (You should have about 2½ cups of broth; if not, add water.) Rinse and dry the pot.

3. Add the oil and butter to the pot and place over medium heat until the butter has melted. Add the onion and cook until softened, 5 to 7 minutes. Stir in the garlic, thyme, oregano, and red pepper flakes and cook until fragrant, about 30 seconds. Stir in the flour and cook for 1 minute.

4. Gradually whisk in the reserved steaming liquid and bottled clam juice, smoothing out any lumps. Stir in the tomatoes with their juice and bay leaf and bring to a boil. Reduce to a gentle simmer and cook until thickened and the flavors meld, about 20 minutes.

5. Stir in the scallops and continue to simmer gently until they are nearly cooked through, about 3 minutes. Stir in the shrimp and sprinkle the cooked clams and mussels over the top. Cover and continue to simmer gently until the shrimp are bright pink and the scallops are milky white, 1 to 2 minutes. Remove the bay leaf. Season with salt and pepper to taste and serve in wide, shallow bowls.

CLEANING MUSSELS

Mussels often contain a weedy beard protruding from the crack between the two shells. It's fairly small and can be difficult to tug out of place. We have found the flat surface of a knife gives some leverage to help remove the pesky beard. Trap the beard between the side of a small paring knife and your thumb and pull to remove it.

TEN-VEGETABLE STEW

GREAT VEGETABLE STEWS MARRY HEARTY vegetables with a richly flavored broth and herbs or spices that complement the vegetables. But all too often, they are little more than a jumble of soggy vegetables devoid of color and flavor. We wanted a hearty, flavorful vegetable stew, one that could be as soul-satisfying in the dead of winter as a beef stew. To get there, we'd need to figure out the best way to build flavor (minus the meat) and determine just which combination of vegetables works best together.

To start, we worked on developing a great base of flavor. We selected a number of aromatics—onion, carrot, celery, and bell pepper—and sautéed them until brown to coax out their natural sweetness. Garlic, thyme, and tomato paste contributed further depth and a little flour would help thicken our stew once the liquid was added. At this point, a little bit of flavorful fond had built up, so we deglazed the pot with wine, which picked up the browned bits and added complexity at the same time. We tried red wine first, but it overpowered the vegetables. White wine proved to be a much better choice, adding brightness, a slight acidity, and depth all at once. After the wine reduced, we were ready to add the other liquid components.

We began our testing with vegetable broth and water. Vegetable broth alone can be overly sweet and since our stew would include a number of vegetables (many of which are naturally sweet), we knew that cutting the broth with water would be necessary. Ultimately, a ratio of nearly equal parts vegetable broth and water proved best.

Now for the real hurdle: What vegetables should be featured in our stew? In many recipes, root vegetables are a major component, not just for their earthy flavor but also because their starch acts as a thickener and gives the stew a rich consistency. We selected a variety of root vegetables and worked our way through them. Carrots made the stew too sweet (and we were already using them for an aromatic), turnips proved to be slightly bitter, and sweet potatoes fell apart during cooking. In the end, we preferred red potatoes, parsnips, and celery root. The red potatoes and celery root held their shape after the long simmering time and added some heartiness, and the parsnips contributed sweet yet earthy flavor. The size we cut these vegetables proved key—too small and they disappeared into the stew, too large and they didn't cook through. In the end, 1-inch pieces were just right.

In addition to the root vegetables, we also wanted to include greens for contrast. Tasters liked both kale and spinach, but the real winner was Swiss chard, which tastes earthy but is still somewhat delicate. We utilized both the stems and leaves, sautéing the stems with the aromatics and the leaves toward the end of the cooking to ensure they didn't disintegrate. However, in spite of our best attempts, the stew was still falling a little short.

In most stews, meat provides substance. But since we were after a vegetarian stew, that wasn't an option here. Mushrooms are a common addition to stews (vegetarian or not), as they are meaty and rich. We decided to give them a shot here. We tried portobellos first, but even with just one small mushroom in the pot, its bold, earthy flavor dominated in a way that tasters disliked. We found that white button mushrooms, the supermarket standard, worked much better. To intensify their flavor and rid them of excess liquid that could water down our stew, we sautéed them first until they

released their juice and then browned them. This, combined with our aromatics, created an especially rich, flavorful fond.

Tasters approved of our mushroom-enriched vegetable stew, but were now begging for a touch of freshness and acidity. Summery zucchini added with the chard leaves at the end of cooking contrasted nicely with the long-cooked vegetables, and a splash of lemon juice and a sprinkle of minced parsley perked up the stew's flavors. At last, we had a vegetable stew that was undeniably hearty (we had managed to squeeze in a whopping 10 vegetables!) and full of flavor.

Hearty Ten-Vegetable Stew
SERVES 6 TO 8

Kale greens or curly-leaf spinach, stemmed and sliced ½ inch thick, can be substituted for the chard leaves (omit the stems); the kale may require up to 5 minutes of additional simmering time in step 5 to become tender.

2	tablespoons vegetable oil
I	pound white mushrooms, wiped clean, trimmed, and sliced thin
	Salt and ground black pepper
½	large bunch Swiss chard (about 8 ounces), stems and leaves separated, stems chopped fine, and leaves sliced ½ inch thick (see the illustrations on page 150)
2	medium onions, minced
I	celery rib, cut into ½-inch pieces
I	carrot, peeled and cut into 1-inch pieces
I	red bell pepper, stemmed, seeded, and cut into ½-inch pieces (see the illustrations on page 226)
6	medium garlic cloves, minced or pressed through a garlic press (about 2 tablespoons)
2	teaspoons minced fresh thyme leaves or ¾ teaspoon dried
2	tablespoons unbleached all-purpose flour

SEEDING ZUCCHINI

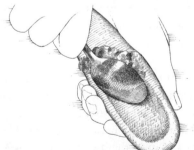

Halve the zucchini lengthwise. Run a small spoon inside each zucchini half to scoop out the seeds.

1 tablespoon tomato paste

½ cup dry white wine

3 cups vegetable broth

2½ cups water

8 ounces red potatoes (about 2 medium), scrubbed and cut into 1-inch pieces

2 parsnips, peeled and cut into 1-inch pieces

8 ounces celery root, peeled and cut into 1-inch pieces

2 bay leaves

1 medium zucchini (about 8 ounces), halved lengthwise, seeded (see the illustration on page 148), and cut into ½-inch pieces

¼ cup minced fresh parsley leaves

1 tablespoon juice from 1 lemon

1. Heat 1 tablespoon of the oil in a large Dutch oven over medium heat until shimmering. Add the mushrooms and ¼ teaspoon salt, cover, and cook until the mushrooms have released their liquid, about 5 minutes. Uncover and continue to cook until the mushrooms are dry and browned, 5 to 10 minutes.

2. Stir in the remaining 1 tablespoon oil, chard stems, onions, celery, carrot, and bell pepper and cook until the vegetables are well browned, 7 to 10 minutes.

3. Stir in the garlic and thyme and cook until fragrant, about 30 seconds. Stir in the flour and tomato paste and cook for 1 minute. Stir in the wine, scraping up the browned bits, and cook until nearly evaporated, about 1 minute.

4. Stir in the broth, water, potatoes, parsnips, celery root, and bay leaves and bring to a boil. Reduce to a gentle simmer, cover the pot partially (leaving about 1 inch of the pot open), and cook until the stew is thickened and the vegetables are tender, about 1 hour. (At this point, the stew can be cooled and refrigerated in an airtight container for up to 2 days. Reheat gently, adding water as needed to loosen its consistency, before continuing.)

5. Stir in the zucchini and chard leaves and continue to simmer until they are just tender, 5 to 10 minutes. Off the heat, remove the bay leaves and stir in the parsley and lemon juice. Season with salt and pepper to taste and serve.

North African Vegetable and Bean Stew

TOO OFTEN, VEGETABLE STEWS LACK THE depth, complexity, and richness of their meat-laden counterparts. But that's not true of stews that are inspired by North African cuisine. The combination of heady, potent spices and hearty, filling vegetables and beans is one that rarely leaves diners hungry. We set out to create a rich-tasting, satisfying vegetable stew in the manner of Moroccan and Tunisian cookery, one that featured a spicy, tomatoey base studded with a balanced selection of leafy and hearty vegetables, meaty beans, and bites of pasta.

We started by testing a number of recipes to determine what we liked best. While they varied widely, almost all delivered on their promise of unique, deep flavors and satisfying textures. Unfortunately, along with great flavor came the difficulty of finding ingredients, such as *harissa* and *ras el hanout*. In addition, many stews required soaking a variety of dried beans or making fresh pasta. We decided to start with our established method for stews (sautéing aromatics and spices, adding broth and cooking vegetables, beans, or pasta, and finishing with flavorful garnishes) and choose appropriate substitutions along the way. We started at the heart of North African cuisine—the spices.

Ras el hanout is a proprietary blend of a spice seller's top spices. Although ras el hanout can vary considerably from store to store, it often includes cinnamon, paprika, nutmeg, cardamom, cumin, and coriander. Given its relative obscurity stateside, and the fact that when you do find it there's no way to know how long it has been on the shelves, we decided to make our own. To test a few different blends, we cobbled together a working recipe for our stew. First, we softened an onion in olive oil, then added a test batch of ras el hanout and a few cloves of garlic. Next, we stirred in a little flour to add body and thickness. Once the spices became fragrant and the flour had lost its raw flavor, we stirred in vegetable broth and simmered the mixture for 20 minutes. Using this method, we tested and tasted a dozen different combinations of spices—some containing every traditional spice and others featuring just a few. Tasters overwhelmingly preferred mixes that contained a modest list of spices, as these produced a cleaner-tasting broth. In the end, cumin, paprika, coriander, and cinnamon proved the winners, offering a warm, complex array of flavors. Next, we tackled the "meat" of our stew.

The recipes we tested contained a large mix of vegetables, beans, and pastas. Our favorites, unfortunately, contained the most labor-intensive ingredients, including dried chickpeas and dried butter beans (lima beans), fresh pasta, and a laundry list of vegetables. Since our stew would also feature beans and pasta, we limited the number of vegetables in the pot. Tomatoes were a given, and for a hearty green, we settled on Swiss chard. We also liked the sweetness contributed by a couple of carrots. We chose to sauté the chopped chard stems with the onion and add the greens toward the end of cooking in order to obtain the best flavor and texture from both. We liked the carrots cut into ½-inch pieces, as they retained some bite and didn't disintegrate into the stew. While tasters appreciated the texture of the carrots and chard, they didn't care for chunks of tomato in the final stew. Wishing to the keep the tomato flavor but ditch the chunks, we tried switching to tomato paste. By stirring in a full 2 tablespoons of paste before adding the broth, we got just the rich tomato flavor we were after.

Next, we set about determining the best way to incorporate the beans and pasta.

Beans play an important role in North African vegetable stews, as they provide much of the protein and hearty texture associated with meat. The most traditional stews we tasted featured both chickpeas and butter beans, which offered a balance of bite, earthiness, and creaminess. With convenience in mind, we settled on canned chickpeas and canned butter beans.

While handmade pasta may be de rigueur in North African cooking, it's a bit more work than we had in mind. We opted for convenience again, looking to dried pasta and experimenting with shapes and sizes. Most of the traditional stews we tasted featured thin, short noodles, but tasters found them difficult to scoop up with a spoon. Instead, they liked smaller, shorter shapes, especially ditalini. With a hearty vegetable and bean stew on the stove, we focused on one last challenging ingredient.

Harissa, like ras el hanout, is a ubiquitous North African ingredient. It's essentially a spicy paste of ground chiles, cumin, coriander, garlic, and olive oil. From using the paste in previous recipes, we knew that heat levels vary among different brands of harissa, so we decided to make our own. We spooned our harissa into the stew until tasters were satisfied with both the heat and spice levels, reserving the rest for diners to add to their bowls. A final shower of parsley provided a dose of freshness to our boldly flavored North African stew.

PREPARING KALE, SWISS CHARD, OR BOK CHOY

1. Cut away the leafy green portion from either side of the stalk or stem using a chef's knife.

2. Stack several leaves on top of one another and either slice the leaves crosswise or chop into pieces (as directed in the recipe). Wash and dry the leaves after they are cut, using a salad spinner.

3. If including the stalks or stems, wash them thoroughly, then trim and cut them into small pieces as directed in the recipe.

North African Vegetable and Bean Stew

SERVES 6 TO 8

You can substitute one 10-ounce bag frozen baby lima beans for the butter beans. Also, you can substitute store-bought harissa if you wish, but be aware that spiciness can vary greatly by brand.

HARISSA

5	tablespoons extra-virgin olive oil
1½	tablespoons sweet paprika
4	medium garlic cloves, minced or pressed through a garlic press (about 4 teaspoons)
2	teaspoons ground coriander
¾	teaspoon ground cumin
¼	teaspoon cayenne pepper
⅛	teaspoon salt

STEW

1	tablespoon extra-virgin olive oil
1	medium onion, minced
½	large bunch Swiss chard (about 8 ounces), stems and leaves separated, stems chopped fine, and leaves sliced ½ inch thick (see the illustrations on page 150)
4	medium garlic cloves, minced or pressed through a garlic press (about 4 teaspoons)
1	teaspoon ground cumin
½	teaspoon sweet paprika
½	teaspoon ground coriander
¼	teaspoon ground cinnamon
2	tablespoons tomato paste
2	tablespoons unbleached all-purpose flour
7	cups vegetable broth
2	carrots, peeled and cut into ½-inch pieces
1	(15-ounce) can chickpeas, drained and rinsed
1	(15-ounce) can butter beans, drained and rinsed
½	cup ditalini
⅓	cup minced fresh parsley leaves
	Salt and ground black pepper

1. **FOR THE HARISSA:** Combine all the ingredients in a medium bowl and microwave on high power until bubbling and fragrant, 15 to 30 seconds. Set aside to cool.

2. **FOR THE STEW:** Heat the oil in a large Dutch oven over medium heat until shimmering. Add the onion and chard stems and cook until softened, 5 to 7 minutes. Stir in the garlic, cumin, paprika, coriander, and cinnamon and cook until fragrant, about 30 seconds. Stir in the tomato paste and flour and cook for 1 minute.

3. Stir in the broth, scraping up any browned bits and smoothing out any lumps. Stir in the carrots and bring to a boil. Reduce to a gentle simmer and cook for 10 minutes. Stir in the chard leaves, chickpeas, butter beans, and pasta and continue to simmer until the vegetables and pasta are tender, 10 to 15 minutes longer.

4. Off the heat, stir in the parsley and ¼ cup of the harissa. Season with salt and pepper to taste and serve, passing the remaining harissa separately.

HEARTY TUSCAN WHITE BEAN STEW

WHITE BEANS PLAY A STARRING ROLE IN innumerable soups and stews, but one of our favorites is Tuscan white bean stew, which boasts creamy beans in a light, velvety broth. Cannellini are the region's most famous legume, and Tuscan cooks go to extremes to ensure these beans cook up tender every time. Simmering the cannellini in rainwater to produce an almost buttery texture is not uncommon, and putting the beans in an empty wine bottle to slow-cook overnight in a fire's dying embers is not unheard of. We set out to make a hearty version of classic Tuscan white bean stew as good as what we'd find in Italy, but we hoped to ditch the fire and rainwater in favor of a more practical approach.

The first task was to sort through all the contradictory advice given for dried-bean cookery. We began with the most hotly contested issue: how long to soak the beans before cooking. Some recipes swear that a lengthy soak leads to beans with a more tender, uniform texture. Others insist that a quick soak—an hour-long rest off the stove covered with just-boiled water—is best. In the past, our own research has shown that no soak at all can sometimes be the way to go too.

To judge for ourselves, we cooked up batches of beans using all three approaches. We found relatively minor differences, the biggest being cooking time: The no-soak beans took 45 minutes longer to soften fully than the beans soaked by the other two methods. Since the beans soaked overnight were, in fact, the most tender and evenly cooked of the bunch and had the least number of exploded beans, that's the method we settled on.

While the beans' interiors were creamy, their skins remained tough. Like length of soaking, when to add salt is a much-debated topic in bean cookery. As beans cook, their starch granules swell with water, softening to a creamy texture and eventually bursting. Adding salt to the cooking water causes the starch granules to swell less, so that fewer reach the point of bursting. But because the beans have a lot of starch granules still intact, the resulting texture is usually described as either mealy or gritty.

Though the texture of the beans cooked in salted water was inferior, their skins were exactly what we wanted: soft and pliable. Was there a different way to use salt to get the same effect? Our

thoughts turned to brining, which we use in the test kitchen to help meat remain moist during cooking. Over the years, we've brined everything from poultry and pork to beef and shrimp. We had a hunch it might work with beans too, so we made a brine by dissolving a few tablespoons of salt in water and left the beans to soak overnight in the solution. Our experiment was a success: The cannellini now boasted tender, almost imperceptible skins with interiors that were buttery soft. As it turns out, when beans are soaked in salted water, rather than being cooked in it, not as much salt enters the beans. Its impact is confined mainly to the skins, creating a softer texture.

However, there were still quite a few exploded beans in the pot. Usually the culprit is vigorously bubbling cooking liquid, so we would need to simmer the beans very gently. Thinking back to the Tuscan technique of cooking beans overnight in a dying fire, we wondered if we might simply try cooking our beans in the oven. In our next test, we brought the beans and water to a simmer on the stovetop, then covered the pot and placed it in a 250-degree oven. This method required a little more time but it worked beautifully, producing perfectly cooked beans that stayed intact.

With tender, creamy beans in our pot, it was time to work on the stew's other flavors. Pancetta is traditional in Tuscan white bean stew, lending depth and flavor. Earthy-tasting kale, another Tuscan favorite, made the stew more substantial; canned diced tomatoes, carrots, celery, onion, and lots of garlic contributed a pungent, vegetal aroma. For extra richness, we replaced some of the water in the stew with chicken broth. We sautéed the onion and celery (reserving the carrots, kale, and tomatoes) with the pancetta, added the beans and liquid, and placed the stew in the oven. The acid in tomatoes can toughen beans, so we rinsed the tomatoes and waited until the beans were sufficiently softened, about 45 minutes, before adding them to the pot, along with the kale and carrots. The final touch: a sprig of rosemary, steeped in the stew just before serving, infused the broth with a delicate herbal aroma.

To make our stew even more substantial, we made garlic toasts and served them on the side. But

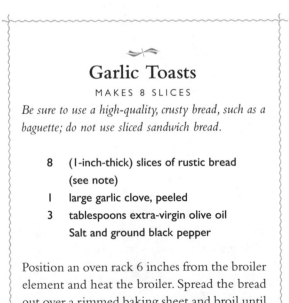

Garlic Toasts

MAKES 8 SLICES

Be sure to use a high-quality, crusty bread, such as a baguette; do not use sliced sandwich bread.

- 8 (1-inch-thick) slices of rustic bread (see note)
- 1 large garlic clove, peeled
- 3 tablespoons extra-virgin olive oil
  Salt and ground black pepper

Position an oven rack 6 inches from the broiler element and heat the broiler. Spread the bread out over a rimmed baking sheet and broil until golden brown on both sides, about 2 minutes per side. Briefly rub one side of each toast with the garlic. Drizzle the toasts with the oil, season with salt and pepper to taste, and serve.

watching tasters lustily dip their bread in the broth gave us an even better idea—setting the toasts in the bowls first, then ladling the stew on top, which slowly "melted" the bread and slightly thickened the broth. Drizzled with fruity extra-virgin olive oil, this hearty stew was pure comfort food.

Hearty Tuscan White Bean Stew
SERVES 8

If you can't find pancetta, substitute 4 ounces of bacon (about 4 slices). The garlic toasts, which are optional, will turn this stew into a more substantial dish.

6	ounces pancetta, chopped fine
1	tablespoon extra-virgin olive oil, plus extra for serving
1	large onion, chopped medium
2	celery ribs, chopped medium
8	medium garlic cloves, minced or pressed through a garlic press (about 8 teaspoons)
5	cups low-sodium chicken broth
3	cups water
1	pound dried cannellini beans, picked over, salt-soaked (see right), and rinsed
2	bay leaves
1	(14.5-ounce) can diced tomatoes, drained and rinsed
½	bunch kale or collard greens (about 8 ounces), stemmed and leaves chopped into 1-inch pieces (see the illustrations on page 150)
2	carrots, peeled and cut into ½-inch pieces
1	sprig fresh rosemary
	Salt and ground black pepper
1	recipe Garlic Toasts (page 152) (optional)

1. Adjust an oven rack to the lower-middle position and heat the oven to 250 degrees. Cook the pancetta and oil together in a large Dutch oven over medium heat until the pancetta is rendered and lightly browned, about 8 minutes. Stir in the onion and celery and cook until the vegetables are softened and lightly browned, 12 to 15 minutes.

2. Stir in the garlic and cook until fragrant, about 30 seconds. Stir in the broth, water, soaked beans, and bay leaves and bring to a boil. Cover the pot, transfer to the oven, and cook until the beans are almost tender, 45 to 60 minutes.

3. Stir in the tomatoes, kale, and carrots and continue to cook in the oven, covered, until the beans and vegetables are fully tender, 30 to 40 minutes longer.

4. Remove the pot from the oven. Submerge the rosemary sprig in the stew, cover, and let it steep off the heat for 15 minutes. Remove the bay leaves and rosemary sprig and season with salt and pepper to taste. If desired, use the back of a spoon to mash some beans against the side of the pot to thicken the stew. (The stew can be cooled and refrigerated in an airtight container for up to 2 days. Reheat gently, adding water as needed to loosen its consistency, before serving.)

5. To serve, place the garlic toasts (if using) into individual bowls, ladle the stew over the top, and drizzle lightly with additional olive oil.

TECHNIQUE: Salt-Soaking Beans

Here in the test kitchen, we've found that soaking dried beans in salt water before cooking is a good idea. The soaking slightly softens the beans and evens out the cooking time so that the beans are less prone to breaking and bursting during cooking. Don't worry if you don't have time to soak the beans (or forgot)—we've come up with a "quick salt-soak" method that works nearly as well (we still slightly prefer the overnight soak if given a choice).

OVERNIGHT SOAKING METHOD: Pick through and rinse the beans. For every pound of beans, dissolve 2 tablespoons salt into 4 quarts cold water. Combine the beans and salt water in a large container and let the beans soak at room temperature for at least 8 hours, or up to 24 hours. Drain the beans, discarding the soaking liquid, and rinse well before cooking.

QUICK SOAKING METHOD: Pick through and rinse the beans. For every pound of beans, dissolve 3 tablespoons salt into 2 quarts boiling water. Combine the beans and hot salt water together in a large container and let the beans soak at room temperature for 1 hour. Drain the beans, discarding the soaking liquid, and rinse well before cooking.

CLASSIC BEEF CHILI

LIKE POLITICS, CHILI SPARKS HEATED DEBATES. Some purists insist that a chili that contains beans or tomatoes is just not chili. Others claim that home-made chili powder is essential or that ground meat is taboo. But there is one kind of chili that almost every American has eaten (or even made) at one time or another. It's the kind of chili you liked as a kid and still see being served at Super Bowl parties. Made with ground meat, tomatoes, beans, and chili powder, this thick, fairly smooth chili is spiced but not spicy, and it will please almost everyone.

Although this simple chili should come together easily, it should not taste as if it did. The flavors should be rich and balanced, the texture thick and hearty. Unfortunately, many "basic" recipes yield a pot of underspiced, underflavored chili reminiscent of Sloppy Joes. Our goal was to develop a no-fuss chili that tasted far better than the sum of its parts.

Most of the recipes for this simple chili begin by sautéing onions and garlic, and tasters also liked a red bell pepper added to these aromatics. After this first step, things became less clear.

Our first experiments followed a formula we had seen in many recipes: 2 pounds ground beef, 3 tablespoons chili powder, 2 teaspoons ground cumin, and 1 teaspoon each red pepper flakes and dried oregano. Most recipes add the spices after the beef has been browned, but we have usually found that ground spices develop a deeper flavor when they come into direct contact with the hot cooking oil. To prevent the spices from burning, we added them to the pot once the aromatics were already in and sautéed them to bloom their flavor. Commercial chili powder is typically 80 percent ground dried red chiles, with the rest a mix of garlic powder, onion powder, oregano, ground cumin, and salt. This combination of flavors worked well, but they needed a boost. We increased the amount of chili powder from 3 to 4 tablespoons, added more cumin and oregano, and tossed in some cayenne for heat. We also tried some more exotic spices, including cinnamon, allspice, and coriander. Only the coriander became part of our working recipe.

It was now time to consider the meat. Two pounds of ground beef seemed ideal when paired with two 15-ounce cans of beans. Tests using 90 percent, 85 percent, and 80 percent lean ground beef showed that there is such a thing as too much fat. Pools of orange oil floated to the top of the chili made with ground chuck (80 percent lean beef). At the other end of the spectrum, the chili made with 90 percent lean beef was a tad bland—not bad, but not as full-flavored as the chili made with 85 percent lean beef, which was our final choice.

Tomatoes were definitely going into the pot, but we had yet to decide on the type and amount. We first tried two small (14.5-ounce) cans of diced tomatoes, which were clearly not enough. What's more, the tomatoes were too chunky, and they were floating in a thin sauce. We tried two 28-ounce cans of diced tomatoes, pureeing the contents of one can in the blender to thicken the sauce. Although the chunkiness was reduced, the sauce was still watery. Next we paired one can of tomato puree with one can of diced tomatoes and, without exception, tasters preferred the thicker consistency. And we were pleased to discover that our chili required no additional liquid.

We tried cooking the chili with the lid on, with the lid off, and with the lid on in the beginning and off at the end. The chili cooked with the lid on was too soupy, that cooked with the lid off too dense. Keeping the lid on for half of the cooking time and then removing it was ideal—the consistency was rich but not too thick. Almost two hours of gentle simmering was sufficient to meld the flavors; shorter cooking times yielded chili that was soupy or bland—or both.

Most recipes add the beans toward the end of cooking, the idea being to let them heat through without causing them to fall apart. But this method often makes for very bland beans floating in a sea of highly flavorful chili. After testing several options, we found it best to add the beans (we liked dark red kidney beans) with the tomatoes. The more time the beans spent in the pot, the better they tasted, and we found that they held their shape just fine.

It was now time to try some of those off-beat additions to the pot that other cooks swear by, including cocoa powder, ground coffee beans, mushrooms, and lima beans. Our conclusion? Each of these ingredients was either weird-tasting or too subtle to make much difference. A sprinkling of garnishes was all our chili needed—tasters liked any combination of cilantro, scallions, onion, avocado, cheese, and sour cream, as well as a squeeze of fresh lime juice. We were finally satisfied that we'd created a beef chili good enough to silence any debate.

Classic Beef Chili

SERVES 6 TO 8

Serve with lime wedges, minced fresh cilantro, sliced scallions, minced onion, diced avocado, shredded cheddar or Monterey Jack cheese, and/or sour cream, as well as Sweet and Easy Cornbread (page 159), if desired.

¼	cup chili powder
I	tablespoon ground cumin
2	teaspoons ground coriander
I	teaspoon red pepper flakes
I	teaspoon dried oregano
½	teaspoon cayenne pepper
	Salt and ground black pepper
2	tablespoons vegetable oil
2	medium onions, minced
I	red bell pepper, stemmed, seeded, and cut into ½-inch pieces (see the illustrations on page 226)
6	medium garlic cloves, minced or pressed through a garlic press (about 2 tablespoons)
2	pounds 85 percent lean ground beef
2	(15-ounce) cans dark red kidney beans, drained and rinsed
I	(28-ounce) can diced tomatoes
I	(28-ounce) can tomato puree
	Water, as needed

1. Combine the chili powder, cumin, coriander, red pepper flakes, oregano, cayenne, and 1 teaspoon salt in a small bowl; set aside.

2. Heat the oil in a large Dutch oven over medium heat until shimmering. Add the onions and bell pepper and cook until softened, 8 to 10 minutes. Stir in the garlic and cook until fragrant, about 30 seconds. Stir in the spice mixture and cook, stirring constantly, until fragrant, about 1 minute (do not let the spices burn).

3. Stir in half of the beef. Increase the heat to medium-high and cook, breaking up the meat with a wooden spoon, until no longer pink, 3 to 5 minutes. Repeat with the remaining beef. Stir in the beans, diced tomatoes with their juice, and tomato puree and bring to a simmer. Cover, reduce to a gentle simmer, and cook, stirring occasionally, for 1 hour.

4. Uncover and continue to simmer gently until the beef is tender and the sauce is dark, rich, and slightly thickened, about 45 minutes longer. (If at any time the chili begins to stick to the bottom of the pot or look too thick, stir in water as needed.) Season with salt and pepper to taste and serve. (The chili can be cooled and refrigerated in an airtight container for up to 2 days. Reheat gently, adding water as needed to loosen its consistency, before serving.)

INGREDIENTS: Chili Powder

While there are numerous applications for chili powder, its most common use is in chili. Considering that most chili recipes rely so heavily on chili powder (ours uses a whopping ¼ cup), we thought it was necessary to gather up as many brands as possible to find the one that made the best chili. To focus on the flavor of the chili powder, we made a bare-bones version of our chili and rated each chili powder for aroma, depth of flavor, and level of spiciness. Tasters concluded that Spice Islands Chili Powder was the clear winner. This well-known supermarket brand was noted by one taster as having "a big flavor that stands out from the others."

THE BEST CHILI POWDER

Spice Islands Chili Powder is our favorite chili powder, with its perfect balance of chili flavor and spiciness.

SPICE ISLANDS

CARNE ADOVADA

VISIT NEW MEXICO, AND YOU'LL LIKELY encounter a little-known chile-based dish that deserves a big reputation: *carne adovada*, literally "marinated meat." Like many New Mexican dishes, it's headlined by local chiles. Meltingly tender chunks of pork butt are braised in an intense, soulful red chile sauce with hints of oregano, onion, and garlic. It's at once smoky and bright, spicy yet sweet.

While it's easy to find recipes for carne adovada, if you don't live in the Southwest, it may not be so easy to find the requisite chiles. We searched out and tested several recipes with the usual inclusions, and the most promising recipe required toasting, seeding, and grinding nearly two dozen dried New Mexico chiles (commonly Anaheims ripened until red). Tasters loved the toasty, fruity notes added by all the chiles, which also thickened the sauce nicely. But we wanted to reproduce those rich and complex flavors using ingredients available in any supermarket.

We began by reaching for a jar of chili powder, which we felt would provide a nice baseline of warmth and depth; store-bought chili powder is mostly ground dried red chiles, with the rest a mix of garlic powder, onion powder, oregano, ground cumin, and salt. First we cubed and browned a boneless pork butt in oil before setting it aside. (We decided to cut the meat into 1½-inch chunks because they felt rustic and substantial.) After softening some onion and garlic in the residual fat, we added ⅓ cup chili powder, about the same amount our research recipes use of freshly roasted and ground dried New Mexico chiles. Then we stirred in some chicken broth, pureed the mixture, and added back the reserved meat to cook through. As with our meaty stews, we found that cooking in the oven, as opposed to the stovetop, ensured that the meat cooked through evenly. After two hours, the meat was tender and the sauce was an attractive rust-red, but the dish tasted utterly flat, and the meat juice had made the sauce runny.

For some smoky depth, we turned to the test kitchen pantry staple, canned chipotle chiles in adobo sauce, which contribute great smoky flavor to a variety of dishes. We tried various quantities before deciding that 1 tablespoon brought the right amount of complexity and heat. Wondering how to replicate the fruity quality of dried chiles, it occurred to us that we could use actual fruit. Since the flavor of chiles is sometimes described as raisiny, we hoped raisins might supply that nuance, but tasters rejected the dots of dried fruit in the sauce. We tried soaking the raisins in hot water to soften them, then made a puree and stirred it in. Tasters liked the agreeably subtle flavor it contributed. To replicate the bitter quality of freshly ground dried chiles, we tried stirring in cocoa powder or unsweetened chocolate. In carne adovada, however, they tasted wrong and out of place. A colleague

WARMING TORTILLAS

Our preferred way to warm tortillas (either flour or corn) is over the open flame of a gas burner. This technique gives them a nice roasted flavor. However, you can also toast them in a skillet one at a time over medium-high heat until soft and speckled with brown spots (20 to 30 seconds per side), or warm them in the microwave. To microwave, simply stack tortillas on a plate, cover with microwave-safe plastic wrap, and microwave on high power until warm and soft, 1 to 2 minutes. Once warmed, keep the tortillas wrapped in foil or a kitchen towel until ready to use, or they will dry out. If your tortillas are very dry, pat each with a little water before warming.

To warm tortillas over the open flame of a gas burner, place each tortilla directly on the cooking grate over a medium flame. Heat until slightly charred around edges, about 30 seconds per side.

suggested we soak the raisins in coffee instead of water, and indeed, a half-cup of coffee brought the flavors into robust, bittersweet balance.

For final touches, we stirred in flour with the spices, which nicely thickened the sauce. Tasters couldn't detect the minuscule amount of oregano—a must in carne adovada—included in the chili powder, so we reinforced it with an additional teaspoon. At the last minute, we stirred in lime juice, lime zest, and cilantro to brighten the otherwise earthy dish. While these ingredients aren't traditional, our tasters felt the flavor of the dish benefited hugely. At last, using easy-to-find ingredients, we'd developed a simple version of carne adovada that rivals the best that New Mexico has to offer.

Carne Adovada

SERVES 6

Boneless pork butt roast is often labeled as boneless Boston butt in the supermarket. You can substitute 1½ teaspoons ground espresso powder dissolved in ½ cup boiling water for the brewed coffee if desired. Serve with rice or warmed tortillas (see page 156).

¼	cup raisins
½	cup brewed coffee, hot
⅓	cup chili powder
3	tablespoons unbleached all-purpose flour
1	teaspoon dried oregano
1	(3½- to 4-pound) boneless pork butt roast, trimmed and cut into 1½-inch pieces (see note)
	Salt and ground black pepper
3	tablespoons vegetable oil
2	medium onions, minced
6	medium garlic cloves, minced or pressed through a garlic press (about 2 tablespoons)
1	tablespoon minced chipotle chile in adobo sauce
2	cups low-sodium chicken broth
1	cup water
¼	cup minced fresh cilantro leaves
1	teaspoon grated zest and 1 tablespoon juice from 1 lime

1. Adjust an oven rack to the lower-middle position and heat the oven to 325 degrees. Combine the raisins and hot coffee in a small bowl, cover, and let sit until the raisins are plump, about 5 minutes. Combine the chili powder, flour, and oregano in a small bowl. Pat the pork dry with paper towels and season with salt and pepper.

2. Heat 1 tablespoon of the oil in a large Dutch oven over medium-high heat until just smoking. Add half of the pork and brown well on all sides, 7 to 10 minutes; transfer to a large bowl. Repeat with 1 tablespoon more oil and the remaining pork; transfer to the bowl.

3. Pour off all but 2 tablespoons of the fat left in the pot, add the onions, and cook over medium heat until softened, 5 to 7 minutes. Stir in the garlic and chipotles and cook until fragrant, about 30 seconds. Stir in the spice mixture and remaining 1 tablespoon oil and cook, stirring constantly, until fragrant, about 1 minute (do not let the spices burn). Stir in the broth, water, and raisin-coffee mixture, scraping up any browned bits.

4. Working in batches, puree the sauce until smooth in a blender, then return it to the pot (or use an immersion blender). Stir in the browned pork with any accumulated juice and bring to a simmer. Cover, transfer the pot to the oven, and cook until the pork is tender and the sauce is thickened, about 2 hours, stirring halfway through cooking.

5. Remove the pot from the oven and stir in the cilantro, lime zest, and lime juice. Season with salt and pepper to taste and serve. (The chili can be cooled and refrigerated in an airtight container for up to 2 days. Reheat gently, adding water as needed to loosen its consistency, before serving.)

CHICKEN MOLE CHILI

LIKE CHILI, MOLE DERIVES ITS COMPLEX flavor from dried chiles and spices. In its native country, Mexico, rich-tasting mole is often paired with mild-mannered chicken and served in tortillas or ladled over white rice—the ideal canvases for mole to display its character. An authentic mole has intricate layers of flavor—besides chiles and spices, moles can include nuts, fruit, and chocolate— but these exotic flavors come with a price: an extensive list of ingredients and a notoriously long and complicated cooking method. Our goal was to translate chicken mole into an easy-to-serve chili that would still have all the deep, nuanced flavor of an authentic mole.

Moles are generally made by cooking each ingredient individually, toasting each item to bring it to its peak of flavor. Next, all the ingredients are combined in a large pot with broth or water and simmered. The mixture is then pureed smooth and returned to the pot to continue cooking until the flavors meld and the chicken is finished cook- ing. While the basic method seemed workable, we automatically nixed toasting the nuts, chiles, etc., separately; the only ingredient in the mole we felt deserved this attention were the dried chiles, which require heat to release their flavor and aroma.

Most authentic mole recipes call for several different types of chiles, such as guajillos, pasillas, anchos, and chipotles. We sought out and tested all of these chiles in various sauces and were pleased to find that we could come up with a delicious mole using just two of the most common: anchos and chipotles. Since canned chipotles in adobo are a test kitchen pantry staple, we were curious how they would compare to the dried chipotles. We tested them side by side and noted little difference. With only one type of dried chile to purchase, our shopping list was already looking more manageable.

Next, we moved on to the nut and seed component of the mole, which is typically some combination of toasted almonds, pumpkin seeds, peanuts, and sesame seeds. We liked the rich, creamy flavors of toasted almonds and sesame seeds. Most recipes call for finely ground almonds, but we didn't like their gritty texture in the otherwise smooth puree. We solved this problem by substituting almond butter for the ground almonds and were pleasantly surprised to find that the butter also gave the sauce a luxurious, velvety texture.

Up to now we had been using semisweet chocolate in the sauce, but wondered if different chocolate types, including authentic Mexican chocolate (which contains cinnamon and sometimes almonds and vanilla), might make a difference. Unsweetened chocolate and cocoa powder stood out as tasting bitter, but semisweet, bittersweet, and Mexican chocolates all worked well. A touch of sugar balanced the bitterness of the chocolate (we liked the complex flavor of dark brown sugar).

Our mole had begun to come together, but it was still missing some of the complexity of the more elaborate recipes. Adding cinnamon, cloves, and some raisins was a step in the right direction. Replacing the water with chicken broth and adding a can of diced tomatoes also helped round out the flavor. These additions were a huge improvement, but the sauce needed more resonance. Hesitant to lengthen our shopping list, we decided to revisit our cooking method, hoping to eke more flavor from our existing ingredients.

We had dismissed the technique of cooking each ingredient separately, but since we were sau- téing the onions and garlic anyway, why not sauté the chiles, chocolate, and spices too? Instead of throwing everything into the pot together, we tried incorporating the ingredients in stages. We started by sautéing the dried anchos in plenty of oil (to preventing burning) until they were dark red and toasted. Sesame seeds were next, followed by minced onion. Once the onion was softened we added the raisins, chocolate, almond butter, garlic, chipotles, and dried spices. As the heat drove off the excess moisture, the mixture cooked down, becom- ing bubbly, rich, and deeply fragrant. We then added the broth and tomatoes.

This technique of sautéing the ingredients in stages only took a few extra minutes but proved to be just the boost the mole needed, drawing out the flavor of the ingredients and intensifying the mole significantly. We were also able to skip the step of toasting the dried ancho chiles in the oven. We simply ripped the untoasted chiles into small pieces, discarding the seeds and stems before sautéing. Later, when brought to a simmer with the broth, the chiles rehydrated and became soft, blending into a smooth sauce when pureed.

With our recipe nearly complete, it was time to turn our attention to incorporating the chicken into the dish to make a chili. After trying a variety of bone-in chicken pieces, tasters thought the deeper flavor and tenderness of shredded dark meat—in particular the meaty thighs—was best suited to the assertive mole. Browning the thighs with the skin on produced flavorful browned bits on the bottom of the pot as well as rendered fat we could use to sauté the mole ingredients.

We saw no reason that the mole couldn't simmer and develop flavor at the same time as the chicken cooked, so after returning the pureed sauce to the pot, we nestled in the browned thighs, making sure to cover them completely with the sauce. Although it is traditionally simmered on the stove, we found that cooking the mole in a 325-degree oven was much more reliable, guaranteeing a predictably even, consistent level of heat and ensuring that the chocolate-thickened mole didn't burn on the bottom of the pot. When the chicken was done, we pulled the meat off the bones and stirred it back into the sauce. After a sprinkling of sesame seeds and scallions, our chicken mole chili was complete—glossy, dark, and rich.

Sweet and Easy Cornbread

SERVES 6 TO 8

The slightly sweet flavor of this cornbread tastes great with chili. Don't use stone-ground or whole grain cornmeal here, or the bread will taste dry and tough.

1½	cups (7½ ounces) unbleached all-purpose flour
1	cup (5 ounces) yellow cornmeal (see note)
2	teaspoons baking powder
¾	teaspoon salt
¼	teaspoon baking soda
1	cup buttermilk
¾	cup fresh corn or frozen corn, thawed
¼	cup packed (1¾ ounces) light brown sugar
2	large eggs
8	tablespoons (1 stick) unsalted butter, melted and cooled

1. Adjust an oven rack to the middle position and heat the oven to 400 degrees. Grease an 8-inch square baking dish. Whisk the flour, cornmeal, baking powder, salt, and baking soda together in a medium bowl.

2. Process the buttermilk, corn, and sugar in a food processor until combined, about 5 seconds. Add the eggs and continue to process until well combined (some corn lumps will remain), about 5 seconds. Fold the buttermilk mixture into the flour mixture with a rubber spatula. Fold in the melted butter until just incorporated (do not overmix).

3. Scrape the batter into the prepared pan and smooth the top. Bake until golden brown and a toothpick inserted into the center comes out clean, 25 to 35 minutes, rotating the pan halfway through baking.

4. Let the cornbread cool in the pan for 10 minutes, then turn out onto a wire rack and let cool for 20 minutes before serving.

Chicken Mole Chili

SERVES 6 TO 8

Ground ancho powder can be substituted for the whole ancho chiles; add 2 tablespoons ground ancho powder to the raisin-chocolate mixture in step 1 and skip the ancho toasting instructions in step 3. Serve with rice, warmed tortillas (see page 156), and/or Sweet and Easy Cornbread (page 159), if desired.

¼	cup raisins
¼	cup almond butter
1	ounce bittersweet, semisweet, or Mexican chocolate, broken into pieces
2	medium garlic cloves, minced or pressed through a garlic press (about 2 teaspoons)
1	teaspoon minced chipotle chile in adobo sauce
½	teaspoon ground cinnamon
⅛	teaspoon ground cloves
4	pounds bone-in, skin-on chicken thighs (10 to 12), trimmed
	Salt and ground black pepper
2	tablespoons vegetable oil
2	ancho chiles (about ½ ounce), stemmed, seeded, and broken into small pieces
2	tablespoons sesame seeds, plus extra for serving
1	medium onion, minced
2	cups low-sodium chicken broth
1	(14.5-ounce) can diced tomatoes
1	teaspoon dark brown sugar, plus extra to taste
2	scallions, sliced thin

1. Adjust an oven rack to the lower-middle position and heat the oven to 325 degrees. Combine the raisins, almond butter, chocolate, garlic, chipotles, cinnamon, and cloves in a small bowl; set aside. Pat the chicken dry with paper towels and season with salt and pepper.

2. Heat 1 tablespoon of the oil in a large Dutch oven over medium-high heat. Add half of the chicken and cook until well browned on both sides, about 10 minutes; transfer to a plate. Repeat with the remaining 1 tablespoon oil and chicken; transfer to the plate. Remove and discard the chicken skin.

3. Pour off all but 2 tablespoons of the fat left in the pot, add the ancho chiles, and cook over medium heat, stirring constantly, until they are dark red and toasted, about 5 minutes. Stir in 2 tablespoons of the sesame seeds and cook until golden, about 1 minute. Stir in the onion and cook until just softened, about 2 minutes.

4. Stir in the raisin-chocolate mixture and cook, stirring constantly, until the chocolate is melted and bubbly, 1 to 2 minutes (do not let the chocolate burn). Stir in the broth, scraping up any browned bits.

5. Stir in the diced tomatoes with their juice and 1 teaspoon of the sugar and bring to a simmer. Transfer the mixture to a food processor (or blender) and process until smooth, about 20 seconds. Return the mixture to the pot and season with salt, pepper, and additional sugar to taste.

6. Nestle the browned chicken with any accumulated juice into the pot, spoon the sauce over the chicken, and bring to a simmer. Cover the pot, transfer to the oven, and cook until chicken is very tender, 1 to 1¼ hours.

7. Remove the chicken from the pot, let it cool slightly, then shred the meat into bite-size pieces, following the illustration on page 75, discarding the bones. Whisk the sauce to re-emulsify, then stir in the shredded chicken and reheat gently over low heat, 1 to 2 minutes. Serve, sprinkling individual portions with the scallions and additional sesame seeds. (The chili can be cooled and refrigerated in an airtight container for up to 2 days. Reheat gently, adding water as needed to loosen its consistency, before serving.)

BLACK BEAN CHILI

RED KIDNEY BEANS SEEM TO HOG THE limelight when it comes to chili, but what about black beans? Black beans are earthy, rich, and packed with flavor. We thought these hearty, substantial beans would make a great base for a meat-free chili, and we aimed to make one that would satisfy vegetarians and carnivores alike.

Since beans were to be the core of our chili, that's where we started testing. The first question was what type to use: canned or dried. While we often use canned beans in chilis, a test pitting canned beans against dried beans made it clear that, in this case, dried beans—with their superior texture and flavor—were the only way to go. Usually we prefer to soak beans in a saltwater solution (or brine them) prior to cooking, as this step softens the tough bean skins and evens out the cooking time, so that fewer beans burst open. But, as with our Brazilian Black Bean and Pork Stew (page 140), a few broken beans wouldn't be a bad thing in this dish; we wanted a thick chili and a portion of burst beans would only contribute to our desired texture.

When it comes to chilis and stews where even cooking is crucial, we usually favor the oven for its uniform, consistent heat. The same held true here. After testing a range of temperatures from 250 to 400 degrees, we determined that 325 worked best. Higher temperatures caused too vigorous a simmer and burst every single bean, while lower temperatures meant too long a cooking time.

When cooking unbrined beans, it's particularly important to use a flavorful liquid to ensure well-seasoned interiors. In this case, we found a combination of equal parts vegetable broth and water gave the beans a flavorful backbone. But we knew the flavor of our chili would also benefit from the brightness and acidity of tomatoes. After testing fresh chopped tomatoes, canned diced tomatoes, and canned crushed tomatoes, tasters preferred the smooth texture of the crushed tomatoes. One 28-ounce can, combined with the single pound of beans we were working with, provided a solid tomato base without overwhelming the beans. Since acidic ingredients can toughen beans by preventing their cells from absorbing water, we added the tomatoes to the pot halfway through cooking. A small amount of baking soda, stirred in at the beginning of cooking, ensured that our beans stayed dark and didn't turn gray or drab.

Confident that we had solved our bean cooking method, we looked for ways to boost the meaty flavor of the chili, and immediately thought of mushrooms. We made three batches of beans, adding a different sliced mushroom to each; we tried white, cremini, and portobello mushrooms. While tasters found the texture of portobellos unappealing here, the cremini and white mushrooms were praised for their meaty texture and the rich, deep flavor they contributed to the chili. Since it was a tie, we opted to go with the more readily available white mushrooms.

However, tasters weren't satisfied with the presence of sliced mushrooms in the chili. We decided to pulse them in the food processor instead, then sautéed them with some onion to drive off moisture and create a flavorful fond on the bottom of the pot. The chopped pieces of mushroom didn't overshadow the beans, but they still provided plenty of flavor, texture, and body.

As for aromatics, in addition to onion, we stirred in a generous quantity of garlic, some chili powder, and a couple of bay leaves. Whole cumin seeds and minced chipotle added depth and smokiness. So far, so good, but something was missing. Looking for another way to deepen the flavor of the chili, we reviewed existing recipes again, hoping for inspiration. We noticed a few called for mustard seeds. It seemed a bit odd for chili, but we were curious and gave it a shot, adding some with the aromatics. We found that the chili now had an appealing pungency and an additional level of complexity that tasters immediately noticed but couldn't identify. We eventually settled on 1 tablespoon of mustard seeds—more than this, and the chili took on a bitter taste. To enhance the flavor of the mustard seeds, we employed the technique of blooming, a common test kitchen practice for bringing out the flavor of dried spices by briefly sautéing them. Sautéing the seeds in oil proved to be a minor disaster, causing them to pop out of the pot. Toasting them in a dry pan, along with the cumin seeds, achieved the same goal but with less drama. One tablespoon of brown sugar further rounded out the mustard flavor.

Finally, for some textural contrast and a bit of sweetness, we added two red bell peppers, cut into ½-inch pieces; stirring them in with the tomatoes preserved their color and texture. With a spritz of lime and a sprinkling of minced cilantro, this rich, hearty chili was so satisfying that no one even missed the meat.

Black Bean Chili

SERVES 6 TO 8

We strongly prefer the texture and flavor of mustard seeds and cumin seeds in this chili; however, ground cumin and dry mustard can be substituted—skip the toasting instructions in step 2 and add ½ teaspoon ground cumin and/or ½ teaspoon dry mustard to the pot with the chili powder in step 3. The baking soda added to the beans helps preserve their dark hue; without it, the beans will turn a muddy, grayish color. Serve with sour cream, shredded cheddar or Monterey Jack cheese, chopped tomatoes, and/or minced onion, as well as Sweet and Easy Cornbread (page 159), if desired.

1	pound white mushrooms, wiped clean, trimmed, and broken into rough pieces
1	tablespoon mustard seeds
2	teaspoons cumin seeds
3	tablespoons vegetable oil
1	medium onion, chopped medium
9	medium garlic cloves, minced or pressed through a garlic press (about 3 tablespoons)
1	tablespoon minced chipotle chile in adobo sauce
3	tablespoons chili powder
2½	cups vegetable broth
2½	cups water, plus extra as needed
1	pound dried black beans, picked over and rinsed
1	tablespoon light brown sugar
⅛	teaspoon baking soda
2	bay leaves
1	(28-ounce) can crushed tomatoes
2	red bell peppers, stemmed, seeded, and cut into ½-inch pieces (see the illustrations on page 226)
½	cup minced fresh cilantro leaves
	Salt and ground black pepper
	Lime wedges, for serving

1. Adjust an oven rack to the lower-middle position and heat the oven to 325 degrees. Pulse the mushrooms in a food processor until uniformly coarsely chopped, about 10 pulses; set aside.

2. Toast the mustard seeds and cumin seeds in a large Dutch oven over medium heat, stirring constantly, until fragrant, about 1 minute. Stir in the oil, onion, and processed mushrooms, cover, and cook until the vegetables have released their liquid, about 5 minutes. Uncover and continue to cook until the vegetables are dry and browned, 5 to 10 minutes.

3. Stir in the garlic and chipotles and cook until fragrant, about 30 seconds. Stir in the chili powder and cook, stirring constantly, until fragrant, about 1 minute (do not let it burn). Stir in the broth, water, beans, sugar, baking soda, and bay leaves and bring to a simmer, skimming any impurities that rise to the surface. Cover, transfer the pot to the oven, and cook for 1 hour.

4. Stir in the crushed tomatoes and bell peppers, cover, and continue to cook in the oven until the beans are fully tender, about 1 hour longer. (If at any time the chili begins to stick to the bottom of the pot or look too thick, stir in additional water as needed.)

5. Remove the pot from the oven and remove the bay leaves. Stir in the cilantro, season with salt and pepper to taste, and serve with the lime wedges. (The chili can be cooled and refrigerated in an airtight container for up to 2 days. Reheat gently, adding water as needed to loosen its consistency, before serving.)

6

ONE-POT PASTA

ONE POT PASTA

WEEKNIGHT BOLOGNESE WITH LINGUINE

BOLOGNESE IS OFTEN CONSIDERED THE KING of Italian meat sauces. The classic Bolognese preparation starts with sautéing finely chopped onion and carrot until softened. Ground beef, pork, and veal are then browned in the pan before a series of liquids (often milk, wine, and pureed tomatoes) are added in stages and slowly simmered. The process can take several hours, but the result is a rich, complex, balanced, and meaty sauce. Wishing for similar results with a fraction of the effort, we hoped to develop a one-pot recipe for authentic-tasting Bolognese that could be prepared on a weeknight. Our biggest challenge would be achieving complex flavor without the long simmering time. In addition, we would need to find a way to cook the pasta in the same pot as the sauce.

The test kitchen's traditional, slow-cooked Bolognese recipe starts by softening onion and carrot in butter in a large Dutch oven; meatloaf mix (a combination of ground beef, pork, and veal) is then added and browned to develop rich meaty flavor. Next, 2 cups of milk, 1½ cups of white wine, and a 28-ounce can of whole tomatoes (processed until almost smooth) are added successively and gently reduced until the pot is almost dry—a process that takes 2 hours.

Our first idea for cutting down on cooking time was to reduce the liquids at a rolling boil. Not surprisingly, this technique left us with stringy meat and a muddied sauce. Next, we tried lowering the amounts of the liquid components. This worked to a point—our cooking time was obviously shorter, but the meat was still tough. It turns out that simmering Bolognese gently over a long period of time accomplishes two things. First, it draws out maximum flavor from the meat and vegetables while evaporating moisture and concentrating the flavors of each liquid. Second, it tenderizes the meat.

But given that ground meat is naturally tender we questioned why anything less than two hours of simmering produced tough meat. Then it hit us: browning the meat to develop flavor created a formidable crust—one that took hours of gentle cooking to become tender again. What if we skipped the browning entirely?

For our next batch we cooked the ground meat for just one minute before adding the milk, followed by the wine and tomatoes. To our delight, the meat was supremely tender after just 45 minutes of simmering. But now we had a new problem: By skipping the browning step, we had lost all of the meaty essence that defines Bolognese.

To boost the meatiness of a dish, we frequently turn to glutamate-rich ingredients that can quickly add savory richness (a trait known as *umami*) to any dish. Among these are cured pork products (salt pork, bacon, and pancetta), anchovies, and dried porcini mushrooms. After experimenting with each, we settled on a winning blend. Tasters preferred the clean flavor of pancetta to both bacon and salt pork. Combining the pancetta with ½ ounce of porcini and a minced anchovy, we had a pungent mix that returned our quick Bolognese to exalted, meaty heights. For maximum flavor, we browned the minced pancetta, porcini, and anchovy in butter before adding the onion and carrot to the pot. This sauce tasted great, but considering that our goal was to make Bolognese easier, it seemed counterproductive to add several new ingredients that each required its own prep. Some simplifying was in order.

Since we already had our food processor out to blend the tomatoes, we decided to put it to work. First, we processed the onion and carrots; after transferring them to a bowl, we added the porcini, pancetta, and anchovy. Thirty seconds was sufficient to turn this bold combo into a finely ground mixture that browned quickly in the hot pot. Finally we had a great-tasting, quick, and easy Bolognese sauce.

To stay true to our one-pot pasta goal, we had to find the best way to cook the noodles directly in the finished sauce. Since dried pasta absorbs considerable liquid as it cooks, we would have to add water to compensate. To determine how much water was needed to achieve al dente linguine and a properly thickened sauce, we added a pound of pasta and varying amounts of water to finished batches of our Bolognese. After adding the pasta and water, we covered the pot and vigorously simmered (again a rolling boil proved disastrous for the sauce) the pasta until al dente. Three cups of water was just right, producing nicely cooked pasta and a starchy, but not gluey, sauce. To save time, we tried adding the linguine at the same time as the processed tomatoes. This adjustment easily recouped a quarter of an hour but prevented the tomatoes from reducing and concentrating. To add back concentrated tomato flavor, we stirred in 2 tablespoons of tomato paste.

Bolognese should offer sweet resonance to balance the richness of the meat and the acidity of the wine and tomatoes. The veal provides much of this sweetness, but since tasters wanted more, we added a couple teaspoons of sugar with the garlic. Rich, meaty, complex, and slightly sweet, our Bolognese sauce delivers on all of the promises of a traditional slow-cooked version. You'd never guess it took one pot and less than an hour to put it on the table.

Weeknight Bolognese with Linguine

SERVES 6

If you can't find meatloaf mix, you can substitute eight ounces each of 85 percent lean ground beef and ground pork. When adding the linguine in step 5, stir gently to avoid breaking the noodles; after a minute or two they will soften enough to be stirred more easily. If necessary, add hot water, 1 tablespoon at a time, to adjust the consistency of the sauce before serving.

2	carrots, peeled and cut into 1-inch pieces
1	medium onion, cut into 1-inch pieces
3	ounces pancetta, cut into 1-inch pieces
½	ounce dried porcini mushrooms, rinsed
1	anchovy fillet, rinsed
1	(28-ounce) can whole tomatoes
2	tablespoons unsalted butter
2	teaspoons sugar
1	medium garlic clove, minced or pressed through a garlic press (about 1 teaspoon)
1	pound meatloaf mix
1½	cups whole milk
2	tablespoons tomato paste
½	cup dry white wine
3	cups water
1	pound linguine
	Salt and ground black pepper
	Grated Parmesan cheese, for serving

1. Pulse the carrots and onion in a food processor until finely chopped, 10 to 15 pulses; transfer to a bowl. Process the pancetta, porcini mushrooms, and anchovy until finely chopped, 30 to 35 seconds; transfer to a separate bowl. Pulse the tomatoes with their juice until mostly smooth, about 8 pulses; transfer to a separate bowl.

2. Melt the butter in a large Dutch oven over medium heat. Add the processed pancetta mixture and cook until browned, about 2 minutes. Stir in the processed carrot mixture and cook until softened, 5 to 7 minutes.

3. Stir in the sugar and garlic and cook until fragrant, about 30 seconds. Stir in the meatloaf mix, breaking up the meat with a wooden spoon, about 1 minute. Stir in the milk, scraping up any browned bits, and simmer until nearly evaporated, 18 to 20 minutes.

4. Stir in the tomato paste and cook for 1 minute. Stir in the wine and simmer until nearly evaporated, 8 to 10 minutes.

5. Stir in the processed tomatoes, water, and linguine and bring to a rapid simmer. Cover and simmer vigorously, stirring often, until the pasta is tender and the sauce is thickened, 12 to 16 minutes. Off the heat, season with salt and pepper to taste and serve with the Parmesan.

WEEKNIGHT BOLOGNESE WITH LINGUINE   **PAGE 166**

CHICKEN EN COCOTTE WITH POTATOES AND CARROTS **PAGE 70**

SHRIMP SCAMPI WITH CAMPANELLE   **PAGE 197**

SPICE-RUBBED FLANK STEAK WITH ROASTED CORN AND BLACK BEAN SALAD   **PAGE 4**

PASTA ROLL-UPS WITH CHICKEN, SUN-DRIED TOMATOES, AND PINE NUTS **PAGE 128**

SAVORY CHICKEN COBBLER WITH CARROTS, MUSHROOMS, AND PEAS **PAGE 100**

ROAST PORK LOIN WITH SWEET POTATOES AND CILANTRO SAUCE **PAGE 33**

EASY OLD-FASHIONED ROAST BEEF WITH CARROTS AND POTATOES **PAGE 30**

174

HALIBUT EN PAPILLOTE WITH ZUCCHINI AND TOMATOES **PAGE 322**

175

BEST BEEF STEW **PAGE 134**

ROASTED CHICKEN BREASTS WITH RED POTATOES, FENNEL, AND CAULIFLOWER **PAGE 48**

SPICY STIR-FRIED SESAME CHICKEN WITH GREEN BEANS AND SHIITAKES **PAGE 218**

RACK OF PORK WITH AUTUMN VEGETABLES **PAGE 300**

MEXICAN LASAGNA WITH PORK, CORN, AND PINTO BEANS **PAGE 98**

180

CHICKEN AND SESAME RICE WITH EDAMAME AND CARROTS **PAGE 76**

BAKED ZITI WITH SAUSAGE AND PEPPERS **PAGE 200**

ITALIAN PORK RAGU WITH ZITI

WHILE WE LOVE THE RICH COMPLEXITY OF Bolognese, sometimes we want a simpler, more rustic sauce that still boasts great meatiness. Enter Italian pork ragu: pork that is slow-cooked with tomatoes and wine until fall-apart tender, at which point it's shredded and returned to the sauce. Served atop a steaming bowl of al dente pasta and crowned with grated cheese, this sauce is an expressive example of Italy's deeply comforting peasant food. And, given its short list of ingredients, we assumed it would be as easy to prepare as it is to enjoy. Imagine our surprise, then, when recipe after recipe produced lackluster results. Most were nothing more than a glorified marinara sauce with a few stray shreds of pork, while others featured tough bites of meat in a sharp, winy sauce. None was worth the hours of simmering required. We wanted a sauce that offered rich meaty flavor, tender pork, and balanced tomato and wine presence. And we wanted to cook the pasta right in the same pot.

We figured determining the right cut of pork was the most important matter, so we decided to start there. First we whipped up a quick tomato sauce consisting of onion, garlic, olive oil, red wine, and diced tomatoes. We then simmered a few of the most readily available pork cuts in batches of this basic sauce. Pork chops from the blade, loin, and sirloin, even when well marbled with fat, ended up dry and tough no matter how little or how long we braised them. Even worse, the chops imparted almost no meatiness to the sauce. Pork loin and tenderloin didn't fare much better. It was clear that we needed a cut of pork with more connective tissue and fat.

We then turned to Boston butt—a fatty, tough cut from the shoulder that becomes tender when cooked slowly. The problem with this roast was its size; the smallest at the supermarket was 4 pounds. Nevertheless, we cut up 2 pounds of this meat into stewlike chunks and proceeded. After about 90 minutes of gentle simmering (we used the oven to provide more hands-off cooking) we tasted the meat, which was tender and flavorful. But although the sauce had better body and meatiness than before,

tasters still weren't satisfied. Moving away from this unwieldy roast, we then tried spareribs, which are fattier still. The braised meat from spareribs was the best yet and the sauce was really starting to taste meaty; it seemed as though the bones had contributed just as much flavor and richness to the sauce as the meat. Unfortunately, spareribs are expensive, and an entire rack weighs three or more pounds— again, more than we needed for a batch of our sauce. Looking for a more practical way to get the flavor we were after, we took a look at bone-in country-style ribs. Country-style ribs (which are cut from the back of the pig, not the belly) are inexpensive and easy to find in a variety of package sizes. These ribs cooked up just as tender and rich as the spareribs, and the resulting sauce had good meatiness. With a promising foundation in place, we focused on perfecting our sauce.

To ensure we had enough sauce for a pound of pasta, we increased the diced tomatoes to three 14.5-ounce cans. To compensate for the additional tomatoes, we also increased the ribs to 2½ pounds and the wine (tasters preferred a dry red) to ½ cup. As good as this sauce was, we knew it could be even better. Many Italian meat sauces include anchovies in the ingredient list (in fact, we'd use them in our one-pot Bolognese recipe, see page 165), as these cured, oil-packed fillets contain high levels of glutamates, compounds that make foods taste richer. We tried adding two anchovies to this sauce, and we were amazed at the difference they made. This sauce was exactly what we were looking for: It was rich and intensely flavored. Finally, we could address the pasta.

Tasters preferred this sauce with ziti, which stood up well to the chunky sauce. Using what we had learned from our one-pot Bolognese, we added the pasta to the sauce along with water and simmered it until tender. After a few tests we found that 3½ cups of water, along with the liquid already in the pot, resulted in perfectly cooked pasta and a well-textured sauce. Substituting a cup of chicken broth for a cup of the water fortified the sauce further. After finishing our sauce with a sprinkling of parsley and a dusting of grated Pecorino, we now had the ultimate one-pot meaty tomato sauce with ziti.

Easy Pork Ragu with Ziti
SERVES 6

You can substitute penne, campanelle, medium shells, farfalle, or orecchiette for the ziti; however, the cup measurements will vary. See page 185 for more information on measuring pasta. If necessary, add hot water, 1 tablespoon at a time, to adjust the consistency of the sauce before serving.

2½	pounds bone-in country-style pork ribs, trimmed
	Salt and ground black pepper
2	tablespoons olive oil
1	medium onion, minced
5	medium garlic cloves, minced or pressed through a garlic press (about 5 teaspoons)
2	anchovy fillets, rinsed and minced
½	cup dry red wine
3	(14.5-ounce) cans diced tomatoes
1	cup low-sodium chicken broth
2½	cups water
1	pound ziti
2	tablespoons minced fresh parsley leaves
	Grated Pecorino Romano or Parmesan cheese, for serving

1. Adjust an oven rack to the lower-middle position and heat the oven to 300 degrees. Pat the pork dry with paper towels and season with salt and pepper.

2. Heat 1 tablespoon of the oil in a large Dutch oven over medium-high heat until just smoking. Add half of the pork and brown on all sides, 7 to 10 minutes; transfer to a large plate. Repeat with the remaining 1 tablespoon oil and remaining pork; transfer to the plate.

3. Add the onion to the fat left in the pot and cook over medium heat until softened, 5 to 7 minutes. Stir in the garlic and anchovies and cook until fragrant, about 30 seconds. Stir in the wine, scraping up any browned bits, and cook until nearly evaporated, about 3 to 4 minutes. Stir in the tomatoes with their juice and broth; bring to a simmer.

4. Return the browned pork with any accumulated juice to the pot. Cover, transfer the pot to the oven, and cook until the meat is very tender, about 1½ hours, turning the pork halfway through cooking.

5. Remove the pot from the oven and transfer the pork to a carving board. Let the pork cool slightly, then shred into bite-size pieces following the illustrations on page 75, discarding the fat and bones.

6. Stir the water, ziti, and ½ teaspoon salt into the pot and bring to a rapid simmer over medium heat. Cover and simmer vigorously, stirring often, until the pasta is just tender and the sauce is thickened, 15 to 18 minutes.

7. Uncover, reduce the heat to low, and stir in the shredded pork. Cook, tossing the pasta gently, until it is well coated with sauce and the pork is warmed through, 1 to 2 minutes. Season with salt and pepper to taste and serve with the cheese.

MUSSELS MARINARA WITH SPAGHETTI

THERE'S A LOT TO LIKE ABOUT MUSSELS: They're quick cooking, flavorful, and relatively inexpensive. And since most mussels at the market nowadays are rope cultured and virtually free of sand and grit, they require minimal prep. All of these characteristics make mussels the perfect foundation for a weeknight one-pot supper. One of our favorite preparations is mussels marinara, where mussels are draped in a spicy tomato sauce and served with crusty bread or pasta. We decided to focus on developing a recipe for the latter. Before choosing the pasta and determining the best way to cook the mussels, we set about developing our sauce.

While the term "marinara" generally conjures images of a thick, smooth tomato sauce, most of the recipes we tested for mussels marinara were brothy and chunky. The few versions that did feature a smooth sauce were generally panned by tasters, who felt this style lacked contrast and texture. After tasting a half-dozen variations on the mussels marinara theme, we found that our ideal sauce was indeed brothy with tender chunks of tomato, relatively spicy, and rich with seafood brininess. Examining our notes, we realized that this sauce had much in common with our puttanesca sauce (see page 186). While testing that recipe we discovered that processing whole tomatoes with their juice produced a better sauce than diced tomatoes, crushed tomatoes, or tomato puree. We made a modified version of our puttanesca sauce, which features two 28-ounce cans whole tomatoes, eight anchovies, six cloves of garlic, and ¾ teaspoon red pepper flakes and ditched the olives and capers, which were clearly out of place in this dish. Using this sauce as the base of our working recipe, we turned our attention to the pasta.

Using our one-pot pasta technique, we added a variety of pasta shapes and sizes (with enough water for them to cook properly) to batches of our sauce and simmered them vigorously until the pasta was tender and the sauce was thickened. Tasters immediately showed a preference for long noodles, which seemed to grab more of the sauce when twirled onto a fork. After testing linguine, spaghetti, vermicelli, cappellini, and bucatini, we settled on spaghetti as the best complement to our marinara sauce. With our pasta of choice and a working tomato sauce recipe, we tackled the true star of this dish: the mussels.

Starting with 2 pounds of mussels (enough for six servings) we examined our options for cooking them. A typical approach for clams and mussels is to steam them open in a large pot using a little water or wine. This method allows the bivalves' liquor to be strained of grit before finishing the dish. This is an important step for clams in particular, but since mussels contain very little sand, we wondered if we could use a different, simpler technique. In keeping with our one-pot approach, we tried adding the mussels directly to the pot as the pasta finished simmering. After a few tests, we found that it took just a couple of minutes for the shells to open and for the mussels to release their briny juice into the pot. This technique resulted in perfectly cooked mussels and pasta, with no additional cooking steps. With our goal of one-pot mussels marinara in sight, we took a final look at the flavors of our sauce.

While tasters liked the texture of our sauce, many found the anchovies and heat to be overpowering. To ensure that the mussels remained in the foreground, we cut the anchovies to just one fillet and reduced the red pepper flakes to ½ teaspoon. This sauce offered better balance but lacked the brininess that tasters expected. Substituting a bottle of clam juice for some of the cooking water was the clear and simple solution; it bolstered the dish's brininess without overpowering the flavor of the mussels. A handful of minced fresh parsley added some color and freshness, and we now had a simple, yet sensational one-pot mussels marinara.

MEASURING PASTA SHAPES

IN OUR ONE-POT PASTA RECIPES, THE ratio of pasta to cooking liquid is critical to success. As the pasta cooks at a vigorous simmer, it absorbs the majority of the liquid and the rest reduces to a saucy consistency. Therefore, if you use more pasta than required, there won't be enough liquid to cook it through. Conversely, if you use less, the resulting sauce will be too thin or soupy. Also, pay close attention to the shape of pasta called for in each recipe, because different pasta shapes and sizes have slightly different cooking times and, therefore, not all shapes are interchangeable. The best method for measuring pasta is to weigh it using a scale. However, if you do not own a scale, we have provided the equivalent cup measurements for various shapes. Use dry measuring cups for the most accurate measurements, and pack them full.

PASTA TYPE	8 OUNCES	12 OUNCES
PENNE	2½ cups	3¾ cups
ZITI	2½ cups	3¾ cups
ORECCHIETTE	2½ cups	3½ cups
CAMPANELLE	3 cups	4½ cups
FARFALLE (BOW TIES)	3 cups	4½ cups
MEDIUM SHELLS	3 cups	4½ cups
ELBOW MACARONI	2 cups	3 cups

Mussels Marinara with Spaghetti

SERVES 6

When adding the spaghetti in step 3, stir gently to avoid breaking the noodles; after a minute or two they will soften enough to be stirred more easily. If necessary, add hot water, 1 tablespoon at a time, to adjust the consistency of the sauce before serving. Drizzle with extra-virgin olive oil and serve with Garlic Toasts (page 152) for dipping in the flavorful sauce.

2	(28-ounce) cans whole tomatoes
3	tablespoons extra-virgin olive oil
I	medium onion, minced
6	medium garlic cloves, minced or pressed through a garlic press (about 2 tablespoons)
I	anchovy fillet, rinsed and minced
½	teaspoon red pepper flakes
2	cups water
I	(8-ounce) bottle clam juice
I	pound spaghetti
2	pounds mussels, scrubbed and debearded (see the illustration on page 147)
¼	cup minced fresh parsley leaves
	Salt and ground black pepper

1. Pulse the tomatoes with their juice, one can at a time, in a food processor until coarsely chopped and no large pieces remain, 6 to 8 pulses; transfer to a large bowl.

2. Heat 2 tablespoons of the oil in a large Dutch oven over medium heat until shimmering. Stir in the onion and cook until softened, 5 to 7 minutes. Stir in the garlic, anchovy, and red pepper flakes and cook until fragrant, about 30 seconds. Stir in the processed tomatoes and simmer gently until the tomatoes no longer taste raw, about 10 minutes.

3. Stir in the water, clam juice, and spaghetti and bring to a rapid simmer. Cover and simmer vigorously, stirring often, for 12 minutes. Stir in the mussels and continue to simmer vigorously, covered, until the pasta is tender and the mussels have opened, about 2 minutes longer.

4. Uncover, reduce the heat to low, and stir in the remaining 1 tablespoon oil and parsley. Cook, tossing the pasta gently, until it is well coated with sauce, 1 to 2 minutes. Season with salt and pepper to taste and serve.

PASTA PUTTANESCA

SAID TO HAVE BEEN CREATED BY NEAPOLITAN ladies of the night, puttanesca is a zesty sauce with an attitude. Many home cooks buy this sauce by the jar, which can be disappointing. Even restaurant versions sometimes fall short, overpowered by one flavor, whether it's too fishy, too garlicky, too briny, or just plain too salty. It can also be unduly heavy or dull and monochromatic. We were searching for a satisfying, lusty sauce with aggressive but well-balanced flavors, and it had to serve as the foundation of an easy one-pot supper. Before plunging into the bold elements of puttanesca, we set about developing a flavorful tomato base.

Unlike classic marinara sauce, which is thick and smooth, puttanesca is a rustic balance of thin, tomatoey broth and tomato chunks. To recreate this style, we tested the full range of canned tomato products. Tomato puree and crushed tomatoes (packed in puree) were quickly ruled out, as they produced thick, marinara-like sauces. Diced tomatoes fared better, offering a decent ratio of tomato chunks to juice, but tasters didn't care for their texture in this application. In the end, we found that pulsing whole canned tomatoes briefly in the food processor delivered tender bites of tomato and the perfect ratio of chunks to juice. To turn our tomatoes into a sauce, we sautéed some minced garlic in olive oil, stirred in the processed tomatoes, and gently simmered them to cook out the raw tomato flavor. Using this as our base, we set about introducing the pungent elements that make puttanesca unique.

Combining anchovies, garlic, olives, capers, and red pepper flakes in one pasta dish might sound like a recipe for disaster. And from our experience testing a number of published recipes, it often is. To strike a balance and create a harmonious whole, we started low (two anchovy fillets, two minced cloves of garlic, ¼ teaspoon red pepper flakes, ¼ cup chopped kalamata olives, and 1 tablespoon rinsed capers) and slowly increased each element until tasters were happy. As expected, our first batch lacked gusto. Next, we tried doubling everything, and while tasters were happy with the olives and capers, they were still missing richness, garlic, and heat. Doubling the anchovies again (now eight fillets), increasing the garlic to six cloves, and bumping the red pepper flakes to ¾ teaspoon did the trick. Tasters loved this sauce for its heady combination of assertive flavors, but they felt the olives and capers were overcooked. Up to this point, we had been sautéing everything in the oil before stirring in the processed tomatoes (hoping that the hot oil would draw maximum flavor from each element). To preserve the texture and brightness of the olives and capers, we instead tried stirring them in at the last minute. This sauce was pungent, balanced, and dotted with satisfying briny bites. Next, we focused on the pasta.

Italians have a strict code about pairing sauces (tomato, cream, thick, or thin) and pasta (long, wide, or tubular) and while they certainly have their reasons, we think taste and texture, not tradition, are the most important factors. To find the perfect complement to our puttanesca, we tried penne, campanelle, ziti, spaghettini, linguine, and pappardelle. Using our one-pot pasta technique of cooking the noodles right in the sauce (rather than boiling them in a separate pot), we added 1 pound of each to a batch of sauce (along with enough water to properly cook the pasta) and simmered until tender. While no shape was a failure, tasters preferred a coiled forkful of spaghettini and sauce to the others. The pasta's long thin strands absorbed the sauce's briny, zesty kick and "grabbed" the tomatoes, olives, and capers when twirled onto a fork, ensuring balanced flavor in each bite. We found 3 cups of water produced perfectly cooked pasta and a nicely textured sauce.

To freshen up this decidedly rich, bold pasta, we added ¼ cup minced fresh parsley at the last minute. Served with freshly grated Parmesan, our one-pot puttanesca was now bright, boldly flavored, and worthy of its sultry namesake.

Pasta Puttanesca
SERVES 6

When adding the spaghettini in step 3, stir gently to avoid breaking the noodles; after a minute or two they will soften enough to be stirred more easily. Thin spaghetti or spaghetti can be substituted for the spaghettini. If necessary, add hot water, 1 tablespoon at a time, to adjust the consistency of the sauce before serving.

2	(28-ounce) cans whole tomatoes
3	tablespoons extra-virgin olive oil
8	anchovy fillets, rinsed and minced
6	medium garlic cloves, minced or pressed through a garlic press (about 2 tablespoons)
¾	teaspoon red pepper flakes
3	cups water
1	pound spaghettini
½	cup pitted kalamata olives, chopped coarse
¼	cup minced fresh parsley leaves
2	tablespoons capers, rinsed
	Salt and ground black pepper
	Grated Parmesan cheese, for serving

1. Pulse the tomatoes with their juice, one can at a time, in a food processor until coarsely chopped and no large pieces remain, 6 to 8 pulses; transfer to a large bowl.

2. Cook 2 tablespoons of the oil, anchovies, garlic, and red pepper flakes in a large Dutch oven over medium-low heat, stirring constantly, until the garlic is fragrant but not browned, 1 to 2 minutes. Stir in the processed tomatoes and simmer gently until the tomatoes no longer taste raw, about 10 minutes.

3. Stir in the water and spaghettini and bring to a rapid simmer. Cover and simmer vigorously, stirring often, until the pasta is tender and the sauce is thickened, 12 to 16 minutes.

4. Uncover, reduce the heat to low, and stir in the remaining 1 tablespoon oil, olives, parsley, and capers. Cook, tossing the pasta gently, until it is well coated with sauce, 1 to 2 minutes. Season with salt and pepper to taste and serve with the Parmesan.

Garlic 101

From pungent and fiery to sweet and nutty, garlic is capable of delivering a range of flavors—depending on how you prep and cook it. Here are our proven methods for getting the right results.

BUYING

Choose loose garlic heads, not those sold in cellophane-wrapped boxes, so you can examine them closely. Pick heads without spots, mold, or sprouting. Squeeze them to make sure they're not rubbery and that there aren't any soft spots or missing cloves. The garlic shouldn't have much of a scent; if it does, you're risking spoilage.

SOFTNECK
Of the two main garlic varieties, your best bet at the supermarket is softneck, since it stores well and is heat tolerant. This variety features a circle of large cloves surrounding a small cluster at the center.

HARDNECK
Distinguished by a stiff center staff surrounded by large, uniform cloves, hardneck garlic has a more intense, complex flavor. But since it's easily damaged and doesn't store as well, wait to buy it at the farmers' market.

ELEPHANT GARLIC
The huge individual cloves of so-called elephant garlic—which is actually a member of the leek family—are often sold alongside regular garlic. We find it far milder than regular garlic and don't recommend it for recipes.

STORING

With proper storage, whole heads of garlic should last at least a few weeks.

DO store heads in a cool, dark place with plenty of air circulation to prevent spoiling and sprouting.

DON'T store cut garlic in oil for more than 24 hours. This may seem like an easy way to preserve leftovers, but since the bacteria that cause botulism grow in exactly this kind of oxygen-free environment, it's actually a health hazard.

PREPPING

How garlic is handled can have a dramatic impact on flavor.

DO remove any green shoots from cloves before chopping. They contain bitter-tasting compounds that persist even after cooking.

DO pay attention to how fine you chop garlic. The finer the mince, the stronger the flavor (see "Manipulating Garlic's Flavor," page 189).

DON'T chop garlic in advance. In tests, we've found that since garlic flavor comes from the compound allicin—which is released and starts to build only when the cloves are ruptured—the longer cut garlic sits, the harsher its flavor.

THREE WAYS TO SKIN A CLOVE
Crushing the clove is the easiest way to remove the skin from garlic you plan to mince. When a whole clove is called for, try the other two tips.

CRUSH: Press against the garlic firmly with the flat side of a chef's knife to loosen the skin.

ROLL: The E-Z-Rol Garlic Peeler ($8.95) relies on hand friction to quickly and efficiently remove the skin from cloves placed inside it.

MICROWAVE: Place the garlic on a microwave-safe plate and cook on high power 10 to 20 seconds; cool and peel.

TWO WAYS TO MAKE GARLIC PASTE
In dishes such as *aïoli* and pesto, a paste adds the most robust garlic flavor and keeps the garlic's texture unobtrusive.

GRATE: Rub cloves against the sharp, fine holes of a rasp-style grater to reduce garlic to a paste.

SALT AND DRAG: Sprinkle a mound of minced garlic with a coarse salt such as kosher. Repeatedly drag the side of a chef's knife over the mixture until it turns into a smooth puree.

WHAT'S THE YIELD?

Because of garlic's intense flavor, the size of the cloves can really make a difference in your cooking. Besides specifying the quantity and size of the cloves, our recipes offer teaspoon or tablespoon measurements for minced garlic (our most common preparation) so there's no doubt that you're using the right amount. Illustrations are true to size.

EXTRA-LARGE CLOVE
1 tablespoon minced

LARGE CLOVE
2 teaspoons minced

MEDIUM CLOVE
1 teaspoon minced

SMALL CLOVE
½ teaspoon minced

COOKING

DO wait to add garlic to the pan until other aromatics or ingredients have softened (push these to the perimeter) to avoid browning and the creation of bitter compounds.

DON'T cook garlic over high heat for much longer than 30 seconds; you want to cook it only until it turns fragrant. And make sure to stir constantly.

DO add garlic to a cold pan when it is the only flavoring and cook it over low to medium heat to give it time to release its flavors and keep it from burning.

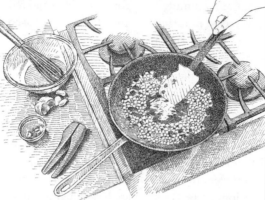

MANIPULATING GARLIC'S FLAVOR

Garlic's pungency emerges only after its cell walls are ruptured, triggering the creation of a compound called allicin. The more a clove is broken down, the more allicin—and the more flavor (and aroma)—are produced. Thus you can control the amount of bite garlic contributes to a recipe by how fine (or coarse) you cut it. Cooking also affects flavor intensity. Garlic is sharpest when raw. When it's heated above 150 degrees, its enzymes are destroyed and no new flavor is produced; only flavor created up to the inactivation temperature remains. This is why toasted or roasted garlic has a mellow, slightly sweet flavor. Alternatively, garlic browned (or overbrowned) at very high temperatures (300 to 350 degrees) results in a bitter flavor. (Garlic chips are the exception, since they are mellowed first, then crisped, which creates a sweet flavor with only hints of bitterness.)

TYPE OF GARLIC	RESULTING FLAVOR
ROASTED WHOLE HEAD	Very mild, sweet, caramel-like
TOASTED WHOLE CLOVE	Mellow and nutty
SLIVERED AND SAUTÉED	Mellow
MINCED AND SAUTÉED	Full and rounded
PRESSED AND SAUTÉED	Very robust, harsh
RAW PASTE	Sharp and fiery

GOOD (AND NOT-SO-GOOD) SUBSTITUTES

Though we almost always prefer a fresh clove to processed garlic, there are times when substitutes can come in handy.

POWDER: Since garlic powder (made from pulverized dehydrated minced garlic) will not burn in the oven, we sometimes prefer it to fresh garlic in spice rubs, breading, and dishes such as roasted potatoes. Substitute ¼ teaspoon garlic powder for each clove of fresh garlic.

PREPEELED: Even if kept unopened in its original packaging, prepeeled garlic lasts only about two weeks before turning yellowish and developing an overly pungent aroma. Still, in tests we found its flavor comparable to that of fresh cloves, if used before yellowing. Make sure to buy prepeeled cloves that look firm and white.

DEHYDRATED MINCED: Because this product takes a long time to rehydrate and packs none of the punch of fresh garlic, we avoid it altogether.

PRESS CREDENTIALS

In our experience, a good garlic press can break down cloves more finely and evenly—and quickly—than the average cook wielding a knife. (Note: The fine mince can lead to stronger garlic taste.) Plus, with a good garlic press, you don't even have to stop and peel the cloves. We squeezed hundreds of cloves with 13 different models to find the best tool for the job: the Kuhn Rikon Easy-Squeeze Garlic Press ($19.95).

TORTELLINI WITH FENNEL, PEAS, AND SPINACH

IT'S A COMMON WEEKNIGHT DINNER scenario: boil up a couple packages of store-bought tortellini, toss with some variety of jarred sauce, and try to cover it all up with a mound of grated Parmesan. This kind of dinner may be easy and quick, but that's about all it has going for it. While we do appreciate the convenience of store-bought tortellini, we're consistently unimpressed by weeknight tortellini recipes that inevitably fall short. The result is typically overcooked pasta floating in a sea of heavy cream sauce. Recognizing the potential of these packaged pasta purses, we committed ourselves to developing a one-pot recipe featuring properly cooked tortellini, fresh vegetables, and a luxurious (but not overly rich), from-scratch sauce.

While some specialty markets sell fresh home-made tortellini, they can be difficult to track down and are always expensive. We wanted an accessible recipe that featured one of the three styles found at the supermarket: fresh, frozen, or dried. We bought a package of each and cooked them according to their directions. The dried tortellini were the clear loser of the group; they took the longest to cook through and had an unappealing rubbery texture. The differences between fresh and frozen were less noticeable, but in the end fresh won for its silkier texture and superior flavor. After sampling the range of fillings commonly found in fresh tortellini, we settled on the simplest, cheese, which would give us the most freedom when choosing flavor combinations and vegetables. To figure out the best way to cook the tortellini, we put together a bare-bones working recipe.

We melted butter in a large Dutch oven (which would easily hold two 9-ounce packages of tortellini) and softened onion and garlic to establish an aromatic base. Next, following our basic one-pot pasta technique, we stirred in 5½ cups of chicken broth (preferred over water) and the tortellini. We simmered the pasta until the liquid had reduced to a lightly thickened sauce, which took about 15 minutes. To our dismay, the tortellini emerged as bloated, mushy spheres. We quickly realized our mistake: In comparing this dish to our other one-pot pastas, we failed to consider the fact that fresh tortellini contains far more moisture than dried pasta. This added moisture means that the pasta absorbs less liquid as it cooks, and thus requires less simmering to become tender. We tested a few more batches of tortellini with 4 cups, 3 cups, and 2 cups of chicken broth, respectively. While 4 cups of broth still produced blown-out pasta, 2 cups left us with just the opposite problem: no sauce and undercooked bites of tortellini. Luckily, the batch with 3 cups of liquid was much closer to our ideal, if just slightly overcooked. After some minor tweaking we finally settled on 2¾ cups broth. This batch of tortellini cooked up tender in about seven minutes, at which point the broth had reduced to a nice sauce. Having ironed out our pasta-cooking method, we addressed the vegetables and flavorings.

As our goal was a fresh-tasting, vibrant dish, we decided to focus on spring vegetables such as artichokes, asparagus, fennel, peas, and spinach. Tasters liked the anise-flavored sweetness of fennel and the delicate elegance of peas and spinach. While artichokes and asparagus both provided welcome texture, tasters found that too many vegetables muddied the flavor of the dish. Since peas and spinach are best when barely cooked, we stirred them in at the last minute. Fennel, on the other hand, benefits from a longer cooking time so it has a chance to become lightly caramelized. We tried swapping ½-inch pieces of fennel for the onion in our recipe, allowing it to slowly soften and brown in the butter before adding the broth and pasta. This approach resulted in a sweet, rich flavor that tasters loved.

For a touch of richness, we stirred in ½ cup cream with the peas and spinach. This small amount gave our broth-based sauce body without dulling the fresh flavors. An ounce of grated Parmesan also helped thicken the sauce and contributed a nutty flavor, while a splash of lemon juice added brightness.

Tasters were really coming around to our reinvention of store-bought tortellini, but felt this sauce was a little too sweet. To counter the sweetness from the cream, fennel, and peas, we decided to add a sprinkling of crisp prosciutto as a garnish. By cooking the prosciutto first and then setting it aside, we were able to incorporate the rendered fat into the dish, which added another layer of flavor and further balanced the sweetness.

Miles away from your average quick-fix tortellini dinner, our dish was a satisfying melange of tender pasta, fresh vegetables, silky sauce, and savory bites of prosciutto.

Tortellini with Fennel, Peas, and Spinach
SERVES 4

Do not substitute frozen or dried tortellini for the fresh tortellini. If necessary, add hot water, 1 tablespoon at a time, to adjust the consistency of the sauce before serving.

- 2 ounces thinly sliced prosciutto, cut into ¼-inch pieces
- 1 tablespoon unsalted butter
- 1 medium fennel bulb (about 12 ounces), trimmed of stalks, cored, and cut into ½-inch pieces (see the illustrations on page 38)
- 3 medium garlic cloves, minced or pressed through a garlic press (about 1 tablespoon)
- 2¾ cups low-sodium chicken broth
- 2 (9-ounce) packages fresh cheese tortellini (see note)
- ½ cup heavy cream
- 5 ounces baby spinach (about 5 cups)
- 1 cup frozen peas
- 1 ounce Parmesan cheese, grated (½ cup), plus extra for serving
- 1 tablespoon juice from 1 lemon
  Salt and ground black pepper

1. Cook the prosciutto in a large Dutch oven over medium heat until browned and crisp, 5 to 7 minutes. Using a slotted spoon, transfer the prosciutto to a paper towel–lined plate; set aside.

2. Melt the butter in the pot over medium heat. Add the fennel and cook until lightly browned, 6 to 9 minutes. Stir in the garlic and cook until fragrant, about 30 seconds. Stir in the broth and tortellini, bring to a rapid simmer, and cook, stirring often, until the tortellini is tender and the sauce is thickened, 6 to 9 minutes.

3. Reduce the heat to low and stir in the cream, spinach, and peas. Cook, stirring gently, until the spinach is wilted and the tortellini is coated in the sauce, 2 to 3 minutes.

4. Off the heat, stir in the Parmesan and lemon juice and season with salt and pepper to taste. Serve, sprinkling individual portions with the prosciutto and additional Parmesan.

PENNE AND CHICKEN WITH BROCCOLI AND BELL PEPPER

FOR A QUICK WEEKNIGHT MEAL, NOTHING beats pasta for ease of preparation. Add some chicken, vegetables, and a flavorful sauce and you've got an instant crowd-pleaser. Penne with chicken and broccoli is one classic option, and when done right, the result is a lightly sauced, perfectly cooked, flavorful penne supper. Unfortunately, this simple combination often produces disappointing results—dry chicken, bland pasta, and overcooked broccoli blanketed by a flavorless cream sauce. We wanted to develop a foolproof method for preparing penne with chicken and broccoli in just one pot, which we could then use to create inspired variations.

Since we already had a basic one-pot technique for simmering pasta right in the sauce, we decided to start with the chicken. Right off the bat, we decided that boneless, skinless chicken breasts were the best choice for this dish; they're easy to prepare and ideal for quick weeknight meals. We tested various cooking methods, including microwaving, poaching, and sautéing. Not surprisingly, microwaving produced bland chicken. Poaching the chicken in the simmering sauce resulted in meat that was tender and juicy, but the flavor was washed out. We had our greatest success with sautéing; the meat was flavorful and the chicken was nicely browned. We turned to our basic stir-fry method, where the chicken is sliced thin and cooked over high heat for a short period of time. This was the clear winner. When the chicken was just cooked through, we set it aside until the sauce and pasta were done, then stirred it back in to warm it.

As for the sauce, we started with a simple chicken broth base. Penne (like other tubular shapes) pairs beautifully with brothy sauces because the sauce binds to the starchy surface of the pasta, both inside and out. By simmering the penne in the sauce, this effect is magnified and the pasta absorbs maximum flavor from the dish's other elements. We found a vigorous simmer was necessary to properly cook the pasta and reduce the liquid to an ideal, saucy consistency. A little white wine, added to the skillet before stirring in the broth and water, provided a balanced acidic note. We also tested adding cream, but tasters favored a lighter, cleaner sauce. Next, we focused on the broccoli.

All too often, broccoli shows up to the table limp and army green, having been negligently

overcooked. Determined to avoid this pitfall, we tested a number of different techniques. Certainly the simplest option was to stir in the broccoli a few minutes before the pasta was done cooking, allowing the simmering liquid to tenderize the florets. And while this method was mostly successful, it proved finicky. If the broccoli was cut too large or small, it was likely to be crunchy or mushy by the time the pasta was tender and the sauce reduced. Sautéing the broccoli before cooking the pasta (and returning it to the pot with the chicken) delivered consistent results, but tasters felt the browned broccoli overpowered the dish. In the end, pan-steaming the broccoli with a splash of water, setting it aside while we prepared the rest of the dish, and then returning it to the pot with the browned chicken proved to be the best option. This broccoli was crisp-tender, vibrant, and delicately flavored. To round out the dish, we added red bell pepper, which provided a burst of sweetness and color, a generous amount of garlic, a touch of red pepper flakes, and a handful of Parmesan. Satisfied with our one-dish approach to this classic, we moved on to develop some interesting and flavorful variations.

For one, we opted for the savory combination of mushrooms and Gorgonzola. Browning white mushrooms left a rich layer of fond in the pot that, once deglazed with white wine, lent flavor to the whole dish. And substituting crumbled Gorgonzola for the Parmesan provided a rich, pungent flavor that tasters loved. Another variation that won rave reviews was a Mediterranean-inspired combination of artichokes, sweet cherry tomatoes, and briny olives. We quartered the cherry tomatoes to help them release their juice and flavor the sauce. Finally, we combined peppery arugula, crunchy, toasted pine nuts, and a healthy dose of lemon for a fresh, light pasta supper.

By choosing easy-to-prep ingredients, combining interesting flavors, and employing an innovative approach to cooking pasta, we were able to reinvent an often-stodgy weeknight menu item. These penne pastas are sure to become instant favorites.

INGREDIENTS: Penne

In the past, domestic brands of dried pasta have repeatedly won top honors with our testers, but now that more specialty brands and Italian imports have hit store shelves, we decided to give fancy pasta another taste. We tried eight brands, with some costing as much as $5 per pound. Though none were deemed unacceptable, there were significant differences among the brands we tasted. Many Italian brands claim to maintain traditional techniques and ingredients, such as slow kneading, mixing cold mountain spring water with hard durum semolina, extruding the dough through traditional bronze cast dies for a coarse texture, and prolonged air-drying. Supposedly, these practices make for stronger flavor and more rustic, sauce-gripping pasta. Yet three expensive imports landed at the bottom of our rankings. Tasters liked three other Italian offerings, but top honors stayed at home with Mueller's Penne Rigate, which offered a "hearty," "wheaty" taste. The bottom line: Money may buy you fancy packaging, but it doesn't buy you better pasta. Pricey Italian imports aren't worth the cost or the trip to a specialty store.

MUELLER'S

THE BEST PENNE

Beating out Italian imports, Mueller's Penne Rigate was praised for its "rich," "slightly sweet" flavor and "good texture."

Penne and Chicken with Broccoli and Bell Pepper

SERVES 4

You can substitute ziti, medium shells, farfalle, campanelle, or orecchiette for the penne; however, the cup measurements will vary. See page 185 for more information on measuring pasta. If necessary, add hot water, 1 tablespoon at a time, to adjust the consistency of the sauce before serving.

¼	cup olive oil
1½	pounds broccoli (1 large bunch), stems discarded, florets cut into bite-size pieces
2	cups water
	Salt and ground black pepper
1	pound boneless, skinless chicken breasts (about 3 medium), trimmed and sliced thin (see illustrations on page 219)
1	medium onion, minced
1	red bell pepper, stemmed, seeded, and cut into ½-inch pieces (see the illustrations on page 226)
6	medium garlic cloves, minced or pressed through a garlic press (about 2 tablespoons)
1	teaspoon minced fresh oregano leaves or ¼ teaspoon dried
⅛	teaspoon red pepper flakes
½	cup dry white wine
2	cups low-sodium chicken broth
8	ounces (2½ cups) penne
2	ounces Parmesan cheese, grated (1 cup), plus extra for serving

1. Heat 1 tablespoon of the oil in a large Dutch oven over medium heat. Add the broccoli, ¼ cup of the water, and a pinch salt. Cover and cook until the broccoli is crisp-tender, 3 to 4 minutes. Uncover and continue to cook until the broccoli is just tender and the liquid has evaporated, 1 to 2 minutes longer. Transfer to a bowl; set aside.

2. Pat the chicken dry with paper towels and season with salt and pepper. Heat 2 tablespoons more oil in the Dutch oven over high heat until just smoking. Add the chicken, break up any clumps, and cook, without stirring, until beginning to brown, about 1 minute. Stir the chicken and continue to cook until just cooked through, 1 to 2 minutes longer. Transfer the chicken to a bowl and cover to keep warm; set aside.

3. Add the remaining 1 tablespoon oil, onion, and bell pepper to the pot and cook over medium heat until softened, 5 to 7 minutes. Stir in the garlic, oregano, and red pepper flakes and cook until fragrant, about 30 seconds. Stir in the wine, scraping up any browned bits, and cook until nearly evaporated, about 1 minute.

4. Stir in the remaining 1¾ cups water, broth, penne, and ½ teaspoon salt and bring to a rapid simmer. Simmer vigorously, stirring often, until the pasta is tender and the sauce is thickened, 15 to 18 minutes.

5. Reduce the heat to low and stir in the cooked broccoli, cooked chicken with any accumulated juice, and Parmesan. Cook, tossing the pasta gently, until it is well coated with sauce, 1 to 2 minutes. Season with salt and pepper to taste and serve with additional Parmesan.

➤ VARIATIONS

Penne and Chicken with Mushrooms and Gorgonzola

Follow the recipe for Penne and Chicken with Broccoli and Bell Pepper, omitting the broccoli and step 1. Substitute 8 ounces white mushrooms, wiped clean, trimmed, and quartered, for the onion and bell pepper in step 3; cook as directed until they have released their moisture and are golden brown, 7 to 10 minutes. Substitute 2 ounces Gorgonzola cheese, crumbled (½ cup), for the Parmesan. Sprinkle with 2 tablespoons minced fresh parsley leaves before serving.

Penne and Chicken with Artichokes, Cherry Tomatoes, and Olives

Follow the recipe for Penne and Chicken with Broccoli and Bell Pepper, omitting the broccoli, step 1, and the bell pepper in step 3. Add 1 (9-ounce) box frozen artichokes, thawed, to the pot halfway through the pasta cooking time in step 4. Stir 2 cups cherry tomatoes (about 12 ounces), quartered, and

½ cup pitted kalamata olives, chopped coarse, into the pasta with the cooked chicken in step 5. Sprinkle with 2 tablespoons minced fresh parsley leaves before serving.

Penne and Chicken with Arugula, Pine Nuts, and Lemon

You can substitute baby spinach for the arugula, if desired.

Follow the recipe for Penne and Chicken with Broccoli and Bell Pepper, omitting the broccoli, step 1, and the bell pepper in step 3. Stir 5 ounces baby arugula (about 5 cups) into the pasta with the cooked chicken in step 5. Stir ¼ cup toasted pine nuts and ½ teaspoon grated zest and 1 tablespoon juice from 1 lemon into the pasta before serving.

PASTA PRIMAVERA

DESPITE THE NAME, PASTA PRIMAVERA originated in the United States, not Italy. This fresh-flavored dish, full of crisp vegetables, was created in the 1970s by the owner of Le Cirque, New York's famed French restaurant. It was dubbed spaghetti primavera—primavera is Italian for "spring"—and became a sensation in a New York minute.

This dish is a sure winner with guests, but for the cook, it's a labor of love. For one thing, it calls for blanching the green vegetables separately to retain their individual character; if the same pot is used for each vegetable, this step can take almost an hour. As if that weren't enough, once the vegetables are blanched, you need five more pots: one to cook the vegetables in garlicky olive oil, one to sauté mushrooms, one to make a fresh tomato sauce flavored with basil, one to make a cream sauce with butter and Parmesan, and one to cook the pasta. While these steps aren't difficult, the timing is complicated—this dish is better suited to a professional kitchen with several cooks. But we love pasta primavera, so we wanted to see if we could simplify the process enough that it would require just one pot but still keep the fresh flavors that are the hallmark of this recipe.

The first issue was to decide which vegetables were essential. Many of the ingredients in the original dish, such as broccoli, green beans, and zucchini, are not actually spring vegetables. We began testing spring vegetables not traditionally used in primavera and soon realized why they were not included. Artichokes were way too much work to prepare. The sweet, anise flavor of fennel overwhelmed the flavors of the other vegetables, and snow peas seemed superfluous, as the original recipe uses shelled peas. Asparagus, on the other hand, was a hit, so we included it along with zucchini, mushrooms, and peas (we liked the convenience and quality of frozen peas).

The next step was cooking and incorporating the vegetables into the dish. Knowing we didn't want to spend extra time blanching each vegetable individually, we searched for a different method. Sautéing the vegetables individually in the skillet worked, but tasters felt that the expected fresh and crisp qualities were now missing. We then tried pan-steaming the green vegetables briefly in a splash of water and a pat of butter until they were crisp, tender, and bright green. Now we were on the right track—this dish was clean and fresh-tasting. We also discovered that we could skip pan-steaming the peas; they only needed a brief stint in the pot when finishing the dish to shake off their frost, leaving their fresh flavor and vibrant color intact. The mushrooms, however, would still need to be browned to cook off their moisture and bring out their flavor. As for the fresh tomato sauce, we took a hint from other stream-lined primavera recipes and skipped this ingredient. Instead, we focused on the cream sauce.

To build flavor in the sauce, garlic and butter proved essential. (Tasters preferred the sweet, rich flavor of butter to the flavor of olive oil.) Using our established one-pot pasta method, we added a combination of vegetable broth and water (3¾ cups total) and our pasta to the pot. We chose the trumpet-shaped campanelle, which stands up well to bites of vegetables; it absorbed most of the liquid as it simmered, and the remainder of the liquid reduced to a nice saucy consistency. Finally, we added the reserved steamed vegetables, peas, and ½ cup cream and let the cream reduce for just a minute or two before stirring in a generous amount of Parmesan cheese and a handful of chopped fresh basil. The sauce was silky and creamy, but some tasters found it a tad too rich. Some fresh lemon juice cut through this rich flavor and gave the dish a brightness that reminded us of spring.

Our recipe was just as delicious as the more laborious original, and we had just one pot to clean, not a sink-full. We had also reduced total preparation and cooking time by more than half. Our primavera is a perfect weeknight meal when you are craving fresh vegetables and pasta.

Pasta Primavera

SERVES 4

We prefer the lighter flavor of vegetable broth here but low-sodium chicken broth can be used instead. You can substitute penne, ziti, medium shells, farfalle, or orecchiette for the campanelle; however, the cup measurements will vary. See page 185 for more information on measuring pasta. If necessary, add hot water, 1 tablespoon at a time, to adjust the consistency of the sauce before serving.

3	tablespoons unsalted butter
8	ounces asparagus (about ½ bunch), tough ends trimmed, cut on the bias into 1-inch lengths
1	large zucchini (about 12 ounces), quartered lengthwise, seeded (see the illustration on page 148), and cut into ½-inch pieces
2	cups water
	Salt and ground black pepper
4	ounces white mushrooms, wiped clean, trimmed, and quartered
3	medium garlic cloves, minced or pressed through a garlic press (about 1 tablespoon)
2	cups vegetable broth
8	ounces (3 cups) campanelle
1	cup frozen peas
½	cup heavy cream
1	ounce Parmesan cheese, grated (½ cup), plus extra for serving
¼	cup chopped fresh basil leaves
1	tablespoon juice from 1 lemon

1. Melt 1 tablespoon of the butter in a large Dutch oven over medium heat. Add the asparagus, zucchini, ¼ cup of the water, and a pinch salt. Cover and cook until crisp-tender, 3 to 4 minutes. Uncover and continue to cook until the vegetables are just tender and the liquid has evaporated, 1 to 2 minutes longer. Transfer to a bowl and cover to keep warm; set aside.

2. Melt the remaining 2 tablespoons butter in the pot over medium heat. Add the mushrooms and cook until golden brown, about 5 minutes. Stir in the garlic and cook until fragrant, about 30 seconds.

3. Stir in the remaining 1¾ cups water, broth, campanelle, and ½ teaspoon salt and bring to a rapid simmer. Simmer vigorously, stirring often, until the pasta is tender and the sauce is thickened, 15 to 18 minutes.

4. Reduce the heat to low and stir in the cooked asparagus and zucchini, peas, cream, and Parmesan. Cook, tossing the pasta gently, until it is well coated with sauce, 1 to 2 minutes. Off the heat, stir in the basil and lemon juice and season with salt and pepper to taste. Serve with additional Parmesan.

INGREDIENTS: Mushrooms

Freshly harvested white button mushrooms have firm caps, stems, and gills that are free of dark spots. That said, some chefs advocate the use of slightly older, blemished mushrooms, claiming that they are more flavorful than pristine, ultra-fresh specimens. To test this claim for ourselves, we sautéed two batches of mushrooms, one fresh from the supermarket and one showing signs of age after a week in the refrigerator. In a side-by-side comparison, the results surprised us. Tasters found that the older mushrooms actually had a deeper, earthier flavor and were substantially more "mushroomy" than the unblemished samples. This is likely because some moisture had evaporated and flavors were concentrated. The takeaway: There's no need to discard old mushrooms. In fact, their imperfections may actually improve the flavor of your dish. Do not, however, use mushrooms that smell fermented or are slimy.

SHRIMP SCAMPI WITH CAMPANELLE

NEARLY EVERY ITALIAN RESTAURANT IN THE United States features a shrimp scampi dish, and for good reason. It's a simply prepared dish full of tender shrimp, al dente bites of pasta, and a garlicky, lemony sauce. When done right, scampi strikes a balance between richness (from a good deal of olive oil) and brightness (from the lemon juice), both of which support an intense—but not overpowering—garlic presence. It's the kind of meal we never get tired of eating. Our challenges would be properly cooking the shrimp, attaining great garlic flavor and a balanced sauce, and of course, cooking everything in just one pot.

We already knew that we wanted to pan-sear the shrimp; this technique produces the ultimate combination of a well-caramelized exterior and a moist, tender interior. We cooked them over high heat in a single layer, without moving them, just long enough for the shrimp to become spotty brown on one side. This allowed us to develop strong shrimp flavor in the skillet without overcooking the shrimp. To promote browning and enhance the flavor of the naturally sweet shrimp, we first tossed them with a little sugar. Once they were almost cooked through, we removed the shrimp and set them aside while we focused on the garlic.

Garlic could be described as the chameleon of the culinary world for its ability to present such a varied array of flavors and aromas depending on how it's prepared. It is at its most powerful when minced and consumed raw. Cooked quickly in hot oil, garlic is pungent and highly aromatic. Slow-cooked over gentle heat (or roasted until very soft), it displays a sweeter, gentler side, accented by a distinct nuttiness. With this full spectrum of garlic flavor in mind, we began by testing ways of infusing it into the oil, which we decided would form our scampi's base. Tests with 2 tablespoons of minced garlic cooked in 2 tablespoons of olive oil over high heat produced a boldly flavored oil that had good garlic presence, but was too spicy for some tasters. Using the same amount of oil and garlic, we tried cooking it slowly over low heat until aromatic and golden. Now the oil boasted a deep garlic flavor and subtle sweetness.

We added red pepper flakes for heat and white wine for acidity, then stirred in clam juice (to enhance the briny flavor of the shrimp), water, and the pasta (we started with penne). Using our one-pot pasta method, we vigorously simmered the pasta until tender, at which point the sauce was reduced and thickened. To finish, we stirred in the seared shrimp and 2 tablespoons of lemon juice. Though the shrimp in this batch were perfectly cooked, their flavor was entirely masked by the clam juice. Substituting chicken broth for the clam juice worked much better, offering some background richness that didn't compete with the shrimp. But we still had a problem: Despite our early efforts at building garlic flavor, it was now too subtle in the finished dish.

We first tried increasing the garlic to 3 tablespoons and, while this helped, our dish still lacked serious garlic punch. We knew that adding raw garlic would add pungency, but were wary of the dish becoming harsh or too spicy. In an attempt to ramp up garlic flavor without overwhelming the dish, we made a paste with salt and two cloves of raw garlic, which we combined with 2 tablespoons of extra-virgin olive oil. Making a paste guarded against the risk of bites of raw garlic in the finished dish. We let this mixture sit while preparing the pasta, and then stirred it into the finished dish at the last minute. Tasters raved about this sauce's rich garlic flavor and gentle heat. Having achieved tender shrimp and big garlic flavor, it was time for some finishing touches.

To balance the robust garlic, we increased the lemon juice to 3 tablespoons and added ½ teaspoon grated zest. Finally, we reexamined our choice of pasta. While penne worked fine, a few tasters felt it was a little pedestrian for this rather sophisticated preparation. We tested myriad medium-shaped pastas before settling on campanelle as our favorite. Campanelle's spiraled shape provided many nooks and crannies to trap the sauce, as well as striking visual appeal. We had finally arrived at our ultimate one-pot shrimp scampi.

Shrimp Scampi with Campanelle

SERVES 4

Be sure not to cook the shrimp through completely in step 2 or they will overcook when returned to the skillet in step 5. You can substitute penne, ziti, medium shells, farfalle, or orecchiette for the campanelle; however, the cup measurements will vary. See page 185 for more information on measuring pasta. If necessary, add hot water, 1 tablespoon at a time, to adjust the consistency of the sauce before serving.

11	medium garlic cloves, 2 cloves minced to a paste (see the illustrations on page 188) and 9 cloves minced or pressed through a garlic press (about 3 tablespoons)
5	tablespoons extra-virgin olive oil
1	pound extra-large shrimp (21 to 25 per pound), peeled and deveined (see the illustration on page 145)
	Salt and ground black pepper
⅛	teaspoon sugar
¼	teaspoon red pepper flakes
½	cup dry white wine
3	cups water
2	cups low-sodium chicken broth
12	ounces (4½ cups) campanelle
3	tablespoons minced fresh parsley leaves
½	teaspoon grated zest and 3 tablespoons juice from 1 lemon

1. Combine the garlic paste and 2 tablespoons of the oil in a small bowl; set aside. In a medium bowl, toss the shrimp with ¼ teaspoon salt, ⅛ teaspoon pepper, and sugar.

2. Heat 1 tablespoon more oil in a 12-inch nonstick skillet over high heat until just smoking. Add the shrimp and cook without stirring until beginning to brown, about 1 minute. Stir the shrimp and continue to cook until they are light pink but not fully cooked through, about 30 seconds. Transfer the shrimp to a bowl and cover to keep warm; set aside.

3. Let the pan cool slightly, about 1 minute. Add the remaining 2 tablespoons oil, minced garlic, and red pepper flakes and cook over low heat, stirring constantly, until the garlic is golden, about 4 minutes. Stir in the wine, increase the heat to medium-high, and simmer until nearly evaporated, 1 to 3 minutes.

4. Stir in the water, broth, campanelle, and ½ teaspoon salt and bring to a rapid simmer. Simmer vigorously, stirring often, until the pasta is tender and the sauce is thickened, 15 to 18 minutes.

5. Reduce the heat to low and stir in the garlic-oil mixture. Cook, tossing the pasta gently, until it is well coated with sauce, 1 to 2 minutes. Off the heat, stir in the shrimp, parsley, lemon zest, and lemon juice. Season with salt and pepper to taste and serve.

SKILLET LASAGNA

LASAGNA IS A CROWD-PLEASER THAT NEVER goes out of style, and second helpings are almost always mandatory. But lasagna is not a dish you can throw together at the last minute. Even with the invention of no-boil noodles, which we'd employed in our Weeknight Meat Lasagna recipe (see page 117), it can still take a good amount of time to make the components and assemble and bake the casserole. Add to that the multitude of dishes that get used (and need to be cleaned) while preparing each ingredient, and making lasagna becomes a serious chore. While lasagna is traditionally made with fully or partially cooked elements that meld together during baking, we wondered if it would be possible to take the same components and cook them on the stovetop all in one skillet, to result in the same flavors and textures. Our plan was simple: We would first brown the meat, then build a thin but flavorful sauce in which to cook the pasta. We would finish the dish by adding ricotta cheese, Parmesan, mozzarella, and any other flavors we thought were necessary. We first examined our pasta options.

No-boil noodles seemed like the ideal option for this type of lasagna, as they are designed to cook directly in a lightly bubbling sauce. Unfortunately, no matter how we incorporated them into this dish, they cooked up either grainy or mushy. Using regular curly-edged lasagna noodles was the only answer. Broken into 2-inch pieces and simmered gently in sauce for about 20 minutes, these noodles became tender but retained a satisfying al dente bite.

Most lasagna sauces simmer for hours, giving the ingredients and flavors a chance to blend, but since speed is a key to weeknight dinner success, we wanted to forgo this step. We limited the time that it took to simmer the sauce to the time that it took to cook the pasta. To rein in the ingredient list, we started with onions and garlic, which gave the sauce its depth. Our lasagna was meant to be a complete meal, so we added some protein. Ground beef was good, but we thought meatloaf mix (a combination of ground beef, pork, and veal sold in one package at most supermarkets) was even better. For a flavor variation, tasters liked a combination of Italian sausage and sweet red pepper.

We next turned to the type of tomatoes we would use in the sauce. We started our tests with tomato puree, but this made a sauce that was a tad too heavy and gloppy; the pasta sat on top of the sauce and cooked unevenly. Adding a little water to the puree created a better medium in which to cook the pasta, but the resulting lasagna was bland. Abandoning tomato puree, we revisited some of our other one-pot pasta recipes and added whole peeled tomatoes pulsed briefly in the food processor. This gave the sauce a slightly chunky and substantial texture—and there was just enough liquid to cook the pasta.

To replicate the cheesiness of traditional lasagna, we stirred in ricotta, shredded mozzarella, and grated Parmesan, but this didn't quite give us the results we were looking for. Once mixed in, the sweet creaminess of the ricotta was lost and the sauce turned into a grainy pink mess. We had success when we stirred in the mozzarella and Parmesan first, then placed dollops of ricotta on top of the lasagna and covered the pan, allowing the mozzarella to melt and the ricotta to heat through but still remain a distinct element. The dots of creamy ricotta also created an attractive pattern over the top of the dish. A sprinkling of freshly chopped basil further enhanced the look and flavor of our skillet lasagna.

With a little creativity and a lot of testing, we proved that lasagna could be made using just one pot. Perhaps even more impressive than the simplicity and practicality of this one-pot recipe is the speed at which it disappeared in the kitchen.

Meaty Skillet Lasagna
SERVES 4

Do not substitute no-boil lasagna noodles for the traditional, curly-edged lasagna noodles here. If you can't find meatloaf mix, you can substitute 8 ounces each 85 percent lean ground beef and ground pork.

3	(14.5-ounce) cans whole tomatoes
1	tablespoon olive oil
1	medium onion, minced
3	medium garlic cloves, minced or pressed through a garlic press (about 1 tablespoon)
1/8	teaspoon red pepper flakes
1	pound meatloaf mix
10	curly-edged lasagna noodles (8½ ounces), broken into 2-inch lengths (see note)
2	ounces mozzarella cheese, shredded (½ cup)
½	ounce Parmesan cheese, grated (¼ cup)
	Salt and ground black pepper
¾	cup whole-milk or part-skim ricotta cheese
3	tablespoons chopped fresh basil leaves

1. Pulse the tomatoes with their juice in a food processor until coarsely chopped and no large pieces remain, 6 to 8 pulses.

2. Heat the oil in a 12-inch nonstick skillet over medium heat until shimmering. Add the onion and cook until softened, 5 to 7 minutes. Stir in the garlic and red pepper flakes and cook until fragrant, about 30 seconds. Stir in the meatloaf mix, breaking up the meat with a wooden spoon, and cook until no longer pink, about 1 minute.

3. Scatter the lasagna pieces into the skillet, pour the processed tomatoes over the pasta, and bring to a rapid simmer. Cover and simmer vigorously, stirring often, until the pasta is tender, about 20 minutes.

4. Off the heat, stir in half of the mozzarella and half of the Parmesan. Season with salt and pepper to taste. Dollop heaping tablespoons of the ricotta over the noodles, then sprinkle with the remaining mozzarella and Parmesan. Cover and let stand off the heat until the cheese melts, 2 to 4 minutes. Sprinkle with the basil and serve.

➤ VARIATION
Skillet Lasagna with Sausage and Peppers

Follow the recipe for Meaty Skillet Lasagna, substituting 1 pound sweet Italian sausage, casings removed, for the meatloaf mix. Add 1 red bell pepper, stemmed, seeded, and chopped coarse (see the illustration on page 226), to the skillet with the onion in step 2.

BAKED ZITI WITH SAUSAGE AND PEPPERS

LIKE LASAGNA, BAKED ZITI IS AN ITALIAN-American classic but the two differ in that baked ziti is inherently simpler and slightly less labor intensive. But as we had learned making our casserole version of Baked Ziti with Ricotta (see page 109), recipes often come up short, with mushy noodles, bland flavors, and an unappealing heaviness. Since we'd had so much success converting lasagna to a skillet dinner, we decided to do the same with baked ziti. We hoped to develop a streamlined recipe for baked ziti using just one skillet. This version would be simple to make and hearty with sausage and peppers.

The sauce for baked ziti should be relatively smooth, with bright tomato flavor. We began our testing with canned crushed tomatoes, which are a mix of tomato chunks and puree. Cooked with extra-virgin olive oil, garlic, and red pepper flakes, this sauce had good flavor, but tasters thought that it was too thick for baked ziti. Having had great success with whole canned tomatoes in other one-pot pastas recipes, we gave them a shot here, briefly processing them in a food processor. These processed whole tomatoes offered fresher tomato flavor than the crushed tomatoes and were just the right consistency for our sauce. Simmering our sauce for 10 minutes rid the tomatoes of their raw flavor and concentrated their sweetness. And since we were adding sausage to our ziti, we realized we could ditch the olive oil and simply use the fat left behind from browning the meat. We rendered and browned ½ pound of crumbled sweet Italian sausage in the skillet before building the sauce.

This sauce had good sausage flavor but tasters were begging for more. It wasn't until we doubled the meat to a full pound that they were satisfied.

With our sauce assembled, it was time to add the pasta. Into our skillet went 8 ounces of ziti and some water (1½ cups turned out to be the right amount). Once the pasta was tender, we stirred in shredded mozzarella and sprinkled more over the top. After a brief stint in a 475-degree oven to melt and brown the cheese, our ziti was ready to sample. We took one bite and were immediately disappointed. First and foremost, despite our best efforts we had managed to overcook the pasta; the result was an unappealing mass of blown-out noodles.

Most baked ziti recipes produce mushy noodles because they make one mistake: cooking the pasta until it's tender. When fully cooked pasta is combined with tomato sauce and then baked, it continues to absorb liquid from the sauce and soften. The result is soggy pasta. In order to prevent this problem in our baked ziti, we made sure to cook the pasta until it was just shy of tender before transferring the skillet to the oven where it could finish cooking. This adjustment greatly improved the texture of the pasta. Now we could address the other complaint from tasters: the sauce.

Traditionally, mozzarella cheese is used in baked ziti to bind the pasta together and add creamy richness. While tasters liked the mozzarella on top of the pasta, they felt it was too bland for use in the sauce. We looked for other ways of getting flavor and creaminess into the dish. We found that adding ⅓ cup of heavy cream to the sauce after the pasta cooked gave us just the right consistency, while a little grated Parmesan cheese really boosted flavor. To ensure that the cheese and cream would be evenly distributed throughout the casserole, we stirred them thoroughly into the pasta before placing the skillet in the oven. For our finishing touch, we added diced red bell pepper and a healthy amount of chopped fresh basil.

Our baked ziti with sausage and peppers was now flavorful, saucy, and satisfying—and simple to prepare. Using just one skillet, we had managed to bring this classic potluck dish quickly and easily to the weeknight dinner table.

199

Baked Ziti with Sausage and Peppers

SERVES 4

You can substitute penne, campanelle, medium shells, far-falle, or orecchiette for the ziti; however, the cup measurements will vary. See page 185 for more information on measuring pasta.

1	(28-ounce) can whole tomatoes
1	pound sweet Italian sausage, casings removed
6	medium garlic cloves, minced or pressed through a garlic press (about 2 tablespoons)
¼	teaspoon red pepper flakes
1½	cups water
8	ounces (2½ cups) ziti
1	red bell pepper, stemmed, seeded, and cut into ½-inch pieces (see the illustrations on page 226)
	Salt and ground black pepper
⅓	cup heavy cream
1	ounce Parmesan cheese, grated (½ cup)
¼	cup chopped fresh basil leaves
6	ounces mozzarella cheese, shredded (1½ cups)

1. Adjust an oven rack to the middle position and heat the oven to 475 degrees. Pulse the tomatoes with their juice in a food processor until coarsely chopped and no large pieces remain, 6 to 8 pulses.

2. Cook the sausage in a 12-inch ovensafe nonstick skillet over medium-high heat, breaking up the meat with a wooden spoon, until lightly browned, 3 to 5 minutes. Stir in the garlic and red pepper flakes and cook until fragrant, about 30 seconds. Stir in the processed tomatoes and simmer gently until the tomatoes no longer taste raw, about 10 minutes.

3. Stir in the water, ziti, bell pepper, and ½ teaspoon salt and bring to a rapid simmer. Cover and simmer vigorously, stirring often, until the pasta is just tender, 14 to 17 minutes.

4. Off the heat, stir in the cream, Parmesan, and basil and season with salt and pepper to taste. Sprinkle the mozzarella evenly over the top. Transfer the skillet to the oven and bake until the cheese has melted and browned, 10 to 15 minutes. Serve.

TEX-MEX MACARONI BAKE

MACARONI BAKES ARE A FAVORITE CHILDHOOD comfort food whose appeal, for many of us, extends well into adulthood. We had already developed a casserole version of what we felt was the Ultimate Chili Mac (see page 115), so now we decided to take our macaroni bake in a slightly different direction, one pointed south to the Lone Star State in pursuit of a Tex-Mex version. We felt this macaroni bake should be relatively spicy, use elbow-shaped pasta, and feature a gooey layer of melted cheese on top. Many recipes we came across in our research were a sorry mix of canned chili and jarred salsa stirred into packaged macaroni and cheese—not an appetizing dinner. But the one recipe almost everyone liked featured spicy ground beef, onions, peppers, and smoky chiles. With this example as our inspiration, we set about creating a one-skillet Tex-Mex macaroni bake featuring meaty chili, perfectly cooked macaroni and vegetables, and just the right amount of heat.

Our first challenges were finding the correct heat level for the chili and determining the ideal proportion of chili to macaroni. We focused on the chili first, and started by sautéing onion and garlic in a 12-inch nonstick skillet with chili powder and a little cayenne pepper (fresh jalapeños added too much heat). This step helped to bloom the flavors of the chili and prevented the spices from tasting harsh. We then added lean ground beef to the skillet; after that, we had to make a decision about the tomato component of our chili.

We rounded up the usual tomato products—whole, diced, crushed, and puree—and made a batch of chili using each. To our surprise, none offered the sweet tomato flavor we were after. We tried stirring in some tomato paste, but its flavor was all wrong here. Taking another look through the pantry we happened upon a can of basic tomato sauce. We whipped up a batch with it and were immediately pleased with the results. Since tomato sauce, unlike other canned tomato products, is cooked and seasoned, it had all of the richness and flavor we were after. With our chili shaping up nicely, we moved on to the macaroni.

After adding 8 ounces of elbow macaroni and 2 cups of water to our chili, we simmered everything together until the pasta was tender. Tasters were happy with the balance of macaroni and chili, so it was time to consider the vegetables. We thought red bell peppers would be a surefire hit, but tasters found that their sweetness, combined with the already sweet tomato sauce, was too cloying. A quick switch to green bell peppers better balanced the flavors. Corn was also a welcome addition, and we chose frozen for its consistent quality and year-round availability. Finally, a can of chopped green chiles provided bright flavor that tasters loved.

It was time to address the cheese and get our macaroni bake into the oven. First we tried cheddar, which had good flavor but a slightly grainy texture. We then stirred in shredded Monterey Jack; this cheese lent a nice creaminess but not enough flavor. The winner ended up being shredded Mexican cheese blend, widely available in supermarkets, which is a combination of cheddar, Monterey Jack, asadero, and queso blanco cheeses. The cheeses helped bind the mixture together and infused our macaroni bake with rich flavor. A brief stint in a hot oven melted the cheese and provided a lightly browned topping for the creamy macaroni and chili underneath. Finished with a sprinkling of fresh cilantro, this Tex-Mex macaroni bake was easy to prepare and sure to please everyone.

Tex-Mex Macaroni Bake

SERVES 4

If you can't find shredded Mexican cheese blend, substitute 1 cup each shredded Monterey Jack cheese and shredded cheddar cheese.

1	tablespoon vegetable oil
1	medium onion, minced
1	green bell pepper, stemmed, seeded, and cut into ½-inch pieces (see the illustrations on page 226)
3	medium garlic cloves, minced or pressed through a garlic press (about 1 tablespoon)
2	tablespoons chili powder
⅛	teaspoon cayenne pepper
1	pound 90 percent lean ground beef
2	cups water
1	(15-ounce) can tomato sauce
8	ounces (2 cups) elbow macaroni
1	cup frozen corn
1	(4.5-ounce can) chopped green chiles
1	(8-ounce) package shredded Mexican cheese blend (2 cups)
	Salt and ground black pepper
2	tablespoons minced fresh cilantro leaves

1. Adjust an oven rack to the middle position and heat the oven to 475 degrees. Heat the oil in a 12-inch ovensafe nonstick skillet over medium heat until shimmering. Add the onion and bell pepper and cook until softened, 5 to 7 minutes.

2. Stir in the garlic, chili powder, and cayenne and cook until fragrant, about 30 seconds. Stir in the beef, breaking up the meat with a wooden spoon, and cook until no longer pink, about 1 minute.

3. Stir in the water, tomato sauce, and macaroni and bring to a rapid simmer. Cover and simmer vigorously, stirring often, until the pasta is tender, 9 to 12 minutes.

4. Off the heat, stir in the corn, chiles, and 1 cup of the cheese and season with salt and pepper to taste. Sprinkle the remaining 1 cup cheese evenly over the top. Transfer the skillet to the oven and bake until the cheese has melted and browned, 10 to 15 minutes. Sprinkle with the cilantro and serve.

CHORIZO AND BLACK BEAN SOPA SECA

THE NAME OF THIS MEXICAN DISH, LITERALLY translated, is "dry soup." But don't let the name fool you. Although it starts off looking like a soup, when completed it is a distinctive pasta dish with robust flavors. We started by doing a little research in order to learn more about sopa seca. Of the dozen recipes we found, the one aspect they all shared was the use of *fideos* as a base. Fideos are thin strands of coiled noodles that have been toasted until golden brown. The distinctive nuttiness they bring to this dish underscores all the other flavors. The fideos are placed in a baking dish, topped with a sauce (the soup part), and baked until all the liquid is absorbed and the pasta is tender (the dry part). But the similarities among the recipes ended there, and the huge variety of liquid and garnish choices made the search for the perfect sopa seca recipe an adventure. In addition to unlocking the mysteries of this unique Mexican specialty, we wanted to prepare all of the components of our recipe in just one skillet.

We decided to address the noodles first. Since fideos are often hard to find, we needed an alternative. We found that regular dried vermicelli, broken in half and toasted in a skillet until golden brown, was the closest match in terms of texture and depth

BREAKING VERMICELLI IN HALF

1. To keep the pasta from flying every which way in the kitchen, roll up the bundle of pasta in a kitchen towel that overlaps the pasta by 3 or 4 inches at both ends.

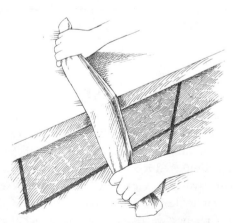

2. Holding both ends firmly, center the rolled bundle over the edge of a table or counter. Push down with both hands to break the pasta in the middle of the bundle.

of flavor. With that important detail taken care of, we moved on to the "soup" of this dish.

The use of tomatoes in the recipes we researched varied greatly. Some called for fresh tomatoes, others canned, and still others listed jarred salsa as the tomato ingredient. We tried all three variations and found that canned diced tomatoes worked the best and yielded the most consistent results. The fresh tomatoes led to inconsistent results due to their varied moisture content. Jarred salsa, which sounded good in theory, overpowered the other ingredients. In addition to the tomato base, sopa seca recipes usually include a liquid component, typically chicken broth or water. Chicken broth was favored over water for the subtle richness and depth of flavor it contributed to the finished dish.

We found that the use of chiles also varied from recipe to recipe. We tried out four options, with our first test using no chiles at all. It was soon obvious, however, that if we wanted a multidimensional sopa seca, chiles were a must. We tried fresh jalapeños and, although they definitely added a spark, some tasters felt they gave the dish too much raw chile flavor. Next up were dried ancho chiles. Many testers liked the smokiness of these chiles, but they required a lengthy soaking period that complicated the cooking process and added too much time to our recipe. Lastly, we tried canned chipotle chiles. These turned out to be the best option: They provided a smoky background similar to that of the ancho chiles, but without the long preparation time, and they added a jalapeño-like spiciness without the raw taste.

Onion and garlic contributed additional flavor, and to make our skillet sopa seca a complete meal, we added chorizo and canned black beans. Lastly, we added the toasted vermicelli back in and simmered the mixture, covered, until most of the liquid was absorbed and the pasta was tender.

After sprinkling shredded Monterey Jack cheese over the noodles, we let the pan sit, covered, until the cheese melted and formed a gooey layer. To finish the dish and add a hit of freshness, we topped it with a sprinkling of cilantro. Our one-dish version of sopa seca now had all the flavor of a traditional one.

Chorizo and Black Bean Sopa Seca

SERVES 4

To make the dish spicier, increase the amount of chipotle chiles to 1 tablespoon. Serve with sour cream, diced avocado, and thinly sliced scallions.

8	ounces vermicelli, broken in half (see the illustrations on page 202)
2	tablespoons vegetable oil
I	medium onion, minced
4	ounces chorizo, halved lengthwise and sliced ¼ inch thick
2	medium garlic cloves, minced or pressed through a garlic press (about 2 teaspoons)
2	teaspoons minced chipotle chile in adobo sauce
2	cups low-sodium chicken broth
I	(15-ounce) can black beans, drained and rinsed
I	(14.5-ounce) can diced tomatoes Salt and ground black pepper
2	ounces Monterey Jack cheese, shredded (½ cup)
¼	cup minced fresh cilantro leaves

1. Toast the vermicelli in 1 tablespoon of the oil in a 12-inch nonstick skillet over medium-high heat, tossing frequently with tongs, until golden, about 4 minutes. Transfer the vermicelli to a paper towel–lined plate; set aside.

2. Add the remaining 1 tablespoon oil and onion to the skillet and cook over medium heat until softened, 5 to 7 minutes. Stir in the chorizo, garlic, and chipotles and cook until fragrant, about 30 seconds.

3. Stir in the toasted vermicelli, broth, beans, and tomatoes with their juice and bring to a rapid simmer. Cover and simmer vigorously, stirring often, until the vermicelli is tender, about 10 minutes.

4. Off the heat, season with salt and pepper to taste and sprinkle the cheese over the top. Cover and let stand until the cheese melts, 2 to 4 minutes. Sprinkle with the cilantro and serve.

INGREDIENTS: Canned Black Beans

Most canned black beans have three main ingredients: beans, water, and salt. Nevertheless, when we sampled six national brands in a blind test, we found out they can taste very different. The three brands that scored highest all have more than 400 milligrams of sodium per ½-cup serving; though simply adding salt to the low-scoring brands that had far less salt didn't help. Tasters also disliked mushy beans. The beans need salt for good flavor, but too much can make them mushy. This is why two of our salty, highly ranked brands include calcium chloride, which counteracts the softening power of sodium. But Bush's Best, our winning brand, does not. How they achieve firm beans with lots of salt and no calcium chloride is proprietary manufacturing information, we're told, but odds are that to preserve more of their firm texture, Bush's quickly processes their beans with less heat than the other brands.

THE BEST CANNED BLACK BEANS

Bush's Best Black Beans won out for their firm texture and salty flavor.

BUSH'S

RAMEN NOODLE DINNERS

INSTANT RAMEN NOODLES HAVE THE reputation of being a mainstay on college campuses across the country. They are cheap (under $1 per package) and they cook quickly (in about 10 minutes), making them a convenient dinner for the thrifty, time-crunched cook. However, in Japan, ramen (or ramen soup) is a much more serious endeavor, with ramen shops on almost every street corner and noodles served in a variety of richly flavored broths. We wanted to take a second look at these quick-cooking noodles and see if we could give them a fresh, new flavor. If we were successful, we would be adding a unique new dish to our one-pot arsenal.

We started by pitching the seasoning packets that come in ramen packages—they're loaded with sodium, not to mention stale, dehydrated ingredients. To create our own flavorful broth in which to simmer the noodles, we sautéed fresh garlic and ginger. To that we added chicken broth and a splash of soy sauce, which made a nice base. It took us a few tries to get the correct ratio of broth to noodles. The noodles needed enough liquid in which to cook, but too much broth diluted the flavors and made the noodles mushy. In the end we settled on 3½ cups of broth and 12 ounces of noodles.

To turn our ramen dish into a substantial meal, we decided to add beef. Tasters approved of flank steak, to which we added shiitake mushrooms and spinach for a classic Asian combination. Before cooking the beef, we sliced it thin and tossed it with a little soy sauce for flavor and to promote browning. We sautéed it briefly over high heat, then set it aside to be returned to the skillet when the noodles were done simmering in the broth.

Finally, we focused on the noodles. For comparison to the supermarket ramen, we sought out dried ramen from an Asian market along with high-end chuka soba noodles (noodles made from all wheat flour or a combination of wheat and buckwheat flours) and fresh egg noodles. The noodles from the Asian market were indistinguishable from their supermarket counterpart. Chuka soba noodles were much thinner and, frankly, didn't have as much flavor as the more common dried ramen noodles. That might be because dried ramen noodles are actually fried as part of the drying process. Frying instills a richer flavor, which in our tests gave them an advantage over the fresh egg noodles. Plus, the ramen noodles instantly soaked up our rich broth when they hit the skillet.

With our basic recipe down, we created a few spin-offs. Thinly sliced pork tenderloin, shredded cabbage, and sliced scallions gave us another dish, while seared shrimp, red bell pepper, roasted peanuts, and hoisin sauce added richness and heft to a kung pao–style shrimp dish. And a vegetarian version with tofu features an interpretation of the flavors found in hot and sour soup.

While many in the test kitchen were originally skeptical about taking ramen noodles this seriously, few could resist slurping up our addictive new dish. The best thing about our ramen suppers (besides their bold flavors and satisfying textures) is that they can be cooked in about the same amount of time as their campus-style counterparts.

Ramen with Beef, Shiitakes, and Spinach
SERVES 4

Do not substitute other types of noodles for the ramen noodles. The sauce in this dish will seem a bit brothy when finished, but the liquid will be absorbed quickly by the noodles when serving.

1	pound flank steak, trimmed and sliced thin across the grain on the bias (see the illustrations on page 215)
8	teaspoons soy sauce
2	tablespoons vegetable oil
8	ounces shiitake mushrooms, wiped clean, stemmed, and sliced thin
3	medium garlic cloves, minced or pressed through a garlic press (about 1 tablespoon)
1	tablespoon minced or grated fresh ginger (see the illustrations on page 216)
3½	cups low-sodium chicken broth
4	(3-ounce) packages ramen noodles, seasoning packets discarded
3	tablespoons Chinese rice cooking wine or dry sherry
2	teaspoons sugar
6	ounces baby spinach (about 6 cups)

1. Pat the beef dry with paper towels and toss with 2 teaspoons of the soy sauce. Heat 1 tablespoon of the oil in a large Dutch oven over high heat until just smoking. Add the beef, break up any clumps, and cook without stirring until beginning to brown, about 1 minute. Stir the beef and continue to cook until it is nearly cooked though, 1 minute longer. Transfer the beef to a bowl and cover to keep warm; set aside.

2. Add the remaining 1 tablespoon oil and mushrooms to the pot and cook over medium-high heat until golden brown, about 5 minutes. Stir in the garlic and ginger and cook until fragrant, about 30 seconds.

3. Stir in the broth. Break the bricks of ramen into small chunks and add to the pot. Bring to a simmer and cook, tossing the ramen constantly with tongs to separate, until the ramen is just tender but there is still liquid in the pan, about 2 minutes.

4. Stir in the remaining 2 tablespoons soy sauce, wine, and sugar. Stir in the spinach, one handful at

a time, until it is wilted and the sauce is thickened. Return the beef with any accumulated juice to the pot and cook until warmed through, about 30 seconds. Serve.

Ramen with Pork, Scallions, and Cabbage
SERVES 4

Do not substitute other types of noodles for the ramen noodles. We found it best to use low-sodium soy sauce here because the oyster sauce is quite salty. The sauce in this dish will seem a bit brothy when finished, but the liquid will be absorbed quickly by the noodles when serving.

1	(1-pound) pork tenderloin, trimmed and sliced thin (see the illustrations on page 223)
8	teaspoons low-sodium soy sauce (see note)
2	tablespoons vegetable oil
1	bunch scallions, white and green parts separated, whites sliced thin and greens cut into 1-inch lengths
6	medium garlic cloves, minced or pressed through a garlic press (about 2 tablespoons)
1	tablespoon minced or grated fresh ginger (see the illustrations on page 216)
⅛	teaspoon red pepper flakes
3½	cups low-sodium chicken broth
4	(3-ounce) packages ramen noodles, seasoning packets discarded
2	tablespoons oyster sauce
2	teaspoons toasted sesame oil
½	pound green cabbage (about ¼ medium head), sliced thin (see the illustrations on page 209)

1. Pat the pork dry with paper towels and toss with 2 teaspoons of the soy sauce. Heat 1 tablespoon of the oil in a large Dutch oven over high heat until just smoking. Add the pork, break up any clumps, and cook without stirring until beginning to brown, about 1 minute. Stir the pork and continue to cook until cooked through, 1 minute longer. Transfer the pork to a bowl and cover to keep warm; set aside.

2. Add the remaining 1 tablespoon oil and scallion whites to the pot and cook over medium-high heat until softened and lightly browned, about

3 minutes. Stir in the garlic, ginger, and red pepper flakes and cook until fragrant, about 30 seconds.

3. Stir in the broth. Break the bricks of ramen into small chunks and add to the pot. Bring to a simmer and cook, tossing the ramen constantly with tongs to separate, until the ramen is just tender but there is still liquid in the pan, about 2 minutes.

4. Stir in the remaining 2 tablespoons soy sauce, oyster sauce, and sesame oil. Stir in the scallion greens and cabbage and cook until the cabbage is wilted and the sauce is thickened, about 1 minute. Return the pork with any accumulated juice to the pot and cook until warmed through, about 30 seconds. Serve.

Kung Pao–Style Shrimp with Ramen
SERVES 4

Do not substitute other types of noodles for the ramen noodles. Be sure not to cook the shrimp through completely in step 1 or they will overcook and turn rubbery when returned to the skillet in step 4. The sauce in this dish will seem a bit brothy when finished, but the liquid will be absorbed quickly by the noodles when serving.

1	pound extra-large shrimp (21 to 25 per pound), peeled and deveined (see the illustration on page 145)
	Salt and ground black pepper
⅛	teaspoon sugar
2	tablespoons vegetable oil
1	red bell pepper, stemmed, seeded, and sliced thin (see the illustrations on page 226)
½	cup roasted unsalted peanuts
3	medium garlic cloves, minced or pressed through a garlic press (about 1 tablespoon)
1	tablespoon minced or grated fresh ginger (see the illustrations on page 216)
1	teaspoon red pepper flakes
3½	cups low-sodium chicken broth
4	(3-ounce) packages ramen noodles, seasoning packets discarded
2	tablespoons hoisin sauce
1	tablespoon rice vinegar
2	teaspoons toasted sesame oil
3	scallions, sliced thin on the bias (see the illustration on page 25)

1. In a medium bowl, toss the shrimp with ¼ teaspoon salt, ⅛ teaspoon pepper, and sugar. Heat 1 tablespoon of the oil in a large Dutch oven over high heat until just smoking. Add the shrimp and cook without stirring until beginning to brown, about 1 minute. Stir the shrimp and continue to cook until they are light pink but not fully cooked through, about 30 seconds. Transfer the shrimp to a bowl and cover to keep warm; set aside.

2. Add the remaining 1 tablespoon oil, bell pepper, and peanuts to the pot and cook over medium heat until the pepper is softened, 2 to 3 minutes. Transfer to the bowl with the shrimp.

3. Add the garlic, ginger, and red pepper flakes to the oil left in the pot and cook until fragrant, about 30 seconds. Stir in the broth. Break the bricks of ramen into small chunks and add to the pot. Bring to a simmer and cook, tossing the ramen constantly with tongs to separate, until the ramen is just tender but there is still liquid in the pan, about 2 minutes.

4. Stir in the hoisin sauce, vinegar, and sesame oil and continue to simmer until the sauce is thickened, about 1 minute. Return the shrimp-pepper mixture to the skillet and cook until heated through, about 30 seconds. Sprinkle with the scallions and serve.

Hot and Sour Ramen with Tofu, Shiitakes, and Spinach

SERVES 4

Do not substitute other types of noodles for the ramen noodles. We prefer the lighter flavor of vegetable broth here; however, low-sodium chicken broth can be substituted. To make the dish spicier, add extra Asian chili-garlic sauce. The sauce in this dish will seem a bit brothy when finished, but the liquid will be absorbed quickly by the noodles when serving.

I (14-ounce) package extra-firm tofu, cut into 1-inch cubes
8 teaspoons soy sauce
2 tablespoons vegetable oil
8 ounces shiitake mushrooms, wiped clean, stemmed, and sliced thin
3 medium garlic cloves, minced or pressed through a garlic press (about 1 tablespoon)
I tablespoon minced or grated fresh ginger (see the illustrations on page 216)

2 teaspoons Asian chili-garlic sauce (see page 230)
3½ cups low-sodium vegetable broth
4 (3-ounce) packages ramen noodles, seasoning packets discarded
3 tablespoons cider vinegar
2 teaspoons sugar
6 ounces baby spinach (about 6 cups)

1. Pat the tofu dry with paper towels and toss with 2 teaspoons of the soy sauce. Heat 1 tablespoon of the oil in a large Dutch oven over high heat until just smoking. Add the tofu and cook until crisp and browned on all sides, 8 to 10 minutes. Transfer the tofu to a bowl and cover to keep warm; set aside.

2. Add the remaining 1 tablespoon oil and mushrooms to the pot and cook over medium-high heat until golden brown, 4 to 5 minutes. Stir in the garlic, ginger, and chili-garlic sauce and cook until fragrant, about 30 seconds.

3. Stir in the broth. Break the bricks of ramen into small chunks and add to the pot. Bring to a simmer and cook, tossing the ramen constantly with tongs to separate, until the ramen is just tender but there is still liquid in the pan, about 2 minutes.

4. Stir in the remaining 2 tablespoons soy sauce, vinegar, and sugar. Stir in the spinach, one handful at a time, until it is wilted and the sauce is thickened. Return the tofu with any accumulated juice to the pot and cook until warmed through, about 30 seconds. Serve.

RICE NOODLES WITH SHRIMP, SHIITAKES, AND SNOW PEAS

SOUTHEAST ASIAN NOODLE DISHES, ESPECIALLY those that hail from Vietnam, are the perfect remedy for a jaded palate. Hot, sweet, bright, and pungent, these preparations wake the senses and provide welcome variety at the dinner table. While we have had memorable take-out versions, we've also been disappointed on more than one occasion. Even more frustrating are the numerous "authentic" recipes we've labored over, only to toss the inedible concoction in the trash. The problems we encounter time and again are gummy noodles, overcooked seafood or meat, and unbalanced sauces. Our goal was to produce a consistently superlative Vietnamese-style rice noodle dish that could be prepared using one pot.

We focused first on the noodles. Flat rice noodles, the type of noodles commonly used in Southeast Asian cuisine, come in a variety of sizes. Wide noodles (½ inch and up), thin noodles (about ⅛ inch thick), and vermicelli-style noodles all have specific recommended uses and cooking times. We decided to use thin noodles for this dish, as they cook quicker than wide noodles but have more resilience than vermicelli-style noodles. We found three different methods for preparing them: soaking them in room-temperature water, soaking them in hot tap water, and boiling them. We began with boiling and quickly realized this was a bad move. Drained and waiting in the colander, the noodles clumped together, and they were soggy and overdone in the finished dish. Noodles soaked in room-temperature water remained fairly stiff no matter how long they sat. We finally tried soaking the noodles in water that had been brought to a boil. These noodles softened and turned limp and pliant, but were not fully tender. Drained, they remained loose and separate and cooked through easily with stir-frying. The result? Noodles that were at once pleasantly tender and chewy. With our noodles ready to go, we focused on creating the right flavor profile.

Sweet, salty, sour, and spicy are all flavor characteristics of Vietnamese cooking, and they should be equally balanced. Although the cooking time for these noodle dishes is short, the ingredient lists generally aren't. Fish sauce and soy sauce supply a salty pungency, sugar gives sweetness, heat comes from chiles (usually in sauce or paste form), lime juice provides acidity, and cilantro, mint, or other more exotic herbs provide citrusy brightness. Garlic and shallots anchor the cuisine, providing heady, robust flavors.

With our basic ingredients in hand, we set off to find out which ones—and in what amounts—were key to success. For 8 ounces of rice noodles

we used 5 tablespoons of fish sauce and 3 tablespoons of soy sauce for a rich, savory foundation. For sweetness and heat, we added 2 tablespoons of sugar and 2 teaspoons of sriracha sauce (a flavorful sauce made from garlic and chiles). To finish the dish we used a full 3 tablespoons of fresh lime juice and ½ cup of cilantro leaves. These amounts may seem excessive but, when properly combined, they create a balanced expression of the flavors of Southeast Asia. As for the garlic, 1 tablespoon minced was our tasters' preference. We found that 3 thinly sliced shallots produced a round, full sweetness and contributed a subtle depth of flavor. To coax the right character out of these two aromatics, we found that cooking them just briefly was critical; they lost their raw flavor but still tasted sharp and sweet.

Among the long list of other ingredients that often turn up in this style of noodle dish, tasters preferred shrimp, shiitake mushrooms, and snow peas. Dried shrimp and preserved vegetables are also common additions, but they can be hard to

INGREDIENTS: Rice Noodles

In Southeast Asia and southern regions of China, delicate pasta made from rice flour and water is used in an array of dishes including soups, stir-fries, and salads. Unlike other pasta, you don't want to boil these delicate noodles. They have a tendency to overcook quickly, resulting in a mushy, sticky mess. We have found it is best to bring water to a boil, then steep the noodles in the water gently off the heat.

FLAT RICE NOODLES
This variety comes in several different widths, from extra-small to extra-large. We use thin noodles (about ⅛ inch wide) for our Rice Noodles with Shrimp, Shiitakes, and Snow Peas.

ROUND RICE NOODLES
Called bun or rice vermicelli, the round noodles also come in a variety of sizes.

find. Fortunately, with so many other bold flavors in the skillet, no one missed them.

Having assembled our key ingredients, we set about finding the best way to combine them in a 12-inch nonstick skillet. Our first instinct was to sear the shrimp to develop their flavor, but eventually we decided there was a better route. Instead, we marinated the shrimp in a few tablespoons of the sauce ingredients and then cooked them briefly at the last minute. We sautéed the shiitakes until golden brown before stirring in the shallots and garlic. To this flavorful base, we then added the drained noodles, shrimp, snow peas, a little chicken broth, and the remaining sauce. After two to three minutes of stirring, the shrimp were cooked through and we added the lime juice and cilantro.

While tasters loved the flavors and contrasting textures of this dish, they found the noodles gummy. To ensure that they retained their pleasantly firm texture, we added them after the shrimp and snow peas were just cooked through. Sweet, spicy, tart, and a little salty, our Vietnamese-inspired rice noodles were an instant hit in the test kitchen.

Rice Noodles with Shrimp, Shiitakes, and Snow Peas

SERVES 4

To make this dish less spicy, reduce the amount of sriracha sauce to 1 teaspoon.

5	tablespoons fish sauce
3	tablespoons soy sauce
2	tablespoons sugar
2	teaspoons sriracha sauce (see page 230)
3	tablespoons vegetable oil
I	pound large shrimp (31 to 40 per pound), peeled and deveined (see the illustration on page 145)
8	ounces (⅛-inch-wide) dried flat rice noodles (see page 207)
8	ounces shiitake mushrooms, wiped clean, stemmed, and sliced thin
3	medium shallots, sliced into thin rings
3	medium garlic cloves, minced or pressed through a garlic press (about I tablespoon)
½	cup low-sodium chicken broth
6	ounces snow peas, tips and strings removed, halved (see the illustration on page 50)
3	tablespoons juice from 2 limes
½	cup loosely packed fresh cilantro leaves

1. Whisk the fish sauce, soy sauce, sugar, sriracha sauce, and 1 tablespoon of the oil together in a small bowl. In a separate bowl, toss the shrimp with 3 tablespoons of the fish sauce mixture and refrigerate for at least 15 minutes or up to 1 hour.

2. Pour 6 cups boiling water into a large bowl, add the noodles, and let stand, stirring occasionally, until the noodles are softened, pliable, and just tender, about 10 minutes. Drain the noodles; set aside.

3. Heat the remaining 2 tablespoons oil in a 12-inch nonstick skillet over high heat until just smoking. Add the mushrooms and cook until golden brown, about 5 minutes. Stir in the shallots and garlic and cook until fragrant, about 30 seconds.

4. Stir in the remaining fish sauce mixture, shrimp, broth, and snow peas and cook until the shrimp are just cooked through, 2 to 3 minutes. Stir in the drained noodles and lime juice and cook, tossing the noodles gently, until they are well coated with sauce, 30 to 60 seconds. Sprinkle with the cilantro and serve.

PORK LO MEIN

PORK LO MEIN IS LIKE FRIED RICE: ORDER IT from your typical take-out joint, and the dish invariably disappoints, with greasy flavors and sodden vegetables. But try to make it at home and you're suddenly faced with an extensive list of hard-to-find ingredients and a pile of dirty dishes. We wanted a streamlined one-pot recipe for pork lo mein, one that would still be a good representation of what any good Chinese home cook could turn out. We wanted chewy noodles tossed in a salty-sweet sauce and accented with bits of smoky *char siu* (barbecued pork) and still-crisp cabbage.

Right off the bat, we knew we'd have to find a suitable replacement for the char siu. This Chinese specialty takes the better part of a day to prepare, and while enterprising cooks might attempt it themselves, it's typically better left in the hands of restaurants and professional kitchens. Since we wanted a streamlined recipe, and we would already be stir-frying the vegetables, why not stir-fry the pork as well? First we considered pork tenderloin, which we've used with great success in stir-fries. The only problem is that tenderloin, while tender, can be a little bland—worlds apart from the richly flavored, well-marbled pork shoulder traditional to char siu. Pork shoulder itself was out—it requires hours of cooking to become fall-apart tender. Pork belly is popular in Chinese cooking, but this fat-streaked meat from the underside of the pig is almost impossible to find at the supermarket. The most sensible option was country-style pork ribs. Though fatty, these meaty ribs from the upper side of the rib cage have the same rich flavor of pork shoulder; plus, they're naturally tender.

Following the protocol for char siu, we wanted to marinate the pork before cooking. To avoid a dish that was overly greasy, we first trimmed the ribs of excess fat and cut them into thin strips that would allow the marinade to penetrate more efficiently. We then soaked the meat in a classic Chinese mixture of hoisin sauce, oyster sauce, soy sauce, and toasted sesame oil. After 15 minutes, we removed the pork from the liquid and seared it quickly over high heat in a nonstick skillet. One bite and it was clear we had the right idea. The meat cooked up tender and juicy on the inside with a crisp, browned exterior.

Pork issues settled, we were ready to tackle the noodles. Lo mein literally translates as "tossed noodles," referring to the way the strands, made from wheat and egg and resembling thick spaghetti, are tossed in sauce. Traditionally the dish calls for fresh noodles, which, unfortunately, cannot be cooked in less than a few quarts of boiling water; otherwise, they become extremely gummy. Since we planned on using our one-pot pasta method of cooking the noodles in the same pot we were using to prepare everything else, fresh noodles were ruled out. We scanned the shelves of our pantry for alternatives and landed on a box of dried linguine. Despite their flat shape, these long Italian strands are similar in width to Chinese noodles. We added 8 ounces of linguine to the pot with 3 cups of water and simmered vigorously until the noodles were tender. We were

SHREDDING CABBAGE

1. Cut the cabbage into quarters and cut away the hard piece of core attached to each quarter.

2. Separate the cored cabbage into stacks of leaves that flatten when pressed lightly.

3A. Use a chef's knife to cut each stack crosswise into thin shreds.

3B. Alternatively, roll the stacked leaves crosswise, fit them into the feed tube of a food processor, and shred them using the shredding disk.

happy to discover that these noodles had the same firm chewiness of fresh Chinese noodles. All that was left was to figure out the vegetables and the sauce.

For the vegetables, we opted for traditional choices—cabbage, scallions, and shiitake mushrooms—stir-frying them in a little vegetable oil with garlic and fresh ginger after cooking the meat. As for the sauce, tasters decided the same mixture we had been using for the meat marinade was also ideal for seasoning the vegetables and noodles. We also stirred in a little Asian chili-garlic sauce for some heat. With chewy noodles coated in a flavorful sauce, tender, browned pork, and crisp, fresh-tasting vegetables, our one-pot pork lo mein really delivers.

Pork Lo Mein

SERVES 4

When adding the linguine in step 5, stir gently to avoid breaking the noodles; after a minute or two they will soften enough to be stirred more easily. To make this dish less spicy, reduce the amount of Asian chili-garlic sauce to 2 teaspoons.

3	tablespoons soy sauce, plus extra as needed
2	tablespoons oyster sauce
2	tablespoons hoisin sauce
1	tablespoon toasted sesame oil
1	pound boneless country-style pork ribs, trimmed and sliced thin crosswise
3	tablespoons vegetable oil
¼	cup Chinese rice cooking wine or dry sherry
8	ounces shiitake mushrooms, wiped clean, stemmed, and halved if large
1	bunch scallions, white and green parts separated, whites sliced thin and greens cut into 1-inch lengths
2	medium garlic cloves, minced or pressed through a garlic press (about 2 teaspoons)
2	teaspoons minced or grated fresh ginger (see the illustrations on page 216)

3	cups water
8	ounces linguine
1	pound napa cabbage (1 small head), quartered, cored, and sliced crosswise into ½-inch strips (see the illustrations on page 209)
1	tablespoon Asian chili-garlic sauce (see page 230)

1. Whisk the soy sauce, oyster sauce, hoisin sauce, and sesame oil together in a medium bowl. In a separate bowl, toss the pork with 3 tablespoons of the soy sauce mixture and refrigerate for at least 15 minutes or up to 1 hour.

2. Heat 1 tablespoon of the vegetable oil in a large Dutch oven over high heat until just smoking. Add half of the pork, break up any clumps, and cook without stirring until beginning to brown, about 1 minute. Stir the pork and continue to cook until just cooked through, 1 to 2 minutes longer.

3. Add 2 tablespoons of the wine and cook until nearly evaporated, 30 to 60 seconds. Transfer the pork to a medium bowl and repeat with 1 tablespoon more vegetable oil, remaining pork, and remaining 2 tablespoons wine; transfer to the bowl.

4. Add the remaining 1 tablespoon vegetable oil to the pot and return to high heat until just smoking. Add the mushrooms and cook until light golden brown, about 5 minutes. Stir in the scallion whites, garlic, and ginger and cook until fragrant, about 30 seconds.

5. Stir in the water and linguine and bring to a rapid simmer. Simmer vigorously, stirring often, until the pasta is tender, 12 to 16 minutes. Stir in the cabbage and continue to cook until the cabbage is wilted and the sauce is thickened, about 2 minutes longer.

6. Reduce the heat to low and stir in the browned pork with any accumulated juice, remaining soy sauce mixture, chili-garlic sauce, and scallion greens. Cook, tossing the noodles gently, until they are well coated with sauce, 1 to 2 minutes. Season with soy sauce to taste and serve.

7

ALL-TIME FAVORITE STIR-FRIES

All-Time Favorite Stir-Fries

BEEF STIR-FRIES

JUICY PIECES OF CARAMELIZED BEEF, CRISP-tender vegetables, and a lively sauce—that's what we look for in a great beef stir-fry. Unfortunately, more often than not, beef stir-fries are pretty mediocre. Steamed, rather than seared beef is common, as are unevenly cooked vegetables. And the sauce? The problems are many, from harsh, uneven flavors to watery or gloppy concoctions. We had already developed a novel approach to stir-frying, including a beef stir-fry (see recipe page 24), but we still wanted to perfect our classic stovetop method. So we started by setting out to make two stovetop beef stir-fries: a classic Chinese-style beef and broccoli with cashews and an exotic Korean-style stir-fry with kimchi (spicy pickled vegetables) and bean sprouts.

Because intense heat is key to a good stir-fry, the cookware you use is critical. Since the shape of woks makes them a lousy match for the American kitchen, we recommend a 12-inch nonstick skillet, which will maximize your heating surface so food will sear, not steam. If you insist on using a wok, choose a flat-bottom model. It won't have as much flat surface area as a skillet, but it will work better on an American stove than a round-bottom wok.

Lean cuts of beef work great for stir-fries, and we quickly decided to go with easy-to-find flank steak. Freezing the beef for at least 15 minutes made it easier to cut the meat across the grain into wide, flat slices that would cook quickly and brown nicely. We determined that a simple marinade (we liked a combination of soy sauce and Chinese rice cooking wine) was all the beef needed for a quick flavor boost. To ensure the beef browned properly, we made sure to drain the meat well before searing.

With the beef marinated, drained, and ready to go, we moved on to the cooking process. First and foremost, we determined that cooking all the beef at once was out of the question. In order to retain the intense heat required for a stir-fry, we cooked the meat in two batches. By adding just a small volume of food at a time, we were able to maintain the heat, as well as give the beef space to sear in the pan. We browned one side without stirring, then stirred once to quickly brown the second side. Although choosing not to "stir-fry" seems counterintuitive and goes against the constant stirring suggested in many recipes, we found that continuous motion detracted from browning.

After the beef was cooked, we removed it from the pan and added the vegetables. For our Chinese beef and broccoli, we found that because broccoli is tough, it wouldn't soften even after several minutes in the pan. Instead, we steamed it by adding a bit of water and covering with a lid; once the broccoli was crisp-tender, the cover came off so excess water could evaporate. For our Korean-style stir-fry, we found we could simply add the kimchi to the hot pan and cook it until it became aromatic, which took a few minutes. We then added the bean sprouts; the remaining cooking time was enough to heat them without compromising their crisp texture.

Most recipes add the aromatics (typically garlic, ginger, and scallions) at the outset of the cooking process. But in batch after batch, by the time our stir-fries were done the aromatics had burned. We found it worked better when we cooked the aromatics after the vegetables. When the vegetables were done, we pushed them to the sides of the pan, added the aromatics and some oil to the center, and cooked until they were fragrant, about 20 seconds.

We were close to finished. We had only one final component: the sauces. We found that our beef and broccoli benefited from a generous amount of oyster sauce, which imparted richness to the dish without overpowering the otherwise simple flavors. Some toasted sesame oil provided an intense nutty flavor that highlighted the flavor of the cashews, while a little brown sugar balanced the salty brininess of the oyster sauce. Chicken broth and Chinese rice cooking wine rounded it out. For our beef and kimchi stir-fry, we kept the sauce relatively simple since the kimchi itself is intensely flavorful: chicken broth provided a good base, and a little soy sauce, sugar, and toasted sesame oil added subtle complexity.

While the flavor of our sauces was good, the consistency needed work—both were too thin and would not adhere properly to the beef and vegetables. We found that adding a little bit of cornstarch to these sauces (2 teaspoons was just enough) helped them to coat the meat and vegetables.

Requiring minimal prep and minimal cleanup, these beef stir-fries come together quickly for a couple of uniquely flavorful one-dish meals.

Classic Beef and Broccoli with Cashews

SERVES 4

To make the flank steak easier to slice, freeze it for 15 minutes. Stir-fries cook quickly, so have everything prepped before you begin cooking. Serve with Simple Steamed White Rice (page 220).

SAUCE

5	tablespoons oyster sauce
2	tablespoons low-sodium chicken broth
1	tablespoon Chinese rice cooking wine or dry sherry
1	tablespoon light brown sugar
2	teaspoons cornstarch
1	teaspoon toasted sesame oil

STIR-FRY

1	pound flank steak, trimmed and sliced thin across the grain on a slight bias (see the illustrations on page 215)
2	teaspoons soy sauce
2	teaspoons Chinese rice cooking wine or dry sherry
6	medium garlic cloves, minced or pressed through a garlic press (about 2 tablespoons)
1	tablespoon minced or grated fresh ginger (see the illustrations on page 216)
2	scallions, minced
2	tablespoons vegetable oil
1¼	pounds broccoli (1 medium bunch), florets cut into 1-inch pieces, stems trimmed and sliced thin (see the illustrations below)
⅓	cup water
½	cup whole roasted, unsalted cashews, toasted

1. FOR THE SAUCE: Whisk all the ingredients together; set aside.

2. FOR THE STIR-FRY: Toss the beef with the soy sauce and rice wine in a medium bowl and marinate for at least 10 minutes or up to 1 hour. In a separate bowl, combine the garlic, ginger, scallions, and 1 teaspoon of the oil.

3. Drain the beef and discard the liquid. Heat 1 teaspoon more oil in a 12-inch nonstick skillet over high heat until just smoking. Add half of the beef to the skillet, break up any clumps, and cook, without stirring, for 1 minute. Stir the beef and continue to cook until browned, 1 to 2 minutes; transfer to a clean bowl. Repeat with 1 teaspoon more oil and the remaining beef; transfer to the bowl.

4. Rinse the skillet clean and dry with paper towels. Add the remaining 1 tablespoon oil to the skillet and place over high heat until just smoking. Add the broccoli florets and stems and cook for 30 seconds. Add the water, cover, and reduce the heat to medium. Steam the broccoli until slightly tender, about 2 minutes. Remove the lid and continue to cook until the broccoli is tender and some of the liquid has evaporated, about 2 minutes.

PREPARING BROCCOLI FOR STIR-FRY

1. Place the head of broccoli upside down on a cutting board and, using a large knife, trim off the florets very close to their heads. Cut the florets into 1-inch pieces.

2. Place the stalk on the cutting board and square it off with the knife, removing the tough outer ⅛-inch peel.

3. Cut the peeled stalk on the bias into ¼-inch-thick slices.

5. Clear the center of the skillet, add the garlic mixture, and cook, mashing the mixture into the pan, until fragrant, about 20 seconds. Stir the garlic mixture into the broccoli.

6. Return the cooked beef with any accumulated juice to the skillet and toss to combine. Whisk the sauce to recombine, then add to the skillet with the cashews. Cook, stirring constantly, until the sauce is thickened, about 30 seconds. Transfer to a platter and serve.

Korean Stir-Fried Beef with Kimchi

SERVES 4

You can find kimchi, a spicy Korean pickled vegetable condiment, in the refrigerated section of Asian markets and some well-stocked supermarkets. Cut large pieces of kimchi into bite-size pieces before stir-frying. To make the flank steak easier to slice, freeze it for 15 minutes. Serve with Simple Steamed White Rice (page 220).

SAUCE

½ cup low-sodium chicken broth

2 tablespoons soy sauce

1 tablespoon sugar

2 teaspoons cornstarch

1 teaspoon toasted sesame oil

STIR-FRY

1 pound flank steak, trimmed and sliced thin across the grain on a slight bias (see the illustrations at right)

2 tablespoons soy sauce

1 teaspoon sugar

3 medium garlic cloves, minced or pressed through a garlic press (about 1 tablespoon)

1 tablespoon minced or grated fresh ginger (see the illustrations on page 216)

2 tablespoons vegetable oil

1 cup cabbage kimchi, drained, 1 tablespoon kimchi liquid reserved (see note)

4 ounces bean sprouts (about 2 cups)

5 scallions, cut into 1½-inch lengths, white and light green pieces cut again lengthwise into 4 thinner strips

1. FOR THE SAUCE: Whisk all the ingredients together; set aside.

2. FOR THE STIR-FRY: Toss the beef with the soy sauce and sugar in a medium bowl and marinate for at least 10 minutes or up to 1 hour. In a separate bowl, combine the garlic, ginger, and 1 teaspoon of the oil.

3. Drain the beef and discard the liquid. Heat 1 teaspoon more oil in a 12-inch nonstick skillet over high heat until just smoking Add half of the beef to the skillet, break up any clumps, and cook, without stirring, for 1 minute. Stir the beef and continue to cook until browned, 1 to 2 minutes; transfer to a clean bowl. Repeat with 1 teaspoon more oil and the remaining beef; transfer to the bowl.

4. Rinse the skillet clean and dry with paper towels. Add the remaining 1 tablespoon oil to the skillet and place over high heat until just smoking. Add the kimchi and kimchi liquid and cook, stirring

SLICING FLANK STEAK THIN

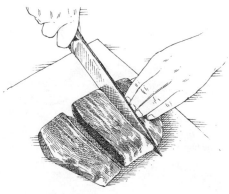

1. Place the partially frozen steak on a clean, dry work surface. Using a sharp chef's knife, slice the steak with the grain into 2-inch-wide pieces.

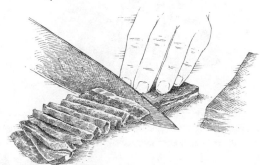

2. Cut each 2-inch piece of flank steak across the grain on a slight bias into very thin slices.

PREPARING GINGER

There are two basic methods used to prepare fresh ginger so that it will evenly distribute throughout a dish.

TO MINCE GINGER:

1. Slice the peeled knob of ginger into thin rounds using a sharp knife. Then fan the rounds out and cut them into thin, matchstick-like strips.

2. Chop the matchsticks crosswise into a fine mince.

TO GRATE GINGER:

Peel a small section of a large piece of ginger. On the small holes of a box grater, grate the peeled portion, using the rest of the ginger as a handle to keep fingers safely away from the grater.

frequently, until aromatic, 1 to 4 minutes. Stir in the bean sprouts.

5. Clear the center of the skillet, add the garlic mixture, and cook, mashing the mixture into the pan, until fragrant, about 20 seconds. Stir the garlic mixture into the vegetables.

6. Return the cooked beef with any accumulated juice to the skillet and toss to combine. Whisk the sauce to recombine, then add to the skillet with the scallions. Cook, stirring constantly, until the sauce is thickened, about 30 seconds. Transfer to a platter and serve.

CHICKEN STIR-FRIES

A CHICKEN STIR-FRY SHOULD BE THE ULTIMATE quick and easy one-dish meal. Boneless, skinless chicken breasts require minimal prep, cook quickly, and pair well with an endless variety of vegetables and sauces. But cooking the chicken just right isn't always so easy—with its relatively small amount of fat, chicken inevitably becomes dry and stringy when cooked over high heat. Perfection in a chicken stir-fry, then, requires split-second timing to avoid either under- or overcooked poultry, neither result being particularly appealing. We were after stir-fries that featured tender, juicy, bite-size pieces of chicken paired with just the right combination of vegetables in simple yet complexly flavored sauces.

We often use a marinade to impart flavor to meat destined for stir-fries, and chicken is no exception. Tossing the pieces of chicken in a simple mixture of soy sauce and Chinese rice cooking wine for 10 minutes before cooking added much-needed flavor to the mild breasts, but did nothing to improve the texture of the meat, which was dry from the high heat despite the short cooking time.

The obvious solution to prevent dry chicken was brining, our favorite method for adding juiciness to poultry. A test of brined boneless breasts did in fact confirm that this method solved the cooking problem. However, a half hour or more of brining time followed by 10 minutes of marinating was out of the question for what is supposed to be a quick dish. It seemed redundant to soak the chicken first in one salty solution (brine), and then another (marinade), so we decided to combine the two, using ¼ cup soy sauce to provide the high salt level in the brine. This turned out to be the secret to great chicken stir-fry. Now we were turning out highly flavored, juicy pieces of chicken—most of the time. Given the finicky nature of high-heat cooking, some batches of chicken still occasionally turned out tough because of overcooking.

We next turned to a traditional Chinese technique called velveting, which involves coating chicken pieces in a thin cornstarch and egg white or oil mixture, then parcooking the chicken in moderately heated oil. The coating forms a barrier on the chicken that keeps precious moisture inside; that extra juiciness makes the chicken seem more tender. Cornstarch mixed with egg white yielded a cakey coating; tasters preferred the more subtle coating provided by cornstarch mixed with oil. This velveted chicken was supple, but it was also pale, and, again, this method seemed far too involved for a quick weeknight dinner.

We wondered if the same method—coating in a cornstarch mixture—would work if we eliminated the parcooking step. It did. This chicken was not only juicy and tender, but it also developed an attractive golden brown coating. Best of all, the entire process took less than five minutes. The only problem was that the coating, which was more of an invisible barrier than a crust, became bloated and slimy when cooked in the sauce. Apparently the cornstarch was absorbing liquid from the sauce, which resulted in the slippery finish. Cutting the cornstarch with flour created a negligible coating—not too thick, not too slimy—that also managed to seal juices inside the chicken. Substituting sesame oil for peanut oil added a rich depth of flavor.

After trying everything from pounding to cubing the chicken, we found that tasters preferred simple flat ½-inch slices, which were all the more easy to cut after freezing the breasts for 15 minutes. These wide, flat slices of chicken browned easily; as with our beef stir-fries (see page 213) we cooked the chicken in two batches, first browning one side, then

EQUIPMENT:
Inexpensive Nonstick Skillets

Nothing takes the challenge out of cooking stir-fries and delicate foods better than a nonstick skillet. But a nonstick skillet's lifespan is always a short one. Its surface inevitably becomes rough, stained, and marred by scratches. Since these pans have to be replaced frequently, we prefer not to spend a lot of money on them. We tested seven contenders under $50 against our longtime (and pricey) favorite, the All-Clad Stainless 12-Inch Nonstick Frying Pan, $159.99, and the Best Buy from our previous testing, the Calphalon Simply Nonstick Omelette Pan, $55. We tested each pan by using them to fry eggs, stir-fry beef and vegetables, and make crêpes. We also ran them through a number of durability tests. The T-Fal Professional Total 12.5-Inch Nonstick Fry Pan aced every cooking test, but a loose handle that resulted from the durability testing was a sign that it's not high-end cookware. Still, at $34.99, it's a bargain, and it was the only pan in the lineup with an exceptionally slick, durable nonstick coating that also turned in a top performance in cooking. As for the All-Clad, it is a solidly built pan and a terrific piece of cookware, but its coating became slightly worn by the end of our tests. Because the All-Clad boasts a lifetime warranty, we still recommend it, but we'll be buying the T-Fal from now on for our own kitchens.

THE BEST INEXPENSIVE NONSTICK SKILLET
The T-Fal Professional Total 12.5-Inch Nonstick Fry Pan ($34.99) has an exceptionally slick, durable nonstick coating and turned in the top performance in cooking.   **T-FAL**

turning them over to quickly brown the second side rather than constantly stirring.

With our chicken just right, it was time to consider the vegetables and sauce. For our first dish, we added green beans and shiitake mushrooms to the chicken. The mushrooms acted like sponges, soaking up the other flavors of the dish, and contributed a pleasantly meaty texture. Tasters thought this combination would hold up well to a spicy sauce, so we added a generous amount of sriracha (an Asian chili sauce) to our base of chicken broth and Chinese rice cooking wine, along with some soy sauce, toasted sesame oil, and a little sugar to balance the heat. A sprinkling of sesame seeds was the perfect finish to this dish. For our second chicken stir-fry, we chose broccoli and water chestnuts as the vegetables, but decided to make ginger the prominent flavor. As an aromatic, as well as a major component of the sauce, ginger gave the dish a sweet and spicy warmth that tasters loved. Soy sauce, oyster sauce, sugar, and red pepper flakes provided a pleasing balance of salty, sweet, and spicy. Adding a small amount of cornstarch to both sauces helped them coat the velveted chicken and vegetables.

In the end, a great chicken stir-fry doesn't really take more time to prepare than a bad one. It does, however, require more attention to detail and knowledge of a few quick tricks.

Spicy Stir-Fried Sesame Chicken with Green Beans and Shiitakes

SERVES 4

To make the chicken easier to slice, freeze it for 15 minutes. For a less spicy stir-fry, reduce the amount of sriracha to 2 teaspoons. Serve with Simple Steamed White Rice (page 220).

SAUCE

½	cup plus 2 tablespoons low-sodium chicken broth
2	tablespoons Chinese rice cooking wine or dry sherry
5	teaspoons sugar
4	teaspoons sriracha sauce (see page 230)
1	tablespoon soy sauce
2	teaspoons sesame seeds, toasted
2	teaspoons toasted sesame oil
1	teaspoon cornstarch
1	medium garlic clove, minced or pressed through a garlic press (about 1 teaspoon)

STIR-FRY

1	pound boneless, skinless chicken breasts, trimmed and sliced thin (see the illustrations on page 219)
1	cup water
¼	cup soy sauce
¼	cup Chinese rice cooking wine or dry sherry
2	tablespoons plus 1 teaspoon toasted sesame oil
1	tablespoon cornstarch
1	tablespoon unbleached all-purpose flour
4	teaspoons sesame seeds, toasted
2	medium garlic cloves, minced or pressed through a garlic press (about 2 teaspoons)
1	teaspoon minced or grated fresh ginger (see the illustrations on page 216)
8	teaspoons vegetable oil
1	pound green beans, trimmed and cut on the bias into 1-inch pieces
8	ounces shiitake mushrooms, wiped clean, stemmed, and sliced ⅛ inch thick

1. FOR THE SAUCE: Whisk all the ingredients together; set aside.

2. FOR THE STIR-FRY: Combine the chicken, water, soy sauce, and rice wine in a medium bowl and marinate for at least 10 minutes or up to 1 hour. Drain the chicken and discard the liquid.

3. Mix 2 tablespoons of the sesame oil, cornstarch, flour, and 1 tablespoon of the sesame seeds together in a medium bowl until smooth, then stir in the drained chicken until evenly coated. In a separate bowl, combine the garlic, ginger, and 1 teaspoon of the vegetable oil.

4. Heat 2 teaspoons more vegetable oil in a 12-inch nonstick skillet over high heat until just smoking. Add half of the chicken, break up any clumps, and cook, without stirring, for 1 minute. Stir the chicken and continue to cook until lightly browned, about 30 seconds; transfer to a clean bowl. Repeat with 2 teaspoons more vegetable oil and the remaining chicken; transfer to the bowl.

5. Add the remaining 1 tablespoon vegetable oil to the skillet and place over high heat until just smoking. Add the green beans and cook for 1 minute. Stir in the mushrooms and cook until the mushrooms are lightly browned and the beans are crisp-tender, 3 to 4 minutes.

6. Clear the center of the skillet, add the garlic mixture and cook, mashing the mixture into the pan, until fragrant, about 20 seconds. Stir the garlic mixture into the vegetables.

7. Return the cooked chicken with any accumulated juice to the skillet and toss to combine. Whisk the sauce to recombine, then add to the skillet. Cook, stirring constantly, until the sauce is thickened, about 30 seconds. Transfer to a platter, sprinkle with the remaining 1 teaspoon sesame oil and remaining 1 teaspoon sesame seeds, and serve.

Gingery Stir-Fried Chicken with Broccoli and Water Chestnuts

SERVES 4

To make the chicken easier to slice, freeze it for 15 minutes. Be sure to rinse the water chestnuts to remove any salty or "tinny" flavors. Serve with Simple Steamed White Rice (page 220).

SAUCE

¾	cup low-sodium chicken broth
2	tablespoons Chinese rice cooking wine or dry sherry
4	teaspoons soy sauce
1	tablespoon oyster sauce
1	tablespoon minced or grated fresh ginger (see the illustrations on page 216)
2	teaspoons cornstarch
1	teaspoon sugar
½	teaspoon toasted sesame oil
¼	teaspoon red pepper flakes

STIR-FRY

1	pound boneless, skinless chicken breasts, trimmed and sliced thin (see the illustrations below)
1⅓	cups water
¼	cup soy sauce
¼	cup Chinese rice cooking wine or dry sherry
2	tablespoons toasted sesame oil
1	tablespoon cornstarch
1	tablespoon unbleached all-purpose flour
1	tablespoon minced or grated fresh ginger (see the illustrations on page 216)
1	medium garlic clove, minced or pressed through a garlic press (about 1 teaspoon)
8	teaspoons vegetable oil
1¼	pounds broccoli (1 medium bunch), florets cut into 1-inch pieces, stems trimmed and sliced thin (see the illustrations on page 214)
1	(8-ounce) can water chestnuts, drained and rinsed

1. FOR THE SAUCE: Whisk all the ingredients together; set aside.

2. FOR THE STIR-FRY: Combine the chicken, 1 cup of the water, soy sauce, and rice wine in a medium bowl and marinate for at least 10 minutes or up to 1 hour. Drain the chicken and discard the liquid.

SLICING CHICKEN BREASTS THIN

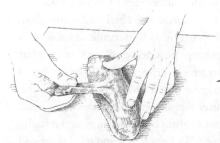

1. Place the partially frozen chicken on a clean, dry work surface. To produce uniform pieces of chicken, separate the tenderloins from the partially frozen boneless, skinless breasts.

2. Slice the breasts across the grain into ½-inch-wide strips that are 1½ to 2 inches long. Center pieces need to be cut in half so they are approximately the same length as the end pieces.

3. Cut tenderloins on the diagonal to produce pieces about the same size as the strips of breast meat.

3. Mix the sesame oil, cornstarch, and flour together in a medium bowl until smooth, then stir in the drained chicken until evenly coated. In a separate bowl, combine the ginger, garlic, and 1 teaspoon of the vegetable oil.

4. Heat 2 teaspoons more vegetable oil in a 12-inch nonstick skillet over high heat until just smoking. Add half of the chicken, break up any clumps, and cook, without stirring, for 1 minute. Stir the chicken and continue to cook until lightly browned, about 30 seconds; transfer to a clean bowl. Repeat with 2 teaspoons more vegetable oil and the remaining chicken; transfer to the bowl.

5. Add the remaining 1 tablespoon vegetable oil to the skillet and place over high heat until just smoking. Add the broccoli florets and stems and cook for 30 seconds. Add the remaining ⅓ cup water, cover, and reduce the heat to medium. Steam the broccoli until slightly tender, about 2 minutes. Remove the lid and continue to cook until the broccoli is tender and some of the liquid has evaporated, about 2 minutes.

6. Clear the center of the skillet, add the garlic mixture and cook, mashing the mixture into the pan, until fragrant, about 20 seconds. Stir the garlic mixture into the broccoli.

7. Return the cooked chicken with any accumulated juice to the skillet. Add the water chestnuts. Whisk the sauce to recombine, then add to the skillet. Cook, stirring constantly, until the sauce is thickened, about 30 seconds. Transfer to a platter and serve.

Simple Steamed White Rice

SERVES 4 TO 6

To rinse the rice, you can either place it in a fine-mesh strainer and rinse under cool water or place it in a medium bowl and repeatedly fill the bowl with water while swishing the rice around, then carefully drain off the water. In either case, you must rinse until the water runs clear.

2   cups long-grain or medium-grain white rice, rinsed

2½   cups water

Bring the rice and water to a boil in a large saucepan, then cover, reduce the heat to low, and cook until the water is just absorbed and there are small holes in the surface of the rice, about 10 minutes. Remove the pot from the heat and let stand, covered, until the rice is tender, about 15 minutes longer. Serve.

ORANGE CHICKEN

WHEN IT COMES TO CHINESE TAKEOUT FOOD, orange-flavored chicken—though far from authentic Chinese fare—is a favorite among American consumers. The chicken is deep-fried and the sauce is sticky and sweet. Sounds like a winning, if decadent, combination. But the reality is that it's never as good as we hope it will be, and instead we're faced with a disappointing combination of ultra-thick breading wrapped around scraps of greasy, tasteless chicken bathed in a sauce that's orange in color only. We wondered if we could take matters into our own hands and make the dish ourselves. We wanted a coating that would be moderately crunchy and maintain its texture beneath a blanket of sauce. We wanted a sauce that wasn't overly sweet; instead, it should have a clear hit of fresh orange flavor, with balanced sweet, sour, and spicy background notes. And finally, we wanted to condense the two pots it normally requires—one to fry the chicken and a second to make the sauce—into just one pot.

We decided to tackle the chicken coating first. A fried-chicken coating (a buttermilk dip followed by a flour–baking powder dip) was somewhat tough and shatteringly crisp. Panko (Japanese bread crumbs) tasted great but wasn't right for this recipe, a cake flour batter slipped off the chicken once fried, and a beer batter coating turned spongy and doughy beneath the sauce. We kept going and tried flour and a whole egg, flour and egg whites, cornstarch and sherry, and even flour and seltzer water. All failed.

Some of the recipes we tested called for velveting the chicken, a process we used with great success in our chicken stir-fries (see page 216), in which the chicken is coated in a thin batter of foamy egg whites or oil mixed with a little cornstarch. While this approach wasn't quite the ticket when it came to deep-frying (the coating was insubstantial and turned soggy), when we separated the ingredients and dunked the chicken first in egg white, then in cornstarch, it worked. Why? Our science editor explained that when egg whites and cornstarch are combined, the starch absorbs water from the whites and creates a sort of glue that, not surprisingly, turns soggy after frying. Our two-step (egg white, then cornstarch) coating created a thin sheath of protein (the egg white) beneath dry cornstarch, which never got the opportunity to swell and absorb water. This dry coating browned and crisped much more readily than a wet, gluey one.

With the basics of the coating in place, we made some minor refinements. A pinch of cayenne gave the chicken some zip, and baking soda was called in to help develop a golden color. (In baking and frying, baking soda has been shown to aid in browning.) The contest between light and dark meat was easily won—thigh meat has richer flavor and is more apt to remain moist when deep-fried than breast meat. A frying temperature of 350 degrees ensured chicken that was crisp but not greasy in just five minutes.

We knew from developing stir-fry recipes that a salty marinade works wonders toward developing flavor and maintaining juiciness in chicken. To marinate chicken for this recipe, soy sauce was a natural choice—it would serve as a brine, seasoning the meat and locking in moisture. Garlic, ginger, brown sugar, white vinegar, chicken broth, and plenty of orange juice rounded out the recipe.

We decided to make extra marinade and use it as the base for our sauce. We added some cornstarch to the extra marinade and then tasted it. Truth be told, it had not even a hint of orange flavor. To bump up the citrus, we tried orange marmalade, frozen orange juice concentrate, reduced fresh orange juice, fresh orange zest, and dried orange zest. The marmalade was bitter, orange juice concentrate and reduced orange juice tasted "fake" and "exceedingly bright," and bottled dried zest was gritty. In the end, a combination of fresh orange juice and fresh zest lent deep, pronounced orange flavor. The slightly bitter, floral taste of the zest plus a healthy dose of cayenne transformed the sauce from sweetly one-dimensional and boring to complex, spicy, and savory. Microwaving the sauce was easy and eliminated the need for another pot on the stove.

Putting the dish together was a snap; we just tossed the fried chicken pieces into the waiting sauce and garnished with strips of orange peel and whole dried red chiles. Now we can look forward to savoring an entire serving of orange-flavored chicken rather than forcing down just one bite.

Orange-Flavored Chicken
SERVES 4

We prefer thigh meat for this recipe; however, 1½ pounds of boneless, skinless chicken breasts can be substituted. Use an instant-read thermometer with a high upper range. The whole dried chiles are added for appearance, not for flavor; they can be omitted. To make the dish spicier, increase the amount of cayenne in the sauce to ½ teaspoon. Serve with Simple Steamed White Rice (page 220).

SAUCE
¾	cup low-sodium chicken broth
1½	teaspoons grated zest, 8 (2-inch-long) strips peel (see the illustration on page 290), and ¾ cup juice from 2 oranges
½	cup packed dark brown sugar
6	tablespoons distilled white vinegar
¼	cup soy sauce
3	medium garlic cloves, minced or pressed through a garlic press (about 1 tablespoon)
1	tablespoon minced or grated fresh ginger (see the illustrations on page 216)
¼	teaspoon cayenne pepper
5	teaspoons cornstarch
8	small whole dried red chiles (optional)

CHICKEN
1½	pounds boneless skinless chicken thighs, trimmed and cut into 1½-inch pieces
3	large egg whites
1	cup cornstarch
½	teaspoon baking soda
¼	teaspoon cayenne pepper
3	cups peanut oil

1. **FOR THE SAUCE:** Whisk the broth, grated orange zest, orange juice, sugar, vinegar, soy sauce, garlic, ginger, and cayenne together in a large microwave-safe bowl until the sugar dissolves. Measure out and reserve 1 cup of the sauce. Whisk the cornstarch into the remaining sauce and microwave on high power, whisking occasionally, until thick and translucent, 3 to 5 minutes. Stir in the chiles (if using) and orange peel strips and cover to keep warm until needed.

2. **FOR THE CHICKEN:** Combine the chicken and reserved 1 cup sauce in a medium bowl, cover, and marinate for at least 30 minutes or up to 1 hour. Drain the chicken, discarding the liquid, then thoroughly pat dry with paper towels.

3. Beat the egg whites in a pie plate with a fork until frothy. In a second pie plate, whisk the cornstarch, baking soda, and cayenne together. Add half of the chicken to the egg whites and coat thoroughly, then transfer the pieces to the cornstarch mixture and coat thoroughly. Place the coated chicken pieces on a wire rack set over a baking sheet; repeat with the remaining chicken.

4. Heat the oil in a large Dutch oven over high heat until it registers 350 degrees on an instant-read thermometer. Carefully add half of the chicken to the hot oil and fry, stirring occasionally, until golden brown on all sides, about 5 minutes. Transfer the chicken to a large paper towel–lined plate. Return the oil to 350 degrees and repeat with the remaining chicken.

5. Reheat the sauce in the microwave if necessary. Add the fried chicken to the hot sauce and toss gently to coat. Serve.

PORK STIR-FRIES

WHILE RECIPES FOR PORK STIR-FRIES ARE EASY to find, a *good* pork stir-fry is not. They typically suffer from the same problems that plague all types of stir-fries: tough, bland meat, nearly raw vegetables, and a greasy, slick, and unbalanced sauce. We wanted to make pork and vegetable stir-fries that combined tender, flavorful pork and perfectly cooked vegetables. We also wanted them to taste true to their Asian heritage, not like generic takeout and, if served with steamed rice, to make a complete meal.

Pork shoulder is often called for in pork stir-fry recipes, but pieces weighing less than several pounds can be difficult to find at the supermarket. In addition, pork shoulder is a cut we typically cook slowly until it becomes tender; to cook it quickly in a stir-fry, we would need to remove the gristle and intramuscular fat. Such a time-consuming step was out of the question for what we wanted (a quick weeknight recipe), so we excluded pork shoulder from our testing. Instead, we tried stir-frying the more sensible options: boneless loin chops and tenderloin, both cut into strips. The loin chops cooked into dry, tight, tough pieces. The tenderloin was the uncontested winner: Tender and yielding, it had the textural qualities of a filet mignon.

We figured the mild pork tenderloin would benefit from a bold flavor boost before hitting the skillet. Tossing the pork slices with either fish sauce or soy sauce worked well, providing a rich saltiness that tasters loved. Because pork tenderloin, like chicken, tends to dry out when stir-fried, we wondered if we could use the velveting technique that worked so well in our chicken stir-fries (see page 216) and apply it to pork. Velveting usually involves coating the meat in a thin mixture of cornstarch and egg whites or oil, then parcooking before stir-frying, but we already found in our chicken stir-fries that we could skip the parcooking step. The velveted pork performed as well as the chicken, browning beautifully over high heat but remaining moist and juicy. Each batch needed to cook for only two minutes.

With the pork out of the skillet and set aside in a bowl, we worked on the vegetables and flavorings. For our first stir-fry, we settled on a Thai-inspired combination of eggplant, onion, garlic, and black pepper. Because eggplant and onion cook at different rates, batch-cooking the vegetables was necessary (batch-cooking also prevented overcrowding, so that the vegetables, too, could brown their way to good flavor). We then added the garlic (a whopping 12 cloves) using our standard stir-fry method, clearing a space in the center of the skillet, where we cooked it long enough to develop its flavor but not long enough to burn. The flavor was assertive, but we felt that the mildness of the pork and eggplant demanded the one-two punch of sautéed garlic and fresh black pepper. Equal amounts of soy and fish sauce added depth, and lime juice lent a shot of bright acidity. Chicken broth provided a liquid element that gave the sauce backbone without diluting its flavor. Finally, just 2 teaspoons of cornstarch provided that clingy, but not gloppy, quality—instead of pooling on the bottom of the plate, the sauce lightly coated the pork and vegetables.

With such a bold-flavored stir-fry under our belts, we decided a lighter, fresher option was in order. Our Chinese cilantro pork bucks tradition and uses cilantro as a vegetable in the stir-fry, rather than as a garnish. We added a full bunch to the skillet—stems and all—with bamboo shoots near the end of cooking. When the cilantro began to wilt, we added the sauce—a balance of sweet and sour flavors with a hint of crushed red pepper—to keep the cilantro's distinctive flavor front and center.

The flavors in these two recipes, as well as the juicy tenderness of the pork, make it easy to see why these decidedly uncommon dishes are some of our favorite stir-fries.

SLICING PORK TENDERLOIN THIN

1. Place the partially frozen pork tenderloin on a clean, dry work surface. Using a sharp chef's knife, slice the pork crosswise into ¼-inch-thick medallions.

2. Slice each medallion into ½-inch-wide strips.

Stir-Fried Pork, Eggplant, and Onion with Garlic and Black Pepper
SERVES 4

This take on a classic Thai stir-fry is not for those with timid palates; it has an intense and slightly salty flavor. To make the pork easier to slice, freeze it for 15 minutes. Leaving the skin on the eggplant keeps the pieces intact during cooking. Serve with Simple Steamed White Rice (see page 220).

SAUCE

½	cup low-sodium chicken broth
¼	cup water
2½	tablespoons light brown sugar
4	teaspoons fish sauce
4	teaspoons soy sauce
2	teaspoons juice from 1 lime
2	teaspoons cornstarch

STIR-FRY

5	tablespoons vegetable oil
1	tablespoon cornstarch
1	tablespoon unbleached all-purpose flour
1	teaspoon fish sauce
1	(1-pound) pork tenderloin, trimmed and sliced thin (see the illustrations at left)
12	medium garlic cloves, minced or pressed through a garlic press (about 4 tablespoons)
2	teaspoons ground black pepper
1	pound eggplant, cut into ¾-inch cubes
1	large onion, sliced pole to pole into ¼-inch wedges
¼	cup coarsely chopped fresh cilantro leaves

1. FOR THE SAUCE: Whisk all the ingredients together; set aside.

2. FOR THE STIR-FRY: Whisk 2 tablespoons of the oil, cornstarch, flour, and fish sauce together in a medium bowl until smooth, then stir in the pork until evenly coated. In a separate bowl, combine the garlic, pepper, and 1 tablespoon more oil.

3. Heat 1 teaspoon more oil in a 12-inch nonstick skillet over high heat until just smoking. Add half of the pork, break up any clumps, and cook, without stirring, for 1 minute. Stir the pork and continue to

cook until lightly browned, about 1 minute; transfer to a clean bowl. Repeat with 1 teaspoon more oil and the remaining pork; transfer to the bowl.

4. Add 1 tablespoon more oil to the skillet and place over high heat until just smoking. Add the eggplant and cook, stirring often, until browned and no longer spongy, 5 to 7 minutes; transfer to the bowl with the pork. Add the remaining 1 teaspoon oil and onion to the skillet and cook over high heat until just softened and lightly browned, about 2 minutes.

5. Clear the center of the skillet, add the garlic mixture and cook, mashing the mixture into the pan, until fragrant, about 1 minute. Stir the garlic mixture into the onion.

6. Return the cooked pork and eggplant with any accumulated juice to the skillet. Whisk the sauce to recombine, then add to the skillet. Cook, stirring constantly, until the sauce is thickened, about 30 seconds. Transfer to a platter, sprinkle with the cilantro, and serve.

Chinese Cilantro Pork

SERVES 4

To make the pork easier to slice, freeze it for 15 minutes. The distinct flavor of this recipe depends on using both the stems and leaves of an entire bunch of cilantro. Be sure to rinse and dry the canned bamboo shoots thoroughly or the packing liquid will ruin the flavor of the sauce. Serve with Simple Steamed White Rice (page 220).

SAUCE

¾	cup low-sodium chicken broth
4	teaspoons soy sauce
4	teaspoons rice vinegar
1	tablespoon sugar
2	teaspoons cornstarch
¼	teaspoon red pepper flakes

STIR-FRY

3	tablespoons vegetable oil
1	tablespoon cornstarch
1	tablespoon unbleached all-purpose flour
2	teaspoons soy sauce
1	(1-pound) pork tenderloin, trimmed and sliced thin (see the illustrations on page 223)
3	medium garlic cloves, minced or pressed through a garlic press (about 1 tablespoon)
1	tablespoon minced or grated fresh ginger (see the illustrations on page 216)
1	large bunch cilantro, stem ends trimmed and cut into 1-inch lengths (see note)
1	(8-ounce) can sliced bamboo shoots, drained, rinsed, and thoroughly patted dry (see note)

1. FOR THE SAUCE: Whisk all the ingredients together; set aside.

2. FOR THE STIR-FRY: Whisk 2 tablespoons of the oil, cornstarch, flour, and soy sauce together in a medium bowl until smooth, then stir in the pork. In a separate bowl, combine the garlic, ginger, and 1 teaspoon more oil.

3. Heat 1 teaspoon more oil in a 12-inch nonstick skillet over high heat until just smoking. Add half of the pork, break up any clumps, and cook, without stirring, for 1 minute. Stir the pork and continue to cook until lightly browned, about 1 minute; transfer to a clean bowl. Repeat with the remaining 1 teaspoon oil and the remaining pork; transfer to the bowl.

4. Add the garlic mixture to the skillet and cook over medium heat, mashing the mixture into the pan, until fragrant, about 20 seconds. Stir in the cilantro, bamboo shoots, and browned pork with any accumulated juice and toss to combine.

5. Whisk the sauce to recombine, then add to the skillet. Cook, stirring constantly, until the sauce is thickened and the cilantro is slightly wilted, about 1 minute. Transfer to a platter and serve.

STIR-FRIED SHRIMP WITH SNOW PEAS AND BELL PEPPER

WITH SEVERAL STIR-FRY RECIPES UNDER OUR belts, we figured we had our basic stir-fry technique mastered: Batch-sear marinated protein and vegetables in a hot skillet, add aromatics, and finish with a flavorful, quick-simmered sauce. It works with just about any type of protein—beef, chicken, and pork—so how could it fail with shrimp?

That was our initial question—before the first tightly curled, rubbery shrimp spirals we choked down demonstrated that meat and shrimp are not interchangeable. That's because shrimp cook faster than meat. Second, marinades seem to roll right off their tightly grained flesh and end up merely burning in the hot skillet. If we wanted perfect shrimp stir-fry, it seemed, we would need to modify our stir-fry technique, customizing it to produce plump, juicy, well-seasoned shrimp in a balanced, flavorful sauce.

The problem with most stir-fry recipes is that they don't account for the fact that home cooks lack high-output, restaurant-style burners that can maintain temperatures hot enough to effectively sear the food before the whole mess overcooks in a cloud of steam. That's where our batch-cooking method comes in: To keep the pan good and hot throughout the process, we use a large, shallow nonstick skillet (which, on a Western range, heats more efficiently than a wok and provides maximum surface area for evaporation), crank up the flame to high, and cook each component separately and in small quantities so that the pieces have a chance to thoroughly brown.

In this case, however, we needed a buffer between the heat and the shrimp. Cooking them shell-on was out (no one likes to peel messy shrimp at the table), but we wondered if the solution was as simple as fabricating an artificial "shell" to help protect the peeled shrimp's delicate meat. One such technique, a traditional Chinese method known as velveting, coats the protein in a starch and egg or oil slurry before cooking to help create a barrier between the meat and the pan. Having already used this technique with chicken and pork, we figured it

would work great here. We tried every iteration of this approach we could think of (cornstarch, flour, whole eggs, egg whites—even a salt and spice powder, as one recipe recommended) to prevent the shrimp from overcooking. Some of the dishes showed slight textural improvements, but the whole lot was generally uninspiring.

If the problem was overcooking, maybe we needed to step back even further from our meat stir-fry technique to reconsider the super-hot fire. Traditionally, high heat serves two purposes: speed and flavorful browning. The time and temperature window for perfectly plump, just-firm shrimp, however, is particularly narrow. An internal temperature of 140 degrees is ideal, but even 20 degrees beyond that and the shrimp turn to rubber erasers. Substantial browning, meanwhile, doesn't occur until well above 300 degrees—a surefire path to overcooking. Since shrimp stir-fries usually call for an assertive sauce (like the hot and sour chili paste and vinegar–based concoctions we were working with) and the vegetables could still develop deep color, we wondered what would happen if we chose not to brown the seafood.

Abandoning the high-heat method, we turned the burner down to medium-low and gently parcooked a batch of shrimp, removed them from the skillet, then turned up the heat to sear the vegetables, sauté the aromatics, and finally finish cooking the shrimp with the sauce. This worked beautifully. Not a single taster was displeased with the shrimp's unbrowned exterior, instead commenting on their supreme tenderness. Reversing the approach—cooking the veggies followed by the aromatics over high, then turning the heat down before adding the shrimp—made the whole process more efficient.

It was time to think more deeply about the marinade. We had been using a pretty standard Chinese rice wine–soy sauce mixture and while this works great for meat, the combination wasn't doing much for the shrimp—in fact, it merely overwhelmed its sweet taste. Instead, we tried another common Chinese texture-boosting technique that we hoped would also improve flavor: soaking the shrimp in a saltwater brine, which both seasons and hydrates the flesh. Their texture became noticeably juicier, but we still wanted more flavor—preferably garlic—in the shrimp themselves. Since garlic's flavor compounds are mostly oil soluble, we opted to lose the water in the brine for a marinade that was oil-based—just oil, salt, ginger, and minced garlic. The salt not only helped the shrimp retain moisture as they cooked, but it also drew flavorful compounds out of the garlic's cells, which then dissolved in the oil and spread evenly around the shellfish. Sure enough, this method worked like a charm.

PREPARING BELL PEPPERS

1. Slice ¼ inch from the top and bottom of the bell pepper, then gently remove the stem from the top slice.

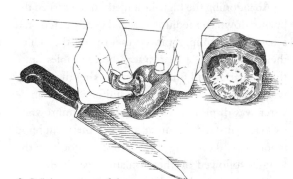

2. Pull the core out of the pepper.

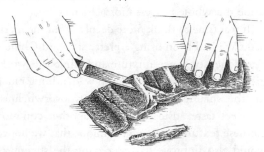

3. Make a slit down one side of the pepper, then lay it flat, skin side down, in one long strip. Slide a sharp knife along the inside of the pepper and remove all ribs and seeds. Cut the flattened pepper into smaller pieces as directed.

As for our sauce, we found that our shrimp stir-fry benefited from a slightly sweet and spicy sauce flavored with garlic and chiles, especially if it was reduced to a consistency that tightly bound to the shrimp. After a few more tests, we had a vinegar-based hot and sour sauce that complemented the shrimp perfectly. By combining Chinese traditions with new techniques, these from-the-sea stir-fries would no longer play second fiddle to their land-based counterparts.

Stir-Fried Shrimp with Snow Peas and Bell Pepper in Hot and Sour Sauce

SERVES 4

Stir-frying the shrimp over medium-low heat keeps them tender; the shrimp are done when they become opaque. Although you don't want to overcook the shrimp in step 5, be sure to bring the sauce to a simmer in order to activate the cornstarch. Serve with Simple Steamed White Rice (page 220).

SAUCE

- 3 tablespoons distilled white vinegar
- 3 tablespoons sugar
- 1 tablespoon Asian chili-garlic sauce (see page 230)
- 1 tablespoon Chinese rice cooking wine or dry sherry
- 1 tablespoon ketchup
- 2 teaspoons toasted sesame oil
- 2 teaspoons cornstarch
- 1 teaspoon soy sauce

STIR-FRY

- 1 pound extra-large shrimp (21 to 25 per pound), peeled and deveined (see the illustration on page 145)
- 3 tablespoons vegetable oil
- 1 tablespoon minced or grated fresh ginger (see the illustrations on page 216)
- 1 medium garlic clove, minced or pressed through a garlic press (about 1 teaspoon), plus 1 medium garlic clove, sliced thin
- ½ teaspoon salt
- 1 large shallot, sliced thin (about ⅓ cup)

½ pound snow peas or sugar snap peas,
    tips and strings removed (see the illustration
    on page 50)

I red bell pepper, stemmed, seeded, and
    cut into ¾-inch pieces (see the illustrations
    on page 226)

1. FOR THE SAUCE: Whisk all the ingredients together; set aside.

2. FOR THE STIR-FRY: Toss the shrimp with 1 tablespoon of the oil, ginger, minced garlic, and salt in a medium bowl and let marinate for 30 minutes or up to 1 hour. In a separate bowl, combine the sliced garlic and shallot.

3. Heat 1 tablespoon more oil in a 12-inch nonstick skillet over high heat until just smoking. Add the snow peas and bell pepper and cook, stirring frequently, until the vegetables begin to brown, 1½ to 2 minutes; transfer to a medium bowl.

4. Add the remaining 1 tablespoon oil to the skillet and heat until just smoking. Add the garlic mixture and cook until fragrant, about 20 seconds. Reduce the heat to medium-low, add the shrimp, and cook, stirring often, until the shrimp are light pink on both sides, 1 to 1½ minutes.

5. Whisk the sauce to recombine and add to the skillet. Increase the heat to high and cook, stirring constantly, until the sauce is thickened and the shrimp are cooked through, 1 to 2 minutes. Return the cooked vegetables to the skillet and toss to combine. Transfer to a platter and serve.

KUNG PAO SHRIMP

KUNG PAO, THE CLASSIC STIR-FRY OF MEAT or shellfish with peanuts and chiles in a rich brown sauce, is a Chinese restaurant standard with an origin that dates back to 19th-century central-western China in the Sichuan province. While most of the original versions of this dish we found use chicken, modern versions of kung pao also feature beef, seafood, tofu, or just vegetables. Shrimp is also a popular variation and the one that intrigued us the most. Unfortunately, the shrimp kung paos we sampled in half a dozen well-reputed restaurants were disappointingly greasy and featured tough, overcooked shrimp. We thought that by carefully examining the key cooking issues—mainly, the preparation of the shrimp and the composition and texture of the sauce—we could come up with something akin to what the Chinese cook at home.

Most Chinese stir-fries go heavy on the vegetables, but kung pao dishes are different. The quantity of vegetables is limited, with the emphasis instead on the shrimp and the nuts. The restaurant versions we tried often included green bell pepper, and some added bamboo shoots, carrots, celery, scallions, and zucchini. We worked our way through these choices and more and settled on a modest amount of red bell pepper for sweetness.

We looked at the shrimp next. Traditionally, they are coated with egg white, cornstarch, and seasonings (to help the sauce adhere), and then fried in a generous quantity of oil. Wanting to simplify this recipe as much as possible, we hoped to use a different method for cooking the shrimp. Since we had just developed a simple technique for stir-frying shrimp without overcooking them (see page 225), we decided to use that approach here: cooking the shrimp over medium-low heat after cooking the vegetables and sautéing the aromatics ensured that they remained tender and juicy. Using extra-large shrimp further ensured that the shellfish wouldn't overcook during their brief stint in the skillet. These shrimp were so juicy and flavorful, not one taster commented on the lack of a browned exterior.

When it came to the sauce, we pictured it deep brown, syrupy in texture, and glistening, with balanced elements of sweet, savory, salty, garlicky, and hot. We tried both chicken broth and water as a base and preferred the broth for the savory underpinning it provided. For a bit of sweetness we added sugar in amounts from 1 tablespoon down to 1 teaspoon, but even a mere teaspoon was overkill. Instead, we chose to add the classic Asian trio of hoisin sauce, oyster sauce, and sesame oil, all good sources of color, flavor depth, and subtle sweetness. An ample supply of garlic gave the sauce authority, and ginger and rice vinegar added brightness. We liked Chinese black rice vinegar (also called Chinkiang vinegar) even better because it was more complex—smoky, salty, plumlike, and slightly sweet. Cornstarch worked well to thicken our sauce, and 1½ teaspoons reliably gelled the sauce to a soft, glazy, shrimp-coating consistency.

For heat, we unanimously chose whole dried chiles, which are traditional for this dish (although red pepper flakes work well also). We coarsely crumbled half of the chiles so that their flavor would better infuse our dish, leaving the rest whole for an attractive presentation. We added the chiles along with the peanuts (tasters demanded a generous ½ cup to ensure nuts in every bite) after cooking the shrimp, but before adding the sauce to the skillet.

Sichuan peppercorns are the other defining flavor in authentic kung pao dishes, but for some reason we had trouble finding recipes that use them. Curious, we dug a bit deeper to find that from 1968 to 2005, it was illegal to bring Sichuan peppercorns into the U.S. (they were thought to be carriers of a disease that could potentially harm citrus crops). Since they're now available (mostly at Asian markets and specialty spice purveyors), we tested different amounts and were horrified that some recipes include handfuls of this potent spice. We found 1 teaspoon, crushed and added with the bell pepper to give the spice a chance to bloom, was just the right amount to provide some well-rounded heat and give this kung pao shrimp the authenticity it demanded. At last, we can skip disappointing take-out versions of this dish and stir-fry our own.

Kung Pao Shrimp
SERVES 4

We prefer black rice vinegar here but plain white rice vinegar can be substituted if necessary. Sichuan peppercorns are an essential flavor in this dish; white or black peppercorns are not acceptable substitutes. This traditional-style kung pao dish is fairly spicy; to make it milder, reduce the number of chiles. Don't eat the whole chiles in the final dish. If you can't find small dried red chiles, substitute 1 teaspoon red pepper flakes. Although you don't want to overcook the shrimp in step 5, be sure to bring the sauce to a simmer in order to activate the cornstarch. Serve with Simple Steamed White Rice (page 220).

SAUCE

- ¾ cup low-sodium chicken broth
- 1 tablespoon oyster sauce
- 1 tablespoon hoisin sauce
- 2 teaspoons black rice vinegar or plain rice vinegar (see page 231)
- 2 teaspoons toasted sesame oil
- 1½ teaspoons cornstarch

STIR-FRY

- 1 pound extra-large shrimp (21 to 25 per pound), peeled and deveined (see the illustration on page 145)
- 2 teaspoons Chinese rice cooking wine or dry sherry
- 3 medium garlic cloves, minced or pressed through a garlic press (about 1 tablespoon)
- 1 teaspoon minced or grated fresh ginger (see the illustrations on page 216)
- 2 scallions, minced
- 5 teaspoons vegetable oil
- 6 small whole dried red chiles (each about 2 inches long) (see note)
- ½ cup roasted unsalted peanuts
- 1 red bell pepper, stemmed, seeded, and cut into ½-inch pieces (see the illustrations on page 226)
- 1 teaspoon Sichuan peppercorns, ground or crushed fine (see page 230) (see note)

1. FOR THE SAUCE: Whisk all the ingredients together; set aside.

2. FOR THE STIR-FRY: Toss the shrimp with the rice wine in a medium bowl and let marinate for 30 minutes (do not overmarinate). In a separate bowl, combine the garlic, ginger, scallions, and 2 teaspoons of the oil. In a third bowl, crumble half of the chiles coarse, then toss with the remaining whole chiles and peanuts.

3. Heat the remaining 1 tablespoon oil in a 12-inch nonstick skillet over high heat until just smoking. Add the bell pepper and Sichuan peppercorns and cook until the pepper is slightly softened

and the ground peppercorns are fragrant, about 1 minute; transfer to a medium bowl.

4. Add the garlic mixture to the skillet and cook, mashing the mixture into the pan, until fragrant, about 20 seconds. Reduce the heat to medium-low, add the shrimp, and cook, stirring often, until the shrimp are light pink on both sides, 1 to 1½ minutes.

5. Stir in the chile-peanut mixture. Whisk the sauce to recombine and add to the skillet. Increase the heat to high and cook, stirring constantly, until the sauce is thickened and the shrimp are cooked through, 1 to 2 minutes. Return the cooked vegetables to the skillet and toss to combine. Transfer to a platter and serve.

Vegetarian Stir-Fry

TAKING THE MEAT OUT OF A STIR-FRY TURNS a one-dish meal into a side dish. At least, that's been our experience with meatless stir-fries. But it doesn't have to be that way. The all-vegetable stir-fry has plenty of contrasting flavor and texture. Our job was to find something substantial enough to anchor the dish firmly in entrée territory.

We reasoned that it wasn't the meat we were missing from the all-veggie stir-fries we've tried over the years, but the meatiness. And with a few strategically chosen vegetables, we were confident we could change the mind of even the most unapologetic carnivore.

Quickly scanning the produce section of the supermarket, it wasn't hard to figure out where to start. If we were looking for meaty heft and texture, then mushrooms were the obvious choice—more specifically, big, hearty portobellos. To capitalize on their bulk and meatiness, we cut them into pieces large enough to stand out from the other vegetables. Though the pan was quite full when we added the mushrooms, they quickly cooked down to a manageable quantity.

The only problem was the gills, which often broke off and muddied the sauce, leaving plenty of "dirty" flavors, according to our tasters. At first we tried cooking the mushrooms on the tops only (to keep the gills from breaking off), but this technique left the mushrooms dried out, leathery, and raw-tasting. Lightly scraping the gills off with a spoon before cooking solved the problem.

Now that we had settled on a cooking technique for our starring vegetable, it was time to move on to the supporting cast—and to more familiar territory. Taking the kitchen's tried-and-true procedure for stir-fries, we simply plugged in the meaty portobellos where the sliced beef or chicken usually went: Cook the portobellos in batches and set them aside; steam-sauté the longer-cooking carrots, and set them aside; quickly stir-fry the snow peas and bok choy, and aromatics (garlic and a generous quantity of ginger); then add everything back to the pan along with a flavorful sauce.

The technique worked without a hitch, but we thought the portobellos could still be more distinct from the other vegetables. Taking a cue from meat stir-fries once again, we experimented with marinades and coatings, but to no avail. Soaking the mushrooms in a soy-based marinade left them soggy, slimy, and difficult to sear. Dipping them in different combinations of egg and cornstarch created a distinct crust initially, but the mushrooms' high moisture content quickly made the crust chewy and wet. A simple sear proved best, but we wondered if an easy-to-prepare glaze (made from the existing sauce ingredients) might help. Adding some soy sauce, chicken broth, and sugar as the mushrooms finished cooking yielded a shiny, flavorful glaze that provided just the boost our mushrooms needed.

Now all we needed was a sauce to complement our "meaty" vegetables. After testing different flavors—savory, sweet, and spicy—we settled on an oyster-based sauce for the mushrooms. The combination of soy and oyster sauces provided umami, that elusive fifth taste that adds another savory layer to recipes and a depth of meaty flavor. A sprinkling of toasted sesame seeds at the end added a pleasing crunch that was a welcome contrast to the meaty portobellos. Now trips to the supermarket don't have to extend beyond the produce section for us to assemble a quick meal that will satisfy the craving for a substantial main course.

Asian Ingredients 101

ASIAN CHILE SAUCES

Used both in cooking and as a condiment, these sauces come in a variety of styles. Sriracha contains garlic and is made from chiles that are ground into a smooth paste. Chili-garlic sauce also contains garlic and is similar to sriracha except that the chiles are coarsely ground. Sambal oelek differs in that it is made purely from ground chiles without the addition of garlic or other spices, thus adding heat but not additional flavor. Once opened these sauces will keep for several months in the refrigerator.

COCONUT MILK

Widely available in cans, coconut milk adds rich flavor and body to soups, curries, and stir-fries. It is available both regular and light; we typically opt for the regular because it adds more body to recipes. Do not confuse coconut milk with cream of coconut, which contains added sugar and is thus much sweeter.

FISH SAUCE

Fish sauce is a salty amber-colored liquid made from fermented fish. It is used as an ingredient and condiment in certain Asian cuisines, most commonly in the foods of Southeast Asia. In very small amounts, it adds a well-rounded, salty flavor to sauces, soups, and marinades. The lighter the color of the fish sauce, the lighter its flavor.

HOISIN SAUCE

Hoisin sauce is a thick reddish brown mixture of soybeans, sugar, vinegar, garlic, chiles, and spices, the most predominant of which is five-spice powder. It is used in many classic Chinese dishes, including barbecued pork, Peking duck, and kung pao shrimp, and as a table condiment, much like ketchup. The ideal hoisin sauce balances sweet, salty, pungent, and spicy elements so that no one flavor dominates.

SICHUAN PEPPERCORNS

From 1968 until 2005, these berries from a spiny shrub indigenous to the Sichuan province of China were banned from the United States (they were thought to be potential carriers of a tree disease that could harm citrus crops). But with their return a few years ago, they are appearing more and more frequently in authentic Sichuan recipes in the States. The peppercorns have purplish-red husks and shiny black seeds. It is preferable to buy Sichuan peppercorns with the shiny black seeds removed, as it's the reddish-brown husks that are used for their aromatic, gently floral fragrance and their telltale numbing effect on the tongue.

MISO

Made from a fermented mixture of soy beans and rice, barley, or rye, miso is incredibly versatile, suitable for use in soups, braises, dressings, and sauces as well as for topping grilled foods. This salty, deep-flavored paste ranges in strength and color from a mild, pale yellow (referred to as white) to stronger-flavored red or brownish black, depending on the fermentation method and ingredients.

OYSTER SAUCE

This thick, salty, and strong brown sauce is a rich, concentrated mixture of oysters, soy sauce, brine, and seasonings. It is used to enhance the flavor of many dishes and stir-fries and is the base for many Asian dipping sauces.

SESAME OIL

Raw sesame oil, which is very mild and light in color, is used mostly for cooking, while toasted sesame oil, which has a deep amber color, is primarily used for seasoning because of its intense, nutty flavor. For the biggest hit of sesame flavor, we prefer to use toasted sesame oil. Just a few drops will give stir-fries, noodle dishes, or salad dressings a deep, rich flavor. Sesame oil stored at room temperature will turn rancid if not used within a few months. Refrigeration will extend its shelf life.

CHILI OIL

This red-hued, spicy oil is made by steeping vegetable oil with hot red chiles. It adds both color and pure, even heat to recipes. It will keep for six months stored at room temperature, but it will hold onto its heat longer if kept in the refrigerator.

CHINESE RICE WINE

This rich-flavored liquid made from fermented glutinous rice or millet is used for both drinking and cooking. It ranges in color from clear to amber and tastes slightly sweet and aromatic. Chinese rice cooking wine is also called yellow wine, Shao Hsing, or Shao Xing. If you can't find Chinese rice cooking wine, dry sherry is a decent substitute.

KIMCHI

Kimchi is a pickled vegetable condiment found at nearly every meal in Korea. It is also a common ingredient in many Korean stews and fried rice dishes. The type of kimchi available depends on the seasonality of ingredients and the region. There are more than 100 different varieties of kimchi; however, the most popular variety consists primarily of napa cabbage, scallions, garlic, and ground chiles in brine (salted water). It is packed in jars, where it is allowed to ferment and build its spicy and pungent flavor.

RICE VINEGAR

Rice vinegar is made from glutinous rice that is broken down into sugars, blended with yeast to ferment into alcohol, and aerated to form vinegar. There are several types of Chinese rice vinegar, but most often you will see plain rice vinegar called for, which is typically clear or pale amber. Because of its sweet-tart flavor, plain rice vinegar is used to accentuate many Asian dishes. It comes in both seasoned and unseasoned versions; we prefer the clean flavor of unseasoned rice vinegar. On occasion we also use black rice vinegar. It adds a complex smoky, salty, plumlike, and slightly sweet flavor to dishes.

SOY SAUCE

Soy sauce is a fermented liquid made from soybeans and roasted grain, usually wheat, but sometimes barley or rice. This Asian condiment should enhance flavor and contribute complexity to food—not just make it salty. We prefer naturally brewed soy sauces to synthetic sauces because the latter are often sweetened with corn syrup and colored with caramel to mimic the flavor and color of fermented soy sauce. "Light" or lower-sodium soy sauces are widely available and are recommended as a healthier alternative for the recipes in this book. But note that even lower-sodium sauces contain a relatively high amount of sodium (almost 900 milligrams of sodium in 2 tablespoons).

MIRIN

This Japanese rice wine has a subtle salty-sweet flavor prized in Asian marinades and glazes. The most traditional method for creating mirin uses glutinous rice, malted rice, and distilled alcohol. Many supermarket brands in this country, however, combine sake or another type of alcohol, with salt, corn syrup, other sweeteners, and sometimes caramel coloring and flavoring. We use mirin to brighten the flavor of stir-fries, teriyaki, and other Asian dishes. If you cannot find mirin, substitute 1 tablespoon dry white wine and ½ teaspoon sugar for every 1 tablespoon of mirin.

Stir-Fried Portobellos with Ginger and Oyster Sauce

SERVES 3 TO 4

If your portobello mushroom caps are smaller than those called for, you may require a few extra. Napa cabbage can be substituted for the bok choy. The skillet will seem crowded when adding the mushrooms in step 3, but they will wilt down substantially as they cook. Serve with Simple Steamed White Rice (page 220). Vegetable broth can be substituted for the chicken broth.

SAUCE

- 1 cup low-sodium chicken broth
- 3 tablespoons oyster sauce
- 1 tablespoon soy sauce
- 1 tablespoon cornstarch
- 2 teaspoons toasted sesame oil

GLAZE

- ¼ cup low-sodium chicken broth
- 2 tablespoons soy sauce
- 2 tablespoons sugar

STIR-FRY

- 4 teaspoons minced or grated fresh ginger (see the illustrations on page 216)
- 2 medium garlic cloves, minced or pressed through a garlic press (about 2 teaspoons)
- ¼ cup vegetable oil
- 6 (6-inch-wide) portobello mushroom caps, gills removed (see the illustration at right), and cut into 2-inch pieces (about 7 cups)
- 4 small carrots, peeled and sliced ¼ inch thick on the bias
- ½ cup low-sodium chicken broth
- 3 ounces snow peas, tips and strings removed (see the illustration on page 50)
- 1 pound bok choy (1 small head), greens cut into ½-inch-wide strips and stalks halved lengthwise and sliced crosswise into ¼-inch-wide pieces (see the illustration on page 150)
- 1 tablespoon sesame seeds, toasted

1. **FOR THE SAUCE:** Whisk all the ingredients together; set aside.

2. **FOR THE GLAZE:** Whisk all the ingredients together; set aside.

3. **FOR THE STIR-FRY:** In a small bowl, combine the ginger, garlic, and 1 teaspoon of the oil. Heat 3 tablespoons more oil in a 12-inch nonstick skillet over medium-high heat until shimmering. Add the mushrooms and cook, without stirring, until browned on one side, 2 to 3 minutes.

4. Flip the mushrooms over, reduce the heat to medium, and continue to cook until tender and browned on the second side, about 5 minutes. Increase the heat to medium-high, add the glaze, and cook until it has thickened and coats the mushrooms, 1 to 2 minutes; transfer to a bowl.

5. Rinse the skillet clean and dry with paper towels. Heat 1 teaspoon more oil in the skillet over medium-high heat until just smoking. Add the carrots and cook until beginning to brown, 1 to 2 minutes. Add the broth, cover, and steam the carrots until just tender, 2 to 3 minutes. Remove the lid and continue to cook until the remaining liquid evaporates, about 30 seconds; transfer to the bowl with the mushrooms.

6. Add the remaining 1 teaspoon oil to the skillet and place over high heat until just smoking. Add

PREPARING PORTOBELLO MUSHROOM CAPS

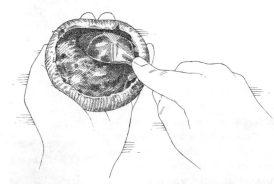

We found that it was necessary to remove the black gills from the portobello mushrooms because they make the stir-fry muddy in appearance. Using a soupspoon, scrape and discard the dark-colored gills from the underside of each mushroom.

the snow peas and bok choy stalks and cook until beginning to brown and soften, 1 to 2 minutes. Stir in the bok choy greens and cook until wilted, about 1 minute.

7. Clear the center of the skillet, add the garlic mixture, and cook, mashing the mixture into the pan, until fragrant, about 20 seconds. Stir the garlic mixture into the vegetables.

8. Return the cooked mushrooms and carrots with any accumulated juices to the skillet and toss to combine. Whisk the sauce to recombine, then add to the skillet. Cook, stirring constantly, until the sauce is thickened and the vegetables are coated, about 1 minute. Transfer to a platter, sprinkle with the sesame seeds, and serve.

MA PAO TOFU

MA PAO DOUFU, OR MA PAO TOFU AS IT'S known in the United States, combines garlic, Asian bean paste, and spicy Sichuan peppercorns with ground pork and tofu to create a dish that's rich, spicy, saucy, and highly addictive. It is a staple on Chinese restaurant menus and is a favorite of many of our test cooks, so gathering opinions about the dish was easy. We were unprepared, though, for the passion it inspired. Ma pao tofu is not a dish to be taken lightly; we would have our work cut out for us if we were going to capture the ideal combination of soft, creamy tofu, flavorful pork, and spicy chili oil to satisfy the experienced palates of our tasters.

Any tofu dish worth its weight should begin with the right kind of tofu. Many stir-fries use firm or extra-firm tofu—they hold up to constant stirring and high heat better than their soft or silken counterparts. (One exception we have found is when pan-frying or deep-frying; in these instances we like the textural contrast that comes from a crispy, fried exterior and a soft, creamy interior.) Given the soft, silky texture of the tofu in the restaurant dishes we tried, we knew firm and extra-firm weren't the way to go. We also dismissed silken tofu, as the tofu in the restaurant samples we tried remained in distinct chunks; silken tofu would have broken up into curds.

That left us with soft tofu. We gave it a test run in a basic working recipe. We sautéed aromatics, added the sauce components, letting them simmer and concentrate in flavor, then added the tofu toward the end, cooking it just long enough to heat through. Tasters agreed, the texture of this tofu wasn't as soft as our favorite restaurant versions. After a little more research, we noticed that some of the recipes referred to ma pao tofu as a braised tofu dish. Would a traditional braising technique over low, slow heat give the soft tofu the proper texture, softening it just as it softens a tough cut of meat? We gave it a shot, adding the soft tofu with the sauce, reducing the heat, and then simmering the tofu for 10 minutes. We noticed a difference in texture but wondered if we could push this approach even further. An additional 10 minutes of simmering gave our tofu a silky, soft texture just like the restaurant versions.

Now we were ready to build a flavor base. While pork is a traditional ingredient in ma pao tofu, we wanted to explore other options. We tasted a meatless version that used fermented black beans, but tasters unanimously dismissed it as lacking. This dish needed the textural contrast of the pork. So we started by browning and cooking through some ground pork, then setting it aside and stirring it into the sauce and tofu at the end, just long enough to heat it through. But tasters felt the browned pork overwhelmed the delicate tofu. For our next test, we added the pork to the aromatics and cooked it over medium heat for a couple minutes, just long enough to cook it through (without browning). Then we set it aside and stirred it in at the end as we had before. This was an improvement, but the pork was a little chewy. Would the pork, like the tofu, benefit from an extended simmer in the sauce? In our next test, we cooked the pork for just a minute, long enough to break it up, then stirred in the sauce, added the tofu, and left the dish to simmer for 20 minutes. This not only yielded tender pork, but also allowed the flavor of the pork to subtly permeate the dish.

Finding the best way to prepare the tofu and pork had been challenging, but determining the exact blend of flavors that give this dish its distinctive taste would prove even more difficult. While most recipes use the heat (and vibrant red color) of readily available chili oil as an integral ingredient, they also rely on more esoteric ingredients like broad bean or chili bean paste to give the sauce meaty depth.

As much as we loved the flavor of the bean paste, we felt a substitute was necessary to keep the recipe accessible. The bean paste added some heat, which could easily be replaced by adding more chili oil, but the rich, salty flavor it possessed would be harder to replicate. Increasing soy sauce helped some, but we needed another source to add complexity. Rooting around our pantry for a solution, we spied fish sauce. Granted, it's a Southeast Asian, not a Chinese, condiment, but just a small amount gives such dishes as pad thai and Vietnamese pho an essential salty complexity. Likewise, a small amount of fish sauce gave this dish the depth it was missing. A teaspoon of ground Sichuan peppercorns gave it the anise flavor and tongue-numbing sensation for which the dish is famous. We added a cornstarch slurry at the end to thicken the sauce and then mixed in two tablespoons of chili oil as a finishing touch.

We knew our efforts had paid off when tasters were too busy eating the ma pao tofu to stop and criticize the dish. While our dish was streamlined enough to make it accessible, the flavor was authentic enough to fool even our most discriminating tasters—and had them coming back for seconds.

Ma Pao Tofu

SERVES 4

Soft tofu is important to the texture of this dish; do not substitute silken, medium, or firm tofu. Sichuan peppercorns are an essential flavor in this dish; white or black peppercorns are not acceptable substitutes. This dish is fairly spicy; to make it milder, reduce the amount of chili oil. Serve with Simple Steamed White Rice (page 220).

SAUCE

2	cups low-sodium chicken broth
½	cup water
4	teaspoons soy sauce
4	teaspoons Chinese rice cooking wine or dry sherry
1	tablespoon fish sauce
2	teaspoons sugar

STIR-FRY

2	(14-ounce) blocks soft tofu, cut into ½-inch cubes (see note)
½	pound ground pork
2	teaspoons soy sauce
3	medium garlic cloves, minced or pressed through a garlic press (about 1 tablespoon)
1	tablespoon minced or grated fresh ginger (see the illustrations on page 216)
1	teaspoon Sichuan peppercorns, ground or crushed fine (see page 230) (see note)
1	tablespoon vegetable oil
3	scallions, white and green parts separated, whites minced, and greens sliced thin on the bias
3	tablespoons cornstarch
3	tablespoons water
2	tablespoons chili oil, plus extra for serving (see page 231)

1. **FOR THE SAUCE:** Whisk all the ingredients together; set aside.

2. **FOR THE STIR-FRY:** Spread the tofu out over several layers of paper towels and let drain for 20 minutes. Meanwhile, toss the pork with the soy sauce in a medium bowl and let marinate for at least 10 minutes or up to 1 hour. In a separate bowl, combine the garlic, ginger, ground Sichuan peppercorns, and 2 teaspoons of the vegetable oil.

3. Heat the remaining 1 teaspoon vegetable oil in a 12-inch nonstick skillet over medium heat until shimmering. Add the scallion whites and cook until softened, about 1 minute. Add the garlic mixture and cook, mashing the mixture into the pan, until fragrant, about 20 seconds.

4. Add the pork, break up the meat into small pieces, and cook until no longer pink, about 1 minute. Whisk the sauce to recombine, then add to the skillet. Gently add the tofu, cover, and simmer gently until the tofu and pork are very tender and the flavor of the sauce has deepened, about 20 minutes.

5. In a small bowl, whisk the cornstarch and water together. Gently whisk the cornstarch mixture into the skillet, being careful not to break up the tofu. Bring to a simmer and cook, stirring often, until the sauce has thickened, 2 to 3 minutes. Stir in the chili oil. Transfer to a platter, sprinkle with the scallion greens, and serve with additional chili oil.

8

30-MINUTE DINNERS

30-Minute Dinners

STEAK WITH POTATOES AND PARSLEY SAUCE

WHILE STEAK AND POTATOES MIGHT SOUND like a mundane dinner, in American chophouses this pairing has been elevated to an art form. The steak is always perfectly cooked, nicely seared and juicy-tender, and the potato wedges are fluffy on the inside with perfectly crisped exteriors. For the home cook, the appeal lies not only in the dish itself, but in the fact that it doesn't require a lot of prep or cooking time. But when the home cook attempts to re-create this duo in his or her own kitchen, all too often the steak is bland and flavorless and the potatoes almost instantly turn soggy sitting in the steak's juice on the plate. We set out to create chophouse-caliber pan-seared steak with crispy potatoes in our own kitchen, relying, of course, on one skillet and getting dinner to the table in just 30 minutes.

We started with the steak. For a perfectly seared steak, we knew from experience that a large, heavy skillet is key for even heat distribution, as is the right level of heat. We quickly discovered that to achieve the perfect crust, we had to make sure of two things: that the oil in the skillet was just smoking before we added the steaks and that the skillet was not overcrowded. If it wasn't hot enough, or if the steaks were jammed too tightly together, the steaks ended up stewing rather than searing. And because moving the steaks releases their liquid, once they were in the pan we let them be. We settled on buying two 1-pound strip steaks and cutting them in half to make four steaks. These larger steaks tend to be thicker, about 1½ inches, which allowed us to get a really good crust on the exterior without overcooking the interior. Getting a deep brown crust on the first side took about five minutes, then we flipped them, reduced the heat, and continued cooking until they were medium-rare (120 to 125 degrees), another 5 to 10 minutes. We undercooked the steaks a bit to allow for carryover cooking.

Next we tackled the potatoes. We quickly settled on red because their tender skin doesn't require peeling. Deep-frying was out—it was too messy and would require another pot. Sautéing the potatoes in the same skillet we had used to sear our steak meant that our potatoes would get a flavor boost from the steak's fat. However, dumping a handful of raw potato wedges into a hot skillet with a modicum of oil left us chewing on charred fries with raw centers. Upping the oil to 4 tablespoons helped us achieve more evenly golden potatoes, but it did little to solve the undercooked middles. We wondered if parcooking the potatoes in the microwave before adding them to the skillet would help. This meant we could jump-start the potatoes while the steaks seared, and then sauté them (in only 2 tablespoons oil) just long enough to finish cooking their interiors and crisp up their exteriors. This worked like a charm, and we found that the microwave also helped make the interiors of the potatoes light and fluffy.

While purists won't want to adorn their steak with anything other than a sprinkling of salt and pepper, our tasters felt an herb sauce would brighten the meal and elevate it to the next level. Inspired by an Argentine chimichurri sauce, we gathered parsley, garlic, olive oil, and red wine vinegar for a quick, fresh sauce that we could throw together in the food processor while the potatoes browned in the skillet.

This meal was quick, perfectly cooked, and it definitely went beyond plain old steak and potatoes.

EQUIPMENT: Kitchen Timer

Timing is everything in the test kitchen, critical to making everything from soft-boiled eggs to long-cooked roasts to finicky cookies, so a good kitchen timer is an essential piece of equipment. While timers are all basically the same, there are some features we deem more important than others. Our favorite is the Polder 3-in-1 Clock, Timer, and Stopwatch. Its compact size, easy-to-read display, and simple, intuitive controls (including 10-hour countdown and 24-hour count-up features) make it one of the most reliable, sensibly designed timers we've ever used. A 36-inch lanyard comfortably loops around the neck, and a convenient back-mounted magnet allows you to affix it wherever you want in the kitchen.

THE BEST KITCHEN TIMER

Polder 3-in-1 Clock, Timer, and Stopwatch ($12) has a lengthy time range, the ability to count up after the alarm goes off, and is easy to use and read.

POLDER

Pan-Seared Steak with Crispy Potatoes and Parsley Sauce

SERVES 4

We prefer this steak cooked to medium-rare, but if you prefer it more or less done, see our guidelines in the chart on page 45.

STEAK AND POTATOES

1½	pounds red potatoes (4 to 5 medium), scrubbed and cut into 1-inch wedges
¼	cup vegetable oil
	Salt and ground black pepper
2	(1-pound) boneless strip steaks, about 1½ inches thick, each steak cut in half crosswise

PARSLEY SAUCE

1	cup fresh parsley leaves
½	cup extra-virgin olive oil
¼	cup chopped red onion
¼	cup red wine vinegar
2	tablespoons water
4	medium garlic cloves, minced or pressed through a garlic press (about 4 teaspoons)
1	teaspoon salt
¼	teaspoon red pepper flakes

1. FOR THE STEAK AND POTATOES: Toss the potatoes with 1 tablespoon of the oil, ¼ teaspoon salt, and ⅛ teaspoon pepper in a microwave-safe bowl. Cover and microwave on high power until the potatoes begin to soften, 5 to 7 minutes, stirring the potatoes halfway through cooking.

2. Meanwhile, pat the steaks dry with paper towels and season with salt and pepper. Heat 1 tablespoon more oil in a 12-inch nonstick skillet over medium-high heat until just smoking. Carefully lay the steaks in the skillet and cook until well browned on the first side, 3 to 5 minutes.

3. Flip the steaks over, reduce the heat to medium, and continue to cook until the steak registers 125 degrees on an instant-read thermometer (for medium-rare), 5 to 7 minutes longer. Transfer the steaks to a plate, tent loosely with aluminum foil, and let rest while finishing the potatoes.

4. Drain the microwaved potatoes. Add the remaining 2 tablespoons oil to the skillet and return to medium heat until shimmering. Add the potatoes and cook until golden brown and tender, about 10 minutes.

5. FOR THE PARSLEY SAUCE: Process all the ingredients in a food processor until well combined, about 20 seconds, stopping to scrape down the bowl as needed. Drizzle the sauce over the steak and potatoes before serving.

SKILLET TAMALE PIE

WITH ITS JUICY, SPICY MIXTURE OF MEAT AND vegetables encased in or topped with a cornmeal crust, a good tamale pie is hard to beat. Classic Tex-Mex comfort food with a kick, tamale pie is also easy to assemble and bake, typically relying on multiple canned or prepared ingredients to make quick work of the prep. But sadly, bad tamale pies tend to be the norm. These are dry and bland, doing little to infuse the components with flavor, and they usually have too much or too little filling. We wanted to develop a great-tasting, quick tamale pie, one with just the right proportion of filling to topping. And instead of fussing with two pots—a skillet and a pie plate—we'd make our pie, start to finish, in just a skillet.

In our research, we found that most recipes use either ground beef or ground pork as the base. We began by testing both options in a working recipe, and the all-beef pie came out on top, as tasters felt it would stand up better to the spicier flavors we had in mind for our pie. So we sautéed some onion and garlic first, then added the meat to the pan. At this point, we looked at the traditional Southwestern ingredients, tomatoes and black beans. Adding a can of each right in with our ground beef helped us keep to our simple-and-quick strategy and brought an authentic touch to the dish.

We had all the right ingredients in place, but we had to work on the Tex-Mex flavor a bit. For a spicy kick, we added some chili powder to the sautéed onion, then stirred in minced fresh cilantro right before the skillet went into the oven, where it would cook just long enough for the flavors to meld.

We were getting there, but the filling needed more substance and cohesion. A cup of shredded cheddar cheese did the trick, bringing the filling together so it was both thicker and more flavorful.

Next we turned to the cornmeal topping. At first, we were torn—should it resemble the moist, savory exterior of real tamales, which are made from *masa*? Or should it be drier and slightly sweeter, more like cornbread, as we'd seen in so many existing tamale pie recipes? We tried both. The tamale-style topping didn't fly with our tasters; it just didn't seem like the right fit for this homey skillet casserole, not to mention we were reluctant to call for a specialty ingredient like masa for an easy weeknight recipe. Well aware that time was of the essence, we decided that the convenience of a cornbread mix had a lot going for it—just pour the mix into a bowl, add milk (and sometimes egg), mix, and bake. As we expected, the moist, tender crumb and subtle sweetness in the cornbread topping was the perfect complement to the spicy filling; it was the clear winner.

Putting together filling and topping was easy. Once we had prepared our filling in the skillet, we simply poured the cornbread batter over the top and spread it in an even layer to the edges of the dish. A moderately high oven temperature of 450 degrees for just 10 to 15 minutes did the best job of getting a golden, light crust and heating the filling. This tamale pie definitely hit the mark.

Skillet Tamale Pie

SERVES 4

Cornbread mixes vary from brand to brand; we like Betty Crocker Golden Corn Muffin and Bread Mix and Jiffy Corn Muffin Mix, but feel free to use your favorite brand. Note that you will need some additional ingredients not listed here to prepare your selected cornbread mix.

- 2 tablespoons vegetable oil
- 1 medium onion, minced
- 2 tablespoons chili powder
  Salt and ground black pepper
- 2 medium garlic cloves, minced or pressed through a garlic press (about 2 teaspoons)
- 1 pound 90 percent lean ground beef
- 1 (15-ounce) can black beans, drained and rinsed
- 1 (14.5-ounce) can diced tomatoes, drained
- 4 ounces cheddar cheese, shredded (1 cup)
- 2 tablespoons minced fresh cilantro leaves
- 1 (6.5- to 8.5-ounce) package cornbread mix (see note)

1. Adjust an oven rack to the middle position and heat the oven to 450 degrees. Heat the oil in a 12-inch ovensafe skillet over medium heat until shimmering. Add the onion, chili powder, and ½ teaspoon salt and cook until the onion is softened, about 5 minutes. Stir in the garlic and cook until fragrant, about 30 seconds.

2. Stir in the ground beef, beans, and tomatoes and bring to a simmer, breaking up the meat with a wooden spoon, about 5 minutes. Off the heat, stir in the cheddar and cilantro and season with salt and pepper to taste.

3. Meanwhile, mix the cornbread batter according to the package instructions. Smooth the filling into an even layer in the skillet. Dollop the corn bread topping evenly over the filling, then spread it into an even layer, covering the filling completely.

4. Bake the pie until the cornbread is golden and has baked through completely in the center, 10 to 15 minutes. Serve.

PAN-SEARED PORK CHOPS WITH DIRTY RICE

PORK CHOPS ARE AN EASY CHOICE FOR A quick dinner, but dinners of plain chops with basic sides like white rice and steamed vegetables can get a little ho-hum. We wanted to come up with a pork chop dinner that was still easy and quick but had a little more oomph. In the South, pork chops are often paired with dirty rice—a side dish of cooked rice, cured meats, vegetables, and seasonings that give the rice a "dirty" appearance. This pork and rice combination is no doubt a success when the cook takes the time to prepare the two components separately, but we wondered if we could make it all in the same skillet to create a boldly flavored, fast one-dish meal. There was only one way to find out.

We began by pan-searing four pork chops in our skillet, then we set them aside while we prepared the rice. We cooked chorizo, cutting it into ¼-inch pieces and browning it in the skillet, along with the traditional dirty rice ingredients of onion and bell pepper, followed by some garlic. After adding some chicken broth and the rice to the pan, we nestled in the browned chops, brought everything to a simmer, and allowed the pork and rice to finish cooking together. After tasting the results, we knew this approach certainly had potential, but there was plenty of room for improvement—the pork was tough and dry, the rice was bland and mushy, and we would need to find some shortcuts if we wanted to make this meal in 30 minutes or less.

We focused on the pork first. Because pork chops tend to be fairly lean, we typically favor bone-in rib chops, which are higher in fat than other types of chops and therefore are less prone to drying out. But even with the extra fat to protect them, the chops were still overcooking from the combination of pan-searing and simmering with the rice. We tried searing them for less time, but this left us with pale, bland chops. We were after moist, juicy chops with the deep flavor that comes only from a well-caramelized exterior. In the end, we found that pan-searing the chops until well browned on just one side—which took about five minutes—gave us the golden, crisp crust we sought (the side of the pork that was getting nestled into the rice lost its crispness anyway), while still ensuring juicy meat and deep flavor.

As for methods for cooking rice quickly in a skillet, many recipes turn to quick-cooking instant rice. But long-grain rice, with its superior texture and flavor, offered a lot more appeal in our minds—if we could get it to work. The long-grain rice would present a challenge to our time limit since it can take up to 25 minutes to cook. The microwave had come in handy before for a number of one-dish suppers where we needed to speed things up and give components a jump on cooking, and we

wondered if it could help here to cook the rice while the pork browned in the skillet. We began our testing with a basic ratio of 2 cups of water to 1 cup of rice. This rice was unevenly cooked and clumpy. After numerous tests, we found that for this method we needed more water than usual. In the end, 2½ cups of water proved best. We added 1¼ cups to the rice before it went into the microwave, and the remaining water was added to the skillet with the rice and pork. This method guaranteed distinct grains of perfectly cooked rice every time.

To add a little more depth to the rice, tasters favored swapping chicken broth for water and adding a modest amount of thyme and cayenne to the pan. We also folded in a bit of sliced scallion for freshness. With our flavorful pork chops and dirty rice recipe ready to go, we could finally say goodbye to our old boring pork chop dinners.

Pan-Seared Pork Chops with Dirty Rice
SERVES 4

If you can't find chorizo sausage, use andouille or linguiça.

2½	cups low-sodium chicken broth
1	cup long-grain white rice, rinsed (see the illustration on page 57)
4	(8- to 10-ounce) bone-in pork rib chops, ¾ to 1 inch thick, trimmed, sides slit (see the illustration on page 241) Salt and ground black pepper
1	tablespoon vegetable oil
4	ounces chorizo (see note), halved lengthwise and cut crosswise into ¼-inch pieces
1	small onion, minced
1	red bell pepper, stemmed, seeded, and chopped fine (see the illustrations on page 226)
6	medium garlic cloves, minced or pressed through a garlic press (about 2 tablespoons)
1	teaspoon minced fresh thyme leaves or ¼ teaspoon dried
¾	teaspoon Cajun spice blend or chili powder
3	scallions, sliced thin

PREPARING PORK CHOPS

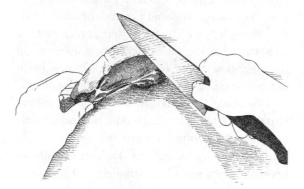

To get pork chops to lie flat and cook evenly, cut two slits about 2 inches apart through the fat and connective tissue.

1. Combine 1¼ cups of the broth and rice in a microwave-safe bowl, cover, and microwave on high power until the liquid is absorbed, about 10 minutes. Fluff the rice with a fork.

2. Meanwhile, pat the pork chops dry with paper towels and season with salt and pepper. Heat the oil in a 12-inch skillet over medium-high heat until just smoking. Carefully lay the pork chops in the skillet and cook until well browned on one side, 4 to 6 minutes. Transfer the pork chops to a plate.

3. Pour off all but 1 tablespoon of the fat from the skillet and return the skillet to medium heat. Add the chorizo, onion, and bell pepper and cook until the vegetables are softened, about 5 minutes. Stir in the garlic, thyme, and Cajun spice blend and cook until fragrant, about 30 seconds.

4. Stir in the remaining 1¼ cups broth and microwaved rice, scraping up any browned bits. Nestle the pork chops into the rice, browned side up, and bring to a simmer. Cover, reduce the heat to medium-low, and cook until the pork chops register 140 to 145 degrees on an instant-read thermometer, the rice is tender, and the liquid is absorbed, 8 to 10 minutes.

5. Transfer the pork chops to a plate, browned side up, brushing any rice that sticks to the chops back into the skillet. Tent the chops loosely with aluminum foil and let rest for 5 minutes. Gently fold the scallions into the rice, season with salt and pepper to taste, and serve with the pork chops.

EASY PORK TACOS

THE CLASSIC CRUNCHY BEEF TACO IS A GREAT go-to recipe for a quick and fun south-of-the-border family meal. But after a few years of regularly making our standby ground beef taco recipe, we wondered if it was time to come up with another taco night option. A fellow test cook mentioned the classic *tacos al pastor*, made with slow-cooked chile-rubbed pork, chopped onions, a sprig or two of cilantro, and a squeeze of fresh lime. We knew slow cooking and shredding pork wasn't an option for a quick weeknight meal, but we were inspired. Could we take these flavors and build a quick pork taco recipe using ground pork?

First, we set out to address the challenge of the chile flavor. Most authentic versions of tacos al pastor use a combination of hard-to-find dried chiles and a laundry list of spices. While dried chiles like anchos and chipotles probably would have worked well, we didn't have the time to soak and rehydrate them given our 30-minute limit. So instead, we opted for chipotle chiles in adobo sauce, which provided a smoky, open-fire flavor along with some subtle lingering heat without requiring any prep. We sautéed a small amount of chopped onion along with the chipotle chiles to give our sauce a base, then stirred in the ground pork and cooked it for five minutes, which was all it took for the pork to cook through. Juicy and rich, our ground pork was proving to be a terrific timesaving stand-in for roast pork. A generous handful of chopped cilantro added fresh floral notes, while a tablespoon of lime juice enlivened the flavors in the sauce.

To top off these tacos, tasters wanted a fresh fruit salsa to lend a bright, cool finish. We considered a few options, but in the end mango was the favorite. In keeping with our goal of requiring minimal ingredients, we looked at the ingredients we were already using to flavor our pork. Could some of these play double duty and also work in our salsa? Some minced onion, a handful of chopped cilantro, and a spritz of fresh lime juice gave our mango salsa all the fresh flavor it needed. Tasters voted that mellower red onion would work better than the white for the salsa, so we opted to use the red with the pork as well to keep our ingredients streamlined.

PEELING A MANGO

Because of their odd shape and slippery texture, mangos are notoriously difficult to peel and pit. Here's how we handle the task.

1. Remove a thin slice from one end of the mango so that it sits flat on a work surface.

2. Hold the mango cut side down and, working from top to bottom, remove the skin in thin strips using a sharp paring knife.

3. Cut down along the side of the flat pit to remove the flesh from one side of the mango. Do the same on the other side of the pit.

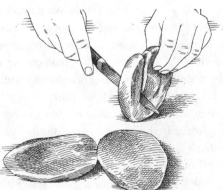

4. Trim around the pit to remove any remaining flesh. The mango flesh can now be chopped or sliced as desired.

It was time to give the tacos a try. We spooned our pork filling into warm corn tortillas and topped them with mango salsa and a garnish of some shredded Monterey Jack cheese. Tasters agreed that we were close, but the filling lacked cohesiveness. On the suggestion of one colleague, for our next batch of tacos we opted to stir the shredded cheese directly into the filling. Problem solved—the cheese melted into the pork filling lending it both flavor and a little creaminess that bound it together.

As we watched tasters come back for seconds, we knew beef taco night had definitely met its match.

Easy Pork Tacos

SERVES 4

We prefer fresh, ripe mangos here, but you can substitute 2 cups frozen mangos, thawed and chopped as directed. If your mangos are unripe (whether fresh or frozen), add sugar to the salsa in step 1 as needed.

2	medium mangos, peeled, pitted, and cut into ¼-inch dice (see the illustrations at left)
1	small red onion, minced
½	cup chopped fresh cilantro leaves
2	tablespoons juice from 1 lime
	Salt and ground black pepper
2	teaspoons vegetable oil
2	teaspoons minced chipotle chile in adobo sauce
1½	pounds ground pork
2	ounces Monterey Jack cheese, shredded (½ cup)
12	(6-inch) corn tortillas

1. Combine the mangos, half of the onion, ¼ cup of the cilantro, 1 tablespoon of the lime juice, ¼ teaspoon salt, and ¼ teaspoon pepper in a medium bowl; set aside.

2. Heat the oil in a 12-inch skillet over medium-high heat until shimmering. Add the remaining onion and chipotles and cook until softened, about 5 minutes. Stir in the pork and cook, breaking up the meat with a wooden spoon, until no longer pink, about 5 minutes. Off the heat, stir in the remaining ¼ cup cilantro, remaining 1 tablespoon lime juice, and cheese. Season with salt and pepper to taste.

3. Stack the tortillas on a plate, cover, and microwave on high power until warm and soft, 1 to 2 minutes. Spoon a small amount of the pork filling into the center of each warm tortilla, top with the mango mixture, and serve.

INDOOR WISCONSIN BRATS AND BEER

GRILLING BURGERS OR FRANKS IS QUICK AND easy for the cook, but you don't always have the time (or the perfect weather) to deal with firing up the grill. And while cooking a few beef patties in a skillet on the stovetop gets the job done for a weeknight dinner that hints at bringing grilling indoors, we were after something more interesting. One of our favorite grilling recipes is a Midwest football season favorite combining, of course, bratwurst and beer. Typically, a disposable aluminum pan filled with cheap lager and sliced onions is placed on one half of the grill and the sausages on the other half. The sausages are then simmered in the onions and beer to finish cooking. The idea is that the beer and onions flavor the bratwurst, which is then nestled into a bun, smothered with the beer-infused onions, and doused with plenty of mustard. Our goal was to bring this full-flavored, crowd-pleasing meal indoors for a one-dish makeover.

We started with the star, the meat. Bratwurst is the classic choice in the grilled version, though knackwurst follows closely (both are fresh sausages that must be thoroughly cooked). Authentic bratwurst is made from a combination of pork and veal seasoned with a variety of spices, including ginger, nutmeg, and caraway. Knackwurst is a combination of beef and pork flavored with cumin and garlic. While our local German butcher supplied the best-quality sausages, we were also able to find suitable options in our local supermarket's deli department.

In the grilled version, the sausages begin by browning on the grill, which deepens flavor and adds visual appeal. For our indoor adaptation, we moved them to a skillet. We found that about five minutes of browning over medium-high heat was enough to intensify the flavor of the sausages and develop a fond in the pan, which we could use to help season the onions. For our skillet version, we simply added the onions and beer to the skillet with the browned sausages and simmered them together until the sausages were cooked through.

The bratwurst tasted great, but the onions were pale and still called for a flavor boost. For starters, we needed to better utilize the flavorful fond left in the skillet from browning the sausages. For our next test, we sliced the onions thin, then tossed them into the hot skillet after removing the sausages. Letting the onions cook long enough to turn golden brown allowed them to become caramelized and much more flavorful. Then we added their beer bath, scraped up the browned bits, and placed the sausages in the pan. We all agreed that these onions, with their slightly sweet, rich caramelized flavor, could definitely hold their own next to the brats.

So the onions and brats were in good shape, but we wanted to see where else we could add flavor without adding time or too many ingredients. What about the beer? We tried dark ales and expensive lagers, but we quickly discovered that their big flavors become overly harsh and bitter when reduced. Cheap, mild lagers remained our favorite, as they maintained a mellow, pleasant flavor when simmered for half an hour.

In most outdoor recipes, once the bratwurst and onions have been cooked, the braising liquid is considered spent and it's dumped on the ground. But the caramelized onions and brats had infused the beer with so much flavor that we couldn't bear to see it go to waste. Cooked down, it did a great job of coating our onions and brats, so we decided to amp up its flavor even further. We began by adding mustard to the cooking liquid; this lent brightness and body. A little bit of sugar, pepper, and some caraway seeds added richness and complexity. In the time it took for the sausages to cook through our liquid had thickened slightly, allowing it to lightly coat the sausages and onions, lending another layer of flavor to the recipe.

With crisp, browned, and flavorful bratwurst and beer-and-mustard infused onions nestled into a bun—and all done in just 30 minutes—we were sure it could hold its own against the grilled version.

Indoor Wisconsin Brats and Beer

SERVES 4

Liberally pricking the sausages with a fork prior to cooking ensures they won't explode. We prefer the mellow flavor of Budweiser or Miller Genuine Draft in this recipe. Note that bratwurst are often bigger than your average hot dog and therefore require a larger than average hot dog roll.

2	tablespoons vegetable oil
I	pound bratwurst (4 to 6 links), pricked all over with a fork
2	medium onions, halved and sliced pole to pole into ¼-inch-thick pieces (see illustration on page 134)
I	teaspoon brown sugar
	Salt and ground black pepper
I	(12-ounce) can or bottle beer (see note)
¼	cup whole grain mustard
½	teaspoon caraway seeds
I	tablespoon minced fresh parsley leaves
4–6	large hot dog rolls

1. Heat the oil in a 12-inch skillet over medium-high heat until shimmering. Brown the bratwurst on all sides, about 5 minutes; transfer to a plate.

2. Add the onions, sugar, and ⅛ teaspoon salt to the fat left in the skillet and cook over medium heat until softened and golden, about 8 minutes. Stir in the beer, mustard, caraway seeds, and ½ teaspoon pepper, scraping up any browned bits, and bring to a simmer.

3. Nestle the sausages into the skillet and reduce the heat to medium–low. Cook until the sausages are no longer pink in the center and the sauce is slightly thickened, about 12 minutes. Off the heat, stir in the parsley. Place the sausages in the rolls, top with the onions, and serve.

CHICKEN FAJITAS

WHAT IS LABELED AS CHICKEN FAJITAS IN most restaurants these days is barely edible, with guacamole, sour cream, and salsa slathered on in a weak attempt to mask the blandness of the key ingredients. We wanted to go back to the basics and come up with a simple combination of smoky roasted vegetables and strips of chicken wrapped up at the table in warm flour tortillas. That said, we also wanted a fajita recipe that could be made quickly (in 30 minutes) without lugging out the grill; we would rely instead on our skillet.

EQUIPMENT: Traditional Skillets

We use our skillets for everything from pan-roasting chicken breasts and cooking burgers and steaks to preparing one-skillet meals. But the variation in price is dizzying—pans can cost anywhere from $30 to $150 or more. Preliminary tests of traditional 12-inch skillets confirmed our suspicions that cheap was not the way to go, but how much do you really need to spend? All of the pans we tested had flared sides and most had uncoated stainless steel cooking surfaces, which we prize for promoting a fond (the browned bits that cling to the interior of the pan when food is sautéed and that help flavor sauces).

The pans tested measured 12 inches in diameter (across the top) or as close to that as we could get. This large size is the most versatile because it can accommodate a big steak or all of the pieces of a cut-up 3-pound chicken. However, the cooking surface in a pan can measure considerably less than the top diameter measurement, meaning the pan has a smaller surface area and less room for the food to brown.

In the end, we concluded that medium-weight pans are ideal. These pans have enough heft for heat retention (which ensures even cooking and browning) and structural integrity, but not so much that they are difficult to manipulate. For its combination of excellent performance, optimum weight and balance, and overall ease of use, the All-Clad Stainless Fry Pan was the hands-down winner.

THE BEST SKILLET
The All-Clad Stainless Fry Pan ($110) browns food perfectly, has a spacious cooking area, and is easy to handle.

ALL-CLAD

While skirt steak, the choice for classic beef fajitas, can get away with foregoing an extra boost of flavor, boneless chicken breasts need all the help they can get. Normally, we would have started our testing with a marinade, but that was obviously out, as was brining, given our 30-minute time limit. For the brightest flavor and simplest, fastest method, we settled on sautéing the chicken plain and tossing the cooked strips in the "marinade" afterward. After a few tests, we settled on a simple mix of oil, cilantro, salt, and sugar, along with plenty of lime juice (4 tablespoons juice to 2 tablespoons oil). This yielded tender, browned chicken with a bright, unadulterated tang.

Our post-marinade added fresh citrus flavor notes to the chicken that tasters approved of, but it still lacked the smokiness and depth we expect in fajitas. After trying numerous unsuccessful flavor additions, we finally hit upon Worcestershire sauce. Though an unlikely choice, Worcestershire has a savory quality known as *umami*, a culinary term that refers to a fifth taste sensation beyond the familiar sweet, sour, bitter, and salty. It was just what our chicken fajita meat needed. A mere 2 teaspoons of Worcestershire added another layer of saltiness and smokiness.

As for vegetables, both bell peppers and onion gave the fajitas some needed contrast, not just in terms of visual appeal but in their bitter and sweet flavors. While the chicken rested, we sautéed the peppers and onions in the same skillet, taking advantage of the flavorful fond left by the meat. Though the incorporated fond lent the vegetables a full flavor that needed minimal enhancement, we experimented with adding a variety of spices to see if we could lend just a bit more complexity. We settled on chili powder, which added a characteristically Southwestern flavor. We added the spice to the pan with the vegetables and poured in ½ cup water to help the process along and prevent the spices from tasting raw and gritty.

We warmed our tortillas quickly in the microwave to save time, and pulled together our favorite toppings, which we could now use to complement—not cover up—our full-flavor fajitas. All that was left to do was assemble them and eat.

Skillet Chicken Fajitas
SERVES 4

To make this dish spicy, add a sliced jalapeño to the skillet with the bell pepper. Serve with salsa, sour cream, chopped avocado, shredded cheese, shredded lettuce, and lime wedges.

4	(5- to 6-ounce) boneless, skinless chicken breasts, trimmed and lightly pounded to a uniform thickness (see the illustration on page 247)
	Salt and ground black pepper
¼	cup vegetable oil
2	red, yellow, or orange bell peppers, stemmed, seeded, and sliced thin (see the illustrations on page 226)
I	medium red onion, halved and sliced thin
½	cup water
I½	teaspoons chili powder
12	(6-inch) flour tortillas
¼	cup juice from 2 limes
2	tablespoons minced fresh cilantro leaves
2	teaspoons Worcestershire sauce
½	teaspoon brown sugar

1. Pat the chicken dry with paper towels and season with salt and pepper. Heat 2 tablespoons of the oil in a 12-inch skillet over medium-high heat until just smoking. Carefully lay the chicken in the skillet and cook until well browned on the first side, 6 to 8 minutes.

2. Flip the chicken over, reduce the heat to medium, and continue to cook until the thickest part of the chicken registers 160 to 165 degrees on an instant-read thermometer, 6 to 8 minutes longer. Transfer the chicken to a carving board, tent loosely with aluminum foil, and let rest while cooking the vegetables.

3. Add the bell peppers, onion, water, chili powder, and ½ teaspoon salt to the fat left in the skillet and cook over medium-high heat, scraping up any browned bits, until the onion is softened, 5 to 7 minutes. Transfer to a serving bowl and cover to keep warm.

4. Meanwhile, stack the tortillas on a plate, cover, and microwave on high power until warm and soft,

1 to 2 minutes. Mix the remaining 2 tablespoons oil, lime juice, cilantro, Worcestershire, sugar, and ¼ teaspoon salt together in a large bowl. Slice the chicken into ¼-inch-thick pieces, toss with the lime juice mixture, and serve with the vegetables and warm tortillas.

➤ VARIATION
Skillet Chicken Fajitas with Zucchini and Red Onion
Follow the recipe for Skillet Chicken Fajitas, substituting 2 medium zucchini (about 1 pound), halved lengthwise and cut into ¼-inch pieces, for the bell peppers.

CHICKEN AND COUSCOUS

WHEN COOKED CORRECTLY, COUSCOUS HAS a supremely fluffy texture, pairs well with a variety of flavors, and because it cooks so quickly, makes a great alternative to longer-cooking rice. Offering a change from the same old chicken and rice dinner, it seemed like a perfect option for an unusual and flavorful skillet supper for a busy weeknight. We wanted a one-dish chicken and couscous meal where the couscous was light and fluffy, the chicken was lightly browned and moist, and the flavors were bright.

The real trick with this dish would be deciding the best way to cook the chicken and couscous in the same skillet without compromising the flavor or integrity of either. After searching through dozens of chicken and couscous recipes with various flavor combinations, we settled on a simple rendition incorporating fennel, red onion, orange, and cilantro.

First, we settled how we would cook the chicken. We kept things simple by following a basic test kitchen method for sautéed chicken breasts. First we browned the chicken over medium-high heat, then reduced the heat and cooked it through. From our previous testing, we had learned when sautéing boneless, skinless chicken breasts (our cut of choice here since they are the least fussy) there are a few

keys to moist, tender meat. Pounding the chicken to an even thickness would allow it to cook and brown more evenly, which in turn is key to sealing in the juice. We knew that lightly dredging the chicken in flour would also encourage the browning without drying out the surface of the chicken. With these techniques in place, our recipe was well on its way.

Once the chicken had cooked, we set it aside and moved on to the couscous and vegetables. We began with the red onion and fennel. They would provide the dish with heft, texture, and a clean vegetal sweetness. We added both to the skillet and cooked them until the onion began to soften and the fennel was crisp-tender.

Next, we stirred the couscous into the vegetables along with garlic and a pinch of cayenne for heat. Toasting the couscous with the oil and aromatics served two purposes: It added a nutty flavor, and it would help keep the grains separate and prevent clumping throughout the cooking process.

We then considered the cooking liquid. Most recipes employ either water or broth to hydrate the couscous. Cooking in water resulted in bland couscous, even with our assortment of aromatics and fennel, so we opted for the more flavorful choice of chicken broth. To incorporate the orange, we found recipes that added orange segments, but this technique was tedious, time-consuming, and failed to provide the amount of orange flavor we wanted. Instead, we supplemented our chicken broth with orange juice, which helped to bring out more of the fennel's flavor and brighten the entire dish. We brought our mixture to a simmer, then let it sit off the heat until the couscous absorbed the liquid and was evenly plump and tender, which took a mere five minutes.

For our final touches, we folded in a few tablespoons of cilantro and then drizzled both the chicken and the couscous with olive oil that we accented with orange juice, cayenne, and cilantro (all ingredients we had already used in the recipe) before serving. Our variation with chickpeas, dried apricots, and cinnamon offers a pleasant sweetness and contrasting touch of spice. Fragrant and flavorful, both recipes are great options for spicing up weeknight dinner menus.

Chicken and Couscous with Fennel and Orange

SERVES 4

Be sure to use regular (or fine-grain) couscous; large-grain couscous, often labeled Israeli-style, takes much longer to cook and won't work in this recipe.

½	cup unbleached all-purpose flour
4	(5- to 6-ounce) boneless, skinless chicken breasts, trimmed and lightly pounded to a uniform thickness (see the illustration below) Salt and ground black pepper
½	cup olive oil
1	medium red onion, halved and sliced thin
1	medium fennel bulb (about 12 ounces), trimmed of stalks, cored, and sliced thin (see the illustrations on page 38)
1	cup couscous (see note)
3	medium garlic cloves, minced or pressed through a garlic press (about 1 tablespoon) Pinch cayenne pepper
1	cup orange juice
¾	cup low-sodium chicken broth
¼	cup minced fresh cilantro leaves

1. Place the flour in a shallow dish. Pat the chicken dry with paper towels and season with salt and black pepper. Working with 1 chicken breast at a time, dredge in the flour, shaking off the excess.

2. Heat 2 tablespoons of the oil in a 12-inch nonstick skillet over medium-high heat until just smoking. Carefully lay the chicken in the skillet and cook until well browned on the first side, 6 to 8 minutes.

3. Flip the chicken over, reduce the heat to medium, and continue to cook until the thickest part of the chicken registers 160 to 165 degrees on an instant-read thermometer, 6 to 8 minutes longer. Transfer the chicken to a plate, tent loosely with aluminum foil, and let rest while cooking the vegetables and couscous.

4. Add 1 tablespoon more oil to the skillet and return to medium-high heat until shimmering. Add the onion, fennel, and ½ teaspoon salt and cook until the onion is softened, about 5 minutes. Stir in the couscous, garlic, and a pinch cayenne and cook until fragrant, about 30 seconds. Stir in ¾ cup of the orange juice and broth, scraping up any browned bits. Bring to a simmer, then remove from the heat, cover, and let sit until the liquid is absorbed, about 5 minutes.

5. Whisk the remaining 5 tablespoons oil, remaining ¼ cup orange juice, 2 tablespoons of the cilantro, and a pinch cayenne together in a small bowl.

6. Gently fold the remaining 2 tablespoons cilantro into the couscous and season with salt and black pepper to taste. Drizzle the orange juice mixture over the chicken and couscous before serving.

➤ VARIATION

Chicken and Couscous with Chickpeas and Apricots

Follow the recipe for Chicken and Couscous with Fennel and Orange, omitting the fennel and cayenne. In step 4, add ½ teaspoon ground cinnamon with the onion and add 1 (15-ounce) can chickpeas, drained and rinsed, and 1 cup dried apricots, chopped coarse, with the orange juice. Add a pinch ground cinnamon to the orange juice mixture in step 5.

POUNDING CHICKEN BREASTS

To ensure that chicken breasts are of even thickness (and thus will cook evenly), you may need to pound them. Place the breasts, smooth side down, on a large sheet of plastic wrap. Cover with a second sheet of plastic wrap and pound gently, making sure that each breast has the same thickness from end to end.

SAUTÉED CHICKEN WITH CHERRY TOMATOES

BONELESS, SKINLESS CHICKEN BREASTS ARE an easy choice for a quick weeknight meal, and we had just developed an appealing alternative to chicken and rice with our Chicken and Couscous with Fennel and Orange (page 247). We weren't done yet—we wanted to find another way to transform plain sautéed chicken breasts into a quick weeknight meal that was flavorful and bright. After a little research, we came across a magazine photo of perfectly browned boneless, skinless breasts paired with a mixture of tomatoes, olives, and feta cheese. This dish was colorful and inviting, and we thought it would make the perfect simple meal for a hot summer night.

Preparing the chicken was easy. We followed our basic method for sautéed chicken breasts, trimming and pounding the chicken to an even thickness, seasoning it with salt and pepper, dredging it in flour before browning it in the skillet, and then lowering the heat to cook it through. This time we included a sprinkling of ground coriander when we seasoned each chicken breast, which would brighten the flavor and complement the fresh tomatoes.

After cooking the chicken breasts, we set them aside so we could whip together the side dish in our skillet. We knew the key ingredients would be fresh cherry tomatoes, rich kalamata olives, and tangy feta, so it was a matter of nailing down the quantities of each, the method of cooking, and finally fine-tuning the flavors.

Garlic and olive oil are a natural pairing with tomatoes, so we started there. We quickly learned that tossing a few cloves of minced garlic, some olive oil, and fresh cherry tomatoes straight into the pan all at once left us with a harsh garlic flavor. Cooking the garlic first over low heat helped, but we had better results from cooking it in hot olive oil over moderately high heat for about 30 seconds. This was enough time to infuse the oil with the garlic's flavor and mellow any harshness in the garlic itself.

Next into the skillet went the cherry tomatoes. We first tried adding them whole, but by the time the skins were adequately wilted, they had begun to burst. For our next attempt, we halved the tomatoes first. This simple step, combined with the high heat of the pan, allowed for some release of the tomatoes' liquid while keeping the skin relatively taut. The tomato juice mingled with the fond in the pan and created a mixture that was part sauce, part side dish.

Thinking we were done at this point, we tossed in the remaining ingredients (olives and feta) and gave the dish a taste. To our surprise, tasters' comments focused on the briny bite of the olives; they wanted a mellower flavor to allow the sweetness of the tomatoes to shine through. Reducing the amount of olives left the mixture too bland, and rinsing them was even worse. Our solution was to add the olives to the skillet along with the tomatoes. The heat calmed the olives' brininess and lent saltiness to the tomatoes. The final result was a salty-sweet combination that tasters loved.

Instead of adding the feta cheese to the hot pan, where it would melt, we poured the tomato-olive mixture onto a serving platter and then sprinkled the cheese over the top. The cool, tangy cheese was the perfect contrast to the warm, sweet tomatoes and briny olives. A sprinkling of shredded mint leaves for color and freshness was the perfect finishing touch to our side dish.

Tasters liked this dish so much that we came up with a variation with a slightly different spin. With chili powder and corn, our second sautéed chicken dinner was as appealing as the original.

Sautéed Chicken with Cherry Tomatoes, Olives, Feta, and Mint
SERVES 4

Fresh basil or cilantro can be substituted for the mint.

½   cup unbleached all-purpose flour
4   (5- to 6-ounce) boneless, skinless chicken breasts, trimmed and lightly pounded to a uniform thickness (see the illustration on page 247)
1   teaspoon ground coriander
    Salt and ground black pepper

3   tablespoons plus 2 teaspoons olive oil
2   medium garlic cloves, minced or pressed through a garlic press (about 2 teaspoons)
2   cups cherry tomatoes (about 12 ounces), halved
½   cup pitted kalamata olives, halved
2   ounces feta cheese, crumbled (½ cup)
¼   cup shredded fresh mint leaves

1. Place the flour in a shallow dish. Pat the chicken dry with paper towels and season with the coriander, salt, and pepper. Working with 1 chicken breast at a time, dredge in the flour, shaking off the excess.

2. Heat 2 tablespoons of the oil in a 12-inch nonstick skillet over medium-high heat until just smoking. Carefully lay the chicken in the skillet and cook until well browned on the first side, 6 to 8 minutes.

3. Flip the chicken over, reduce the heat to medium, and continue to cook until the thickest part of the chicken registers 160 to 165 degrees on an instant-read thermometer, 6 to 8 minutes longer. Transfer the chicken to a plate, tent loosely with aluminum foil, and let rest while cooking the vegetables.

4. Add 2 teaspoons more oil and garlic to the skillet and return to medium-high heat until fragrant, 30 to 60 seconds. Stir in the tomatoes and olives, scraping up any browned bits, and cook until the tomatoes are just softened, about 2 minutes.

5. Off the heat, stir in the remaining 1 tablespoon oil, transfer to a large serving platter, and sprinkle with the feta and mint. Serve with the chicken.

➤ VARIATION

Sautéed Chicken with Cherry Tomatoes and Toasted Corn

Three cups thawed frozen corn can be substituted for the fresh corn. Do not stir the corn when cooking in step 4 or it will not brown well.

½   cup unbleached all-purpose flour
4   (5- to 6-ounce) boneless, skinless chicken breasts, trimmed and lightly pounded to a uniform thickness (see the illustration on page 247)
1   teaspoon chili powder

    Salt and ground black pepper
3   tablespoons plus 2 teaspoons olive oil
4   ears corn, husk and silk removed, kernels cut from the cob (about 3 cups) (see the illustration on page 5) (see note)
1   medium shallot, minced (about 3 tablespoons)
2   medium garlic cloves, minced or pressed through a garlic press (about 2 teaspoons)
2   cups cherry tomatoes (about 12 ounces), halved
¼   cup minced fresh cilantro leaves
2   tablespoons juice from 1 lime

1. Place the flour in a shallow dish. Pat the chicken dry with paper towels and season with the chili powder, salt, and pepper. Working with 1 chicken breast at a time, dredge in the flour, shaking off the excess.

2. Heat 2 tablespoons of the oil in a 12-inch nonstick skillet over medium-high heat until just smoking. Carefully lay the chicken in the skillet and cook until well browned on the first side, 6 to 8 minutes.

3. Flip the chicken over, reduce the heat to medium, and continue to cook until the thickest part of the chicken registers 160 to 165 degrees on an instant-read thermometer, 6 to 8 minutes longer. Transfer the chicken to a plate, tent loosely with aluminum foil, and let rest while cooking the vegetables.

4. Add 2 teaspoons more oil to the skillet and return to medium-high heat until shimmering. Add the corn and cook, without stirring, until well browned and toasted, about 8 minutes. Stir in the shallot and garlic and cook until fragrant, about 30 seconds. Stir in the tomatoes, scraping up any browned bits, and cook until the tomatoes are just softened, about 2 minutes.

5. Off the heat, stir in the remaining 1 tablespoon oil, cilantro, and lime juice and season with salt and pepper to taste. Transfer to a large serving platter and serve with the chicken.

The Best Kitchen Tools 101

Countless gadgets promise convenience but deliver disappointment and lost drawer space. Here are 17 tools that really work.

MEASURING CUPS AND SPOONS

WHY YOU NEED THEM: Inaccurate measuring of ingredients is one of the most common reasons recipes fail. Just ask any of us in the test kitchen: The need for a collection of measuring cups and spoons that efficiently and accurately measure ingredients is not debatable.

THE BEST DRY MEASURING CUPS: AMCO Basic Ingredient 4-Piece Measuring Cup Set ($11.50)

WHY WE LIKE THEM: This stainless steel set measured with perfect—truly perfect—accuracy and offered moderate weight, great balance, and long, level, clearly marked handles.

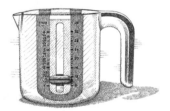

THE BEST LIQUID MEASURING CUP: Cuisipro Deluxe Liquid Measuring Cup, 2-cup ($10.95) and 4-cup ($14.95)

WHY WE LIKE IT: Unlike other liquid measuring cups, which require you to crouch down to see if the liquid meets the line at eye level, this clear plastic cup can be read from above. It's durable, has easy-to-read markings, is dishwasher- and microwave-safe, and is available in 2- and 4-cup sizes.

THE BEST MEASURING SPOONS: Cuisipro Stainless Steel Oval Measuring Spoons ($13.95)

WHY WE LIKE THEM: The handles and bowl are flush, which facilitates the leveling of dry ingredients. Deep bowls make measuring liquids easier. And they're slim enough to be scooped into narrow spice jars.

VEGETABLE PEELERS

WHY YOU NEED THEM: Most people have some kind of peeler that does an OK job on carrots and potatoes. But for other peeling jobs—say, the thick peel of a winter squash or the delicate skin of a pear—we rely on vegetable peelers that have maneuverable blades.

THE BEST VEGETABLE PEELER: Messermeister Pro-Touch Swivel Peeler ($6.95)

WHY WE LIKE IT: Remarkably sharp and light, this peeler has a smooth motion and remains comfortable to use, so hand strain is never a problem—even after peeling piles of apples or potatoes.

THE BEST SERRATED PEELER: Messermeister Serrated Swivel Peeler ($6.95)

WHY WE LIKE IT: While not an everyday tool, this peeler has a sharp serrated blade that cleanly pulls the skin off difficult-to-peel produce such as tomatoes and easy-to-bruise peaches.

HEATPROOF RUBBER SPATULA

WHY YOU NEED IT: Nothing is better suited to a multitude of tasks, from cleaning out the corners of bowls and pots to stirring batters, icing cakes, or folding egg whites. With the introduction of heat-resistant models, the tool is even more indispensable.

THE BEST RUBBER SPATULA: Rubbermaid Professional 13.5-Inch High Heat Scraper ($18.99)

WHY WE LIKE IT: The wide, firm blade is rigid enough to mix the stiffest batter yet flexible enough to reach into the tightest of spaces. Unlike some rubber spatulas, the Rubbermaid doesn't stain or carry odors—even when used to stir chili. Rubbermaid's high-heat material is truly heatproof, something we've proved time and time again by leaving them in hot skillets and soup pots.

GRATERS

WHY YOU NEED THEM: A sharp box grater is indispensable for many tasks, from uniformly grating blocks of cheddar cheese to shredding potatoes. A finely textured rasp-style grater—so called because it's modeled after the woodworker's filelike tool—is portable, allowing you to grate or zest at the stove or table.

THE BEST GRATERS: OXO Good Grips Box Grater ($17.95); Microplane Classic 40020 Grater/Zester ($14.95)

WHY WE LIKE THEM: This razor-sharp box grater requires little effort or pressure to get results. It also comes with a handy container marked with cup measurements that snaps onto the bottom. The handheld grater has razor-sharp teeth that can finely grate Parmesan in a flash. In addition to cheese, it can handle shallots, garlic, ginger, nutmeg, chocolate, and citrus zest.

TONGS

WHY YOU NEED THEM: Acting like an extension of the hand, tongs let you lift, flip, turn, and rotate most any type of food, from small shrimp to a 5-pound rib roast, all without burning your fingers.

THE BEST TONGS: OXO Good Grips 12-Inch Locking Tongs ($12.95)

WHY WE LIKE THEM: These stainless steel tongs have rubber grips that help secure them in your hand. While they can open wide enough to pick up large items, they have springs that enable them to pick up the smallest of vegetables.

INSTANT-READ THERMOMETER

WHY YOU NEED IT: With an instant-read thermometer, you'll never again overcook a steak or undercook a chicken. We use them for everything from sauces and breads to cheesecakes.

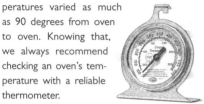

THE BEST INSTANT-READ THERMOMETER: ThermoWorks Splash-Proof Super-Fast Thermapen ($96)

WHY WE LIKE IT: In the test kitchen, we call it the Ferrari of thermometers. Besides providing an accurate read each time, its qualities include a quick response time, thin probe, and large display. It can register temperatures from –40 to 450 degrees and is water resistant.

OVEN THERMOMETER

WHY YOU NEED IT: While we calibrate the test kitchen ovens every two months, a survey of our ovens at home found that temperatures varied as much as 90 degrees from oven to oven. Knowing that, we always recommend checking an oven's temperature with a reliable thermometer.

THE BEST OVEN THERMOMETER: Cooper-Atkins Oven Thermometer ($6.12)

WHY WE LIKE IT: This thermometer has clearly marked numbers for easy readability, has a stable base as well as a hook, and a temperature range up to 600 degrees.

PEPPER MILL

WHY YOU NEED IT: Because the preground stuff sold in bottles is insipid when compared with freshly ground. But grinding pepper shouldn't be a wrist-wrenching chore.

THE BEST PEPPER MILL: Unicorn Magnum Plus Peppermill ($45)

WHY WE LIKE IT: Whether set to coarse or fine, it quickly yields a consistent grind and requires little wrist action to operate. Its large capacity hopper requires infrequent filling. Best of all, it's easy to fill—no taking apart.

COLANDER

WHY YOU NEED IT: How else are you going to drain pasta and vegetables?

THE BEST COLANDER: RSVP International Endurance Precision Pierced 5-Quart Colander ($32.95)

WHY WE LIKE IT: This large-capacity colander contains minute, meshlike perforations that drain in seconds. A wide base means it can sit in the sink without tipping or spilling.

SALAD SPINNER

WHY YOU NEED IT: Wet greens can't be dressed properly. We also use a salad spinner to wash and dry herbs.

THE BEST SALAD SPINNER: OXO Good Grips Salad Spinner ($29.99)

WHY WE LIKE IT: Its sturdy, leakproof bowl allows us to wash greens right in the bowl rather than in the sink. Its top-mounted pump knob requires little effort to use. We like that the top locks into place for storage, and a nonskid bottom holds the spinner in place.

FINE-MESH STRAINER

WHY YOU NEED IT: A strainer is essential for such tasks as dusting a tart with powdered sugar or turning cooked raspberries into a seedless sauce. It also makes an excellent stand-in for a sifter.

THE BEST FINE-MESH STRAINER: CIA Masters Collection 6¾-Inch Fine Mesh Strainer ($27.49)

WHY WE LIKE IT: This strainer sits securely in large and medium bowls and produces smooth sauces.

WHISK

WHY YOU NEED IT: Useful not only for whipping cream and egg whites, a whisk can also mix batters and make pan sauces and gravies.

THE BEST WHISK: Best Manufacturers 12-Inch Standard French Whip ($10.50)

WHY WE LIKE IT: This long whisk boasts an agile set of tines and a comfortable handle that is light enough to keep the whisk from tipping out of short saucepans.

GARLIC PRESS

WHY YOU NEED IT: A garlic press does a better job of mincing than one can do by hand—producing a fuller, less acrid flavor that is more evenly distributed throughout a dish.

THE BEST GARLIC PRESS: Kuhn Rikon Easy-Squeeze Garlic Press ($19.95)

WHY WE LIKE IT: Its long, curved handle and short distance between the pivot point and the plunger help make pressing less work.

KITCHEN SHEARS

WHY YOU NEED THEM: Our favorite tool for cutting up and trimming chickens, versatile kitchen shears are ideal for trimming pie dough, snipping herbs, and cutting parchment paper rounds. Try severing twine without them.

THE BEST KITCHEN SHEARS: Messermeister Take-Apart Shears ($19.95)

WHY WE LIKE THEM: They're precise, super-sharp, and agile. We like their slip-resistant handles and the fact that they can be taken apart and cleaned thoroughly.

CHICKEN AND WHITE BEAN PANZANELLA SALAD

THE IDEA OF USING BREAD AS ONE OF THE major components in a salad (and we're not talking croutons) may be unfamiliar to some, but bread salad, or *panzanella*, is not uncommon in Italy. There, stale bread is typically combined with fresh ingredients—tomatoes, onions, and basil—and a simple oil and vinegar dressing. The result is a simple meal that is light yet satisfying, one that is far more than the sum of its parts. We wanted to take this classic recipe one step further and create a complete one-dish meal by including juicy pieces of chicken, white beans, fresh arugula, and shaved Parmesan.

For the chicken, we immediately decided to use boneless, skinless breasts. Taking a cue from our previous 30-minute suppers involving chicken, we trimmed and pounded the breasts to an even thickness, seasoned them with salt and pepper, and browned them in the skillet. Dredging the chicken in flour would have helped create a perfect golden crust but we decided it wasn't necessary for this recipe (and skipping the step would save us time) because we were going to chop the chicken after it cooked and incorporate it with so many other flavorful components. After sautéing the chicken, we set it aside and turned our focus to the bread.

We knew the quality of the bread would be fundamental to the success of this dish, so we tried several varieties. Sliced supermarket sandwich bread was immediately out. Its overly smooth texture meant it turned to mush when tossed with the vinaigrette (at this point a simple combination of red wine vinegar and extra-virgin olive oil), and its slightly sweet flavor clashed with the savory flavors of the salad. We thought breads containing dried fruits or nuts might add a nice touch to our salad, but in fact, their garnishes seemed random and out of place. In the end, a high-quality rustic loaf or baguette worked the best. The sturdy texture and strong wheaty flavor paired well with the other flavors and it held up reasonably well once dressed.

Panzanella traditionally relies on stale bread, which helps the bread hold up once dressed, but many people don't typically have stale bread on hand, so we set out to make our recipe to work with fresh bread. We needed to keep our recipe streamlined and limited to one pan, so toasting the bread on its own in the oven was out. At this point, cooking the chicken through was compromising a lot of our time, so we considered ways to combine cooking the chicken and the bread. What if we quickly browned the chicken in the skillet, then placed the cubes of bread in the skillet, underneath the chicken, and moved it all to the oven? Though a little far-fetched, it certainly seemed like the most efficient approach possible, so we gave it a shot. We were surprised at how well it worked. After less than 15 minutes, the chicken was cooked through and the bread had toasted nicely, and at the same time it had absorbed the flavorful drippings from the chicken.

Now all we needed to do was put the finishing touches on our vinaigrette and assemble the salad. Keeping with our Mediterranean theme, we started with a basic red wine vinegar and extra-virgin olive oil combination, seasoned it with salt and pepper, and added some chopped basil for freshness. We tossed the dressing with the bread and pieces of tender chicken, adding our arugula, tomatoes, white beans (canned for convenience), red onion, and Parmesan shavings—all traditional Mediterranean ingredients that worked well here.

After a few forkfuls, we agreed our salad was very close, but everyone had two small complaints: they wanted a bit more flavor, and they thought the bread was too dry. In reviewing our method, an idea came to mind: Why not mix the tomatoes and beans with the dressing and let them marinate while the chicken and bread were in the oven? We whipped up another batch of salad with this new method and found that not only did the dressing give the tomatoes and beans more flavor, but the salt in the dressing drew out the tomato juice, thereby creating a more flavorful, juicy dressing. The vinaigrette now lent the bread cubes the moisture they needed and wilted the arugula just slightly, creating a flavorful and cohesive dish. We found that letting the salad sit for 5 to 10 minutes before serving helped improved the final texture even more.

Skillet Chicken and White Bean Panzanella Salad

SERVES 4 TO 6

Be sure to use high-quality bread here—it is important for both flavor and texture in the salad. Do not discard the seeds or juice as you chop the tomatoes because they add important moisture to the recipe.

6	ounces French or Italian bread, cut or torn into ½- to ¾-inch cubes (about 4 cups) (see note)
½	cup extra-virgin olive oil
	Salt and ground black pepper
3	(5- to 6-ounce) boneless, skinless chicken breasts, trimmed and lightly pounded to a uniform thickness (see the illustration on page 247)
3	tablespoons red wine vinegar
1½	pounds tomatoes, cored and chopped medium, seeds and juice reserved (see note)
1	(15-ounce) can cannellini beans, drained and rinsed
1	small red onion, halved and sliced thin
¼	cup chopped fresh basil leaves
3	ounces baby arugula (about 3 cups)
2	ounces Parmesan cheese, shaved into thin strips using a vegetable peeler (½ cup) (see the illustration below)

MAKING PARMESAN SHAVINGS

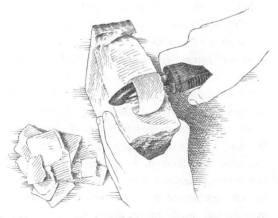

To achieve paper-thin slices of Parmesan, employ your vegetable peeler. Run the peeler over a block of Parmesan, using a light touch for thin shavings.

1. Adjust an oven rack to the lowest position and heat the oven to 450 degrees. Toss the bread cubes with 1 tablespoon of the oil, ¼ teaspoon salt, and a pinch pepper.

2. Pat the chicken dry with paper towels and season with salt and pepper. Heat 1 tablespoon more oil in a 12-inch ovensafe skillet over medium-high heat until just smoking. Carefully lay the chicken in the skillet and brown lightly on both sides, about 2 minutes per side; transfer to a plate.

3. Off the heat, spread the bread cubes evenly into the skillet. Lay the chicken on top of the bread and transfer the skillet to the oven. Bake until the thickest part of the breast registers 160 to 165 degrees on an instant-read thermometer and the bread is browned in spots, 12 to 15 minutes.

4. Meanwhile, whisk the remaining 6 tablespoons olive oil, vinegar, and ¼ teaspoon salt together in a large bowl. Stir in the tomatoes with their seeds and juice, beans, onion, and basil and set aside to allow the flavors to develop.

5. Transfer the chicken to a carving board, let cool slightly, then cut into 1-inch chunks. Gently fold the chicken, toasted bread cubes, and arugula into the tomato mixture. Season with salt and pepper to taste, sprinkle with the Parmesan, and let sit for 5 to 10 minutes before serving.

SALMON WITH ASPARAGUS

FISH IS AN IDEAL CHOICE FOR A QUICK weeknight meal—it cooks in a matter of minutes, and with a flavorful choice such as salmon, it requires little adornment. Salmon is a rich, buttery, and satisfying fish that appeals to adults and kids alike, and while there are many ways to prepare it, we wanted to use salmon as the basis for a quick skillet supper using a pan-searing method. In the test kitchen we've found pan-searing is the best way to take advantage of salmon's high fat content and produce a flavorful, caramelized crust. To make it a meal, asparagus, a classic match for salmon, came to mind as the perfect accompaniment. We hoped that a simple skillet method might deliver crisp, nicely browned spears to serve alongside our salmon with a wedge of lemon.

We decided to tackle the salmon first. While we normally prefer to buy a whole center-cut fillet and cut it into four uniform pieces that cook at the same rate, for this recipe we opted to buy individual fillets to save prep and cleanup time. We began by patting the salmon fillets dry with paper towels to ensure a good sear, then seasoned them liberally with salt and pepper. For cooking fish, we knew a nonstick skillet was a must to avoid the common issue of the fish sticking to the pan. The real question concerned the heat level. Knowing that we were after a good caramelized crust, we heated 2 tablespoons of oil over medium-high heat until it was just smoking. We placed the salmon in the skillet (skin side up), and after just five minutes it had a nicely browned crust and was ready to flip and cook through on the second side. After some trial and error, we found it best to reduce the heat to medium and cook it three minutes more on the second side, just until it had turned from translucent to opaque. Any longer and the salmon quickly went from velvety and moist to dry and chalky.

With our heat level and timing down, the salmon had an irresistibly supple texture that was right on, but the fish was overly greasy. Realizing that the salmon's high fat content was the cause, we cooked up another batch, this time using less oil. We found that a modest amount—just 1 tablespoon—was enough to brown the fish and achieve that caramelized crisp crust. The salmon was cooked in just about eight minutes, so we had plenty of time left on the clock to cook the asparagus. We transferred the salmon to a platter to rest and turned our attention to the asparagus.

After wiping out our skillet (the fishy oil left in the pan would have ruined the more delicate flavor of the asparagus), we began testing different sizes of spears. The thinner spears were eliminated; they overcooked long before they could get a proper sear. Selecting thicker spears got us pointed in the right direction, but we were still a long way from getting them to brown properly. Over moderate heat, the spears took so long to develop a crisp, browned

exterior that they overcooked. But cranking up the temperature was not the answer either—cooked this way, the spears skipped browning altogether and went straight to spotty and blackened while the interior didn't cook through.

We knew that parcooking the asparagus first—a common cooking method to keep vegetables looking vibrant—would enhance browning, but we did not have the time nor the extra pot at our disposal. We wondered if simply covering the pan at the start of the cooking would retain enough and have the same effect as parcooking. Indeed it did—after several more rounds of asparagus, we hit on a winning method. We cooked the asparagus, covered, over medium heat using a combination of oil and butter. The butter, with a makeup that is 20 percent water, added enough moisture to start steaming the asparagus at the outset, and soon the asparagus began to release its own moisture. After five minutes, we uncovered the pan and cranked up the heat. We found that placing the asparagus with half the tips pointing in one direction and half pointing in the opposite ensured a tidy fit and even cooking.

At this point the asparagus was bright green and just barely softened. Once the lid was removed, however, it was a race against the clock to try to get all the spears turned and browned all over before they overcooked and turned limp. But we made a fortunate discovery. Citing the pleasing contrast of textures, tasters actually preferred the spears that were browned on one side only and remained bright green on the other—and these half-browned spears didn't have the chance to overcook.

With all the components cooked and ready to go, it was time to assemble the meal. We were pleased with the distinct elements of the dish, but found that a squeeze of lemon was not enough to pull the meal together. Instead, we turned to a simple vinaigrette made with shallot, olive oil, lemon juice, Dijon, and a generous handful of chopped herbs. We could make the vinaigrette while the salmon and asparagus cooked, so no time was added to our recipe. Drizzled over the salmon and asparagus, the vinaigrette added a final burst of freshness that brought our quick dinner together.

Salmon with Asparagus and Herb Vinaigrette

SERVES 4

To ensure even cooking, make sure to buy salmon fillets of equal size and thickness. This recipe works best with asparagus that is at least ½ inch thick near the base. Do not use pencil-thin asparagus because it cannot withstand the heat and will overcook too easily.

4   (6-ounce) center-cut salmon fillets, about
    1½ inches thick
    Salt and ground black pepper
6   tablespoons olive oil
1   tablespoon unsalted butter
2   pounds thick asparagus (about 2 bunches),
    tough ends trimmed
2   tablespoons juice from 1 lemon
1   small shallot, minced (about 1 tablespoon)
1   teaspoon Dijon mustard
1   tablespoon chopped fresh parsley, basil, or
    mint leaves

1. Pat the salmon dry with paper towels and season with salt and pepper. Heat 1 tablespoon of the oil in a 12-inch nonstick skillet over medium-high until just smoking. Carefully lay the salmon in the skillet, skin side up, and cook until well browned on the first side, about 5 minutes.

2. Flip the salmon over, reduce the heat to medium, and continue to cook until all but the very center of each fillet has turned from translucent to opaque, about 3 minutes longer. Transfer the salmon to a platter, tent loosely with aluminum foil, and let rest while cooking the asparagus.

3. Wipe out the skillet with paper towels, add the butter and 1 tablespoon more oil and return it to medium heat until the butter has melted. Add half of the asparagus to the skillet with tips pointed in one direction and the remaining spears with tips pointed in the opposite direction. Sprinkle with ¼ teaspoon salt and gently shake the asparagus into an even layer.

4. Cover and cook until the spears are bright green but still crisp, about 5 minutes. Uncover, increase the heat to high, and continue to cook until the spears are tender and well browned along one side, 5 to 7 minutes, using tongs to move the spears from the center of the pan to the edge of the pan to ensure all are browned.

5. Meanwhile, whisk the remaining ¼ cup oil, lemon juice, shallot, mustard, and parsley together in a small bowl and season with salt and pepper to taste.

6. Transfer the asparagus to the platter with the salmon. Drizzle the salmon and asparagus with the herb vinaigrette and serve.

SKILLET-BRAISED COD PROVENÇAL

IT'S EASY TO GET STUCK IN A RUT WHEN IT comes to preparing cod since just about every cookbook focuses either on traditional Boston baked cod (or one of its many variations) or breaded and fried cod. We were after a fresher approach, our sights set on a highly flavorful but easy braised cod recipe—no bread crumbs or vats of oil required. Turning to the flavors of Provence for inspiration, we envisioned fish that was tender, moist, and flavorful, napped in an aromatic, garlicky tomato sauce that we could mop up with a good loaf of crusty bread.

The handful of recipes we tested produced tough, dry cod, dull and muddy flavors, and a sauce that was too thick or too thin, too sweet or too greasy. The biggest challenge would be cooking the cod to perfection, as it is a meaty but lean fish prone to drying out.

We first focused on the sauce in which the cod would be braised. We started by sautéing a sliced onion in extra-virgin olive oil, then added a generous four cloves of garlic and sautéed them briefly. Turning next to the tomatoes, the base of the braising liquid, we considered the most likely options: crushed, diced, or pureed canned tomatoes (we stuck with canned since they are consistent year-round). Crushed and pureed tomatoes produced thick, sweet, overbearing sauces reminiscent of bad Italian restaurant food. Canned diced tomatoes, though more promising, presented the opposite problem: they contain a fair amount of liquid, and the resulting sauce was too thin. We found that draining the diced tomatoes before adding them to the sauce was the answer. This sauce coated the cod perfectly.

Tasters were now happy with the texture of the sauce, but the flavor was lacking. A splash of white wine gave the sauce brightness and complexity. Our next thought was to add niçoise olives, which appear in many Provençal recipes. However, tasters agreed that their intense briny flavor overwhelmed the sauce (and the fish). On a whim we added sliced fennel along with the onion, and this was just what our sauce needed. It added a clean, refreshing punch with its subtle anise flavor. With our sauce in good shape, we turned our attention to cooking the cod.

We found the key to braising our fish was two-fold: Low heat ensured nothing burned, and a skillet with a tight-fitting lid trapped the heat so that the sauce gently simmered and the fish cooked properly. We nestled the cod into the simmering sauce, then cooked it over medium-low heat, covered, for just 10 minutes. The fish emerged succulent and moist, and the sauce had good body.

As for seasonings, the combination of dried herbs known as herbes de Provence (a combination of lavender, marjoram, basil, fennel seed, rosemary, sage, summer savory, and thyme) seemed like a natural. But tasters said that the dried herbs were too strong and gave the sauce a flavor that bordered on medicinal. We realized dried herbs needed a longer-cooking dish to allow their flavors to mellow out. A simple combination of fresh thyme and parsley worked far better here, and a final drizzle of fruity extra-virgin olive oil rounded out the flavors.

Skillet-Braised Cod Provençal

SERVES 4

Halibut, snapper, tilapia, bluefish, monkfish, and sea bass fillets are all good substitutes for the cod. Serve with a loaf of crusty bread to sop up the extra sauce.

2 tablespoons extra-virgin olive oil, plus extra for serving

1 medium onion, halved and sliced thin

1 medium fennel bulb (about 12 ounces), trimmed of stalks, cored, and sliced thin (see the illustrations on page 38)

Salt and ground black pepper

4 medium garlic cloves, minced or pressed though a garlic press (about 4 teaspoons)

1 (14.5-ounce) can diced tomatoes, drained

½ cup dry white wine or vermouth

1 teaspoon chopped fresh thyme leaves or ¼ teaspoon dried

4 (6-ounce) skinless cod fillets, about 1½ inches thick

2 tablespoons minced fresh parsley leaves

1. Heat the oil in a 12-inch nonstick skillet over medium-high heat until shimmering. Add the onion, fennel, and ½ teaspoon salt and cook until the vegetables have softened, about 5 minutes. Stir in the garlic and cook until fragrant, about 30 seconds. Stir in the tomatoes, wine, and thyme and bring to a simmer.

2. Pat the cod dry with paper towels and season with salt and pepper. Nestle the cod into the skillet and spoon some of the sauce over the fish. Cover, reduce the heat to medium-low, and cook until the fish flakes apart when gently prodded with a paring knife, about 10 minutes.

3. Transfer the fish to individual plates. Stir the parsley into the sauce and season with salt and pepper to taste. Spoon the sauce over the fish and serve with additional extra-virgin olive oil.

➤ VARIATIONS

Skillet-Braised Cod with Peperonata

Follow the recipe for Skillet-Braised Cod Provençal, substituting 2 red bell peppers, stemmed, seeded, and cut into thin strips, for the fennel. Add 2 teaspoons sweet paprika to the skillet with the garlic. Substitute 2 tablespoons minced fresh basil leaves for the parsley. Lightly sprinkle with balsamic or sherry vinegar before serving.

Skillet-Braised Cod Veracruz

Follow the recipe for Skillet-Braised Cod Provençal, omitting the fennel. Add 1 teaspoon chili powder and ½ teaspoon cumin to the skillet with the garlic. Add ¼ cup pimento-stuffed green olives, sliced thin, to the skillet with the tomatoes. Substitute 2 tablespoons minced fresh cilantro for the parsley.

SHRIMP AND ORZO

THOUGH CASSEROLE-STYLE DISHES ARE relatively hands-off once they go in the oven, they do require some time investment in terms of prep, and that factor combined with their oven stint means they don't typically make for a quick 30-minutes-or-less meal. However, one of our favorite casseroles—a Greek-inspired dish of baked shrimp and creamy orzo in a garlicky tomato sauce with feta—struck us as having the potential to transform into a simple skillet dinner. With a little tweaking, could we turn this casserole into a quick one-dish meal?

For this dish, orzo, a tiny rice-shaped pasta, is typically simmered until tender, then transferred to a baking dish with the other ingredients and placed in the oven. While this approach makes sense when cooking a large casserole, we thought for our quicker skillet meal we could use a different technique. Some previous test kitchen experience had taught us that orzo can also be cooked "pilaf-style," sautéed briefly in oil with aromatics and seasonings for deeper flavor before liquid is added. And, if diligently stirred as it simmers, the orzo will release starches into the cooking liquid and create a creamy sauce—not quite as creamy as risotto perhaps, but rich and velvety nevertheless. This technique cooked the orzo in about 14 minutes, leaving us plenty of room on both ends for prep and cooking the shrimp.

We wanted to limit the vegetables to a select few to keep preparation brief. Tomatoes were a given, adding bright flavor and acidity. We opted for canned diced tomatoes for their simplicity and the fact they held their shape, adding texture to the dish. Red onion seemed like a natural for adding depth and body, as did the crisp, sweet crunch of red bell peppers. Sautéed until just beginning to brown, the vegetables added flavor and a bit of bite.

As for seasoning, a healthy dose of garlic seemed essential, in keeping with the Mediterranean spirit of our recipe. A pinch of saffron suffused the pasta with a sunny orange hue and its warm flavor. A handful of fresh herbs seemed apropos as well, and after testing a slew of options, tasters favored a simple combination of oregano and scallions. The oregano lent the casserole a decidedly Greek edge while the scallions, sprinkled raw over the top, added a sharp bite.

We were finally ready to tackle the shrimp. First off, because we were short on time and looking for the simplest approach, we wanted to finish cooking the recipe on the stovetop. After testing various sizes of shrimp, we settled on large shrimp (31 to 40 per pound), left whole, because they stayed moist longer than smaller shrimp. As for the cooking method, we thought searing the shrimp in a smoking skillet might deepen flavor and add color but, surprisingly, tasters thought the sweet caramelized aspect clashed with the light, bright flavors of the pilaf. Nestling the raw shrimp right into the pilaf, covering the pan, and then cooking it all together proved a better bet. The shrimp maintained their clean, fresh flavor and were perfectly cooked in just five minutes.

Our last component was the feta. The cheese's salty, briny bite proved to be a perfect counterpoint to the sweetness of the shrimp and the fruitiness of the tomato and bell pepper. We crumbled the cheese and scattered it over the finished dish for our first test, but in the end we found it actually tasted better warm, so we let it cook along with the shrimp. This was the perfect finish to a quick skillet meal sure to put a fresh spin onto our dinner routine.

INGREDIENTS: Feta Cheese

In Greece, salty, crumbly curds of feta are still made from methods dating back to the Trojan War, and in 2005 the European Union ruled that only cheese produced in that country from at least 70 percent sheep's milk can rightfully bear the name. Here in the United States, domestic and imported imitators abound, and we wanted to see how they compare to the real deal. We tasted five brands—two Greek fetas, one French version, and two American cheeses. Tasters lamented the lack of "funky," "grassy" tang in the domestic cheeses (all of which were made with 100 percent cow's milk), preferring the "barnyard" taste of the sheep and goat's milk imports. In the end, Mt. Vikos Traditional Feta (a combination of sheep and goat's milk), a true feta from the mother country, won out.

THE BEST FETA
Mt. Vikos Traditional Feta from Greece was the clear favorite for its floral, funky flavor that was not too salty.

MT. VIKOS

INGREDIENTS: Shrimp

Virtually all of the shrimp sold today in supermarkets have been previously frozen, either in large blocks of ice or with a method called "individually quick frozen," or IQF for short. Supermarkets simply defrost the shrimp before displaying them on ice at the fish counter, where they look as though they are freshly plucked from the sea. As a general rule, we highly recommend purchasing bags of still-frozen, shell-on IQF shrimp and defrosting them as needed at home, since there is no telling how long "fresh" shrimp may have been kept on ice at the market. IQF shrimp also have a better flavor and texture than shrimp frozen in blocks. IQF shrimp are available both with and without their shells, but we find the shell-on shrimp to be firmer and sweeter. Also, shrimp should be the only ingredient listed on the bag. Some packagers add sodium-based chemicals as preservatives, but we find these shrimp have a strange translucency and unpleasant, rubbery texture.

Shrimp are sold by size (small, medium, large, and extra-large) as well as by the number needed to make 1 pound, usually given in a range. Choosing shrimp by the numerical rating is more accurate than choosing them by the size label, because that varies from store to store. Here's how the two sizing systems generally compare:

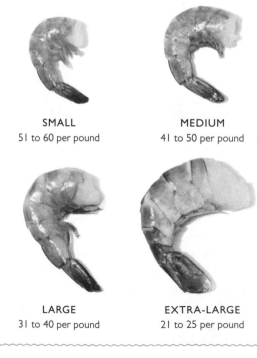

SMALL
51 to 60 per pound

MEDIUM
41 to 50 per pound

LARGE
31 to 40 per pound

EXTRA-LARGE
21 to 25 per pound

Shrimp and Orzo
SERVES 4

If you don't have saffron, substitute ¼ teaspoon ground turmeric.

1	pound large shrimp (31 to 40 per pound), peeled and deveined (see the illustration on page 145)
	Salt and ground black pepper
1	tablespoon extra-virgin olive oil
1	medium red onion, minced
1	large red bell pepper, stemmed, seeded, and cut into ½-inch pieces (see the illustrations on page 226)
6	medium garlic cloves, minced or pressed through a garlic press (about 2 tablespoons)
2	teaspoons minced fresh oregano leaves or ½ teaspoon dried
1½	cups orzo
	Pinch saffron threads, crumbled
3	cups low-sodium chicken broth
1	(28-ounce) can diced tomatoes, drained with ½ cup juice reserved
4	ounces feta cheese, crumbled (1 cup)
3	scallions, sliced thin
	Lemon wedges, for serving

1. Pat the shrimp dry with paper towels and season with salt and pepper; set aside.

2. Heat the oil in a 12-inch nonstick skillet over medium heat until shimmering. Add the onion, bell pepper, and ½ teaspoon salt and cook until softened, about 5 minutes. Stir in the garlic and oregano and cook until fragrant, about 30 seconds. Stir in the orzo and saffron and cook, stirring frequently, until the orzo is coated with oil and lightly browned, about 2 minutes.

3. Stir in the broth, tomatoes, and reserved tomato juice, bring to a simmer, and cook, stirring occasionally, until the orzo is mostly tender yet still slightly firm at the center, about 12 minutes.

4. Stir in the shrimp and sprinkle the feta over top. Cover and continue to cook until the orzo is tender and the shrimp are cooked through, about 5 minutes. Sprinkle with the scallions and serve with the lemon wedges.

CHEESY SKILLET POLENTA AND EGGPLANT BAKE

SUCCESSFULLY TRANSFORMING ONE OF OUR favorite casseroles of shrimp and creamy orzo into a skillet dinner (see page 257) inspired us to look further into our casserole recipes and see what other dishes might work for a quick skillet meal. Our Rustic Sausage and Spinach Polenta Casserole (page 108) had been a big hit with tasters, but it still took around 45 minutes to make. Could we come up with a similarly satisfying, comforting polenta dish that could be made more quickly in a skillet? We imagined our skillet baked polenta would be a sophisticated dish, with a layer of soft polenta covered by savory toppings and a touch of flavorful cheese. We thought this could be a perfect vegetarian entrée when served with a simple green salad.

We knew that if we wanted to precook any of our topping ingredients, we would have to do it before making the polenta to keep our cooking to one skillet, so we started there. We were immediately drawn to the idea of using eggplant in some fashion. Its nutty flavor is a classic pairing with polenta and it is a vegetable that adds a certain heft and meatiness to meatless dishes. After cooking a few batches of the vegetable, which we cut into manageable ¾-inch pieces, we realized the key to achieving good eggplant flavor was to brown the pieces well in a generous amount of oil (with very little stirring so it wouldn't fall apart) and cook them until just tender. We then added garlic for depth and bite and chopped cherry tomatoes for an acidic, bright component that would also help give our topping a saucy aspect. We added them to the skillet and cooked until they were just beginning to wilt. We found that quartering the tomatoes allowed them to release more juice while they cooked, which created a saucier topping that tasters favored. With our topping ready, we set it aside so we could focus on the polenta itself.

Traditional polenta made from scratch takes at least 30 minutes to cook, so once again we turned, as we had in our casserole recipe, to quick-cooking instant polenta. We knew that the polenta had to be added very slowly to boiling salted water to prevent clumping. We also knew it was vital to whisk the polenta constantly as it cooked to ensure it would not end up lumpy, or worse, as one solid mass. To give the flavor of the polenta a boost, we tried cooking it in milk rather than water. While the milk rounded out the flavor of the polenta nicely, it also added an unwelcome slimy texture, so we stuck with water. It took just three to four minutes over moderate heat to cook the polenta. We finished by stirring in ¾ cup Parmesan cheese, which helped enrich the flavor.

With the polenta cooked, we smoothed it out over the bottom of our skillet, spread the cooked eggplant-tomato mixture over the top, and sprinkled on fontina and pine nuts, a combination that added texture and gooey appeal. After just six minutes under the broiler, the cheese was melted and the nuts were toasty and flavorful. Garnished with a bit of fresh basil, our polenta bake was not only elegant and delicious, but we could get it on the table in just 30 minutes.

Cheesy Skillet Polenta and Eggplant Bake
SERVES 4

Leaving the skin on the eggplant keeps the pieces intact during cooking. Be sure to use instant polenta here; traditional polenta cannot be substituted.

¼	cup olive oil
1	medium eggplant (1 pound), trimmed and cut into ¾-inch pieces
	Salt and ground black pepper
3	medium garlic cloves, minced or pressed through a garlic press (about 1 tablespoon)
2	cups cherry tomatoes (about 12 ounces), quartered
4	cups water
1	cup instant polenta (see note)
1½	ounces Parmesan cheese, grated (¾ cup)
4	ounces fontina cheese, shredded (1 cup)
¼	cup pine nuts, toasted
⅓	cup chopped fresh basil leaves

1. Position an oven rack 6 inches from the broiler element and heat the broiler.

2. Heat the oil in a 12-inch broiler-safe nonstick skillet over medium-high heat until shimmering. Add the eggplant and ¼ teaspoon salt and cook until it begins brown, about 4 minutes. Reduce the heat to medium and continue to cook until the eggplant is tender, about 4 minutes.

3. Stir in the garlic and cook until fragrant, about 30 seconds. Stir in the tomatoes and cook until just beginning to wilt, 2 to 3 minutes. Season with salt and pepper to taste and transfer to a bowl.

4. Add the water to the skillet and bring to a boil over medium-high heat. Stir in 1 teaspoon salt, then very slowly whisk in the polenta. Reduce the heat to medium and cook, whisking constantly, until very thick, 3 to 4 minutes. Off the heat, stir in the Parmesan and season with salt and pepper to taste.

5. Smooth the polenta into an even layer in the skillet. Spoon the eggplant mixture evenly over the polenta, leaving a ½-inch border around the edge. Sprinkle with the fontina and pine nuts. Broil until the cheese is melted and beginning to brown, about 6 minutes. Sprinkle with the basil and serve.

THICK AND HEARTY FRITTATA

A FRITTATA IS A QUICK RECIPE BY DESIGN— an easy eggs-for-dinner meal that can be almost infinitely varied just by changing the fillings. When it comes to the cooking, frittatas are more forgiving than their omelet cousins, but they are certainly not foolproof. Tough, rubbery, and overstuffed frittatas are all too common, so we set out to create a recipe that yielded a perfect frittata every time, one that was firm yet moist, with a pleasing balance of egg to filling and a supportive, browned exterior.

We knew from test kitchen experience that avoiding excess moisture is key with any egg dish, so we would have to start by sautéing any watery vegetables that would go into our frittata before combining them with the eggs. After cooking the filling in our skillet (we would work out what exactly we wanted to include in our filling later),

we could simply pour the beaten eggs over the top and proceed.

Once we added the eggs to the skillet, we knew the cooking method could go in one of three directions: we could cook the frittata fully on the stovetop, fully in the oven, or start it on the stovetop and finish it in the oven. We first tried cooking a working frittata fully on the stovetop, but no matter what we did, varying both time and temperature, the underside always ended up tough and overcooked. Cooking the frittata fully in the oven proved problematic as well. Again, we tried cooking at different temperatures and for different lengths of time, but the results were either too dry or unevenly cooked. A combination of stovetop and oven showed the most promise. We began by cooking the frittata almost fully on top of the stove and then slid the skillet in the oven to finish up.

We learned quickly during the stovetop stage that dumping the eggs in the skillet and leaving them alone wasn't acceptable—the results were unevenly cooked and rubbery. Stirring the eggs on the stovetop until large curds began forming solved the problem; it evenly distributed the eggs as they began cooking, leading to more tender eggs and a frittata that was properly cooked throughout. We discovered that for even cooking it was also important to make sure the eggs were set on the bottom before they left the stovetop.

Now we had to iron out the details of the oven stage. A few tests proved residual heat was at play when the skillet was out of the oven, so if we waited to pull our skillet until the eggs were done, after the frittata sat for a few minutes the eggs ended up overcooked. It was best to pull our skillet from the oven when the eggs were still slightly wet and runny so that the residual heat would just cook them through.

The last remaining problem was that the top of our frittata didn't show the browning that is the trademark of a good frittata. Modifying our stovetop-to-oven method slightly, we tried finishing the frittata under the broiler. This worked best of all. The resulting frittata was evenly cooked, lightly browned, and firm without being too dry— exactly what we had been seeking.

With our method down pat, we finessed the fillings to create a few combination options. First we tested a number of cheeses. Parmesan was too dry, but Gruyère, goat cheese, and fontina all worked well. Cubing the cheese (or crumbling, in the case of goat cheese) rather than shredding it added a nice change in texture. Though not traditional for a frittata, we also tried adding half-and-half to the eggs before pouring them in the skillet. It lent a nice touch of creaminess so we kept it in. We then tried adding various meats and vegetables and came up with several combinations. Asparagus, ham, and Gruyère formed a winning variation, as did leek, prosciutto, and goat cheese. Tasters also enjoyed the earthy combination of broccoli rabe and sun-dried tomatoes with nutty fontina. In less than 15 minutes we had perfectly puffed and browned frittatas on the table.

Asparagus, Ham, and Gruyère Frittata

SERVES 4 TO 6

Although we prefer the strong flavor of Gruyère in this recipe, you can substitute Swiss if desired. Because broilers vary so much in intensity, watch the frittata carefully as it cooks.

12	large eggs
3	tablespoons half-and-half
½	teaspoon salt
¼	teaspoon ground black pepper
3	ounces Gruyère cheese, cut into ¼-inch cubes (¾ cup)
2	teaspoons olive oil
½	pound asparagus (about ½ bunch), tough ends trimmed, sliced thin on the bias
4	ounces thick-sliced deli ham, chopped fine
I	medium shallot, minced (about 3 tablespoons)

1. Position an oven rack 6 inches from the broiler element and heat the broiler. Whisk the eggs, half-and-half, salt, and pepper together in a medium bowl, then stir in the cheese.

2. Heat the oil in a 12-inch broiler-safe nonstick skillet over medium heat until shimmering. Add the asparagus and cook until lightly browned and crisp-tender, 2 to 4 minutes. Stir in the ham and shallot and cook until the shallot softens, about 2 minutes.

3. Add the egg mixture and cook, using a rubber spatula to stir and scrape the bottom of the skillet, until large curds form and the spatula begins to leave a wake but the eggs are still very wet, about 2 minutes. Shake the skillet to distribute the eggs evenly and continue to cook, without stirring, to set the bottom, about 30 seconds.

4. Slide the skillet under the broiler and cook until the surface is puffed and spotty brown, yet the center remains slightly wet and runny when cut into with a paring knife, 3 to 4 minutes.

5. Remove the skillet from the broiler and let stand until the eggs in the middle are just set, about 5 minutes. Use a rubber spatula to loosen the frittata from the skillet, then slide it onto a cutting board. Slice into wedges and serve.

➤ VARIATIONS

Leek, Prosciutto, and Goat Cheese Frittata

Thinly sliced deli ham can be substituted for the prosciutto. Because broilers vary so much in intensity, watch the frittata carefully as it cooks.

12	large eggs
3	tablespoons half-and-half
	Salt and ground black pepper
3	ounces thinly sliced prosciutto, chopped coarse
¼	cup minced fresh basil leaves
2	ounces goat cheese, crumbled (½ cup)
2	tablespoons unsalted butter
2	medium leeks, white and light green parts only, halved lengthwise, sliced thin crosswise, and rinsed thoroughly (see the illustrations on page 138)

1. Position an oven rack 6 inches from the broiler element and heat the broiler. Whisk the eggs, half-and-half, ½ teaspoon salt, and ¼ teaspoon pepper together in a medium bowl, then stir in the prosciutto, basil, and half of the goat cheese.

2. Melt the butter in a 12-inch broiler-safe nonstick skillet over medium-low heat. Add the leeks and a pinch salt, cover, and cook until softened, 8 to 10 minutes.

3. Uncover the skillet and increase the heat to

medium. Add the egg mixture and cook, using a rubber spatula to stir and scrape the bottom of the skillet, until large curds form and the spatula begins to leave a wake but the eggs are still very wet, about 2 minutes. Shake the skillet to distribute the eggs evenly and continue to cook, without stirring, to set the bottom, about 30 seconds.

4. Dot the remaining goat cheese evenly over the top. Slide the skillet under the broiler and cook until the surface is puffed and spotty brown, yet the center remains slightly wet and runny when cut into with a paring knife, 3 to 4 minutes.

5. Remove the skillet from the broiler and let stand until the eggs in the middle are just set, about 5 minutes. Use a rubber spatula to loosen the frittata from the skillet, then slide onto a cutting board. Slice into wedges and serve.

Broccoli Rabe, Sun-Dried Tomato, and Fontina Frittata

Be sure to use oil-packed sun-dried tomatoes here or the tomatoes will remain tough and chewy in the frittata. Because broilers vary so much in intensity, watch the frittata carefully as it cooks.

12	large eggs
3	tablespoons half-and-half
	Salt and ground black pepper
3	ounces Italian fontina cheese, cut into ¼-inch cubes (¾ cup)
¼	cup oil-packed sun-dried tomatoes, patted dry and minced
2	teaspoons olive oil
8	ounces broccoli rabe, trimmed and cut into 1-inch pieces
1	medium garlic clove, minced or pressed through a garlic press (about 1 teaspoon)
⅛	teaspoon red pepper flakes

1. Position an oven rack 6 inches from the broiler element and heat the broiler. Whisk the eggs, half-and-half, ½ teaspoon salt, and ¼ teaspoon pepper together, then stir in the fontina and sun-dried tomatoes.

2. Heat the oil in a 12-inch broiler-safe nonstick skillet over medium heat until shimmering. Add the broccoli rabe and a pinch salt and cook until just beginning to brown and soften, 6 to 8 minutes. Stir in the garlic and red pepper flakes and cook until fragrant, about 30 seconds.

3. Add the egg mixture and cook, using a rubber spatula to stir and scrape the bottom of the skillet, until large curds form and the spatula begins to leave a wake but the eggs are still very wet, about 2 minutes. Shake the skillet to distribute the eggs evenly and continue to cook, without stirring, to set the bottom, about 30 seconds.

4. Slide the skillet under the broiler and cook until the surface is puffed and spotty brown, yet the center remains slightly wet and runny when cut into with a paring knife, 3 to 4 minutes.

5. Remove the skillet from the broiler and let stand until the eggs in the middle are just set, about 5 minutes. Use a rubber spatula to loosen the frittata from the skillet, then slide onto a cutting board. Slice into wedges and serve.

INGREDIENTS: Gruyère Cheese

Though it is known mainly for its use in recipes like fondue and French onion soup, Gruyère is also a table cheese, revered for its creamy texture and savory flavor. Both Switzerland and France make authentic versions, crafted from raw cow's milk and aged for the better part of a year in government-designated regions. Though labeled "Gruyère," domestic cheeses of this type are made from pasteurized cow's milk, are aged for fewer months, and bear little resemblance to the real thing. In a blind taste test of nine brands, tasters overwhelmingly panned the two domestics, likening one to "plastic." Imported Gruyères, on the other hand, received raves. The two top picks in the lineup were reserve cheeses aged 10 or more months to develop stronger flavor: Emmi Le Gruyère Reserve and a Gruyère Salé from a Boston-area cheese shop.

THE BEST GRUYÈRE CHEESE

Emmi Le Gruyère Reserve was described as "grassy," "salty," and "nicely dry."

EMMI

9

SLOW-COOKER DISHES WORTH THE WAIT

Slow-Cooker Dishes Worth The Wait

SLOW-COOKER BEEF STEW

RECIPES FOR SLOW-COOKER BEEF STEW SEEM to fall into two camps. In one, the meat, vegetables, and seasoning are simply dumped into a pot and left to their own devices. Effortless, yes. But flavorful? We'd have to say no. The second type of stew, the one in which the meat is browned before it goes into the slow cooker, is the more flavorful stew. Here the foundation for flavor is built on the browned bits left behind (the fond), the backbone of the stew's sauce. But this browning, which needs to be done in batches so the meat doesn't steam, can take a good chunk of time—not that appealing to time-pressed cooks. In developing a recipe for slow-cooker beef stew, we wanted to find a way to maximize flavor, while minimizing both time and labor.

We knew that in order to justify jettisoning the browning step, we needed to come up with a flavor replacement for the fond. We tried an array of "browning sauces," such as Gravy Master and Kitchen Bouquet, as well as bouillon cubes and different combinations of beef and chicken broth. After extensive testing, we landed on a winning solution: We used a combination of soy sauce (its salty elements reinforced the beefy flavor and added deep color) and tomato paste, which we had successfully used in our traditional beef stew recipe (see page 131) to beef up the flavor. Next, we had to determine what to do with the aromatics. Traditionally, we would sauté the onions and garlic to enhance their flavor and soften their texture before adding them to the slow cooker. But this was a one-dish supper and we didn't want to deal with the extra pan and step, so we tried adding the aromatics raw to the slow cooker. The result was, unsurprisingly, crunchy, sour onions. In lieu of sautéing, we settled on microwaving the aromatics to not only soften them but also develop additional flavor notes. We tossed them with a little oil and microwaved them just until the onions were soft. Adding the tomato paste to the bowl at the same time allowed us to deepen its flavor as well. Then we added them to the slow cooker and proceeded with our working recipe.

There were, however, some in the test kitchen who were having a hard time coming to grips with this unconventional, unbrowned approach to a full-flavored stew. To make sure that everyone was on board with our new technique, we conducted a blind taste test of three stews side by side: browned beef stew, unbrowned beef stew with no flavor replacement, and unbrowned beef stew with our fond replacement of cooked aromatics, tomato paste, and soy sauce. Unaware of the different methods used, the majority of tasters favored the third stew. We were happy that taste buds, rather than preconceived notions, settled the controversy. Our third stew was rich and full-bodied, and we had saved a good amount of time.

Satisfied with our faux fond, we moved on to address one troubling issue that resulted from not browning the meat: greasiness. Browning helps to render fat, so our stew made with unbrowned meat had a grease slick on top. Following the lead of our traditional beef stew, up until now we had been using a chuck-eye roast trimmed and cut into 1½-inch pieces. Wondering if a leaner roast would solve our problem, we tested five stews made with different cuts of beef: top round, bottom round, eye round, rump roast, and top sirloin. But they were all too lean, resulting in flavorless, dry meat. We decided that we didn't mind using a spoon to skim a bit of grease from the stew if that was what it would take to get maximum flavor, so we returned to the chuck-eye roast.

The next dilemma was how to thicken our stew. While many slow-cooker recipes turn to a slurry (a starch stirred together with liquid) of either flour or cornstarch, we knew from previous experience that this would only lead to a stew that tasted starchy. Instant tapioca, stirred in at the onset of cooking, was a better choice. The stew was now thick without being tacky, there was no raw, starchy aftertaste, and it required no last-minute fussing.

Moving on, we wanted to find a way to prevent the vegetables from disintegrating as they simmered away for hours in the slow cooker. Stealing a trick often used in grilling, we insulated the potatoes and carrots by wrapping them in a foil packet. Then we placed the packet on top of the beef in the slow cooker. It may have looked a bit odd, but when we opened the packet and poured the tender vegetables and their juices back into the stew at the end of cooking, the results were amazing. The carrots were perfectly cooked and the potatoes were intact. Adding frozen peas at the same time ensured they were just heated through.

We were so pleased with our recipe that we thought we'd try a variation with an Asian spin. Adding ginger and dry sherry to our flavor base was a solid first step. Because we liked the texture, heft, and sweetness of the carrots, we kept them in the recipe, but we opted to replace the potatoes and peas with a combination of snow peas, water chestnuts, and sliced scallions.

MAKING A FOIL PACKET

For most recipes in this chapter, we discovered that the best way to prevent vegetables from overcooking was to wrap them in an aluminum foil packet, or "hobo pack." Keeping the vegetables out of the cooking liquid slows down their cooking time and prevents their flavors from fading. Here's how you do it:

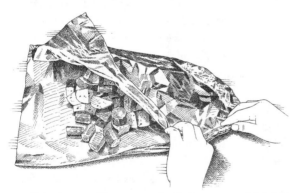

1. Place the vegetables on one side of a large piece of foil. Fold the foil over, shaping it into a packet that will fit into your slow cooker, then crimp to seal the edges.

2. Place the foil packet directly on top of the soup or stew, pressing gently as needed to make it fit inside the cooker.

Slow-Cooker Beef Stew

SERVES 6 TO 8

Feel free to add a pound of parsnips, peeled and cut into 1-inch pieces, to the aluminum foil packet along with the carrots and potatoes.

- 3 medium onions, minced
- ¼ cup tomato paste
- 6 medium garlic cloves, minced or pressed through a garlic press (about 2 tablespoons)
- 1 tablespoon minced fresh thyme leaves or 1 teaspoon dried
- 2 tablespoons vegetable oil
- 1½ cups low-sodium chicken broth, plus extra as needed
- 1½ cups beef broth, plus extra as needed
- ⅓ cup soy sauce
- 3 tablespoons Minute tapioca
- 2 bay leaves
- 1 (5-pound) boneless beef chuck-eye roast, trimmed and cut into 1½-inch pieces (see the illustrations on page 133) Salt and ground black pepper
- 1½ pounds red potatoes (about 5 medium), scrubbed and cut into 1-inch chunks
- 1 pound carrots (about 6 medium), peeled and sliced 1 inch thick
- 2 cups frozen peas

1. Microwave the onions, tomato paste, garlic, thyme, and 1 tablespoon of the oil together in a medium bowl on high power, stirring occasionally, until the onions are softened, about 5 minutes; transfer to a slow cooker.

2. Stir the chicken and beef broths, soy sauce, tapioca, and bay leaves into the slow cooker. Season the beef with salt and pepper and nestle into the slow cooker. Toss the potatoes and carrots with the remaining 1 tablespoon oil, season with salt and pepper to taste, and wrap in a foil packet following the illustrations at left. Lay the foil packet on top of the stew. Cover and cook until the meat is tender, 9 to 11 hours on low or 5 to 7 hours on high.

3. Transfer the vegetable packet to a plate. Let the stew settle for 5 minutes, then remove as much fat as possible from the surface using a large spoon.

4. Discard the bay leaves and stir in the peas. Carefully open the vegetable packet (watch for steam) and stir the vegetables with any accumulated juice into the stew. Let the stew sit until everything is heated through, about 5 minutes. (Adjust the stew consistency with additional hot broth as needed.) Season with salt and pepper to taste and serve.

➤ VARIATION

Slow-Cooker Asian-Style Beef Stew
Follow the recipe for Slow-Cooker Beef Stew, omitting the potatoes and peas. Microwave 3 tablespoons minced or grated fresh ginger with the onion mixture in step 1. Increase the amount of tapioca to ¼ cup and add ⅓ cup dry sherry to the slow cooker in step 2. Before serving, microwave 8 ounces snow peas with 1 tablespoon vegetable oil on high power until tender, 3 to 5 minutes. Stir the snow peas, 1 (8-ounce) can water chestnuts, drained and patted dry, and 1 tablespoon brown sugar into the stew with the other vegetables in step 4. Sprinkle with 4 thinly sliced scallions and serve with additional soy sauce.

INGREDIENTS: Soy Sauce

Most of us rarely give a second thought when it comes to soy sauce. There are many brands to choose from at the supermarket, so we sought to narrow the field.

We tasted 12 soy sauces three different ways: plain, drizzled over warm rice, and cooked in a simple teriyaki glaze over chicken thighs. The brands varied in origin—some were domestic, while imports hailed from China and Japan—and cost, with $6.49 being the highest price. Fortunately, our overall winner, Lee Kum Kee Tabletop Soy Sauce, came in at a much lower price ($1.99 for a 5.1-ounce bottle). Tasters praised Lee Kum Kee for a "salty, sweet, pleasant" flavor with a "great aroma." Lee Kum Kee is our top pick for cooking, but the pricey $6.49 soy sauce, Ohsawa Nama Shoyu Organic Unpasteurized Soy Sauce, is a great choice for dipping sauces.

THE BEST SOY SAUCE
Lee Kum Kee Tabletop Soy Sauce, with its depth and balance, is our favorite.

LEE KUM KEE

SLOW-COOKER BEEF GOULASH

BEEF GOULASH MAY NOT HAVE A NAME THAT rolls easily off the tongue, but that shouldn't keep you from adding it to your recipe file. The epitome of Hungarian comfort food, goulash is a stew made with chunks of beef and robustly flavored with Hungarian paprika. When made correctly, it's rich and satisfying. Stick-to-your-ribs ingredients like beef, onions, garlic, and paprika are the constants in this dish. Although we had already perfected a traditional recipe (see page 135), we quickly learned it's not a dish you can easily get right in the slow cooker. Our first attempts turned out watery and bland. We refused to admit defeat, however, so we set about formulating a new way of slow-cooking this traditional dish. Our goal? A simple but delicious goulash with tender, flavorful beef and onions in a rich, intensely flavored sauce, prepared this time in our slow cooker.

After developing our recipe for Slow-Cooker Beef Stew (page 266), we knew that chuck roast is the best choice for stewing in the slow cooker because it is a cut that actually benefits from an extended cooking time, becoming tender and flavorful after several hours of simmering. And, in keeping with the findings from our beef stew testing, we also knew we could add the meat to the slow cooker without browning it first (eliminating the need for a skillet), provided we find a way to replace the fond, the bits in the pot left behind from browning that infuse the dish with flavor.

To begin, we cooked the onions in the microwave with tomato paste and an ample quantity of good-quality Hungarian paprika, giving the flavors a chance to meld and eliminating the harsh flavor of raw onions. The tomato paste and paprika contributed the deep rust color traditional to goulash—a rich hue that, we were surprised to find, withstood the lengthy time in the slow cooker. Then, we added the unusual ingredient that had served us well in our beef stew recipe: soy sauce, which contributed a salty, meaty flavor. Because we weren't browning the meat, we found it necessary to skim some fat off the top of our goulash at the end of cooking, but

267

this simple step was a small price to pay for tender, flavorful beef.

Although onions are a must, the recipes we looked at were divided on the question of garlic. Tasters, however, were not. Everyone in the test kitchen liked garlic in this stew. Six cloves added depth and also balanced the sweetness of the paprika and onions. The quantity of paprika was the next problem to solve. Too much and the goulash tasted bitter, almost burned. Too little and we ended up with a goulash that paled in comparison to our standard stovetop recipe. We settled on ¼ cup, which provided the perfect amount of flavor and color without overpowering the other ingredients.

Recipes uncovered in our research used an assortment of liquids, including water, beef broth, and chicken broth. We found that water created a bland stew, and beef broth, though a success in our traditional goulash recipe, where we added it toward the end of cooking, contributed a bitter edge to the goulash after the long stint spent in the slow cooker. Chicken broth proved to be the best option, lending the stew body and just enough richness without competing with the other flavorings. Some recipes also include wine, although authentic ones do not. We tried varying amounts of red wine, and tasters felt that its flavor was overpowering. Goulash should be soft and mellow; while red wine added complexity, it also made the stew acidic and a bit harsh. A few sources suggested white wine, but tasters were again unimpressed, so we stuck with tradition and left the wine out. Our recipe was coming together.

Many Hungarian goulash recipes do not include sour cream, which seems more popular in German and Austrian versions. Nevertheless, some of our tasters felt that sour cream nicely mellowed and enriched this stew, so we decided to make it optional by serving sour cream alongside the goulash at the table.

Goulash is traditionally served over buttered egg noodles or spaetzle. Though spaetzle provides interesting texture, egg noodles require almost no effort to cook and are our first choice.

Slow-Cooker Beef Goulash
SERVES 6 TO 8

Be sure to use sweet paprika, often labeled as Hungarian paprika, to achieve the correct flavor for this dish. Serve with sour cream and buttered egg noodles.

1½	pounds onions, minced
¼	cup sweet paprika (see note)
¼	cup tomato paste
3	tablespoons vegetable oil
6	medium garlic cloves, minced or pressed through a garlic press (about 2 tablespoons)
1	teaspoon caraway seeds
2	cups low-sodium chicken broth, plus extra as needed
⅓	cup soy sauce
¼	cup Minute tapioca
2	bay leaves
1	(4-pound) boneless beef chuck-eye roast, trimmed and cut into 1½-inch pieces (see the illustrations on page 133) Salt and ground black pepper
2	tablespoons minced fresh parsley leaves

1. Microwave the onions, paprika, tomato paste, oil, garlic, and caraway seeds together in a medium bowl on high power, stirring occasionally, until the onions are softened, about 5 minutes; transfer to a slow cooker.

2. Stir the broth, soy sauce, tapioca, and bay leaves into the slow cooker. Season the beef with salt and pepper and nestle into the slow cooker. Cover and cook until the beef is tender, 9 to 11 hours on low or 5 to 7 hours on high.

3. Let the stew settle for 5 minutes, then remove as much fat as possible from the surface using a large spoon. Discard the bay leaves. (Adjust the stew consistency with additional hot broth as needed.) Stir in the parsley, season with salt and pepper to taste, and serve.

Slow Cooking 101

The low, moist heat of the slow cooker makes it ideal for the long, hands-off cooking of soups, stews, and chilis. But learning how to extract maximum flavor from recipes in the slow cooker has taken some effort and lots of testing. Over the years we've learned a few things. First, all slow cookers are not created equal, which is why these recipes have a range of cooking times. The key when it comes to timing is to get to know your slow cooker and whether it runs slow (and low) or fast (and hot). And second, a little advance prep can go a long way in building a flavorful base for a soup or stew. It is a rare recipe where raw ingredients can simply be dumped into a slow cooker with good results. Here are a few things we've learned that will help you turn out rich and flavorful soups and stews in your slow cooker.

KNOW YOUR SLOW COOKER

Through years of slow-cooker recipe development, we've learned that not all slow cookers are the same—some run hot (and fast) while others run cool (and slow). And since all slow-cooker recipes come with a time range, knowing how your individual slow cooker runs will be helpful in determining which end of the range will likely yield the best results. We have done all of our testing using our winning slow cooker (see below), but if you are using a different brand you might find that you need slightly altered cooking times. One quick way to determine how hot or cool your cooker runs is to perform a simple water test. Place 4 quarts of room temperature water in your slow cooker, cover it, and cook on either high or low for six hours, then measure the temperature of the water. Ideally, the water should register between 195 and 205 degrees on an instant-read thermometer. If your cooker runs hotter or cooler, be ready to check the food for doneness either earlier or later than our recipes indicate. Also, we've found that some cookers run hot or cool on just one of the settings (either low or high), so consider checking both if you find you are having problems.

PREP-AHEAD TIPS

Our slow-cooker recipes require a bit of prep work before the ingredients can be added to the slow cooker. Here are some things you can do up to a day in advance to streamline your prep:

1. Microwave the aromatics as described (in step 1 and/or 2 of most recipes), then transfer them to an airtight container and refrigerate.
2. Peel and cut any vegetables as directed (except potatoes, which discolor after being cut) and refrigerate.
3. Trim and cut the meat as directed. Refrigerate it separately from the microwaved aromatics in an airtight container.

THE BEST SLOW COOKER

After testing a number of slow cookers, we found our favorite in the Crock-Pot Touchscreen Slow Cooker ($129.99), which has a 6.5-quart capacity. It had the best control panel, which was simple to set and clearly indicated that the cooker has been programmed. It has a clear glass lid, so it's easy to see the food as it cooks. Also, the insert has handles, which makes it easy to remove the insert from the cooker.

CROCK-POT

FOUR TIPS FOR SUCCESS

1. PUMP UP THE AROMATICS

To keep the flavor of slow-cooker recipes from being washed out, we use a hefty amount of onions and other aromatics to build a flavor base. We often use more aromatics, spices, and herbs in a slow-cooker recipe than you would expect, because the long cooking time and moist heat dulls their impact. And when appropriate, we also season at the end of cooking with fresh herbs to brighten the flavor.

2. COOK YOUR AROMATICS

While many slow-cooker recipes recommend simply dumping the raw aromatics into the slow cooker, we have found that this technique results in a flat-tasting dish (not to mention crunchy onions). Instead, we like to cook the aromatics, often with a little tomato paste for deeper

flavor, before adding them to the slow cooker. Because our goal in this book is to keep hands-on time and cookware to a minimum, we simply microwave our aromatics with a little oil until they are softened.

3. TRIM AWAY EXCESS FAT

During the extended cooking time in the slow cooker, beef and chicken can release a large amount of fat. Trimming and removing excess fat and skin from meat and poultry before adding them to the slow cooker reduces the amount of fat that can be rendered and prevents the dish from becoming greasy. And once the dish has finished cooking, it's also helpful to skim any residual fat off the surface with a large spoon.

4. KEEP THE LID ON

Slow cookers rely on their lids to retain heat and moisture and maintain their cooking temperature. After placing the lid on the slow cooker to begin cooking, we have found that it is important to avoid lifting the lid until the cooking time is finished—doing so can release heat and extend the cooking time significantly.

Slow-Cooker Beef Chili

GROUND BEEF CHILI IS A NATURAL FOR THE slow cooker but, despite the myriad recipes for it, most that we tested turned out watery and bland. How hard could it be to produce a great chili in a slow cooker? We were looking for a hearty all-American chili, with rich flavors and a thick, substantial texture—perfect as a foil for all those wonderful accompaniments such as a dollop of sour cream or a sprinkling of cheese (which are half the reason for making chili in the first place). We already had a good head start with our Classic Beef Chili recipe (page 155), so we set out to see how well it would translate to the slow cooker.

Most slow-cooker chili recipes begin by cooking and draining ground meat, then sautéing onions, garlic, and peppers. Hoping to keep our recipe simple and shorten prep time, our first order of business was to determine if we really needed to cook the meat before it went into the slow cooker. We learned some tricks in our slow-cooker beef stew testing that allowed us to bypass browning (see page 265) by closely replicating the flavor of fond with microwaved aromatics and tomato paste, so we followed that method here. Pitting chili made with browned beef against one made with uncooked beef and the faux-fond method, we found little discernible difference between the two.

Ready to zero in on flavors, we tested varying amounts of onion, garlic, peppers, celery, and carrots. Tasters liked a hefty quantity of onion and garlic, but disliked the others; they made the chili taste too vegetal and sweet. Having selected the aromatics we would microwave with tomato paste and our spices, we now began the more difficult task of getting the proportions of spice, meat, and liquid in perfect balance.

We started with the ingredient quantities used in our traditional chili recipe. It calls for 2 pounds ground beef, ¼ cup chili powder, 1 tablespoon ground cumin, 1 teaspoon of both red pepper flakes and dried oregano, and ½ teaspoon cayenne. The addition of tomatoes and beans to chili is often the subject of much debate concerning their rightful (or unwanted) presence in chili. But once again, since we were focusing on flavor and texture, we planned to include both. Our stovetop recipe includes 2 cans of kidney beans, one (28-ounce) can each of diced tomatoes and tomato puree, so we gave it a try and sat back while the slow cooker did its work.

After our first test, we found the balance between the meat, beans, and tomatoes was spot on. We were surprised that the juice from the tomatoes was all the liquid our slow-cooker version needed. And just as in our traditional recipe, we found we could add the beans at the beginning of cooking with the tomatoes; they remained intact despite the lengthy cooking time. They also tasted better than beans that had been added toward the end of cooking. Tasters preferred dark red kidney beans since they kept their shape better than light red kidney beans, the other common choice.

In our traditional recipe, we use 85 percent lean ground beef, but it was giving us a slightly greasy chili in this case that required skimming. While we weren't against that small extra step, we wondered if using a leaner meat would avoid the problem in the first place. We ran another test with our working recipe, this time using 90 percent lean ground beef. Unfortunately, this chili was dry and devoid of flavor. The recipe with ground beef with just a little more fat was such a big improvement that it was worth the extra step of skimming the fat.

However, even with the right type of meat, the chili still had a sandier texture than we wanted due to the long cooking time. We often use a panade, a mixture of milk and bread, when making meatloaf and meatballs to keep ground meat moist, so why not try it here? Simply combining the meat with a panade and putting it in the slow cooker wasn't enough; a chili prepared this way had a mushy texture. We discovered that microwaving the raw meat–panade mixture before putting it in the slow cooker helped firm it up and gave us the proper texture. And microwaving it along with our onion mixture kept things streamlined and easy.

With the core components of our recipe all set, we needed to make some minor tweaks to the seasoning. The amount of chili powder, oregano, and cumin were all fine as is, but the heat level wasn't translating quite right after the long cooking time. After some tinkering, we decided to decrease the amount of red pepper flakes to ½ teaspoon and omit the cayenne entirely in favor of another form of heat that would also add some smokiness: canned chipotle chile in adobo sauce. Just 2 teaspoons added the complex background flavor that our slow-cooker chili had been lacking.

As with our slow-cooker beef stews (see pages 265–267), we found that a little soy sauce further enhanced the beefy flavor of our slow-cooker beef chili. Now we were close, and adding a tablespoon of dark brown sugar lent our recipe a nice sweetness that balanced out our new additions of soy sauce and chipotle chiles.

Although we all agreed that garnishes of avocado, cheese, and cool sour cream are a great addition to chili if you have the time, we found that lime wedges, passed separately at the table, were a simple and sufficient garnish to brighten the flavor of the chili and accentuate the heat of the spices.

Slow-Cooker Beef Chili

SERVES 6 TO 8

Do not use beef any leaner than 85 percent or its texture will turn dry and sandy as it cooks. Serve with lime wedges, minced fresh cilantro, minced onion or scallions, diced avocado, shredded cheddar or Monterey Jack cheese, sour cream, rice, and/or warmed tortillas.

2	slices high-quality white sandwich bread, torn into quarters
¼	cup whole milk
2	pounds 85 percent lean ground beef (see note)
	Salt and ground black pepper
1½	pounds onions, minced
¼	cup chili powder
¼	cup tomato paste
3	tablespoons vegetable oil
6	medium garlic cloves, minced or pressed through a garlic press (about 2 tablespoons)
1	tablespoon ground cumin
1	teaspoon dried oregano
½	teaspoon red pepper flakes
2	(15-ounce) cans dark red kidney beans, drained and rinsed
1	(28-ounce) can diced tomatoes
1	(28-ounce) can tomato puree
3	tablespoons soy sauce
1	tablespoon dark brown sugar
2	teaspoons minced chipotle chile in adobo sauce

1. Mash the bread and milk into a paste in a large bowl using a fork, then mix in the ground beef, ½ teaspoon salt, and ½ teaspoon pepper with your hands. In a large microwave-safe bowl, combine the onions, chili powder, tomato paste, oil, garlic, cumin, oregano, and red pepper flakes. Place the meat mixture on top of the onion, and microwave on high power, stirring occasionally, until the onions are softened and the meat is no longer pink, 10 to 15 minutes.

2. Transfer the beef-onion mixture to a slow cooker. Using a potato masher, break apart any large pieces of meat. Stir in the beans, tomatoes with their juice, tomato puree, soy sauce, sugar, and chipotles into the slow cooker. Cover and cook until the beef is tender, 6 to 8 hours on low or 3 to 5 hours on high.

3. Let the chili settle for 5 minutes, then remove as much fat as possible from the surface using a large spoon. Break up any remaining large pieces of beef with a spoon, season with salt and pepper to taste, and serve.

✒ VARIATIONS

Slow-Cooker Three-Alarm Beef Chili

Since habanero chiles vary in intensity, you may need to adjust the heat of the chili with additional chipotles and hot sauce.

Follow the recipe for Slow-Cooker Beef Chili, microwaving 3 habanero chiles, minced, with the onion mixture in step 1. Increase the amount of minced chipotles to 1 tablespoon. Season with additional chipotles and hot sauce to taste and serve with sliced pickled banana peppers, chopped fine.

Slow-Cooker Moroccan Beef Chili with Chickpeas and Raisins

Follow the recipe for Slow-Cooker Beef Chili, substituting 1 tablespoon sweet paprika, 1 tablespoon ground ginger, ½ teaspoon cayenne pepper, and ½ teaspoon ground cinnamon for the chili powder and red pepper flakes. Substitute 2 (15-ounce) cans chickpeas, drained and rinsed, for the kidney beans and omit the chipotles. After removing the fat in step 3, stir in 1 cup raisins and let sit until heated through, about 5 minutes. Before serving, stir in 1 tablespoon lemon juice and 1 teaspoon grated lemon zest.

SLOW-COOKER CHILI CON CARNE

IF YOU'RE FROM TEXAS, CHILI MEANS ONE thing: Hearty chunks of beef simmered with dried chiles in water or broth—no tomatoes or beans in sight. Although many authentic recipes for this type of chili, also called chili con carne, demand a mix of dried chiles in place of supermarket chili powder, we were hoping to find an easier way to infuse our chili with rich, deep flavor and heat. This Lone Star State classic seemed like a natural for the slow cooker—hours of simmering would render the meat incredibly tender, and a streamlined ingredient list would keep the process fairly straightforward.

Since chili con carne is all about the meat, that's where we started. We opted to use chuck-eye roast; it's a cut that we find flavorful, tender, and juicy, and it takes just 10 minutes to trim the meat and cut it into large pieces. As with our previous slow-cooker recipes that also use chuck-eye roast, we knew we could save on prep time by not browning the meat; instead, we cooked our aromatics and tomato paste together in the microwave to develop rich flavor. We also knew that we could augment the flavor with soy sauce, which adds depth; although this ingredient was a tad unconventional for chili, we found that it worked just fine.

As for the aromatics and spices, we found that tasters enjoyed the sweetness provided by cooked onions, even though they were not standard in most traditional chili con carne recipes. A hefty amount of garlic—eight cloves—provided a punch of flavor. As for the spices, dried chiles are the authentic choice, but for a simple slow-cooker chili, the work involved in toasting and seeding them seemed excessive. Instead we utilized the test kitchen's technique for blooming spices in hot oil to help enhance the flavor of store-bought chili powder. Combined in the microwave with the onions, the chili powder contributed ample fragrance. A little cumin and dried oregano rounded out our flavor base.

At this point the flavors were nearly there, but the chili still needed a bit more complexity. We thought of the deep, smoky flavor of chipotle chile packed in adobo sauce, which had served us well in our Slow-Cooker Beef Chili recipe (page 271).

We were now ready to look more closely at the liquid component of the chili. Up until this point we had been using water, as most recipes suggested, though we were eager to see the effects of substituting a more flavorful broth. Beef broth overwhelmed the already meaty flavor of the chili and vegetable broth made the chili taste too sweet. Chicken broth, however, was a great success, enriching the chili without making its presence known.

While testing broths we also found most tasters requested the addition of (gasp) tomatoes. With several options available, we tried diced tomatoes, tomato puree, and crushed tomatoes; the tomato puree beat out the others, contributing acidity and flavor, and blending into the chili better than diced or crushed tomatoes. However, now that we had added the tomato puree, our chili was thinner than we liked. Unable to rely on evaporation to thicken the chili due to the covered slow cooker, we felt the use of a thickener was the next best solution. Flour and cornstarch both made the chili taste starchy, but

PEELING GARLIC

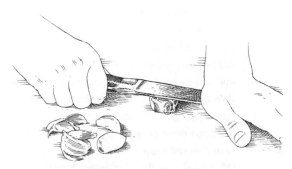

Unless whole cloves are needed, we crush garlic cloves with the side of a chef's knife to loosen the skins and make them easier to remove from the clove.

tapioca gave our chili just the right texture without contributing any off-flavors.

The chili was almost complete, but some tasters were left wondering about beans. While authentic chili con carne doesn't include them, in the end we liked the creaminess that they brought to our slow-cooker version, and their starch helped balance the spices. As with our Slow-Cooker Beef Chili (page 271), we found that the beans held up well and had the best flavor when we added them at the onset of cooking.

With some dark brown sugar stirred in for a hint of sweetness, our slow-cooked chili con carne was finally complete. While our version may not be completely authentic, judging by the smiles on our tasters' faces, that was just fine.

Slow-Cooker Chili con Carne

SERVES 6 TO 8

Adjust the heat of the chili by adding more or less chipotles. Serve with lime wedges, minced fresh cilantro, minced onion or scallions, diced avocado, shredded cheddar or Monterey Jack cheese, sour cream, rice, and/or warmed tortillas.

1½	pounds onions, minced
¼	cup chili powder
¼	cup tomato paste
8	medium garlic cloves, minced or pressed through a garlic press (about 8 teaspoons)
2	tablespoons vegetable oil
2	tablespoons ground cumin
1	teaspoon dried oregano
1	(28-ounce) can tomato puree
2	(15-ounce) cans dark red kidney beans, drained and rinsed
2	cups low-sodium chicken broth
¼	cup Minute tapioca
3	tablespoons soy sauce
2	tablespoons minced chipotle chile in adobo sauce
2	tablespoons dark brown sugar, plus extra as needed
1	(5-pound) boneless beef chuck-eye roast, trimmed and cut into 1½-inch pieces (see the illustrations on page 133) Salt and ground black pepper

1. Microwave the onions, chili powder, tomato paste, garlic, oil, cumin, and oregano together in a medium bowl on high power, stirring occasionally, until the onions are softened, about 5 minutes; transfer to a slow cooker.

2. Stir the tomato puree, beans, broth, tapioca, soy sauce, chipotles, and brown sugar into the slow cooker. Season the beef with salt and pepper and nestle into the slow cooker. Cover and cook until the meat is tender, 9 to 11 hours on low or 5 to 7 hours on high.

3. Let the chili settle for 5 minutes, then remove as much fat as possible from the surface using a large spoon. Season with salt, pepper, and brown sugar to taste and serve.

SLOW-COOKER KOREAN BRAISED SHORT RIBS

ONE OF OUR FAVORITE KOREAN DISHES IS *kalbi*, grilled beef short ribs marinated in a sweet soy mixture with garlic, scallions, and pears. This mouth-watering dish is a staple in Korean restaurants and is taken just as seriously as Americans view their burgers and steaks. Since short ribs are also well suited to braising, we wondered if we might have luck transferring the flavors of our favorite Korean dish from the grill to the slow cooker. We knew that the texture of the ribs would benefit from the slow, moist heat, but we were concerned about the bold flavor of the marinade being diluted by the stewing liquid required in the slow cooker. Could we find the secret for tender braised ribs with intense Korean barbecued flavor?

Short ribs are a tough cut of meat that usually requires a long, slow braise to achieve melting, fork-tender perfection. In the test kitchen, we use English-style ribs for braises. Their single bone and thick layer of meat make for hefty, uniform portions. Browning the ribs in a skillet is usually the first step to intensify the meat's flavor, but we wanted to avoid the mess and cleanup of an added step (and dish). While we were interested in saving time, however, we didn't want to do so at the expense of flavor.

We looked at the bones sticking out of the ribs and wondered if they could be the key to increasing flavor in our slow-cooker braise.

Restaurant chefs know that roasting bones is key to making flavorful stock, since bones carry lots of flavor, and roasted bones carry even more. Could we remove the meat from the rib bones and brown the bones to add flavor to our braise? Roasting the bones in the oven would take too much time, but we wondered if we could "roast" the bones in the microwave. We laid them in a baking dish and hit start; after about 15 minutes, the bones looked like they'd spent hours in an oven and, indeed, they added unequivocal depth to the sauce.

Now that we had found a way to add flavor to our dish without browning the meat, we focused on the liquid component. Since the key to authentic Korean ribs is finding the right marinade, we lined up the ingredients for inspection: soy sauce, sugar, rice vinegar, garlic, and scallions. In previous test kitchen work, we have discovered that soy sauce acts as a brine and helps tenderize meat, but it also helps enhance beefy flavor—something that would be an added bonus since we chose not to brown the meat. For more flavor we added sesame oil and ginger. Finally, we added the "secret" ingredient: pureed pear. Many kalbi recipes add pureed pear to the marinade, claiming it acts as a tenderizer. Since tenderness was less of a concern with moist heat cooking than grilling, we didn't necessarily need a tenderizer, but we opted to include the pear for the traditional sweetness and fruity flavor it imparted in our sauce.

For a glossy, velvety consistency, we rejected cornstarch (gluey) and flour (starchy) in favor of instant tapioca, which we added with the chicken broth. Only one problem remained: Short ribs ooze fat as they cook. To remedy this, many recipes chill them overnight so that the gelled fat can be scraped from the cooking liquid and discarded. We didn't want to add a day to our cooking, so we simply fished out the ribs and set them aside, discarded the bones, let the sauce settle, and skimmed as much fat as we could from the top—an easy fix. At last our sauce had sheen, body, and layers of flavor.

After several hours of cooking, we were amazed by the richness of the sauce and the depth of flavors. The short ribs were unbelievably tender, smothered in a marinade with just the right balance of salty soy and sweet pear notes. While we knew the ribs would be delicious served in traditional lettuce wraps with rice, the tender ribs and sturdy sauce seemed to beg for the hearty vegetables we usually associate with braised meats. Taking a cue from our Slow-Cooker Beef Stew (page 266), we added a foil packet of carrots and potatoes to the slow cooker for our final test and were rewarded with a satisfying one-dish meal brimming with tangy Korean flair.

PREPARING THE SHORT RIBS FOR THE SLOW COOKER

1. Using a sharp knife, cut the meat away from the bone, staying as close to the bone as possible, using a sawing motion.

2. Before adding the bones to the slow cooker, microwave them for 10 to 15 minutes to give them a deep "roasted" flavor.

Slow-Cooker Korean Braised Short Ribs

SERVES 4

Buy English-style short ribs that have at least 1 inch of meat on top of the bone; avoid ribs that have little meat or large bones.

5	pounds beef short ribs (6 to 8 English-style ribs)
1	pear, peeled, halved, cored, and chopped coarse
½	cup soy sauce
6	medium garlic cloves, minced or pressed through a garlic press (about 2 tablespoons)
3	scallions, sliced thin
4	teaspoons minced or grated fresh ginger (see the illustrations on page 216)
1	tablespoon rice vinegar
1	cup low-sodium chicken broth
3	tablespoons Minute tapioca
	Salt and ground black pepper
1	pound carrots (about 6 medium), peeled, halved lengthwise, and sliced 1 inch thick
1	pound red potatoes (about 3 medium), scrubbed and cut into 1-inch chunks
1	tablespoon vegetable oil
2	tablespoons minced fresh cilantro leaves

1. Following the illustrations on page 274, cut the meat from the bones and set aside. Arrange the bones in a baking dish and microwave on high power (in batches if necessary) until the bones are well browned, 10 to 15 minutes; transfer to a slow cooker.

2. Process the pear, soy sauce, garlic, scallions, ginger, and vinegar in a food processor until smooth, 20 to 30 seconds; transfer to the slow cooker. Stir the broth and tapioca into the slow cooker. Season the meat with salt and pepper and nestle into the slow cooker.

3. Toss the carrots and potatoes with the oil, season with salt and pepper to taste, and wrap in an aluminum foil packet following the illustrations on page 266. Lay the foil packet on top of the stew. Cover and cook until the beef is tender, 9 to 11 hours on low or 5 to 7 hours on high.

4. Transfer the foil packet to a plate. Transfer the beef to a serving platter and tent loosely with foil. Let the braising liquid settle for 5 minutes, then remove as much fat as possible from the surface using a large spoon. Discard the bones, stir in the cilantro, and season with salt and pepper to taste.

5. Carefully open the vegetable packet (watch for steam), drain away any accumulated liquid, and transfer to a serving bowl. Spoon the sauce over the ribs and serve with the vegetables.

SLOW-COOKER CARNE ADOVADA

WHEN IT COMES TO MAKING CHILI, TEXAS doesn't have the market cornered. New Mexico's *carne adovada*, which literally translates to "marinated meat," may give other chili a run for its money when it comes to tender meat and deep flavor. Here in the test kitchen, it has quickly become a favorite, so much so that we had already developed a recipe using the stovetop and oven (see page 156), so we knew it had all the makings of a natural slow-cooker dish. With the help of the slow cooker, we would cook chunks of pork butt until they became mouth-wateringly tender, and infused with the intense flavors of red chiles, oregano, onion, and garlic. The only thing lost in translation for this version we hoped would be time spent standing at the stove.

The first step in taking our recipe to the slow cooker was to change our approach to the pork. We knew we had the right cut of meat for a long-simmering chili—boneless pork butt. This well-marbled roast stays tender in the slow cooker as the fat melts and keeps the meat moist, but would it be as flavorful without a browned crust? Since we were trying to limit our prep time as much as possible, the browning step would have to go. We had already successfully eliminated this step from several other slow-cooker recipes, so we already knew that we would need to make up for the missing fond through a mixture of aromatics and spices. Since chilis traditionally have both in spades, we had a hunch that the dish wouldn't be lacking in flavor.

We settled on two onions and six cloves of garlic to build a base of flavor for the chili. While we didn't want to add them raw to the slow cooker, we knew from prior testing that we could forgo browning the onions by microwaving them with assertive spices to intensify their flavor. In this case, ¼ cup chili powder would do the job (incidentally, about the same amount our research recipes use of freshly roasted and ground dried New Mexico chiles—but with far less work and mess). To deepen the meaty flavor in our slow-cooker version, we added 2 tablespoons of tomato paste. A teaspoon of dried oregano rounded out the spice brigade for our dish.

With a strong lineup of aromatics and spices, it was time to find the right braising medium for our slow-cooked pork. We started by adding chicken broth and then topped off the liquid with ½ cup of brewed coffee, a trick we'd used in our more traditional stovetop-to-oven version, to replicate the slightly bitter quality of freshly ground dried chiles. We added the pork, which we had cut into 1½-inch chunks and seasoned with salt and pepper, and set the slow cooker for six hours on high. When we returned to the pork several hours later, the meat was tender and the sauce was an attractive rust-red, but the flavor and texture of the sauce left something to be desired.

While we had adjusted for the bitter quality that dried chiles contribute to the dish, we hadn't compensated for the fruity quality they add as well. Since the flavor of chiles is sometimes described as "raisiny," in our earlier version we had actually added raisins and met with great success. But we were afraid the raisin texture would seem jarring in the slow-cooker chili. Unlike our first version, we wouldn't be pureeing the sauce in the slow-cooker version, so any lumps and inconsistencies in texture would be apparent in the final dish. But happily, tasters liked the agreeably subtle flavor the raisins contributed and, after just 10 minutes in the slow cooker, they softened enough to be unobtrusive in the chili.

Finally, we needed to find a way to thicken the sauce without sacrificing flavor. While some stovetop versions cook a roux of flour and oil in the Dutch oven and then add broth to successfully (and tastefully) increase the heartiness of the chili, we found that adding a slurry of flour or cornstarch to the slow-cooker merely resulted in an unappealing starchiness that was woefully out of place. The solution was ¼ cup of tapioca stirred into the braising liquid. At the last minute, we stirred in lime juice, lime zest, and cilantro to brighten the otherwise earthy dish.

When we tucked into the fragrant red chili, we were happy to find it hit the spot—and it took a minimum of effort to get there.

Slow-Cooker Carne Adovada
SERVES 6 TO 8

Boneless pork butt roast is often labeled as boneless Boston butt in the supermarket. You can substitute 1½ teaspoons ground espresso powder dissolved in ½ cup boiling water for the brewed coffee if desired. Serve with lime wedges, minced fresh cilantro, minced onion or scallions, diced avocado, shredded cheddar or Monterey Jack cheese, sour cream, and/or warm corn tortillas.

2	medium onions, minced
¼	cup chili powder
6	medium garlic cloves, minced or pressed through a garlic press (about 2 tablespoons)
2	tablespoons vegetable oil
2	tablespoons tomato paste
I	teaspoon dried oregano
2	cups low-sodium chicken broth
½	cup brewed coffee
¼	cup Minute tapioca
I	tablespoon minced chipotle chile in adobo sauce
I	tablespoon brown sugar, plus extra as needed
I	(4-pound) boneless pork butt roast, trimmed and cut into 1½-inch pieces
	Salt and ground black pepper
½	cup raisins
¼	cup minced fresh cilantro leaves
I	tablespoon juice plus I teaspoon grated zest from I lime, plus extra juice as needed

1. Microwave the onions, chili powder, garlic, oil, tomato paste, and oregano together in a medium bowl on high power, stirring occasionally, until the onions are softened, about 5 minutes; transfer to a slow cooker.

2. Stir the broth, coffee, tapioca, chipotles, and sugar into the slow cooker. Season the pork with salt and pepper and nestle into the slow cooker. Cover and cook until the pork is tender, 9 to 11 hours on low or 5 to 7 hours on high.

3. Let the chili settle for 5 minutes, then remove as much fat as possible from the surface using a large spoon. Stir in the raisins and let sit until heated through, about 10 minutes. Stir in the cilantro, lime zest, and lime juice. Season with salt, pepper, sugar, and lime juice to taste and serve.

SLOW-COOKER PORK STEW WITH FENNEL AND PRUNES

WHILE BEEF STEWS MAY REIGN SUPREME IN this country, pork stews are quite common in other parts of the world. A simple yet elegant example is a French stew that combines braised pork with carrots, prunes, brandy, and a touch of cream. Having developed a traditional version of this stew (see page 137), we wondered if it would successfully translate to the slow cooker. We wanted all the qualities of the Dutch oven version—tender pork, creamy carrots, and sweet prunes balanced by a rich, savory broth—but with even more walk-away time.

We already knew that a boneless pork shoulder roast (known as Boston butt in most markets) would make the best pork stew, owing to the generous fat that would melt during slow cooking and keep the meat moist. Once the pork was cubed and seasoned with salt and pepper, we set it aside, opting to forego the step of browning the meat; not only did this make our recipe easier, but it also prevented a crust from forming on the meat, which tasters felt would interfere with the creamy richness of the stew. After setting aside the meat, we followed our usual step for slow-cooker recipes of microwaving the aromatics—in this case leeks and garlic—with some oil until they softened. This quick and easy step provided a sweet, aromatic backdrop for the stew.

Confident with our techniques for preparing the meat and aromatics, we considered the types and quantities of liquids to use for our braise. Based on the size of our roast, we estimated that we would need a full 4 cups of liquid to properly braise the pork and provide ample liquid for serving the stew. Brandy would be the defining flavor of our braising liquid, complemented by chicken broth for a savory element and cream for richness. We knew getting this formula right would require a careful balancing act.

Starting with 1 cup of brandy (enough to shine through the other ingredients in this flavorful braise), we added 3 cups of chicken broth and 1 cup of cream, ratios we had settled on for our earlier recipe. But since the slow cooker doesn't allow for evaporation (and we weren't deglazing a pan) this combination was too heavy on the brandy and too brothy. So we tried decreasing the brandy to ½ cup and decreasing the broth to 2½ cups.

EQUIPMENT: Ladles

A ladle makes serving soups and stews, whether prepared in your slow cooker or a Dutch oven or stockpot, easy and mess-free. We like a ladle with a handle about 9 to 10 inches in length; ladles with shorter handles will sink into deeper pots, and ladles with longer handles are too cumbersome to maneuver easily. The handle should be slightly offset; without this slight bend in the handle, cleanly transferring the ladle's contents into a bowl is nearly impossible. Our favorite ladle is the Rösle Ladle with Pouring Rim, which, as its name implies, has a drip-prevention pouring rim that keeps even wiggly noodles in place all the way to your bowl.

THE BEST LADLE
The Rösle Ladle with Pouring Rim ($29.95) includes an offset hook handle, a deep bowl, and a spill-prevention pouring rim.

RÖSLE

This reproportioning left us with the right amount of liquid and a good distribution of flavors. The resulting stew was an improvement, but the cream still had that overly sweet, "cooked" flavor. Holding the cream and adding it at the end of cooking allowed the cream to retain its fresh flavor without overwhelming the other ingredients.

Since we wanted this dish to be chock-full of flavor and texture (two qualities that often fade in the slow cooker) we decided that our choice of vegetables wasn't enough to give the dish the complexity we wanted. Prunes provided sweetness and carrots contributed an earthy flavor and creamy texture, but we wanted another vegetable to further round out the flavors and provide a savory element. We settled on fennel as we had in our stovetop-to-oven version; we loved the way it perfumed and infused the stew with its subtle anise flavor. Combined with the cream, the brandy, and the pork, it was a hit. Because fennel and carrots cook at a much faster pace than the pork, we added them to the slow cooker in a foil packet that sat atop the meat, where the vegetables could gently steam and retain their fresh flavors. The prunes were best added at the very end of cooking to prevent them from breaking down and disintegrating into the stew. Freshly minced tarragon, as well as some lemon juice, added a welcome complexity to the finished dish.

We figured it was time to cue up "La Vie en Rose," because our finished stew needed only a glass of hearty Burgundy to transport us to France with ease and elegance any night of the week.

⤖

Slow-Cooker Pork Stew with Fennel and Prunes

SERVES 6 TO 8

Boneless pork butt roast is often labeled as boneless Boston butt in the supermarket. Fresh tarragon is important for the flavor of this stew; do not substitute dried tarragon. Serve with buttered egg noodles or rice.

2   medium leeks, white and light green parts only, halved lengthwise, sliced ½ inch thick, and rinsed thoroughly (see the illustrations on page 138)

3   medium garlic cloves, minced or pressed through a garlic press (about 1 tablespoon)

2   tablespoons vegetable oil

2½   cups low-sodium chicken broth, plus extra as needed

½   cup brandy

3   tablespoons Minute tapioca

2   bay leaves

1   (4-pound) boneless pork butt roast, trimmed and cut into 1½-inch pieces
Salt and ground black pepper

1   pound carrots (about 6 medium), peeled, halved lengthwise, and sliced 1 inch thick

1   medium fennel bulb (about 12 ounces), trimmed of stalks, cored, and cut into ½-inch-thick strips (see the illustrations on page 38)

1½   cups prunes, quartered

1   cup heavy cream

2   tablespoons minced fresh tarragon leaves (see note)

1   tablespoon juice from 1 lemon

1. Microwave the leeks, garlic, and 1 tablespoon of the oil together in a medium bowl on high power, stirring occasionally, until the leeks are softened, about 5 minutes; transfer to a slow cooker.

2. Stir the broth, brandy, tapioca, and bay leaves into the slow cooker. Season the pork with salt and pepper and nestle into the slow cooker. Toss the carrots and fennel with the remaining 1 tablespoon oil, season with salt and pepper to taste, and wrap in an aluminum foil packet following the illustrations on page 266. Lay the foil packet on top of the stew. Cover and cook until the pork is tender, 9 to 11 hours on low or 5 to 7 hours on high.

3. Transfer the foil packet to a plate. Let the stew settle for 5 minutes, then remove as much fat as possible from the surface using a large spoon. Discard the bay leaves.

4. Carefully open the vegetable packet (watch for steam) and stir the vegetables with any accumulated juice into the stew. Stir in the prunes and cream and let sit until heated through, about 5 minutes. (Adjust the stew consistency with additional hot broth as needed.) Stir in the tarragon and lemon juice, season with salt and pepper to taste, and serve.

SLOW-COOKER MEXICAN-STYLE PORK AND HOMINY STEW

POZOLE IS THE MEXICAN NAME FOR BOTH hominy (dried field corn kernels treated with lime and boiled until tender but still chewy) and a stew made with hominy and pork. There are three varieties of this stew: red (made with dried red chiles), green (with tomatillos and fresh green chiles), and white (without chiles). But they all should have a complex, richly flavored broth with lots of body. The meat, which is shredded, must be exceedingly tender, while the hominy should be chewy and sweet. Although pozole has become more popular in the United States, especially in the Southwest, most American cooks balk at preparing such traditional recipes, many of which take 12 hours or more to execute. With its long simmering time, though, pozole seemed a natural for our slow cooker, and we quickly honed in on the red variety since its deep, rich flavor seemed like it would translate well to the slow cooker. Streamlining the prep work and simplifying the recipe would be the challenging part. The meat seemed like the place to start.

Traditional pozole uses offal, cuts like pig's head and unsmoked pig's feet—certainly specialty items in most areas of the United States. In lieu of the unique cuts traditionally used, we settled on boneless pork butt, not only because of its availability and reasonable price, but also because it's ideal for braising, yielding moist, tender meat. Traditionally, pozole differs from other meat stews in that the meat is shredded rather than cubed. The meat is usually stewed in large chunks until it is tender enough to pull apart by hand. Shredding the meat, however, would mean an additional, time-consuming and messy step. Instead, we cut the pork into 1½-inch chunks; small enough to fit perfectly on our spoons, but big enough to withstand the extended time in the slow cooker.

Pozole differs from most stews in another regard. While stew meat is typically browned to enhance the flavor of both the meat and the stewing liquid, in many pozole recipes the meat is simply added raw to the simmering liquid. The reason is simple: Browning creates a firmer, crustier texture on the outside of each piece of meat, which in turn makes the shredding process more difficult. In terms of cutting down on prep time, we couldn't have asked for a better dish. But as with our other slow-cooker recipes that skip the browning process, we needed to rely on other ingredients to provide a strong base of flavor. A full ⅓ cup soy sauce, stirred into the cooking liquid, was the key to mimicking the "browned" flavor. And we already knew that microwaving the aromatics—in this case onions, garlic (we found five cloves was just right), and tomato paste—is a viable option for softening them and deepening flavor when time is at a premium.

Next, it was time to decide on the liquid and other seasonings. We tested water and chicken broth. Although the water was fine, the broth was superior, adding not only depth of flavor but body to the stewing liquid. While some versions of red pozole reserve tomatoes as part of the garnish, our tasters liked the tomatoes cooked right into the stew where they added a lively flavor and pleasing texture. Since oregano is a signature ingredient in pozole, we added a full 2 tablespoons to make its presence known. The last aromatic component—the red chiles—is also the most important. While we started with a variety of chiles and followed a process of rehydrating,

INGREDIENTS: Hominy

Hominy is made from dried corn kernels that have been soaked (or cooked) in an alkali solution (commonly limewater or calcium hydroxide) to remove the germ and hull. It has a slightly chewy texture and toasted corn flavor, and is widely used in soups, stews, and chilis throughout the Southern United States and South America. Given its sturdy texture, hominy can easily withstand hours of simmering and is perfectly suited for the slow cooker. It is sold both dried and canned; however, we prefer the convenience of canned hominy, which only requires a quick rinse before using.

pureeing, and sautéing them, we found that, in the end, using store-bought chili powder was much easier and its flavor held up better during the hours of slow cooking. Microwaving the chili powder with the aromatics helped its flavor bloom and become more intense.

Finally, we addressed the issue of the hominy. Since we were streamlining prep work, using canned hominy seemed like a no-brainer. Canned hominy comes in white and yellow varieties, depending on the type of field corn used; either type works well in this stew. Flavor isn't much of an issue, as both are sweet and "corny" tasting. We determined that adding the canned hominy at the beginning of cooking allowed it to soak up some of the flavorful broth. We also found that the hominy could serve double duty when we decided that we wanted a thicker consistency for our stew; pureeing a can of hominy with some chicken broth gave our stew a thicker texture, as well as a solid base of corn flavor.

Our pozole recipe turned out to be remarkably simple. With minimal prep and plenty of walk-away time, our slow-cooker pozole gave us a unique and flavorful addition to our slow-cooking repertoire.

Slow-Cooker Mexican-Style Pork and Hominy Stew

SERVES 6 TO 8

Boneless pork butt roast is often labeled as boneless Boston butt in the supermarket. Serve with lime wedges, minced fresh cilantro, minced onion or scallions, diced avocado, shredded cheddar or Monterey Jack cheese, sour cream, rice, and/or warmed tortillas.

3	(15-ounce) cans white or yellow hominy, drained and rinsed
3	cups low-sodium chicken broth, plus extra as needed
1½	pounds onions, minced
¼	cup tomato paste
¼	cup vegetable oil
6	medium garlic cloves, minced or pressed through a garlic press (about 2 tablespoons)
2	tablespoons chili powder
2	tablespoons minced fresh oregano leaves or 2 teaspoons dried
1	(14.5-ounce) can diced tomatoes
⅓	cup soy sauce
1	(4-pound) boneless pork butt roast, trimmed and cut into 1½-inch pieces Salt and ground black pepper
1	pound carrots (about 6 medium), peeled, halved lengthwise, and sliced 1 inch thick
¼	cup minced fresh cilantro leaves
1	tablespoon juice from 1 lime

1. Puree 1 can of the hominy and 2 cups of the broth in a blender until smooth, 1 to 2 minutes; transfer to a slow cooker.

2. Microwave the onions, tomato paste, 3 tablespoons of the oil, garlic, chili powder, and oregano together in a medium bowl on high power, stirring occasionally, until the onions are softened, about 5 minutes; transfer to the slow cooker.

3. Stir the remaining 2 cans hominy, remaining 1 cup broth, tomatoes with their juice, and soy sauce into the slow cooker. Season the pork with salt and pepper and nestle into the slow cooker. Toss the carrots with the remaining 1 tablespoon oil, season with salt and pepper to taste, and wrap in an aluminum foil packet following the illustrations on page 266. Lay the foil packet on top of the stew. Cover and cook until the pork is tender, 9 to 11 hours on low or 5 to 7 hours on high.

4. Transfer the foil packet to a plate. Let the stew settle for 5 minutes, then remove as much fat as possible from the surface using a large spoon. Carefully open the vegetable packet (watch for steam) and stir the carrots with any accumulated juice into the stew. Let sit until heated through, about 5 minutes. (Adjust the stew consistency with additional hot broth as needed.) Stir in the cilantro and lime juice, season with salt and pepper to taste, and serve.

EASY SLOW-COOKER CHICKEN CURRY

ROBUSTLY FLAVORED CURRIES, WHETHER THEY are made with vegetables or meat, are central to Indian cuisine. When made well, these dishes showcase complex layers of flavor and at the same time are light and clean-tasting. Curry powder, the key ingredient, is actually a blend of up to 20 different spices and herbs, and it is what makes these dishes complex and engaging. However, we find that it's easy for curries to become overpowering, with cloyingly thick sauces. We wanted to create a chicken curry recipe that was mild but flavor-packed, with a light but substantial sauce that would hold its own when served over couscous or rice. And perhaps most importantly, we wanted to keep things simple by preparing our recipe in the slow cooker.

We began with the chicken. Based on prior test kitchen experience, we already knew a few things about cooking chicken in the slow cooker. First, boneless, skinless chicken thighs are the cut of choice when the meat is to be shredded before serving because they remain more moist and tender than chicken breasts. Second, instead of browning the chicken, we found that flavorful aromatics cooked briefly in the microwave can effectively mimic the flavor of searing without the headache or mess.

Moving on to the flavors of curry, we found the hassle and expense of making our own curry powder was not worth the effort or cost—a good-quality store-bought yellow curry powder can do the job just fine. To balance and round out the flavor of the store-bought curry powder, we added a small amount of garam masala. Garam masala is a mixture of "warm" spices, including coriander, black pepper, cumin, cardamom, and cinnamon, and is typically used to finish Indian dishes. In this case, however, we preferred to add it at the onset of cooking along with the curry powder. Coaxing the maximum flavor from dried spices typically requires blooming them in hot oil; for our recipe we achieved similar results by microwaving the curry powder and garam masala in oil along with the aromatics. This step not only added multiple layers of flavor to the curry, but it also

gave us a strong foundation for our faux fond. For aromatics, we found that a traditional combination of onions, garlic, ginger, and jalapeño chiles worked well and provided a great flavor base for our curry.

These first attempts at developing a well-rounded curry were promising, but the flavor still fell a bit flat, so we turned to tomatoes, a classic Indian curry ingredient. We tried adding diced tomatoes with their juice, but the flavor of the resulting stew was diluted. Next we tried crushed tomatoes and microwaved them along with the aromatics with the hope of coaxing out more flavor. This, too, fell short of our expectations. The solution turned out to be as simple as adding tomato paste to the rest of the aromatics and to finish the curry with fresh diced tomatoes. The tomato paste lent flavor and body to the stew and cooking the paste in the microwave intensified its flavor. The fresh tomatoes added at the end provided acidity and brightness.

Coconut milk, a star ingredient in curries of many origins, adds incredible richness to a stew, but because of its relatively high fat content, we were reluctant to add it at the beginning of the cooking process. When exposed to high heat, the fat in coconut milk has a tendency to separate, leaving behind an oil slick. However, we found that stirring it in at the end didn't give it time to fully flavor the stew.

INGREDIENTS: Curry Powder

Though blends can vary dramatically, curry powders come in two basic styles: mild or sweet and a hotter version called Madras. The former combines as many as 20 different ground spices, herbs, and seeds. We tasted six of these curry powders, mixed into a simple rice pilaf and in a plain vegetable curry. Our favorite was Penzeys Sweet Curry Powder, though Durkee Curry Powder came in a close second.

THE BEST CURRY POWDER

Neither too sweet nor too hot, Penzeys Sweet Curry Powder sets the standard with its "user-friendly balance" of "sweet" and "earthy" notes.

PENZEYS

After adding the coconut milk to the slow cooker starting on low heat with all the other ingredients (including 2 cups of water, which helped protect the milk), we were pleased to see that the coconut milk held together, lending great flavor and richness to the curry.

Coconut milk alone, however, was not enough to provide the rich, suave texture we wanted. We made one more batch, this time stirring in instant tapioca, which gave our curry just the right amount of body without a starchy or floury taste.

Chickpeas, added at the same time as the coconut milk and tapioca, added contrasting texture and further heartiness. Toward the end of cooking, we added golden raisins and allowed them to plump in the sauce. And lastly, to brighten the flavors, we finished our classic Indian curry with green peas and fresh cilantro leaves.

Easy Slow-Cooker Chicken Curry

SERVES 6 TO 8

This curry relies on the richness of regular coconut milk; do not substitute light or reduced-fat coconut milk. While we prefer the subtle sweetness of golden raisins, dark raisins are a good substitute. Serve with couscous or rice.

2	medium onions, minced
2	jalapeño chiles, stemmed, seeded, and minced
3	tablespoons vegetable oil
6	medium garlic cloves, minced or pressed through a garlic press (about 2 tablespoons)
2	tablespoons minced or grated fresh ginger (see the illustrations on page 216)
2	tablespoons curry powder
1	tablespoon tomato paste
1	teaspoon garam masala
2	(15-ounce) cans chickpeas, drained and rinsed
2	cups water, plus extra as needed
1	(14-ounce) can coconut milk (see note)
3	tablespoons Minute tapioca
3	pounds boneless, skinless chicken thighs (about 12 thighs), trimmed
	Salt and ground black pepper
12	ounces plum tomatoes (3 to 4), cored and chopped fine

½	cup golden raisins
1	cup frozen peas
¼	cup minced fresh cilantro leaves
	Lime wedges, for serving

1. Microwave the onions, jalapeños, oil, garlic, ginger, curry, tomato paste, and garam masala together in a medium bowl on high power, stirring occasionally, until the vegetables are softened, about 5 minutes; transfer to a slow cooker.

2. Stir the chickpeas, water, coconut milk, and tapioca into the slow cooker. Season the chicken with salt and pepper and nestle into the slow cooker. Cover and cook until the chicken is tender, 4 to 6 hours on low.

3. Transfer the chicken to a carving board, let cool slightly, then shred into bite-size pieces following the illustration on page 75. Let the stew settle for 5 minutes, then remove as much fat as possible from the surface using a large spoon.

4. Stir in the tomatoes and raisins, cover, and cook on high until heated through, about 10 minutes. Stir in the shredded chicken and peas and let sit until heated through, about 5 minutes. (Adjust the stew consistency with additional hot water as needed.) Stir in the cilantro, season with salt and pepper to taste, and serve with the lime wedges.

SLOW-COOKER MOROCCAN CHICKEN STEW

MOROCCAN CUISINE OFFERS A FEAST FOR THE senses. Drawing on influences from diverse surrounding cultures, Moroccan stews (or tagines, as they're commonly called) are highly aromatic and flavorful. Characterized by brilliant earthy hues and a blend of sweet and savory ingredients, they can be at once intriguing and intimidating. Traditional ingredient lists are often quite extensive, calling for cumin, saffron, coriander, and chiles of all sorts, in addition to complex, robust spice pastes that require shopping reconnaissance missions just to get started. Our plan for this recipe was to duplicate the complex flavors of a traditional Moroccan chicken tagine in the slow cooker, without using a laundry list of exotic ingredients.

Starting with the chicken, we quickly settled on thighs, which we knew would remain moist and tender over the long cooking time, and the richer flavor of dark meat would pair well with the heartier flavors and thicker sauce of the stew. Because we would be shredding the chicken at the end of cooking, we chose boneless, skinless thighs, which would make this step a snap. While browning is a traditional step to add flavor to the stew, we knew from some of our other slow-cooker recipes that we could skip this process as long as we compensated for the loss of flavor with plenty of aromatics and other bold ingredients.

Moving on to the aromatics, we found that two onions and a few garlic cloves provided the right background notes. We knew simply adding these ingredients raw to the slow cooker would yield a sour, overly vegetal flavor, so we opted to microwave them in olive oil with the spices to soften both the flavors and textures of the aromatics and bloom the spices. Knowing that the choice of spices would be critical, we started with three that are common in many Moroccan recipes: cardamom, cinnamon, and paprika. We opted to add a stick of cinnamon to the pot rather than ground to infuse the dish with just a light cinnamon flavor. Cardamom, pungent and aromatic with lemony undertones, nicely balanced the warm cinnamon. Some sweet paprika along with a little cayenne pepper for heat rounded out our spices. Tomato paste added a depth of flavor that was lost from not browning the chicken. To these basic aromatics, we added thyme and bay leaves.

To temper the pungent spices, we added dried apricots for sweetness and used chicken broth as our stewing medium, adding ½ cup of dry white wine for brightness. Now we had a stew packed with great flavors and a balanced contrast between hot and sweet notes. Next we decided to add chickpeas, a common ingredient in Moroccan cuisine. Their tender texture and nutty flavor added yet another dimension to the stew. For ease, we wanted to use canned chickpeas (especially since they weren't the centerpiece of our stew), but we worried that

their texture would suffer if we added them at the beginning of cooking. Since the chicken required a relatively short amount of time in the slow cooker, however, the chickpeas retained their integrity. The apricots, on the other hand, did not fare as well. While the flavor they contributed was indelible, they lost all discernible texture over the course of several hours in the slow cooker. We solved the problem by adding half of the apricots at the beginning of cooking (so their flavor could fully infuse the stew) and stirring in the remaining half at the end (so their texture did not suffer).

Our stew was almost complete, but the consistency of the sauce still needed some work. Many slow-cooker stew recipes turn to a slurry (a starch stirred together with liquid) of either flour or cornstarch, which has to be stirred in at the end of the cooking time. While both of these options worked to thicken the sauce, they imparted a starchy taste. As in other slow-cooker recipes, we turned to instant tapioca, which thickened the sauce without making it gloppy or contributing any discernible flavor. A sprinkle of fresh cilantro and a squeeze of lemon brightened our stew, providing the finishing touch. With its exotic flavors and heady aromas, this simple stew has all the intrigue and complexity of a Casablanca classic, without being daunting.

CHOPPING DRIED FRUIT

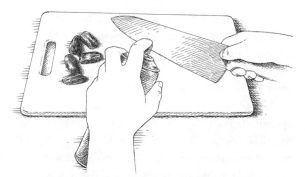

Dried fruit, especially apricots (or dates), very often sticks to the knife when you try to chop it. To avoid this problem, coat the blade with a thin film of vegetable oil spray just before you begin chopping any dried fruit. The chopped fruit won't cling to the blade, and the knife will stay relatively clean.

Slow-Cooker Moroccan Chicken Stew

SERVES 6 TO 8

Be sure to use sweet paprika, often labeled Hungarian paprika, in this recipe. Serve with rice or couscous.

2   medium onions, minced
3   medium garlic cloves, minced or pressed through a garlic press (about 1 tablespoon)
1   tablespoon tomato paste
1   tablespoon vegetable oil
1½ teaspoons sweet paprika
½   teaspoon ground cardamom
¼   teaspoon cayenne pepper
4   cups low-sodium chicken broth, plus extra as needed
½   cup dry white wine
2   (15-ounce) cans chickpeas, drained and rinsed
1   cup dried apricots, chopped medium (see the illustration on page 283)
3   tablespoons Minute tapioca
2   bay leaves
1   cinnamon stick
3   pounds boneless, skinless chicken thighs (about 12 thighs), trimmed
    Salt and ground black pepper
2   tablespoons minced fresh cilantro leaves
    Light brown sugar
    Lemon wedges, for serving

1. Microwave the onions, garlic, tomato paste, oil, paprika, cardamom, and cayenne together in a medium bowl on high power, stirring occasionally, until the onions are softened, about 5 minutes; transfer to a slow cooker.

2. Stir the broth, wine, chickpeas, half of the apricots, tapioca, bay leaves, and cinnamon stick into the slow cooker. Season the chicken with salt and pepper and nestle into the slow cooker. Cover and cook until the chicken is tender, 4 to 6 hours on low.

3. Transfer the chicken to a carving board, let cool slightly, then shred into bite-size pieces following the illustration on page 75. Let the stew settle for 5 minutes, then remove as much fat as possible from the surface using a large spoon. Discard the bay leaves and cinnamon stick.

4. Stir in the remaining apricots, cover, and cook on high until softened, 5 to 10 minutes. Stir in the shredded chicken and let sit until heated through, about 5 minutes. (Adjust the stew consistency with additional hot broth as needed.) Stir in the cilantro, season with salt, pepper, and sugar to taste, and serve with the lemon wedges.

SLOW-COOKER CHICKEN PROVENÇAL

CHICKEN PROVENÇAL MAY REPRESENT THE best of French peasant cooking—chicken on the bone is slowly simmered with tomatoes, garlic, herbs, and olives—but it is not a very well-known dish here in the United States, and even less known as a slow-cooker recipe. We soon discovered why. The handful of recipes we tested produced rubbery, dry chicken, dull and muddy flavors, and a sauce that was either too thick or too thin, too sweet or too greasy. Could we successfully create a slow-cooker version of this traditional, flavorful dish? We headed to the test kitchen to find out.

The chicken was our natural starting point. Most recipes we reviewed begin with browning a cut-up whole chicken, then removing it from the pot, sautéing some aromatic vegetables, deglazing the pot with white wine or dry vermouth, adding stock, tomatoes, olives, and herbs, and finally simmering the chicken in the slow cooker until it is cooked. When we followed this method, just to give us a reference point, we not surprisingly encountered problems. The skin, although crisp after browning, turned soggy and unappealing after braising in the slow cooker. Second, the wings contained mostly inedible skin and very little meat. Finally, with all this skin in the slow cooker, we were left with a greasy sauce. So we tried again, this time using bone-in chicken pieces, and only thighs (we knew that breasts tend to dry out in the slow cooker). The meat came out tender, moist, and flavorful and the sauce was much less greasy, especially since we removed the skin from the chicken prior to cooking.

We also eliminated the step of browning the chicken, since doing so would require an extra pan and extra time. We had learned from developing other slow-cooker recipes that adding tomato paste to the aromatics mimics the roasted flavor of seared meat. Microwaving the aromatics with the tomato paste and some oregano effectively cooked the elements and allowed their flavors to subtly infuse the stew, making the steps of sautéing the aromatics and deglazing the pan unnecessary. However, while we weren't deglazing, we still wanted the flavor that wine contributes, so we added dry white wine (which tasters preferred over vermouth) directly to the pot.

Our final tests with the chicken focused on timing. Chicken is notorious for drying out with extended cooking, even in the moist environment of a slow cooker. After several rubbery results, we found the optimal cooking time and temperature was four to six hours on low. Any longer and the chicken overcooked, and cooking the chicken on high for half that time turned out inconsistent results.

With the chicken issues squared away, we turned our attention to the sauce. Onions, lots of garlic, and tomato paste were already set as the foundation. Tomato sauce and pureed canned tomatoes produced thick, sweet, overbearing sauces reminiscent of bad Italian restaurant fare. Canned diced tomatoes, though more promising, presented the opposite problem: even when drained they contain a fair amount of liquid, and the resulting sauce was too thin. We found a happy medium in crushed tomatoes—this sauce coated the chicken without overwhelming it. Whole niçoise olives appeared in nearly every recipe we found, but tasters complained about the pits. No problem—pitted niçoise olives are readily available in the supermarket.

Next we considered olive oil, a signature ingredient of Provençal cuisine. Stirring in 2 tablespoons at the end perfectly perfumed the dish. The final items on our list, fresh parsley and a garnish of lemon, were welcome additions. The parsley was best added at the end, sprinkled in with the olives, and we liked serving the dish with lemon wedges so each guest could season to his or her taste. These last light, fresh touches emphasized how far we'd come from the heavy, greasy versions of the recipe. We had restored a classic to the status it deserves.

Slow-Cooker Chicken Provençal

SERVES 6

You can substitute pitted kalamata olives for the pitted niçoise olives. Serve with rice or hunks of crusty bread.

1½	pounds onions, minced
12	medium garlic cloves, minced or pressed through a garlic press (about 4 tablespoons)
2	tablespoons tomato paste
2	tablespoons vegetable oil
2	teaspoons minced fresh oregano leaves or ½ teaspoon dried
1	(28-ounce) can crushed tomatoes
½	cup dry white wine
2	bay leaves
12	bone-in chicken thighs (about 4½ pounds), skin removed and trimmed Salt and ground black pepper
½	cup pitted niçoise olives (see the illustration on page 289), chopped coarse
¼	cup minced fresh parsley leaves
2	tablespoons extra-virgin olive oil, plus extra for serving Lemon wedges, for serving

1. Microwave the onions, garlic, tomato paste, vegetable oil, and oregano in a medium bowl on high power, stirring occasionally, until the onions are softened, about 5 minutes; transfer to a slow cooker.

2. Stir the tomatoes, wine, and bay leaves into the slow cooker. Season the chicken with salt and pepper and nestle into the slow cooker. Cover and cook until the chicken is tender, 4 to 6 hours on low.

3. Transfer the chicken to a serving platter and tent loosely with aluminum foil. Let the braising liquid settle for 5 minutes, then remove as much fat as possible from the surface using a large spoon.

4. Discard the bay leaves, stir in the olives, parsley, and olive oil, and season with salt and pepper to taste. Spoon 1 cup of the sauce over the chicken and serve with additional olive oil, lemon wedges, and remaining sauce.

SLOW-COOKER COUNTRY CAPTAIN CHICKEN

LEGEND HAS IT THAT THIS CURRIED CHICKEN dish is named for a British sea captain who brought the recipe back from his travels in India. Now a Southern classic, it features chicken in a fragrant sauce of tomatoes, green peppers, onions, and curry powder, bolstered by garnishes of almonds and fruit. We were willing to bet that this combination of flavors was bold enough to withstand hours in a slow cooker, so we set about developing a recipe. While our goal was to pack tons of flavor into our slow-cooker country captain, we wanted to do it with a modicum of preparation. With such a host of bold flavors, we felt confident that we could streamline the cooking process without making sacrifices. Many country captain recipes insist on browning the chicken before adding it to the slow cooker; we felt this step was unnecessary, given the potency of the contributing flavors in the stew. Taking a cue from our other slow-cooker recipes, we used the microwave to bloom the curry powder, sweet paprika, and cayenne pepper in oil, along with onion, garlic, and green pepper. Microwaving these ingredients allowed them to release more flavor into the stew, and tomato paste provided depth, making up for any flavor lost by not browning the chicken.

The next task was to decide between white and dark meat. Tasters rejected all the stews made with breast meat (the meat was bone dry every time no matter what we tried). As we'd found in our other slow-cooker chicken dishes, the thigh meat was moist and meaty. Thighs are sold in two forms—boneless, skinless and bone-in, skin-on. The stews made with bone-in, skin-on thighs had moist, tender meat and richer overall flavor than the boneless, skinless thighs. However, we did find that chicken skin provides nothing but grease when it comes to slow-cooking, so we removed the skin and trimmed the thighs before adding them to the slow cooker.

Unlike tough cuts of meat, which typically need as many as 12 hours to become tender, chicken will overcook—even in a slow cooker. Many recipes called for eight hours of cooking on the low setting, but this left us with chicken that was dry and lacking in flavor. We found that four to six hours was a much better option; long enough for all the flavors of the stew to meld, but short enough that the chicken remained flavorful, tender, and juicy.

Although the chicken tasted great, the long, slow cooking was taking a toll on the seasonings; the curry flavor had faded, and not a hint of sweetness remained in the raisins and mango. Bumping up the curry to a whopping 2 tablespoons was an easy fix. Simmering the fruit for six hours left it bloated and bland, and while we could have added the fruit near the end of the cooking time as we did with our chicken curry recipe (see page 282), we thought of a more clever and efficient solution. We swapped the mango and raisins for a jar of mango chutney, which added just the right amount of sweet-tart flavor. A chopped Granny Smith apple and a sprinkling of toasted almonds added fresh crispness and a welcome crunch to our slow-cooker country captain chicken, providing the perfect finishing touch.

Slow-Cooker Country Captain Chicken

SERVES 6

Mango chutney (sometimes called Major Grey's chutney) is made from a cooked mixture of unripe green mangos with sugar, vinegar, and aromatic spices; don't omit the chutney in this recipe as it is crucial to the flavor of the stew. Serve with rice or couscous.

2	medium onions, minced
I	green bell pepper, stemmed, seeded, and cut into ½-inch pieces (see the illustrations on page 226)
5	tablespoons tomato paste
2	tablespoons curry powder
4	medium garlic cloves, minced or pressed through a garlic press (about 4 teaspoons)
I	tablespoon vegetable oil
I	tablespoon minced fresh thyme leaves or I teaspoon dried
I ½	teaspoons sweet paprika
¼	teaspoon cayenne pepper
I	(14.5-ounce) can diced tomatoes
I	cup mango chutney (see note)

¾   cup low-sodium chicken broth
12 bone-in chicken thighs (about 4½ pounds),
    skin removed and trimmed
    Salt and ground black pepper
2   tablespoons minced fresh parsley leaves
1   Granny Smith apple, cored and cut into
    ½-inch pieces
¼   cup sliced almonds, toasted

1. Microwave the onions, bell pepper, tomato paste, curry powder, garlic, oil, thyme, paprika, and cayenne together in a medium bowl on high power, stirring occasionally, until the vegetables are softened, about 5 minutes; transfer to a slow cooker.

2. Stir the tomatoes with their juice, chutney, and broth into the slow cooker. Season the chicken with salt and pepper and nestle into the slow cooker. Cover and cook until the chicken is tender, 4 to 6 hours on low.

3. Transfer the chicken to a serving platter and tent loosely with aluminum foil. Let the braising liquid settle for 5 minutes, then remove as much fat as possible from the surface using a large spoon.

4. Stir in the parsley and season with salt and pepper to taste. Spoon 1 cup of the sauce over the chicken and sprinkle with the apple and almonds. Serve with the remaining sauce.

SLOW-COOKER RED LENTIL STEW

SINCE SLOW COOKERS EXCEL AT RETAINING moisture and using gentle, even heat to cook food, several test cooks pointed out it would be the perfect vessel for making a red lentil stew. The spicy Indian stew known as *dal* (which can be served as a main course, side, or spread for *naan* or other flatbread) develops its trademark consistency—a thick, coarse puree—when red lentils cook and break down. The right amount of moisture is key to getting the correct texture for dal. We decided to develop a slow-cooker recipe for dal that would be substantial enough to qualify as a hearty vegetarian entrée when served with rice. We wanted our recipe to be simple yet embody the complex flavors of Indian cuisine. So naturally, we started with the spices.

Not wanting to make an unbearably spicy dal, we sought out a basic blend of spices with heat in mind as a more subtle component in the mix. We settled on a combination of coriander, cumin, cinnamon, turmeric, cardamom, and finally, red pepper flakes. This medley offered a pleasing blend of deep and bright flavors that remained vibrant throughout the cooking process. We also tried adding garam masala—a blend of spices including coriander, cloves, cardamom, cumin, cinnamon, black pepper, and nutmeg—but found it resulted in too many competing flavors.

Many of the recipes we found called for adding the aromatics raw or skipping them altogether, relying entirely on spices and garnishes such as chutney for flavor. We felt this dish would benefit from the addition of onion, garlic, and ginger, but adding them to the dish raw overwhelmed the other flavors. We decided to first bloom the spices in oil in the microwave, along with the onion, garlic, and ginger, before adding them to the slow cooker with the lentils and liquid. Traditionally, additional spices are toasted in a separate pan with oil or clarified butter to make a mixture called *tarka* and then stirred into the lentils at the end of cooking to fortify the flavor of the finished dish. But our method of blooming the spices in the microwave boosted their flavor more easily without employing a sauté pan and additional fat.

Proper dal should have a porridgelike consistency, which comes from cooking the lentils for the appropriate amount of time with the right amount of water. Achieving the right balance was easier said than done, and it took us several tries to get the lentils to their ideal consistency while cooking off all the excess water, particularly since a slow cooker doesn't allow for much evaporation. Whittling the water amount down gradually while keeping the amount of lentils the same, we were close with a 2 to 1 ratio of water to lentils. After a few more tweaks we landed on 4 cups of water to 2¼ cups of lentils. A can of coconut milk gave the dal richness and great flavor to balance the earthiness of the ground spices.

Wanting our dal to have a bit more substance, we decided to add chopped carrots with the lentils at the beginning of cooking. Near the end of cooking, we stirred in chopped raw tomato for sweetness and acidity, then added green peas a few minutes later.

For a garnish, we added cilantro for color and freshness. The result was an authentic, well-balanced dal with both fragrant spice and rich, creamy texture.

Slow-Cooker Red Lentil Stew

SERVES 6

You cannot substitute brown lentils for the red lentils here; red lentils have a very different texture. The addition of coconut milk provides a lush, creamy texture and rich flavor; do not substitute light coconut milk. Serve this stew with rice for a hearty, vegetarian main course.

2	medium onions, minced
6	medium garlic cloves, minced or pressed through a garlic press (about 2 tablespoons)
2	tablespoons vegetable oil
1	tablespoon minced or grated fresh ginger (see the illustration on page 216)
½	teaspoon ground coriander
½	teaspoon ground cumin
½	teaspoon ground cinnamon
½	teaspoon ground turmeric
⅛	teaspoon ground cardamom
⅛	teaspoon red pepper flakes
4	cups water, plus extra as needed
1	(14-ounce) can coconut milk (see note)
1	pound red lentils (2¼ cups), picked over and rinsed (see note)
1	pound carrots (about 6 medium), peeled and chopped medium
1	pound plum tomatoes (4 to 6), cored and chopped medium
1	cup frozen peas
¼	cup minced fresh cilantro leaves
	Salt and ground black pepper

1. Microwave the onions, garlic, oil, ginger, coriander, cumin, cinnamon, turmeric, cardamom, and red pepper flakes together in a medium bowl on high power, stirring occasionally, until the onions are softened, about 5 minutes; transfer to a slow cooker.

2. Stir the water, coconut milk, lentils, and carrots into the slow cooker. Cover and cook until the lentils are tender, 6 to 8 hours on low or 3 to 5 hours on high.

3. Stir in the tomatoes, cover, and cook on high until heated through, about 10 minutes. Stir in the peas and let sit until heated through, about 5 minutes. (Adjust the stew consistency with additional hot water as needed.) Stir in the cilantro, season with salt and pepper to taste, and serve.

SLOW-COOKER ARTICHOKE AND CHICKPEA TAGINE

TAGINES ARE A NORTH AFRICAN SPECIALTY— exotically spiced, assertively flavored stews slow-cooked in earthenware vessels of the same name. Vegetable tagines aren't as well known as meat or poultry tagines, but they can be equally as satisfying and flavorful. Native to the Mediterranean region and a popular ingredient in Moroccan cuisine, artichokes seemed like the perfect vegetable centerpiece to a meat-free tagine. Their intense, earthy flavor could make the ideal counterpoint to the zesty, bright flavors typical of this specialty. We also liked the idea of adding chickpeas, another mainstay of Mediterranean cooking, as they could contribute heartiness and a rich, nutty flavor. We envisioned a stew overflowing with big chunks of artichokes and tender chickpeas, enlivened with pungent garlic, warm spices, briny olives, and tangy lemon. Since chickpeas are such hearty beans, we thought this tagine would translate perfectly to a slow cooker.

Starting with the artichokes, we considered our options: fresh, frozen, jarred, and canned. Fresh artichokes were quickly scratched off the list. Though they tasted great, fresh artichokes were just too time-consuming to prepare. Canned artichokes were too watery no matter how well we drained them (or even if we browned them), so they were also eliminated. Jarred artichokes, which are packed in vinaigrette, seemed like a possibility, as the flavors of the marinade might complement the traditional tagine herbs and spices. We couldn't have been more wrong—the marinade dominated our tagine, even when we thoroughly rinsed the artichokes. We moved on to frozen artichokes. After thawing them and draining off the excess liquid, we patted them dry to remove any remaining moisture. The purer flavor of the frozen variety was our clear winner.

With the artichokes settled, we moved on to building the rest of the stew. Though we generally like canned chickpeas, which had served us well for our Easy Slow-Cooker Chicken Curry (page 282) and Slow-Cooker Moroccan Chicken Stew (page 284), in this vegetarian recipe they are the star ingredient so we needed to incorporate the most flavor and texture possible. Since dried chickpeas offer more nutty flavor and a firmer texture than canned, we opted for the former. One pound of chickpeas provided good heartiness. For more substance and a stronger vegetable presence, we added two bell peppers, cut into matchsticks for visual appeal. Tasters preferred the sweet flavor of red or yellow bell peppers over the more overtly vegetal green peppers. We knew the matchsticks wouldn't hold up in the stew after a long day of cooking, so we opted to parcook them in the microwave and then add them to the stew near the end of cooking.

At this point, we referred to our Slow-Cooker Moroccan Chicken Stew to help us narrow down the aromatics, cooking liquid, and spices. Onions were essential; their pungency mellowed into a sweet, subtle flavor when cooked. As for the garlic, we ultimately needed eight cloves, which offered the ideal amount of headiness and depth. For the liquid component, we used a few cups of chicken broth for rich, well-rounded flavor (although vegetable broth could be substituted to keep the dish vegetarian).

The lemon flavor in authentic tagines comes from preserved lemons, which are difficult to find and impossible to make at home quickly. However, we found that including several strips of lemon zest with the chickpeas and broth contributed similar flavor to our tagine. Some grated lemon zest also imparted bright flavor. For the olives we tried several kinds of green and black Mediterranean olives, and tasters preferred the flavor of kalamata olives.

As for the spices, garam masala—a spice blend of coriander, cloves, cardamom, cumin, cinnamon, black pepper, and nutmeg—gave us the complexity and warmth we were seeking. Paprika gave the stew sweetness and a deep, exotic red hue. Tasters wanted more pronounced sweetness however, so we decided to incorporate some dried fruit into the tagine. Dates, figs, and apricots all offered interesting flavor, but ultimately we liked the appearance and subdued sweetness of golden raisins the best.

Our stew was close to finished, but it tasted a little lean. Looking for ways to enrich it, we landed on yogurt. We stirred ½ cup plain whole-milk yogurt into the pot, and it was good, but plain whole-milk Greek yogurt, with its fuller, richer flavor, was even better. To prevent the yogurt from curdling, we spooned a portion of the tagine's liquid into the yogurt to gently warm it, then stirred the mixture into the pot (a process called tempering). Two spoonfuls of honey stirred in with the broth balanced the sweet and savory, and minced cilantro provided a note of freshness.

At last, we had a vegetable tagine that tasted every bit as bright and exotic as its meat-laden counterparts—and was just as satisfying.

PITTING OLIVES

Removing the pits from olives by hand is not an easy job; if you can't find pitted olives at the supermarket, use this method.

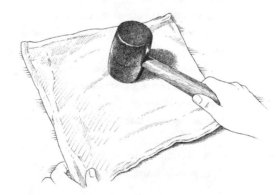

Cover a cutting board with a clean kitchen towel and spread the olives on top, about 1 inch apart from each other. Place a second clean towel over the olives. Using a mallet, pound all of the olives firmly for 10 to 15 seconds, being careful not to split the pits. Remove the top towel and, using your fingers, press the pit out of each olive.

Slow-Cooker Artichoke and Chickpea Tagine

SERVES 6

Frozen artichokes are generally packaged already quartered; if yours are not, cut the artichoke hearts into quarters before using. Dried chickpeas are essential to the texture of this dish; do not substitute canned chickpeas. Serve with rice or couscous.

- 2 medium onions, minced
- 8 medium garlic cloves, minced or pressed through a garlic press (about 8 teaspoons)
- 3 tablespoons extra-virgin olive oil, plus extra for serving
- 4 teaspoons sweet paprika
- 2 teaspoons garam masala
- 6 cups low-sodium chicken broth, plus extra as needed
- 1 pound dried chickpeas (2½ cups), picked over, salt-soaked (see page 153), and rinsed (see note)
- 4 (3-inch-long) strips zest (see the illustration at right) and 1 teaspoon grated zest from 2 lemons
- 2 red or yellow bell peppers, stemmed, seeded, and cut into matchsticks (see the illustrations on page 226)
- 2 (9-ounce) boxes frozen artichokes, thawed (see note)
- ½ cup pitted kalamata olives (see the illustration on page 289), chopped coarse
- ½ cup golden raisins
- ½ cup plain whole-milk Greek yogurt
- ½ cup minced fresh cilantro leaves
- 2 tablespoons honey
    Salt and ground black pepper

1. Microwave the onions, garlic, 2 tablespoons of the oil, paprika, and garam masala together in a medium bowl on high power, stirring occasionally, until the onions are softened, about 5 minutes; transfer to a slow cooker.

2. Stir the broth, chickpeas, and lemon zest strips into the slow cooker. Cover and cook until the chickpeas are tender, 9 to 11 hours on low or 5 to 7 hours on high.

3. Discard the lemon zest strips. Microwave the bell peppers with the remaining 1 tablespoon oil in a medium bowl on high power, stirring occasionally, until tender, about 5 minutes. Stir the softened bell peppers, artichokes, olives, and raisins into the stew, cover, and cook on high until heated through, about 10 minutes.

4. In a bowl, combine ¼ cup of the hot stewing liquid with the yogurt (to temper), then stir the mixture into the stew. Stir in the cilantro, honey, and grated lemon zest. (Adjust the stew consistency with additional hot broth as needed.) Season with salt and pepper to taste and serve with extra-virgin olive oil.

REMOVING LARGE STRIPS OF CITRUS ZEST

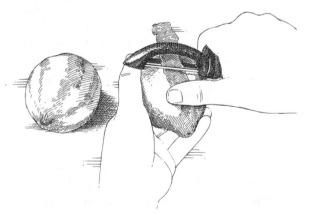

Run a vegetable peeler from pole to pole to remove long, wide strips of zest. Be careful not to remove the white pith, which has a bitter flavor.

10

COOKING FOR COMPANY

Cooking for Company

Roasted Prime Rib and Potatoes

A PRIME RIB IS A LITTLE LIKE A TURKEY: MOST cooks probably cook it only once a year for a special occasion, and in the case of prime rib it's often for Christmas. And because it is an expensive cut, home cooks usually play it safe, sticking to a standard roasting technique, probably learned from their mothers, of using a certain temperature for a set number of minutes per pound of meat. The results are dependable but less than stellar: typically the outer band of the roast is overcooked by the time the center is medium-rare. Not to say this roast still isn't good—prime rib's precious marbling of fat helps tremendously, melting and tenderizing the meat as it cooks—but we wondered if we could do better.

After a little research we found prime rib recipes calling for temperatures ranging from 250 degrees to 425 degrees, and a few recommended an initial high-temperature sear (450 to 500 degrees) followed by reducing the oven temperature to a more moderate 350 degrees to cook the meat through. We started our testing by giving all the options a try. All the prime ribs roasted at oven temperatures exceeding 300 looked pretty much the same: well-done around the exterior, medium toward the center, and a pink medium-rare at the center. Meanwhile, the roast cooked at 250 degrees emerged from the oven with a raw-looking, fatty exterior. Our expectations were low, so we were surprised to discover when we carved the first slice that this roast was beautiful on the inside, all the way from the outer edge to the center. This was the juiciest and most tender of all the roasts we had cooked.

To develop a rich brown crust on large cuts, we usually either pan-sear them before roasting, or we increase the oven temperature for the last few minutes. Prime rib's uneven shape made the stovetop option a little messy and awkward, so we gave the latter method a shot. The results were good: the low heat kept the roast moist during most of the cooking, and a blast of heat at the end melted the flabby external fat and browned the roast.

Now that we had the cooking technique down, we considered sauces or another way to boost the flavor of the meat. Slathering the roast with flavorful herb paste before it went in the oven struck us as a great option. A paste, one that was substantial, would infuse the interior of the meat and also create a satisfying crust that would lend great visual appeal to the centerpiece of our meal.

However, we had problems when we started incorporating the herb paste. A mixture of chopped rosemary and thyme, some olive oil, salt, and pepper went into the oven on top of our prime rib, but it ended up burnt at the bottom of the pan by the end of the roasting time. Our crust needed a binder. We tried eggs, but they imparted a flavor that was out of place on our prime rib. And while the bite of Dijon mustard was a perfect fit with the fresh herbs and sugar lent a nice balance, neither did much to keep the crust together (nevertheless, we kept them both for flavor). In the end, adding a little flour to the mix kept the herb crust firmly in place.

Our crust was now staying put, but it was so substantial that it was getting a little charred. We wondered if we should wait to add the herb paste and reverse the order of the oven temperature, so that the paste could bake for less time and at a more gentle temperature. For our next test, we started the roast naked at 450 degrees. After an hour, when much of the fat was rendered and the roast was well browned (we still wanted browning for flavor), we applied the herb paste and reduced the oven temperature to 250 to finish cooking, which took another 1½ hours. Results: a well-rendered exterior, fragrant herb crust, and a roast that was still plenty juicy and rosy pink. Now we just needed a side dish.

Roasted potatoes seemed like a classic choice here. Red potatoes are our favorite for roasting since they hold their shape and, since they only needed a short stint in a hot oven, we found it easiest to cook them in the 30 minutes of resting time the roast required to allow its juices to redistribute. We found that halving the potatoes and placing them cut side down allowed for maximum contact with the bottom of the roasting pan, resulting in great browning. After transferring the roast to a carving board, we cranked the oven back up to 450 degrees, put the potatoes in the now-vacant roasting pan, and returned the pan to the oven until the potatoes were tender within and crisp on the exterior. When it came to seasoning, salt and pepper was all the potatoes required—they picked up all the flavor they needed from the drippings in the bottom of the roasting pan. This meal was elegant, packed with flavor, and so simple that we now felt sure other special occasions—not just Christmas—would necessitate a prime rib dinner.

HOW TO CARVE PRIME RIB

Carving a bone-in roast as large (and expensive) as a prime rib can be a bit intimidating, but when developing our recipe for Herb-Roasted Prime Rib and Potatoes, we got plenty of practice. Here's the best way to remove the bone and carve this centerpiece roast into perfect slices.

1. Holding the roast in place with a carving fork, remove the meat from the bone by cutting parallel to the rib bones.

2. Place the now-boneless roast cut side down and cut the meat across the grain into ½-inch-thick slices.

Herb-Roasted Prime Rib and Potatoes

SERVES 8 TO 10

Ask your butcher for the first cut of a rib roast (the loin end), with ribs 9 or 10 through 12; it's much less fatty than the second cut (the chuck end; see page 295 for more about the first and second cut). Also, be sure to remove any butcher's twine before cooking. We prefer to use small red potatoes measuring about 1 inch in diameter in this recipe, but you can substitute larger red potatoes, cut into ¾-inch chunks. We prefer this roast cooked to medium-rare, but if you prefer it more or less done, see our guidelines in the chart on page 45.

I	(7-pound) beef standing rib roast, with 3 or 4 ribs (see note)
	Salt and ground black pepper
3	tablespoons minced fresh thyme leaves
3	tablespoons minced fresh rosemary leaves
2	tablespoons Dijon mustard
2	tablespoons olive oil
I	tablespoon unbleached all-purpose flour
I	teaspoon sugar
3	pounds small red potatoes (about 18), scrubbed and cut in half

1. Adjust an oven rack to the lowest position and heat the oven to 450 degrees. Place a V-rack inside a large roasting pan and coat it with vegetable oil spray.

2. Pat the roast dry with paper towels, season with salt and pepper, and place in the prepared V-rack. Roast until well browned, about 1 hour. Meanwhile, combine the thyme, rosemary, mustard, oil, flour, and sugar in a small bowl.

3. Remove the roasting pan from the oven and reduce the oven temperature to 250 degrees. Spread the herb paste evenly over the top of the roast. Continue to roast the beef until it registers 125 degrees on an instant-read thermometer (for medium-rare), about 1½ hours.

4. Transfer the roast to a carving board and let rest for 30 minutes. Increase the oven temperature

to 450 degrees. Remove the V-rack from the roasting pan, then pour off all but 3 tablespoons of the fat left in the pan. Toss the potatoes with salt and pepper and arrange them, cut side down, in the pan. Roast until the potatoes are tender and golden brown, about 30 minutes.

5. Transfer the potatoes to a serving bowl or platter and cover to keep warm. Following the illustrations on page 294, carve the meat off the bones, then cut it into ½-inch-thick slices. Serve with the potatoes.

TO MAKE AHEAD

The herb paste in step 2 can refrigerated in an airtight container for up to 1 day. The potatoes can be prepped, covered with water, and refrigerated for up to 1 day; drain and thoroughly pat dry before cooking. The prime rib can be arranged in the roasting and allowed to sit at room temperature for up to 1 hour before roasting.

INGREDIENTS: Rib Roasts

A whole rib roast (aka prime rib) consists of ribs 6 through 12. Butchers tend to cut the roast in two. We prefer the cut from further back on the cow, closest to the loin. This cut is referred to as the first cut, the loin end, or sometimes the small end because the meat and ribs get larger as they move up toward the shoulder. The first cut can include anywhere from two to four ribs. The first cut, whether you have one that is fewer ribs or more, is more desirable because it contains the large, single rib-eye muscle and is less fatty. The less desirable cut, which is still an excellent roast, is closer to the chuck (or shoulder) end and is sometimes called the second cut. The closer to the chuck, the less tender the roast becomes.

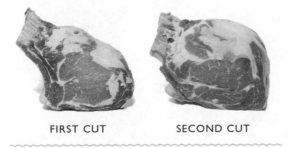

FIRST CUT   **SECOND CUT**

BEEF TENDERLOIN WITH POTATO FANS

WHEN COOKING TO IMPRESS A CROWD, FEW cuts can top a whole beef tenderloin. This elegant roast cooks relatively quickly, and its rich, buttery slices are incredibly fork-tender. But given its high price tag, it's a cut home cooks can find intimidating. We wanted to settle the best way to cook a perfect beef tenderloin. If we could add an equally impressive side dish that could be cooked alongside, we'd have the perfect dinner to serve company.

We started our testing with a trip to our butcher. A whole beef tenderloin can be purchased "unpeeled," which means it has an thick layer of exterior fat left attached, but more often it is sold "peeled," or stripped of this fat. We found the peeled roasts were the more economical choice once you factor in usable meat (stripped of the fat) and time spent if you have to strip the fat from an unpeeled tenderloin.

With our peeled tenderloin in hand, we were ready to start roasting. The problem is that while the tenderloin's sleek, boneless form makes for quick cooking, it is shaped like a torpedo—thick at one end and gradually tapering at the other—which leads to uneven roasting. To fix this, we folded the tip end underneath and tied it in place, which bulked up that end to almost the same thickness as the more substantial butt end. We also tied the roast at 1½-inch intervals, further guaranteeing uniformity. We knew from experience that if left as is, the translucent silver skin encasing the tenderloin would shrink during cooking and cause the meat to bow, so we made sure to cut it at several points.

To determine the ideal roasting temperature, we tested two extremes, roasting one tenderloin at 200 degrees and the other at 500. As expected, the roast cooked at 500 degrees not only created a smoky kitchen from the rendering fat (despite its being a lean roast, this is still an issue), but it was also overcooked at each end and around the perimeter. However, the high oven heat did have one upside: It had given our tenderloin a thick, flavorful crust, which is critical for boosting the appeal of this ultra-tender but otherwise mildly flavored cut. That was a trait missing from our tenderloin cooked at 200 degrees; despite its even, rosy pink interior, that roast lacked the all-important crust.

We didn't want our roast to take all day, so we decided to work our way down from the top. A 450-degree oven still gave us smoke and uneven cooking, so we moved down to 425 degrees. This roast emerged from the oven looking beautiful, and it took just 45 minutes. We felt like we had found the winner, but we decided to run just one more test. Often we cook roasts at two temperatures, a low temperature to gently cook through the interior and a briefer stint at a higher temperature to develop a crust. So we roasted another tenderloin, which we started in a 200-degree oven, increasing to 425 degrees at the end of cooking to develop a crust. To our surprise, this roast looked and tasted almost identical to the roast cooked at 425 the whole time. Because the slow-roasted tenderloin was a hair more fussy and took about twice as long, we settled on the high-heat method and moved on to the side dish.

Since the flavor of tenderloin is relatively mild, we knew it would play well with a side dish that had a strong presence. So far the meal required little kitchen work other than tying the roast, freeing us up to spend a few extra minutes on creating a flavorful, unique side. Not long ago the test kitchen had developed a recipe for baked potato fans, which combine the fluffy interior of a baked potato, the

crisp, golden exterior of an oven fry, and a cheesy spiced topping—all with a distinctive, fanned-out presentation. They struck us as a perfect fit here, and with the tenderloin occupying the center of a rack set in a large rimmed baking sheet, we had two vacant aisles on either side; 10 potatoes (one for each guest), lined up in two diagonal rows, fit perfectly.

The fanning of the potatoes is done by slicing almost all the way through a whole potato crosswise at narrow intervals along its length. Leaving the bottom of the potato intact allows the slices to gently fan open like an accordion as the potato bakes. The skin crisps while the fans create openings into which seasonings, cheese, and bread crumbs can be sprinkled before a final pass in the oven.

Our previous testing had figured out most of the tricky details already. For the type of potato, we had tried red potatoes, but they dried out in the oven, and Yukon Golds were better but still too dry. The russet was the right choice here, as its starchy flesh translated into a fluffy texture when baked.

We cut our russets crosswise into ¼-inch slices, but did not slice all the way through. At first this was a challenge, but after some experimentation we hit upon two tricks that made it nearly foolproof. Slicing off a thin layer lengthwise from each potato created a stable base, or bottom, and placing a chopstick on either side prevented the knife from slicing all the way through. To avoid sticking between each slice, caused by the starch in the potatoes, it was key to give them a quick rinse after slicing. And finally,

PREPPING BAKED POTATO FANS

1. Trim a ¼-inch lengthwise slice from each potato to create a base that will allow it to sit flat, then trim a ¼-inch slice off both ends to give the slices extra room to fan out during baking.

2. Place a chopstick snugly on either side of the potato, running lengthwise. Slice the potatoes crosswise at ¼-inch intervals, leaving the bottom ¼ inch of potato intact (the chopsticks will stop your knife from cutting through).

3. Gently flex the fans open while rinsing under cold running water to rid the potatoes of excess starch, which can impede fanning.

taking a slice off of each end of the potato would give the remaining slices more room to fan out as they baked.

In our original recipe, the prepped potatoes were parcooked in the microwave (a less drying environment than the oven), baked for about 30 minutes in a 450-degree oven, then garnished with the topping and finished under the broiler. So our trick would be to find a way to get perfect baked potato fans cooked along with our beef, and at the same time keep our method as straightforward as possible.

We thought perhaps we could simply cook entrée and side together start to finish, but we were surprised to find the potatoes still hadn't cooked through by the time the beef was done. Following our original recipe, we parcooked the potatoes in the microwave, then cooked them through (without the topping) alongside the beef. By the time the beef was cooked through, the potatoes were crispy outside and tender inside. We then removed the beef from the rack to rest and topped our potatoes with a combination of Parmesan (for nutty flavor), Monterey Jack (because it melts well), and home-made bread crumbs mixed with a little melted butter. Fresh garlic didn't have enough time to cook and mellow, but garlic powder (mixed with some sweet paprika) worked nicely. As a final step, while the beef rested, we added the topping and broiled the potatoes to make the topping irresistibly crunchy.

This was a truly impressive dinner to feed a crowd, and not only was it surprisingly simple to prepare, but perhaps the biggest achievement was that there was only one pan to clean up.

Classic Beef Tenderloin with Crispy Baked Potato Fans

SERVES 10

Unpeeled whole beef tenderloins are cheaper by the pound than peeled but have a thick layer of exterior fat that must be removed; we prefer to buy peeled beef tenderloins that already have this fat removed. To ensure that the potatoes fan out evenly, look for uniformly shaped potatoes. We prefer this roast cooked to medium-rare, but if you prefer it more or less done, see our guidelines in the chart on page 45. Serve with Horseradish Sauce (page 298).

POTATOES

2	slices hearty white sandwich bread, torn into quarters
8	tablespoons (1 stick) unsalted butter, melted
4	ounces Monterey Jack cheese, shredded (1 cup)
1	ounce Parmesan cheese, grated (½ cup)
1	teaspoon paprika
1	teaspoon garlic powder
	Salt and ground black pepper
10	medium russet potatoes (7 to 9 ounces each), scrubbed
6	tablespoons extra-virgin olive oil

BEEF

1	whole peeled beef tenderloin (5 to 6 pounds), silver skin cut, tip end tucked under, and tied (see the illustrations below) (see note)
2	tablespoons olive oil
	Salt and ground black pepper

PREPARING A WHOLE BEEF TENDERLOIN

1. To keep the meat from bowing as it cooks, slide a knife under the silver skin and flick the blade upward. Do this at 5 or 6 spots along the length of the roast.

2. To ensure that the tenderloin roasts more evenly, fold 6 inches of the thin tip end under the roast.

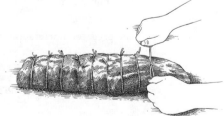

3. For more even cooking and evenly sized slices, use 12-inch lengths of kitchen twine to tie the roast every 1½ inches.

1. **FOR THE POTATOES:** Adjust an oven rack to the lower-middle position and heat the oven to 200 degrees. Pulse the bread in a food processor until coarsely ground, about 8 pulses. Bake the bread crumbs on a large rimmed baking sheet until dry, about 20 minutes. Let the bread crumbs cool slightly, then toss with the butter, cheeses, paprika, garlic powder, ½ teaspoon salt, and ½ teaspoon pepper in a large bowl.

2. Increase the oven to 425 degrees. Place a wire rack inside an aluminum foil–lined rimmed baking sheet and coat it with vegetable oil spray. Following the illustrations on page 296, trim a ¼-inch slice off the length and off both ends of each potato. Place the potatoes on their cut base, then cut the potatoes into fans by slicing them crosswise at ¼-inch intervals, leaving the bottom ¼ inch of the potato intact. Gently rinse the potatoes fans under running water, then let drain.

3. Working with half of the potatoes at time, place them, sliced side down, on a large microwave-safe plate and microwave on high power until slightly soft, 6 to 12 minutes, flipping them halfway through cooking. Brush the potatoes thoroughly with the oil (skin and flesh) and season with salt and pepper to taste.

4. **FOR THE BEEF:** Pat the roast dry with paper towels, coat with the oil, and season with salt and pepper. Lay the roast down the center of the rack on the prepared baking sheet. Arrange the potato fans, sliced side up, on the baking sheet on either side of the beef, angling the potatoes as needed to fit.

5. Roast until the beef registers 120 to 125 degrees on an instant-read thermometer (for medium-rare) and the skin of the potatoes is crisp and the potatoes are beginning to brown, 45 to 60 minutes. Remove the baking sheet from the oven. Transfer the roast to a carving board and let rest for 20 minutes.

6. Meanwhile, position an oven rack 9 inches from the broiler element and heat the broiler. Carefully top the potatoes with the processed bread mixture, pressing gently to adhere. Return the potatoes to the oven and broil until the topping is deep golden brown, about 3 minutes. Remove from the oven and tent loosely with foil to keep warm.

7. Remove the twine from the beef and cut the meat crosswise into ½-inch-thick slices. Serve with the potatoes.

TO MAKE AHEAD

The bread-crumb topping in step 1 can be refrigerated in a zipper-lock bag for up to 2 days. The potato fans can be prepped through step 2, covered with water, and refrigerated for up to 1 day; drain before proceeding with step 3. The beef and potato fans can be arranged on the baking sheet and allowed to sit at room temperature for up to 1 hour before roasting.

Horseradish Sauce

MAKES ABOUT 1 ¾ CUPS

Brands of prepared horseradish can vary dramatically in flavor and intensity; season with additional horseradish to taste.

1	cup sour cream
¼	cup mayonnaise
½	cup prepared horseradish, plus extra to taste
½	teaspoon sugar
	Salt and ground black pepper

Mix all the ingredients together in a serving bowl. Season with additional horseradish, salt, and pepper to taste. Cover with plastic wrap and refrigerate for 30 minutes before serving.

RACK OF PORK WITH AUTUMN VEGETABLES

WITH ITS FRENCHED BONES RISING AROUND the circular perimeter, stuffing in the shallow center, and ornate finishes like the paper frills that look like little hats perched on the tips of the bones, a crown roast of pork makes quite a centerpiece. This traditional roast consists of two center-cut, bone-in pork loins trussed together to form a ring. But beyond the spectacle, it typically has little to offer in the way of flavor and is typically overcooked and dry. And let's be honest: to the modern eye, there is something a little silly and ostentatious about the crown roast, like an overly groomed poodle. But on the flip side, a plain pork roast isn't very exciting for a special occasion. We wondered, was there something between the two? The answer, we realized, is a rack of pork.

Though we would be roasting the same cut of pork as a crown roast (two bone-in loin roasts), we would have several advantages right out of the gate. To fashion racks into a crown roast, the chine bone (the backbone) is often removed, robbing the meat of a source of much-needed flavor. Meanwhile, cooking separate racks does not require complete removal of the chine bone; you only need to remove its tip and slice the bone between each rib for easy carving. Also, a crown roast is prone to uneven cooking, as the bones, pointed upward, brown while the loin steams in the juice below. Roasting the racks separately would give us a better opportunity to brown the roast on all sides and cook it more evenly.

Our first task was to get the racks of pork to taste as good as they looked, a challenging task given today's lean pork. Although we have traditionally brined pork in a saltwater solution to keep it flavorful and moist, when dealing with a larger roast (and in this case, two roasts) it's tricky to fit a big container of pork and brine in the refrigerator. Since the roasts need to be rinsed after brining, it is a messy endeavor as well. Another option is to salt the meat overnight. When salt is applied to raw meat, juice inside the meat is drawn to the surface. The salt then dissolves in the exuded liquid, forming a sort of brine that is eventually reabsorbed by the meat. The result? Juicy, evenly seasoned meat. And because the pork is reabsorbing its own juice (not plain water, as in a brine), it has an appealingly pure pork flavor. We rubbed the pork roasts with 3 tablespoons kosher salt (we find its coarse texture makes it easier to sprinkle evenly than table salt), wrapped them with plastic wrap, and stashed them in the refrigerator for several hours (they would be fine refrigerated for up to a day).

Next we addressed oven temperatures, testing increments ranging from 250 to 450 degrees. Higher temperatures resulted in tougher, drier meat that was unevenly cooked. Given the relative leanness of the pork, a gentle 250-degree oven produced the best results. But while this meat was juicy and moist, the exterior was somewhat pale and unattractive. Raising the heat to 450 degrees for the final 20 minutes of cooking allowed for a gradual increase in temperature that browned the crust without losing significant moisture in the meat. Rubbing the racks with a light herb paste of chopped thyme or rosemary further improved their appearance and flavor.

Since we were cooking the racks on a V-rack set in a roasting pan (to allow for air circulation), the bottom of the pan provided empty real estate we could use for a side dish. We felt the roasted racks of pork had an autumn-harvest feel, so we considered vegetables that would fit this theme. Brussels sprouts came to mind first, but the gentle, low heat of the oven caused them to steam rather than roast, giving them a cabbage-y off-flavor. Butternut squash, however, worked perfectly and it complemented the pork's natural sweetness. Tasters also liked potatoes and shallots in the mix. Red potatoes were our choice here since they would hold their shape well, and because they take longer to cook than the squash, we found it best to cut them into slightly smaller pieces than the squash. The shallots we peeled and halved.

After about an hour and a half, the pork was done and the vegetables were tender, but the vegetables were not as brown and flavorful as we wanted. Returning them to the oven for 20 minutes while the racks rested gave us well-browned vegetables to present alongside the attractive roasts.

As a final finishing touch, we whipped up a fresh herb sauce for the pork while the meat was resting and the vegetables were finishing up. Starting with a few of the ingredients we were already using—olive oil, minced thyme, and shallot—we whisked in sherry vinegar, some additional herbs (basil and parsley) for another hit of freshness, and a little honey to balance the acidity. This modern take on crown roast was an impressive centerpiece, and it didn't hurt that it tasted as good as it looked.

Rack of Pork with Autumn Vegetables

SERVES 10

If your butcher frenches the racks for you, make sure to scrape the rib bones with a paring knife to remove any scraps of meat or fat they might have missed. Kosher salt is preferable to table salt for salting the meat, since its coarse texture makes it easier to sprinkle evenly, but you can use 1 tablespoon table salt instead.

PORK AND VEGETABLES

- 2 (5-pound) bone-in pork loin roasts, with 5 to 6 ribs each, tip of chine removed, chine bone cut between each rib, bones frenched and scraped clean (see the illustrations at left) Kosher salt (see note)
- 1 medium butternut squash (about 2 pounds), peeled, seeded, and cut into 1-inch pieces
- 2 pounds red potatoes (about 6 medium), scrubbed and cut into ¾-inch chunks
- 8 ounces large shallots (about 6), peeled and halved
- 6 tablespoons olive oil Ground black pepper
- 3 medium garlic cloves, minced or pressed through a garlic press (about 1 tablespoon)
- 2 tablespoons minced fresh thyme, sage, or rosemary leaves

SAUCE

- ¼ cup olive oil
- 1 medium shallot, minced (about 3 tablespoons)
- 2 tablespoons sherry vinegar
- 2 teaspoons minced fresh thyme leaves
- 3 tablespoons minced fresh basil leaves
- 2 tablespoons minced fresh parsley leaves
- 2 teaspoons honey Salt and ground black pepper

1. FOR THE PORK AND VEGETABLES: Rub each roast evenly with 1½ tablespoons kosher salt, wrap tightly with plastic wrap, and refrigerate at least 6 hours or up to 24 hours.

2. Adjust an oven rack to the lower-middle position and heat the oven to 250 degrees. Place a V-rack inside a large roasting pan and coat it with vegetable oil spray. Toss the squash, potatoes, and shallots with ¼ cup of the oil and season with salt and pepper to taste. Spread the vegetables into the roasting pan underneath the V-rack.

3. Combine the garlic, thyme, 2 teaspoons pepper, and remaining 2 tablespoons oil in a small bowl to make a thick paste. Pat the pork dry with paper towels, then rub evenly with the paste. Place the loins in the prepared V-rack. Roast until the pork registers 120 degrees on an instant-read thermometer, 1¼ to 1½ hours.

4. Increase the oven temperature to 450 degrees and continue to roast the pork until it registers 140 to 145 degrees on an instant-read thermometer, about 20 minutes longer. Transfer the roasts to a carving board and let rest for 20 minutes.

5. While the pork rests, remove the V-rack from the roasting pan and stir the vegetables. Return the vegetables to the oven and continue to roast until they are fully tender and well browned, 15 to 20 minutes. Transfer to a serving bowl or platter and cover to keep warm.

6. FOR THE SAUCE: Whisk all the sauce ingredients together in a small serving bowl and season with salt and pepper to taste.

7. Carve the roasts, cutting between each rib. Serve with the vegetables, passing the sauce separately.

TO MAKE AHEAD

The squash and shallots can be prepped and refrigerated in an airtight container for up to 1 day. The potatoes can be prepped, covered with water, and refrigerated for up to 1 day; drain and thoroughly pat dry before proceeding with step 2. The pork and potatoes can be arranged in the roasting pan and allowed to sit at room temperature for up to 1 hour before roasting. The sauce can be refrigerated in an airtight container for up to 3 hours before serving.

PREPARING A RACK OF PORK

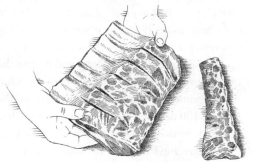

1. So that chops can be easily carved from the roast, have the butcher remove the tip of the chine bone and slice the chine bone between each rib. When you pull the roast apart, you should be able to see the cuts between the individual chops.

2. Before the ribs can be frenched, the fatty piece that covers the ribs must be removed. You can ask your butcher to do this, or you can do it yourself.

3. Use a paring knife to remove the meat from between each rib. If possible, have the butcher do this step as well.

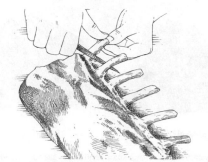

4. Scrape the bones with the paring knife to remove any remaining pieces of meat or fat.

GLAZED HAM WITH CARROTS AND FENNEL

IT'S EASY TO UNDERSTAND WHY HAM IS served at just about every major holiday. Since it is already cooked and cured, all a supermarket ham needs is a glaze and some time in the oven and you're good to go. So why is it that all too often we are served ham that tastes like salty jerky with a sticky, saccharine exterior? Ideally, ham is moist and tender and the glaze complements—but doesn't overwhelm—the meat. We've cooked hundreds of hams here over the years and have had our share of disasters, so we decided to reexamine this topic to settle what really works—and what doesn't.

Supermarket hams come boneless, semiboneless, bone-in, whole, and half. Each of these types is available unsliced or presliced (often labeled "spiral-sliced"). We favor bone-in hams that have been spiral-sliced, as they offer the best flavor with the least amount of post-cooking carving. A whole ham is the entire leg of the animal, so unless you are feeding a very large crowd, we recommend a half ham. Half hams are available in two cuts: shank end (the bottom part of the leg) and sirloin end (the portion of the leg closer to the rump). If labeling is unclear, it's easy to identify half hams by shape—shank hams have a pointed end much smaller than the larger end, whereas the sirloin end is rounded. A few basics tests proved the shank end is the better choice for ease of carving since the bone is relatively straight compared with the odder-shaped bones in the sirloin end.

Reading labels is also important. Typically, supermarket hams are wet-cured, a process that involves soaking the ham in or injecting it with a brine. During this process, the ham absorbs water and gains weight. Not surprisingly, we found hams that gained the least water weight (labeled "ham with natural juices") taste the best. Avoid labels that read "ham with water added" or "ham and water products."

Now, we know what you're thinking: If a spiral-sliced ham is already cooked, why do you have to cook it? Well, truth be told, there is nothing you have to do to serve a cured and cooked ham other than cut it off the bone. When ham is the centerpiece of a holiday dinner, however, most

301

people prefer to have it served warm, and often with a glaze. After roasting a number of hams to internal temperatures ranging from 100 to 160 degrees, we found the ham was best heated to a temperature somewhere between 110 and 120 degrees. This was enough to take the chill off the meat without drying it out; any higher (which many sources suggest) and we ended up with dry meat.

Most recipes we found cooked the ham in a 350-degree oven until it reached its target temperature, but we found that even at this relatively modest temperature, the resulting ham was tough, with a parched exterior. After numerous tests, we found that a 250-degree oven yielded much better results; this low temperature lessened the differential between the exterior and the interior as the ham cooked. We also found that placing the ham in hot tap water for 90 minutes prior to cooking took the chill off the exterior of the ham, further ensuring that it would heat evenly.

While many cooks set the ham directly in the roasting pan, we discovered that roasting the ham in an oven bag reduced the amount of moisture lost in a 10-pound ham by as much as 50 percent. A few tests proved that aluminum foil worked fine when we couldn't get our hands on an oven bag, but we had to add three to four minutes of cooking time per pound of meat (between 21 and 40 minutes for a 7- to 10-pound ham).

Almost all supermarket hams come with a packet of premixed glaze and instructions to brush it on the ham while cooking. Glaze is a good idea, but tasters agreed that the stuff in the packets tasted awful. We knew we'd be far better off making our own glaze strictly with pantry ingredients. A combination of maple syrup and orange marmalade (two popular ham flavorings) was already close to the right glaze consistency; it was just a little loose. A few minutes of simmering in the microwave was all it needed. The addition of a little butter added richness and body, and some tangy Dijon mustard balanced the sweetness (and was also a classic flavor match for the ham). Since ham is so salty, we didn't add any additional salt to the glaze, just some ground black pepper and a little cinnamon.

This small amount of effort was all that was required to make a flavorful glaze that was heads and tails above the saccharine stuff in the packets. But now that we had a great glaze, we needed to figure out how to apply it. Since we were cooking our ham inside an oven bag, it wasn't as simple as occasionally opening the oven door and giving the ham a quick brushing. We found our best approach was to wait until the internal temperature of the ham reached 100 degrees, then we cut open the bag and increased the oven temperature to 350. We then applied the glaze and baked the ham for 10 minutes. After removing the ham from the oven, we applied another layer, which gave our finished ham a good, shiny finish. We still had a little glaze left over, so we decided this was a perfect opportunity to create a sauce for passing at the table. To give our remaining glaze a bit more depth, we combined it with the ham's drippings left behind in the oven bag, and while this boosted the glaze's flavor and turned it into a more savory sauce, it did make it a bit looser than we wanted. The solution was simple: a few more minutes in the microwave solved the problem.

Finally, we tested whether or not the ham needed to rest before serving. Because a 15-minute rest allowed the internal temperature to increase by 5 to 15 degrees, we settled on letting it rest and simply decreased the baking time.

To round out the meal, we decided to roast some vegetables alongside the ham. Since we would need to feed a crowd, carrots seemed a good option; relatively inexpensive and readily available, carrots become exceptionally sweet and appealing when roasted. Pairing the carrots with anise-flavored fennel added further depth of flavor and an upscale

CHOOSING A SPIRAL-SLICED HAM

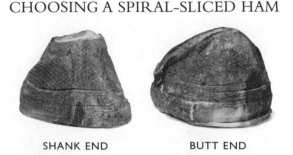

SHANK END BUTT END

For easy carving, look for a shank-end spiral-sliced ham, which has a tapered, pointed end opposite the cut side. The sirloin, or butt, end has a rounded, blunt end.

flare. In addition to salt and pepper, we tossed the vegetables with a few garlic cloves (left whole), minced thyme, and olive oil before adding them to the roasting with the ham.

When it came time to cook everything together, we ran into problems. With the low oven temperature and enough vegetables for 16 people in our pan, the crowded vegetables were far from cooked through by the time the ham was done. Parcooking the vegetables in the microwave before adding them to the pan with the ham gave them a jump start, but they needed exposure to high, dry heat to develop flavor. So while the ham was resting, we cranked the heat to 450 and returned the vegetables to the oven. This final stint ensured vegetables that were fully tender and flavorful.

Requiring minimal work of the home cook and delivering juicy meat and flavorful results, this ham and roasted vegetable dinner was ready for Christmas, Easter, or any holiday celebration.

Maple-Orange Glazed Spiral-Sliced Ham with Carrots and Fennel

SERVES 16

Make sure the plastic or foil covering the ham is intact and waterproof before covering the ham with warm water in step 1; if there is a hole in the covering, wrap the ham in several layers of plastic wrap. In step 3, instead of using a plastic oven bag, the ham may be placed cut side down in the roasting pan and covered tightly with aluminum foil, but you will need to add 3 to 4 minutes per pound to the heating time in step 4. If using an oven bag, be sure to cut slits in the bag so it does not burst. If the stem ends of your carrots are very thick, slice them in half lengthwise first to ensure even cooking.

HAM AND VEGETABLES

1	(7- to 10-pound) spiral-sliced bone-in half ham, preferably shank end, plastic or foil covering intact (see note)
4	pounds carrots (about 24 medium), peeled and cut into 2-inch lengths

TRIMMING THE OVEN BAG

Use scissors to trim the oven bag, leaving 1 inch above the tie.

3	large fennel bulbs (about 3 pounds), trimmed of stalks, cored, and cut into ½-inch-thick strips (see the illustrations on page 38)
4	medium garlic cloves, peeled
¼	cup water
¼	cup olive oil
1	tablespoon minced fresh thyme leaves
	Salt and ground black pepper
1	large plastic oven bag (see note)

GLAZE

¾	cup maple syrup
½	cup orange marmalade
2	tablespoons unsalted butter, melted
1	tablespoon Dijon mustard
1	teaspoon ground black pepper
¼	teaspoon ground cinnamon

1. FOR THE HAM AND VEGETABLES: Place the wrapped ham in a stockpot or large container, cover with hot tap water, and let sit for 45 minutes. Drain, cover again with hot tap water, and let sit for 45 minutes longer.

2. Meanwhile, combine the carrots, fennel, garlic, and water in a large microwave-safe bowl. Cover and microwave on high power until the vegetables have softened, 10 to 15 minutes. Drain the vegetables well, then toss with the oil and thyme and season with salt and pepper to taste.

CARVING A SPIRAL-SLICED HAM

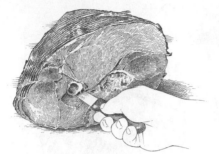

1. With the tip of a paring or carving knife, cut around the bone to loosen the attached slices.

2. Using a long carving knife, slice horizontally above the bone and through the spiral-cut slices, toward the back of the ham.

3. Pull the cut portion away from the bone and cut between the slices to separate them fully.

4. Beginning at the tapered end, slice above the bone to remove the remaining chunk of meat. Flip the ham over and repeat the procedure for the other side.

3. Adjust an oven rack to the lowest position and heat the oven to 250 degrees. Unwrap the ham, discarding the plastic disk covering the bone. Place the ham in an oven bag. Gather the top of the bag tightly so the bag fits snugly around the ham and trim the excess plastic following the illustration on page 303.

4. Place the bagged ham, cut side down, in a large roasting pan and cut 4 slits in the top of the bag. Arrange the vegetables in the roasting pan around the ham. Bake until the ham registers 100 degrees on an instant-read thermometer, 1 to 1½ hours (about 10 minutes per pound).

5. FOR THE GLAZE: Whisk all the glaze ingredients together in a medium microwave-safe bowl. Microwave on high power until the mixture thickens slightly, 3 to 5 minutes. Cover to keep warm and set aside. (The glaze will thicken as it cools between bastings; rewarm as needed to loosen.)

6. Remove the ham from the oven and increase the oven temperature to 350 degrees. Cut open the oven bag and roll back the sides to expose the ham. Brush the ham with one-third of the glaze and continue to cook until the glaze becomes sticky, about 10 minutes longer.

7. Remove the roasting pan from the oven and increase the oven temperature to 450 degrees. Transfer the ham to a carving board, reserving ⅓ cup of the juice left in the bag, and discard the bag. Brush the ham with half of the remaining glaze, tent loosely with foil, and let rest for 20 minutes.

8. While the ham rests, stir the vegetables and continue to roast until fully tender, about 20 minutes. Transfer to a serving bowl or platter and cover to keep warm.

9. Whisk the reserved juice into the remaining glaze and microwave on high power until thickened and saucy, 1 to 2 minutes. Transfer to a serving bowl and cover to keep warm. Carve the ham following the illustrations at left and serve with the roasted vegetables, passing the sauce separately.

TO MAKE-AHEAD

The carrots and fennel can be prepped and refrigerated in an airtight container for up to 1 day. The glaze ingredients can be combined and held at room temperature for several hours before microwaving in step 5.

PROVENÇAL BEEF STEW

STEWS ARE IDEAL FOR FEEDING A GROUP with little fuss: After you assemble the stew and put it in the oven, you have several hours of walk-away time to clean up, prepare for guests, or enjoy a glass or two of wine. Stews also hold well, so they can be made days ahead and reheated. But most stews, while appealing, seem a bit commonplace for a special occasion. Enter daube Provençal, a dressed-up beef stew that hails from Nice, France, and features a varied mix of ingredients, including olives, tomatoes, oranges, mushrooms, anchovies, garlic, and red wine (all native to the local region). This stew has a sunny flavor that makes it anything but commonplace.

Our game plan was to scale up the ingredients of our classic beef stew recipe (see page 131), adapting the cooking technique as needed for a larger batch, and then incorporating the ingredients that are the hallmark of daube Provençal.

The first issue we faced was choosing the right cooking vessel. While the large Dutch oven we use for regular stews was fine for browning the meat for this recipe, it wasn't large enough to cook the stew. We had already learned that beef stew requires the slow, gentle heat of the oven and we found that a stockpot, with its tall, narrow shape, just isn't ideal for the oven; its depth and small surface area kept the large batch of stew from cooking evenly and the sauce from reducing properly. Our solution? A roasting pan. It exposed a larger area of the stew to the oven's heat, thereby keeping the entire stew at the proper simmering temperature for the duration of the cooking time.

With our cookware settled, we moved on to the recipe itself. A typical beef stew serves about six people and calls for roughly 3½ pounds of chuck-eye roast. We wanted our stew to serve a crowd of 12 to 14 people, so we determined that 7 pounds of meat, trimmed and cut into substantial 2-inch chunks (as in traditional daube recipes), was the right amount. Browning the meat was our first step, and we noted that several Provençal recipes called for browning the beef in olive oil rather than rendered pork fat or vegetable oil (the fats common to most other beef stew recipes). And in fact, we found that we liked the Mediterranean flavor of olive oil here; we just had to make sure to keep an eye on the pot

to make sure it didn't scorch (olive oil has a lower smoke point than the other oils).

One timesaving discovery we made early on was that it wasn't necessary to brown *all* the meat. The browned bits (fond) left in the pot after browning the meat are important for flavoring the dish, but we found just half of our meat, browned in two batches, provided plenty of flavor for our stew. So we started our recipe by setting aside half of the raw beef in the roasting pan, then browned the remainder of the meat in the Dutch oven. We transferred the browned meat to the roasting pan, deglazed the Dutch oven with some red wine, added a touch of flour (to thicken the stew) and tomato paste (for deep, slow-cooked flavor), then poured in all the cooking liquid (we found that equal parts store-bought chicken and beef broth provided the most balanced flavor) and brought it to a simmer. This sauce went into the roasting pan with the meat (along with some carrots), and the roasting pan went into the oven.

With our basic technique settled, we could focus on building the Provençal flavor of the stew, working our way through the list of traditional inclusions. Tasters loved the earthiness contributed by dried porcini. Niçoise olives lent a briny and authentic local flavor and tomatoes (we opted for canned for their year-round dependability) brought brightness and texture. Orange peel contributed a subtle floral element, while herbs, particularly thyme and bay leaves, are a natural addition to anything from Provence. Seven garlic cloves, sliced thin and added straight to the cooking liquid, imbued the whole dish with their aroma.

Things were going well, but tasters weren't enthusiastic about every ingredient we tried. When we broached the subject of anchovies, some tasters were unwilling to even consider them, claiming that these pungent fish have no place in beef stew. But when we made our stew without the anchovies, tasters complained that the stew lacked depth of flavor. Over the next couple of days, we quietly added the anchovies back in one at a time, maxing out at five fillets. Tasters praised the rich, earthy flavors of this stew and we just kept the secret ingredient to ourselves.

Pig's trotters (i.e., pig's feet), a standard ingredient in many older recipes, contribute gelatin, which lends the sauce body, and pork meat and fat, which provide flavor. But the protests against a foot in the stew were too much; this time we caved. We substituted salt pork and adjusted the amount of salt in the stew to accommodate it. The salt pork, like the anchovies, added a noticeable, welcome richness. Just two pieces did the job well, and we removed and discarded them before serving, once they had given up their flavor to the stew.

Red wine is also a key ingredient in daube Provençal. Thus far we had been using three-quarters of a bottle of wine, but the flavor was barely noticeable amid the other ingredients. Could we add more? Conservatively, we began adding more wine, being careful not to sacrifice the integrity of the other flavors. In the end, we discovered that this stew was bold enough to accommodate a full bottle and a half. The wine (we liked Cabernet Sauvignon, but Côtes du Rhône and Zinfandel worked well too) gave the sauce rich, round flavors and a velvety texture.

To thicken the stew, we had been following our established technique and sprinkling flour into the pot to cook with the vegetables and tomato paste. But simply scaling up the flour amount wasn't enough, in large part because the unbrowned meat was releasing a lot more moisture as it cooked. Starting with ½ cup flour, we increased the flour in increments and eventually settled on a full cup. The result was immediately noticeable. The extra flour created a braising liquid that thickened to the consistency of a luxurious sauce.

After 3½ hours in the oven, our stew offered tender, flavorful beef swathed in a velvety sauce with all the bright and briny flavors of Provence. With a touch of parsley stirred in before serving, this was an elegant, perfect rendition of a French classic, ideal for our next large dinner party.

Provençal Beef Stew

SERVES 12 TO 14

You will need a roasting pan that measures about 18 by 13 inches with 4-inch-high sides for this recipe; alternatively, you can use 2 disposable aluminum roasting pans with these same dimensions, one nested inside the other and supported by a baking sheet. We tie the salt pork with twine in order to make it easy to identify (and thus remove) after cooking. You can substitute 6 ounces of uncooked bacon for the salt pork (make sure to remove it before serving). Cabernet Sauvignon is our favorite wine for this recipe, but Côtes du Rhône and Zinfandel also work. If niçoise olives are not available, kalamata olives can be substituted. The pan of stew will be heavy so use caution when handling. Serve with polenta, buttered egg noodles, or boiled potatoes.

2	pounds carrots (about 12 medium), peeled and sliced 1 inch thick
2	(3-ounce) pieces salt pork, rind removed, tied tightly with kitchen twine
7	(3-inch-long) strips orange zest from 1 orange (see page 290), trimmed of white pith and cut into thin matchsticks
7	medium garlic cloves, peeled and sliced thin
5	anchovy fillets, rinsed and minced
8	sprigs fresh thyme, tied together with kitchen twine
3	bay leaves
7	pounds boneless beef chuck-eye roast, trimmed and cut into 2-inch pieces (see the illustrations on page 133)
1½	cups pitted niçoise olives (see the illustration on page 289), patted dry and chopped coarse
	Salt and ground black pepper
7	tablespoons olive oil
2	pounds onions (about 4 medium), halved and sliced pole to pole into ⅛-inch-thick pieces (see the illustration on page 134)
1	ounce dried porcini mushrooms, rinsed and minced
1	cup unbleached all-purpose flour
¼	cup tomato paste
4⅔	cups dry red wine (about 1½ bottles)
2	cups low-sodium chicken broth
2	cups beef broth
1	(28-ounce) can whole tomatoes, drained and chopped into ½-inch pieces
⅓	cup minced fresh parsley leaves

1. Adjust an oven rack to the lower-middle position and heat the oven to 325 degrees. Place the carrots, salt pork, orange zest, garlic, anchovies, thyme bundle, bay leaves, half of the meat, and half of the olives in a large roasting pan; set aside.

2. Pat the remaining meat dry with paper towels and season with salt and pepper. Heat 1 tablespoon of the oil in a large Dutch oven over medium-high heat until just smoking. Add one-half of the meat and brown well on all sides, 7 to 10 minutes; transfer to the roasting pan. Repeat with 1 tablespoon more oil and the remaining meat; transfer to the roasting pan.

3. Add the remaining 5 tablespoons oil to the pot and heat over medium heat until shimmering. Add the onions, mushrooms, and 1 teaspoon salt and cook until softened, 7 to 10 minutes. Stir in the flour and tomato paste and cook for 1 minute. Gradually whisk in the wine, scraping up any browned bits and smoothing out any lumps. Gradually whisk in the chicken broth and beef broth and bring to a boil. Pour the mixture into the roasting pan and stir to combine.

4. Cover the pan tightly with aluminum foil. Place the roasting pan in the oven and cook until the meat is tender and the sauce is thickened and glossy, 3¼ to 3¾ hours.

5. Remove the stew from the oven and remove the salt pork, thyme bundle, and bay leaves. Stir in the tomatoes and remaining olives, cover, and let sit for 10 minutes. Stir in the parsley, season with salt and pepper to taste, and serve.

TO MAKE AHEAD

The stew can be prepared through step 4, then cooled for 45 minutes. Cover the roasting pan tightly with foil and refrigerate for up to 2 days. (We think storing and reheating the stew in the roasting pan is best because it minimizes handling so the tender pieces of meat stay intact. If tight on space, you can transfer the stew to an airtight container; return it to the roasting pan before continuing.) To serve, remove any fat that has collected on top and re-cover the pan tightly with foil. Reheat the stew in a 425-degree oven until hot, 1 to 1½ hours. Add water as needed to adjust the stew's consistency and continue with step 5 as directed.

LAMB TAGINE

HAVING JUST DEVELOPED A RECIPE FOR Provençal Beef Stew (page 306), we realized there were a multitude of other stews that could work equally well as an elegant entrée to serve a crowd. As we considered other options, we thought of tagines, exotically spiced, assertively flavored stews that are a specialty of Morocco. Typically slow cooked in earthenware vessels of the same name, tagines are highly aromatic and usually feature a blend of sweet and savory ingredients. Although tagines can include all manner of meats, vegetables, and fruit (usually dried), one of our upscale favorites combines moist, succulent chunks of lamb with apricots, as well as a heady mixture of ground spices, garlic, and cilantro. With its balance of sweet, savory, and bold flavors, it seemed like a great dish to further round out our cooking-for-company recipe collection.

Traditionally, tagine recipes require time-consuming cooking methods, a special pot (the tagine), and hard-to-find ingredients. But we weren't intimidated; we knew that at its most elemental level, a tagine is really just a stew. Our goal for this recipe was to develop a dish that kept the authentic flavors of Morocco but eliminated most of the fuss. This meant shortening the ingredient list and forgoing the tagine as our cookware. We also wanted a batch suitably sized for company, so we knew our vessel of choice would be a roasting pan, which we had found in earlier testing worked well when cooking larger batches of stew. A roasting pan allows for enough of the surface area of the stew to be exposed so that in the oven the components cook evenly and the liquid is able to reduce properly.

When making lamb stews in the past, we have used both the meat and the bones from lamb shoulder chops for maximum flavor. But given the abundance of flavors in a tagine, we wondered if we could simplify the process and use boneless lamb shoulder meat here instead. After giving it a try in a basic working recipe, we were happy to find that no one missed the subtle complexity provided by the bones.

As with our large batch of Provençal Beef Stew, we found it wasn't necessary to brown all of the meat; the fond produced by browning half of the lamb gave the tagine plenty of deep flavor. Our process here was also similar to the beef stew. After browning half the meat (in two batches) in a large Dutch oven, we set it aside in the roasting pan along with the unbrowned meat. Then we could build the rest of the stew in the Dutch oven, transfer it to the roasting pan, and put the whole thing in the oven.

We focused on the spices next. Sweet, warm spices are typically used in North African cooking. Ground cinnamon and ginger were quickly voted in by tasters, as was cumin. Most everyone liked the addition of some fragrant coriander, but they were divided about cayenne, so we decided to make that spice optional.

Although some sources we found suggested tossing the meat with the spices before browning it, we found that this caused the spices to burn. On the other extreme, some recipes add the spices with the liquid, but the spices in these instances still tasted raw and sharp after the stew was done, and the stew lacked depth. In the test kitchen we often bloom dried spices in oil, a step that greatly enhances their flavor. So after we had browned the meat, we sautéed some garlic and onions in oil, then we added some flour (for thickening the stew) and the spices to the pot. One minute of sautéing was all it took to bring their flavor to the next level. We found that it was best to use a strong hand with the garlic given all the other bold flavors in our bold stew, and we eventually settled on nine cloves.

As for cooking liquid, some traditional recipes call for lamb stock, but we wondered how store-bought broths, a far less fussy option, would perform. After testing store-bought chicken broth, store-bought beef broth, and a combination of the two, we found we liked the store-bought chicken broth the best. It added body to the stew but didn't compete with the distinct lamb flavor.

Tomatoes are another constant in most tagines. We found that canned diced tomatoes provided an acidic contrast that heightened the other flavors and also stayed relatively intact throughout cooking, adding texture as well. We tested several other vegetables, including summer squash, sweet potatoes, and potatoes. All were delicious, but we eventually decided none were essential to our recipe; the tomatoes and onions could carry the day. We did like the addition of chickpeas, another common tagine ingredient. The test kitchen has found that canned chickpeas are in most situations as good as their dried counterpart, though we did decide to add them at the end. This way their skins retained more bite and remained more distinct, resulting in a tagine with a cleaner flavor and some textural contrast.

As for fruits, we already knew apricots were our favored choice, but we nevertheless tested a variety of other options. Prunes, raisins, and dried currants all worked well, so we made them alternate choices. Some cilantro added at the end was all it needed.

Once we moved our roasting pan with the stew into the oven, aside from a few periodic stirs it was conveniently hands-off. While the heady aroma of our Lamb Tagine filled the house, we were happily free to entertain our guests.

Lamb Tagine
SERVES 12 TO 14

You will need a roasting pan that measures about 18 by 13 inches with 4-inch-high sides for this recipe; alternatively, you can use 2 disposable aluminum roasting pans with these same dimensions, one nested inside the other and supported by a baking sheet. If you can't find boneless lamb shoulder, you can purchase blade or arm chops and remove the meat yourself. Buy 12½ pounds of chops to yield the 7 pounds of boneless meat needed for this recipe. Prunes, raisins, golden raisins, or dried currants can be substituted for the apricots. The pan of stew will be heavy so use caution when handling. Serve with couscous or rice.

2   cups dried apricots (about 12 ounces), chopped coarse (see the illustration on page 283)

3   bay leaves

7   pounds boneless lamb shoulder, trimmed and cut into 1½-inch pieces (see note)
    Salt and ground black pepper

¼   cup olive oil

2   pounds onions (about 4 medium), chopped medium

9   medium garlic cloves, minced or pressed through a garlic press (about 3 tablespoons)

6   tablespoons unbleached all-purpose flour

1   tablespoon ground cumin

2   teaspoons ground cinnamon

2   teaspoons ground ginger

1	teaspoon ground coriander
¼	teaspoon cayenne pepper (optional)
4½	cups low-sodium chicken broth
1	(28-ounce) can diced tomatoes
2	(15-ounce) cans chickpeas, drained and rinsed
½	cup minced fresh cilantro leaves

1. Adjust an oven rack to the lower-middle position and heat the oven to 325 degrees. Place the apricots, bay leaves, and half of the meat in a large roasting pan; set aside.

2. Pat the remaining meat dry with paper towels and season with salt and pepper. Heat 1 tablespoon of the oil in a large Dutch oven over medium-high heat until just smoking. Add half of the meat and brown well on all sides, 7 to 10 minutes; transfer to the roasting pan. Repeat with 1 tablespoon more oil and the remaining meat; transfer to the roasting pan.

3. Add the remaining 2 tablespoons oil to the pot and heat over medium heat until shimmering. Add the onions and ½ teaspoon salt and cook until softened, 7 to 10 minutes. Stir in the garlic and cook until fragrant, about 30 seconds. Stir in the flour, cumin, cinnamon, ginger, coriander, and cayenne (if using) and cook for 1 minute.

4. Slowly whisk in the broth, scraping up any browned bits and smoothing out any lumps. Stir in the tomatoes with their juice and bring to a boil. Pour the mixture into the roasting pan and stir to combine.

5. Cover the pan tightly with aluminum foil. Place the roasting pan in the oven and cook for 2 hours. Stir in the chickpeas and continue to cook in the oven, covered, until the meat is tender and the sauce is thickened, 45 to 60 minutes longer.

6. Remove the stew from the oven and remove and discard the bay leaves. Stir in the cilantro, season with salt and pepper to taste, and serve.

TO MAKE AHEAD

The tagine can be prepared through step 5, then cooled for 45 minutes. Cover the roasting pan tightly with foil and refrigerate for up to 2 days. (We think storing and reheating the stew in the roasting pan is best because it minimizes handling so the tender pieces of meat stay intact. If tight on space, you can transfer the stew to an airtight container; return it to the roasting pan before continuing.) To serve, remove any fat that has collected on top and re-cover the pan tightly with foil. Reheat the stew in a 425-degree oven until hot, 1 to 1½ hours. Add water as needed to adjust the stew's consistency and continue with step 6 as directed.

CORNISH GAME HENS WITH RICE STUFFING

EVEN THOUGH CORNISH HENS ARE RELATIVELY cheap (about $4.25 each in our supermarket) and cook quickly enough for a weeknight supper (less than 30 minutes), most people think of them as festive fare. And for good reason: They make a stunning presentation, and they stuff beautifully. But cooking Cornish hens to perfection is not an easy task—the white meat and dark meat cook at different rates, browning can be difficult (since these small birds cook quickly), and stuffing them can be a challenge. And because most Cornish hens are mass-produced and not premium quality, we were faced with the added challenge of trying to deepen their flavor. Despite these issues, we were determined to develop a recipe for really great stuffed and roasted Cornish game hens that would be a perfect one-dish dinner for a special-occasion meal.

First, we looked at our cooking vessel. We had set our sights on cooking eight hens, and the roasting pan seemed like a logical choice to hold them. But we quickly found you might as well steam Cornish hens as roast eight of them in a high-sided roasting pan. The pan sides shielded the birds from oven heat, and their snug fit in the pan further prevented browning. So our first move was to get the birds out of the roasting pan and onto a wire rack set over a baking sheet.

From our initial testing, we also found rotating the birds was crucial for moist, juicy breast meat. Though the unturned birds were more deeply browned, their breast meat was too dry. But because Cornish hens are in the oven for such a relatively short time and because there are several of them, multiple turns were out of the question. One turn, from breast side down to breast side up, was our limit.

After roasting groups of Cornish hens at temperatures ranging from 350 degrees to 500 degrees, as well as roasting them at a high temperature to start and then finishing low—and then starting low and finishing high—we found that every scenario had its problems. Eventually we settled on starting at 400 degrees and turning up to 450 degrees during the last few minutes. This gave us an oven that was hot enough to encourage good browning on the birds, but not so hot as to burn drippings and cause significant smoking.

But even at our relatively high cooking temperatures, the Cornish hens simply didn't spend enough time in the oven to develop the deep mahogany color we sought. We felt a glaze could fix the color problem and at the same time boost the flavor of our recipe. We tested a few different glaze bases on several batches of hens: soy sauce, a balsamic vinegar–brown sugar mixture, and jam thinned with a little soy sauce. We applied the glazes twice: right before they were turned and once again after the oven temperature was increased to 450 degrees. Because the high oven heat caramelized the sugar in these glazes, all of the birds colored more beautifully than any of our unglazed birds. But the balsamic vinegar glaze was our favorite; it gave the hens a pleasant burnished look. We found that cooking the mixture in the microwave was an easy way to thicken the glaze to the right consistency and saved us from washing another pan.

Now our Cornish hens looked outstanding, but how they tasted was a different story. All of the Cornish game hens at our local supermarket are mass-produced, which translated to mediocre-tasting meat. But brining the birds for just 30 minutes in a saltwater solution seasoned the meat and made it juicy, transforming them into birds we would proudly serve to guests.

For the stuffing, we wanted something that was simple but flavorful and felt elegant without requiring expensive or esoteric ingredients. Wild rice blend (a blend of regular and wild rice) had better flavor and texture than other varieties of rice and could stand on its own as a side dish. The addition of fruit and nuts (we quickly settled on toasted pecans and dried cranberries) gave the stuffing textural and

flavor variation. For aromatics, sautéed onion and celery, plus fresh parsley and thyme, served to infuse the stuffing with deep flavor.

Our final challenge was determining how to roast these stuffed birds without overcooking them, since the stuffing can take longer than the birds to come up to a safe temperature. In fact, in the test kitchen we generally eschew stuffing poultry for this very reason, but the small size of a game hen means there is less lag time between the stuffed cavity and the meat compared to a 20-pound Thanksgiving turkey, so we had hope it would work out. Although we're certain that slightly overcooking a stuffed bird is inevitable, a few things helped. Brining protected the birds from drying out, and starting the birds breast side down slowed the cooking of the breast meat, which cooks more quickly than the thigh and leg meat. And heating the stuffing before spooning it into the birds' cavities shortened the gap in time between when the birds were done and when the stuffing had reached a safe temperature.

Although we were aware that trussing might not be ideal because it would slow down the roasting of the hens' legs and thighs, stuffing the bird created the need to close the cavity. But luckily, we discovered that simply tying the hens' legs together was all that was needed to improve their looks and secure the stuffing without impeding the roasting.

Though there was a little labor and time involved with our recipe, it was a special-occasion meal that looked so great on the plate we felt we'd be game to make it the next opportunity we had.

Roasted Cornish Game Hens with Wild Rice Stuffing

SERVES 8

We like to use a wild rice blend for the stuffing because it offers an interesting variety of flavors and textures. There are lots of brands and styles of wild rice blends available, and all will work well here. We use table salt in the brine, but kosher salt will also work. To use kosher salt in the brine, see page 34 for conversion information. If using kosher chicken skip step 1, don't rinse the chicken in step 3, and season with salt in step 3.

HENS

I	cup table salt (see note)
8	(1¼- to 1½-pound) Cornish game hens, giblets removed

STUFFING

1⅓	cups wild rice blend (see note)
3	tablespoons unsalted butter
I	medium onion, minced
I	celery rib, chopped fine
⅓	cup pecans, toasted and chopped coarse
⅓	cup dried cranberries
3	tablespoons minced fresh parsley leaves
I	tablespoon minced fresh thyme leaves
	Salt and ground black pepper

GLAZE

1⅓	cups packed dark brown sugar
I	cup balsamic vinegar
I	teaspoon salt

1. **For the hens:** Dissolve the salt in 4 quarts cold water in a large container. Submerge the hens in the brine, cover, and refrigerate for 30 minutes or up to 1 hour.

2. **For the stuffing:** Cook the wild rice blend according to the package instructions, omitting any additional flavorings or fat; transfer to a large microwave-safe bowl. Melt the butter in a medium saucepan over medium heat. Add the onion and celery and cook until softened, 5 to 7 minutes; add to the bowl with the rice. Stir in the pecans, cranberries, parsley, and thyme and season with salt and pepper to taste.

3. Adjust an oven rack to the middle position and heat the oven to 400 degrees. Place a wire rack inside an aluminum foil–lined rimmed baking sheet. Remove the hens from the brine, rinse well, and pat dry with paper towels.

4. Microwave the stuffing on high power, covered, until very hot, about 2 minutes. Following the illustrations at right, spoon ½ cup of the hot stuffing into the cavity of each hen, then tie the legs together with kitchen twine. Tuck the wings following the

illustration on page 70, then season with pepper. Arrange the hens, breast side down, on the prepared wire rack. Roast until the backs are golden brown, about 25 minutes.

5. **For the glaze:** Whisk all the glaze ingredients together in a liquid measuring cup and microwave on high power until the mixture thickens and reduces to about 1⅓ cups, about 10 minutes. Measure out and reserve ⅓ cup of the glaze separately for serving. Cover the remaining glaze to keep warm. (The glaze will thicken as it cools between bastings; rewarm as needed to loosen.)

6. Remove the hens from the oven and brush with one-third of the remaining glaze. Flip the hens

PREPARING STUFFED CORNISH HENS

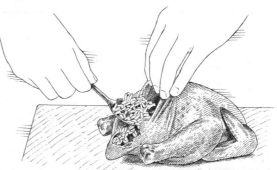

1. Spoon ½ cup of the hot stuffing into the cavity of each hen.

2. Tie the legs of each hen together with twine.

breast side up and brush with half of the remaining glaze. Continue to roast until the stuffed cavity registers 150 degrees on an instant-read thermometer, 15 to 20 minutes longer.

7. Increase the oven temperature to 450 degrees. Brush the hens with the remaining glaze and continue to roast until the hens are spotty brown and the cavity registers 160 to 165 degrees, 5 to 10 minutes longer. Remove the hens from the oven, transfer to a carving board or platter, and brush with the reserved glaze. Let rest 10 minutes before serving.

TO MAKE AHEAD

The stuffing can be prepared through step 2 and refrigerated in an airtight container for up to 1 day. The glaze ingredients can be combined and held at room temperature for several hours before microwaving in step 5.

LASAGNA DI CARNEVALE

A WELL-MADE VERSION OF CLASSIC ITALIAN-American lasagna, with tender noodles balanced by mozzarella and ricotta cheese and flavorful red sauce, is an ideal comfort food casserole, but it's not exactly elegant. In Naples, they claim a lasagna that is a little more upscale and festive. With tiny meatballs, tomato sauce, and mozzarella cheese, *lasagna di Carnevale* is traditionally made to celebrate Carnevale, a festival that takes place just before Lent. We wanted to make this Neapolitan-style lasagna with its distinct layers, moderate amount of deeply flavored sauce (less than what you'd see in classic Italian-American lasagna), and tender meatballs. But we had no intention of making a traditional Neapolitan recipe, since they typically use upward of 25 ingredients and take an entire day to prepare. We wanted to devise a recipe with these classic tastes but without the backbreaking labor.

Our first task was to make sense of the cheese component. Various Neapolitan recipes call for mozzarella, ricotta (sometimes mixed with whole eggs or egg yolks), and/or a hard grating cheese (usually Parmesan, but sometimes Pecorino Romano). After trying the various combinations, we realized that in this type of lasagna, ricotta caused "lasagna meltdown"—the loss of shape and distinct layering. Even with the addition of whole eggs or yolks as a thickener, ricotta proved too watery because of the meatballs; the meatballs disrupted the simple, even layering and thus required a cheese with more binding power to keep our lasagna from falling apart.

Mozzarella seemed like a much better option, as it offered plenty of creaminess and a stringiness that could bind the layers to each other. Fresh mozzarella, however, had too much moisture to be effective. When it melted, it released so much liquid that the lasagna became mushy and watery. In addition, the delicate flavor of expensive fresh mozzarella was lost in the baking process. So after a few disastrous attempts, we turned to fresh mozzarella's shrink-wrapped cousin, whole-milk mozzarella, and had much better results. We also found that a small amount of either Parmesan or Pecorino Romano provided a pleasantly sharp contrast to the somewhat mild mozzarella.

With the cheese question resolved, we turned our focus to the meatballs. Here again we looked to traditional Italian recipes for inspiration, then tried to simplify. We seasoned ground beef with herbs, cheese, eggs, and bread crumbs. However, instead of rolling out whole, large meatballs, we pinched off small bits of the mixture to create mini-meatballs that would allow for more even layering. We tried pinching them off directly into hot oil, which worked fine but required us to stand over the oil frying for upwards of four batches of mini-meatballs. There had to be an easier way. Could we bake them? For our next test, we formed all the meatballs and placed them on a baking sheet. After just eight minutes in a 450-degree oven, they were done and ready for our lasagna. And since our aim was to simplify matters, we decided to add the meatballs straight to the sauce so that we could cut back on the layering steps.

Many traditional recipes simmer whole tomatoes or tomato puree for hours to make a rich, complex sauce, but we decided for our easier recipe we would go with a quick-cooking sauce made with crushed tomatoes. Simmering canned crushed tomatoes for 10 minutes was enough to give our sauce the proper consistency.

Next we focused our attention on the choice of noodles and the layering process. In the test kitchen, we often make lasagna with no-boil noodles. They really simplify the process and produce great results, so we thought we would give them a try here. We made our working recipe, layering the cheeses and meatball sauce with no-boil noodles, only to find out that the no-boil noodles were a no-go. They emerged from the oven with a tough, cardboardlike texture. Thinking that soaking the noodles in hot water would help them to soften, we gave it a try. No luck. Our lightly sauced lasagna (with about half of the sauce you'd find in the more familiar lasagna style) simply did not have enough moisture for the noodles to absorb and become tender as the lasagna cooked. It was clear that this type of lasagna would require a more traditional type of noodle.

Many Italian lasagna recipes call for fresh pasta. Tasters liked the thinness of the fresh noodles, but they voted unanimously against making them from scratch—after all, we were trying to simplify our lasagna-making process, not complicate it. We then tried several brands of fresh pasta from our local markets, but they varied dramatically, not only in thickness and dimensions, but also in quality. Traditional dried lasagna noodles—the type that require boiling before assembling the lasagna—turned out to be our favorite, in part because they were the most reliable, but also because tasters were happiest with the lasagna they produced. The only key to working with these noodles is that you must boil them until soft and then rinse them with cold water to stop them from cooking further and becoming mushy. This step also rinses away some of the starch, preventing them from sticking together.

In terms of the actual layering procedure, we found it helpful to grease the baking pan with cooking spray. We then spread a small amount of tomato sauce (without any meatballs) over the dish's bottom to moisten the bottom layer of pasta and added the first layer of noodles. After that, we spread sauce and meatballs evenly over the noodles, covered them with shredded mozzarella, then sprinkled on grated Parmesan. We then built more layers using this same process. After a few tests

we realized that the tomato sauce and meatballs tended to dry out when not covered by pasta, so we settled on making the two cheeses our final layer. They browned nicely during baking and gave our lasagna good visual appeal.

After just 20 minutes in a 400-degree oven, the lasagna was ready to eat (although we do recommend letting it cool for 10 minutes before serving). This lasagna is certainly just as satisfying as traditional Neapolitan versions but quicker to assemble. The best part is that you and your guests don't have to wait for Carnevale or visit Italy to enjoy it!

Lasagna di Carnevale
SERVES 6 TO 8

Do not substitute no-boil noodles for the traditional noodles here; they will not work in this dish. The size of the noodles varies by brand; if the noodles are short (such as DeCecco) you will layer them crosswise in the dish, but if they are long (such as Barilla and Ronzoni) you will layer them lengthwise in the dish. Regardless of which brand of noodle you are using, there should be 3 noodles per layer.

1	pound 85 percent lean ground beef
6	ounces Parmesan or Pecorino Romano cheese, grated (3 cups)
½	cup plain dried bread crumbs
2	large eggs, lightly beaten
½	cup minced fresh basil or parsley leaves
	Salt and ground black pepper
3	tablespoons olive oil
2	medium garlic cloves, minced or pressed through a garlic press (about 2 teaspoons)
1	(28-ounce) can crushed tomatoes
12	dried lasagna noodles (see note)
1	pound whole-milk mozzarella cheese, shredded (4 cups)

1. Adjust an oven rack to the middle position and heat the oven to 450 degrees. Spray a large rimmed baking sheet with vegetable oil spray. Mix the beef, 1 cup of the cheese, bread crumbs, eggs, 5 tablespoons of the basil, 1 teaspoon salt, and ½ teaspoon pepper together in a large bowl using your hands until uniform.

2. Pinch off grape-size pieces of the mixture, roll them into small meatballs, and arrange on the prepared baking sheet. Bake the meatballs until just cooked through and lightly browned, 8 to 10 minutes. Transfer the meatballs to a paper towel–lined platter and set aside. Reduce the oven to 400 degrees.

3. Meanwhile, heat the oil and garlic in a medium saucepan over medium heat until the garlic starts to sizzle, about 2 minutes. Stir in the tomatoes and simmer until the sauce thickens slightly, 10 to 15 minutes. Off the heat, stir in the remaining 3 tablespoons basil and season with salt and pepper to taste. Stir in the meatballs and cover to keep warm.

4. Bring 4 quarts water to a boil in a large pot. Stir in 1 tablespoon salt and noodles and cook, stirring often, until al dente. Drain and rinse the noodles under cold water. Spread the noodles out in a single layer over clean kitchen towels. (Do not use paper towels; they will stick to the noodles.)

4. Spray a 13 by 9-inch baking dish with vegetable oil spray. Smear 3 tablespoons of the tomato sauce (without any meatballs) over the bottom of the pan. Layer 3 noodles into the pan; the noodles can touch but not overlap. Spread about 1½ cups of the tomato sauce with meatballs evenly over the noodles. Sprinkle evenly with 1 cup of the mozzarella and ½ cup of the Parmesan.

5. Repeat the layering of noodles, tomato sauce with meatballs, and cheeses twice more. For the final layer, cover the noodles with the remaining 1 cup mozzarella and sprinkle with the remaining ½ cup Parmesan.

6. Bake until the filling is bubbling and the cheese is spotty brown, 20 to 25 minutes. Let the lasagna cool for 10 minutes before serving.

TO MAKE AHEAD

The lasagna can be assembled through step 5, then covered with plastic wrap and refrigerated for up to 2 days. Remove the plastic wrap and cover the lasagna tightly with aluminum foil that has been sprayed with vegetable oil spray (or use nonstick foil). Bake the lasagna covered for 10 minutes, then remove the foil and continue to bake as directed in step 6.

LOBSTER FETTUCCINE

LOBSTER IS A CLASSIC CHOICE FOR A celebratory meal. Most home cooks boil the crustaceans and serve them whole with a side of drawn butter, and while dismantling a lobster with beer and bibs is an important tradition, it's a casual one. Meanwhile, more refined preparations, such as lobster ravioli, are usually left to restaurant chefs because of the work involved. But the duo of pasta and a creamy sauce is an ideal showcase for the sweet, rich flavor of lobster, so we set out to bring these components together in an elegant pasta dish that didn't require a day's worth of prep. We decided to skip filling pasta and instead combine tender chunks of lobster with a cream sauce and al dente noodles. We quickly settled on fettuccine, the usual partner for cream sauces because it holds on to sauce exceptionally well, and then set out to make a foolproof recipe for an elegant pasta dinner.

To get started, we immediately turned to our already developed method for one-pot pastas (see pages 165–210). This technique creates a loose, overly liquidy sauce, then calls for adding the dry pasta and simmering rapidly. As the pasta cooks, it absorbs some of the liquid, and the remainder of the liquid becomes thickened (partly through reduction and partly from starch released from the pasta) to become the sauce. If done right, by the time the pasta is tender, you also have a velvety, flavorful sauce, and because the pasta is cooked with the aromatics and sauce, the pasta absorbs maximum flavor. (There's also the plus that you have just one pot to clean when it's all over.) Our plan was to stir in cooked lobster meat once the pasta was done—this, we hoped, would ensure tender, not overcooked, chunks of lobster in our final dish.

We started our sauce with a base of sautéed onion, but we also liked the addition of a head of fennel; the slight anise flavor gave the sauce refinement. For additional aromatics, we kept the flavor clean with a modest quantity of minced thyme and garlic, and a tiny bit of cayenne for a subtle heat that would contrast with the overall richness of the dish. We then deglazed the pan with some sherry, a natural pairing with lobster and cream. Now it was

Lobster 101

HARD-SHELL VERSUS SOFT-SHELL LOBSTERS

During the year, lobsters go through a molting stage in order to grow into a larger shell. If caught during this stage, the lobsters are called soft-shell. You can tell they are soft-shell just by squeezing them—if squeezed, their soft sides will yield to pressure. Does this matter? Yes and no. Soft-shell lobsters have less meat and are considered to be less flavorful. For most of us, though, soft-shell lobsters taste just fine. The only thing to keep in mind is that they cook faster than hard-shell lobsters do.

THE BEST WAY TO COOK LOBSTER

We found that the best way to cook a lobster, hands down, is steaming. There is no difference in taste between boiled and steamed lobsters, but boiling often leaves lobsters waterlogged. Below are steaming instructions and a chart with cooking times and meat yields for different sizes and types of lobster. For the Lobster Fettuccine with Fennel, Tarragon, and Cream recipe, you'll need a total of 2 pounds (32 ounces) of cooked lobster meat.

HOW TO STEAM LOBSTERS

Fit a large Dutch oven with a steamer basket and add water to the pot until it just touches the bottom of the basket. Bring the water to a boil over high heat, then add the lobsters to the steamer basket. Following the times in the chart, cover and steam the lobsters until they are bright red and fully cooked. Be sure to check the pot periodically to make sure the water has not boiled dry; add more water as needed. Remove the lobsters from the steamer basket and let them cool slightly before shelling. (Once shelled, the cooked lobster meat can be refrigerated in an airtight container for up to 2 days.)

APPROXIMATE STEAMING TIMES AND MEAT YIELDS FOR LOBSTER

LOBSTER SIZE	COOKING TIME	MEAT YIELD
1 LB.		
SOFT-SHELL	8 to 9 min.	about 3 oz.
HARD-SHELL	10 to 11 min.	4 to 4½ oz.
1¼ LBS.		
SOFT-SHELL	11 to 12 min.	3½ to 4 oz.
HARD-SHELL	13 to 14 min.	5½ to 6 oz.
1½ LBS.		
SOFT-SHELL	13 to 14 min.	5½ to 6 oz.
HARD-SHELL	15 to 16 min.	7½ to 8 oz.
1¾ LBS.–2 LBS.		
SOFT-SHELL	17 to 18 min.	6¼ to 6½ oz.
HARD-SHELL	about 19 min.	8½ to 9 oz.

REMOVING MEAT FROM STEAMED LOBSTERS

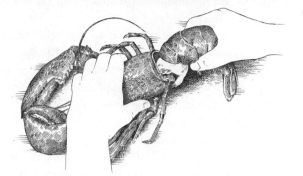

1. After the cooked lobster has cooled slightly, twist the tail and claw appendages to remove them from the body. Discard the body.

2. Twist the tail flippers off the tail, then use a fork or your finger to push the tail meat out through the wide end of the tail.

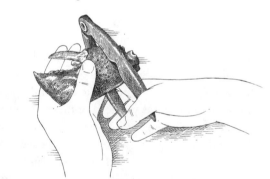

3. Use lobster crackers or a mallet to break open the claw and remove the meat.

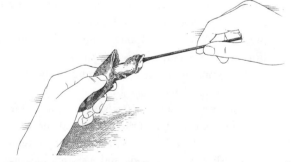

4. Crack open the claw appendage's connecting joint and remove the meat with a cocktail fork.

time to add the liquid that would create the sauce and cook the pasta.

The right pasta-to-liquid ratio is crucial when making one-pot pastas. We found that 10 cups of liquid was the right quantity to cook our 2 pounds of pasta and leave us with the appropriate sauciness after it had reduced and thickened. We already knew cream would be one of the liquid components. We briefly considered incorporating a homemade lobster stock to boost the lobster flavor, but while we were willing to put in extra time for a special dinner, we weren't up for the all-day project of making our own stock. Instead, store-bought chicken broth added a savory anchor for the sweetness and delicacy of the rest of the dish. Cutting the cream and broth with water was also key to getting the sauce just right. After some experimentation we settled on using 4 cups each broth and water and 2 cups cream.

We then added our pasta to the pot with the sauce, brought the liquid to a rapid simmer, and cooked the mixture until the pasta was tender, which took about 15 minutes. Once it was done, it was time to stir in the lobster.

One side-by-side test proved we liked the flavor of lobster meat we steamed ourselves over lobster meat we purchased already cooked, and steaming and shelling four lobsters was a simple procedure. It also helped that we could take care of this steaming step up to two days ahead of time. (If you have a hard time finding live lobsters, or don't want to deal with cooking them yourself, precooked lobster meat, which can be found at a good fish market or even a local supermarket, will still work fine.) To ensure the lobster meat didn't get rubbery or fall apart, we waited until the pasta was tender and our sauce velvety before adding it in large bite-size pieces, cooking it just long enough to let it heat it through and become coated in the sauce.

To complement the fennel and give the dish an herbal presence, we added fresh minced tarragon to the pot with the lobster. Finally, a tablespoon of fresh lemon juice brightened the flavors and cut through the richness. Dotted with sweet bites of lobster, this pasta dish feels luxurious and elegant; and better yet, no one will suspect how simple it is to prepare.

Lobster Fettuccine with Fennel, Tarragon, and Cream
SERVES 8 TO 10

You can either buy cooked lobster meat or steam and shell your own lobsters; see page 315 for more information on how to steam lobsters. Be sure to use dried fettuccine in this recipe; fresh fettuccine will not work. When adding the fettuccine in step 2, stir gently to avoid breaking the noodles; after a minute or two they will soften enough to allow for easier stirring. Be ready to serve the pasta as soon as it is finished; the sauce will turn thick and clumpy if held for too long. Warm serving bowls (warmed in a 200-degree oven) will help extend the serving time for the pasta.

3	tablespoons olive oil
1	medium onion, minced
1	medium fennel bulb (about 12 ounces), trimmed of stalks, cored, and chopped fine (see the illustrations on page 38)
	Salt and ground black pepper
1	tablespoon minced fresh thyme leaves
3	medium garlic cloves, minced or pressed through a garlic press (about 1 tablespoon)
¼	teaspoon cayenne pepper
¾	cup dry sherry
4	cups low-sodium chicken broth
4	cups water
2	cups heavy cream
2	pounds fettuccine (see note)
2	pounds cooked lobster meat, cut into ⅓-inch pieces
3	tablespoon minced fresh tarragon leaves
1	tablespoon juice from 1 lemon
	Grated Parmesan cheese, for serving (optional)

1. Heat the oil in a large Dutch oven over medium heat until shimmering. Add the onion, fennel, and ½ teaspoon salt and cook until softened, 5 to 7 minutes. Stir in the thyme, garlic, and cayenne and cook until fragrant, about 30 seconds. Stir in the sherry and simmer until it has nearly evaporated, about 4 minutes.

2. Stir in the broth, water, and cream. Stir in the pasta and bring to a rapid simmer. Simmer

vigorously, stirring often, until the fettuccine is tender, 12 to 16 minutes.

3. Reduce the heat to low and add the lobster and tarragon. Cook, gently tossing to combine, until the lobster is just warmed through, about 3 minutes. Off the heat, stir in the lemon juice and season with salt and pepper to taste. Serve immediately in warmed bowls, passing the Parmesan separately (if using).

TO MAKE AHEAD

Though this recipe must be cooked just before serving, it can be helpful to have all of the ingredients prepped and measured out ahead of time. All of the ingredients (except for the minced fresh tarragon) can be prepped, measured, and stored (in the refrigerator if perishable) for up to 1 day.

Paella

DESPITE ITS CURRENT REPUTATION AS A colorful Spanish restaurant staple geared toward serving a crowd, paella hasn't always been categorized as a party food. Developed by agricultural workers just outside of Valencia, Spain, as a means of cooking large quantities of rice, traditional paella was not fancy. Cooked in flat-bottomed pans over an open fire and flavored with local, easy-to-find ingredients such as snails, rabbit, and green beans, this utilitarian dish was a far cry from what we know as paella today. Paella has evolved into a big production piece with a commanding list of ingredients, ranging from artichokes, green beans, broad beans, bell peppers, peas, and pork to chorizo, chicken, lobster, scallops, calamari, fish, mussels, clams, and shrimp. We set out to create a recipe that alluded to the simplicity of the earliest versions but could be made in a reasonable amount of time, with a manageable number of easy-to-find ingredients, and without requiring a special paella pan. All the same, we wanted a dish that could hold its own as the centerpiece.

While none of the recipes we found in our research were perfect, some did offer important clues. One was that if the rice and proteins were to cook uniformly, they had to be arranged in a not-too-thick, relatively even layer. Crowding or mounding the ingredients in a pile was a sure-fire route to disaster, a point quickly proven when we tried to make a recipe for eight in a 12-inch skillet. So what was the best paella pan replacement? A Dutch oven was the answer: It fit perfectly on the stovetop, gave our ingredients enough room, and offered the best distribution and retention of heat.

Looking over various recipes, there seemed to be five key steps: browning the sturdier proteins, sautéing the aromatics, toasting the rice, adding liquid to steam the rice, and, last, cooking the seafood. As for proteins, we settled on chorizo, chicken, shrimp (preferred over scallops or calamari), and mussels (favored over clams). We ruled out lobster (too much work), diced pork (flavorful chorizo sausage would be enough), fish (flakes too easily and gets lost in the rice), and rabbit and snails (too unconventional).

We began by browning the chicken and chorizo, which would give the meat a head start and lend necessary flavor to the fat used to sauté the onion and garlic later on. While many recipes call for bone-in, skin-on chicken pieces, to save time we opted for boneless, skinless thighs (richer in flavor and less prone to drying out than breasts). We seared both sides of some halved chicken thighs in olive oil, not cooking them all the way through to make sure they would be tender and juicy once added back in with the rice to cook through.

Spanish cuisine uses the trio of onions, tomatoes, and garlic—called *sofrito*—as the building block for its rice dishes. We began by sautéing one finely diced onion until soft and stirring in a large dose (2 tablespoons) of minced garlic. Traditionally, the final ingredient, tomato, is added in seeded, grated form. To avoid the mess (as well as skinned fingers), we used a can of drained diced tomatoes instead, mincing the pieces for a similarly fine consistency and cooking the resulting pulp until thick and slightly darkened.

With the sofrito complete, we could now focus on the rice. Long-grain rice seemed out of place (a paella is not supposed to be light and fluffy) and medium-grain rice didn't seem quite right. Out of the short-grain varieties, Valencia, the traditional choice for paella, was preferred for its creamy but still distinct grains, with Italian Arborio following closely behind. Two cups of rice cooked to the right volume to feed eight. We sautéed the rice in the sofrito just long enough to become slightly toasted and coated with the flavorful base, and then it was time to add the liquid. For its clean, full-bodied flavor, tasters preferred rice cooked in straight chicken broth to clam juice or a combination of the two. Replacing some of the broth with a bit of white wine provided an additional layer of flavor.

Saffron gives paella its colored hue and adds a distinctive earthy flavor. Most recipes call for steeping the saffron threads in a pot of simmering liquid, but, to save time and keep this a one-pot dish, we added cold liquid along with ½ teaspoon of saffron (plus two bay leaves and the browned chicken and chorizo) to the rice and brought everything to a boil. After a few quick stirs to make sure the saffron was distributed evenly, we covered the pot and turned things down to a simmer, leaving the paella untouched until the rice had soaked up most of the liquid.

Unfortunately this all-stovetop steaming method had a major flaw. While the rice in the middle of the pot was cooked perfectly, grains along the edges were partially undercooked. Our solution was simple: we transferred the pot to the oven to finish cooking. Once the rice came up to a simmer, we placed the pot in a 350-degree oven and 15 minutes later the grains had evenly absorbed nearly all of the liquid. At this point, the rice needed another 10 or so minutes to cook, so it was the perfect window to add the seafood and return the pot to the oven.

The mussels, placed in the pot hinged end down so that they could open readily, cooked in about 10 minutes. When the shrimp were added raw along with the mussels, they were perfectly juicy at the 10-minute mark but they were also bland. To fix this issue, we briefly marinated the raw shrimp in olive oil, salt, pepper, and minced garlic.

Now all the paella lacked was a few vegetables. Peas and bell pepper were the most vibrant, least fussy choices. We chose to scatter the peas over the rice toward the end of cooking, which ensured they would retain their bright green hue. In paella, bell pepper often gets lost when mixed with the sofrito

or when stirred into the rice. Wanting to make it a more prominent component, we decided to use strips of sautéed red bell pepper as a garnish.

At this point, we could easily have called it a day, but several people demanded soccarat, the crusty brown layer of rice that develops on the bottom of a perfectly cooked batch of paella. Curious to see if we could get this to work in a Dutch oven, we waited until the dish was completely cooked and then removed the lid and put the pot back on the stove. After only about five minutes, a spoon inserted into the depths of the rice revealed nicely caramelized grains. Before we let anyone dig in, we allowed the paella to rest, covered, so the rice could continue to firm up and absorb excess moisture. After adding a garnish of parsley and lemon, we were done. Our final recipe had all the flavor and sparkle of this world-famous Spanish dish—minus the hefty workload.

Paella
SERVES 6 TO 8

This recipe requires a Dutch oven that is 11 to 12 inches in diameter with at least a 6-quart capacity. With minor modifications, it can also be made in a paella pan (see the variation "Paella Using a Paella Pan or Skillet" on page 320). Spanish chorizo is the sausage of choice for paella, but Mexican chorizo or linguiça is an acceptable substitute. Soccarat, a layer of crusty browned rice that forms on the bottom of the pan, is a traditional part of paella, but we've made it optional; if desired, see instructions for how to make a soccarat at the end of step 6.

1	pound extra-large shrimp (21 to 25 per pound), peeled and deveined (see the illustration on page 145)
2	tablespoons olive oil, plus extra as needed
9	medium garlic cloves, minced or pressed through a garlic press (about 3 tablespoons) Salt and ground black pepper
1	pound boneless, skinless chicken thighs (about 4 thighs), trimmed and halved crosswise

I   red bell pepper, stemmed, seeded, and cut
    into ½-inch-wide strips (see the illustrations
    on page 226)

8   ounces Spanish chorizo, sliced ½ inch thick
    on the bias

I   medium onion, minced

I   (14.5-ounce) can diced tomatoes, drained,
    minced, and drained again

3   cups low-sodium chicken broth

2   cups Valencia or Arborio rice

⅓   cup dry white wine

½   teaspoon saffron threads, crumbled

2   bay leaves

12 mussels (about 6 ounces), scrubbed and
    debearded (see the illustration on page 147)

½   cup frozen peas, thawed

2   tablespoons minced fresh parsley leaves
    Lemon wedges, for serving

1. Adjust an oven rack to the lower-middle position and heat the oven to 350 degrees. Toss the shrimp with 1 tablespoon oil, 1 teaspoon of the garlic, ¼ teaspoon salt, and ¼ teaspoon pepper in a medium bowl; cover and refrigerate until needed. Season the chicken thighs with salt and pepper.

2. Heat 2 teaspoons oil in a large Dutch oven over medium-high heat until shimmering. Add the bell pepper and cook until the skin begins to blister and turn spotty black, about 3 minutes; transfer to a plate.

3. Add 1 teaspoon oil to the pot and place over medium-high heat until shimmering. Brown the chicken on both sides, 6 to 8 minutes; transfer to a bowl. Reduce the heat to medium, add the chorizo, and cook, stirring frequently, until deeply browned and the fat begins to render, about 4 minutes; transfer to the bowl with the chicken.

4. Add enough oil to the fat left in the pot to equal 2 tablespoons, add the onion, and cook over medium heat until softened, 5 to 7 minutes. Stir in the remaining 8 teaspoons garlic and cook until fragrant, about 30 seconds. Stir in the tomatoes and cook until the mixture begins to thicken, about 3 minutes.

5. Stir in the chicken broth, rice, wine, saffron, bay leaves, and ½ teaspoon salt. Return the chicken and chorizo to the pot, increase the heat to medium-high, and bring to a boil. Cover the pot, transfer to the oven, and cook until the rice absorbs almost all of the liquid, about 15 minutes.

6. Remove the pot from the oven. Scatter the shrimp and bell pepper over the rice, insert the

INGREDIENTS: Saffron

Cultivated from the crocus flower, saffron is a delicate red thread pulled from the stigma (the female part of the crocus) by hand at harvest each October. Because each flower yields only three stigmas, it can take the *mondadoras* (petal strippers) up to 200 hours to yield only 1 pound of saffron—which explains why it is the most expensive spice in the world. Once harvested, the saffron threads are roasted over a gentle charcoal or gas fire to dry and then stored in a dark place free of humidity.

Saffron is available in two forms—threads and powder. Conventional wisdom says that deep, dark red threads are better than yellow or orange threads. We held a small tasting of broths infused with different saffron samples and the threads with considerable spots of yellow and orange did in fact yield the weakest-colored and flattest-tasting broths. The reddest threads yielded intensely flavorful broths.

Conventional wisdom also cautions against using powdered saffron. Some sources say that inferior threads are used to produce the powder and that coloring agents may be added. While this may be true, we found powdered saffron purchased from a reputable source to be just as flavorful and fragrant as even the highest-quality threads. (Note that you will need about one-third to one-half the volume measurement of threads.)

POWDERED SAFFRON   **SAFFRON THREADS**

mussels into the rice (hinged side down), and sprinkle with the peas. Cover, return to the oven, and cook until the shrimp are opaque and the mussels have opened, 10 to 12 minutes. (If a soccarat is desired, remove the pot from the oven, uncover, and cook over medium-high heat for 3 to 6 minutes, rotating the pot as needed for even browning.)

7. Let the paella sit, covered, for 5 minutes. Remove and discard the bay leaves and any mussels that have not opened. Sprinkle with the parsley and serve with lemon wedges.

➤ VARIATION

Paella Using a Paella Pan or Skillet

A paella pan makes for an attractive and impressive presentation. Use one that is 14 to 15 inches in diameter. A 14-inch ovensafe skillet will work as well, but do not attempt to use anything smaller because the contents will not fit.

Follow the recipe for Paella, increasing the chicken broth to 3¼ cups and the wine to ½ cup. Before placing the pan in the oven, cover tightly with aluminum foil.

TO MAKE AHEAD

Though this recipe must be cooked just before serving, it can be helpful to have all of the ingredients prepped and measured out ahead of time. All of the ingredients (except for the minced fresh parsley) can be prepped, measured, and stored (in the refrigerator if perishable) for up to 1 day.

INGREDIENTS: Valencia Rice

Our top choice for our paella recipe, this short- to medium-grain Spanish rice was praised for its balance of textures: separate and chewy, but with a bit of creaminess. Grown in many regions of Spain, it gets its name from the province of Valencia, the largest rice-growing region of Spain. Unfortunately, Valencia rice is not available at every supermarket. If you have trouble locating Valencia rice, Arborio rice (the Italian rice used for risotto) is an acceptable substitute.

HALIBUT EN PAPILLOTE

COOKING *EN PAPILLOTE*—WHERE THE FOOD IS baked in a tightly sealed, artfully folded parchment package that is slit open just before serving for dramatic presentation—may seem as outdated or showy as beef Wellington or pheasant under glass. But there's a practical reason the technique has held its own through countless culinary fads and fashions. It's an easy, mess-free way to enhance delicate flavor, particularly that of fish, since the food is allowed to steam in its own juices. The fish cooks quickly in the moist environment, and because there's no water added to dilute flavors, it's a more flavorful method than ordinary poaching. If you throw vegetables into the package, it adds up to a light but satisfying, and visually appealing, "one-pouch" meal.

But fish en papillote, while delicate and simple in flavor, is not trouble-free in terms of technique. Without the right blend of flavorings, the fish can taste so lean and bland you might as well be dining on diet food. Also, not all vegetables pair well with fish, and careful consideration must be given to their size and their required cooking time, as you can otherwise wind up with fish surrounded by crunchy and undercooked or mushy and overcooked vegetables. We wanted to create an approach worthy of this technique's haute cuisine roots that also produced moist, flaky fish and tender-firm vegetables all flavored by the rich, aromatic goodness of their mingled juices.

All the classic recipes call for cutting parchment paper into attractive shapes such as teardrops, hearts, and butterflies. The fish is placed between two of these identical shapes, which are then painstakingly crimped together. The results make for a dramatic visual—the paper balloons and browns in the oven, to be slit open just before serving. After some experimentation with parchment, we found that we could achieve the same results as the fussy recipes without a talent for origami. We folded a piece of parchment in half, trimming the corners so it unfolded into a rough heart shape. The vegetables and fish went on one side of the heart, the other half was folded over the fish, and the two sides were folded together to complete the package. With only one shape to cut per fish bundle, eight packets came together quickly, with no awkward parchment pieces to match up, and only one seam to crimp per packet.

Our method settled, our next step was to figure out what type of fish worked best. After trying a variety of fish fillets, we determined that tasters favored flaky, mild white fish, like halibut and red snapper, over more assertively flavored fish like salmon or tuna. In the moist atmosphere of the pouch, the oilier fish had a more concentrated flavor that tasters felt would overpower the flavors of the milder vegetables; better to save them for poaching or grilling.

Next we needed to determine the best vegetables for the situation. Since the fish and vegetables would have to cook at the same rate, we knew there would be some limitations. Dense vegetables like potatoes were immediately out of the running because they took far too long to cook through, as were absorbent vegetables like eggplant, which would simply cook to mush. Broccoli seemed a little bold for an otherwise delicate dish. Light, clean-tasting zucchini, sliced into thin rounds, was a winner. For sweetness, color, and some more moisture to encourage steaming, we also settled on chopped tomatoes.

Determining when the fish was done proved more challenging: It was hard to nick and peek when the fish was sealed tightly in parchment. The old rule of thumb for fish—10 minutes of cooking time per inch of thickness—failed in this case, as the fish was barely opaque within that period. After experimenting with oven temperatures, we found that 1-inch-thick fillets cooked best at 450 degrees for 15 minutes. While this seemed like an excessive length of time at such high heat, we found the fish cooked in this manner was flaky and moist since it was well insulated within the sealed packets, and the vegetables were likewise perfectly cooked.

But now that we had the textures just right, we were ending up with diluted flavor. The solution was to salt and drain the zucchini in a colander before assembling the packet; the moisture from the tomatoes was all we needed for the perfect steamy environment. Cooking the packets on two rimmed baking sheets (four packets per baking sheet) gave the packets the contact they needed with the hot baking sheet to concentrate the liquid within and

evenly steam the contents. We put one baking sheet on the upper-middle rack and the other on the lower-middle, switching and rotating them halfway through to ensure the two cooked at the same rate.

To boost the flavor of our meal and add a little richness, we turned to a compound butter flavored with garlic, red pepper flakes, and oregano for an assertive kick. For a finishing touch, a sprinkling of chopped basil lent a pleasant fragrance. The flavored butters basted the fish as it cooked and mingled with the juices given off by the vegetables, leaving behind an aromatic, full-flavored sauce that perfectly complemented the fish.

For a variation, carrots and leeks replaced the zucchini and tomatoes. We topped it with thyme and a lemon zest butter, and sprinkled it with parsley

MAKING THIN FISH FILLETS THICKER

If some of your fillets are thin (such as the tail piece), you can make them thicker so that they cook at the same rate as the others.

1. With a sharp knife, cut halfway through the flesh crosswise 2 to 3 inches from tail end. This will create a seam to fold the tail under.

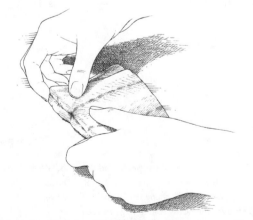

2. Fold the tail end under the thicker end to create a fillet of relatively even thickness.

for a clean finish. Both recipes were so light, fresh, and easy to prepare, they more than did justice to the classic method.

Halibut en Papillote with Zucchini and Tomatoes

SERVES 8

Haddock, red snapper, sea bass, and cod can be substituted for the halibut, as long as the fillets measure 1 to 1¼ inches thick. You will need 8 pieces of 16 by 14-inch parchment paper for this recipe, but it's a good idea to have extra around for practice; do not substitute waxed paper. Dry the vegetables and fish well before assembling the packets as excess moisture can weaken and tear the paper. Cut open each packet promptly after baking to prevent overcooking.

4　medium zucchini (about 2 pounds), trimmed and sliced ¼ inch thick
　　Salt and ground black pepper
8　tablespoons (1 stick) unsalted butter, softened
4　medium garlic cloves, minced or pressed through a garlic press (about 4 teaspoons)
2　teaspoons minced fresh oregano leaves
¼　teaspoon red pepper flakes
4　plum tomatoes (about 1 pound), cored, seeded, and chopped into ½-inch pieces
8　16 by 14-inch sheets parchment paper
8　skinless halibut fillets, 1 to ¼ inches thick (about 6 ounces each)
½　cup chopped fresh basil leaves
　　Lemon wedges, for serving

MAKING FISH EN PAPILLOTE

1. Fold a 16 by 14-inch sheet of parchment in half widthwise. Trim 3 of the corners so that when the paper is unfolded, it has a rough heart shape with a flat bottom and straightened sides.

2. Unfold the paper and pile the vegetables on one side of the heart, close to the fold. Place a piece of fish on top of the vegetables and spread 1 tablespoon of the butter over the top.

3. Refold the paper heart over the fish and align the paper edges.

4. Starting at the top of the heart, fold the outer 1 inch of the edge of parchment over into a tight, triangular-shape fold. Run your thumb over the newly folded edge to seal, then repeat at ¾-inch intervals to seal the fish securely into a parchment pouch.

5. When finished crimping, fold the final tailpiece of crimped parchment underneath to seal.

6. Before serving, use scissors to cut an X in the top of the parchment and sprinkle the fresh herbs over the cooked fish.

1. Toss the zucchini with 1 teaspoon salt and let drain in a colander for 30 minutes. Spread the zucchini out over several layers of paper towels and thoroughly blot dry. In a small bowl, mash the softened butter, garlic, oregano, red pepper flakes, ½ teaspoon salt, and ¼ teaspoon pepper together. In a separate bowl, season the tomatoes lightly with salt and pepper to taste.

2. Following the illustrations on page 322, fold and cut the parchment into 8 rough heart shapes. Adjust the oven racks to the lower-middle and upper-middle positions and heat the oven to 450 degrees.

3. Spread the pieces of parchment out over a clean, dry counter (or work in batches if counter space is tight). Neatly shingle the zucchini into a small pile on one side of each parchment sheet. Spoon ¼ cup of the tomatoes on top of each zucchini pile. Pat the fish dry with paper towels, season with salt and pepper, and lay on top of the tomatoes. Spread 1 tablespoon of the butter mixture evenly over the top of each piece of fish.

4. Fold the cut edges of the parchment over to make tidy airtight packets. Place the packets on 2 large rimmed baking sheets. Bake for 15 minutes, switching and rotating the pans halfway through the cooking time.

5. Working quickly, cut an X in the top of each packet with scissors and sprinkle the basil over the fish. Using a stiff spatula, gently transfer the packets to individual plates and serve with lemon wedges.

Halibut en Papillote with Leeks and Carrots

SERVES 8

Haddock, red snapper, sea bass, and cod can be substituted for the halibut, as long as the fillets measure 1 to 1¼ inches thick. You will need 8 pieces of 16 by 14-inch parchment paper for this recipe, but it's a good idea to have extra around for practice; do not substitute waxed paper. Dry the vegetables and fish well before assembling the packets as excess moisture can weaken and tear the paper. Cut open each packet promptly after baking to prevent overcooking.

8	tablespoons (1 stick) unsalted butter, softened
4	medium garlic cloves, minced or pressed through a garlic press (about 4 teaspoons)
2	teaspoons grated zest from 1 lemon
2	teaspoons minced fresh thyme leaves
	Salt and ground black pepper
3	medium leeks, white and light green parts only, cut into matchsticks (see the illustrations below), rinsed thoroughly (about 4½ cups)
4	carrots, peeled and cut into matchsticks (see the illustrations on page 324)
8	16 by 14-inch sheets parchment paper
8	skinless halibut fillets, 1 to ¼ inches thick (about 6 ounces each)
¼	cup minced fresh parsley leaves
	Lemon wedges, for serving

CUTTING LEEKS INTO MATCHSTICKS

1. Trim away the dark green leafy tops and root end. Cut the leek into manageable 2-inch segments.

2. Cut each segment in half lengthwise, then pull the leek apart into smaller stacks consisting of 3 or 4 layers.

3. Cut the smaller stacks thin into ⅛-inch-thick matchsticks, then rinse and dry them thoroughly.

1. In a small bowl, mash the butter, garlic, zest, thyme, ½ teaspoon salt, and ¼ teaspoon pepper together. Thoroughly pat the leeks dry with paper towels, then toss with the carrots in a large bowl and season lightly with salt and pepper.

2. Following the illustrations on page 322, fold and cut the parchment into 8 rough heart shapes. Adjust the oven racks to the lower-middle and upper-middle positions and heat the oven to 450 degrees.

3. Spread the pieces of parchment out over a clean, dry counter (or work in batches if counter space is tight). Neatly pile the leek-carrot mixture on one side of each parchment sheet. Pat the fish dry with paper towels, season with salt and pepper, and lay on top of the vegetables. Spread 1 tablespoon of the butter mixture evenly over the top of each piece of fish.

4. Fold the cut edges of the parchment over to make tidy, airtight packets. Place the packets on 2 large rimmed baking sheets. Bake for 15 minutes, switching and rotating the pans halfway through the cooking time.

5. Working quickly, cut an X in the top of each packet with scissors and sprinkle the basil over the fish. Using a stiff spatula, gently transfer the packets to individual plates and serve with lemon wedges.

TO MAKE AHEAD

All of the ingredients can be prepped and refrigerated in airtight containers for up to 1 day. Once assembled, the packets can only be held for 30 minutes before cooking; otherwise the moisture from the vegetables and fish will weaken and tear the parchment. If you substitute heavy-duty aluminum foil for the parchment, however, the packets can be assembled and refrigerated for up to 5 hours before baking; increase the baking time by 2 to 5 minutes.

CUTTING CARROTS INTO MATCHSTICKS

1. Start by slicing the carrot on the bias into 2-inch-long ovals.

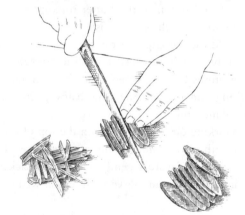

2. Slice the ovals lengthwise into ¼-inch-thick matchsticks. To be efficient, you can stack or shingle several ovals on top of one another before cutting the matchsticks.

INDEX

A Note on Conversions

SOME SAY COOKING IS A SCIENCE AND AN ART. We would say that geography has a hand in it, too. Flour milled in the United Kingdom and elsewhere will feel and taste different from flour milled in the United States. So, while we cannot promise that the loaf of bread you bake in Canada or England will taste the same as a loaf baked in the States, we can offer guidelines for converting weights and measures. We also recommend that you rely on your instincts when making our recipes. Refer to the visual cues provided. If the bread dough hasn't "come together in a ball," as described, you may need to add more flour—even if the recipe doesn't tell you so. You be the judge.

The recipes in this book were developed using standard U.S. measures following U.S. government guidelines. The charts below offer equivalents for U.S., metric, and Imperial (U.K.) measures. All conversions are approximate and have been rounded up or down to the nearest whole number. For example:

EXAMPLE:

1 teaspoon = 4.9292 milliliters, rounded up to 5 milliliters

1 ounce = 28.3495 grams, rounded down to 28 grams

Volume Conversions

U.S.	METRIC
1 teaspoon	5 milliliters
2 teaspoons	10 milliliters
1 tablespoon	15 milliliters
2 tablespoons	30 milliliters
¼ cup	59 milliliters
⅓ cup	79 milliliters
½ cup	118 milliliters
¾ cup	177 milliliters
1 cup	237 milliliters
1¼ cups	296 milliliters
1½ cups	355 milliliters
2 cups	473 milliliters
2½ cups	592 milliliters
3 cups	710 milliliters
4 cups (1 quart)	0.946 liter
1.06 quarts	1 liter
4 quarts (1 gallon)	3.8 liters

Weight Conversions

OUNCES	GRAMS
½	14
¾	21
1	28
1½	43
2	57
2½	71
3	85
3½	99
4	113
4½	128
5	142
6	170
7	198
8	227
9	255
10	283
12	340
16 (1 pound)	454

Conversions for Ingredients Commonly Used in Baking

Baking is an exacting science. Because measuring by weight is far more accurate than measuring by volume, and thus more likely to achieve reliable results, in our recipes we provide ounce measures in addition to cup measures for many ingredients. Refer to the chart below to convert these measures into grams.

INGREDIENT	OUNCES	GRAMS
Flour		
1 cup all-purpose flour*	5	142
1 cup whole wheat flour	5½	156
Sugar		
1 cup granulated (white) sugar	7	198
1 cup packed brown sugar (light or dark)	7	198
1 cup confectioners' sugar	4	113
Cocoa Powder		
1 cup cocoa powder	3	85
Butter†		
4 tablespoons (½ stick, or ¼ cup)	2	57
8 tablespoons (1 stick, or ½ cup)	4	113
16 tablespoons (2 sticks, or 1 cup)	8	227

* U.S. all-purpose flour, the most frequently used flour in this book, does not contain leaveners, as some European flours do. These leavened flours are called self-rising or self-raising. If you are using self-rising flour, take this into consideration before adding leavening to a recipe.

† In the United States, butter is sold both salted and unsalted. We generally recommend unsalted butter. If you are using salted butter, take this into consideration before adding salt to a recipe.

Oven Temperatures

FAHRENHEIT	CELSIUS	GAS MARK (IMPERIAL)
225	105	¼
250	120	½
275	130	1
300	150	2
325	165	3
350	180	4
375	190	5
400	200	6
425	220	7
450	230	8
475	245	9

Converting Temperatures from an Instant-Read Thermometer

We include doneness temperatures in many of our recipes, such as those for poultry, meat, and bread. We recommend an instant-read thermometer for the job. Refer to the table above to convert Fahrenheit degrees to Celsius. Or, for temperatures not represented in the chart, use this simple formula:

Subtract 32 degrees from the Fahrenheit reading, then divide the result by 1.8 to find the Celsius reading.

EXAMPLE:

"Roast until the thickest part of a chicken thigh registers 175 degrees on an instant-read thermometer." To convert:

$175°F - 32 = 143$
$143 \div 1.8 = 79.44°C$, rounded down to 79°C